Here are some basic map concepts that will help you to get the m̶ maps in this textbook.

- Always look at the scale, which allows you to determine the distance in miles or kilometers between locations on the map.

- Examine the legend carefully. It explains the colors and symbols used on the map.

- Note the locations of mountains, rivers, oceans, and other geographic features and consider how these would affect such human activities as agriculture, commerce, travel, and warfare.

- Read the map caption thoroughly. It provides important information, sometimes not covered in the text itself.

- Many of the maps showing premodern political boundaries and labels also carry a *spot map*. This smaller map identifies the contemporary, political boundaries of the area and allows you to gain a better understanding of the breadth of empires and the evolution of nations. In addition, an occasional *spot map* showing a detail of a larger map appears in the text.

www.wadsworth.com

www.wadsworth.com is the World Wide Web site for Wadsworth and is your direct source to dozens of on-line resources.

At *www.wadsworth.com* you can find out about supplements, demonstration software, and student resources. You can also send email to many of our authors and preview new publications and exciting new technologies.

www.wadsworth.com
Changing the way the world learns®

Western Civilization

A HISTORY OF EUROPEAN SOCIETY

Volume I: To 1715

SECOND EDITION

Western Civilization

Civilization

A HISTORY OF EUROPEAN SOCIETY

Volume I: To 1715

SECOND EDITION

Steven C. Hause
Washington University–St. Louis

William Maltby
University of Missouri–St. Louis

THOMSON
★
WADSWORTH

Australia • Canada • Mexico • Singapore • Spain
United Kingdom • United States

THOMSON

WADSWORTH

Publisher: *Clark Baxter*
Senior Assistant Editor: *Julie Yardley*
Editorial Assistant: *Anne Gittinger*
Senior Technology Project Manager: *Melinda Newfarmer*
Marketing Manager: *Lori Grebe Cook*
Marketing Assistant: *Mary Ho*
Advertising Project Managers: *Brian Chaffee and Stacey Purviance*
Project Manager, Editorial Production: *Kimberly Adams*
Print/Media Buyer: *Barbara Britton*

Permissions Editor: *Sarah Harkrader*
Production Service: *Graphic World Inc.*
Text Designer: *Ellen Pettengell*
Art Editor: *Graphic World Inc.*
Copy Editor: *Graphic World Inc.*
Illustrator: *Graphic World Inc.*
Cover Designer: *Ellen Pettengell*
Cover Image: *The Construction of the Tower at Babylon 13th Century, A. K. G., Berlin/SuperStock.*
Cover Printer: *Quebecor World/Dubuque*
Compositor: *Graphic World Inc.*
Printer: *Quebecor World/Dubuque*

For more information about our products, contact us at:
Thomson Learning Academic Resource Center
1-800-423-0563

For permission to use material from this text or product,
submit a request online at
http://www.thomsonrights.com.

Any additional questions about permissions can be
submitted by email to thomsonrights@thomson.com.

Thomson Wadsworth
10 Davis Drive
Belmont, CA 94002-3098
USA

Asia
Thomson Learning
5 Shenton Way #01-01
UIC Building
Singapore 068808

Australia/New Zealand
Thomson Learning
102 Dodds Street
Southbank, Victoria 3006
Australia

Canada
Nelson
1120 Birchmount Road
Toronto, Ontario M1K 5G4

Canada
Europe/Middle East/Africa
Thomson Learning
High Holborn House
50/51 Bedford Row
London WC1R 4LR
United Kingdom

Latin America
Thomson Learning
Seneca, 53
Colonia Polanco
11560 Mexico D.F.
Mexico

Spain/Portugal
Paraninfo
Calle Magallanes, 25
28015 Madrid, Spain

Library of Congress Control Number: 2004107731

ISBN 0-534-62120-1

Contents in Brief

Contents in Detail

Chapter 3

Chapter 4

Chapter 5

Chapter 6

Chapter 16

Maps

Documents

Tables

Preface

Every Western civilization textbook has an individual character. The special concern of this text is revealed in its subtitle, *A History of European Society*. The authors share an interest in the varieties of social history—of women, the family, and the daily lives of ordinary people—that have changed historical studies in recent years. We have tried to weave a synthesis of this contemporary social history scholarship throughout the text. We have sought to locate our social history in the traditional concerns of a Western civilization textbook, rooted in economic and political context and related to historical issues of differing cultures. War and technological developments—phenomena that influenced and were influenced by social and economic structures—are not treated in isolation but rather as phenomena with profound implications for everyday life. We have tried to provide insight into popular culture without sacrificing the traditional emphasis on the intellectual, scientific, and religious interests of the elite and without forgetting that popular culture and elite culture are often the same.

Our attempt to combine traditional breadth and a focus on social history has led us to integrate a large quantity of supporting materials and historical sources into the text. In addition to the maps, illustrations, and documents that usually serve this purpose, we have chosen to add a number of statistical tables and graphs needed to document social and economic history. These are closely integrated into the text so that their basic meaning is clear and their raw data can illuminate discussion.

Learning History through Narrative and Historical Analysis

Fundamentally, of course, the development of Western civilization is a story, and we tell it as a narrative. But unlike ancient bards and other storytellers, historians must also explain, analyze, and teach the characteristics of the different historical eras. The chapters into which the book is divided must explain why and how each historical era developed these characteristics.

Sometimes a chapter must focus on evaluating and explaining interactions, such as the events leading to a war or revolution; and sometimes a chapter must focus on showing what actually happened—telling the narrative story of important changes and developments. Both are skills that students of history will seek to develop as they refine their understanding of the past.

Guideposts. Most of the reviewers who helped guide our work agree that students can easily get lost in the wealth of information within a chapter. We share with our colleagues a keen desire that students learn to love history as much as we do. The sooner they spot both the forest and the trees in each chapter, the sooner real understanding begins to take root. To help our readers, we have added a **Chapter Outline** and **Focus Questions** at the beginning of each chapter and **Review Questions** at the end. We have also added a descriptive word or two—**topic heads**—at the beginning of appropriate paragraphs. We hope these unobtrusive guideposts will help students study, learn, and perform well on their exams by making it clear whenever the focus of a section shifts from one topic to the next. We have also included **pronunciation guides** following foreign terms and names to help students read and remember unfamiliar material. Acknowledging that pronunciations of foreign terms differ over time and that their sounds can be difficult to communicate in text, we nevertheless hope that by offering a starting point for the instructor to modify aurally as needed, we have given students an essential tool for participating in discussions.

The West in the World. The study of Western civilization inevitably, and increasingly, bears on changing notions of the idea of the West and the many points of contact between the West and the rest of the world. This edition opens with a discussion of the place of the West in a global, geographical context, and brief recurring essays throughout the text explore points of contact. However, we have also taken special care throughout the text to compare civilizations when doing so can help readers see the uniqueness and the similarities of major cultures. For example, a box in Chapter 1 discusses (and shows) the differences between the major monuments created for the rulers of Egypt and Mesopotamia.

Learning History through Primary Source Documents

For first-time readers, we want to bring to attention the documents that complement the narrative. Each chapter includes a broad range of letters, treaties, poems, broadsides, declarations, and other written sources—primary source documents similar to the material that most instructors use to supplement their courses. The purpose of such documents is to make the descriptions more vivid, to substantiate the analysis yet provoke questions, and to introduce readers to the raw materials of historical study. As often as possible, we have embedded with a document an illustration or two that illuminates the primary document. For example, in Chapter 2, images from artifacts of the period show Greek athletes performing events that a Pindar ode to the winner of the ancient Olympic games praises. For a comprehensive list, see page xxi.

Learning History through Tables

This edition is filled with numerous tables of historical data. Most of these tables illustrate the details of everyday life and help students to see the human faces hidden just behind each column of numbers. Until very recently, of course, the great majority of Europeans were illiterate and unable to leave behind a written record of their lives. By examining parish, municipal, and other records, we are able to piece together information such as wages and prices in ancient Rome, life expectancy in the Middle Ages, the incidence of abandoned children in major cities, and other telling details of everyday life.

For example, Table 18.3 in Chapter 18 shows that 45 percent of a worker's family income in late eighteenth-century Berlin was spent on bread, 12 percent was spent on other vegetable products, and 15 percent on meat and dairy products. The table clearly shows that for many centuries bread was the major source of nutrition for peasants and workers, rather than the side dish it has become today. The recurring bread riots discussed in the text reflect the real deprivation when the price of bread rose and ordinary people starved; the numbers make such a crisis starkly plain. For a comprehensive list, see page xxv.

Learning History through Art

Some of the richest views of history presented in Western civilization textbooks have come from seeing the art and architecture of the past. More re-cently, of course, television and the Internet have created a generation of visual learners. Without losing faith in the power of words, we have included more than 600 photographs in the book, most in full color. Each image bears directly on the discussion in the pages on which they appear. And those that are not embedded in a document or table include a caption of some length that complements the text. For example, an illustration in Chapter 18 shows a coach stop in a small eighteenth-century town. Students will enjoy the picture on their own—but many will also want to speculate on how long it will take to fix the broken wheel on one of the stagecoaches and to think further about the pace of transportation in eighteenth-century Europe.

Learning History through Maps

Geography and history are interrelated subjects, and maps are essential components of basic historical study. At the elementary level, it makes an enormous difference to the history of Europe that England is an island or that Germany and Poland have no natural barrier between them. At a more sophisticated level, a linguistic geography of central and eastern Europe shows the complexity of political conflicts in that region. All of the book's maps, more than 100, appear in full color, and most include such topographic features as mountains and rivers. These features make it clear, for example, how the mountainous terrain of the Peloponnesian Peninsula encouraged the development of independent city-states in ancient Greece. For a comprehensive list, see page xix.

Spot Maps. In addition, overlapped on maps of the ancient period through the eighteenth century are small maps showing contemporary political boundaries. For example, overlapped on the map of the ancient Middle East in Chapter 1 is a small spot map showing the political boundaries of the contemporary middle east—an area as important today as it was in ancient times.

Learning History through Timelines

One of the most common concerns of students who confront large amounts of historical material for the first time is an anxiety about dates. Dates are essential to constructing a sequence of events, and an understanding of change over time can come only with the help of the dates that mark time. Furthermore, a date can mark the aberration in a period, the event, invention, or discovery that heralds a development a hundred years later. Yet too many dates become a burden to readers. To address this problem, each chapter ends with a timeline to assist students in keeping events in their correct relationship without memorizing all of the dates in the text.

ACKNOWLEDGMENTS

We owe our gratitude to all those who helped us in the preparation of this second edition of *Western Civilization: A History of European Society*. We would like to thank all those at Wadsworth Publishing who have assisted us in producing this book: Clark Baxter, our editor and publisher who suggested the book and carried it into production; Julie Yardley, assistant editor, who put the supplement package together; Kim Adams, project manager; Lori Grebe Cook, marketing manager; and Melinda Newfarmer, technology project manager. We especially want to thank our reviewers: Kathryn Abbott, Western Kentucky University; William Abbott, Fairfield University; Gerald D. Anderson, North Dakota State University; Roz L. Ashby, Yavapai College; Robert Barnes, Arizona State University; David Bartley, Indiana Wesleyan University; Anthony Bedford, Modesto Junior College; Rodney E. Bell, University of South Dakota; Melissa Bonafont, Austin Texas Community College; Jerry Brookshire, Middle Tennessee State University; Richard Camp, California State University–Northridge; Marybeth Carlson, University of Dayton; Elizabeth Carney, Clemson University; Sherri Cole, Arizona Western College; Jeffrey Cox, University of Iowa; Kevin Cramer, Indiana University–Purdue University, Indianapolis; Frederic Crawford, Middle Tennessee State University; Philip B. Crow; Leslie Derfler, Florida Atlantic University; Linda S. Frey, University of Montana; Charlotte M. Gradie, Sacred Heart University; Sarah Gravelle, University of Detroit; Stephen Haliczer, Northern Illinois University; Barry Hankins, Baylor University; William Hartel, Marietta College; John A. Heitmann, University of Dayton; Mack Holt, George Mason University; David Hudson, California State University, Fresno; Frank Josserand, Southwest Texas State University; Gary Kates, Trinity University; Charles Killinger, Valencia Community College; Michael Kulikowski, University of Tennessee; Paul Leuschen, University of Arkansas; Eleanor Long, Hinds Community College; William Matheny, Liberty University; Olivia H. McIntyre, Eckerd College; David L. Longfellow, Baylor University; Bill Mackey, University of Alaska–Anchorage; Tom McMullen, Georgia Southern University; Paul L. Maier, Western Michigan University; Larry Marvin, St. Louis University; Carol Bresnahan Menning, University of Toledo; Jeffrey Merrick, University of Wisconsin–Milwaukee; Dennis Mihelich, Creighton University; Charles G. Nauert, Jr., University of Missouri–Columbia; Elizabeth Neumeyer, Kellogg Community College; Thomas C. Owen, Louisiana State University; William E. Painter, University of North Texas; Kathleen Paul, University of Southern Florida; Mark D. Potter, University of Wyoming; Dermot Quinn, Seton Hall University; Nancy Rachels, Hillsborough Community College; Elsa Rapp, Montgomery County Community College; Miriam Raub Vivian, California State University–Bakersfield; Richard R. Rivers, Macomb Community College; Kenneth W. Rock, Colorado State University; Karl A. Roider, Louisiana State University; Leonard Rosenband, Utah State University; Joyce E. Salisbury, University of Wisconsin–Green Bay; Claire A. Sanders, Texas Christian University; Jerry Sandvick, North Hennepin Community College; Thomas P. Schlunz, University of New Orleans; Donna Simpson, Wheeling Jesuit University; Elisabeth Sommer, Grand Valley State University; Ira Spar, Ramapo College of New Jersey; Jake W. Spidle, University of New Mexico; Roger D. Tate, Somerset Community College; Jackson Taylor, Jr., University of Mississippi; Timothy M. Teeter, Georgia Southern University; Lee Shai Weissbach, University of Louisville; Pamela West, Jefferson State Community College; Richard Weigel, Western Kentucky University; Richard S. Williams, Washington State University.

ABOUT THE AUTHORS

Steven C. Hause is Senior Scholar in the Humanities and Co-Director of European Studies at Washington University–St. Louis. He is also Professor of History Emeritus at the University of Missouri–St. Louis, where he held the Thomas Jefferson Professorship and won the Chancellor's Award for Excellence in Teaching (1996) and the Pierre Laclede Honors College Teacher of the Year Award (1989). He is the author and co-author of three previous books on the history of the women's rights movement in modern France, which have won four research prizes: *Women's Suffrage and Social Politics in the French Third Republic*, with Anne R. Kenney (Princeton University Press, 1984); *Hubertine Auclert, the French Suffragette* (Yale University Press, 1987); and *Feminisms of the Belle Epoque*, with Jennifer Waelti-Walters (University of Nebraska Press, 1994). His current research focuses on the Protestant minority in modern France. His essays have appeared in several journals, including *American Historical Review* and *French Historical Studies*.

William S. Maltby is Professor of History Emeritus at the University of Missouri–St. Louis, where he taught for more than 30 years. Among his publications are *The Black Legend in England: The Development of Anti-Spanish Sentiment, 1558–1660* (Duke University Press, 1971); *Alba: A Biography of Fernando Alvarez de Toledo, Third Duke of Alba, 1507–1582* (University of California Press, 1983); *The Reign of Charles V* (Palgrave Macmillan, 2002), and articles on various aspects of Early Modern European history. From 1977 to 1997, he also served as Executive Director of the Center for Reformation Research and as editor of several volumes and series of volumes on the history of the Reformation.

The West in the World

MEDITERRANEAN GEOGRAPHY AND CLIMATE

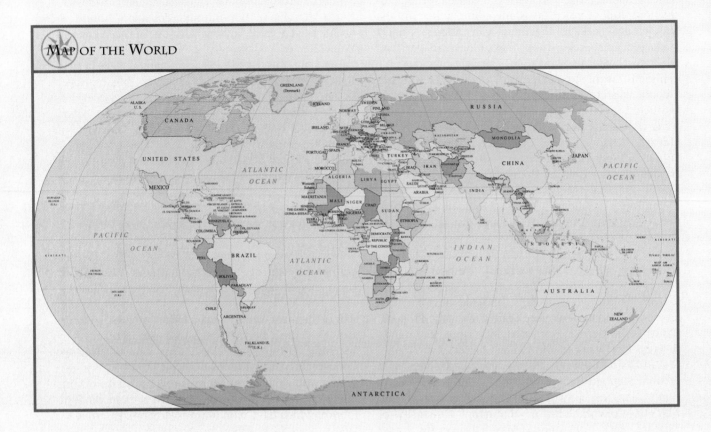

MAP OF THE WORLD

All societies are to some extent the products of their environment. For example, climate and geography determine the foods they eat, and this affects how they organize their economic and social lives. Seas, rivers, and mountain ranges either hinder or encourage communications and, in so doing, set the limits within which cultural borrowing occurs. In some cases, climate and geography present obstacles that can be overcome only through the modification of social and cultural institutions. From its earliest beginnings, the West depended on cereal grains such as wheat, barley, and millet. They were as important to its development as rice to the countries of East Asia or maize to the cultures of Mesoamerica. The Mediterranean Sea, together with the great river valleys of Europe and the Middle East, facilitated communication and for many centuries defined the limits of economic and cultural exchange. Any discussion of how Western society developed should begin with a description of these basic geographical features.

The Mediterranean Region

The western third of the Eurasian landmass is as hospitable to human beings as any region on the face of the globe. It is separated from Africa by the Mediterranean Sea, a deep saltwater trench more than 2,000 miles in length whose width—thanks to the Iberian, Italian, and Balkan peninsulas—varies from 500 to only a few miles. To the north, the sea is partially sheltered from arctic winds by the mountainous spine of the continent. On the southwest flank, the Atlas Mountains hold back the desert, but for a thousand miles from Gabes to Sinai, the Sahara touches shore.

Climate. The Mediterranean climate is warm and dry, with an annual rainfall that varies from less than 10 inches in the Egyptian desert to more than 30 inches in a few favored spots, such as the Po valley of northern Italy. Summers are hot, with high temperatures in the eighties and nineties (Fahrenheit). An area of Atlantic high pressure, normally centered over the Azores from

May until October, ensures cloudless skies. Rain falls mainly in the autumn and early spring, and the winters are typically moderate, with snow common only at the higher elevations.

Abundant sunshine and scarce rainfall create a high evaporation rate. About 20 percent of the water lost from the Mediterranean each year through evaporation is made up by rainfall. Another 5 percent comes from rivers, of which the Nile is by far the most important, and an insignificant 3 percent comes from the Black Sea via the Bosporus. The rest pours in from the Atlantic through the Strait of Gibraltar. This vast influx of water influences Mediterranean navigation. The surface current entering the strait runs at approximately 6 knots. (A knot is the standard measure of speed at sea, equivalent to 1 nautical mile per hour. A nautical mile equals about 1.16 land miles.) It is re-

inforced for most of the year by strong westerlies blowing off the Atlantic. Therefore, driving ships by oars or sails to pass into the open ocean is extremely difficult.

Navigation. Like most seas, the Mediterranean has eased communication for those who lived along its shores. Its mild weather and weak tides are envied by mariners, but its peculiarities must be respected. Once waters from the Atlantic enter the Mediterranean, the powerful current runs along the North African coast for its entire length, creating a counterclockwise pattern of circulation that washes westward along the northern coasts until it exits again at Gibraltar. Because it has become saltier through evaporation, the old water is heavier than the new and exits far below the incoming torrent. It is not felt by ships.

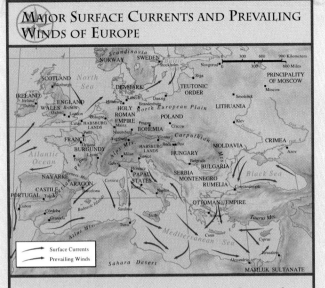

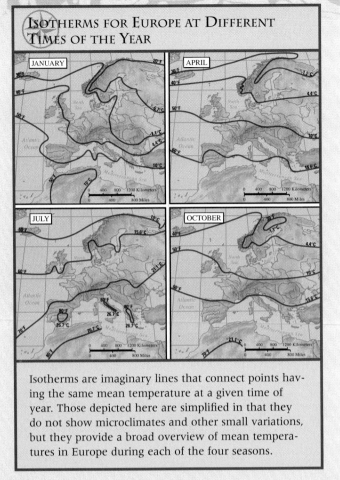

These currents and the prevailing north to northwest winds determined shipping routes until the age of steam and ensured that at sea the shortest distance between two points was almost never a straight line. Their influence on commerce and naval strategy was therefore great, but they were not the only navigational peculiarity of the Mediterranean basin. Although idyllic looking in travel posters, the Mediterranean can be dangerous. From October to April it is beset with land winds whose names—*mistral, bora, sirocco*—are ominous to sailors. Sometimes blowing at 30 or 40 knots, they are difficult to predict and raise high, chaotic seas with disconcerting speed. The captains of fragile oared galleys or clumsy sailing ships usually preferred to spend the winter months in port.

Topographically, much of the land that surrounds the Mediterranean is rocky and mountainous. On the Italian and Greek peninsulas, along the northwest African coast, and in Palestine, only the narrow coastal plains and the even narrower river valleys are suitable for large-scale cultivation. In prehistoric times, most of these regions were wooded, but as the population of humans and their livestock increased, the forests were destroyed and intensive grazing by sheep and goats depleted the ground cover. Long before the dawn of recorded history, this process created the landscape that exists today: relatively small patches of cultivation interspersed with steep rocky hillsides, arid semidesert, and impenetrable scrub. Wood for building or fuel is scarce, and the management of water supplies has been a constant preoccupation of farmers and town dwellers alike for millennia.

The European Mainland

The Iberian Peninsula and Anatolia, the Asian part of modern Turkey, are high plateaus surrounded by rugged mountains. With elevations of as much as 3,000 feet above sea level, these plains can be cold in winter and, except for autumn, are almost always dry, with annual rainfall averaging between 10 and 20 inches. Wood and water are scarce here as well, and erosion caused by thousands of years of overgrazing has only made matters worse.

To the north, beyond the rugged barrier of the Alps, the Pyrenees, and the mountainous Balkan Peninsula, the climate is very different. Northwestern Europe, although at the same latitude as Newfoundland and Labrador, is mild and moist. Its weather is moderated by the Atlantic Ocean and, in particular, by the Gulf Stream, a warm water current that rises in the Caribbean and washes the shore of England and France. Pleasant summers with temperatures that usually do not exceed 80°

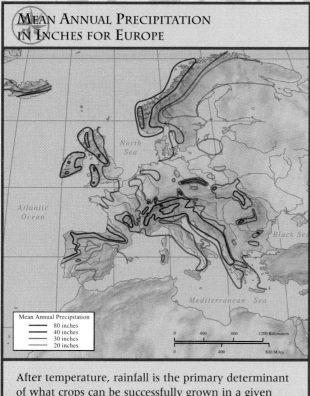

MEAN ANNUAL PRECIPITATION IN INCHES FOR EUROPE

North Sea

Atlantic Ocean

Black Sea

Mediterranean Sea

Mean Annual Precipitation
—— 80 inches
—— 40 inches
—— 30 inches
—— 20 inches

0   400   800   1200 Kilometers

0   400   800 Miles

After temperature, rainfall is the primary determinant of what crops can be successfully grown in a given area. From 20 to 40 inches of rain per year is probably optimal, although the season in which it falls is important, too.

Fahrenheit follow long wet winters during which prolonged freezes are rare. Palm trees, although not native to the region, can be grown on France's Breton peninsula or along the southwestern coasts of the British Isles. The prevailing winds are westerly, bringing abundant rainfall even in the summer months as Atlantic squalls, forced northward by high pressure over the Iberian Peninsula, drop their moisture on the land.

Much of western Europe is flat or gently rolling, with deep, easily worked soils that were once covered by deciduous forests. The land blends almost imperceptibly into the North European Plain, which stretches from the marshes of the Netherlands eastward into Russia. In Russia and Poland, moderate summers, harsh winters, and often unpredictable rainfall provide a typical continental climate. Large areas of central Europe, meanwhile, are hilly. A series of wooded uplands from the Argonne and Vosges on the west to the Carpathians on the east are drained by navigable rivers, the most important of which are the Rhine and the Danube. Both rise in the highlands of southwest Germany, but whereas the Danube flows eastward into the Black Sea through the rich plains of Hungary and Walachia, the Rhine flows northward to its broad estuary on the North Sea. The Rhine provides rapid access from the Alpine foothills and central Germany to the Atlantic.

The North Sea, like the present contours of the Baltic coast, is relatively modern. As recently as 4000 BCE, Great Britain was connected to the European mainland while the Baltic depression was just that—a broad marshy region surrounding a brackish lake with no outlet to the sea. The rise in ocean levels at the end of the last Ice Age inundated both areas and produced the present coastline. Beyond the newly formed sea lies Scandinavia, a wintry region with only small amounts of arable land, but with usable ports; abundant fish; and vast resources in timber, copper, and iron.

To its first inhabitants, the European subcontinent must have seemed an earthly paradise. Its climate is for the most part moderate. In prehistoric times its plains and forests teemed with wild game and its lakes, streams, and estuaries offered a rich harvest of fish and other edible marine organisms. Large tracts of well-watered and easily worked soils held the promise of intensive agriculture on a scale rarely achieved in other parts of the globe. From earliest times, the European subcontinent was home to a wide variety of human cultures.

Question: What advantages of climate and geography would help Europe become one of the world's centers of civilization?

FOCUS QUESTIONS

- How did the development of agriculture influence populations, social structure, and the status of women?
- What constitutes a civilization, and how did civilizations arise in the ancient Middle East?
- What were the social, economic, and legal structures of ancient Middle Eastern societies?
- What were their religious beliefs?
- How did the religious, intellectual, and artistic achievements of the ancient Middle East influence the development of Western civilization?

Chapter 1

THE ANCIENT MIDDLE EAST: MESOPOTAMIA, EGYPT, PHOENICIA, ISRAEL

About 10,000 years ago in what is now southeastern Turkey, a woman, or perhaps a group of women working together, discovered how to cross-pollinate three types of wild edible grasses that grew in the region. It was almost certainly women who did this because men in that age did not often concern themselves with gathering or nurturing plants. This early example of selective breeding ranks among the great technical achievements of all time. It required careful observation and exquisite care in transferring the live pollen from one plant to another to produce modern bread wheat whose hardiness and greater yields helped create an agriculture that could sustain large numbers of people. The cultivation of crops, together with the domestication of animals, marked the beginning of the Neolithic revolution. Humans began to settle in permanent towns and villages, and in time, many of these settlements coalesced into great civilizations.

Chapter 1 discusses life in the **Paleolithic** or Old Stone Age before examining the **Neolithic revolution** and its material consequences—including its impact on diet, **demography** (population statistics), and the advent of organized warfare. This chapter then covers two great ancient civilizations, Mesopotamia and Egypt, each of which profoundly affected the development of the West. Progressing to the land *between* Egypt and Mesopotamia, this chapter concludes with the ancient society of Phoenicia, whose people invented the alphabet from which we derive our own, and Israel, whose religious ideas became the basis of the three great western faiths: Judaism, Christianity, and Islam.

THE FIRST EUROPEANS: THE PALEOLITHIC ERA TO C. 10,000 BCE

Few subjects are more controversial than the origins of the human species. During the long series of Ice Ages, a race of tool-making bipeds inhabited the fringes of the European ice pack. Known conventionally as Neanderthals because their remains were first discovered at Neanderthal in Germany, these bipeds were heavier, stronger, and hairier than *Homo sapiens* (the Latin name for modern human beings). Neanderthals hunted the great herd animals of the day: mammoth, bison, wooly rhinoceros, and reindeer. They lived in caves, buried their dead in ways that suggest some form of religious belief, and knew how to make stone tools and weapons—thus the name for this period, the Old Stone or Paleolithic Age.

About 30,000 years ago, *Homo sapiens,* a people physically identical to modern men and women, abruptly superseded the Neanderthals. Most modern scholars believe that the new arrivals came from Africa, but nearly everything about human origins is controversial. Soon after the arrival of *Homo sapiens* the Neanderthals vanished. Their extinction remains mysterious, for *Homo sapiens* were no more advanced in culture or technology than the Neanderthals and were physically rather weak and puny by comparison.

Some have suggested that the Neanderthals fell victim to an epidemic disease or could not adapt to warmer weather after the retreat of the glaciers. They may have found it difficult to hunt the faster, more solitary animals of modern times after the extinction of their traditional prey. Both races were hunter-gatherers, so-called because they hunted game and gathered plants for food.

Paleolithic Work and Trade. The first humans lived on a protein-rich diet of game and fish supplemented by fruit, berries, nuts, and wild plants. Constantly on the move, they lived in caves or temporary shelters that they constructed from wood or bones and covered with the skins of the animals they killed. They made stone tools and weapons that became steadily more sophisticated over time—axes, arrows, daggers, spears, whetstones for sharpening them, and trowels for digging up plants. As they roamed, they came in contact with other groups and engaged in the interchange of goods and

FIGURE 1.1 *Prehistoric Stone Tool (c. 400,000 BCE).* Until people learned to work with metals, they made most of their cutting and chopping tools and most of their edged weapons from flint or similar stone. By striking the stone's surface repeatedly with another stone, the toolmaker detached flakes and formed a cutting edge. Bone or wood could then be used to detach even smaller flakes to make the edge sharper. Makers shaped the larger detached flakes into smaller pieces like arrowheads. This hand ax (meaning an ax used with the hand rather than fitted to a wooden shaft) was found at Hoxne, England. Nothing is known about the people who shaped or used it, but excavations where this ax was found uncovered extensive flint-working areas on the edge of an ancient river as well as animal bones, including elephant, rhinoceros, and lion.

FIGURE 1.2 *Leaf-Shaped Spear Point (c. 14,000 BCE).* Suitable flints often had to be brought from great distances and were among the most important trade goods in prehistoric times. This spear point was made from flint brought from a part of France far from Volgu, France, where it was found. The point's shape and the shallow parallel-sided scars are left by the removal of long thin flakes struck off using an antler or wooden hammer. To make the spear, Paleolithic people typically fit the thinned base of a point into a slot at the top of a wooden shaft and held it in place with a cord. Made by *Homo sapiens* rather than Neanderthals, it illustrates how the best stone weapons could be harder and sharper than those made by early metal workers of the later Bronze Age.

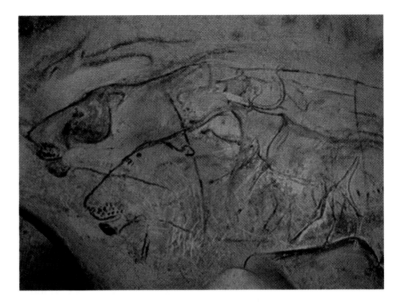

FIGURE 1.3 *Paleolithic Cave Painting (c. 28,000 BCE). Detail from the Lion Panel in the Hillaire Chamber, the Cave of Chauvet-Pont-d'Arc, France.* Early human cultures in France and northern Spain covered the walls of hundreds of caves with beautiful, lifelike pictures of animals. In this detail (2 yards) from the oldest drawings yet found, an artist drew three big lions on top of earlier figures of lions. The one in the background, standing out after scraping, is represented only by the beginning of its back line, its ear, and the top of its face. On the other two, one can see how stump drawing [shading] was used and the whiskers put in. The fine engravings in the foreground are cave bear scratches, which shows that the bears came back to the cave after the people had made their drawings.

ideas—an interchange that anthropologists call **cultural borrowing.** Excavations have uncovered tools made of stone from distant geographical sources, which indicates early trade between groups.

Paleolithic Society. If the hunter-gatherer societies of modern times are an indication, early peoples probably lived in **extended families.** Extended families may contain not only parents and children but also other biological relatives—aunts, uncles, nieces, nephews, and cousins. **Nuclear families** contain only parents and children. If they survived and prospered, families eventually became tribes. A **tribe** is composed of several nuclear and extended families that claim common descent. Because every member's cooperative effort is important in a small group, the social structure may have been more egalitarian than hierarchical. Paleolithic groups divided their responsibilities in a straightforward manner. Men hunted, fished, and perhaps made tools. Women cared for the children, tended the fire, and gathered berries and wild plants. Status derived from superior skill in any of these activities. When a tribe was headed by a chief, his primary role was probably to organize hunts.

Art and Religion. Among the most extraordinary achievements of these paleographic cultures was their art. Magnificent wall paintings, usually of animals, decorate the caves they inhabited from Spain to southern Russia. Many groups also produced small clay figurines with exaggerated female features. This suggests the widespread worship of a fertility goddess, but Paleolithic religious beliefs remain unclear. The purpose of the paintings is also unknown. They may have involved a form of magic designed to bring game animals under the hunter's power, or they may have been purely decorative. In any case, the technical skill of the artists was anything but primitive.

THE NEOLITHIC REVOLUTION (C. 10,000–3500 BCE)

Hunting and gathering remained the chief economic activity for a long time. Long before the advent of agriculture, pottery, or writing, Neolithic peoples developed the bow and arrow as well as the basic tools still used to hook or net fish and trap game. The **domestication** (taming and breeding) of animals probably began at an early date with the use of hunting dogs but later extended to raising and herding sheep, goats, and cattle as a reliable source of protein when game was scarce. Shortly thereafter, the first efforts were made to cultivate edible plants. The domestication of animals and the invention of agriculture marked one of the great turning points in human history.

Agriculture—The Beginning of the Neolithic Revolution

Wheat. Several species of edible grasses are native to the upper reaches of the Tigris and Euphrates valleys,

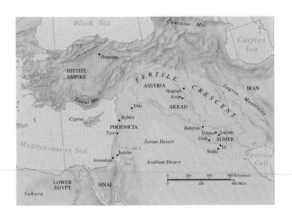

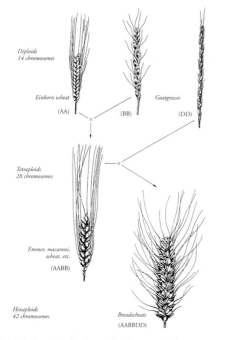

FIGURE 1.4 *The Evolution of Modern Wheat.* Early farmers cross-pollinated einkorn wheat (upper left) with inedible goat grasses to create emmer wheat (lower left) and modern bread wheats (lower right), which are far more efficient sources of food. Emmer wheat is related to the durum wheat from which we have macaroni. (The letters in parentheses represent sets of chromosomes and show the combinations of the new strains.)

including wild barley and two varieties of wheat. Einkorn (one-corn), a variety of wheat with a single row of seeds per stalk, produces only modest yields; emmer, with multiple rows on each stem, is more productive. When the two grains are crossbred with other grasses, the result is modern bread wheat, a grain with vastly improved yields.

Why did agriculture begin in Mesopotamia? Perhaps only in the upper Tigris and Euphrates valleys did the seeds of this particular combination of grasses meet a warm climate and well-watered soils. How people learned the techniques of cross-pollination and of converting these seeds into gruel or bread is unknown, but once learned, the value of systematic cultivation, or farming, became apparent. The invention of agriculture marked the beginning of the Neolithic Age.

Migration, contact among cultures, and cultural borrowing facilitated the diffusion of agricultural techniques. By 7000 BCE, farming was well established from Iran to Palestine. It spread into the Nile valley and the Aegean by 5000 BCE and from the Balkans up the Danube and into central Europe in the years that followed. Radiocarbon dating has established the existence of farming settlements in the Netherlands by 4000 BCE and in Britain by 3200 BCE.

Farming developed in response to a general increase in population that upset the old Paleolithic ecology. Human competition for dwindling resources became more intense as game grew more scarce and elusive. Herding and the cultivation of row crops were soon essential to survival. As the human population continued to grow, even herding diminished because it provides fewer calories per unit of land than row crops. Neolithic farmers increasingly restricted the raising of animals to tracts otherwise unsuitable for cultivation. Although other sources of food would always supplement crop raising, it gradually emerged as the primary activity wherever land could be tilled for planting. The cultivation of plants, beginning with grains and expanding to include beans, peas, olives, and eventually grapes, made food supplies far more predictable than in a hunting or herding economy and greatly increased the number of calories that a given area of land could produce. The invention of the wheel and the wooden plow, both of which came into common use around 3000 BCE, further enhanced the efficient use of land. Farming therefore promoted demographic growth both absolutely and in the density of population that a given area could support.

Neolithic Health and Diet. On the negative side, populations expand to meet the availability of resources, and Neolithic communities soon reached their ecological limits. Grain yields on unfertilized land typically range from three to twelve bushels per acre with a probable average of five. If societies could not expand the area under cultivation, they reached a balance that barely sustained life.

The transition to a farming economy often resulted in diets that were deficient in protein and other important elements. Bread became the proverbial staff of life, largely because land planted with grain supports more people. The nuts, animal proteins, and wild fruits typical of the Paleolithic diet became luxuries to be eaten only on special occasions. As a result, Neolithic farmers were shorter and less healthy than their Paleolithic ancestors (as their skeletal remains indicate). Although beans, peas, and lentils became valuable sources of protein, ordinary people consumed as much as 80 percent of their calories in the form of carbohydrates from bread, or more often, from gruel made by boiling ground grain in water or milk.

Caloric intake varied widely. An adult male engaged in heavy labor requires a minimum of 3,700 calories per day. Although we cannot measure a typical diet in Neolithic or ancient times, we can estimate that the average peasant or laborer probably made do on far less, perhaps only 2,500 to 2,700 calories per day. Moreover, because grain harvests depend on good weather and are susceptible to destruction by pests, shortfalls were common. In years of famine, caloric intake dropped below the level of subsistence.

TABLE 1.1 THE DOMESTICATION OF ANIMALS IN THE NEOLITHIC PERIOD

Analysis of the bones left at Neolithic sites provides clues to the domestication of animals and an insight into the Neolithic diet. The figures in the table come from Tarnabod (a site of the Bordrogkereztur culture) and Budapest-Andor utca (the Baden culture), both in Hungary, and Ćmielow, Poland (a site of the Beaker people).

The number of animal bones that researchers have found at each site appears under the name of the site; the percentage that each set of bones represents in the total appears in parentheses. For example, 61.3% of the bones found at Tarnabod are domesticated cattle bones, and 9.1% are aurochs bones, a species of wild cattle now extinct.

The disparity in the total percentage of wild animal bones (7.5% at Ćmielow, for instance) versus the percentage of domestic animal bones (92.5% at Ćmielow) tells us that wild animals formed a declining part of the Neolithic diet. Local variations existed in the species of domesticated animals. All three cultures used copper tools. Although hard evidence is available only for Ćmielow, they probably grew emmer wheat, barley, flax, and wheat.

Questions: What animals were easiest to domesticate? Why do you suppose this is? What common types of animals do not appear in this table? Again, why do you think they do not appear here? At what site does the smallest percentage of domesticated animal remains appear? What do you conclude about that culture?

| | 3200–3000 BCE | 2900–2400 BCE | |
	TARNABOD, HUNGARY	BUDAPEST-ANDOR, HUNGARY	ĆMIELOW, POLAND
Domestic Animals			
Cattle	562 (61.3%)	160 (32.1%)	1,578 (57.7%)
Dog	3 (0.3%)	6 (1.2%)	111 (4.1%)
Pig	109 (11.9%)	105 (21.0%)	566 (20.7%)
Sheep and goat	69 (7.5%)	194 (8.9%)	276 (10.1%)
Total	743 (81.0%)	465 (93.2%)	**2,531 (92.5%)**
Wild Animals			
Aurochs	83 (9.1%)	4 (0.8%)	0
Horse	0	0	58 (2.1%)
Pig	31 (3.4%)	4 (0.8%)	43 (1.6%)
Red deer	43 (4.7%)	13 (2.6%)	36 (1.3%)
Roe deer	12 (1.3%)	4 (0.8%)	45 (1.6%)
Other	5 (0.5%)	9 (1.8%)	23 (0.8%)
Total	174 (19.0%)	34 (6.8%)	**205 (7.5%)**

Source: Adapted from Murray, Jacqueline, *The First European Agriculture* (Edinburgh: Edinburgh University Press, 1970, pp. 306, 362–363).

The permanence of farming settlements also encouraged the spread of disease. The hunter-gatherers of Paleolithic times had lived in small groups, camped in caves or temporary shelters, and moved frequently in pursuit of game—a way of life that virtually precluded epidemics. Farming, however, is by definition sedentary. Fields and orchards require constant attention and therefore permanent shelter. Early farmers built houses of sun-dried brick or of reeds and wood and placed them close together to promote security and cooperation. Such villages encouraged the accumulation of refuse and human waste. Water supplies became contaminated, and disease-bearing rats, flies, lice, and cockroaches became the village or town dweller's constant companions.

Neolithic Demography. Inadequate nutrition and susceptibility to epidemic disease created the so-called **biological old regime,** a demographic pattern that prevailed in Europe until the middle of the nineteenth century. Although few people literally starved to death, disease kept death rates high while poor nutrition kept birth rates low. Malnutrition also raises the age of first menstruation and can prevent ovulation in mature women, thereby reducing the rate of conception. When conception did occur, poor maternal diet led to a high rate of stillbirths and complications during pregnancy. If a baby were brought to term and survived the primitive obstetrics of the age, there remained the possibility that the mother would be too malnourished to nurse the newborn. Statistics are unavailable, but infant mortality probably ranged from 30 to 70 percent in the first 2 years of life.

The age distribution of Neolithic and ancient populations therefore bore little resemblance to that of a modern industrial society. The young far outnumbered the old, and most people had shorter working lives than their modern counterparts. Their reproductive lifetimes were also shorter, and in people of mature years (aged 35 to 50), men may have outnumbered women, primarily because so many women died in childbirth. The life expectancy for either gender may not have been much more than 30 years at birth, but those who survived their fifties had almost as good a chance as their modern counterparts of reaching an advanced age. This pattern, like the conditions that produced it, would also persist until the industrial revolution of modern times.

The Neolithic Concept of Property and Its Social Implications

The Social Order. The invention of agriculture expanded the idea of personal property to include land and domesticated animals. In Paleolithic times, people owned their tools, weapons, and clothing, but not the animals, plant foods, or land on which they depended for survival. The primary measure of individual worth was a person's ability to hunt or gather, skills from which the entire tribe presumably benefited. The Neolithic world, however, measured status in terms of ownership of flocks, herds, and fields. This change affected the structure of human societies in three important ways. First, because luck and management skills vary widely, certain individuals amassed greater wealth than others. To gain the maximum advantage from their wealth, they found it necessary to use, and often to exploit, the labor of their poorer neighbors. Thus, although a measure of cooperation in agricultural and construction tasks could be found at the village level, social stratification characterized Neolithic society.

Subordination of Women. The emergence of property seems also to have affected the status of women. Little is known about the lives of women in Paleolithic times, but most theorists agree that, with the development of herds and landed property, controlling female sexuality became important in ways that would have been unnecessary in a community of hunter-gatherers. The issue was inheritance. The long-term survival of a Neolithic family depended on the preservation and augmentation of its wealth. Women were expected to provide heirs who were the biological children of their partners. The result was the development of a double standard by which women had to be pure and seen to be pure by the entire community. If anthropologists are correct, the subjugation of women and the evolution of characteristically feminine behaviors were an outgrowth of the Neolithic revolution.

Warfare. Finally, the Neolithic age marked the beginning of warfare, the systematic use of force by one community against another. Whereas Paleolithic hunters may have fought one another on occasion, Neolithic peoples fought to defend their property—their homes, livestock, and cultivated land—against the predatory behavior of

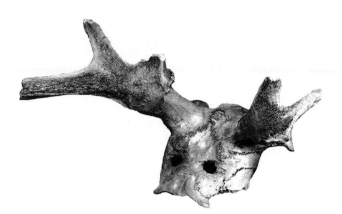

FIGURE 1.5 *Red Deer Antler Headdress, 9,500 years old.* Hunters may have worn headdresses like this one as a disguise, but it is more likely that these antlers were part of a costume worn on special occasions, perhaps during religious ceremonies. The lines of cut marks made by flint tools show that its makers deliberately removed the skin from the skulls, broke off the antlers and the bones forming the top of the nose, and trimmed the edges of the remaining skull. A leather thong, looped through the two holes in the back of skull, held the antlers to the head.

neighboring peoples. Dealing with population growth by annexing the land of others was all too easy and resulted in frequent aggression. War, in turn, made possible the development of slavery. To a hunter-gatherer, slaves are unnecessary, but to herders and agriculturalists, slave labor makes possible the expansion of herds and the cultivation of more land: under typical circumstances, slaves produce more than they consume.

Power and Government. At first, Neolithic communities seem to have been organized along tribal lines, a structure inherited from their hunting and gathering ancestors when they settled down to till the land. Most inhabitants shared a common ancestor, and **chieftainship** was probably the dominant form of social organization. The function of the chief in agricultural societies was far more complex than in the days of hunting and gathering, involving not only military leadership but also the management of goods and labor. Efficiency in operations such as harvesting and sheep shearing requires cooperation and direction. In return, the chief demanded a share of each individual's agricultural surplus, which he then stored for redistribution during hard times while holding back a portion for his own use.

Specialization and Work. The chief's role in the management and allocation of resources explains the storehouses that early rulers constructed. As agriculture developed, crops became more varied. In the Mediterranean basin, for example, wheat, wine, and olives became the basic triad of products on which society depended. One farmer might have a grove of olive trees but no land capable of growing wheat, whereas another

▼FIGURE **1.6** *Stonehenge (c. 3100–1550 BCE).* The greatest of western Europe's prehistoric circles stands on England's Salisbury Plain. A place of worship and burial, Stonehenge may also have served as an astronomical calendar, but its true purpose is uncertain. We do know that prehistoric builders constructed Stonehenge in several stages. About 3100 BCE, they built the *henge*—a circular, raised earth plateau inside a ditch. Approximately 1,000 years later, the builders set Bluestones in a double circle inside the henge; transported from a quarry in the mountains of Wales 240 miles away, each stone weighed about 4 tons. Somewhat later the Stonehenge builders arranged thirty Sarsen stones in an outer circle of about 100 feet in diameter; brought from a quarry 20 miles away, these larger Sarsen stones each weighed about 50 tons. As seen here in the surviving portion of the outer circle, the Sarsen lintels (horizontal slabs) connected continuously, end-to-end, with tongue-and-groove joints. Pegs on the tops of the uprights—note the round protrusion on the upright stone toward the center of the picture—fit into prepared holes in the lintels and held them in place (mortise and tenon joints). The builders created the joints and shaped the stones by pounding them with stone hammers. Inside the outer Sarsen circle, the builders arranged five trilithons (a trilithon is a pair of uprights with a lintel) in the shape of a horseshoe. Its axis lay on the sunrise of the summer solstice. A heel stone, set outside the henge, marked the axis and the path to the center. The prevalence of these large-scale construction projects, whatever their purpose, and the care in selecting the right combination of building materials, indicates that Neolithic societies could, and did, achieve high levels of organization and technological sophistication.

would be blessed with well-drained, south-facing hillsides producing the best grapes for wine. A chief acted to encourage agricultural specialization and an efficient use of group resources. He could collect oil from one and grapes from another and barter both to a third farmer in return for his surplus wheat. Different commodities prevailed in different regions, but the principle was the same. In the absence of merchants or organized markets, the chief fulfilled an important role in the distribution of goods and services. Although specialization in Neolithic times was rarely total, prudent farmers knew that diversification offered a measure of security that **monoculture,** or the growing of only one crop, can never provide. If the major crop failed, they needed something else to fall back on, and even a modest degree of specialization can increase efficiency and raise a community's standard of living.

Religion and Monumental Architecture. Chiefs may also have had religious duties, although organized priesthoods evolved in some early societies. Chiefs almost certainly organized the building of communal burial places in the Aegean and along the Atlantic and North Sea coasts from Iberia to Scandinavia. Originally simple **dolmens** formed of a giant stone or megalith laid upon other stones, these tombs gradually evolved into domed chambers that were entered through long masonry passages. Graves of this kind are often found in the vicinity of stone circles such as Stonehenge.

Neolithic Advances in Technology

Pottery. Specialization and effective distribution can also encourage the development of technology. Pottery appeared soon after the Neolithic revolution as a way to store grains or liquids. Women probably made the first pots at home and fired them in a communal oven, but the invention of the potter's wheel allowed for "throwing" pots with unprecedented speed and efficiency. Because the new method required great skill, those who mastered it tended to become specialists, that is, artisans who were paid for their work in food or other commodities.

Metallurgy: The Beginning of the Bronze Age (3500 BCE). The advent of metallurgy provides a more dramatic example of occupational specialization. Before 6000 BCE, Neolithic people used pure copper, which is sometimes found in nature, for jewelry and personal items. By 4500 BCE, they were smelting copper from ores and hammering the heated metal into tools and weapons. These complex processes appear to have evolved separately and independently in the Middle East and in the Balkans, where copper deposits were common. Smelting and forging depended on the development of ovens that could achieve both a controlled air flow and temperatures of more than 2000° Fahrenheit. An analysis of pottery from these areas reveals that potters had developed such ovens to facilitate glazing.

By 3500 BCE, bronze—a mixture of copper and tin—was in general use throughout the West for the manufacture of tools and weapons. Bronze is harder than copper and holds a better edge. Stone is more durable and can be sharper than either bronze or copper, but the process of forming stone tools by hand is labor-intensive and therefore inefficient. The Neolithic Age was now over, and the Bronze Age had begun. It lasted until the invention of ironworking ushered in the Iron Age in about 1200 BCE.

Because the skills involved in working bronze were highly specialized, smiths devoted themselves exclusively to forging wares, which they sold or bartered for necessities. This implies a sophisticated trading network and system of governance stable enough to protect it, but in the absence of written records, evidence is lacking. Transferring weapons manufacture from the individual to the specialist, however, promoted the large-scale production of metal weapons and may have enhanced the power of chiefs by enabling them to amass large armories.

THE EMERGENCE OF CIVILIZATIONS

When survival—as opposed to the demands of ritual—required a major cooperative effort, some societies evolved into civilizations. A term loaded with subjective meanings, for our purposes, **civilization** refers to the establishment of a political and cultural unity over a large geographical area. It implies high population densities and the production of substantial wealth requiring elaborate social, commercial, and administrative structures.

In most cases, civilization also meant the development of mathematics and a written language. Both

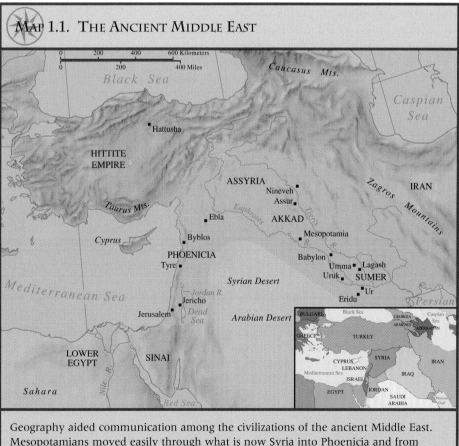

MAP 1.1. THE ANCIENT MIDDLE EAST

Geography aided communication among the civilizations of the ancient Middle East. Mesopotamians moved easily through what is now Syria into Phoenicia and from there to Egypt. Egyptians used the same route, while the Hittites had access to both Egypt and Mesopotamia through the same corridor.

were needed for land surveys, administration, and the distribution of goods and services in a complex society. As chiefs became kings, the record of taxes and tributes paid, of lands annexed, and of the provisions consumed by their ever-larger armies acquired great significance. The desire to record the ruler's glorious deeds for posterity came slightly later but was nevertheless important. Writing gives names to individuals and permits the dead to speak in their own words. Without it, there is no history.

The emergence of societies at this level of complexity affected even those areas not directly under a society's control. Great civilizations are magnets that draw other cultures into their orbits. As peoples on the periphery pay tribute to or trade with the larger market, cultural borrowing accelerates. Then, as civilizations expand, they come into conflict with one another and bring neighboring peoples into their systems of war and diplomacy. By 3000 BCE, at least two such civilizations had begun to emerge: one in the valley of the Tigris and Euphrates Rivers, the other in the valley of the Nile.

THE ANCIENT MIDDLE EAST

Sometimes known as the Fertile Crescent, the ancient Middle East includes Mesopotamia and the eastern shores of the Mediterranean to the borders of Egypt. The writing, mathematics, and religious faiths of Western civilization originated here. The broad valley of the Tigris and Euphrates Rivers (center right on the accompanying map) is known as Mesopotamia, the heart of one of the first great civilizations. For 1,500 years, the rulers of different regions or cities (Sumer, Akkad, Babylon, Assyria) conquered all or part of Mesopotamia without substantially altering its basic culture. The coastal region centered on the Phoenician city-states served as a corridor between Mesopotamia and Egypt and was on various occasions ruled by one or the other of these great civilizations.

Mesopotamia

Geography. *Mesopotamia,* in Greek, means the land between the rivers, in this case the Tigris and the Euphrates. It is a hot, fertile flood plain, most of which is within the borders of modern Iraq. Summer high temperatures reach 110° to 120° Fahrenheit, and no rain falls from May through late October. Winters are more moderate, but only Assyria in the north receives enough rainfall to support agriculture without irrigation. In the lower valley, everything depends on water supplied by the two rivers.

Of the two, the Tigris carries by far the larger volume of water. The Euphrates on the west has fewer tributaries and loses more of its flow to evaporation as it passes

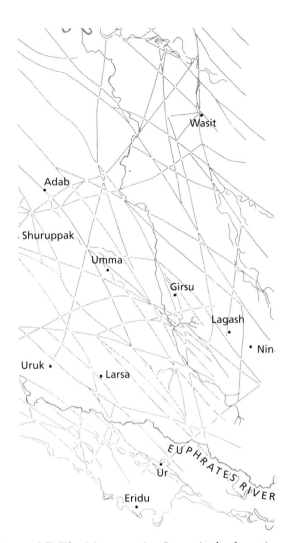

FIGURE 1.7 *The Mesopotamian Levee (embankment) System.* Then as now, levees protected croplands and cities from floodwaters. Here, satellite imagery reveals many of the more important levees in the lower Tigris and Euphrates valley (modern Iraq) constructed during the Sumerian and Babylonian epochs. These ancient levees follow not only the rivers but major irrigation channels. The extent of the levees indicates the high level of social organization and technological sophistication that led to survival in the land between the rivers.

through the dry plains of what is now Syria and northwestern Iraq. In April and May, snow melting in the Zagros Mountains causes massive flooding throughout the region. This provides needed water and deposits a rich layer of alluvial silt, but the inundation presents enormous problems of management. Communities must control the floods not only to protect human settlement but to preserve water for irrigation during the rainless summer. To make matters worse, both rivers create natural embankments or levees that inhibit the flow of tributaries and that over time have raised the water level above that of the surrounding countryside. If spring floods wash the embankments away, the rivers change their courses, often with disastrous results. The biblical story of Noah and the Flood originated in Mesopotamia, although there were probably many floods rather than just one (see Document 1.1).

The first known settlements in the region were village cultures speaking a Semitic language distantly related to the more modern Hebrew or Arabic. They grew wheat and barley and by 4500 BCE had established themselves as far south as Akkad near the modern Iraqi capital of Baghdad. Although Semitic peoples from the west and southwest continued to migrate into the region until the Arab invasions of the ninth century CE, by 3000 BCE, a non-Semitic people who may have come originally from India—the Sumerians—had achieved dominance in the lower valley.

The Sumerians. The Sumerians introduced large-scale irrigation and built the first true cities, usually on a tributary of one of the rivers. Many of them grew into city-states that dominated a territory of perhaps a hundred square miles. The inhabitants cultivated cereals, especially barley, and had learned the secret of making beer. Sumerian homes of sun-baked brick were originally small and circular, like a peasant's hut, but gradually expanded to become large, one-story structures with square or rectangular rooms surrounding a central courtyard.

The Sumerian Social Order. The organization of the Sumerian city-states provided a model for their Akkadian and Babylonian successors. Each city had a king who ruled with the assistance of a palace bureaucracy. A city council, elected by free citizens, had legislative and judicial responsibilities, although the precise division of powers is unknown. The royal family and its retainers owned large tracts of land. An organized priesthood also held extensive properties to support their service in the great raised temple, or **ziggurat,** that dominated the town (see *Two Faiths: Their Prayers and Monuments*). Private families—most of them extended, multigenerational, and organized on patriarchal lines—owned the rest of the land. Although rarely rich, these freeholders enjoyed full civil rights and participated in the city's representative assembly. The greatest threat to their independence was debt, which could lead to enslavement. Still, although slavery in payment of debt was common and the temple or palace sometimes acquired slaves through war, Sumer was not a slave-based economy.

Sumerian cities warred continually over the allocation of land and water. At first the local kings were probably war chiefs. As the need to mobilize the city's resources for war grew, they acquired new responsibilities for the allocation of goods and labor and their powers became hereditary. Like chiefs in other societies, they stood at the center of a system of clientage that involved their families and their servants, as well as officials, commoners, and priests.

Clientage. As the basic form of social organization in many cultures, clientage was destined to become a powerful force in the history of the West. **Clientage** is best defined as a system of mutual dependency in which a

DOCUMENT 1.1

THE FLOOD FROM *THE EPIC OF GILGAMESH*

The great Mesopotamian epic based on the adventures of Gilgamesh contains an account of the flood that strongly resembles the biblical account in Genesis. Here Utnapishtim, the Mesopotamian equivalent of Noah, tells his story to the hero Gilgamesh.

In those days the world teemed, the people multiplied, the world bellowed like a wild bull, and the great god was aroused by the clamor. Enlil heard the clamor and said to the gods in council, "the uproar of mankind is intolerable and sleep is no longer possible by reason of the babel." So the gods agreed to exterminate mankind. Enlil did this, but Ea [the god of the waters] because of his oath warned me in a dream . . ."tear down your house and build a boat, abandon possessions and look for life, despise worldly goods and save your soul alive . . . then take up into the boat the seed of all living creatures . . ." [After Utnapishtim did this] for six days and six nights the winds blew, torrent and tempest and flood overwhelmed the world, tempest and flood raged together like warring hosts. When the seventh day dawned the storm from the south subsided, the sea grew calm, the flood was stilled; I looked at the face of the world and there was silence, all mankind was turned to clay. The surface of the sea stretched as flat as a rooftop; I opened a hatch and the light fell on my face . . . I looked for land in vain, but fourteen leagues distant there appeared a mountain, and there the boat grounded; on the mountain of Nisir the boat held fast. . . .

When the seventh day dawned I loosed a dove and let her go. She flew away, but finding no resting place she returned. Then I loosed a swallow, and she flew away but finding no resting place she returned. I loosed a raven, she saw that the waters had retreated, she ate, she flew around, she cawed, and she did not come back. Then I threw everything open to the four winds. I made a sacrifice and poured out a libation on the mountain top.

From *The Epic of Gilgamesh*, trans. N. K. Sandars, rev. ed. (Harmondsworth, England. Penguin Classics, 1964).

Question: What does the writer mean by "all mankind was turned to clay"?

FIGURE 1.8 This fragment in Akkadian of the *Epic of Gilgamesh* tells the Babylonian legend of the flood and comes from the great library established at Nineveh by the Assyrian King Ashurbanipal (669–626 BCE). Like all cuneiform writing, it was created by pressing a wedge-shaped stylus into a slab of wet mud and then baking it or allowing it to dry.

wood, stone, copper ingots, and precious metals. Iron and steel were as yet unknown. Later, in the time of Hammurabi (c. 1750 BCE), Babylonian rulers attempted to bring some of these trading companies under government regulation.

The First Writing. We know more about the Sumerians only because they were the first Western people to create a written language. Their political and economic relationships had reached a level of complexity that required permanent record-keeping. Although the Sumerian language was apparently unrelated to any other and was used only for religious purposes after about 2000 BCE, all later Mesopotamian cultures adopted its cuneiform system of writing. **Cuneiform** refers to the wedge-shaped marks left by a stylus when it is pressed into a wet clay tablet. Sumer was rich in mud, and slabs of clay were perfect for recording taxes, land transfers, and legal agreements. When the document was ready, the tablet could be baked until hard and stored for future reference.

Power Struggles and Warfare in Mesopotamia

Throughout its history, Mesopotamia's wealth and lack of natural defenses made it a tempting prize for conquerors. For 1,500 years, the rulers of different regions in succession conquered all or part of Mesopotamia. Using force and the careful manipulation of alliances, they established dynasties that ended when their descendants fell prey either to internal divisive forces or to invasions by people from the surrounding highlands.

Sumer. Even with written records, political relations among the Sumerian city-states are difficult to reconstruct. As populations increased, struggles over boundaries and trading rights grew more violent. By 2300 BCE, intercity conflicts engulfed the region as kings claimed rulership over more than one city, or, all of Sumer—although

powerful individual protects the interests of others in return for their political or economic support. A system that can be informal or sanctioned by law, clientage in Sumer appears to have been both. Informal ties of dependency existed together with a separate class of free individuals who, defined by the law as clients, leased the use of small parcels of land in return for labor and a share of their produce. Their patrons—kings, officials, or temple priests—retained title to the land and a compelling hold on their client's political loyalties. Sumerian clients had full rights as citizens, but they could not be expected to vote against those who controlled their economic lives.

Trade. The organization of trade, like that of agriculture, reflected this social structure. For centuries, Mesopotamian business rested on the extended family or what would today be called family corporations. Some groups ran caravans to every part of the Middle East or shipped goods by sea via the Persian Gulf. They exported textiles, copper implements, and other products of Mesopotamian craftsmanship and imported there may never have been a Sumerian Empire of any significant length. According to the inscriptions of King Lugalzagesi of Umma (c. 2375 BCE), he achieved control over the entire region only to have it taken from him by a non-Sumerian, Sargon of Akkad.

Akkad. The Akkadian triumph marked the beginning of a new imperial age. The unification of southern and central Mesopotamia gave Sargon (reigned c. 2350–2300 BCE) the means to conquer the north together with Syria. Although Akkadian rule was brief, it transmitted elements of Mesopotamian culture throughout the Middle East, and Akkadian, a Semitic language, became standard throughout the Tigris and Euphrates valleys. But the brevity of Sargon's triumph set a pattern for the political future.

Babylon. After the overthrow of Sargon's descendants by a desert people known as the Guti and a brief revival of Sumerian power under the Third Dynasty of Ur, Babylon became the chief political and cultural center of the region. Under **Hammurabi** (ruled c. 1792–1750 BCE) the Babylonians achieved hegemony over all of Mesopotamia, but a series of invasions after 1600 BCE led to a long period of political disorder. The invaders, the most important of whom were **Hittites,** an Indo-European people from the area around Hattusha in south-central Asia, introduced fighting from wheeled chariots, a tactic that soon spread throughout the Middle East. Because the Hittites did not seek to alter local institutions, their influence was otherwise impermanent; however, a rivalry soon developed between Babylon and Assyria, a kingdom in the northern part of the valley centered first on the city of Ashur and later on Nineveh.

Assyria. A fierce people who spoke a dialect of Akkadian, the Assyrians may have been the first people to coordinate the use of cavalry, infantry, and missile weapons. Not only were their armies well organized, but their grasp of logistics appears to have surpassed that of other ancient empires. Although a highly civilized people whose literary and artistic achievements continued the traditions of Sumer and Babylon, they waged psychological warfare by cultivating a reputation for horrific cruelty. They eventually defeated the Babylonians and after 933 restored the achievements of Sargon by establishing an empire that stretched from Egypt to Persia.

Mesopotamian Culture, Law, and Religion

In spite of violent political alterations, Mesopotamia remained culturally homogeneous for nearly 3,000 years. While capitals and dynasties rose and fell, the land between the rivers remained captive to the annual floods and consequent need for cooperation, superlative engineering, and frequent redistribution of land. The Mesopotamians' highest intellectual achievements were therefore practical.

Mathematics. The Mesopotamians were the first great mathematicians whose place-value system of notation is the basis of all modern numeral systems. They used a numerical system based on sixty (instead of the modern ten) and produced reference tables for multiplication, division, square roots, cube roots, and other functions. Their greatest achievement, the place-value system in which the value of each digit is determined by its position after the base—instead of by a separate name—made describing large numbers possible.

The Legal Code of Hammurabi. The Babylonians also created one of the first comprehensive legal codes. Named after Hammurabi, it was almost certainly a compendium of existing laws rather than new legislation and reflected a legal tradition that had been developing for centuries. Its basic principles were retribution in kind and the sanctity of contracts. In criminal cases this meant literally "an eye for an eye, a tooth for a tooth"—if the social status of the parties were equal. If not, a defendant of higher status could usually escape by paying a fine. Blood feuds, private retribution, and other features of tribal law, however, were forbidden. This same sense of retributive justice extended to the punishment of fraud and negligence. A builder whose house collapsed and killed its occupants could be executed; tavern keepers who watered their drinks were drowned. Craftsmen had to replace poor workmanship at their own expense, and farmers who failed to keep their ditches and levees in good repair were sold into slavery if they could not compensate the victims of their carelessness. Contracts governed everything from marriage to interest rates and could not be broken without paying a heavy fine.

An almost oppressive sense of social responsibility drove Hammurabi's Code. The ecology of Mesopotamia was both fragile and largely manmade. Only elaborate regulation could prevent disaster, and the law is explicit on many aspects of trade, agriculture, and manufacturing. Courts and city councils heard a variety of cases—demonstrating the continuing importance of local government even after the establishment of an empire—and also took an interest in personal, family issues, including marriage.

As in most ancient cultures, parents arranged the marriages of their children. The parents of the bride provided her with a dowry, which she was entitled to keep in the event of widowhood or divorce. Husbands could demand a divorce at any time but had to pay maintenance and child support unless they could demonstrate that the wife had failed in her duties.

SELECTIONS FROM HAMMURABI'S CODE

In this translation, *Seignior* refers to both nobles and free citizens. The distinction is important because Mesopotamian law, like many early legal systems, prescribed different penalties and obligations on the basis of social class.

If a seignior has destroyed the eye of a member of the aristocracy, they shall destroy his eye. If he has destroyed the eye of a commoner or broken the bone of a commoner, he shall pay one mina of silver. If he has destroyed the eye of a seignior's slave or broken the bone of a seignior's slave, he shall pay one-half of his value.

If an obligation came due against a seignior and he sold the services of his wife, his son, or his daughter, or he has been bound over for service, they shall work in the house of their purchaser or obligee for three years with their freedom reestablished in the fourth year. . . .

If outlaws have congregated in the establishment of a woman wine seller and she has not arrested those outlaws and did not take them to the palace, that wine seller shall be put to death. . . .

If a woman so hated her husband that she has declared, "You may not have me," her record shall be investigated at her city council, and if she was careful and was not at fault, even though her husband has been going out and disparaging her greatly, that woman, without incurring any blame at all, may take her dowry and go off to her father's house. If she was not careful, but was a gadabout, thus neglecting her house and humiliating her husband, they shall throw that woman in the water.

Question: From the excerpt, what can you conclude about a woman's right to own property?

Those duties, like all other aspects of the marriage arrangement, were spelled out in a detailed contract that entitled husbands to satisfy their creditors by selling wives and children into slavery, usually for no more than 2 or 3 years. The system was patriarchal, but a wife could sue for divorce on grounds of cruelty, neglect, or her husband's false accusation of adultery. If, however, adultery were proved, the guilty couple would be tied together and drowned; if the aggrieved husband forgave his wife, her lover would be pardoned as well. Because there were no lawyers, women, like men, were expected to plead their own cases—a right often denied them in more modern legal systems. To reduce litigation, Hammurabi's Code decreed the death penalty for those who brought false accusations or frivolous suits.

Religion. Mesopotamian religion was not based on ethical commandments from the gods (although like most lawgivers, Hammurabi claimed divine sanction for his code). The Sumerians had worshipped more than 3,000 deities, many of whom acquired human form and a rich mythology around their adventures. Most Mesopotamian gods represented natural forces or the spirits of particular localities. The chief god of Babylon was its city god, Marduk, and the Assyrians accorded similar honors to Ashur. Both were thought of as creators who had brought the universe out of primal chaos. Other gods and goddesses were still worshipped, but in an apparent step toward **monotheism** (the belief in one god), they were increasingly described as agents of Marduk or Ashur and eventually as manifestations of a single god.

The power of the gods was absolute. Humans depended on their whims and could hope to propitiate them only through the ceremonies of the priests. The problem of the righteous sufferer was therefore a recurring theme in Babylonian literature. Even death offered no hope of relief. In the greatest of all Babylonian epics, the hero **Gilgamesh,** inspired by the death of his friend Enkidu, wrestles with the problem of the hereafter. His discoveries are not reassuring. The nether world is a grim place, and neither the legendary Gilgamesh nor any other Mesopotamian could imagine a personal salvation. If their extensive literature is an indication, the peoples of ancient Mesopotamia knew how to enjoy life, but a grim fatalism tempered their enjoyment (see *Two Faiths: Their Prayers and Monuments*). In the land between the rivers, with its terrible inundations and vulnerability to invaders, it could hardly have been otherwise.

ANCIENT EGYPT

Geography

While the Sumerians were establishing themselves in Mesopotamia, another great civilization was developing in the valley of the Nile. In central Africa, Uganda's Lake Victoria, more than 3,000 miles from the shores of the Mediterranean, streams running from a cluster of great lakes merge their waters to form the White Nile. The lakes serve as a reservoir, and the river's volume remains constant with the seasons as it flows north to meet the Blue Nile at Khartoum. The Blue Nile is smaller than the White, but its sources are north of Addis Adaba in the Ethiopian highlands, where the monsoon rains of June and the melting mountain snow become a torrent. This annual flood, which reaches the lower Nile valley in July or August, provides both the moisture and the rich layer of black silt that support Egyptian life.

From the confluence of the two rivers, the Nile makes a wide sweep to the west before flowing northward through a valley more than more than 350 miles long but rarely more than 10 miles wide. The historic land of Egypt is a narrow well-watered passageway between the Mediterranean and the heart of Africa. To the west lies the vast emptiness of the Libyan desert; to the east, a line of parched and rugged hills mark the shores of the Red Sea. Open country is found only near the river's mouth, a vast alluvial delta through which, in antiquity at least, seven main channels provided access to the Mediterranean Sea. Summer temperatures in the valley are not as hot as those of Mesopotamia, but little or no rain falls and, without the river, life would be insupportable.

As in Mesopotamia, the key to Egyptian agriculture was the proper management of the annual flood. The Nile is more predictable and less violent than the Tigris or Euphrates, but the construction of levees, catchments, and an extensive network of ditches was essential both to protect settlements and to preserve water after the flood subsided in the fall. Such projects, as well as the preservation and distribution of grain during the dry months, required a high level of organization. That may in turn have led to the centralized, hierarchical character of ancient Egyptian society, but the point is arguable. Little is known of politics before the advent of the First Dynasty around 3100 BCE. At that time, the kings of the First Dynasty or their immediate predecessors united the two lands of Upper (southern) and Lower (northern) Egypt and laid the foundations of a political culture that would endure for nearly three millennia. The essential characteristics of Egyptian society were in place when the Third Dynasty assumed power in 2686 BCE and began the Old Kingdom.

Political History

Historical Periods. The history of ancient Egypt is conventionally divided into three kingdoms and no fewer than twenty-six dynasties: the Old Kingdom (2686–2181 BCE), the Middle Kingdom (2133–1786 BCE), and the New Kingdom (1567–525 BCE). The terms *old*, *middle*, and *new* do not necessarily reflect progress. Some of Egypt's greatest achievements—for example, the construction of the pyramids at Giza—came during the predynastic period and the Old Kingdom. The Intermediate Periods between these kingdoms were troubled times during which provincial governors, known to the Greeks as *nomarchs*, increased their power at the expense of the central government. Periodically one would gain ascendancy over the others and establish a dynasty that served as the cornerstone of a new kingdom.

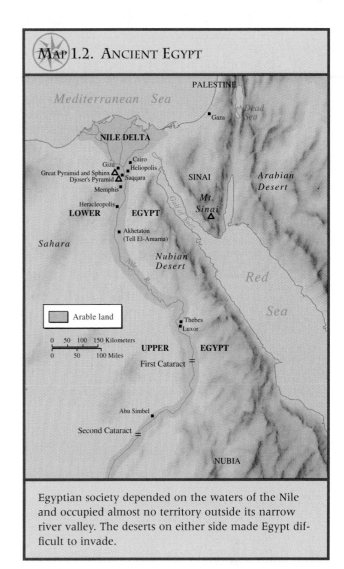

MAP 1.2. ANCIENT EGYPT

Egyptian society depended on the waters of the Nile and occupied almost no territory outside its narrow river valley. The deserts on either side made Egypt difficult to invade.

The Old and Middle Kingdoms. The Old Kingdom ended when massive crop failures coincided with the political collapse of the Sixth Dynasty. After an anarchic Intermediate Period of more than 100 years, Amenemhet I, the ruler of Thebes in Upper Egypt, reunited the country and established the Middle Kingdom. During the Twelfth Dynasty (c. 1991–1786 BCE), Egypt found itself under military pressure in both the north and south and, for the first time in its history, created a standing army. Expeditions into Palestine, Syria, and Libya helped stabilize the north while massive fortresses were built in Upper Egypt as protection against the growing power of Kerma, an expansionist state in what is now Sudan. The Middle Kingdom dissolved when a series of foreign dynasties known as the Hyksos supplanted the native Egyptian rulers. From the late 1700s BCE, Egypt's wealth attracted an influx of immigrants from Palestine and other parts of the Middle East. The Hyksos rulers were probably drawn from these groups. They

Two Faiths: Their Prayers and Monuments

The Mesopotamians believed that the gods were hostile, demanding, and inscrutable. Denying them due respect brought immediate and terrible punishment in this world, but they promised no reward in the next. In contrast, Egyptian beliefs centered on an afterlife. The following illustrations and documents show two very different spiritual worlds.

A Mesopotamian Prayer

This fragment from a longer prayer displays the characteristic Mesopotamian sense that the gods were not only demanding, but fickle, and that the worshipper could never be certain of finding favor with them.

> *The sin, which I have committed, I know not.*
> *The iniquity, which I have done, I know not.*
> *The iniquity, which I have done, I know not.*
> *The offence, which I committed, I know not.*
> *The transgression I have done, I know not.*
> *The lord, in the anger of his heart, hath looked upon me.*
> *The god, in the wrath of his heart, hath visited me.*
> *The goddess hath become angry with me, and hath grievously*
> *   stricken me.*
> *The known or unknown god hath straightened me.*
> *The known or unknown goddess hath brought affliction upon*
> *   me.*
> *I sought for help, but no one taketh my hand.*
> *I wept, but no one came to my side.*
> *May the known and unknown god be pacified!*
> *May the known and unknown goddess be pacified!*

From "Penitential Psalms," in *Assyrian and Babylonian Literature*, trans. R. F. Harper (New York: D. Appleton, 1901).

An Egyptian Prayer

This prayer or incantation was found on coffins during the Middle Kingdom. It reveals none of the Mesopotamian fear of arbitrary punishment but provides a graphic vision of life after death as well as a fine sample of Egyptian religious imagery. The Eastern Doors mark the entry into paradise. Re is the Sun god, and Shu is the god of air who raised Heaven above the Earth and planted trees to support it. A *cubit* measures between 17 and 21 inches.

> *Going in and Out of the Eastern Doors of Heaven among the Followers of Re. I know the Eastern Souls.*
>
> *I know the central door from which Re issues in the east. Its south is the pool of kha-birds, in the place where Re sails with the breeze; its north is the waters of ro-fowl, in the place where Re sails with rowing. I am the keeper of the halyard of the boat of the god; I am the oarsman who does not weary in the barque of Re.*
>
> *I know those two sycamores of turquoise between which Re comes forth, the two which came from the sowing of Shu at every eastern door at which Re rises.*
>
> *I know the Field of Reeds of Re. The wall which is around it is of metal. The height of its barley is four cubits; its beard is one cubit; and its stalk is three cubits. Its emmer is seven cubits; its beard is two cubits, and its stalk is five cubits. It is the horizon dwellers, nine cubits in height, who reap it by the side of the Eastern Souls.*
>
> *I know the Eastern Souls. They are Har-akhti, The Khurrer-Calf, and the Morning Star.*

From *Ancient Near Eastern Texts Related to the Old Testament*, vol. 1, 2nd ed. James B. Pritchard (Princeton, NJ: Princeton University Press, 1955).

---

came to power by infiltrating high office instead of by invading, but their success was deeply resented.

The New Kingdom. The restoration of a native dynasty in 1567 BCE marked the beginning of the New Kingdom. A series of warlike pharaohs destroyed the capital of Kerma and briefly extended their authority to the banks of the Euphrates. Ramses II (1279–1213 BCE) fought the Hittite empire to a truce. Ramses III remained strong enough to protect Egypt against a series of threatening population movements in the early

twelfth century BCE. Thereafter, the power of the monarchy declined, perhaps because the gold and silver imports that sustained its armies began to shrink. After 525 BCE, Egypt fell first to the Persians and then to the Macedonians under Alexander the Great in 323 BCE.

Characteristics of Egyptian Society

The Pharaoh. The society that survived these changes bore little resemblance to that of Mesopotamia. Its most unusual feature was the absolute power it ac-

Although pyramids and ziggurats are superficially similar, their purposes were different. The ziggurat was a stepped pyramid dedicated to the god or goddess who was patron of the city. Like the later pyramids of Central America, it drew the eyes of the worshipper upward to a platform at the top where priests performed sacrifices and conducted religious ceremonies. The pyramids of Egyptian pharaohs were covered in smooth stone that could not be scaled. Their purpose was to ensure the resurrection of the god-king in the lands of the west so that the eternal cycle of floods and harvests might continue. The pyramid had to be oriented precisely and contained not only the embalmed remains of the dead ruler but also the possessions he would he would need in the afterlife.

A Mesopotamian Ziggurat. Begun in the twenty-second century BCE and restored in modern times, the structure is built of burnt bricks set in bitumen (a naturally occurring petroleum-based substance similar to asphalt). Its base measures 210 × 150 feet, and its original height was about 40 feet. On the northeast face, shown here, three staircases lead upward to the bedchamber of Nanna, the Moon God and patron of the city of Ur. The sloping walls are not straight, but they are built on a slight convex curve so that they do not appear to sag.

The Pyramids at Giza. The largest of the pyramids, that of Cheops or Khufu (c. 2570 BCE) on the right, measures 480 feet in height. The middle one is that of Khefren (c. 2530 BCE), and the pyramid of Menkaure (c. 2465 BCE) is on the left.

corded to the king, or **pharaoh,** a Middle Kingdom title meaning "great house." His authority in life was absolute. In practice, he was expected to act according to *ma'at,* a concept of justice or social order based on the balance or reconciliation of conflicting principles. The king could not appear arbitrary or irresponsible, and because Egyptian society was conservative, precedent further limited his actions. If ma'at were not preserved, dynasties could fall, but the historical circumstances in which this happened are generally unknown.

When the king died, his spirit, or *ka,* would take its place in the divine pantheon and become one with Osiris, god of the dead. To facilitate this passage, the Egyptians built vast funeral monuments—the **pyramids**—to hold the dead ruler's mummified remains and serve as the center of a temple complex dedicated to his worship. The largest pyramids were built at Giza during the Old Kingdom by the Fourth Dynasty (2613–2494 BCE) monarchs—Khufu (Cheops), Khefren, and Menkaure (see *Two Faiths: Their Prayers and Monuments*). Constructed of between 80 million and 100 million cubic feet of cut and fitted stone, they are among the largest structures ever built. Projects on this scale were a measure of the king's wealth and power. Scholars believe that early rulers, acting in the common interest to tame the Nile, first conscripted and directed workers. Later kings retained this right to labor services, and conscript labor rather than slaves probably built the pyramids as well as the massive fortifications constructed in Upper Egypt to protect the kingdom from Nubian invasions. Shifts in the course of the river have obliterated similar works in the Nile delta.

Such projects could be seen as an appalling waste of resources, but they may have served a vital economic and social purpose. They certainly provided sustenance for thousands of workers, especially during the months of flood from July to November, when farmers could not till their fields. As such, they were an important mechanism for the distribution and redistribution of wealth. Furthermore, by centralizing the direction of a project's arts and crafts under royal patronage, the quality of both improved and led to technological advances that might not otherwise have occurred.

The Social Order. The character of Egyptian society is difficult to reconstruct, in part because no legal code comparable to that of Hammurabi has been found. Little is known, for example, about how land was owned or held. In theory, all land belonged to the king, and royal officials administered much of it for the king's benefit. In practice, the king granted income-producing lands to high officials, and much was perhaps held on long-term leases that could, in some circumstances, be bought and sold. Tenants, who seem to have enjoyed a high degree of security, worked most of these properties. The nature of their tenures is unknown, as are the conditions under which property or tenures could be inherited. All landholders, however, had to pay an annual tribute in kind to the ruler. Detailed records of assessment reveal a competent and often ruthless bureaucracy at work in even the humblest of villages. Heavy taxation encouraged the growth of tax-exempt foundations for the support of temples and other religious activities. Some of these foundations were vast, but others supported only a small temple whose priest and his acolytes (assistants who may have been family members) farmed the land.

Bureaucrats with multiple titles and responsibilities supervised the construction of pyramids and other public projects. Many supervisors combined priestly, secular, and military offices, which suggests that managerial competence was valued above specialized skills. Some high officials were royal relatives, whereas others were drawn from what may have been a hereditary caste of scribes and civil servants. The establishment of a standing army during the Middle Kingdom encouraged the emergence of professional soldiers, but no military aristocracy existed. From laborer to soldier to official, all were paid in food, drink, and various commodities, including gold (the Egyptians did not coin money until long after the end of the New Kingdom).

Slaves, most of whom had been captured in war, worked in the fields and households of the rich or in royal mines and quarries. They belonged by law to the pharaoh, who in turn granted them to private individuals or the great trusts that managed the temples. Slaves could hold property in their own right and were frequently manumitted, or freed, through a simple declaration by their owners. They were neither numerous nor central to the workings of the economy, except perhaps in the expansionist period when the New Kingdom pharaohs conquered much of Phoenicia and Syria (c. 1560–1299 BCE).

The vast majority of Egyptians were humble farmers whose lives probably resembled that of today's *fellahin.* They lived in small villages built of mud bricks, spent their days working in the fields, and drew precious water by means of the *shaduf,* a bucket swung from a counterbalanced beam. They paid taxes, performed conscript labor, and perhaps, served in the army. The idea of conscription was so pervasive that even after death people expected to labor in the fields of Osiris and placed small clay figurines of slaves in their tombs to help them with the work.

Egyptian Agriculture. Crops varied remarkably. Barley and wheat were the staples, and the average person's diet included large quantities of bread and beer with broad or fava beans for protein, onions for flavor, and the tender stalks of the young papyrus plant for an occasional salad. Papyrus was primarily valued because its fibers could be formed into a kind of paper—an Egyptian invention that takes its name from the plant. (Modern paper uses wood pulp and is derived from a process developed originally in China.) Wines for upper-class consumption were produced in the delta and painstakingly classified according to source and quality. Beef, too, was a delta product and formed an important part of a wealthy person's diet along with game birds, mutton, and pork. Poultry was common, as were many different kinds of fruit. Cotton, so closely associated with the Egyptian economy in modern times, was not introduced until about 500 BCE, and most Egyptians wore simple linen garments made from locally grown flax.

Health. Famines and epidemics were rare, and the life expectancy of ancient Egyptians was about 35 or 36 years, a figure somewhat higher than that for most other societies before the industrial revolution. An extensive medical literature reflects the Egyptian reputation as the greatest doctors of antiquity. Rules for diagnosis and treatment, lists of remedies, and careful instructions for surgical operations on every part of the body have been preserved. The Egyptian practice of embalming the dead and removing their organs contributed to a knowledge of anatomy unequaled by any other ancient culture.

FIGURE 1.9 *An Egyptian Couple Farming.* This wall painting from the nineteenth dynasty (c. 1297–1185 BCE) shows the farmer Sennedjem and his wife working in the fields. Sennedjem plows with the aid of two oxen while his wife follows behind sowing grain. A grove of date palms is shown in the foreground (at the bottom of the picture). The inscriptions behind them are an example of hieroglyphics. In the New Kingdom, even relatively humble people aspired to tombs of their own, and Sennedjem apparently arranged to have this picture painted on the walls of his own burial chamber.

Egyptian Trade. Egypt was not as heavily urbanized a society as Mesopotamia. Traders operating at the village level served the modest needs of the countryside, and royal officials conducted long-distance commerce. The major cities, including Thebes, the capital of Upper Egypt, and Memphis, near the present site of Cairo, were centers of government and ceremony.

Official expeditions visited mines and collected the gold and copper that were among Egypt's most important exports. Copper was used domestically for tools and weapons, but the Egyptians did not adopt the use of bronze until about 1500 BCE, long after it was common elsewhere. Egypt was self-sufficient in most commodities, with the exception of wood—the chief import. The Nile valley contained few trees, and those that existed were of species unsuitable for boat building or for the exquisite cabinetry favored by the royal court. Long before the First Dynasty, ships sailed to Byblos on the coast of Lebanon and returned with cargos of rare timber. This trade was the probable primary vehicle for cultural and demographic contacts with Asia.

The People. The appearance of its people reflected Egypt's role as a link between Asia and Africa. In Upper Egypt, the predominant physical type was slender with dark skin and African features. The people of the delta were heavier, with broad skulls and lighter complexions that indicated Asian or European origins. But representatives of both types were found everywhere, and the Egyptians as a whole seem to have been indifferent to racial or ethnic classifications. No apparent connection was made between rank and skin color. Immigrants from Palestine to the north and Nubia in the south were found in the army as well as civilian society and often achieved high office. The Egyptian language, too, contained a mixture of African and Semitic elements.

Status of Women. The absence of a surviving legal code and the shortage of court records make evaluating the true status of women in Egyptian society difficult, but several factors seem to have operated in their behalf. The identity of a child's mother, not the father, established heredity, and the matrilineal inheritance of private property, a practice dating from predynastic times, was far more common in Egypt than in other parts of the ancient Middle East.

In art, women were sometimes portrayed as equal to their husbands. They could hold property, initiate divorce, and undertake contractual obligations in their own right. The women of the royal family owned vast estates and seem to have exerted an influence on politics. At least one queen ruled Old Kingdom Egypt in her own name, and two women ruled in the New Kingdom— Tawosre and **Hatshepsut** (c. 1503–1482 BCE), who devoted her reign to the development of commerce and commissioned some of the finest monuments of Egyptian architecture. No evidence exists that women served as scribes or as officials in the royal administration, but the respect accorded women of the royal family may also have affected attitudes toward women throughout the country. In general, the status of women in Egyptian society was higher than that in most other ancient cultures.

Egyptian Culture, Science, and Religion

Written Language. Writing evolved in Egypt and in Mesopotamia at about the same time, but the two systems were different. Egyptian writing is known as **hieroglyphics** and in its earliest form consisted of lifelike pictures representing specific objects or actions. By a process similar to word association, certain hieroglyphs acquired additional meanings, and by about 2700 BCE, seventy-eight of them were being used phonetically to represent consonants or groups of consonants. As in the Semitic languages, Egyptian writing had no vowels. Symbols representing both the object or idea and its pronunciation were often used simultaneously to avoid confusion, and spelling was not standardized. Although Egyptian can be read vertically or horizontally in any direction, the hieroglyphic figures always face the beginning of the line.

Hieroglyphics appeared primarily in formal inscriptions on stone or papyrus. For contracts, correspondence, and other everyday documents, professional scribes wrote with reed pens on papyrus in a script known as *hieratic*. Based on hieroglyphics, *hieratic* became more cursive over time. Most of Egyptian literature, including poems and popular romances, as well as learned treatises, was circulated in this form.

Mathematics. The Egyptian number system, like our own, was based on ten. (The Greeks adopted it from the Egyptians and passed it on to other European peoples.) But the Egyptians never developed a place-value system of notation, so they needed a bewildering combination of symbols to express numbers that were not multiples of ten. Generally less sophisticated in mathematics than Mesopotamians, ancient Egyptians could multiply and divide only by doubling, but this appears to have been sufficient for their needs. They understood squares and square roots, and they knew, at an early date, the approximate value of π. The need for land surveys after each annual flood forced the Egyptians to become skilled measurers, and the construction of the pyramids reveals an impressive grasp of geometry.

Architecture. Pyramids after the Fourth Dynasty grew smaller and less expensive, but the Egyptian penchant for public works, temples, and funerary monuments continued until the Hellenistic (Greek) era. The Egyptians were superior craftsmen in stone and could convert even the hardest granites into works of art. As architects they seem to have invented post-and-lintel construction in masonry. Their temples, whether cut into the limestone cliffs of the Nile valley or freestanding, are graced with magnificent galleries and porticoes supported by stone columns, many of which were decorated or inscribed with writing. The Egyptians also built spacious palaces for the kings and their officials, but few of these structures survived the centuries intact.

Religion. Although few cultures have devoted more attention to religion and philosophy, or produced a larger body of speculative literature, the ancient Egyptian ideas are difficult to describe. This is in part because they saw no need to demonstrate the logical connection between different statements. Asserting principles or retelling illustrative myths was enough; analysis was left to the wit or imagination of the reader. If an oral tradition supplemented these utterances or provided a methodological guide to their interpretation, it has been lost. The surviving literature is therefore rich, complex, and allusive, but to literal-minded moderns, full of contradictions.

The earliest Egyptian gods and goddesses were nature spirits peculiar to a village or region. They usually took the forms of animals, such as the vulture goddess Nekhbet who became the patroness of Upper Egypt and her Lower Egyptian counterpart, the cobra goddess Buto. The effigies of both adorned the pharaoh's crown as a symbol of imperial unity. This animal imagery may reflect totemic beliefs of great antiquity, but in time the deities acquired human bodies while retaining their animal heads.

Eventually, new deities emerged who personified abstract qualities. Ma'at, the principle of justice and equilibrium, became the goddess of good order; Sia was the god of intelligence. None of this involved the displacement of other gods; the Egyptians, like other societies with polytheistic religions, sought to include and revere every conceivable aspect of the divine.

The Egyptians long resisted monotheism. Perhaps they believed it was too simple a concept to account for the complexity of the universe. When the New Kingdom pharaoh **Akhenaton** (reigned c. 1379–1362 BCE) banned all cults save that of Aton, the Sun disk (formerly an aspect of Re-Horus), the people rejected his ideas as heretical and abandoned them soon after his death. Some writers view Akhenaton as an early pioneer of monotheism, but little reason can be found to believe that his views had much influence either in Egypt or elsewhere. Akhenaton's greatest legacy was probably artistic, for he and his queen, Nefertiti, were great patrons, and the art of the Amarna Age, named after the new capital he constructed at Tell el-Amarna, was magnificent.

Of the many facets of Egyptian religion, the one that most intrigued outsiders was its concern with eternal life. Broadly speaking, the Egyptians thought of eternal life as a continuation of life on Earth, spent somewhere beyond the "roads of the west" (see *Two Faiths: Their Prayers and Monuments*). They also believed that, like the pharaoh, the virtuous dead would merge their identities with Osiris. This was possible because the human soul had many aspects or manifestations, including the *akh,* which emerged only after death. The fate of the wicked was not reassuring. Their sins were weighed in a scale against the feather of ma'at, and if the scale tipped, their souls were thrown to the monstrous, crocodile-like "devourer of hearts."

Science. The works attributed by Greek scholars to Hermes Trismegistus (Hermes the Thrice-Great, or Thoth) may be a compilation of ancient Egyptian sources on astronomy, astrology, and natural magic, although their origins remain the subject of controversy. It is indisputable, however, that the Greeks admired the Egyptians for their medical and scientific wisdom and would borrow heavily from them, especially after Ptolemy established a Greco-Egyptian dynasty in 323 BCE.

Egyptian culture, for all its concern with the unseen world, was at another level deeply practical. Its institutions, like its engineering, endured. Conservative, inward-looking, and less aggressive than many empires, it served as a bridge not only between Africa and Europe but also between historic times and an almost unimaginably distant past. Growing involvement with the outside world after about 900 BCE was in some ways a tragedy for the Egyptians as the country fell to a succession of foreign rulers. Most of them, whether Persian, Greek, or Roman, were content to preserve Egyptian institutions; only the triumph of Islam in the seventh century CE brought fundamental change. By this time, much of the Egyptian achievement had been incorporated, often unconsciously, into the development of the West.

CANAAN, PHOENICIA, AND PHILISTIA

The eastern shore of the Mediterranean has been inhabited since earliest times. Neanderthal and Cro-Magnon remains are found in close proximity to one another in the caves of Mt. Carmel, and agriculture was established on the eastern shore before it was introduced to Egypt or Mesopotamia. The Bible calls it "the land of milk and honey." The climate is benign, with mild winters and enough rainfall to support the Mediterranean triad of crops—wheat, olives, and grapes. But Canaan, a term that describes the entire region, was also a corridor and at times a disputed frontier between the civilizations of Mesopotamia and Egypt. Its inhabitants never enjoyed the political stability of the great river empires. The eastern shore of the Mediterranean was a world of small, aggressive city-states whose wealth and strategic position attracted the unwelcome attention of stronger powers.

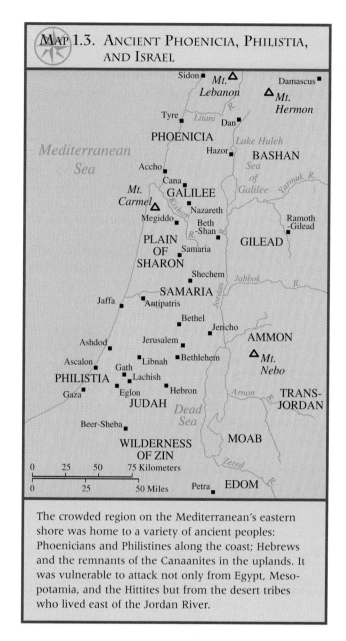

MAP 1.3. ANCIENT PHOENICIA, PHILISTIA, AND ISRAEL

The crowded region on the Mediterranean's eastern shore was home to a variety of ancient peoples: Phoenicians and Philistines along the coast; Hebrews and the remnants of the Canaanites in the uplands. It was vulnerable to attack not only from Egypt, Mesopotamia, and the Hittites but from the desert tribes who lived east of the Jordan River.

Ancient Palestine

Phoenicia. The first Phoenicians, as they were known to the Greeks, spoke a variety of Semitic dialects and moved into the northern coastal region of Canaan during the fourth millennium, superseding or blending with an earlier Neolithic population. Their first urban foundations, at Sidon, Byblos, and Ras Shamra (Ugarit), date from around 3000 BCE. Politically, Phoenician towns were governed by a hereditary king assisted by a council of elders. In practice, they were probably **oligarchies** in which policy was decided by the wealthy merchants who served on the council, but little is known of their civic life or even of their religious practices.

Trade. From the beginning, these and a host of other cities traded actively with both Egypt and Sumer. Their inhabitants were sailors, shipbuilders, and merchants who played a vital role in the process of cultural exchange. The Phoenicians were also skilled craftsmen. Carved furniture of wood and ivory was an obvious specialty, given the forests of cedar and other valuable woods that covered the nearby hills, but metalworking was equally important. The Phoenicians exported fine gold and copper jewelry, bronze tools, and weapons over a wide area. Around 1500 BCE, they seem to have invented the process of casting glass around a core of sand. Decorative glassware remained an important export throughout antiquity, and the Phoenician's descendants likely invented glassblowing in Roman times. The women of Sidon were known for their remarkable textiles incorporating the purple dye that symbolized royalty throughout the ancient world. The dye was extracted with great difficulty from the shell of the murex snail, a creature abundant in the harbors of Sidon and Tyre (Lebanon).

The First Alphabet. The Phoenicians are credited with inventing the first true alphabet, a phonetic script with twenty-two abstract symbols representing the consonants. Vowels, as in the other Semitic languages, were omitted. Their system is regarded as the greatest of all Phoenician contributions to Western culture because it could be mastered without the kind of extensive education given to professional scribes in Egypt or Mesopotamia. Literacy was now available to nearly everyone, but because the Phoenicians normally wrote with ink on papyrus, most of their records have perished.

The Philistines. Political crises were common. Phoenicia was invaded and at times ruled by both Egypt and the Hittites of Asia Minor. In 1190 BCE, a mysterious group known as the Sea People attacked the Egyptian delta. They were driven out but eventually established themselves along the coast south of Jaffa. They appear to have come from somewhere in the Aegean or western Asia Minor and to have brought with them the use of iron weapons. Little of their language has survived. Their gods appear to have been Canaanite deities adopted on arrival. The Sea People were great fighters and ironsmiths who dominated the iron trade in the Middle East for many years. Politically, their towns of Gaza, Ashkelon, Ashdod, Gath, and Eglon formed a powerful league known as Philistia or the Philistine confederacy. The Bible calls these people **Philistines,** and the Romans used Palestine, a term derived from that name, to describe the entire region.

The Hebrews. While the Philistines annexed the southern coast, the Hebrews, recently escaped from Egypt, invaded the Canaanite highlands. They fought bitterly with the Philistines, but after establishing a united kingdom of Israel that stretched from the Negev desert to Galilee, they formed an alliance of sorts with the Phoenicians of Tyre.

The Philistine and Hebrew incursions were related to broader population movements in the eastern Mediterranean. They coincide roughly with the displacement of the Ionians in Greece and a successful assault on the western portion of the Hittite empire by the Phrygians, a people who may have come from the same region as the Philistines. In Canaan proper, both Philistines and Hebrews were forced to contend with other peoples pushing in from the Arabian Desert and the country beyond the Jordan River.

Phoenician Colonies, Trade, and Exploration. Canaan was becoming crowded. The newcomers encountered a land that may already have been reaching its ecological limits after several millennia of human settlement. The closely spaced Phoenician cities now saw their territories greatly reduced, and with that their ability to feed their people. Led by Tyre, the Phoenicians began planting colonies from one end of the Mediterranean to the other. The first was at Utica in North Africa, supposedly founded by 1101 BCE. In the next three centuries, dozens of others were established in Cyprus, Sicily, Sardinia, and Spain. At least twenty-six such communities were in North Africa, the most important of which was Carthage, founded about 800 BCE near the present site of Tunis.

Like the colonies later established by the Greeks, those of the Phoenicians retained commercial and perhaps sentimental ties to their founding city but were for all practical purposes independent city-states. They did not normally try to establish control over large territories. They served as commercial stations that extracted wealth from the interior in return for goods from the civilizations of the eastern Mediterranean. They were also useful as safe harbors for Phoenician traders.

FIGURE 1.10 *A Phoenician Clay Mask.* Designed to frighten away evil spirits, this 7-inch mask was found in a tomb at the site of the Phoenician colony of Tharros, Sardinia, and imported from Carthage in the sixth century BCE. The Phoenicians typically buried their dead in tombs with their feet pointing toward an east-facing entrance. Written spells and gifts such as terra-cotta figures invoked the god's protection. Phoenician contacts with Sardinia trace back to around 1000 BCE, but it was not until the eighth century BCE that they established permanent colonies on the island. One of the most important was Tharros, a major trading center.

By the seventh century BCE, Phoenician ships had reached Britain in search of precious tin, and Phoenician caravan routes based in the North African colonies had penetrated the regions south of the Sahara. The Carthaginians later claimed to have circumnavigated Africa, and at the very beginnings of the age of colonization, Hiram I of Tyre and his ally Solomon of Israel sent triennial expeditions to Ophir, a place now thought to have been on the coast of India. Wherever they went, the Phoenicians carried their system of writing together with the ideas and products of a dozen other cultures. Though their history was all too often neglected or written by their enemies, they played a vital role in the establishment of Mediterranean civilization.

ANCIENT ISRAEL

The history of ancient Israel is based on the collection of writings known as the Bible and on the archeological record compiled by hundreds of excavations. The age and complexity of these sources, together with their importance to the religious beliefs of Jews, Christians, and Muslims alike, have led to great controversy, but the basic outline of that history is accepted by a majority of scholars.

Historical Development

The *Hapiru*, who entered Canaan around 1200 BCE, came from Egypt. The name is thought to mean outsider or marauder and is the probable root of the term *Hebrew*. The invaders were a Semitic group of mixed ancestry whose forebears had left Mesopotamia some 600 years earlier during Babylon's conquest of Sumeria. According to tradition, their patriarch Abraham came from Ur. They lived for several generations as pastoralists in the trans–Jordan highlands and then emigrated to Egypt, probably at about the time of the Hyksos domination. With the revival of the New Kingdom under native Egyptian dynasties, the situation of the Semitic immigrants became more difficult. Oppressed by a pharaoh (or pharaohs) whose identity remains the subject of controversy, a group of them fled to Sinai under the leadership of **Moses.** Moses, whose Egyptian name helps confirm the biblical story of his origins, molded the refugees into the people of Israel and transmitted to them the Ten Commandments, the ethical code that forms the basis of Judaism, Christianity, and Islam.

According to the Bible, the Israelites spent 40 years in the Sinai desert before beginning the conquest of the Canaanite Highlands. The period between 1200 and 1020 BCE appears to have been one of constant struggle between the Hebrews and the other peoples of the region. As described in the Book of Judges, the people of Israel were at this time a loose confederacy of tribes united by a common religion and military necessity. After they subdued the Canaanite highlanders, Saul (reigned c. 1020–1000 BCE) established a monarchy of sorts in response to a military threat from the Philistines, but it was not until after his death that David (ruled 1000–961 BCE) consolidated the territories between Beersheba and the Sea of Galilee into the kingdom of Israel.

Under David's son Solomon (reigned 961–922 BCE), Israel became a regional power. Commerce flourished, and the king used his wealth to construct a lavish palace as well as the First Temple at Jerusalem, a structure heavily influenced by Phoenician models. But Solomon's glory came at a price. Heavy taxation and religious disputes led to rebellion after his death, and Israel divided into two kingdoms: Israel in the north and Judah in the south. Israel was a loosely knit, aristocratic monarchy occupying the land later known as Samaria. Judah, with its walled capital of Jerusalem, was poorer but more cohesive. Both, in the end, would fall prey to more powerful neighbors.

Invasions. The danger came from the north. In what is now Syria, remnants of the Hittite empire had survived as petty states. Many of them were annexed in the twelfth century by the Aramaeans, a Semitic people whose most important center was Damascus. The Aramaic language would become the vernacular of the Middle East—it was the language, for example, in which Jesus preached. However, Syria remained politically unstable. Assyria, once more in an expansionist phase and enriched by the conquest of Mesopotamia, filled the vacuum. The ministates of the region could not long expect to resist such a juggernaut. For a time, an alliance between Israel and Damascus held the Assyrians at bay, but by 722 BCE, both had fallen to the armies of the Assyrian conquerors Tiglath-pileser and Sargon II. Sennacherib (ruled 705–682 BCE) annexed Philistia and Phoenicia, after which Esarhaddon (ruled 680–689 BCE) and Assurbanipal (reigned 669–c. 627 BCE), the greatest and most cultivated of the Assyrian emperors, conquered Egypt. The tiny kingdom of Judah survived only by allying itself with the conquerors.

Babylonian Captivity and Diaspora. The end came in 587 BCE. A resurgent Babylonia had destroyed Assyria by allying itself with the Medes and adopting Assyrian military tactics. In a general settling of scores, the Babylonian king Nebuchadnezzar II then sacked Jerusalem, destroyed the temple, and carried the Judaean leadership off to captivity in Babylon. Many of these people returned after the Persians conquered Babylon in 539 BCE, but the Israelites or Jews, a name derived from the kingdom of Judah, did not establish another independent state until 142 BCE. Judaea and Samaria would be ruled for 400 years by Persians and by Hellenistic Greeks, while thousands of Jews, faced with the desolation of their homeland, dispersed to the corners of the known world.

Religion of Israel

Ancient Israel was not a material success. Its people were never numerous or rich, and it was only briefly a regional power. Its contributions to art and technology were negligible, yet few societies have had a greater influence on those that followed. The reason for this paradox is that the Jews developed a religion that was unlike anything else in the ancient world. It was not wholly without precedent, for ideas were borrowed from Mesopotamian and perhaps from Egyptian sources. Moreover, although inspired by revelations that can be dated with some accuracy, its basic practices evolved over time. But if the history of the beliefs themselves can be traced like those of any other religion, the Jewish concept of the divine was nevertheless revolutionary.

One God. Its central feature was its **monotheism:** a vision of one God who was indivisible. Yahweh, the God of the Jews, could not be represented or understood in visual terms, nor could he be described. The name is formed from the Hebrew word *YHWH* and appears to be a derivative of the verb "to be," indicating that the deity is eternal and changeless. Creator of the universe and absolute in power, the God of Israel was at the same time a personal god who acted in history and took an interest in the lives of individual Jews.

Ethical Behavior. Above all, the worship of Yahweh demanded ethical behavior on the part of the worshipper. This was extraordinary, because while the Mesopotamians had emphasized the helplessness of humans and Akhenaton had thought of a single, all-powerful god, the idea that a god might be served by good deeds as well as by ritual and sacrifice was new.

A Covenant with God. The ethical concept was founded on the idea of a covenant or agreement made first between God and Abraham and reaffirmed at the time of the exodus from Egypt (see *Biblical Sources of Judaism*). In return for God's favor, the Hebrews would worship Him only and obey His laws. Failure to observe them could bring terrible punishment. The fall of Jerusalem to Nebuchadnezzar was thought to be an example of what could happen if the Jews lapsed in their devotion, and a rich prophetic tradition developed that called upon the people of Israel to avoid God's wrath by behaving in an ethical manner. The Jews thus became the first people to write long narratives of human events as opposed to mere chronologies and king lists. Much of the Jewish Bible is devoted to the interaction between God and the children of Israel and is intended to provide a record of God's judgments that will help His followers to discern the divine will. Therefore, although not history

as the Greeks would write it, the Bible remains the first attempt to provide a coherent account of past events.

The Mosaic Code of Law. The primary expression of Yahweh's will is found in the Ten Commandments and in the subsequent elaboration of the **Mosaic Law.** The Ten Commandments, brought down by Moses from Mt. Sinai and delivered to the people of Israel before their entry into Canaan, formed the basis of an elaborate legal and moral code that governed virtually every aspect of life and conduct. Like the concept of God, the law evolved over time. Refined and amplified by generations of priests, prophets, and teachers, it remains to this day the foundation of Jewish life.

Certain features of Mosaic Law—such as the principle of an eye for an eye, a tooth for a tooth—recall Babylonian precedents, but it went much further by seeking to govern both private and public behavior. Dietary regulations were set forth in great detail along with rules for sexual conduct and the proper form of religious observances. Although legalistic in form, Mosaic Law offered a comprehensive guide to ethical behavior whose force transcended social or political sanctions (see *Biblical Sources of Judaism*). It was intended not only as legislation but also as a prescription for the godly life. This concept of righteousness as an essential duty, together with many of the specific ethical principles enshrined in the *Torah,* or first five books of the Jewish Bible, would later be adopted by both Christianity and Islam. The influence of Mosaic Law on Western thought and society has therefore been incalculable.

Social Order. The society that produced these revolutionary concepts was not in other respects much different from its neighbors. From a federation of nomadic herdsmen initially organized into twelve tribes, the earliest Jews evolved into settled agriculturalists after their arrival in Canaan. Tribal practices such as the communal ownership of resources gave way to a system in which families generally owned land and water as private property. Inevitably, some families were more successful than others, and many became substantial landholders with tenants and perhaps a few slaves. As in Mesopotamia, these families were often extended and always patriarchal in organization. A gradual process of urbanization increased the importance of crafts and trade, but the basic family structure remained.

Status of Women. In earliest times, fathers held absolute authority over wives and children. As ethical standards evolved, patriarchy was increasingly tempered by a sense of responsibility and mercy. However, the status of women was lower in ancient Israel than among the Hittites, the Egyptians, or the Mesopotamians. Under the Judges who ruled Israel from the invasion of Canaan to the emergence of the monarchy, women presided as priestesses over certain festivals. As

BIBLICAL SOURCES OF JUDAISM

The three passages that follow are taken from the *Torah*, the first five books of what Christians call the Old Testament. They illustrate three major themes within ancient, and indeed, modern Judaism: the belief and trust in a special relationship between the God of Israel and the Jewish people, a strong emphasis on ethical behavior, and the minute regulation of private life by Mosaic Law.

The Covenant (Exod. 19:1–9)

This passage describes the making of the covenant between the Hebrews and their God that forms the basis of the Jewish religion and the concept of the Jews as a chosen people.

On the third new moon after the Israelites had gone out of the land of Egypt, on that very day, they came into the wilderness of Sinai. . . . Israel camped there in front of the mountain. Then Moses went up to God, the LORD called to him from the mountain, saying, "Thus you shall say to the house of Jacob, and tell the Israelites: You have seen what I did to the Egyptians, and how I bore you on eagle's wings and brought you to myself. Now, therefore, if you obey my voice and keep my covenant, you shall be my treasured possession out of all the peoples. Indeed, the whole earth is mine, but you shall be for me a priestly kingdom and a holy nation. These are the words that you shall speak to the Israelites." So Moses came, summoned the elders of the people, and set before them all these words that the LORD had commanded him. The people all answered as one: "Everything that the LORD has spoken we will do." Moses reported the words of the people to the LORD. Then the LORD said to Moses, "I am going to come to you in a dense cloud, in order that the people may hear when I speak to you and so trust you ever after.

The Prophet Isaiah: Social Justice (Isa. 1:11–17)

This passage, attributed to Isaiah of Jerusalem in the mid-eighth century BCE, demonstrates the increasing emphasis on social justice in Hebrew religious thought.

What to me is the multitude of your sacrifices? says the LORD. I have had enough of burnt offerings of rams and the fat of fed beasts; I do not delight in the blood of bulls, or of lambs, or of he-goats. When you come to appear before me, who requires of you this trampling of my courts? Bring no more vain offerings; incense is an abomination to me. New moon and sabbath and the calling of assemblies—I cannot endure iniquity and solemn assembly. Your new moons and your appointed feasts my soul hates; they have become a burden to me, I am weary of bearing them. When you spread forth your hands I will hide my eyes from you; even though you make many prayers, I will not listen; your hands are full of blood. Wash yourselves; make yourselves clean; remove the evil of your doings from before my eyes; cease to do evil, learn to do good; seek justice, correct oppression; defend the fatherless, plead for the widow.

Leviticus: The Impurity of Women (Lev. 15:12–22)

These passages of the Mosaic Law are part of a much longer section concerned with impurity; that is, those conditions under which performing religious rituals is not permissible. Note that, although men, too, could be impure, the purification of women took longer and the amount of time required for purification after the birth of a girl was twice as long as that following the birth of a boy.

If a man has an emission of semen, he shall bathe his whole body in water, and be unclean until the evening. Everything made of cloth or skin on which the semen falls shall be washed with water and be unclean until the evening. If a man lies with a woman and has an emission of semen, both of them shall bathe in water and be unclean until the evening. When a woman has a discharge of blood that is her regular discharge from her body, she shall be in her impurity for seven days, and whoever touches her shall be unclean until the evening. Everything on which she lies during her impurity shall be unclean; everything also on which she sits shall be unclean. Whoever touches her bed shall wash his clothes, and bathe in water, and be unclean until the evening. Whoever touches anything on which she sits shall wash his clothes and bathe in water, and be unclean until the evening.

---

interpretation of Mosaic Law evolved, women's participation in religious life was restricted (see *Biblical Sources of Judaism*). The worship of Yahweh demanded purity as well as holiness, and women were regarded as ritually impure during menstruation and after childbirth. They were also exempted from regular prayer and other rituals on the theory that they should not be distracted from child care. In effect, they were excluded from direct participation in all public rites and were segregated from men even as observers because their presence was thought to be distracting. The proper role of women was in the home, which was central to religious life.

Families arranged marriages for their children and sealed them by contract as in Babylon, but only men could initiate divorce. No provision was made for a dowry, which usually meant that a man could divorce his wife without financial loss. Divorce was nevertheless uncommon because Mosaic Law and Jewish custom placed a premium on the family. Polygyny and concubinage, although permitted, were rare for economic reasons, and adultery was punishable by death.

Within the home, women received more respect than their legal position might indicate. They had the right to name the children and were responsible for their early instruction in moral and practical matters. Theory aside, they often controlled the everyday life of the household. Furthermore, Jewish literature reveals none of the contempt for women and their capacities sometimes found in the writings of ancient Greece. The Bible abounds in heroic women, such as Esther, Rachel, and Deborah, and the Book of Proverbs holds the value of a good woman as "beyond rubies." But the patriarchal nature of Jewish society coupled with the divine origin of Mosaic Law would have a profound impact on subsequent history. Christianity, Islam, and modern Judaism absorbed from the Bible the idea that women's exclusion from many aspects of public and religious life was ordained by God.

Children. The Mosaic emphasis on family placed a high value on children. The law forbade infanticide, a practice common in other ancient cultures, and prescribed child-rearing practices. On the eighth day after birth, male children were circumcised as a sign of their covenant with God. They received religious instruction from their fathers and at age 13 assumed the full religious responsibilities of an adult. Eldest sons, who were especially honored, had extra responsibilities. Both boys and girls were expected to help in the fields and in the home, but gender roles were carefully preserved. Boys learned their father's trade or cared for the livestock. Girls gleaned (gathered up grains that remained in the fields) after the harvest and kept the house supplied with water from wells that, in town at least, were usually communal. What remained in the fields after gleaning was left for the poor.

Charity. The obligation to assist the poor and helpless—symbolized by this minor, yet divinely established, injunction—was central to the Jewish conception of righteousness. A comprehensive ideal of charity and communal responsibility gradually evolved from such precepts and, like monotheism itself, spread throughout Western society long after Israel as a political entity had ceased to exist.

CONCLUSION

For all their differences, the ancient societies of the Near East formed part of a larger, interconnected world in which the Mediterranean Sea facilitated cultural borrowing through trade and migration. Conditions in the great river valleys of Egypt and Mesopotamia had demanded the organization of resources on an unprecedented scale. Writing and mathematics were invented to facilitate that organization. These developments marked the beginning of Western civilization, for writing enabled people to transmit the memory of their achievements to others. The Phoenician invention of the alphabet simplified the process of communication and was quickly adopted by other cultures. Trade, warfare, and colonization spread Egyptian and Mesopotamian ideas throughout the Mediterranean world. Among the chief beneficiaries of this cultural ferment were the Greeks, who would adopt and modify some of the mathematical, scientific, and philosophical theories of the Near East for their own purposes and transmit them to the modern world. The transmission of Jewish religious ideas took longer, but the vision of a single deity whose worship demands righteousness and ethical behavior would one day become the foundation of Christianity and Islam as well as modern Judaism.

Review Questions

- What was "the biological old regime," and how did it arise from the invention of agriculture?
- How did the status of women in Mesopotamia compare with their status in Egypt and ancient Israel? In what ways could women exert their influence?
- Why did the civilizations of the ancient Middle East develop writing, mathematics, and eventually alphabets?
- Why was ancient Egypt more politically stable than Mesopotamia?
- How did the religion of ancient Israel differ from that of other ancient societies, and how did it influence the later development of Christianity and Islam?

For Further Study

Readings

Burl, Aubrey, *Great Stone Circles: Fable, Fiction, Facts* (New Haven, CT: Yale, 1999). A no-nonsense analysis of twelve sites, including Stonehenge.

Cohen, Mark N., *The Food Crisis in Prehistory: Overpopulation and the Origins of Agriculture* (New Haven, CT: Yale, 1977). A standard work on the beginnings of the Neolithic Revolution.

Markoe, Glenn E. *The Phoenicians* (Berkeley: University of California Press, 2000). A, brief but thorough and up-to-date survey.

Niditch, Susan, *Ancient Israelite Religion* (New York: Oxford, 1997). Places religious issues in their historic context.

Web Site

http://www.fordham.edu/halsall/ancient/asbook.html
   The Internet Ancient History Sourcebook offers a broad range of materials and information on all of the ancient societies discussed in the text.

THE ANCIENT MIDDLE EAST

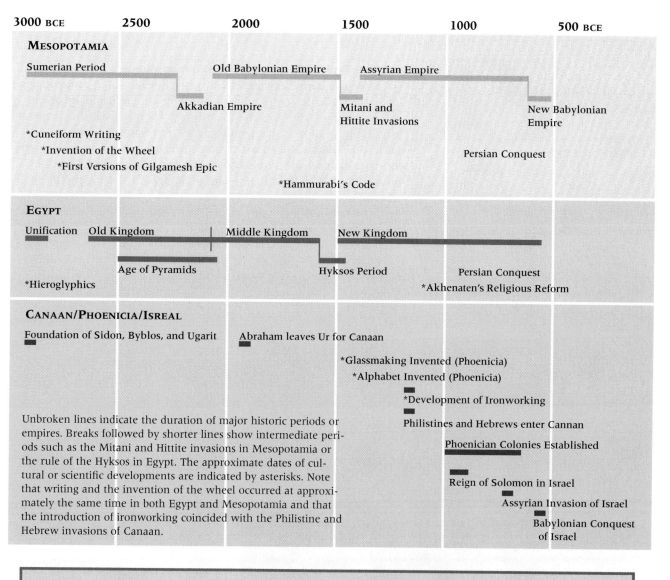

| 3000 BCE | 2500 | 2000 | 1500 | 1000 | 500 BCE |

MESOPOTAMIA

Sumerian Period

Old Babylonian Empire

Assyrian Empire

Akkadian Empire

Mitani and Hittite Invasions

New Babylonian Empire

*Cuneiform Writing

*Invention of the Wheel

*First Versions of Gilgamesh Epic

Persian Conquest

*Hammurabi's Code

EGYPT

Unification   Old Kingdom   Middle Kingdom   New Kingdom

Age of Pyramids   Hyksos Period   Persian Conquest

*Hieroglyphics   *Akhenaten's Religious Reform

CANAAN/PHOENICIA/ISREAL

Foundation of Sidon, Byblos, and Ugarit   Abraham leaves Ur for Canaan

*Glassmaking Invented (Phoenicia)

*Alphabet Invented (Phoenicia)

*Development of Ironworking

Philistines and Hebrews enter Cannan

Phoenician Colonies Established

Reign of Solomon in Israel

Assyrian Invasion of Israel

Babylonian Conquest of Israel

Unbroken lines indicate the duration of major historic periods or empires. Breaks followed by shorter lines show intermediate periods such as the Mitani and Hittite invasions in Mesopotamia or the rule of the Hyksos in Egypt. The approximate dates of cultural or scientific developments are indicated by asterisks. Note that writing and the invention of the wheel occurred at approximately the same time in both Egypt and Mesopotamia and that the introduction of ironworking coincided with the Philistine and Hebrew invasions of Canaan.

FOCUS QUESTIONS

- How did geography shape the development of independent city-states in ancient Greece?
- How did changes in Greek military tactics influence the political development of democracy?
- How did the Greeks and Persians come into conflict, and why did the Greeks win?
- What were the causes of the Peloponnesian Wars, and why did Athens, with all its relative wealth and naval power, lose?

Chapter 2

ANCIENT GREECE TO THE END OF THE PELOPONNESIAN WARS

As the first year of the great Peloponnesian War drew to a close, the Athenian statesman Pericles delivered a funeral oration to honor those who had died in the struggle. Praising the men who died and the city for which they fought, the speech was designed to lift the spirits of a people at war. Extolling Athens for its hymns, games, and dramatic spectacles that made it the source of all that was good in life, its openness to strangers and free inquiry that made it "the school of Greece," the speech reflected the fundamental Greek belief in the value of the *polis*. To the ancient Greeks, life centered on the city-state or **polis,** which provided far more than a place to live. Its rituals and institutions formed their personal character and made them who they were. Other ancient peoples, the Phoenicians, for example, had lived in city-states, but the Greeks developed from their concept of the polis a unique and immensely vital culture—a culture that in many ways became the foundation of Western civilization as a whole.

Chapter 2 traces the development of Greek society from Minoan times to the end of the Peloponnesian Wars. The heart of that process—the evolution of the polis—takes us from a group of simple fortified settlements to the great cities of the fifth century BCE, from a long period of dominance by aristocratic elites, through the rule of tyrants, to the emergence of the first true democracies in recorded history. We will survey the social institutions common to Greek society as a whole and look at daily life in two very different *poleis* (the plural of polis)—democratic Athens and conservative, aristocratic Sparta. This chapter ends with the two great crises of ancient Greek history: the Persian War, which preserved Greek independence, and the Peloponnesian Wars, which set the stage for its eventual loss.

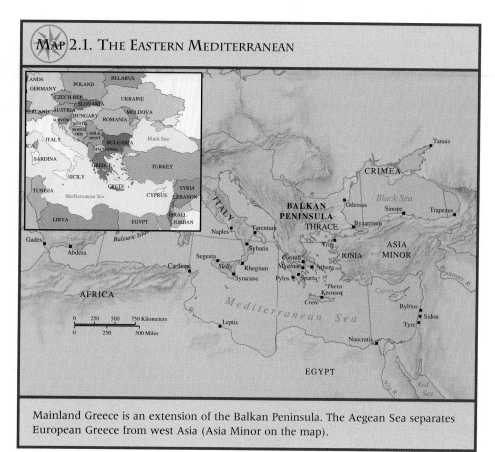

MAP 2.1. THE EASTERN MEDITERRANEAN

Mainland Greece is an extension of the Balkan Peninsula. The Aegean Sea separates European Greece from west Asia (Asia Minor on the map).

EARLY AEGEAN CULTURES TO 800 BCE

The eastern Mediterranean Sea was like a great lake that facilitated trade, communication, and cultural borrowing. The societies that surrounded it, Phoenicians, Egyptians, Greeks, and many others, shared similar diets, ideas, and institutions. The Greeks, for example, took their alphabet from the Phoenicians and some of their philosophical and scientific ideas from Egypt; their social organization into city-states bore a superficial resemblance to the Phoenician city-state.

Minoan Crete—The First Aegean Civilization (3000–1400 BCE). The Aegean Sea, with its innumerable islands, has been a crossroads of trade and communication since the first sailors ventured forth. To the south is Crete, the navigational center of the eastern Mediterranean in ancient times. Approximately 150 miles long and no more than 35 miles wide, it lies across the southern end of the Aegean Sea, about 60 miles from the southernmost extremity of the Greek mainland and not more than 120 miles from the coast of west Asia. Africa is only 200 miles to the south. But the importance of Crete was determined less by raw distances than by wind and current. Ships westbound from Egypt

had to follow the currents north along the Phoenician coast and then west to Crete before proceeding to the ports of Italy or North Africa. Phoenician ships on the way to Carthage or the Strait of Gibraltar did the same, passing either to the north or the south of the island. Most preferred Crete's northern shore because it offered more sandy inlets where their ships could anchor for the night or be hauled ashore for repairs and cleaning. The same harbors offered easy access to the Greek mainland, the Ionian islands of the Aegean, and Troy. Crete was therefore a natural and convenient way station for the transshipment of Egyptian and Phoenician goods.

A people of unknown origins arrived on the island of Crete before 4000 BCE. They found not only a strategic location but a land that was well suited for Neolithic agriculture. Crete's mountains rise to more than 8,000 feet, but the island has rich valleys and coastal plains that provide abundant grain. The climate is generally mild. Perfection is marred only by summer droughts, winter gales, and devastating earthquakes that are perhaps the most conspicuous feature of the island's history.

The civilization that developed on Crete arose at about the same time as those of Egypt and Mesopotamia. It is usually called **Minoan,** after Minos, a legendary ruler who became part of Greek mythology as a creature who was half man and half bull. Minoan (Min-o'-un) society's chief characteristics were the early manufacture of bronze and the construction of enormous palaces that combined political, religious, and economic functions. The Minoans constructed four main palace complexes—at Knossos, Phaistos, Zakros, and Mallia—and the ruins of other large houses are found throughout the island. All are built around large rectangular courts that the Minoans apparently used for religious and public ceremonies. Minoan builders covered their walls with thin layers of shiny gypsum or decorated them with naturalistic wall paintings. The upper levels of the palaces had decorative staircases and colonnades that resembled those of Egyptian temples. Below, they built innumerable storerooms and a system of drains for the removal of wastes and rainwater. So elaborate was the floor plan that *Labyrinth*, the Greek name for the palace at Knossos after the heraldic *labrys*, or two-headed axe of the Minoan royal house, became the common word for a maze.

FIGURE 2.1 *Bull Leaping at Knossos.* This fresco from the east wing of the palace at Knossos portrays a man holding the horns of a bull while a woman somersaults over its back and another woman waits to catch her. Whether this was a sport, a religious ritual, or both is not known. But the presence of women in such an activity indicates a measure of gender equality that would not be found among the Greeks.

The presence of such vast storage facilities indicates that Minoan rulers played an important part in the distribution of goods, but little is known of Minoan social or political life. The early language of Crete, written at first in hieroglyphic characters derived from Egyptian models, has not yet been deciphered. A later linear script is equally unreadable. Only the so-called Linear B, dating from the last period of Minoan history, has been translated and reveals an early form of the Greek language, probably introduced by a new Mycenaean dynasty from the mainland that seized control of the island around 1400 BCE.

Minoan religious beliefs are also obscure. Wall paintings and statuary portray women in priestly roles, and the dominant cult was almost certainly that of the Earth Mother, the fertility goddess whose worship in the Mediterranean basin dates from Paleolithic times. Other paintings show young women and men vaulting over the heads of bulls and doing gymnastic routines on their backs. This dangerous sport probably had religious significance and was performed in the palace courtyards, but its exact purpose is unknown. In any case, the prominence of women in Minoan art and the range of activities in which they were portrayed indicate a measure of gender equality that would not be found among the Greeks.

Troy. At the northern end of the Aegean Sea stood Troy, the earliest of whose nine cities, each one built upon the ruins of its predecessors, dates from before 3000 BCE. Built on a ridge, Troy overlooked the southern entry to the Dardanelles, or Hellespont, the long narrow waterway through which ships must pass to enter the Sea of Marmara, the Bosporus, and the Black Sea. The current in the strait runs southward at about 3 knots (approximately 3.5 mph), and the prevailing winds are from the north, making the strait passable only under the most favorable of conditions to early ships powered solely by oarsmen and small sails. Fortunately, a small harbor just inside its mouth allowed ships to lie at anchor while they awaited a favorable wind or offloaded Aegean goods for transshipment by land. Troy controlled the harbor as well as that part of the Dardanelles offering the best crossing point on the land route from Europe and Asia. The city had obvious strategic importance and grew rich from the tolls it extracted from passing merchants.

The Mycenaeans—Precursors of the Ancient Greeks (2000–1200 BCE). Mainland Greece is an extension of the Balkan Peninsula bounded by the Aegean Sea on the east and the Adriatic Sea on the west. It is, as it was in antiquity, a rugged land—mountainous, rocky, and dry, with much of the rainfall coming in the autumn and winter months. Large areas suitable for cultivation are rare, and the narrow Greek valleys provide only modest amounts of rich land. Deforestation, largely the

result of overgrazing, was already well advanced by the fifth century BCE. For much of its history the relative poverty and rugged geography of Greece protected it from foreign conquest. The same dubious blessings made it difficult, if not impossible, for any one settlement to achieve regional dominance. The result was a society outward-looking, commercial, and fiercely resistant to the need for unity.

The **Mycenaeans** (My-see′-nee-uns), so-called after Mycenae, one of their many cities on the Greek mainland, spoke an early form of Greek and may have occupied Macedonia or Thessaly before establishing themselves on the Greek mainland. Their chief centers—apart from Mycenae and its companion fortress, Tiryns, in the Peloponnese—were Athens on the rich peninsula of Attica and Thebes in the Boeotian (boh-ee′-shun) plain. All were flourishing by 2000 BCE.

Kings or chieftains ruled each of the Mycenaean communities and apparently distributed commodities in the traditional way. They carried on an extensive trade with Crete and Egypt and built vast palaces and tombs using cut stones of as much as 100 tons apiece. The palaces, although similar in function to those on Crete, were heavily fortified and more symmetrical in design, but with the same spacious apartments and colonnaded porches on the upper levels. Below were vast storerooms, some of them heated to keep major exports such as olive oil from congealing in the winter cold. The Mycenaeans kept voluminous accounts of commercial transactions, and their careful, hardheaded organization of vast enterprises characterized Mycenaean life.

The earliest tombs were shaft graves of a kind found in many other parts of Europe: underground burial chambers reached by a horizontal stone-lined passage. Later, vast **corbeled** vaults became common; in a corbeled vault, each stone in the upper walls of the tomb extends slightly beyond the one below it to form a kind of domed ceiling. The Mycenaeans buried their dead with magnificent treasures, for they collected art and luxury goods from other cultures as well as from their own. They were also skilled metalworkers. Their bronze armor and weapons, like their gold jewelry and face masks, were among the finest produced in the ancient world.

Aside from their material culture, the Mycenaeans remain something of a mystery. **Homer,** the semimythical poet who stands at the beginnings of Greek culture, made them the heroes of his *The Iliad.* This great epic, discussed in more detail later, tells the story of the Mycenaeans' successful siege of Troy, an event partially supported by archaeological evidence. The society he de-

FIGURE 2.2 *The Upper-Body Armor of a Mycenaean Warrior.* This bronze cuirass and helmet from the fifteenth century BCE consists of a collar, shoulder pads, a breast-plate, and an articulated midsection made from three broad bronze belts to protect the wearer's midsection while permitting freedom of movement. It was found in a Mycenaean tomb at Dendra.

scribes, however, is unlike that revealed by Mycenaean ruins. Homer's Mycenaeans cremate, rather than entomb, their dead and fight as individual champions. Homer probably described a much later world—that of the ninth century BCE in which he lived—and attributed its values to his Mycenaean predecessors. By the time Homer wrote, the Aegean world bore little resemblance to that of the Minoans and Mycenaeans.

The Dark Age Migrations (1200–800 BCE)

The population movements that began around 1200 BCE inaugurated a kind of dark age about which little is known. Greeks of the classical age believed that the Dorians, a Greek-speaking people from the north, swept into the peninsula and established themselves in the Peloponnese and other Mycenaean centers. Recent scholarship casts doubt on this theory; some historians believe that a Dorian population already lived in the peninsula and came to power by taking advantage of disunity among the Mycenaeans. In any case, the Dorians destroyed Mycenae but apparently bypassed Athens, which became the conduit for a vast eastward migration. Thousands of refugees, their lands taken by newcomers, fled to Attica, the region surrounding Athens. Taking ships from Athens, they colonized the islands of the Aegean and the southwestern coast of Asia. The migration of these Ionian Greeks displaced other peoples, who flowed eastward into southwest Asia. The Phrygians who toppled the weakened fragments of the Hittite Empire and the Philistines who descended on the Canaanite coast were almost certainly among them, for all of these events occurred at about the same time.

By the ninth century BCE, the Greek world was divided into two major subgroups: the Dorians, who dominated most of the peninsula, and the Ionians, who inhabited the regions of Attica, Euboea (you-be'-a) and the Aegean islands. They spoke different Greek dialects but shared many aspects of a common culture. Both groups thought of the Greek-speaking world as **Hellas** and referred to themselves as **Hellenes.**

THE DEVELOPMENT OF THE GREEK POLIS TO 500 BCE

The Dorians and Ionians tended to settle in high places that they could fortify against their enemies. After expelling some of the existing population and subjugating others, each community—and there were scores of them—claimed full sovereign rights and vigorously defended its independence against all comers. Some communities had minuscule populations and armies numbering no more than 80 or 100 men. Even the largest, including Athens and Corinth, were small by modern standards. Many of the settlements did not possess enough land to support their populations. Cooperation among them was always fragile and warfare endemic. The mountainous terrain of Greece with its many valleys and no permanent roads enhanced a community's isolation. Furthermore, security from threats outside the Greek peninsula during this period made possible the political decentralization within. The Greek city-states developed after the Hittites had fallen and when Egypt was in decline. The great Asian empires were not yet a threat.

These early communities were the precursors of the polis (poh'-lis), the basis of Greek political and social life. Each polis, whether Dorian or Ionian, claimed the

FIGURE 2.3 *The Site of an Early Polis.* The ancient acropolis of Corinth, shown here with ruins at the top, provides a sense of how the early poleis must have looked. Corinth became a large city, but the first settlement would have been small enough to fit on this inaccessible but secure site.

primary loyalty of its inhabitants. Composed in theory of those who shared a common ancestry and worshipped the same gods, the polis molded the character of its inhabitants and operated as the focus of their lives. In practice, this meant that only those born to one of the local tribes or clans could claim citizenship. Foreigners, including Greeks born in another polis, might be allowed residency but had no political rights. A god or goddess served as each city's patron, and the rites and ceremonies for that god or goddess formed an important part of civic culture. To Greeks of the later classical period, the polis was far more than a city-state; it was the only form of social organization in which the individual's full potential could be achieved. To live apart from the polis was to live as a beast.

Governments in the Early Poleis. Until about 750 BCE, the governments of these communities reflected their quasi-tribal origins. Membership in a recognized tribe or clan entitled a man and his family to the protection of the polis and obligated him to support it, but it did not necessarily give him a voice in its governance. Actual power rested in the hands of those who demonstrated prowess on the battlefield. Some communities had a king. This form of government was called a **monarchy,** a Greek term meaning "rule by one." Kings might inherit their thrones or be elected, but they always governed with the assistance of a council of warrior aristocrats. Other governments were **aristocratic**— another Greek word meaning, literally, "rule by the best." Warriors descended from families that had played a leading role in the city's foundation held power by hereditary right. The best fighters generally had the greatest personal influence. In either system, birth and military prowess granted more status than wealth did. Warfare between the early cities, aimed largely at seizing or destroying a neighboring polis' crops, reflected

FIGURE 2.4 *Hoplite Warfare.* This vase painting from the seventh century BCE is one of the few surviving portraits of Hoplites at war. The helmets and armor portrayed were too expensive for the poorer citizens who therefore served as archers or support troops. As in the Homeric era, heraldic devices similar to those of the Western middle ages decorate the shields and identify the warriors. On the left a piper leads another phalanx into battle.

the organization of society. Individual champions fought one another with sword and lance, while tactics in the larger sense were unknown. It was a primitive form of warfare suited only to a simple society. As the Greek cities grew, armies became larger and the usefulness of individual champions declined.

The Hoplite Phalanx and the Beginnings of Democracy. The period of aristocratic dominance came to an end with the adoption of the hoplite (hop'-lite) phalanx, a new tactical system that required the participation of every able-bodied freeman who could afford arms and armor. The **hoplite phalanx** was a formation of trained spearmen who fought shoulder to shoulder in a rectangle that was normally eight ranks deep. As long as no one broke ranks, the phalanx was almost invincible against a frontal attack by horse or foot and could clear the field of traditional infantry at will. Only another band of hoplites could stand against them. Grounding the sides of the formation against natural or humanmade obstacles, an easy task in the rugged Greek countryside, prevented flanking attacks by cavalry. Missile weapons (arrows or thrown javelins) presented only a minor threat because the hoplite's bronze armor was heavy and enemy archers usually had to fight in the open. After the first volley, the phalanx could cover the distance of a bowshot in the time it took to fire a second or third arrow, and the archers would be forced to flee in disorder. The major weakness of the formation was its immobility. Maneuvering was difficult and pursuit impossible without breaking ranks. Keeping ranks reduced the number of casualties but made it difficult to achieve decisive results. Breaking the formation usually resulted in catastrophe.

The adoption of the hoplite phalanx forced cities to adopt more representative forms of government. Men who fought for the polis could not be denied a say in its governance. Whereas slaves, women, and foreigners—meaning those who had been born in another polis—were excluded from public life, all male citizens now expected to participate in matters of justice and public policy. Even those too poor to equip themselves as hoplites served as support troops or rowed in the city's galleys, for many Greek cities maintained a navy as well. Although wealth and heredity still counted, the new warfare greatly increased the number of those who participated in public life. In some of the poleis it marked the beginnings of democracy.

The Age of Tyrants. Still, **democracy,** Greek for "rule by the people," grew slowly, for the aristocrats resisted change. Efforts to maintain their traditional privileges caused disorder in every polis, and the late eighth and early seventh centuries BCE were times of civic conflict. When the leader of a faction, whether popular or aristocratic, triumphed over his adversaries, he became a **tyrant,** or dictator. The more capable tyrants served a useful, if unappreciated, historical purpose. They developed new administrative structures and, by weakening old loyalties based on tribe or district, focused a broader patriotism on the polis. Nearly every city accepted a tyrant at one time or another because rule by one man was better than endless civil war, but most Greeks regarded tyrannical rule as an aberration, a temporary suspension of the laws rather than a permanent institution. Most cities eventually overthrew their tyrants and replaced them with some form of government that represented the will of the community. This might be a narrowly based oligarchy, as at Corinth, or a true democracy of the kind that evolved gradually at Athens. **Oligarchy** means "rule by the few." In most cases, this meant rule by the wealthy, whose eligibility for office depended on property qualifications.

Tyrants and the Physical Landscape of the Polis. Built around an *acropolis*—the high point selected as a place of refuge by the original inhabitants—the typical polis contained the acropolis and *agora*—an open space that served as the economic center, marketplace, and social center of the town—inside walled fortifications. The polis' rural farming district lay outside the walls. On the acropolis they established the first rude temples in honor of the city's gods. The tyrants, many of whom were great builders whose temples and public works gave form to the cities of the classical age, replaced the early temples with new, more magnificent structures and banished private

FIGURE 2.5 *The Acropolis and the Agora.* This model shows the two main public spaces of a large Greek polis, in this case Athens at its peak. The acropolis (in the background) on its high hill contained the Parthenon and other centers of public worship. The agora (foreground), with its long colonnades, served as a public market, but temples and other public buildings are shown within it. In reality, ancient Athens was not this tidy. The thousands of homes and private shops that made up the rest of the city are not portrayed.

buildings to the area around the base of the hill. With rare exceptions, Greeks built simple homes and spent much of their daily lives in the streets or in the agora. This space, perhaps as much as any other factor, accounts for the vitality of Greek politics and intellectual life; the life of the citizen was one of constant interaction with his fellows.

The more ambitious tyrants not only built temples but remodeled such public spaces as the agora. They strengthened the defensive walls that surrounded their cities and worked to improve the quality and quantity of the water supply. Some went even further. Corinth, one of the wealthiest Greek cities, bestrides the narrow isthmus that separates the Saronic Gulf from the Gulf of Corinth. The Corinthian tyrant Periander built a stone trackway across the isthmus, allowing entire ships to be hauled from the Aegean to the Adriatic. Merchants willing to pay a substantial toll could thereby save a voyage of several hundred miles.

The Age of Colonization (750–600 BCE). The troubled situation that gave birth to the tyrants also produced the great age of Greek colonization. Good farmland had always been scarce in Greece. Most farms were small and practiced **subsistence agriculture.** This means that the owners raised a variety of crops, nearly all of which went to support their own households. If they produced a surplus, they sold the excess crops in the agora. Farm owners were, of course, full citizens, and some of the wealthier townsmen owned farms in

the countryside that they managed with the help of small numbers of slaves. Their efforts helped, but did not produce enough to feed the city's population of craftsmen, merchants, and wage laborers in the construction or shipbuilding trades. By 850 BCE, most Greek cities had long outgrown their agricultural resources and were importing food, especially from Egypt.

The resulting competition for scarce resources intensified conflicts among the poleis and probably inspired the development of the hoplite phalanx. Internally, the shortage of arable land brought social tensions that threatened the stability of the state and encouraged tyranny. But even tyrants could only redistribute wealth; they could not create it. Fortunately, Greece had an extensive coastline with good harbors and a seafaring population. A polis could preserve its independence if it followed the Phoenician example and established colonies in other parts of the Mediterranean world as an outlet for surplus population.

The process seems to have begun around 750 BCE with the establishment of a trading community in the Bay of Naples. Its founders intended it to provide access to the copper of Etruria, but the colonies established during the next 50 years in eastern Sicily were almost purely agrarian. Some of the colonists were merchants or political exiles, but most were poor people who sought only enough land to feed their families. Settlements then spread throughout southern Italy and westward into France, where in 600 BCE the Ionic town of Phocaea founded Massalia, the present-day Marseilles. Other cities founded colonies around the shores of the Black Sea. These colonies, in what is now the southern Ukraine, soon played an important role in supplying the Greek peninsula with grain.

Some Italian colonies, such as Sybaris on the Italian Gulf of Taranto, grew wealthy through trade. Although originally founded to exploit a rich agricultural plain, Sybaris became a point of transshipment for goods from the Adriatic to the Tyrrhenian Sea, thereby avoiding the treacherous Strait of Messina. Other colonies, such as Syracuse in Sicily, owed their wealth to agriculture, but Syracuse grew larger than its parent Corinth and became a major power in the fifth century BCE. Virtually all of these towns came into conflict with the Phoenicians and Carthaginians who had settled in Spain, Africa, and western Sicily. In some cases they displaced native peoples who took refuge in inaccessible regions away from the coasts. By 600 BCE, at least 500 new Greek poleis had been established from Spain to the Crimea on the Black Sea.

The term *polis* appropriately describes the new cities, for they were not colonies in the modern sense, but fully independent states. City governments on the Greek mainland organized the colonizing expeditions and appointed their leaders, but when the colonists arrived in

SELECTION FROM HESIOD'S *WORKS AND DAYS*

Hesiod (fl. late eighth century BCE) was one of the first Greek poets and a landowner from Boeotia, a relatively wealthy area northwest of Athens. In this fragment from a long poem, Hesiod instructs his ne'er-do-well brother, Perses, on the life of a Greek landowner. Using the movements of the constellations in the night sky (Orion, the Pleiades, and so on) to judge the seasons, he advises when to plant, harvest, or put to sea, as well as how to safeguard property against thieves and damage. The poem is an unforgettable description of rural life in an age when farmers went to sea to sell their produce abroad. Zephyr is the god of the winds, Demeter the goddess of harvests, and Dionysus the god of wine. Note that Hesiod, like most ancients, believed in watering his wine.

When the thistle blooms and the chirping cicada
sits on trees and pours down shrill song
from frenziedly quivering wings in the toilsome summer
then goats are fatter than ever and wine is at its best
women's lust knows no bounds and men are all dried up,
because the dog star parches their heads and knees
and the heat sears their skin. Then, ah then,
I wish you a shady ledge and your choice wine,
bread baked in the dusk and mid-August goat milk
and meat from a free-roving heifer that has never calved—
and from firstling kids. Drink sparkling wine,
sitting in the shade with your appetite sated,
and face Zephyr's breeze as it blows from mountain peaks.
Pour three measures of water fetched from a clear spring,
One that flows unchecked, and a fourth of wine.
As soon as mighty Orion rises above the horizon
exhort your slaves to thresh Demeter's holy grain
in a windy, well-rounded threshing floor.
Measure it first and then store it in bins.
But when your grain is tightly stored inside the house
then hire an unmarried worker and look for a female
servant with no children—nursing women are a burden.

Keep a dog with sharp teeth and feed it well,
wary of the day-sleepers who might rob you.
Bring in a lasting supply of hay and fodder
for your oxen and your mules. Once this is done let your
slaves rest their weary knees and unyoke the oxen.
When Orion and the dog star rise to the middle of the
sky and rosy-fingered dawn looks upon Arcturus,
then Perses, gather your grapes and bring them home
and leave them in the sun for ten days and nights,
in the shade for five, and on the sixth day
draw the gift of joyous Dionysos into your vats.
When the Pleiades, the Hyades, and mighty Orion set,
remember the time has come to plow again—
and may the earth nurse for you a full year's supply,
And if longing seizes you for sailing the stormy seas,
when the Pleiades flee mighty Orion
and plunge into the misty deep
and all the gusty winds are raging,
then do not take your ship on the wine-dark sea
but, as I bid you, remember to work the land.
Haul your ship onto land and secure it to the ground
with stones on all sides to stay the blast of rain and wind,
and pull the plug to avoid rotting caused by rain water.
Store up the tackle compactly inside your house
and neatly fold the sails, the wings of a seafaring ship.
Hang your rudder above the fireplace
and wait until the time to sail comes again.

Source: Hesiod, *Theogony, Works and Days, Shield*, ed. and trans. A. N. Athanassakis (Baltimore: John Hopkins University Press, 1983). Copyright © 1983 Johns Hopkins University Press. Used by permission.

Questions: Why do you think the Greeks planted their crops and planned their voyages by the movements of the stars? What does this passage reveal about Hesiod's attitude toward women?

their new homes, they governed themselves. For the most part, governing institutions tended to parallel those in the older Greek cities. Some, like Syracuse, became tyrannies while others achieved a measure of democracy. Few of the new settlements, however, maintained close ties with their city of origin. Most of them continued to venerate the divine patron of their founding city and some extended special privileges to citizens of the founding city, but "mother" cities competed with their "colonies" for trade and on occasion fought them. Still, all of these new cities regarded themselves as part of Hellas.

THE ROOTS OF GREEK CULTURE

Greek values as well as Greek literary and artistic inspiration stemmed from two basic sources: the Homeric poems and the mythology that had grown up around the adventures of the gods. Together, these wellsprings of the Greek tradition provided a rich fund of themes and motifs that illustrated in graphic terms what it meant to be Greek. The influence of that tradition had little to do with religious teachings as they are now understood. The behavior of the gods—and of Homer's

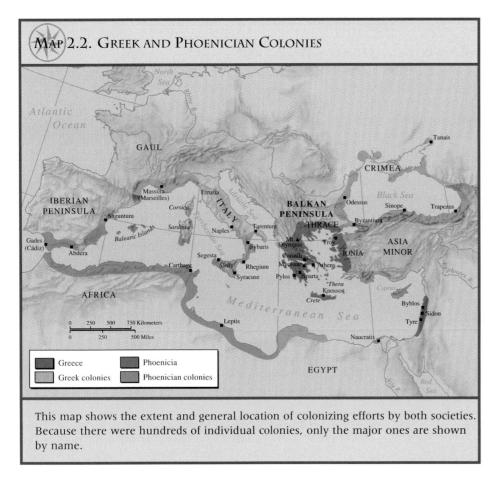

MAP 2.2. GREEK AND PHOENICIAN COLONIES

This map shows the extent and general location of colonizing efforts by both societies. Because there were hundreds of individual colonies, only the major ones are shown by name.

The Greeks thought of their deities in human terms, although the gods were immortal and possessed superhuman powers. The adventures of the gods inspired a vast mythology that, together with the poems of Homer, provided themes for later Greek art and literature. **Myths** are stories that explain the distantly remembered past or the existence of natural phenomena such as earthquakes, the seasons, or astronomical constellations. They reflect the values of the society that produces them and therefore play a vital part in educating the young. Because the gods' behavior was often capricious and immoral, Greek ethical principles derived not from divine precepts but from commonsense notions of how to get along with one's neighbors.

Greek religion offered little or no hope of personal immortality, although some heroes—was often highly improper, and Greek religion offered few ethical prescriptions. The ancient tales did not preach, but even when they taught by bad example they offered a precious guide to values, social attitudes, and conduct. For this reason, each polis sought to encourage the arts to the best of its financial ability. They were the means by which citizens were created and common values reaffirmed.

Greek Religion. The Greeks based their religion on an extended family of twelve gods who were believed to inhabit Mt. Olympus in northeastern Greece. The greatest were Zeus, the father of the Gods; his consort, Hera; and his brother Poseidon, the god of the sea and of earthquakes. Hestia, the goddess of hearths, and Demeter, the goddess of the harvest who was often associated with the earlier Earth Mother, were his sisters. Zeus's children included Aphrodite, goddess of love; Ares, god of war; and Apollo, god of the Sun, music, and poetry. Athena was goddess of wisdom and the fine arts and Hephaestus, god of fire and metallurgy. Hermes, with winged feet, was their messenger, but he also served as god of commerce and of other matters that involved cleverness or trickery. Perhaps the most popular of the deities was Artemis, the virgin nature goddess who symbolized chastity and to whom women prayed for help in childbirth.

believed that the dead inhabited a dark, unpleasant realm beneath the ground. Perhaps as a result, some Greeks buried their dead and others cremated them. Worship meant offering prayers and sacrifices in return for the protection of the gods or to secure the goodwill of lesser spirits who ruled over particular localities such as springs or fields. Ordinary men and women performed these rituals, often on behalf of their families. Public officials sacrificed to the patron god or goddess of their city on special occasions. There was no priestly caste, although individuals of both sexes sometimes lived within the grounds of shrines and temples and dedicated themselves to their maintenance. By the eighth century BCE, centers of worship open to all Greeks had been established at several locations. The shrine of Apollo at Delphi was home to the Delphic oracle, whose cryptic predictions were widely sought until Roman times. Olympia, dedicated to Zeus, and the shrine of Poseidon at Corinth were famous for athletic contests held annually in the gods' honor.

Olympic Games and the Competitive Spirit. Common shrines, and above all the **Olympic games,** provided unifying elements in a culture that would for centuries remain politically fragmented. According to tradition the first games were held in 776 BCE and involved saw athletics as an essential component of the good life. Physical fitness prepared them for war, but competition lay at the heart of their concept of personal worth, and athletic success was seen as almost godlike.

Homeric Values. The epic poems attributed to Homer form the other main source of Greek cultural values. The Greeks believed that in addition to *The Iliad,* Homer (fl. 850 BCE) also wrote **The Odyssey.** Modern scholars suspect that both were compiled from an earlier body of oral tradition soon after the Greeks adopted the alphabet and that *The Iliad* and *The Odyssey* had different authors. The two epics are certainly very different, but both teach moral lessons that permeated Greek culture. *The Iliad* adopts a tragic form appropriate to a tale of war and heroism (see Document 2.2), whereas *The Odyssey* is an entertaining series of adventure stories that stress the importance of cleverness, cunning, and strength of character. The Greeks valued these practical talents as much as the qualities stressed by *The Iliad*—courage, persistence, and dignity. Educated Greeks memorized long passages from both epics as part of their cultural education, and themes taken from both inspired much of the Greek literature and art that would follow.

LIFE IN THE POLIS: ATHENS AND SPARTA

No two Greek cities were precisely alike, especially in their governmental institutions, but most of the larger ones probably resembled Athens in their economic and social makeup. We know the most about Athens because it was the largest city in ancient Greece and produced more literature than any of its fellows. At the other political extreme was Sparta, the great rival of Athens. Most Greeks thought of Sparta as an institutional relic of earlier times. In fact, its system of life and government was a response to historical circumstances that had few parallels in the Greek world. It is important precisely because it was atypical and because Sparta became a major power during the Persian and Peloponnesian Wars.

The Democratic Polis of Athens (c. 700–461 BCE)

Although Athens, on the Attic Peninsula, became the cultural center of classical Greece, its initial development was slow. Until 594 BCE it was governed by an aristocratic council known as the *Areopagus* (ar-ee-op'-uh-gus), which elected nine magistrates, or *archons* (ar'-kahns), annually. Membership in the Areopagus was hereditary, and there was no written law. The archons, who were always aristocrats, interpreted legal issues to suit themselves.

only a foot race. In time the Olympics became a 7-day event that included nine other events. They were held every 4 years. The Greeks used these 4-year periods, or **Olympiads,** to date historical events. The games drew men from every part of the Greek world and provided a peaceful arena for the competitive spirit that was a great part of ancient Greek life until the Roman emperor Theodosius abolished them in 393 CE. Poets praised the winners, and their grateful communities showered them with gifts. All able-bodied Greek men participated in sports (women were not permitted to compete), for they

GREEK MYTHOLOGY

Greek myths became important not only to the ancient Greeks but to the development of Western culture. Romans built their literature on that of the Greeks and, until the early twentieth century, Westerners used the **classics** (as the literature of ancient Greece and Rome is called) as the core of their educational system. Today, the influence of Greek myths may be most apparent in the history of Western art. For centuries, these ancient stories inspired Western artists to capture the power, drama, and mystery of Greek myths—as this seventeenth-century painting of the myth of Prometheus aptly illustrates.

Question: What does the myth of Prometheus reveal about Greek attitudes toward the intentions of the gods, the hope of human happiness, and the character of women?

The Myth of Prometheus

Prometheus (Proh-mee´-thee-us) was one of the Titans, a race of giant, divine beings. Taking pity on the bleak existence of early mortals, Prometheus stole fire from the gods and gave it to mankind. Zeus was furious. He sent to Earth the first woman, Pandora, with a closed jar. When, out of curiosity, Pandora opened the jar, *hard work, greed, violence,* and *disease* flew out to subvert human happiness. Zeus then sent Hephaestus (Heh-fee´-stuss, Vulcan in Roman mythology), the god of metals and blacksmith to the gods, to punish Prometheus by chaining him to a rock at the furthest ends of the Earth. There, a giant eagle would gnaw forever on his immortal liver. In this painting (c. 1623), the Dutch artist, Dirck van Baburen (c. 1590–1624), paints a purposeful Hephaestus chaining a horrified Prometheus, while on the right, Hermes, messenger of the gods, looks on almost in delight, and the eagle hovers menacingly at the upper left. For most Greeks, the Prometheus myth worked on many levels, none of them optimistic.

Agrarian and Social Crisis. Aristocratic dominance and the gradual depletion of the soil eventually produced an agrarian crisis. Most Athenians, like most Greeks, were small farmers who grew wheat and barley and tried to maintain a few vines and olive trees. Wheat yields probably averaged about 5 bushels per acre; barley, 10. Such yields are normal for unfertilized, unirrigated soils in almost any region and are generally enough to guarantee subsistence but little more. When yields began declining in the early seventh century BCE, Attic farmers had to borrow from the aristocrats to survive. Inevitably, harvests failed to improve, and citizens who defaulted were enslaved and sometimes sold abroad by their creditors.

Dissatisfaction with this state of affairs, and with the endless blood feuds among aristocratic clans, led to a short-lived tyranny in 632 BCE. Eleven years later, a semilegendary figure named Draco (Dray´-coh) passed laws against aristocratic violence so harsh that *draconian* has become a byword for severity. However, the agrarian problem remained. Political tensions remained high until the election of **Solon** as the sole archon in 594 BCE.

Solon's Reforms. Solon (Soh´-lun) canceled outstanding debts, freed many slaves, and forbade the use of a citizen's person as collateral. He created a written constitution and broadened the social base of the Athenian government by creating a popularly elected Council of 400 as a check on the powers of the Areopagus. His economic ideas were less successful. While trying to encourage commerce and industry, Solon prohibited the export of wheat and encouraged that of olive oil. Consequently, the larger landholders, seeing profit in olives and other cash crops, took wheat land out of production and Athens became permanently dependent on imported grain, most of which came from the rich plains north of the Black Sea. This meant that, in later years, Athenian

FIGURE 2.6 *Harvesting Olives.* This vase painting shows farmers harvesting olives for olive oil, a staple commodity in the Mediterranean world. As part of his reforms, Solon encouraged the growing of olives as a cash crop instead of grain. Olives and olive oil remain a major Greek export today.

survival required control of the Dardanelles or Hellespont, the narrow strait that separates Europe from Asia and provided access to the Greek ports of the Crimea. Solon had no intention of serving for life and retired when he had completed his reforms.

Athenian Tyrants—Pisistratus and Hippias.
Solon's social measures, although popular, failed to prevent the emergence of Pisistratus (Pi-sis'-tra-tus), a tyrant briefly in 560 BCE and then from 546 BCE to his death in 527 BCE. Using his mastery of electoral politics within Solon's constitutional measures, Pisistratus, like the tyrants of other cities, worked tirelessly to break the remaining power of the aristocratic families. Through taxation and dues for more and more public festivals, he weakened the aristocrats financially and he sent magistrates into the countryside to interfere in their legal disputes. Public works flourished, and projects such as temple construction and the remodeling of the agora provided work for thousands. Pisistratus was succeeded by his son Hippias (Hip'-ee-us), who became a tyrant in the more conventional sense of the word. The Athenians overthrew him with Spartan assistance in 510 BCE and replaced him with Cleisthenes (Klis'-thuh-neez)

Cleisthenes and the Advent of Athenian Democracy.
Cleisthenes laid the foundations of the democratic system that lasted throughout the classical age. He expanded the number of *demes* (deems), or wards, which served as the primary units of local government, and divided them into ten tribes instead of four. The composition of these tribes is uncertain. Each tribe elected 50 members to a Council of 500. This body (less than 1 percent of the population) prepared legislation and supervised finances and foreign affairs, but final authority over legislation and questions of war and peace rested with an assembly of all male citizens that met at least forty times a year. The assembly could also

vote to **ostracize**—exile from the city for 10 years without a formal trial—dangerous or unpopular politicians.

To ensure impartiality, the city now chose magistrates (judges and governing officials) by lot from a list of volunteers who were not paid for their public service. The city elected its military commander presumably on the basis of merit. In an effort to ensure competence, the Athenians subjected officials to a stringent review of their actions at the end of each year. Plato (see Chapter 3) and others who sympathized with aristocracy found the entire democratic system absurd, but Pericles and his associates in the popular party liberalized it even further after 461 BCE.

Athens represented an extreme level of democratic government, but the breadth of its public participation was not unique. A number of other Greek cities adopted democratic forms of government, although in some cases, representative institutions quickly fell under the control of the wealthy and became oligarchies. Although widely criticized by philosophers, democracy in Athens worked remarkably well for almost 200 years and provided the basis for local government even after the city lost its freedom to the Macedonians in 338 BCE. At the very least, democracy guaranteed intense involvement by the entire population of male citizens in the life of the polis. Population estimates vary, but classical Athens probably had between 40,000 and 50,000 male citizens in both town and country. Any one of them could be part of its political, military, and judicial processes.

Life in the Athenian Polis.
In material terms, the Athenian way of life was remarkably simple. Athenians, like other Greeks, ate bread garnished with oil, onions, or garlic and drank wine that was usually watered and flavored with sweeteners, pine resin, or other substances. Beans and various fruits supplemented this otherwise meager diet. Meat was expensive and normally consumed in small quantities. Even the largest Athenian houses, although often built of stone, were small by Egyptian or Mesopotamian standards, but their arrangement was similar. Square or rectangular rooms surrounded a central courtyard, which might contain a private well. Some houses had second stories. Merchants and artisans often conducted their business from rooms on the street side of their dwellings. Housing for the many poor, being more cheaply built, has not been well preserved.

Slavery.
Athens probably had at least 40,000 to 50,000 slaves of both sexes who worked as artisans, domestic servants, or laborers. A large number worked in the mines. As in the rest of the ancient world, slavery among the Greeks had begun with the taking of captives in war, but by the classical age, Greeks were purchasing barbarian (that is, non-Greek) slaves from itinerant traders. Still, no great slave-worked estates

THE OLYMPIC GAMES

According to legend, King Ifitos of Elis and nearby Olympia asked Apollo's oracle at Delphi how to end the wars that were devastating the Peloponnese. Apollo's reply advised Ifitos to restore the "sports contests" at Olympia. Ifitos established the Olympic games and signed, along with Sparta's Lycurgus and Pisa's Cleisthenes, the longest-standing (1,200 years) peace accord in history—the Olympic Truce. Throughout the duration of the Olympic Truce, from the seventh day prior to the opening of the Games to the seventh day following the closing, all conflicts ceased, allowing athletes, artists, and spectators to travel to Olympia, participate in the Games, and return to their homelands in safety. The city of Elis organized the games every 4 years during the month of July or August. Elean citizens, chosen by lot, supervised the events and enforced their elaborate regulations and rules of sportsmanship. Winners were crowned at the games with a wreath of wild olive leaves and honored by their cities with poems, special privileges, and often high political office when they returned home. At first, spectators (men only) watched from the hillside, but the Eleans eventually built a true stadium seating 45,000 people. The games lasted 5 days and gradually expanded to include ten events, most of which, like the javelin throw, had military applications. The Eleans also organized a separate set of athletic games for women, who competed wearing short tunics.

Discus and Javelin Throwers. These red-figure vases from c. 520–510 BCE portray two Olympic events. The one on the left shows a discus thrower beginning his warm-up. The one on the right shows a javelin thrower. Ancient illustrations of these events indicate that they were probably conducted in the same way as their modern Olympic counterparts and that the technique used by the athletes has not changed.

▶*Horse and Chariot Racing.* **Horse racing**, which included several events, was an aristocratic sport. The Greeks loved horses, but few could afford to maintain them. The **chariot race** was the most spectacular event and must have required great strength and skill. Some of the most important historical personages participated, driving their own chariots, while wealthy owners, some of whom were women, hired trainers, riders, and drivers. Then as now, the *hippodrome*, or race track, was a place to display wealth and political power. This vase shows the *tethrippon* or *quadriga*, an event for four-horse chariots that was introduced in 680 BCE.

existed, and even the richest citizens seem to have owned only a few. Slave artisans who toiled outside their master's home normally received wages, a fixed portion of which was returned to their owner. This practice tended to depress the pay rates of free workers and ensured that many citizens lived no better than the slaves. As in Mesopotamia, killing a slave was a crime, and the law guaranteed slaves their freedom *(manumission)* if they could raise their price of purchase.

In addition to slaves and free citizens, Athens boasted a large population of foreigners. The city was a commercial center that, although located a few miles from

The Foot Race. In the beginning the games lasted 1 day and featured only one event, the foot race—a 600-foot sprint called a *stadion* (hence our word *stadium*). The event came to include the *diaulos,* a 1,200-foot run. As this vase painting indicates, the athletes ran naked.

Pindar's Ode to an Athlete

Following his Olympic success, an athlete's native city often commissioned a poem to honor him, as was the case with this poem. Pindar (c. 518–438 BCE), best known for his odes honoring successful athletes, was a native of Thebes and one of the greatest lyric poets of ancient Greece. As he does here, Pindar often included a brief warning against *hubris,* the fatal pride that leads men to challenge the gods.

"For Phylakidas of Aegina, Winner in the Trial of Strength"

> In the struggle of the games he has won
> The glory of his desire,
> Whose hair is tied with thick garlands
> For victory with his hands
> Or swiftness of foot.
> Men's valor is judged by their fates,
> But two things alone
> Look after the sweetest grace of life
> Among the fine flowers of wealth.
> If a man fares well and hears his good name spoken,
> Seek not to become a Zeus!
> You have everything, if a share
> Of those beautiful things come to you.
> Mortal ends befit mortal men.
> For you Phylakidas, at the Isthmus
> A double success is planted and thrives,
> And at Nemea for you and your brother Pytheas
> In the Trial of Strength. My heart tastes song.

Source: Pindar, *The Odes of Pindar,* trans. C. M. Bowra (Harmondsworth, England: Penguin Books, 1969, p. 47). Copyright © The Estate of C. M. Bowra, 1969. Reproduced by permission of Penguin Books Ltd.

the coast, had a bustling port at Piraeus. Unlike some Greeks, the Athenians welcomed foreign ideas—and capital investment. Although foreign residents could not participate in public life or own real estate, they were well treated and many became wealthy. The merchants among them controlled much of the city's commerce.

The Status of Women in Athens. As in other societies, historical sources are apt to be legal documents or literary works written from the male point of view. These documents do not always reflect the real experiences of women and sometimes present a misleading image of powerlessness and even irrelevance. Thus, their true

SELECTION FROM HOMER'S *THE ILIAD*

Homer's great epic of the Trojan War—*The Iliad*—defined Greek values and ideals for later generations. Those values are humanistic; that is, Homer's heroes strive for excellence in human rather than religious terms. But underlying all their actions is a sense that, even for the greatest of mortals, the order of the universe is unsafe. This passage reflects the tragic side of Greek consciousness. Priam, the aging King of Troy, having seen his son Hector killed by the Greek warrior Achilles, goes to Achilles to ask him to return Hector's body for burial.

Priam had set Achilles thinking about his own father and brought him to the verge of tears. Taking the old man's hand, he gently put him from him; and overcome by their memories, they both broke down. Priam, crouching at Achilles's feet, wept bitterly for man-slaying Hector, and Achilles wept for his father, and then again for Patroclus. The house was filled with the sounds of their lamentation. But presently when he had had enough of tears and recovered his composure, the excellent Achilles leapt from his chair, and in compassion for the man's grey head and grey beard, took him by the arm and raised him. Then he spoke to him from his heart: "You are indeed a man of sorrows and have suffered much. How could you dare to come by yourself to the Achaean ships into the presence of a man who has killed so many of your gallant sons? You have a heart of iron. But pray be seated now, here on this chair, and let us leave our sorrows, bitter though they are, locked up in our own hearts, for weeping is cold comfort and does little good. We men are wretched things, and the gods, who have no cares themselves, have woven sorrow into the very pattern of our lives."

Source: Homer, *The Iliad*, trans. E. V. Rieu (Harmondsworth, England: Penguin Books, 1950).

Question: What cultural values and attitudes is Homer trying to convey in this passage?

rifices, or the theater, where male relatives accompanied them. It is thought that men also did the shopping to keep their wives and daughters from coming into contact with strangers. Women were even expected to avoid certain areas within the home. The *andron,* a room where men received their male guests, was strictly off-limits to women, and in many Greek houses it had a separate entrance to the street.

Underlying these practices was the conviction, voiced frequently by Greek writers, that women were incapable of controlling their sexuality. A woman suspected of having a child by someone other than her lawful husband endangered the status of her other children, who might lose their citizenship if challenged in court by an enemy. For this reason, the head of a family had the right to kill any man who seduced his wife, daughter, or any other female relative under his protection. As one offended husband said in a famous case: "The lawgiver [Solon] prescribed death for adultery because he who achieves his ends by persuasion thereby corrupts the mind as well as the body of the woman . . . [he] gains access to all a man's possessions, and casts doubt on his children's parentage." The adulterous woman could not, however, be killed because she was legally and morally irresponsible. If married, her husband could divorce her; if single, she ruined her prospects for finding a husband and spent the rest of her life as a virtual prisoner in the house of her father or guardian. Despite these sanctions, adultery may not have been as uncommon as scholars once believed.

By modern standards, women of middle- and upper-class families remained virtual prisoners. They were married early, often at age 14 or 15, to much older men who were chosen for them by their families. Women almost never received a formal education, although a few upper-class women, like the sister of the statesman Cimon, were well educated. Much of their time was spent spinning and sewing because Greek clothing was simple and could easily be manufactured at home. This does not mean, however, that Greek women were without influence. They managed their husband's household, controlled the domestic slaves, and raised the children. Their husband's economic survival depended on their efforts, and literary sources indicate that the men of the family consulted them regularly on both business matters and on the political issues of the day. Child-rearing made them, as in most societies, the guardians of societal values, not only for the children but for their husbands as well. In Greece, as elsewhere, a propertied widow might enjoy considerable influence if she did not remarry.

From a modern perspective, poor and foreign women led more interesting lives. Many worked or sold goods in the marketplace, activities that were essential to the sur-

status has been the subject of much controversy. Nevertheless, Greek women did not enjoy the same legal and personal status as their Egyptian counterparts.

Theoretically, even Greek women who had been born to citizen families had no political rights. Men exercised women's judicial rights for them because female status was that of permanent legal minor. Women did have dowries, which protected them to some extent if they were divorced or widowed, but divorce seems to have been rare. The Athenians, like most ancient Greeks, made extraordinary efforts to segregate the sexes. Respectable women of the citizen class stayed at home except for occasional attendance at festivals, sac-

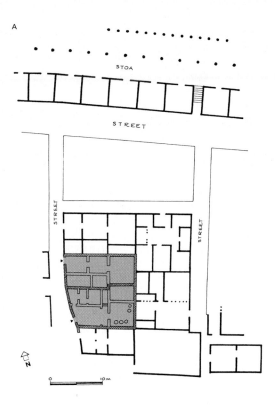

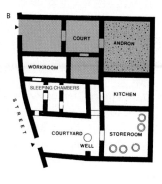

FIGURE 2.7 *Plan of a Greek House.* This house was part of a residential block on the south slope of the Areopagus in Athens. Judging by its size and location near the center of town, it probably belonged to a prosperous tradesman. The drawing on the left shows its location relative to other buildings in the block and to the agora. The stalls of the agora are shown at the top together with the *stoa*, or covered portico, that protected them from sun and rain. The drawing to the right shows the probable function of the rooms. The shaded area was used only by men. Note that the men's and women's areas of the house had separate entrances (arrows) and that no interior access appears between them.

vival of their families and that guaranteed them a freedom of movement unknown to their wealthier sisters. Such women, however, normally lacked the protection of an economically stable and politically privileged family.

Prostitution. Segregation of the sexes led to an acceptance of male extramarital relations with slave and foreign women. Prostitution was common, and at the higher levels of society, Athenian men valued courtesans, or *hetairai* (het-eye'-ree), as companions at banquets and other social occasions from which respectable women were excluded. Courtesans were often highly educated. Some—such as Aspasia, the mistress of the fifth-century statesman Pericles—achieved considerable fame and could hold their own in intellectual discourse, but they were still regarded as prostitutes. Aspasia ended her days as the madam of an Athens brothel.

Homosexuality. Homosexuality, too, was regarded by many Greeks as normal, and in some cases praiseworthy (see *Greek Attitudes Toward Sex and Marriage*). Soldiers, for example, were thought to fight more bravely when accompanied by their male lovers. Many of these relationships formed in the *gymnasia,* where men of the citizen class trained for war or athletics. It was not uncommon for a youth to become sexually involved with an older man who then served as his mentor in intellectual as well as athletic matters. Such

arrangements were widely accepted. The Greeks, however, did not view homosexuality as an orientation that precluded sexual relations with women or a conventional family life. Furthermore, homosexual promiscuity could ruin a man's reputation or lead to exile, and many regarded it as inferior to married love.

As in many other cultures, Greek men and women may have belonged in effect to separate societies that met only in bed. If true, this would also account for the widespread acceptance of lesbianism. Greek men may not have cared about sex between women because it did not raise the issue of inheritance. The term *lesbian* comes from the Ionic island of Lesbos, home of Sappho (c. 610–580 BCE), a woman and the greatest of Greek lyric poets. Europeans of a later age found her erotic poems to other women scandalous (see Document 2.3), and their renown has perhaps unfairly eclipsed the much wider range of her work in the minds of all but the most determined classicists.

Although Athenians, like other Greeks, were remarkably open about sexual matters, they did not abandon themselves to debauchery. Self-control remained the essence of the ideal citizen, and the Greeks admired sexual restraint as much as they admired moderation in the consumption of food and drink and physical fitness. A man who wasted his wealth and corrupted his body was of no value to the polis, which was always at risk and demanded nothing less than excellence in those who would defend it.

GREEK ATTITUDES TOWARD SEX AND MARRIAGE

Greek attitudes toward sex and marriage arose out of the culture's perception of women as morally and intellectually inferior to men—a perception we see clearly in Xenophon's *Oeconomicus (Household Management)*. In Plutarch's *Dialogue on Love*, the character Protogenes uses the same perception to defend homosexuality, but the dialogue shows that the Greeks were as conflicted about this issue as are the cultures of today. Sappho's poem to her lover Atthis (see Document 2.3) is a fine example of lyric poetry and a graphic illustration that, although the law tolerated lesbian relationships, women could rarely be masters of their own emotional fate.

Xenophon's "The Role of the Athenian Wife" from Oeconomicus (Household Management)

In this excerpt, Ischomachus tells Socrates how he began to train his 15-year-old bride. Like most Greek husbands, Ischomachus would have been far older than his wife. His patronizing views reflect conventional Athenian thinking.

Well Socrates, as soon as I had tamed her and she was relaxed enough to talk, I asked her the following question: "Tell me, my dear," said I, "do you understand why I married you and why your parents gave you to me? You know as well as I do that neither of us would have had trouble finding someone else to share our beds. But after thinking about it carefully, it was you I chose and me your parents chose as the best partners we could find for

our home and children. Now if God sends us children, we shall think about how best to raise them, for we share an interest in securing the best allies and support for our old age."

My wife answered, "But how can I help? What am I capable of doing? It is on you that everything depends. My duty, my mother said, is to be well behaved."

"Oh, by Zeus," said I, "my father said the same to me. But the best behavior in a man and woman is that which will keep up their property and increase it as far as may be done by honest and legal means. . . ."

"It seems to me that God adapted women's nature to indoor and man's to outdoor work. . . . As Nature has entrusted woman with guarding the household supplies, and a timid nature is no disadvantage in such a job, it has endowed women with more fear than man. It is more proper for a woman to stay in the house than out of doors and less so for a man to be indoors instead of out. . . . You must stay indoors and send out the servants whose work is outside and supervise those who work indoors, receive what is brought in, give out what is to be spent, plan ahead for what is to be stored and ensure that provisions for a year are not used up in a month. . . . Many of your duties will give you pleasure: for instance, if you teach spinning and weaving to a slave who did not know how to do this when you got her, you double your usefulness to yourself."

From Xenophon "Oeconomicus" in Julia O'Faolain and Lauro Martines, *Not in God's Image: Women in History from the Greeks to the Victorians* (London: Temple Smith, 1973).

The Military Polis of Sparta (c. 700–500 BCE)

South of Athens, in a remote valley of the Peloponnese, lay Sparta—a polis very different from, and one-fourth the size of, Athens. Sparta produced few poets and no philosophers. Its unwalled capital, built on a raised mound to keep it from the floodwaters of the river Eurotas (You-ro'-tas), was said to resemble an overgrown village. The Spartans engaged in no commerce to speak of and lived almost entirely from the proceeds of agriculture. Long after other Greeks had adopted coinage, they continued to use iron bars as their only currency. Because the Spartans wrote little, we know them chiefly through the writings of foreign political theorists. By all accounts, Sparta was a military state—grim, poor, rigidly conservative, and distinguished only by its magnificent army and the single-minded discipline of its citizens.

Early History. The first Spartans were probably a band of Dorians who established their polis on the ruins of an earlier society. Under a dual monarchy in which two hereditary kings exerted equal powers in war and religious matters, the Spartans displaced an earlier ruling class that was probably Dorian as well, allowing these *perioikoi* (per-ee'-ee-kee) to retain property and personal freedom within their own communities. The original pre-Dorian inhabitants became serfs, or in Spartan terms, **helots** (hell'-uts). Bound to the properties on which they worked, they differed from slaves only in that they do not seem to have been sold as individuals. Around 725 BCE, Sparta conquered the neighboring polis of Messenia and reduced its inhabitants to serfdom as well. Helots now outnumbered Spartans by a probable ratio of 10-to-1. The conquest of Messenia and the serfdom of its inhabitants made Sparta agriculturally self-sufficient, a situation almost unique among the Greek states. It even provided a modest surplus for export, although Spartan citizens were forbidden to engage directly in trade. Unfortunately, their success forced the Spartans to live as an armed minority surrounded by a hostile population. In the Second

Plutarch's Dialogue on Love

Debates (or *dialogues*) over the relative merits of homosexual and heterosexual love were commonplace in ancient Greece. Plutarch, this debate's author, lived in the first century CE. He was an avid propagandist for Hellenic values, and his works are thought to reflect the attitudes of the age. Here, Protogenes, who believes that women are incapable of true feeling or intellect, argues that love is almost by definition homosexual. His friend Daphnaeus, who apparently represents Plutarch, vehemently disagrees.

"Do you call marriage and the union of man and wife shameful?" interposed Daphnaeus, "there can be no bond more sacred."

"Such unions are necessary for the propagation of the race," said Protogenes, "and so our lawgivers have been careful to endow them with sanctity and exalt them before the populace. But of true Love the women's apartment has no shred. For my part I deny that the word "love" can be applied to the sentiment you feel for women and girls, no more than flies can be said to 'love' milk, or bees honey, or victualers and cooks can be said to have amorous feelings for the beeves and fowl they fatten in the dark. . . ." A noble love which attaches to a youthful [male] spirit issues in excellence upon the path of friendship. From these desires for women, even if they turn out well, one may enjoy only physical pleasure and the satisfaction of a ripe body."

[After much argument, Daphnaeus responds:] "If we examine the truth of the matter, Protogenes, the passion for boys and for women derives from one and the same Love, but if you insist on distinguishing between them for argument's sake, you will find that the Love of boys does not comport himself decently; he is like a late issue, born unseasonably, illegitimate, and shady, who drives out the elder and legitimate love. It was only yesterday, my friend, or the day before, after lads began to strip and bare themselves for exercise that it crept surreptitiously into the gymnasia with its allurements and embraces, and then, little by little, when it had fledged its wings full in the palaestras, it could no longer be held in check; now it abuses and befouls that noble conjugal Love which assures immortality to our mortal kind, for by procreation it rekindles our nature when it is extinguished.

"Protogenes denies there is pleasure in the Love of boys: he does so out of shame and fear. He must have some decent pretext for attachment to his young beauties, and so he speaks of friendship and excellence. He covers himself with athlete's dust, takes cold baths, raises his eyebrows, and declares he is chastely philosophizing—to outward view and because of the law. But when night falls and all is quiet then 'sweet is the fruit when the keeper is gone.' "

Source: Plutarch, "Dialogue on Love," in ed. and trans. Moses Hadas, *On Love, the Family, and the Good Life: Selected Essays of Plutarch* (New York: Mentor Books, 1957, pp. 307–308).

Messenian War (c. 650 BCE) the helots of both communities rose against their masters and, with the help of some neighboring cities, came close to destroying the Spartan state. The survival of an independent Sparta required a complete reorganization of their society.

Lycurgus and New Spartan Government. The Spartans attributed their reorganization to the legendary figure of Lycurgus (Lie-kur'-gus), but the new practices almost certainly evolved over time. By the fifth century BCE, the monarchy's influence had become severely limited. A Council of Elders, composed of twenty-eight men over the age of 60, advised them and served as a kind of appellate court in reviewing their legal decisions. The *ephors* (eff'-ors), a committee of five, ran the government. They conducted foreign policy, watched over the helots, and could, if necessary, override the military decisions of the kings. Both groups were elected by an assembly composed of all Spartan males over the age of 30, the ephors for 1-year terms,

the councillors for life. Unlike Athens, Sparta restricted citizenship to those who owned land. Although the citizen assembly voted by acclamation on all important matters, the ephors usually negotiated the decisions in advance before presenting them to the meetings for ratification. There seems to have been little of the vigorous public debate that characterized Athenian society.

Life in the Spartan Polis. The aristocratic character of Spartan government struck Greeks as old-fashioned, but they admired its effectiveness and stability. The social system over which the government presided was stranger. From the sixth century BCE onward, everything in a Spartan's life was subordinated to the security of the polis (see Document 2.4). Infants who appeared physically unfit were killed. At age 7, males were taken from their mothers and trained to fight, endure pain, and survive without supplies in a hostile countryside. At age 20, they entered a *phiditia* (fid-ish'-ee-a), a kind of barracks community where they would live for most of their

SAPPHO'S "TO ATTHIS"

In this lyric, Sappho, a poetess from the island of Lesbos, laments her parting from a woman she loved. It is evident that the families of the two women, or some other third party, perhaps a husband, has forced their separation.

So I shall never see Atthis again,
and really I long to be dead,
although she too cried bitterly
when she left and said to me,
"Ah, what a nightmare we suffered
Sappho, I swear I go unwillingly."
And I answered, "Go, and be happy.
But remember me, for surely you
know how I worshipped you. If not,
then I want you to remember all
the exquisite days we shared;
how when near me you would adorn
your hanging locks with violets and

tiny roses and your sapling throat
with necklets of a hundred blossoms;
how your young flesh was rich with kingly
myrrh as you leaned near my breasts on
the soft couch where delicate girls
served all that an Ionian could desire;
how we went to every hill, brook,
and holy place; and when early spring
filled the woods with noises of birds
and a choir of nightingales—we two
in solitude were wandering there."

Source: Sappho, "To Atthis," in Willis Barnstone, *Greek Lyric Poetry* (New York: Bantam Books, 1962). By permission of Willis Barnstone.

Question: What point does Sappho make about the situation of women in Greek society?

---

lives. The phiditias dined in public on Hyacinthian Street in the same mess tents they used in war. These dinners, rather than the life of the agora, provided Spartan males with most of their social interaction.

Although allowed to marry, younger Spartans could visit their wives only in secret, and family life in the ordinary sense was discouraged. Because the Spartans wrote little, we know nothing of their attitude toward homosexuality, but, as Greeks who found them odd in every other respect did not mention it, it must have been similar to that of the Athenians. Their military obligation ended only at the age of 60. To the Spartan, eternal vigilance was the price of survival. Unlike most Greeks, they periodically expelled foreigners from the state as a security precaution. Trade and agricultural work were forbidden them; fitness, discipline, and courage were prized.

The Status of Women in Sparta. Spartan women were renowned throughout Greece for their independence and assertiveness. They appeared in public, rode horses, and said what they thought. Because the Spartan warrior paid dues to his phiditia from the proceeds of land worked by the helots, that work was supervised to some extent by Spartan women. Although not expected to fight, women received extensive physical training on the theory that a strong mother produces strong children. Spartan women dressed simply and wore no jewelry. They could hold land in their own right and were capable of dealing with hostile and rebellious helots. Their courage, like that of the Spartan men, was legendary.

Spartan Foreign Policy. The constant threat of helot insurrection made Spartans wary of foreign entanglements, and the Spartans followed a policy that was traditionally defensive and inward-looking. This changed in the course of the fifth century BCE, when the Persian invasion and the subsequent expansion of Athens forced them to take a more active role. They would eventually be drawn into a fatal rivalry with the Athenians, whose army was inferior but whose superior navy and greater wealth made them formidable antagonists. The story of those struggles forms the political background of the Greek classical age.

THE PERSIAN WAR (499–479 BCE)

Greek isolation from the turbulent politics of the Asian land mass came to an abrupt end with the advent of the Persian War of 499–479 BCE. The tiny states whose competition with one another had long since become traditional now faced the greatest military power the world had yet known.

The Persian Empire. The Persians were an Indo-European people from the Iranian highlands who emerged in the sixth century BCE as the dominant power in the vast region between Mesopotamia and India. By the end of the sixth century BCE, the ruling elite had adopted **Zoroastrianism,** a religion preached

XENOPHON'S DESCRIPTION OF A SPARTAN CHILDHOOD FROM "THE CONSTITUTION OF THE LACEDAEMONIANS"

This passage from Xenophon is one of several descriptions of Spartan values as perceived by other Greeks, many of whom were both attracted and repelled by them.

In other Greek cities, parents who profess to give their sons the best education place their boys under the care and control of a moral tutor as soon as they can understand what is said to them, and send them to a school to learn letters, music, and the exercises of the wrestling ground. Moreover, they soften the children's feet by giving them sandals, and pamper their bodies with changes of clothing; and it is customary to allow them as much food as they can eat.

Lycurgus, on the contrary, instead of leaving each father to appoint a slave to act as tutor, gave the duty of controlling the boys to a member of the class from which the highest offices are filled, in fact to the "Warden" as he is called. He gave this person authority to punish them severely in case of misconduct. He also assigned to him a staff of youths provided with whips to chastise them when necessary. . . . Instead of softening their feet with sandals he required them to harden their feet by going without shoes. He believed that if this habit were cultivated it would enable them to climb hills more easily and descend steep slopes with less danger. And instead of letting them be pampered in the matter of clothing, he introduced the custom of wearing one garment throughout the year, believing

that they would thus be better prepared to face changes of heat and cold. As to the food, he required the prefect to bring with him such a moderate amount of it that the boys would never suffer from repletion and would know what it was to go with their hunger unsatisfied; for he believed that those who underwent this training would be better able to continue working on an empty stomach if necessary, and would be capable of carrying on longer without extra food. . . .

He allowed them to alleviate their hunger by stealing something. It was not on account of a difficulty in providing for them that he encouraged them to get their food by cunning. . . . Obviously, a man who intends to take to thieving must spend sleepless nights and play the deceiver and lie in ambush by day, and moreover, if he means to make a capture, he must have spies ready. There can be no doubt then, that all this education was planned by him in order to make the boys more resourceful in getting supplies and be better fighting men.

Source: Xenophon, "The Constitution of the Lacedemonians," in *Scripta Minora.* Loeb Classical Library (Cambridge, MA: Harvard University Press, 1925).

Question: What was the purpose of the education described in this passage?

---

by the prophet and reformer Zoroaster (sometimes called Zarathustra). A dualistic system in which Ahura Mazda, the god of light, truth, and goodness contends eternally with Ahriman, the god of darkness and evil, Zoroastrianism condemned images of the gods and maintained the highest of ethical precepts. Its radical distinction between good and evil influenced early Christianity, and Ahriman has been seen by some as a prototype of the Christian Satan.

Under **Cyrus I "the Great"** (c. 585–529 BCE) the Persians conquered Babylon, together with Egypt, Syria, Palestine, and most of southwest Asia. Like the Assyrians, the Persians used cavalry, many of them armed with bows, to pin down the enemy's infantry until their own infantry could destroy them. But unlike the Assyrians, Persian government of conquered peoples was generally benign. It avoided atrocities, except in cases of outright rebellion, and asked only that new subjects pay tribute and provide troops for the army. Because the Persians typically preserved local institutions, many parts of the former Assyrian Empire welcomed them as liberators.

Origins of the Persian–Greek Conflict. Greek involvement with the Persian Empire began when Cyrus the Great conquered the kingdom of Lydia in 546 BCE. Located in southwestern Asia, Lydia was heavily influenced by Greek culture and famous for its wealth. The Lydians are credited with the invention of modern coinage. Under the fabulously wealthy king Croesus (Kree'-sus), Lydia established a loose dominance over the Ionian communities of the western Aegean. When Lydia fell, the Persians assumed control of its Greek dependencies. In 499 BCE, several Ionian states rebelled against local rulers backed by Persia and asked mainland Greeks to help. Sparta, worried about the internal threat of helot rebellion, refused, but Athens and the Euboean city of Eretria (Air-uh-tree'-ya) sent twenty-five ships. Athenian rhetoric stressed their city's ancient and sentimental ties to Ionia, but the Athenians also feared a threat to their vital supply of grain imported from the Crimea if Persia controlled the approaches to the Black Sea.

In a short-lived triumph, the Ionians and their allies managed to burn Sardis, the Lydian capital. Persia soon reestablished control over southwestern Asia and in 490 BCE dispatched a retaliatory expedition against Eretria and Athens. The Persians destroyed Eretria, but Athens fought and defeated the Persian army at

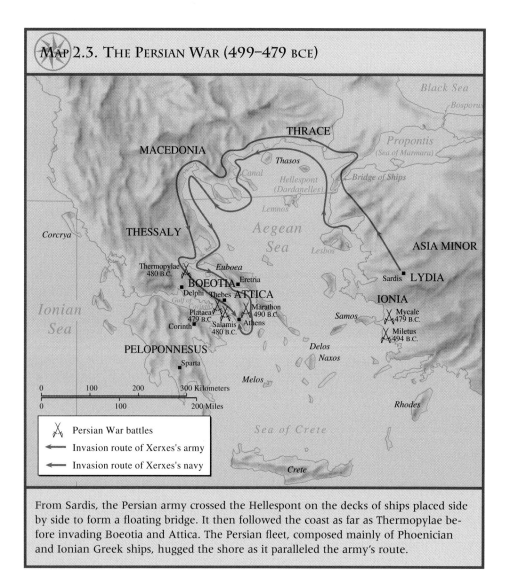

MAP 2.3. THE PERSIAN WAR (499–479 BCE)

Persian War battles

← Invasion route of Xerxes's army

← Invasion route of Xerxes's navy

From Sardis, the Persian army crossed the Hellespont on the decks of ships placed side by side to form a floating bridge. It then followed the coast as far as Thermopylae before invading Boeotia and Attica. The Persian fleet, composed mainly of Phoenician and Ionian Greek ships, hugged the shore as it paralleled the army's route.

a metal prow for ramming. Although far superior to earlier galleys, triremes were expensive, and only the discovery of new silver deposits at Laureion in Attica made their construction possible.

Athens needed the ships because Greek defensive strategy was essentially naval. But the main Persian army was marching south toward Athens along the European shore after crossing the Dardanelles from southwest Asia. The army depended for its supplies on a fleet of perhaps 300 triremes manned by Persia's Phoenician and Ionian allies. At the narrow pass of Thermopylae (Thur-mop'-uh-lee), Themistocles hoped to delay the Persian land forces long enough for adverse weather and a naval action at nearby Artemisium to deplete the Persian fleet (see Document 2.5).

The Spartans, under their king Leonidas (Lee-a-nye'-duss), coordinated a heroic defense at Thermopylae but fell when the invaders found a way to flank the Spartan position. Offshore, the Greeks fought an indecisive naval battle with a Persian force that, as Themistocles predicted, had been weakened by a series of earlier storms. Still, these actions provided time to evacuate Athens and take the Greek fleet to a position near the island of Salamis. The Athenians and their allies hoped that by forcing a sea battle in the narrow waters between the island and the mainland they could compensate for the greater speed and maneuverability of the Persian fleet.

Marathon. The marathon as a modern Olympic event commemorates the achievement of a courier who brought the news to Athens, 22 miles away. This victory, achieved in the absence of the feared Persian cavalry, gave the Greeks confidence in their ability to defeat an enemy who until then had been regarded as invincible.

The Persian Invasion of the Greek Mainland.

That confidence was tested in 480 BCE, when the new Persian emperor, **Xerxes** (Zurk'-seez), launched a full-scale invasion of Greece by land and sea. It was a measure of Greek disunity that only thirty-one cities out of several hundred attempted to resist. Sparta and Athens took the lead. **Themistocles** (Theh-mis'-tuh-cleez), who dominated Athenian politics at the time and advocated sea power, used his influence to build a fleet of 200 triremes in anticipation of a Persian attack. The **trireme** was a large, complex warship with three ranks of oarsmen and

Battle of Salamis.

Xerxes's army entered the deserted city of Athens and burned it. Shortly thereafter the Greek triremes destroyed half of his fleet in the battle of Salamis (Sal'-a-mis), one of the greatest naval engagements in history. As Themistocles had foreseen, the Persians crowded into the narrow strait and could not maneuver properly. The Greek ships, although slower, carried more fighting men and found it easy to ram and overwhelm their opponents as they came in.

▶ FIGURE 2.8 *Persian Guard of the Period of the Persian Wars.* Part of a larger frieze made of polychrome glazed bricks depicting rows of guards, perhaps the "immortals" who made up the king's personal bodyguard. From the Palace of Darius I (522–486 BCE) at Susa.

Salamis marked the turning point of the war. Without the support of his fleet, Xerxes could not supply his troops. Leaving a garrison to winter at Plataea in Greece, Xerxes and the main portion of his army returned to Persia. The Greeks defeated this garrison in the summer of 479 BCE and the Persians fled, never to return. At the same time, a fleet under Spartan command dislodged the enemy from the Ionian coast in the battle of Mycale (Mik'-uh-lee).

THE PELOPONNESIAN WARS (460–404 BCE)

The Persian threat had been repelled but not extinguished. Under the direction of Themistocles, the Athenians began to rebuild their city, fortifying its port at Piraeus and constructing the Long Walls that protected the road connecting the two. After Themistocles was ostracized in 472 BCE (the great enemy of the Persians ended his life as a Persian governor in southwest Asia), his successor, Cimon (Kee'-mon), continued the work. Then, in the winter of 478–477 BCE, Athens, as the leading Greek naval power, joined with a number of its allies to form the **Delian League** (taking its name from the Ionian island of Delos), an association dedicated to protecting the cities of the Aegean from Persians and pirates. Although Sparta had led the war on land, it did not join, preferring instead to concentrate on the helot problem and on strengthening its own **Peloponnesian League.** By 467 BCE, the Athenian navy and its Delian allies had secured the coasts of southwest Asia and achieved unquestioned dominance at sea. Greece was now divided into two increasingly competitive alliance systems.

The Delian and Peloponnesian Leagues. The size of its fleet made Athens the dominant partner in the Delian League, and although the Athenians initially maintained the rhetoric of friendship, they used the alliance to further their own purposes. Under Cimon's leadership, Athens sought to control grain supplies in the Aegean and to improve its access to ship's timber and precious metals by seizing new territory. Heavy tributes swelled the Athenian treasury. Some of the conquered land was distributed to poor citizens of Athens, and wealthier Athenians acquired property in allied cities without regard for local law. The true nature of the league was revealed when the island of Thasos tried to withdraw from it in 465 BCE. Athens treated the withdrawal as a rebellion and laid siege to the island for 2 years. League members and some Athenians began to think of the league as an Athenian empire.

Corinth, Athen's chief commercial rival and an ally of Sparta, had long argued against what it saw as the Athenian imperialism. Now both Delians and Peloponnesians began to fear that Athens sought nothing less than political hegemony over the Greek world. As long as Cimon, an admirer of Sparta, controlled Athenian policy, every effort was made to avoid open conflict with the Peloponnesian League. But he, too, was ostracized in 461 BCE and war followed immediately.

Pericles and Further Democratic Reform in Athens. The removal of Cimon coincided with a further democratization of Athenian government under the leadership of Ephialtes (Ef-ee'-all-teez) and his younger colleague **Pericles** (Per'-i-kleez) (c. 495–429 BCE). The Persian War and its aftermath had for the first time involved large numbers of poor citizens in combat, especially in the navy. Although theoretically equal, in practice the poor were barred from holding office because they could not afford to live without pay while serving on juries or in the Council. After the war, their claims to full participation in civic life could no longer be ignored, and Pericles, who would play a dominant role in Athenian politics for more than 30 years, built his career on changes that further liberalized the system created by Cleisthenes.

Realizing that most people could not afford to serve the polis, the reformers adopted the policy of paying men for public service, from deme representatives on the Council to members of a jury, a measure paid for by the wealth accumulated in Cimon's day. Citizenship, which now became more valuable than ever, was restricted for the first time to men with two citizen parents, but by 450 BCE Athens had become a participatory democracy in which every male citizen could play a role. Some have held that this democratization contributed to the tremen-

A Trireme—A Modern Reconstruction

The *trireme* was the basic Greek warship of the Persian and Peloponnesian Wars. A development from earlier designs, its distinguishing feature was the addition of a third rank of rowers, seated nearest the water, who provided greater speed and ramming power. The Trireme Trust reconstructed the trireme *Olympias,* shown here in several photographs, on the basis of ancient evidence, and the Greek navy commissioned her to service in 1987.

The Ram. This image shows the formidable ram at the bow (front) of the ship. When enemies reinforced their hulls against the ram, as they did during the Peloponnesian Wars, the triremes began to carry marines; using grappling irons to pull an enemy ship alongside, the marines boarded it and fought hand-to-hand with javelin and sword. The painted eye is found on many vessels in the Mediterranean today. In folklore, it helps the ship find its way and ward off danger.

The Olympias. Like triremes at the battle of Salamis, the *Olympias* is propelled by 170 rowers arranged on three vertical decks. Ancient sources indicate a rowing speed of 7 knots (c. 8 mph), but this speed is not sustainable over long distances. Square sails rigged on two masts supply the power for long voyages. The trireme was meant for battle; its advantage during the Persian War lay in its rowers' ability to quickly maneuver the trireme, ram the wooden hulls of Persian ships, and abandon them to sink. The *triarch,* or commander, sits in the stern (back) behind the two tillers that control the steering oars. There is one steering oar on each side of the ship, and at full power each steering oar requires two steersmen. One can imagine the coordination among commander, rowers, and steersmen that success in battle would require.

The Arrangement of the Trireme's Oars. This photo from the ship's side shows how the three tiers of oars were arranged. The top rank of rowers sat on benches that extended outboard from the hull. Most rowers on Greek warships were not slaves, but free citizens of the poorer classes.

dous flowering of high culture in the classical or Periclean age (see Chapter 3); others have held that it fueled the increasingly aggressive and reckless character of Athenian policy. The two arguments are not incompatible.

The Beginning of the Peloponnesian Wars. In the First Peloponnesian War (460–445 BCE) the Delian League defeated both the Peloponnesians and their Persian allies, but when several Delian allies rebelled against the arrogance of Athenian leadership, Pericles agreed to a 30 years' peace. He balanced his skills as an orator and popular leader with prudence, but the peace, which enabled Athens to recover its strength and reorganize its empire, lasted only 14 years. In 435 BCE, war broke out between Corinth and Corcyra. Corcyra was a former Corinthian colony in the Adriatic that had

HERODOTUS'S THE SPARTANS AT THERMOPYLAE FROM *THE HISTORIES*

"Tell them in Sparta, you who've read, that we obeyed their orders and are dead." The archetypal story of heroism in the face of great odds—the doomed defense of the pass at Thermopylae by a handful of Spartans and their Thespian and Theban allies against the entire Persian army—not only captured the imagination of the Greeks but lingers today in that 19th-century rhyme. This account from Herodotus, the great historian of the Persian War, dramatically contrasted free Greeks, willingly fighting for their native soil, with servile Asians driven into battle with whips.

As the Persian army advanced to the assault, the Greeks under Leonidas, knowing that the fight would be their last, pressed forward into the wider part of the pass. . . . Many of the invaders fell; behind them their company commanders plied their whips, driving the men remorselessly on. Many fell into the sea and were drowned, and still more were trampled to death by their friends. No one could count the number of the dead. The Greeks, who knew that the enemy were on their way round by the mountain track and that death was inevitable, fought with reckless desperation. . . . By this time most of their spears were broken, and they were killing Persians with their swords.

In the course of that fight Leonidas fell, having fought like a man indeed. Many distinguished Spartans were killed at his side. . . . There was a bitter struggle over the body of Leonidas; four times the Greeks drove the enemy off, and at last by their valor succeeded in dragging it away. So it went until the fresh troops with Ephialtes [the Greek who had revealed the secret track to the Persians] were close at hand; and then when the Greeks knew that they had come, the character of the fighting changed. They withdrew again into the narrow neck of the pass, behind the walls, and took up a position in a single compact body . . . on the little hill at the entrance to the pass, where the stone lion in memory of Leonidas stands today. Here they resisted to the last, with their swords if they had them, and if not, with their hands and teeth, until the Persians coming on in front over the ruins of the wall and closing in from behind, finally overwhelmed them.

Source: Herodotus, *The Histories*, trans. Aubrey de Sélincourt (Baltimore: Penguin Books, 1954, pp. 492–493).

Question: What does this passage say about the Greeks' perception of themselves and why they believed the struggle with Persia was essential?

---

been neutral in the First Peloponnesian War. The Athenians feared the loss of their naval dominance if Corcyra's powerful fleet fell into Corinthian hands. When Athens allied itself with Corcyra, Corinth protested to the Peloponnesian League, claiming again that the Athenians wanted total hegemony over all the Greeks. Attempts at negotiation failed, and in 431 BCE the Spartans invaded the Attica peninsula.

The Second Peloponnesian War. Realizing that the Spartans could not be defeated on land, Pericles allowed them to occupy the Athenian countryside. People from the rural demes crowded into the city. Although the Athenians mounted cavalry raids against Spartan garrisons, the major thrust of its policy was to launch amphibious expeditions against Sparta's allies. Pericles reasoned that because Athens was wealthy and its fleet controlled the seas, the city could survive on imports for up to 5 years before further tribute had to be demanded from members of the Delian League. Sparta's Peloponnesian allies were more vulnerable and would, he thought, sue for peace within 3 years.

The Plague at Athens. Unfortunately, a great plague struck Athens in the second year of the war (432 BCE)

and killed one-third of the people gathered there. The historian Thucydides (Thoo-sid'-uh-deez) described the symptoms of the disease in great detail, but they do not correspond precisely to anything in modern medicine. An enraged public drove Pericles from office. They recalled him, but he died soon after of the pestilence, and the city eventually abandoned his defensive policies. The more aggressive strategy advocated by Cleon, who followed Pericles as leader of the popular faction, at first succeeded. The Athenians fomented popular revolutions in a number of cities and supported democratic factions within them while the Spartans predictably backed their opponents. The Athenians then fortified Pylos on the western coast of Messenia and defeated a Spartan fleet that had been sent to drive them out. More than 400 Spartans had to take refuge on a nearby island. This was a significant

Pericles

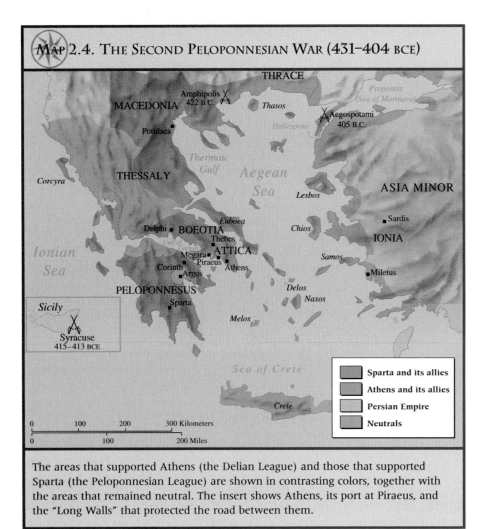

MAP 2.4. THE SECOND PELOPONNESIAN WAR (431–404 BCE)

The areas that supported Athens (the Delian League) and those that supported Sparta (the Peloponnesian League) are shown in contrasting colors, together with the areas that remained neutral. The insert shows Athens, its port at Piraeus, and the "Long Walls" that protected the road between them.

When Cleon died in the unsuccessful attempt to relieve Amphipolis, **Alcibiades** (Al-suh-bye'-ah-deez), an unscrupulous young aristocrat who had been a pupil of the philosopher Socrates, succeeded him as the dominant voice in Athenian politics. Under his guidance, Athens supported a Persian governor and his son in their revolt against the king. Persia, which had remained neutral, now had reason to back Sparta if hostilities resumed. Then in 415 BCE, Alcibiades convinced the Athenians to mount a great expedition against Sicily. It was a brazen attempt to acquire new resources by broadening the scope of the war, and it failed. Syracuse alone proved equal to Athens in wealth, population, and naval preparedness, and the rest of Sicily backed Syracuse. The Sicilians, with their superior cavalry, disrupted the Athenian siege and defeated their army on land. In 413 BCE, they destroyed the Athenian fleet. The Athenians lost 200 ships, more than 4,500 of their own men, and perhaps 20,000 of their allies.

Although Athens rebuilt its fleet and continued the struggle, its allies deserted one by one. The Spartans, backed by Persian money, launched a series of naval campaigns against them. Most were unsuccessful, but in 405 BCE, they destroyed a newly rebuilt Athenian fleet at Aegospotami (Eg-goss-pot'-a-mee). Lysander, the Spartan commander, cut off his enemy's grain supplies by seizing the Dardanelles. Faced with starvation, the Athenians surrendered unconditionally in 404 BCE. The Peloponnesian Wars were over.

CONCLUSION

Bearing little resemblance to the civilizations created in the river valleys of Egypt or Mesopotamia, early Greek society did not develop out of a common effort to mold a hostile environment. Nor did it ever achieve true economic or political unity. Greek society rested on a common culture rooted in Homeric values and devoted to the survival and life of the separate and independent

portion of Sparta's fighting elite. Without a navy and facing yet another helot revolt, the Spartans were desperate to recover their men and sued for peace.

Once again, overconfidence betrayed the Athenians. Dreaming of total victory, they refused to negotiate. Instead they attacked the nearby city of Megara and then invaded the rich agricultural region of Boeotia (Boh-ee'-sha). Both efforts failed, and several of their allies went over to the Spartans. Thus strengthened, the Spartan general Brasidas captured Amphipolis, the most important Athenian base in the northwestern Aegean. When relief efforts failed, it was the Athenian's turn to ask for a truce.

The Sicilian Expedition and End of the Wars.
The resulting peace of Nicias (421 BCE) accomplished little, in part because several important cities on both sides of the dispute refused to accept it. Hostilities continued, although Athens and Sparta remained only indirectly involved. Both sides attempted through diplomacy to lure away each other's allies, but internal factions and instability hampered Athens in its efforts.

polis. But while the polis became the site of the first democracies, its insular, competitive psychology made it difficult, if not impossible, for the Greeks to unite or to live at peace with one another. Even while driving off the Persians, much of the Greek world had sided with the enemy out of rivalry with either Athens, Sparta, or one of their allies. The failure of Athens—or Sparta—to forge an effective Panhellenic alliance created a power vacuum that would eventually be filled by the Macedonians, a people who, although related to the Greeks, did not share the culture of the polis. As a result, the independence of the polis would be gravely compromised. Athens itself fell under the control of the Thirty Tyrants, a group of collaborators who ruled with Spartan support. The Athenian empire disintegrated and its trade diminished, although it remained the cultural heart of the Greek world for centuries to come.

As the next chapter reveals, ancient Greece stands at the beginning of Western civilization. Its aesthetic ideals and its commitment to human self-development, competition, and linear thought transformed everything it touched and laid the foundations of the first characteristically Western culture. The struggles of the fifth century BCE coincided with the greatest intellectual and artistic achievements of classical Greek civilization, but they also marked the beginning of its end.

Review Questions

- Based on the Documents in this chapter, how did Greek mythology and the poems attributed to Homer influence the development of Greek culture?
- Using Athens as an example, how would you describe the development of the polis from its origins to the emergence of a democratic system of government?
- Why did Sparta developed into a conservative military state?
- How did the Delian League become a kind of Athenian empire, and how did this development contribute to the coming of the Peloponnesian Wars?

For Further Study

Readings

Davies, John Kenyon, *Democracy and Classical Greece*, 2nd ed. (Cambridge, MA: Harvard, 1993). Covers politics and more from 479 BCE to the struggle between Athens and Thebes.

Garlan, Yvon, *Slavery in Ancient Greece*, trans. J. Lloyd (Ithaca, NY: Cornell, 1988).

Just, Roger, *Women in Athenian Law and Life* (New York: Routledge, 1988). A comprehensive treatment.

Osborne, Robin, *Greece in the Making, 1200–479 BCE* (New York: Routledge, 1996). The origins of Greek society from the time of the migrations.

Sansone, David, *Greek Athletics and the Genesis of Sport* (Berkeley: University of California Press, 1988).

Websites

http://www.fordham.edu/halsall/ancient/asbook.html
The Ancient History Sourcebook. The section *Ancient Greece* contains information on every aspect of Greek life from the Minoans to Philip II of Macedon plus complete texts of the major ancient Greek historians, including Herodotus and Thucydides.

http://homepage.mac.com/cparada/GML/index.html
Greek Mythology Link by Carlos Parada. A vast compendium of text, images, and maps. Terrific scholarship and resource.

 InfoTrac College Edition

Visit the source collections at *http://infotrac.thomson learning.com* and use the search function with the following key terms.

Using Key Terms, enter the search terms:
Greek history   *Peloponnesian War*

Using the Subject Guide, enter the search term:
Greek mythology

Visit the Western Civilization Companion Web Site for resources specific to this textbook:
http://history.wadsworth.com/hause02/

The CD in the back of this book and the Western Civilization Resource Center at *http://history. wadsworth.com/western/* offer a variety of tools to help you succeed in this course, including access to quizzes; images; documents; interactive simulations, maps, and timelines; movie explorations; and a wealth of other sources.

EARLY GREECE AND ITS NEIGHBORS

The Eastern Mediterranean linked the ancient world and provided a matrix for the growth of civilizations in Greece and the Middle East. Notice their simultaneous events—their beginnings, conquests, and migrations. The reasons behind the connections, as well as their relationship, if any, to the beginnings of the Iron Age, remain unclear. Notice too the competition between Greeks and Phoenicians for colonies, and Phoenicia's head start. In Greece proper, the long period often referred to as the Greek Dark Ages ended in the eighth century with the introduction of the alphabet (the beginnings of Greek literature) and the Hoplite phalanx.

3500 BCE	1400 BCE	1200 BCE	800 BCE	700 BCE	600 BCE	500 BCE	400 BCE

GREECE

*Beginnings of Minoan Civilization on Crete

*Mycenaean Conquest of Crete (1400) →

Greek Dark Ages (c. 1200–800)

Dorian and Ionian
   Migrations

Phrygians Defeat Hittites
   *Introduction of an Alphabet
   *Homer's *The Iliad* (fl. 850)

Hoplite Phalanx introduced
*Hesiod's *Works and Days*

Age of Greek Colonization
*First Greek Colony at Naples Opens
   *Sappho's Poems
      *Greek Colony Founded at Marseilles
*Spartans Conquer Messenia

Age of the Tyrants
*Second Messenian War at Sparta
      *Cleisthenes Makes Democratic
         Reforms at Athens
      The Persian War

**The Peloponnesian Wars
(460–404 BCE)**

MIDDLE EAST

*Beginnings of Egyptian Civilization
*Beginnings of Mesopotamian Civilization

Hebrew and Philistine Migrations
*Introduction of Ironworking
   *First Phoenician Colony founded at Utica
   *Reigh of Solomon in Israel
      *Assyria Conquers Israel
   *Phoenicians found Carthage

Persians Conquer Mesopotamia and Egypt

Chapter 3

GREEK CULTURE AND ITS HELLENISTIC DIFFUSION

*I*n 327 BCE, at Bactra in what is now Uzbekistan, Alexander the Great married Roxana, a princess from Sogdiana, dividing a loaf of bread with her according to the local custom. Alexander had never been much interested in women. He had led his army of Greeks and Macedonians to the furthest limits of the known world, conquering Egypt, Mesopotamia, and the Persian Empire. This marriage had nothing to do with love or even with politics in the normal dynastic sense. It was to be a visible symbol of the unity between east and west, a unity that Alexander believed necessary if his conquests were to be preserved. By all accounts, the wedding ceremony offended his Greek followers without greatly impressing his new Asian subjects. Alexander died 3 years later far away in Babylon. Shortly thereafter, his generals murdered Roxana and their infant son in an effort to simplify the problem of Alexander's inheritance; although this piece of political theater ended badly, it was not entirely without meaning.

For all its violence and insecurity, the age of the Persian and Peloponnesian Wars had been for the Greeks, and in particular for Athens, a time of unparalleled creativity. The intensity of life in the midst of almost perpetual crisis called forth their best efforts, not only in war and politics but also in art, literature, and philosophy. The conquests of Alexander spread Greek culture and values to the limits of the known world. The process, however, was one of diffusion rather than imposition. The peoples of the Middle East retained their own identities while adopting Greek ideas, and the Greeks changed through contacts with ancient civilizations whose cultural norms differed radically from their own. The result was a rich and cosmopolitan fusion that is usually referred to as the *Hellenistic Age*.

Chapter 3 begins with a discussion of the art, literature, and thought produced by Greek civilization at its peak. It then describes how Philip II of Macedon took advantage of Greek disunity to lay the foundations of a Macedonian empire, and how his son Alexander the Great expanded that empire to the borders of India. It concludes with a description of the three great Hellenistic kingdoms that were created after Alexander's death and of the vibrant culture they produced.

ART AND LITERATURE IN CLASSICAL GREECE (530–320 BCE)

Greek Drama. Nowhere were Greek values, social attitudes, and conduct more evident than in drama. Plays, like athletic contests, accompanied many religious festivals. Actors who were often paid by the city performed the plays during the day in open-air amphitheaters that had been constructed at public expense. Men wearing masks played all of the roles, both male and female, and spoke their lines in verse. A male chorus provided explanation and commentary. In fifth-century Athens, as many 30,000 people might attend a single performance. The first plays were tragedies, a dramatic form thought to have been invented by the Athenian Thespis around 530 BCE. The themes of Attic tragedy (the form of tragic drama developed in Attica, or the region of Athens) came with rare exceptions from mythology or from Homer and drew their dramatic power from irreconcilable conflicts, often between the demands of the gods and those of the state or family. In these plays, the hero, who might be either male or female, sometimes prevails, although only after great suffering. More often he or she is undone by an unsuspected personal flaw or by *hubris,* the pride born of overconfidence. To the audience these dramas provided not only *catharsis,* a Greek word meaning emotional release, but a warning to the arrogant and to those who would make important decisions without regard to their moral complexity.

Among the greatest of the Greek dramatists were **Aeschylus** (Es'-ki-lus, c. 525–456 BCE), whose tragedies are the first to have been preserved, and **Sophocles** (Sahf'-uh-kleez, c. 495–406 BCE), whose *Antigone, Oedipus Rex, Electra,* and other works continue to inspire modern authors. **Euripides** (You-rip'-uh-deez, c. 484–406 BCE) was more popular in the fourth century BCE than in his own time. His later plays diluted the original tragic formula and led the way to more personal and unheroic themes. Comedy displays a similar progression. The plays of **Aristophanes** (Air-iss-toff'-uh-neez, c. 450–388 BCE) and his contemporaries, usually known as the *Old Comedy,* provided political satire with a razor's edge. As

FIGURE 3.1 *The Theater at Epidaurus.* The best preserved Greek theater is at Epidaurus in the northeast corner of the Peloponnesian Peninsula. It was built to provide entertainment for those who visited the city's famous temple of Asclepius, god of healing. The stone seats are built into the side of a hill. A low sill of white limestone marks off the orchestra and stage, but no attempt has been made to restore the backdrops, stage sets, and other structures behind it. The acoustics are so good that, without raising his or her voice, an actor can be heard in the rear seats.

the third century BCE progressed, comedy lost its public focus and turned to love stories and domestic situations whose plots continue to inspire modern scriptwriters.

The Invention of History in Classical Greece. The Greeks may also be said to have invented history. Earlier peoples preserved king lists and inscriptions that recorded the doings of royalty. The Hebrews chronicled their history to illuminate God's purposes, but the Greeks made history a branch of literature. The first writer to do this was **Herodotus** (Huh-rod'-uh-tus, c. 484–420 BCE), whose history of the Persian War was written specifically "to preserve the memory of the past by putting on record the astonishing achievements both of our own and of the Asiatic peoples; secondly, and more particularly, to show how the two races came into conflict." The result is both history and anthropology—an entertaining tour of the ancient world, its cultures, and its myths. The story of the war itself comes only toward the end of the book. However, his portraits of individual leaders are unforgettable, and he deserves his title, "the father of history."

The history of the Peloponnesian Wars by the Athenian **Thucydides** (Thoo-sid'-uh-deez, c. 460–404 BCE) is different. Exiled for his role as a naval commander in the ill-fated attempt to relieve Amphipolis, Thucydides was determined to understand the past because he believed that human nature was constant and that history therefore repeats itself. If one knows the past, it should be possible to avoid similar mistakes in the future (see Document 3.1). Other cultures had believed that history moves in cycles and that, as the biblical author of Ecclesiastes said in a notable departure from Jewish tradition, "there is no new thing under the sun." But the Greeks, beginning with Thucydides, used this ancient notion to justify the systematic study of history. It was among the most original of their achievements. Many of the better Roman historians studied history to avoid the mistakes of the past, and the idea, revived during the Renaissance, remained influential until well into the twentieth century.

Architecture in Classical Greece. Greek art, too, served public purposes. Although a fine aesthetic sense extended to everyday objects such as jewelry, armor, and decorated pottery, the greatest artistic achievement of ancient Greece was its monumental sculpture and architecture. The Greeks built temples to the gods who protected the *polis* or to house the oracles whom they consulted on all important occasions. These structures, whose function was as much civic as religious, were subtle adaptations of earlier Egyptian or Minoan ideas. Construction was basic post-and-lintel; the genius lay in the proportions and the details. An inner sanctuary that housed the statue of the deity formed the heart of the temple. It was surrounded by a colonnade supporting a sloped roof with triangular pediments at each end. Greek architects made the columns, which might or might not have decorated capitals, wider at the middle and tapered them gently toward the top to counteract the optical illusion known as *parallax*, thereby making them appear straight. The frieze, the entablature, and the pediments were decorated with sculptured reliefs of gods, goddesses, and heroes.

Sculpture in Classical Greece. Greek sculpture was concerned almost exclusively with the portrayal of the human figure. Early statues had a formal, abstract quality, with a power and dignity that reflected their subjects: gods, goddesses, heroes, and athletes. Male figures were almost invariably nudes, a preference that reflected the Greek willingness to appear naked in games and on the battlefield and that non-Greeks found shocking. In the early, or **archaic** period, female figures were invariably clothed. Gradually, during the sixth century BCE, sculptors began to work toward a more lifelike image.

By the fifth century BCE, sculptors such as **Phidias** (Fid'-ee-us) had achieved a level of skill that has never been surpassed, but realism was not their goal. Faces and figures reflect an idealized vision of human beauty rarely seen in nature. Female nudes, reflecting a sensuality hitherto seen only in the portrayal of men, became common. The aesthetic conventions developed by Phidias and the fourth-century BCE master **Praxiteles** (Prax-sit'-uh-leez) became the basis of later Hellenistic and Roman

tastes. Like the conventions of Greek architecture, they have been restored to temporary dominance by classic revivals in more modern times and remain an underlying part of the Western visual tradition.

Unfortunately, that vision may be historically misleading. Most of Greek art was destroyed by the early Christians, who saw it as idolatrous if not obscene, and modern taste has been formed largely by Roman copies. Painting, which to many ancient Greeks was more important than sculpture, has been lost entirely. The Greeks loved color, and statues preserved only in their undecorated state were once brilliantly painted. Some even had precious stones for eyes. The overall impression must have been very unlike the serene appearance that later generations associated with classicism, and the more refined modern critics of the eighteenth and nineteenth centuries would probably have found the statues gaudy.

FIGURE 3.2 *The Parthenon, on the Acropolis of Athens.* The most famous—and one of the largest—temples constructed in ancient Greece, the Parthenon was designed by the architect Ictinus in partnership with Callicrates and dedicated in 432 BCE to Athena Parthenos, the patron goddess of Athens. Sparta invaded Athens in the following year as part of the second Peloponnesian War. The use of the Doric order is unusually graceful. The magnificent sculptures that once adorned the pediments were carried away by the British and may now be seen in the British Museum.

GREEK THOUGHT FROM THE PRE-SOCRATICS TO ARISTOTLE (C. 550–322 BCE)

The earliest Greek thought concerned the nature of the physical universe, or physics, and was formulated in terms that suggest Egyptian or Mesopotamian influence. According to tradition, the sixth-century BCE philosopher **Thales** (Thay'-leez) of Miletus introduced geometry and astronomy to Greece after visiting Egypt. He may also have encountered there the idea that the universe was based ultimately upon water. But Greek thought developed differently from that of the Egyptians in several important respects. From the beginning, perhaps because of the structure of their language, the Greeks sought to demonstrate in the clearest possible way the logical connection between statements. This in turn forced them to confront the problem of **epistemology,** or how we know what we know. Can our physical senses be trusted, or can we understand the world only through the intellect? Logic, epistemology, and physics remain among the central concerns of Western thought to this day.

The Pre-Socratic Philosophers. The Pre-Socratics (the philosophers who preceded Socrates) concerned

themselves primarily with the physical world. Most of them believed that the senses provide an unreliable guide to reality and therefore tried to look beneath appearances to discover the true basis of matter. With one exception, they believed that basis to be a permanent and unchanging **element** or elements. The opposing view of **Heraclitus** (Hair-uh-cly'-tus, c. 500 BCE)—that the universe was in a constant state of movement—at first found few supporters. Some, like Thales, argued that all matter was ultimately composed of water; others believed that the basic element was earth. Eventually, **Empedocles** (Em-ped'-uh-cleez) of Acragas (c. 490–430 BCE) named the four basic elements as earth, air, fire, and water. Later accepted by Aristotle, this theory served as the basis for scientific investigation of the physical universe until the scientific revolution of modern times. An alternative view, proposed at about the same time by Leucippus (Loo-sip'-us) of Miletus and his

FIGURE 3.3 *The Architectural Orders.* The capitals at the top of a Greek column were always made in one of three designs or architectural orders. The Ionic order is shown at the left; the simpler Doric in the middle; and the Corinthian, with its decoration of acanthus leaves, on the right. The Romans adopted these orders as the European architects from the Renaissance to the present did.

THE EVOLUTION OF GREEK SCULPTURE

Greek sculpture changed dramatically during the Persian and Peloponnesian Wars. Works from the sixth century BCE are generally referred to as Archaic. The figures usually appear in a full frontal pose or in profile and have a static, formal look. Male figures normally appear nude or nearly so; women are fully clothed. By the middle of the fifth century, the figures have become three dimensional and natural, although still idealized. Sculptors still sought to portray perfect beauty in a serene atmosphere. Women were often portrayed in the nude. A century later, in the time of Alexander the Great, serenity has been banished. The sculptors of the age used their technical mastery to show emotion and violent movement.

▶ The figure on the left is a *kore* (masc. *koros*) from the Athenian acropolis, c. 520 BCE. Figures of this kind were used as tomb markers or votive statues and are one of the most common forms of early Greek sculpture. Although more delicately modeled than most, this piece is still formal, two-dimensional, and somewhat abstract. On the right is a Roman copy of the famous Aphrodite by Praxiteles. Although the statue reflects a certain classical serenity, the sensuality is, by earlier Greek standards, remarkable. In archaic times, only male figures were portrayed in the nude.

pupil **Democritus** (Dem-mock'-ruh-tus), held that everything was composed of atoms, invisible particles that combined and separated to produce the various forms of matter. Like the arguments of Heraclitus, it found little support.

If these early philosophers speculated on ethical matters, their writings on the subject have been lost, but the proper conduct of life was vitally important to people who lacked a moral code based on divine revelation. **Pythagoras** (Pith-ag'-oh-rus), who founded a school at Croton in Italy around the year 500 BCE, taught ethics based in part on his belief in the religious cult of Orpheus. In the course of his studies, he discovered the mathematical basis of musical harmony and decided that the fundamental organizing principle of the universe was numerical. This idea, like his theory that the Earth revolved around the sun, would prove interesting to later thinkers.

The Sophists. By the fifth century BCE, most people were learning the practical arts of rhetoric and persuasion, as well as ethics, from the **Sophists.** These itinerant teachers charged high fees for their services but offered nothing less than a prescription for success in private and public life. Their teachings varied, but most were **subjectivists.** As **Protagoras,** the most famous of them, said, "Man is the measure." He meant that the individual's personal experience, however imperfect in an absolute sense, is the only conceivable basis for knowledge or judgment. Everything is relative to the individual's perception.

The implications of this view were profoundly disturbing. Extreme Sophists held that truth was objectively unknowable. Law and even the polis were based on convention and mutual agreement, not fundamental principles. Some went so far as to claim that justice was merely the interest of the strong and that the gods had been invented by clever men as a means of social control.

Socrates. Socrates (Sock'-ruh-teez, c. 470–399 BCE) wrote nothing. Wandering the streets of Athens, he asked questions intended to reveal the responder's underlying assumptions about human values and institutions. Using logic and irony, he would then question the validity of those assumptions. His purpose, unlike that of the Sophists whom he otherwise resembled, was to find an **objective** basis for ethical and political behavior. He made no promises and took no fees, but his questions were rarely open-ended and made people feel foolish.

Socrates

Socrates tried the patience of the Athenians severely. In 399 BCE, they executed him for corrupting the youth of Athens and inventing new gods. The charges were largely specious and reflected Athenian wariness of challenges to the polis—Socrates, although himself of humble origins, favored aristocracy as the ideal form of government and mocked democratic notions then in favor.

Plato. As a young man from an aristocratic Athenian family, **Plato** (Play'-toe, 428–347 BCE) toyed with the idea of a political career until the aftermath of the Sicilian expedition and the execution of Socrates convinced him that politics was incompatible with a good conscience. Around the year 387 BCE, he founded The Academy on the out-

skirts of Athens, a kind of institute for advanced studies in mathematics, the physical sciences, and philosophy.

Plato had been a student of Socrates and made him the leading character in a series of famous **dialogues**—philosophical arguments in dramatic form—that became a model of philosophic writing for centuries to come. The character Socrates reflects the author's views. With the exception of the *Timaeus,* a later dialogue that deals with cosmology and mathematics, most of Plato's dialogues explore questions of ethics, education, government, and religion. The *Republic* describes the ideal state, in which philosophers rule according to the highest principles of wisdom, whereas the dialogue *Protagoras* argues against the relativism of the Sophists.

Platonic Idealism. The underlying principle of Plato's dialogues is the **theory of forms** (see Document 3.2). Plato argued that the form of a thing has an objective reality of its own. This "universal" or idea of a thing exists apart from any object perceived by the senses and can be understood only by the intellect. Because the senses are deceptive, understanding can be achieved only through the knowledge of forms. When extended to such universal qualities as justice or beauty, the theory of forms becomes the basis for absolute standards that can be applied to human conduct, both public and private. To Plato, the relativism of the Sophists was an illusion. Platonic Idealism (also known as Realism, because it affirms the reality of ideas) was one pole of the epistemological debate that would occupy Western philosophy for centuries. Subjectivism was the other. Because the argument dealt with what was real and what was knowable, the position of philosophers on epistemology influenced and in some cases determined their view of everything else.

Aristotle and the Study of Logic and Science. Aristotle (Air'-us-stot-uhl, 384–322 BCE) was the most famous of Plato's pupils. After studying at Plato's Academy until Plato's death, Aristotle served as tutor to the future conqueror Alexander the Great. In 336 BCE, Aristotle established his own school at Athens—the Lyceum. His followers were known in later years as the Peripatetics after the covered walkway or *peripatos* under which they met. Most of the enormous body of work attributed to him appears to be derived from lecture notes and other materials collected by the Peripatetics in the course of their studies.

Although he accepted Plato's theory of forms, Aristotle rejected the notion that they were wholly separate from empirical reality. He relied heavily upon observation, especially in his scientific work. His basic viewpoint, however, remained, like Plato's, teleological. Both thinkers, in other words, believed that things could be understood only in relation to their end or purpose *(telos* in Greek). To Aristotle, for example, actions must be judged in terms of

PLATO'S PARABLE OF THE CAVE FROM *THE REPUBLIC*

The parable of the cave describes in graphic terms the difference between sense perceptions and reality, which can be perceived only through thought. The cave is a metaphor for the world of sense impressions in which nothing is as it appears, and to Plato all people are prisoners within it. The author is speaking to his friend Glaucon.

"Picture men dwelling in a sort of subterranean cavern with a long entrance open to the light on its entire width. Conceive of them as having their legs and necks fettered from childhood, so that they remain in the same spot, able to look forward only, and prevented by the fetters from turning their heads. Picture further the light from a fire burning higher up and at a distance behind them, and between the fire and the prisoners and above them a road along which a low wall has been built, as the exhibitors of puppet-shows have partitions before the men themselves above which they show the puppets."

"All that I see," he said.

"See also, then, men carrying past the wall implements of all kinds that rise above the wall, and human images and shapes of animals as well, wrought in stone and wood and every material, some of these bearers presumably speaking and others silent."

"A strange image you speak of," he said, *"and strange prisoners."*

"Like to us," I said: *"for, to begin with, tell me do you think that these men would have seen anything of themselves or of one another except the shadows cast from the fire on the wall of the cave that fronted them?"*

"How could they," he said, *"if they were compelled to hold their heads unmoved through life."*

"And again, would not the same be true of the objects carried past them? . . . Then in every way such prisoners would deem reality to be nothing else than the shadows of artificial objects."

From Plato, *The Republic,* trans. Paul Shorey (Cambridge, MA: Harvard University Press, 1963).

Question: If Plato is correct in arguing that our senses deceive us, how is it possible for humans to acquire knowledge?

---

the result they produce, an ethical principle that in medieval times would form the basis of natural law. In politics, this led him to an impassioned defense of the polis as the best form of social organization. Although these contributions to ethics and politics were enormously important, Aristotle's greatest influence lay elsewhere.

Logic. The process by which statements are formed and relate to one another, that is, **logic,** was central to Greek discourse. Aristotle was the first to analyze this process and, in so doing, codified a logical method that dominated formal thought until the twentieth century. Its basis is the **syllogism,** an argument that in its simplest form says that if all A is B and all C is A, then all C must be B. A traditional example is: "All men are mortal. Socrates is a man. Therefore, Socrates is Mortal." Aristotle went far beyond this, and his six treatises on logic, known collectively as the *Organon,* describe many types of syllogisms, the formation and categorization of statements, and the nature of language itself.

Science. In the physical sciences, Aristotle's influence dominated thought until the scientific revolution of the sixteenth and seventeenth centuries. He wrote extensively on biology, physics, and human psychology and was responsible for collecting and transmitting much of what is known about the Pre-Socratic philosophers. His method was to observe natural phenomena and to understand them in terms of what he called the "four causes." These were not causes in the modern sense but rather aspects of a problem that had to be considered in its solution. The four causes are the matter out of which a thing is made (material cause), its form or shape (formal cause), the purpose it is intended to fulfill (final cause), and the force that brings it into being (efficient cause).

These causes are discovered by logical inference from empirical observations. Aristotle made no effort to create predictive mathematical models based on these inferences and did not attempt to verify them through experiment. His method was therefore unlike that of modern science and produced different results. Scientists no longer believe that the process by which a physical change occurs can be fully explained by its final cause or teleological purpose. Since the seventeenth century they have asked different questions and have rejected most of Aristotle's conclusions about the behavior of matter. Still, Aristotle's observations and hypotheses set the agenda for more than

ARISTOTLE'S DESCRIPTION OF THE CIRCULATORY SYSTEM FROM "HISTORY OF ANIMALS"

This brief excerpt demonstrates the careful observation that made Aristotle's works influential until the scientific revolution of the seventeenth century. Although Aristotle describes the connection between the heart and lungs, he does not infer from this the circulation of the blood, in part because he makes no attempt to relate morphology (anatomical structure) to function.

1. *The heart has three cavities: it lies above the lungs, near the division of the trachea. It has a fat and thick membrane by which it is united to the great vein and the aorta.*

2. *The greatest [of the cavities] is that on the right, the least on the left, the middle one is of intermediate size. They are all perforated toward the lungs.*

3. *Near the principal cavity it is attached to the great vein by which also the mesenterium is united, and in the middle it is attached to the aorta. Passages lead from the lungs to the heart, and they are divided in the same way as the trachea,* following the passages from the trachea throughout the whole lungs.

4. *The lung has more blood than all the other parts, for the whole lung is spongy, and through each perforation branches of the great vein proceed. Those persons are deceived who say that the lungs are empty, drawing their conclusions from dissected animals from which all blood has escaped. Of all the viscera, the heart also contains blood, and in the lungs the blood is not in the lungs themselves but in the veins by which they are perforated. But in the heart itself the blood is in each of the cavities, but the thinnest blood is in the middle cavity.*

5. *Beneath the lungs is that division of the trunk which is called the diaphragm, It is united to the ribs, the hypochondriac region, and the spine. In the center is a smooth membranous part, and there are veins extending through it.*

From Aristotle, "History of Animals," in *Source Book of Medical History,* ed. Logan Clendenning (New York: Dover, 1960, pp. 36–37).

Question: How does Aristotle's refusal to describe how this anatomical system actually worked reflect the basic stance of nearly every Greek scientific philosopher with the exception of Heraclitus?

1,000 years of speculation, while his teleological bias and preoccupation with qualitative descriptions (the material and formal causes) was a compelling, if not always productive, influence on later thought. His insistence on careful observation and logically constructed argument remains a part of the scientific tradition today. No other thinker has had such a powerful impact on later generations.

THE MACEDONIAN CONQUESTS TO 323 BCE

Aristotle lived in the twilight of classical Greek civilization. Although he probably did little to inspire them, the exploits of his pupil Alexander of Macedon, known as **Alexander the Great,** changed the political structure of the Greek world and spread Greek values and ideas throughout the Middle East. Inevitably, those values were changed and diluted in the process, and the culture that emerged from the Macedonian conquests was at the same time more cosmopolitan and less intense than that of the ancient polis.

The Decline of Greece

The Theban Hegemony. The end of the Peloponnesian Wars had left the Greek states under the political influence of Sparta. The Spartans, like the Athenians before them, soon made themselves hated by interfering with the internal policies of their allies. Athens and Thebes combined against them, and in 371 BCE a Theban army under the command of **Epaminondas** (Epp-pam'-in-on-dus, c. 410–362 BCE) defeated the Spartans at Leuctra. Sparta's role as a major power ended, and a new era of military innovation began. Epaminondas had given careful thought to a peculiarity of hoplite warfare. Hoplites carried their shields on the left. In combat they shifted toward the right, away from the point of impact. This threw the phalanx out of balance, but the consequent strengthening of its right side meant that the right frequently won the battle. Epaminondas took advantage of this oddity and weighted his phalanx heavily to the left and held back the right. This unbalanced formation, supported by cavalry on his right flank, enabled him to crush the Spartans at their strongest point and envelop them. The use of deep formations, effectively supported

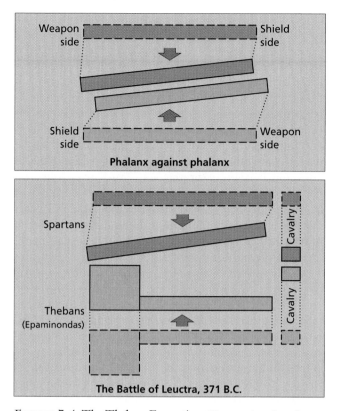

FIGURE 3.4 *The Theban Formation.* The top drawing shows the traditional pattern of hoplite warfare with the shield side of each formation slowly giving way as the battle develops. The bottom drawing shows how Epaminondas weighted his formation at Leuctra to crush the Spartans at their strongest point (the "weapon side," or right).

for the first time by cavalry, would be greatly expanded by the Macedonians.

Although supported by the relative wealth of Boeotia, Theban hegemony lasted no longer than that of the Spartans. The Athenians had revived their alliance system in the years immediately before Leuctra and, fearing Theban ambition, soon turned it against Epaminondas. By 362 BCE, the Peloponnesians had also reconstituted their confederacy, and although Epaminondas defeated the combined forces of Athens and Sparta at Mantinea, he died in the battle. Deprived of his leadership, Theban military power declined. Without the stimulus of threats from Thebes or Sparta, the "second" Athenian Empire collapsed and Greece reverted to its traditional state of disorganization.

Economic and Political Decline of Greece. A century of warfare had brought economic decline and social tension to the Greek cities. The Carthaginians encroached upon their overseas markets while the Greek colonies in Italy became, of necessity, more self-sufficient. As exports diminished, thousands of Greeks sought employment as mercenaries. One such group found itself stranded

in Mesopotamia when the schemes of their Persian employer miscarried. A leader of the expedition, the Athenian writer and military theorist Xenophon (c. 431–350 BCE) left a vivid account of their march to the Black Sea coast and safety. Xenophon and the career of Epaminondas show that Greek fighting men had lost nothing of their skill and valor. The artistic and intellectual achievements of the fourth century BCE demonstrate that the culture was alive and well. But for all its evident vigor, Greece had become a political vacuum.

Philip II of Macedon and the End of Greek Independence. The Macedonians filled that vacuum. Ancient Macedonia occupied the broad plain at the head of the Thermaic Gulf in northeastern Greece. Its people spoke a dialect of Greek, but their social and political institutions differed from those of the poleis. The population was almost entirely rural and, by Greek standards, widely scattered. Rich pastures encouraged the raising of horses. Macedonian society was therefore dominated by a landholding aristocracy that fought on horseback, usually against the neighboring hill tribes whose raids posed a constant threat to the country's borders. Hereditary kings tried to rule with or without cooperation from the aristocracy, and internal strife was common. To other Greeks, the Macedonians seemed primitive, but their homeland was rich in timber, minerals, and agricultural resources. Many believed that if Macedon could achieve stability, it would one day become a major power.

Philip II (382–336 BCE) achieved that goal. Philip was a younger son of the Macedonian royal family who, while a hostage at Thebes, had observed the military reforms of Epaminondas. His brother died in 359 BCE and left Philip as regent for the youthful heir, Amyntas IV. Cunning and energetic, Philip used his position to remove political rivals and suppress the local hill tribes. In 357 through 356 BCE, he seized Amphipolis and then Mt. Pangaeus with its rich deposits of gold and silver. At about this time he also usurped his nephew's throne.

With his political base secure, and fortified by the wealth of Mt. Pangaeus, Philip moved to extend his power over Greece as a whole. Through warfare, bribery, and skilled diplomacy, Philip played upon the disunity of the Greeks. The Athenian orator **Demosthenes** (Duh-mahs'-thuh-neeze) tried to rally them with his *Philippics,* a series of speeches attacking Philip as a ruthless barbarian, but by this time it was too late for them to mount an effective resistance. In 338 BCE, Philip defeated a poorly organized army of Thebans and Athenians at Chaeronea and became master of the Greek world. For the most part, Philip wore his new authority lightly. He secured a measure of acceptance by not interfering in local politics, but his plan to lead the united Greeks against Persia did not materialize in his lifetime.

Military Legacy of Philip II. Philip II left a formidable legacy. Not only did he unite the Greeks, but he also created the army with which his son Alexander III, "the Great," would conquer most of the known world. The heart of the Macedonian army remained some 2,000 cavalry armed with sword and spear, the so-called companions of the king. They were supported by infantry drawn up in the Macedonian phalanx, a formation that differed substantially from that of the hoplites. The peasants of Macedonia could not afford hoplite equipment, and their geographical isolation made intensive training difficult. Philip solved these problems by arranging his men in deep formations and arming them with spears longer than those used by the hoplites. By fighting in tightly closed ranks, the Macedonians could thereby present an almost impenetrable front without the need for highly specialized combat skills.

Hoplites were added to the Macedonian ranks as Philip's system of alliances grew. He also recruited mercenary horsemen from Thessaly, which bordered Macedon on the south, and supplemented his infantry with slingers, bowmen, and javelin throwers. The genius of Philip (and Alexander) lay in the ability to coordinate these varied elements and to make even the cavalry fight as a disciplined tactical unit instead of as individual champions. But the Macedonians were equally attentive to the problems of siege craft. Philip introduced to the Aegean world the techniques and siege engines developed by Dionysius, the Tyrant of Syracuse, and used them successfully against Perinthus and Byzantium. He was planning an attack on the Persian Empire when he was assassinated in 336 BCE, possibly at the instigation of his wife.

Alexander the Great

In 10 years (334–324 BCE), Philip's son Alexander used this formidable army to conquer the Persian Empire and extend his authority from Greece to Egypt and from Egypt to India. Alexander's military exploits have rarely been equaled, but his character remains something of a mystery. After putting down a rebellion among the Greeks, the 22-year-old Alexander marched into Asia Minor at the head of about 37,000 men. In 334 BCE, he defeated the Persians at the Granicus River in what is now Turkey, and in the following year, he gained control of the Ionian cities of the eastern Aegean. In 333, his victory over a superior force under the Persian

Alexander

emperor Darius at Issus in present-day Syria opened the way to Phoenicia and Egypt. When Tyre and Gaza fell to the siege engines of the Greeks, Egypt surrendered and Darius offered him everything west of the Euphrates River in return for peace. Alexander, now pharaoh of Egypt, refused. After establishing a new Egyptian capital, which he named Alexandria after himself, he invaded Mesopotamia. Another victory over the Persians at Gaugamela in present-day Iraq (331 BCE) opened the way to Babylon and ultimately to the Persian capitals of Susa and Persepolis (present-day Iran), where he was named Emperor of Persia. After Darius was assassinated by one of his own governors, Alexander spent 3 years fighting in the east before his army mutinied and forced him to turn toward home. By this time he had penetrated into what is now India.

Nearly all of Alexander's major battles, on the Granicus in Asia Minor, at Issus in Syria, at Gaugamela on the upper Tigris, and on the Hydaspes in India, were brilliant cavalry actions in which the infantry played only a secondary role. His sieges were consistently successful, and his ability to hold a multiethnic army together on hard campaigns in unfamiliar territory attests to an extraordinary capacity for leadership. Even after the Macedonians mutinied and demanded to return home, he preserved their loyalty by officially making them his kinsmen.

His purposes, however, are not entirely clear. Many of his contemporaries saw only personal ambition. Arrian, the chronicler of his campaigns, said, "if he had found no one else to strive with he would have striven with himself." Others, including Plutarch, detected more noble motives (see *Alexander the Great*). Alexander's publicists encouraged the notion of a vast state based on universal brotherhood. He proclaimed the equality of all subjects regardless of religion or ethnicity and gave this policy tangible form by marrying Roxana, a princess from Sogdiana in central Asia.

He may also have hoped to spread the benefits of Hellenic culture, but he seems to have stressed this only in dealing with Greeks. Not all Greeks were convinced. They resented his acceptance of foreign customs and his tendency to claim divine attributes when dealing with easterners. His idealism, if such it was, was accompanied by utter ruthlessness and by a casual brutality aggravated by heavy drinking. When he died in 323 BCE at the age of 32, he left no successors and only the most general plan for the governance of his realms.

THE HELLENISTIC KINGDOMS (323–330 BCE)

The Division of Alexander's Empire. Alexander's death led to a prolonged struggle among the Macedonian generals. Although Roxana was pregnant when he died,

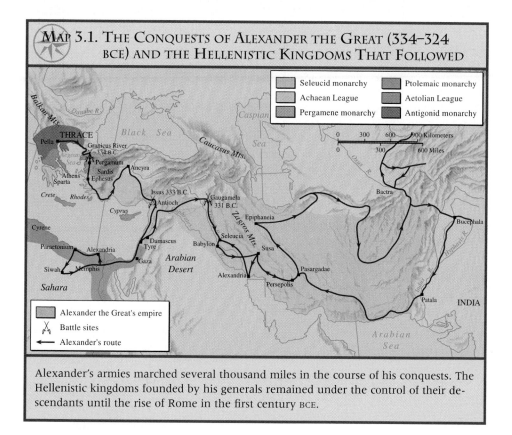

MAP 3.1. THE CONQUESTS OF ALEXANDER THE GREAT (334–324 BCE) AND THE HELLENISTIC KINGDOMS THAT FOLLOWED

Seleucid monarchy
Achaean League
Pergamene monarchy
Ptolemaic monarchy
Aetolian League
Antigonid monarchy

Alexander the Great's empire
Battle sites
Alexander's route

Alexander's armies marched several thousand miles in the course of his conquests. The Hellenistic kingdoms founded by his generals remained under the control of their descendants until the rise of Rome in the first century BCE.

there was no immediate successor. The commanders at first divided the empire into governorships, with the intention of preserving it for the conqueror's unborn heir, but they soon fell to fighting among themselves. In the civil wars that followed, Roxana and her son, together with several of the generals, were murdered. Three main successor states under Alexander's generals Antigonus, Seleucus, and Ptolemy emerged from the shambles. Macedon, much of Asia Minor, and a dominant position in the Greek alliance fell to Antigonus (382–301 BCE). The descendants of Ptolemy (d. 283 BCE) ruled Egypt as its Thirty-Third Dynasty until the death of Cleopatra in 30 BCE, while Seleucus (d. 281 BCE) established an empire based on Syria and Mesopotamia.

All three dynasties, the **Antigonids** (An-tig'-o-nids), the **Ptolemies** (Tol'-uh-meez), and the **Seleucids** (Se-loo'-sids), are called **Hellenistic,** as is the entire period from their founding to the death of Cleopatra VII of Egypt in 30 BCE. The term itself was coined in the nineteenth century and seems to have implied a dilution of Greek values, particularly those of the polis. If so, it is unduly patronizing. The Hellenistic period was one of unprecedented cultural borrowing and transmission. Ideas, religions, and artistic motifs from Egypt and the Middle East fused with those of the Greeks and spread throughout the Mediterranean world. Science, philosophy, and the arts flourished. But the term is unfortunate for another reason. It implies a uniformity that did not exist. Politically and socially, the successor kingdoms differed widely from one another. If the kingdoms shared a certain veneer of Greek culture, their problems were unique and for more than a century they maintained a rivalry that sometimes degenerated into open war.

Foreign Policies of the Hellenistic Monarchies. The chief foreign policy goal of the Ptolemies was to protect the Nile delta from foreign invasion. This required the maintenance of a large navy and, from the Egyptian point of view, control over Phoenicia and the Syrian coast, which supplied the fleet with timber and naval stores. The Seleucids resisted Ptolemaic claims to Syria because they needed the Mediterranean ports to maintain their trade with the west. After a series of wars, the Seleucids ultimately gained control of both Syria and Palestine, but not before the Antigonids, too, became entangled in the web of Ptolemaic diplomacy. Fearing an alliance between the Seleucids and the Antigonids, the Ptolemies supported the growth of Pergamum as a buffer state between the two kingdoms and, whenever possible, stirred up anti-Macedonian sentiment in Greece. This usually meant support for one of the two leagues of city-states that formed in third-century Greece: the Aetolian League in the west central part of the Greek peninsula and the Achaean League, headed by Corinth, in northern Peloponnese. Egyptian policy collapsed when, in about 230 BCE, the Ptolemies also formed an alliance with Sparta. The frightened Achaeans turned to the Antigonids for help, and the Ptolemies, under attack by the Seleucid king, Antiochus III, "the Great," could do nothing to protect the Aetolians. In the end Antiochus conquered Syria, Phoenicia, and Palestine, and the Aetolians allied themselves with a new power then emerging in the west: Rome.

The struggles among the Hellenistic kingdoms, although occasionally dramatic, seem to have had little impact on everyday life. The most important social and economic effect was a periodic influx of slaves into the labor market as one side or the other succeeded in taking large numbers of captives. As a result, slavery became increasingly important to the Hellenistic economy, forcing free laborers into marginal occupations or

ALEXANDER THE GREAT

Alexander's character and motives mystified his contemporaries. Two very different pictures of the conqueror can be found in works by the same author. It is not impossible, of course, that the self-indulgent violence described by Plutarch in his *Life of Alexander* could coexist with motives of the highest kind. But was Alexander's devotion to universal brotherhood a propaganda ploy designed to further his personal ambitions? Those who knew him could not be sure.

A Positive View of Alexander's Conquests

Plutarch, who wrote the important *Life of Alexander*, believed in the conqueror's "civilizing" mission and dedication to the universal brotherhood of humankind. In this *Oratio* (speech) he makes the best possible case for his hero's motives.

Alexander did not follow Aristotle's advice to treat the Greeks as a leader, the barbarians as a master, cultivating the former as friends and kinsmen, and treating the latter as animals or plants. Had he done so his kingdom would have been filled with warfare, banishments and secret plots, but he regarded himself as divinely sent to mediate and govern the world. And those whom he failed to win over by persuasion he overpowered in arms, bringing them

together from every land, combining, as it were in a loving cup, their lives, customs, marriages, and manners of living. . . .

For he did not cross Asia like a robber, nor did he have it in mind to ravage and despoil it for the booty and loot presented by such an unheard-of stroke of fortune. . . . Instead he conducted himself as he did out of a desire to subject all the races in the world to one rule and one form of government, making all mankind a single people. Had not the divinity that sent Alexander recalled his soul so soon, there would have been a single law, as it were, watching over all mankind, and all men would have looked to one form of justice as their common source of light. But now, that portion of the world that never beheld Alexander has remained as if deprived of the sun.

From Plutarch, "De Alexandri Magni Fortuna ast Virtute, Oratio I," in *Sources in Western Civilization: Ancient Greece*, ed. and trans. Truesdell S. Brown (New York: The Free Press [Simon & Schuster], 1965, pp. 199–200).

Alexander Murders a Friend

Plutarch was well aware of another side of Alexander's personality. In this extract from his *Life of Alexander*, the conqueror appears as violent, drunken, and superstitious. It also

outright unemployment. By the end of the third century BCE, the cities of all three kingdoms were struggling with the social problems created by poverty.

Greece under the Antigonids

In the Antigonid kingdom, life went on largely as before, although without the endless warfare of Greek against Greek that had characterized the classical period. Under Macedonian rule the states retained their separate identities, but loss of control over foreign and military affairs blunted the intensity of their political life. Not even the formation of the Achaean and Aetolian leagues could restore it. Economic decline continued. Poor yields as a result of erosion and soil exhaustion forced landowners to compensate by experimenting with fertilizers and new agricultural techniques. These methods were modestly successful, but for small farmers their cost was prohibitive. Large estates, many of them worked by slaves, became more common. For thousands of Greeks, service as mercenaries or as administrators in the other Hellenistic kingdoms remained the most promising route to success.

The Seleucid Monarchy

The Seleucid kingdom absorbed most of these ambitious folk. Alexander had established almost seventy Greek cities in what had been the Persian Empire. He sought to provide homes for his veterans and for those fleeing overpopulation in their native land. He also hoped to establish trustworthy centers of administration in a vast region populated by dozens of different ethnic and religious groups. The Seleucids greatly expanded this policy. The new cities tried to duplicate as far as possible the life of the polis. In the years after Alexander's death, the wealth extracted from his conquests paid for the construction of temples, theaters, and other public buildings in the Greek style. Greek law and Greek political institutions were imposed, but these cities, for all their magnificence, remained cultural hybrids thronged with people of many cultures. Unlike the citizens of a polis, they had neither gods nor ancestors in common.

The Greco-Macedonian Elite. The Seleucids respected the cultural and religious sensibilities of their subjects but preferred to rely on Greek or Macedonian reveals that the tension between the Macedonians and Alexander's new Asian subjects was far greater than the *Oratio* seems to suggest.

After the company had drunk a good deal somebody began to sing the verses of a man named Pranichus . . . which had been written to make fun of some Macedonian commanders who had recently been defeated by the barbarians. The older members of the party took offense at this . . . but Alexander and those sitting near him listened with obvious pleasure and told the man to continue. Cleitus, who had already drunk too much and was rough and hot-tempered by nature, became angrier than ever and shouted that it was not right for Macedonians to be insulted in the presence of barbarians and enemies, even if they had met with misfortune, for they were better men than those who had been laughing at them. Alexander retorted that if Cleitus was trying to disguise cowardice as misfortune, he must be pleading his own case. At this Cleitus sprang to his feet and shouted back, "Yes, it was my cowardice that saved your life, you who call yourself the son of the gods, when you were turning your back to Spithridate's sword. And it is the blood of these Macedonians . . . which [has] made you so great that you disown your own father and claim to be the son of Ammon (the Egyptian god)!"

These words made Alexander furious. "You scum," he cried out, "do you think you can keep on speaking of me like this and stir up

the Macedonians and not pay for it?" "Oh, but we Macedonians did pay for it," Cleitus retorted. "Just think of the rewards we got for all our efforts . . ." [After much more of this] Alexander could no longer control his rage: he hurled one of the apples on the table, hit him, then looked around for his dagger. One of his bodyguards . . . had already removed it out of harm's way, and the others crowded around him and begged him to be quiet . . . As Cleitus still refused to give way . . . Alexander seized a spear from one of his guard, faced Cleitus as he was drawing aside the curtain of the doorway and ran him through. With a roar of pain and a groan. When [Alexander] came to himself and saw his friends standing around him speechless, he snatched the weapon out of the dead body and would have plunged it into his own throat if the guards had not forestalled him by seizing his hands and carrying him by force to his chamber.

There he spent the rest of the night and the whole of the following day in an agony of remorse. At last he lay exhausted by grief, uttering deep groans but unable to speak a word, until his friends, alarmed at his silence, forced their way into his room, He paid no attention to what any of them said, except when Aristander the diviner reminded him . . . that these events had long ago been ordained by fate . . . He seemed to accept this assurance.

From Plutarch, "Life of Alexander," in *The Age of Alexander*, trans. Ian Scott-Kilvert (Harmondsworth, UK: Penguin Books, 1973).

soldiers and administrators for the day-to-day business of governing. The Greek population of the cities, reinforced until the second century BCE by emigration from Greece, formed a dominant, although not especially cohesive, elite. Their own origins were diverse and their perspective essentially careerist. They formed few emotional ties to their new homes and were usually prepared to go elsewhere if opportunity knocked. The Syrians, Persians, and Babylonians, who made up the bulk of the population, adopted a few Greek ideas and customs while retaining their own cultural identities.

Seleucid Society. The result was a cosmopolitan society held together largely by military force. The cities remained unstable amalgams of contending ethnic and religious groups. They had their own administrations and popular assemblies but were legally the possessions of the king and had to deal with him through emissaries to protect their interests. Riots were common. *Koine*, a universal Greek dialect, evolved as the language of trade and administration but never fully displaced Aramaic or the other tongues of the ancient Middle East. In the countryside, Greek influence re-

mained negligible. Village societies retained their traditional structure even when they became part of the royal domain and paid taxes directly to the crown. Royal grants allotted some of them to the cities while others became legally subject to a variety of private landholders. The forms of land tenure, taxation, and provincial administration were highly diverse.

The Seleucid Empire survived for nearly 300 years, largely because its cities and provinces had no common basis for resistance to the crown, and because—until the coming of the Romans—it faced no serious outside threats. The conflicts with the Ptolemies over Palestine and Syria and with the Antigonids over portions of Asia Minor were largely settled by the early second century BCE. Border provinces, especially in the east and in Asia Minor, sometimes broke away, but the royal administration was generally competent. If the empire failed to attract the loyalty of its subjects, its cosmopolitanism offered at least some of them increased opportunities for profit.

Trade and the Economy. Until the disorders of the first century BCE, the eastern empire enjoyed relative

DOCUMENT 3.4

A HELLENISTIC MARRIAGE CONTRACT

This marriage contract, dated 311 BCE, between Heracleides and Demetria, a Greek couple from the island of Cos on the shores of Asia Minor, demonstrates how the status of women had improved since the days of classical Athenian law. It not only mentions Demetria's mother but also takes the infidelities of the husband as seriously as those of his wife.

Heracleides takes Demetria of Cos as his lawful wife. He receives her from her father, Leptines of Cos, and from her mother, Philotis. He is a free man and she a free woman. She brings with her clothes and jewels worth 1000 drachmas. Heracleides will provide Demetria with all the requirements of a free woman. They shall live in whatever place seems best to Leptines and Heracleides.

If Demetria is found to have done something which disgraces her husband, she shall lose everything she brought with her. And Heracleides shall accuse her before three men chosen by the pair of them. Heracleides shall not be permitted to wrong Demetria by keeping another woman or having children by another woman, nor to harm Demetria in any way under any pretext. If Heracleides is found to have done such a thing, Demetria shall accuse him before three men whom they shall have selected together. Heracleides shall then pay Demetria back the 1000 drachmas she brought as dowry and a further 1000 drachmas in Alexandrian silver as recompense.

From Préaux, Claire, "Le Statut de la femme à l'époque hellénistique, principalment en Égypte," in Julia O'Faolain and Lauro Martines, *Not in God's Image: Women in History from the Greeks to the Victorians* (London: Temple Smith, 1973).

Question: What are the major differences between the legal status of Demetria as a married women and that of the Athenian women described in Chapter 2?

prosperity. The Seleucids imposed no internal trade barriers and guaranteed the safety of caravans as a matter of policy. Even when its leaders were fighting over Alexander's inheritance, the entire Hellenistic world had been open to commerce. A merchant in Damascus or Babylon could trade unimpeded with Greece or Egypt. The more adventurous sent their goods into India or traded with Carthaginians and Romans in the west. Perhaps the most enduring of Alexander's legacies was the creation of a great world market in goods and ideas. This, more than anything else, led to what traditionalists called a dilution of Greek values. Under the influence of Syria and Egypt, Greek legal traditions and even the status of women began to change (see Document 3.4).

The Jews in the Seleucid Empire. Hellenistic culture, for all its richness and sophistication, was not uni-

versally admired. Among those who resisted it most persistently were the Jews. The dispersions of the sixth century BCE had created a vast Jewish exile population. The largest of these communities were in Alexandria and Babylon, but virtually every city in the ancient world had Jewish residents. Most were artisans or small tradesmen. While some eventually assimilated to one degree or another, others gathered together in close-knit communities to preserve their religious and cultural identity.

In Israel and Judaea, a remnant of impoverished peasants held on, reinforced after the Persian conquest of Babylon by small numbers of the devout who sought to return to their homeland. In 516 BCE they rebuilt the Temple at Jerusalem. Not as grand as the Temple of Solomon, it served as the center of Jewish faith and aspirations until the Romans destroyed it in 70 CE.

The Talmud. The glue that held the many Jewish communities together was the teaching of prophets and devotion to the Law, as symbolized by the gradual evolution of **the Talmud** from the fifth century BCE onward. The Prophets, many of whose writings have been preserved in the Bible, exhorted the Jews to remain faithful. The Talmud is a collection of commentaries by rabbis (the Jewish word for teachers), who sought to uncover the full meaning of the Mosaic Law and apply it to every conceivable circumstance. This process of commentary, which continues today, was central to the development of mature Judaism, but certain aspects of it were not unopposed. The biblical books of Jonah and of Ruth may be veiled protests against what many saw as an increasingly narrow and overly proscriptive faith.

The Maccabee Revolt. In general, the Hellenistic monarchies followed a policy of tolerance and granted Jewish communities a measure of autonomy that allowed them to govern themselves by their own law. The conflict between Hellenism and Hebraism was nevertheless fundamental. A life lived according to divinely revealed law was incompatible with the Greek love of speculation and with aesthetic standards based on the beauties of nature and the perfection of the human body. That conflict became violent when the Seleucid monarch, Antiochus IV Epiphanes (c. 215–164 BCE), violated the principal of tolerance by introducing the worship of Zeus to the temple at Jerusalem. A revolt led by the **Maccabees,** the five sons of the priest Mattathias, resulted in the restoration of an independent Jewish state.

Pharisees and Sadducees. In later years the dynasty founded by the Maccabees embarked upon a policy of expansion and forced conversions to Judaism. This was opposed by the **Pharisees,** who sought a return to the Law and to traditional Jewish values. A bloody civil war between the Pharisees and the Sadducees, as the supporters of the dynasty were known, ended only with

The Jewish Struggle against Hellenism under the Seleucids

The First and Second Book of Maccabees tells the story of the struggle against the hellenizing policies of Antiochus Epiphanes from the standpoint of observant Jews. The books are not found in the Hebrew Bible but are accepted by Catholic Christians as part of the Biblical canon and by Protestants as part of the *Apocrypha*. This translation is taken from the *Apocrypha*. Although each book has a different author, they follow roughly the same chronology.

The Hellenizing of Jewish Culture
(2 Macc. 4:7–15)

Jason obtained the high priesthood by corruption, promising the king in his petition 360 talents of silver and 80 talents from other revenues. When the king had consented and he had taken office, he immediately brought his countrymen over to the Greek way of living. He set aside the royal ordinances especially favoring the Jews . . . and abrogating the lawful ways of living he introduced new customs contrary to the Law. For he willingly established a gymnasium right under the citadel, and he made the finest of the young men wear the Greek hat. And to such a pitch did the cultivation of Greek fashions and the coming-in of foreign customs rise . . . that the priests were no longer earnest about the services of the altar, but disdaining the sacrifices, they hurried to take part in the unlawful exercises of the wrestling school, after the summons to the discus throwing, regarding as worthless the things their forefathers valued, and thinking Greek standards the finest.

The Revolt of the Maccabees
(1 Macc. 2:23–27, 42–48)

[After Antiochus ordered that the people of a Jewish town sacrifice to Zeus] a Jew went up before the eyes of all of them to offer sacrifice as the king commanded . . . And Mattathias saw him and was filled with zeal, and his heart was stirred, and he was very properly roused to anger, and ran up and slaughtered him upon the altar. At the same time he killed the king's officer who was trying to compel them to sacrifice, and he tore down the altar . . . Then Mattathias cried out in a loud voice in the town and said "Let everybody who is zealous for the Law and stands by the agreement come out after me.

Then they were joined by a company of Hasideans, warlike Israelites, every one a volunteer for the Law. And all who had fled to escape harsh treatment joined them and reinforced them . . . And Mattathias and his friends went about and tore down the altars, and forcibly circumcised all the uncircumcised children they found within the limits of Israel. And they drove the arrogant before them, and the work prospered in their hands. So they rescued the Law from the hands of the heathen and their kings, and would not let the sinners triumph.

From *The Apocrypha*, trans. Edgar J. Goodspeed (New York: Random House, 1959).

Question: What was the cause of the Jewish revolt against the Seleucids?

Roman intervention in 64 BCE and the abolition of the monarchy in the following year. Although political independence was lost, the danger of Hellenism had been avoided. The Romans made no effort to interfere with the Jewish faith, and the Pharisees emerged as the dominant faction in religious life—both at home and in the scattered communities of the dispersion.

Egypt under the Ptolemies

Egypt under the Ptolemies contrasted vividly with the decentralized empire of the Seleucids. Egypt was a far more homogeneous society than that of the old Persian Empire, and Ptolemy I (d. c. 282 BCE) had little difficulty in substituting his own rule for that of the pharaohs. After reaching an accommodation with the country's religious leaders, he established a royal despotism that reached into every corner of Egyptian life. With the exception of three Greek cities, only one of which was established by the Ptolemies, all of the country's land had

long been regarded as the property of the king. A large and efficient bureaucracy managed royal monopolies in essential goods and collected more than 200 different taxes. The most important of these monopolies was in grain. Royal officials distributed seed to the peasants in return for a substantial percentage of their yields. They then stored the grain and released it to the export market when prices were high. Grain was Egypt's leading export, and the profits from this trade were immense. The crown also held a complete monopoly on the production of vegetable oils (which it protected with a 50 percent duty on imported olive oil) and partial monopolies on virtually every other commodity from meat to papyrus. Policy was based on extracting the maximum amount of wealth from the country. By the middle of the second century BCE, many peasants had become desperate, but being in a narrow valley surrounded by desert, they had nowhere to flee. The Ptolemies continued to pile up a great treasury until the fall of the dynasty in 30 BCE.

The City of Alexandria. The Ptolemies lavished much of that wealth on their capital at Alexandria. The city had been founded on the shores of the Mediterranean by Alexander. A causeway connected the narrow offshore island of Pharos to the mainland, forming two spacious harbors, one of which was linked to nearby Lake Mareotis by a canal. A second canal connected the lake with the western branch of the Nile. This enormous port soon formed the nucleus of the Mediterranean's largest city. Under the first and second Ptolemies, the population of Alexandria grew to nearly 500,000 Greeks, Macedonians, Egyptians, and Jews. Its people drew their water supply from vast cisterns built beneath the city, and a lighthouse, said to have been more than 400 feet tall, was constructed on Pharos.

The cosmopolitan nature of its population and the patronage of the Ptolemies made Alexandria the cultural and intellectual center of the Hellenistic world. Its center was the Museum, which was a kind of research institute, and a library that collected materials from every literate culture known to the Greeks. The crown used some of its vast revenues to subsidize these institutions as well as the scholars who attended them, and the learned flocked to Alexandria from all over the Mediterranean basin.

HELLENISTIC SCIENCE, PHILOSOPHY, AND RELIGION (323–100 BCE)

The encouragement of the Ptolemies and the intellectual foundations laid down by Aristotle made the third century BCE a period of extraordinary achievement in science, mathematics, engineering, and navigation. Nothing like it would be seen again until the scientific revolution of the sixteenth and seventeenth centuries.

Hellenistic Science and Technology

Mathematics and Cosmology. Some of the work done at Alexandria was scholarship—the compilation and transmission of earlier ideas. The *Elements of Geometry,* composed early in the century by **Euclid** (You'-klid), contained little that was completely new but became the basis of geometric instruction until modern times. Hellenistic speculations on cosmography (the study of the universe) and physics were more original. **Aristarchus** (Air-is-tar'-kus) **of Samos** (c. 310–230 BCE) disputed Aristotle's theory that the Earth was the center of the universe. He reasoned, without benefit of telescopes or other instruments, that the sun was larger than the Earth and that the planets were far more distant from one another than Aristotle had imagined. The

sun must therefore be the center around which the Earth and planets revolved. **Eratosthenes** (Air-uh-tahs'-thuhn-eez) **of Cyrene** (c. 276–194 BCE), a mathematician who spent most of his life as head of the Library at Alexandria, founded mathematical geography. Among other things, he calculated the circumference of the Earth to within 50 miles of modern estimates and devised a calendar that used leap years.

Like much of Hellenistic science, these theories bore little fruit until scholars revived them in the sixteenth century. Roman and medieval scholars accepted the view of **Ptolemy of Alexandria** (fl.127–145 CE), who believed with Aristotle that the Earth was the center of the universe. The authority of Aristotle in Roman and medieval times was too great to permit the acceptance of a **heliocentric,** or sun-centered, universe without independent proof, and the telescopes and navigational instruments needed to support the theories of Aristarchus and Eratosthenes had not yet been invented. In physics, cosmology, and biology, where Theophrastus (d. c. 287 BCE) used the methods of Aristotle to classify plants and animals discovered in the east, the inspiration of Hellenistic science was largely Greek.

Physics. The achievements of **Archimedes** (Ar-ki-mee'-deez) **of Syracuse** (c. 287–212 BCE) stand at the beginning of modern physics. Archimedes, who studied at Alexandria and who was a friend of Eratosthenes, spent most of his life in his native city. A close associate and perhaps a relative of the ruling dynasty, he was valued for his work on catapults; compound pulleys; and the screw of Archimedes, a helical device for lifting water out of wells, mineshafts, and the hulls of ships. Most of these devices had both military and civilian applications, but Archimedes regarded them as little better than toys. He is best known for his work *On Plane Equilibriums,* which describes the basic principle of levers, and for his discovery that solids can be weighed by measuring the amount of liquid they displace.

Medicine. In medicine, however, two ancient traditions merged. The Greek Hippocratic tradition was based on the teachings of **Hippocrates,** a semimythical figure who is supposed to have lived on the island of Cos in the fifth century BCE. The Hippocratic Oath attributed to him is still revered by doctors (see Document 3.5). The main feature of the Hippocratic tradition was the theory of the humors. Until late in the eighteenth century, most doctors believed that the human body contained four humors: blood, black bile, yellow bile, and phlegm. Good health depended on keeping these humors in perfect balance, and medication was typically prescribed if one or more of them were either deficient or present in excess. An excess of blood, for example, could be reduced by bleeding.

The Alexandrians added Egyptian surgery and anatomy to the Hippocratic tradition and passed their findings on to the Romans. They also passed on a fun-

THE HIPPOCRATIC OATH

The origins of the Hippocratic oath are unclear. Hippocrates was supposed to have imposed the oath upon his students, but it may have appeared at any time between the fifth century BCE and the first century CE. Latin and Arabic versions appear throughout the Middle Ages. The first part of the text closely resembles an indenture between master and apprentice. The second deals with medical ethics, but some of the points mentioned do not accord with ancient Greek practice. Other literature attributed to Hippocrates and his school describes various techniques of abortion. Moreover, the Greeks did not object to suicide. Some scholars believe that these prohibitions appeared in the oath after the appearance of Christianity. The oath taken by modern physicians at their medical school graduations differs from the one quoted here in two important respects. The prohibition against sexual relations with patients is more clearly stated, and the distinction between medicine and surgery has been abandoned. Until the nineteenth century, surgeons were a separate—and inferior—profession. The names in the invocation are those of the various gods responsible for health and healing.

I swear by Apollo Physician, by Asclepius, by Health, by Panacea, and by all the gods and goddesses, making them by witnesses, that I will carry out, according to my ability and judgment, this oath and this indenture. To hold my teacher in this art equal to my own parents; to make him partner in my livelihood; when he is in need of money to share mine with him; to consider his family as my own brothers, and to teach them this art, if they want to learn it, without fee or indenture; to impart precept, oral instruction, and all other instruction to my own sons, the sons of my teacher, and to indentured pupils who have taken the physician's oath, but to nobody else. I will use treatment to help the sick according to my ability and judgment, but never with a view to injury and wrongdoing. Neither will I administer a poison to anybody when asked to do so, nor will I suggest such a course. Similarly I will not give a woman a pessary to cause abortion. But I will keep pure and holy both my life and my art. I will not use the knife, not even, verily, on sufferers from stone, but I will give place to such as are craftsmen therein. Into whatsoever houses I enter, I will enter to help the sick, and I will abstain from all intentional wrong-doing and harm, especially from abusing the bodies of man or woman, bond or free. And whatsoever I shall see or hear in the course of my profession, as well as outside my profession in my intercourse with men, if it be what should be published abroad, I will never divulge, holding such things to be holy secrets. Now if I carry out this oath, and break it not, may I gain for ever reputation among all men for my life and for my art; but if I forswear myself, may the opposite befall me.

From "The Hippocratic Oath," in Logan Clendening, ed., *Source-Book of Medical History* (New York: Dover, 1960, pp. 14–15).

Questions: How does the Oath protect the medical profession? How does it protect the patient?

damental difference of opinion that would bedevil Western medicine until the nineteenth century. By 280 BCE, the physicians of Alexandria had become either **Dogmatics,** who studied anatomy in the hope of understanding how the body worked, or **Empirics,** who stressed the practical arts of diagnosis and cure. A third group, less reputable to modern eyes but popular in their own day, practiced magic.

Hellenistic Literature and Art

Literature. Greeks of the classical era had derived much of their identity from the polis and assumed that the good life could be lived only within its social framework. In the great empires of Hellenistic times, that framework no longer existed. For the Greco-Macedonian elite, cut off from their homelands and living essentially as mercenaries, the gratifications of private life gradually replaced those of the organic community. For the non-Greek masses with their long history of subjection to alien empires, there was no issue: only the individual and the family mattered. The arts reflected this new individualism. Hellenistic drama abandoned the great themes of tragic conflict in favor of domestic comedies that dealt with love stories and other events on a personal level. The works of **Menander** (c. 300 BCE) are typical of this genre. Poetry, much of it written by and for women, explored personal themes in elegant short verses known as epigrams, many of which were collected in antholologies.

Hellenistic Art. Painting and sculpture flourished as never before. Ancient commentators claimed that painting especially reached unprecedented levels of excellence. Owing to the perishable nature of the colors, all of it has been lost. In sculpture, much of which has been preserved in Roman copies, many of the best artists abandoned the serene classicism of Phidias and Praxiteles and sought to express emotion through the dramatic arrangement of their figures, agonized facial expressions, and exaggerated muscular tension. The famous statue of Laocoön and his sons is an outstanding example. Others chose humble figures from everyday

FIGURE 3.5 *Laocoön and His Sons.* This monumental sculpture from Pergamum is an example of the way in which Hellenistic artists used formal arrangement, exaggerated musculature, and agonized facial expressions to portray emotion. The serene classicism of Praxiteles and his contemporaries has been abandoned. Even the theme, an episode from *The Iliad* in which the gods sent serpents to destroy the Trojan priest Laocoön and his children, is chosen for its emotional impact. The work as shown is probably a Roman copy.

life and portrayed them in sympathetic detail. Whatever their subject, the artists of the Hellenistic age achieved new heights of technical virtuosity that would astonish and at times dismay the critics of a later age.

Hellenistic Thought and Religion

Philosophy. Hellenistic philosophy, too, reflected this shift in values, abandoning political theory in favor of individualistic prescriptions for the good life. The philosophic school known as the **Cynics** carried this tendency further than anyone else. They argued that the best life was lived closest to nature and that wisdom lay in abandoning worldly goods and ambition. **Diogenes** (Dye-ahj'-uh-neez, d. 320 BCE), their most effective spokesman, delighted in exposing the folly and vanity of others. Popular legend has it that he lived in a tub and carried a lantern with which he hoped—unsuccessfully—to find an honest man.

The Stoics. Among those attracted to the teachings of the Cynics was **Zeno** (c. 335–263 BCE). A native of Phoenician Cyprus, Zeno established a school at Athens named the Stoa after the portico in the Agora where his disciples met. The **Stoics,** as they were called, believed that living in harmony with nature was essential. They identified nature with the divine principle or *logos.* Each human being and each object had the logos within it and acted according to a divine, predetermined plan. This plan, although good in itself, might not always work in the best interests of a particular individual. Sickness, death, and misfortune were all part of a providential order that could not be escaped but only endured.

Those who believed in this theory found it paradoxically liberating. To the Stoic, only moral qualities such as prudence, courage, folly, and intemperance were good or bad. Wealth, pleasure, beauty, and health were morally indifferent because they were essentially states of mind—the products of feeling or passion. The wise person, regardless of condition, should realize that it is not what happens but how one reacts to it that determines the good life. The goal of wisdom was therefore *apatheia,* or indifference to what is morally neutral, coupled with ethical behavior and the cultivation of personal qualities that are morally good. According to the Stoics, anyone could achieve this goal. Men and women, slaves and princes, all possessed the same divine spark. Although the conditions of their lives might differ, they were all inherently equal.

Unlike the teachings of the Cynics, Stoicism was based on physical and epistemological principles derived at some distance from Aristotle. It offered not only an ethical code but also a means of understanding and accepting an often-hostile universe. Of all the philosophical schools of late antiquity, it was the most popular among educated people. It became the dominant belief among the Roman upper classes and would strongly influence the development of Christian theology.

Epicureanism. Stoicism's chief rival was **Epicureanism.** Epicurus (Ep-i-cure'-us, 341–270 BCE) was born to an Athenian family on the island of Samos and established a school at Athens known among other things for being open to women. Epicurus argued, as Leucippus and Democritus had done, that the universe was composed of atoms that combined and recombined in an infinite variety of patterns. Growth and dissolution were inevitable, but Epicurus rejected the kind of providential order claimed by the Stoics. In the absence of such an order, the greatest good from the human point of view was pleasure, and the search for pleasure should be the philosopher's primary goal. By pleasure, Epicurus meant peace of mind and the absence of pain, not the active pursuit of dissipation. He sought a quiet life, removed from the troubles of the world and governed by the

FIGURE 3.6 *Alexander and Diogenes.* This painting by the nineteenth-century French painter Nicolas Andre Monsiau illustrates a famous story that remained a popular subject for centuries. Alexander the Great, conqueror of the world, supposedly went to the Cynic philosopher and asked him if there was anything he could do for him. Diogenes, who had no home and lived by begging, said, "Yes, you could stand a little less between me and the sun." The tale illustrates that power is useless to the truly ethical person, at least as "ethical" was defined by Cynic philosophy.

principle of moderation in all things. Even the gods should not be feared, but emulated in their Olympian detachment from the things of this world. Epicureanism, too, had its followers, but detachment from the world did not always recommend itself to those with practical responsibilities.

Hellenistic Religion. Like all philosophical schools, Stoicism and Epicureanism appealed primarily to the educated. The mass of people in the Hellenistic world found solace in religion. This in itself was a relatively new development, at least among the Greeks, for the gods of Olympus had offered little to their worshipers beyond a conditional protection from their wrath. In the classical age, while the learned took refuge in philosophy, ordinary men and women had resorted to superstition and a helpless resignation to *Tyche,* or fate.

For many in the Hellenistic kingdoms, Tyche retained her powers, but others embraced what are called **mystery religions.** Mystery religions claimed to guarantee personal immortality, often through the intervention of a god or goddess who came to Earth in human form and suffered for the sins of humankind. Most, although not all, had eastern roots. Among the more important were the cult of Serapis, encouraged by Ptolemy I, and the far more ancient veneration of Isis.

Because the Romans adopted most of these religions they are discussed at greater length in Chapter 6.

CONCLUSION

Unlike that of the Jews, the culture of ancient Greece was profoundly humanistic in the sense that Greek thinkers emphasized the cultivation of virtue and the good life within a social instead of a religious framework. Greek artists concentrated almost exclusively on the human form, while poets found inspiration in the heroic dignity of men and women in the face of tragedy. This intense concentration on the human experience was coupled with an extraordinary spirit of inquiry. Other ancient societies, notably the Egyptians and Mesopotamians, had rich speculative traditions, but the Greeks were unique in insisting on a rigorous form of logic in which the connections between each part of a statement had to be made perfectly clear.

These habits of thought, together with a mass of learning and speculation drawn from the most diverse sources, were the Greek legacy to Western society. From the beginning the Greeks were borrowers. They had a rare ability to absorb the ideas and beliefs of others without threatening their own sense of what it meant to be Greek. When, in the Hellenistic age, they penetrated to the edges of the known world, this tendency accelerated. Elements from every ancient culture were adopted and transformed according to their own needs and preconceptions. In so doing they imposed a kind of intellectual unity that, if it distorted some things and neglected others, was passed on intact to the Romans and from the Romans to the modern Western world. For good or ill, the ancient world is viewed through Greek eyes.

Review Questions

- What public purposes were Greek art and literature intended to serve?
- What fundamental questions raised by ancient Greek philosophers remain important today?
- How did the Hellenistic age achieve the partial integration of Greek and non-Greek cultures in both politics and thought?
- What was the basis of the conflict between Judaism and Hellenism?

For Further Study

Readings

Boardman, John, *Greek Art*, 4th ed. (New York: Thames and Hudson, 1996). A classic.

Hamilton, J. R., *Alexander the Great* (Pittsburgh: University of Pittsburgh Press, 1973). A good, accessible biography.

Lesky, Albin, *History of Greek Literature*, trans. J. Willis and C. de Heer (New York: Crowell, 1963). Still the standard treatment of a very broad subject.

Lloyd, G. E. R., *Greek Science after Aristotle* (New York: Norton, 1973). An outstanding brief survey of an important topic.

Sharples, R. W., *Stoics, Epicureans, and Sceptics. An Introduction to Hellenistic Philosophy* (London: Routledge, 1996). A clear explanation of Hellenistic thought in 154 pages.

Walbank, F. W., *The Hellenistic World*, rev. ed. (Cambridge, MA: Harvard, 1993). The standard survey of the Hellenistic era.

InfoTrac College Edition

Visit the source collections at *http://infotrac.thomson learning.com* and use the search function with the following key terms.

Using Key Terms, enter the search terms:
Greek history   *Alexander the Great*
Archimedes

Web Sites

www.fordham.edu/halsall/ancient/asbook.html
   Internet Ancient History Sourcebook. Maintained by Fordham University, this site contains sections on Greek art, literature, and the Hellenistic era, as well as a good selection of documents and literary sources.

www.nlm.nih.gov/hmd/greek/index.html
   Greek Medicine is a site maintained by the National Library of Medicine and the National Institutes of Health. It contains material on Greek medicine from earliest times through the Hellenistic period, including Hippocrates and the Hippocratic Oath.

Visit the Western Civilization Companion Web Site for resources specific to this textbook:
http://history.wadsworth.com/hause02/

 The CD in the back of this book and the Western Civilization Resource Center at *http://history. wadsworth.com/western/* offer a variety of tools to help you succeed in this course, including access to quizzes; images; documents; interactive simulations, maps, and timelines; movie explorations; and a wealth of other sources.

CLASSICAL AND HELLENISTIC GREECE

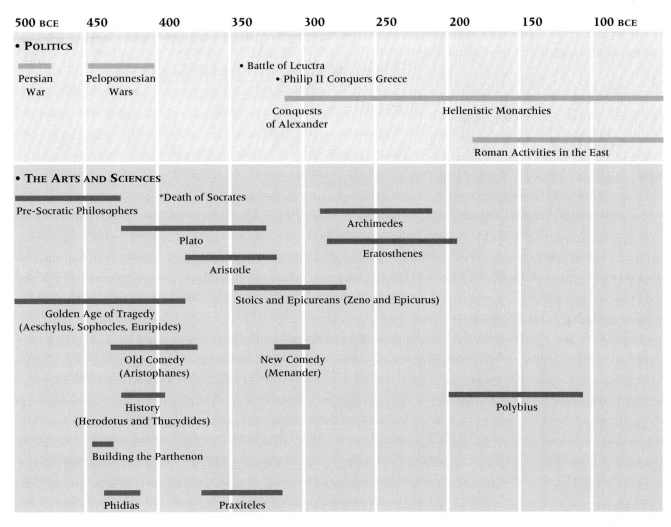

| 500 BCE | 450 | 400 | 350 | 300 | 250 | 200 | 150 | 100 BCE |

• POLITICS

Persian War

Peloponnesian Wars

• Battle of Leuctra
• Philip II Conquers Greece

Conquests of Alexander

Hellenistic Monarchies

Roman Activities in the East

• THE ARTS AND SCIENCES

Pre-Socratic Philosophers

*Death of Socrates

Plato

Aristotle

Archimedes

Eratosthenes

Stoics and Epicureans (Zeno and Epicurus)

Golden Age of Tragedy
(Aeschylus, Sophocles, Euripides)

Old Comedy
(Aristophanes)

New Comedy
(Menander)

History
(Herodotus and Thucydides)

Polybius

Building the Parthenon

Phidias   Praxiteles

The conquests of Alexander and the Hellenistic monarchies established thereafter and shown in relation to the Persian and Peloponnesian Wars and the emergence of Rome as an imperial power. Under the heading Arts and Sciences, both movements and the life spans of individual artists and thinkers are shown by lines.

Chapter 4

THE RISE OF THE ROMAN REPUBLIC

*I*n 457 BCE, a delegation from the Roman Senate approached Cincinnatus as he worked on his tiny 3-acre farm and ordered him to come with them to the city. Wiping the sweat from his brow, Cincinnatus put on his ceremonial toga and accompanied them. The Senate informed him that a Roman army had been surrounded by the *Aequi* (Ek'-why), a hostile neighboring people. It was the job of Cincinnatus to defeat the Aequi, and he was hereby appointed dictator for that purpose. As dictator, he would control the entire resources of the state, for a term of 6 months. Cincinnatus raised an army, defeated the Aequi, and received a **triumph** in which the enemy commanders marched before his chariot on a procession through Rome. Fifteen days after the original summons, he resigned his office and returned to his farm.

This story, from the historian Livy (Liv'-ee), may not be true in all its details, but to Romans it symbolized the best in their tradition. Ideally, all Romans would, like Cincinnatus, drop what they were doing, defend their city with ferocious competence, and retire to private life with no expectation of reward. Although not all did retire gracefully, enough of them answered the call of public service to make Rome first the master of Italy and then the master of the known world.

Chapter 4 shows how Rome grew from a modest settlement to become the center of a great empire. After describing ancient Italy and the society of early Rome, it will explain how the Romans developed a unique political and military system out of the social conflict known as the "Struggle of the Orders." The effectiveness of that system, together with a wise political strategy, gave Rome control over the Italian peninsula by 270 BCE. But the growth of Roman power threatened Carthage, the leading naval power in the western Mediterranean. In a series of bitter wars, Rome, too, developed a navy and defeated the Carthaginians. The Romans then turned their attention to Macedon and Greece. The chapter concludes with how and why Rome intervened in Greek affairs and how the outcome of that intervention brought it an empire that encompassed the Mediterranean and transformed the society of Rome itself.

ANCIENT ITALY TO C. 500 BCE

Geography. The long, boot-shaped Italian peninsula bisects the Mediterranean. At first glance it seems especially favored by nature. Its central location lends it strategic and commercial importance, and its climate is generally milder and wetter than that of Greece. Agricultural yields are higher, and some of the upland regions, which in Greece have become a moonscape of rocks and dry scrub, can support grazing. These advantages, however, are relative. The development of prehistoric Italy was at first hindered by natural obstacles of every kind. The Apennines, a mountain range that in its central portions reaches nearly 10,000 feet in height, dominate the Italian peninsula for most of its length. On the east, the mountains drop precipitously to the Adriatic Sea. Few good harbors can be found on the

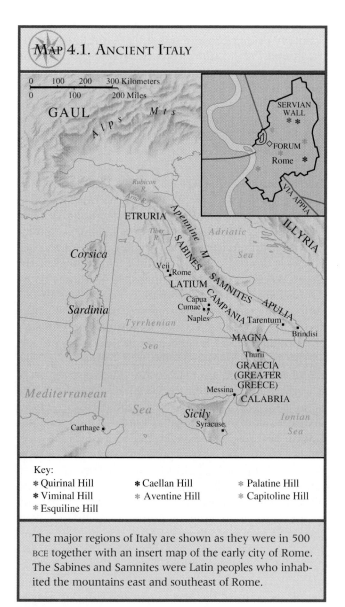

MAP 4.1. ANCIENT ITALY

Key:
* Quirinal Hill   * Caellan Hill   * Palatine Hill
* Viminal Hill   * Aventine Hill   * Capitoline Hill
* Esquiline Hill

The major regions of Italy are shown as they were in 500 BCE together with an insert map of the early city of Rome. The Sabines and Samnites were Latin peoples who inhabited the mountains east and southeast of Rome.

Italian shore of the Adriatic, and arable land is scarce except in Apulia, the region immediately southeast of Mt. Garganus, which protrudes like a spur into the Adriatic.

The western coast, also lacking in good harbors, is more hospitable. The valleys of the Arno and the Tiber are suitable for agriculture and open out onto an extensive coastal plain that, although potentially fertile, was in early times marshy and subject to floods. Further south, around the Bay of Naples, lies the rich plain of Campania, whose soil is the gift of volcanic deposits from Mt. Vesuvius. Another active volcano, Mt. Etna, dominates the eastern part of Sicily, the large, wedge-shaped island immediately southwest of the mainland. As a consequence of climatic change, Sicily today is dry and relatively poor, but until the sixteenth century CE it supplied much of Italy with grain.

At the opposite end of the peninsula, between the westward curve of the Apennines and the great northern barrier of the Alps, is the valley of the Po River, which flows eastward into the Adriatic. The Po valley is now among the world's richest agricultural and industrial regions, but its wealth is largely the fruit of human effort. As recently as the fourth century BCE, it was a wild marshland, not yet tamed by 2,000 years of digging canals and building levees.

Greek Colonization. Beginning in the eighth century BCE, Greek colonists had established themselves in the richest of the southern coastal lands. Eastern Sicily, Apulia, and Campania, as well as Calabria (the heel of the boot) and the shores of the Gulf of Taranto (its arch), were soon dominated by *poleis* of the Aegean type, rich and vigorous, but as combative and incapable of unified action as their models. At the same time, the Carthaginians colonized western Sicily and contended violently with their Greek neighbors for land and trade. Of the original inhabitants of these areas, some became slaves or tenants of the colonists while others retreated to the interior and retained their tribal cultures.

The Etruscans. A variety of tribes, Latins, Umbrians, and Samnites (Sam'-nights)—each speaking its own Italic or other Indo-European language—inhabited Latium, the central part of the peninsula. The Etruscans dominated the region between the Tiber and the Arno. Their language can be only partially deciphered, but their alphabet was similar to that of the Greeks and their art seems also to have been derived from Greek models. Most of what is known about the Etruscans comes from archaeology, and little has survived from the days when Etruscan power was at its height. Above all, the Etruscans were city dwellers. Their economy was based heavily on trade and manufacturing, and although they were also accomplished farmers, they preferred to live in town whenever possible. They constructed their twelve main cities according to engineering and religious principles that would profoundly influence the Romans. Where terrain permitted, the Etruscans favored a symmetrical city plan that was unlike anything devised by the Greeks. Elaborate tunnels of dressed stone drained low-lying areas or brought fresh water for the consumption of the townspeople, and buildings featured arches and vaulted ceilings, construction techniques that appear to have been invented by Etruscans.

This sophistication did not extend to political structures. None of the Etruscan cities became democracies. Etruscan society was rigidly stratified with a handful of wealthy families dominating each of the twelve cities through legally enforceable clientage and the ownership of many slaves. In war, the rich fought on horseback under their king, who may have been elected. By the fifth century BCE, the Etruscans had replaced their kings with aristocratic magistrates and adopted the hoplite tactics of the Greeks. But if the political evolution of the Etruscans differed from that of the Greeks, in another respect they closely resembled them: the twelve cities were almost incapable of united action. At an early date they formed a league, which was chiefly religious and athletic in purpose. The cities also celebrated certain religious festivals in common, but they fought incessantly among themselves and their merchants competed for each other's markets as well as for those of the Greek and Carthaginian colonies to the south.

THE ORIGINS OF ROME (C. 700–295 BCE)

The Tiber is the largest river in central Italy. Its valley, running roughly from north to south, is strategically important because it provides the easiest land route for travelers—and armies—moving between the Po valley and southern Italy. The last point at which the river can be easily crossed lies about 15 miles from its mouth, where the valley is broad and marshy.

Seven low hills in the immediate area provide a refuge from floods and invaders alike. In the eighth century BCE, a tribe of people who spoke an early version of Latin occupied the Palatine hill. Shortly afterward, a related group took up residence on the nearby Aventine hill. These two settlements formed the nucleus of ancient Rome. They were part of a larger group of Italic communities that formed themselves into **a Latin league** for political and religious purposes, but their common ties did not prevent them from fighting among themselves.

Blessed with rich land and abundant water, the early Romans were nevertheless too few to preserve full autonomy in the face of Etruscan influence. The nearest of the Etruscan cities was Veii (Vay'-eye), only 12 miles away, and almost from the first, the Romans found themselves under the influence of their more powerful neighbors. Some of the first kings of Rome bore Etruscan

names, and reportedly the Romans did not depose the last of them and establish a Roman Republic ruled by two magistrates until 509 BCE (although it could have been a generation later).

Rome and the Etruscans. The true nature of the relationship between Rome and the Etruscans is unclear. Rome's early history was written by Livy (Titus Livius, c. 59 BCE–17 CE), a memorable stylist who sometimes used legends when documented facts were unavailable. Writing immediately after the fall of the Republic, he hoped to rekindle ancient virtue by preserving the city's foundation myths. Livy's account is vivid, but leaves much to be desired in terms of explanation and analysis. If, as he claimed, the Romans elected their kings, Etruscan rule may reflect nothing more than the cultural dominance of a more advanced society over its neighbors. It may have been a kind of Etruscan protectorate backed by military force and strengthened by a substantial Etruscan presence within the Roman population.

In any event, Etruscan influence contributed greatly to Roman civilization. The Romans adopted the Etruscan alphabet, although not the language itself, and learned most of what they knew about metalworking, civic planning, and architecture from their northern neighbors. Many religious customs described by Livy, together with a number of Roman political institutions, have Etruscan roots as well.

Early Expansion (509–338 BCE). Under the kings, Rome used its dominant position in the Latin league to subdue the Sabines and other Italic communities along the lower Tiber, absorbing their populations and granting citizenship to the leading families. This enlightened policy, a marked contrast to the exclusiveness of the Greek poleis, was largely responsible for Rome's successful expansion. The prospect of fair treatment discouraged fanatic resistance among the city's enemies and made accepting Roman **hegemony** (dominance without direct rule) far easier for its neighbors.

The policy continued after the formation of the Republic. The Romans expelled the Etruscans as part of a larger movement that involved Rome's Greek and Latin neighbors. The capture of the Etruscan city of Veii, after an extensive siege in 396 BCE, almost doubled Roman territory. Nine years later, however, disaster struck. The Gauls, a Celtic people from central Europe, descended on the peninsula and burned Rome in 387 BCE. The action was a tremendous psychological blow. The Gauls, with their vast numbers and sheer ferocity, appalled the Romans. Sometimes fighting naked, the Gauls seemed to live exclusively on meat and alcohol. Fortunately, they made no effort to consolidate their victory and retired to the sparsely inhabited valley of the Po. There they settled down to a more-or-less ordered agricultural life and began the long process of clearing and draining the region. In later times, the Romans called it *Cisalpine Gaul.*

Among the more serious consequences of the Gallic invasion was that it undermined the loyalty of Rome's Latin allies. The Latin league rebelled against Roman hegemony. But the Romans recovered quickly, and by 338 BCE, they had again subdued all of Latium. Once more, the Romans showed a restraint and a grasp of political realities that were all too rare in the ancient world. They gave the towns nearest Rome full citizenship. Others, farther away, were granted **municipal status,** which meant that their citizens could marry or trade with Romans but had no voting rights outside their own communities. The specific provisions of these agreements were tailored to individual circumstances and were open-ended in the sense that Rome always held out the prospect of new privileges in return for good behavior. Some towns merely enrolled as allies, but all save those that received citizenship retained self-government. The one universally enforced rule was that none of the federated communities could make similar agreements with each other.

To ensure communication and provide for the common defense, the Romans built the first of a series of paved, all-weather roads linking Rome with her allies—the Appian Way. They would follow this policy of road building until the empire ended. Because all roads led to Rome, these highways had the effect of separating the allies from one another while allowing Rome to intervene militarily in case of rebellion or some other threat. Surfaced in stone and often lined with trees, a few of the roads are still used today.

The Samnite Wars (343–295 BCE). These political alliances proved effective in the next great crisis. The consolidation of Latium threatened the Samnites, a warlike people who inhabited the uplands between Rome and the Greek settlements around the Bay of Naples. Joined by the Gauls and by the Etruscans, whose power was now greatly reduced, the Samnites launched a series of bitter struggles that ended with the Roman victory at Sentinium in 295 BCE. Although a few of Rome's Latin allies deserted, the coalition as a whole held firm.

The Roman Military System. The Roman military system achieved maturity during the Samnite Wars. Under the monarchy, the Romans had learned to use hoplites flanked by cavalry (soldiers on horseback) from the Etruscans. Their greater success resulted largely from a superior discipline rooted ultimately in cultural values. The Romans prized self-discipline, determination, and a sense of duty to the community above all else, but they were not indifferent to practical concerns. After about 400 BCE, they paid their troops while on duty, a practice unknown to contemporary Greeks. The Samnites, who were as tough as the Romans and who enjoyed the defensive advantage of a rugged, mountainous terrain, forced them to change tactics. To achieve greater maneuverability, the Romans abandoned the phalanx in favor of a smaller unit known as a *maniple.* A maniple contained 100 to 120 foot soldiers and was commanded by an officer known in later days as a *centurion.* Thirty maniples, plus five in reserve, made up a *legion* (3,400 to 3,700 men). In battle, the maniples were arranged in three lines, with a space between each unit large enough to permit the forward ranks to move back or the rear ranks to move forward as needed. Such a formation required discipline and control, while permitting an almost infinite number of tactical combinations regardless of the terrain. The new

FIGURE 4.1 *The Appian Way.* Begun about 312 BCE, the Appian Way was the first of the great paved highways built to link Rome with its allies and eventually with the farthest reaches of its empire. It ran south from Rome to Capua, near Naples, and was later extended to Brundisium (modern Brindisi) on the heel of the Italian boot. From there, travelers could take ships to Greece. Near Rome, the road was lined with tombs. To build a road like this, the Romans first laid down a base of compact earth and covered it with a surface of small stones set in mortar. They then added another layer of gravel before setting the surface stones. Low retaining walls and ditches on both sides completed the project. As this modern photo demonstrates, Roman engineering was built to last.

LIVY ON ROMAN TACTICS AT THE TIME OF THE SAMNITE WARS, FROM HIS "HISTORY OF ROME"

Titus Livius (59 BCE–17 CE), known as Livy, was the greatest historian of ancient Rome. Writing with the patronage of the Emperor Augustus, Livy compiled a history of Rome from its origins to 9 BCE. This work consisted of 142 books; only 35 of these (plus fragments) have survived. Livy was a conservative analyst who stressed the traditional strengths of Rome, such as the citizen army. The following excerpt from Livy's history explains how the Romans used their military organization during the Samnite Wars (343–259 BCE) of the early Republic.

The foremost line consisted of the hastati, *forming 15 maniples [companies] stationed a short distance from each other. This front line . . . consisted of the flower of the young men who were growing ripe for service. Behind them were stationed an equal number of maniples, called* principes, *made up of men of a more stalwart age. . . . This body of 30 maniples was called the* antepilani *because behind the standards there were stationed 15 other companies, each of which was divided into three sections, the first section being called the* pilius. *The company consisted of three* vexilla *[banners]. A single* vexillum *had 60 soldiers, two centurions, and one* vexillarius, *or color-bearer; the company numbered 186 men. The first* vexillum *led the* triarii, *veterans of proven courage; the second, the* rorarii, *or skirmishers, younger and less distinguished men; the third, the* accensi, *who were least to be depended upon and were therefore assigned to the rearmost line.*

When an army had been drawn up in these ranks, the hastati *were the first of all to engage. If the* hastati *failed to repulse the enemy, they slowly retired through the intervals between the companies of the* principes, *who then took up the fight, the* hastati *following in their rear. The* triarii, *meanwhile, were kneeling under their standards with left leg advanced, their shields leaning against their shoulders, and their spears planted in the ground with points obliquely upward, as if their battle line were fortified by a bristling palisade. If the* principes *were also unsuccessful, they slowly retired from the battle line to the* triarii *(which has given rise to the proverbial saying, when people are in great trouble, "matters have come down to the* triarii"*). When the* triarii *had admitted the* hastati *and* principes *through the intervals between their companies, they rose up and, instantly closing their companies up, blocked the lanes, as it were, and in one compact mass fell on the enemy, there being no more reserves left behind them. The enemy, who had pursued the others as though they had defeated them, saw with the greatest dread a new line suddenly rising up with increased numbers.*

From Livy, "History of Rome," book 8, from *Roman Civilization*, 3rd ed., 2 vols. Naphtali Lewis and Meyer Rheinhold, eds. Copyright © 1990, Columbia University Press. By permission.

Question: What was the major military advantage of the Roman army over the Grecian hoplite phalanx?

---

system, which in its basic outlines lasted until the end of the fourth century CE, brought success in the Battle of Sentinum and served them well as they faced further threats. The Romans had to defend themselves against a series of powerful neighbors, but each victory made them new enemies. The defeat of the Samnites and their allies awakened the Greek cities of the south. The Romans now controlled all of Italy from the borders of Campania to the Po, and the Greeks feared that such a concentration of power would lead to their downfall. Bickering and complaining to the last, the Greeks nevertheless united enough to hire the greatest mercenary of the age to defend their interests.

The Pyrrhic Wars. Pyrrhus (Peer'-us) of Epirus was ruler of a small state in what is now Albania. Backed by Greek wealth and supported by a contingent of war elephants, he twice defeated the Romans but suffered such heavy casualties that he retreated to Sicily in 278 BCE, saying that if he won another such victory he would be ruined. These wars gave rise to the term *Pyrrhic victory*, meaning a victory that is not worth winning because its

cost is too high. Nevertheless, he returned again in 275 BCE only to be defeated, marking the end of Greek independence on the Italian mainland. The Romans incorporated the Greek cities, too, into their system. The Republic now controlled all Italy south of the Po.

SOCIETY AND ECONOMY IN EARLY ROME TO 264 BCE

Agriculture. The city of Rome that conquered Italy was similar in its social arrangements to the classical Greek *polis*. A majority of early Romans engaged in small-scale farming. Although their plots of land probably averaged no more than 2 or 3 acres—they regarded 20 acres as a substantial estate—the intensive cultivation of many different crops provided them with a measure of self-sufficiency. Wherever possible, they planted grain between rows of vines or olive trees and replaced it with beans or other legumes in alternate years. The Romans practiced crop rotation and were careful to enrich the

FIGURE 4.2 (a) *A Roman Aqueduct: The Pont du Gard Near Nîmes, France.* For most of their length, Roman aqueducts were stone-lined ditches or covered tunnels that ran for many miles to bring clean water from mountain springs to a city. The Romans trusted neither the purity of river water nor the regularity of its flow. When the aqueduct had to bridge a river, Roman engineers built structures of this kind using an arch construction that had been unknown to the Greeks. The Etruscans built the first aqueducts, but the Romans constructed far more of them to serve their major cities. The Pont du Gard is the largest section of the Roman aqueduct built to serve Nemausus (Nîmes). It is built of limestone blocks weighing up to 6 tons each, fitted together without mortar and secured with iron clamps. Begun about 19 BCE, it was completed in the reign of the emperor Trajan (98 BCE–117 CE). (b) The map shows the entire route of the aqueduct that brought 44 million gallons of water a day to the residents of Nemausus. It runs 50 km from the springs at the Fountaine d'Eure to Nîmes at a gradient of only 17 meters. The Pont du Gard spans the valley of the Gardon.

soil through composting and animal fertilizers. Because grazing land was scarce, there was never enough manure. They raised sheep for their wool and milk, whereas cattle served mainly as draft animals. Everyone tried to maintain a miniature orchard of apples, pears, or figs.

This kind of farming required skill and a great deal of effort in virtually every month of the year. Fields had to be plowed at least three times, then hoed frequently during the growing season to reduce soil temperature and preserve moisture. Water was always a problem in the hot, dry Italian summer and often had to be carried from some distance to irrigate the garden vegetables. The Romans built massive stone-lined **aqueducts** to carry a steady supply of water to the towns from springs or other sources in the hills. The water arrived under pressure and fed into fountains, where it could be collected by the public. In the countryside, however, farmers usually had to carry their water by hand. Compost piles helped compensate for the shortage of manure. Roman farmers used every bit of organic matter available, but compost needed water as well as frequent turning with the pitchfork. The successful cultivation of vineyards and fruit trees demanded clever techniques for grafting and pruning. A measure of the labor involved may be gathered from the box on Roman agriculture.

The Roman Diet. Heroic efforts produced a balanced but simple diet: wheat or barley gruel supplemented by olives, cabbage, and beans. Milk, cheese, fruit, and baked bread provided variety, but the Romans ate meat—usually pork—only on special occasions. Sheep, goats, and cattle were too valuable to be slaughtered for their meat but sometimes found their way to the table after serving as burnt offerings to the gods. Hogs, which could root in the oak forests or in other waste spaces, provided not only hams and sausages but also that greatest of all Roman delicacies: roast suckling pig.

The Family. Roman farms were usually worked by the owner and his *familia* (fah-mill'-ee-uh)—the legal definition of which, although precise, was remarkably inclusive. *Familia* meant the nuclear family as well as the entire household, including dependent relatives and slaves. Most plots could support only the owner, his wife, and his children, but the labor-intensive character of Italian agriculture favored the growth of extended families whenever sufficient land was available. It also encouraged slavery, even on properties that seem small by modern standards. The early Republic had no great slave-worked estates of the kind that became common in the second century BCE, but many

The Rise of the Roman Republic 83

ROMAN AGRICULTURE

Cato on Farm Management

Marcus Porcius Cato (234–149 BCE) was the first Latin writer of prose. Although he wrote in the second century BCE, his fervent traditionalism led him to value the social ideals of a

Threshing Grain. This mosaic from about 200 CE shows a typical scene from the Roman agricultural year. Men are using horses and cattle to separate the grains from the chaff by trampling the harvested wheat underfoot. A lady, perhaps the mistress of the villa shown at the top, provides encouragement. From the Tripoli Museum, Libya.

far earlier time, and he devoted much of his political career to a vigorous attack on luxury and the importation of foreign ideas. He directed his *De agri cultura*, the earliest of many Roman tracts on farming by Roman authors, to men like himself who had farmed modest acreage with the help of an overseer and a few slaves. He did not intend it for the owners of opulent estates. It includes a wealth of technical information on every aspect of farming and advice on management. The following passages reflect a hard-bitten attitude that must have been common among Romans in the earliest days of the Republic.

Sell worn-out oxen, blemished cattle, blemished sheep, wool, hides, an old slave, a sickly slave, and whatever else is superfluous. The master should be in the selling habit, not the buying habit. . . .

On feast days, old ditches might have been cleaned, road work done, brambles cut, the garden spaded, a meadow cleared, faggots bundled, thorns rooted out, spelt ground, and general cleaning done. When the slaves were sick, such large rations should not have been issued.

When the weather is bad and no other work can be done, clear out manure for the compost heap; clean thoroughly the ox stalls, sheep pens, barnyard, and farmstead; and mend wine-jars with lead, or hoop them with thoroughly dried oak wood. . . . In rainy weather try to find something to do indoors. Clean up rather than be idle. Remember that even though work stops, expenses run on.

From Cato, *De agricultura*, trans. W. D. Hooper and H. D. Ash, Loeb Classical Library (Cambridge, MA: Harvard University Press, 1934).

Question: How would you compare Cato's advice to Hesiod's on page 37?

families found that owning a few extra workers was a good investment.

Slavery. Some slaves were war captives, but in the early Republic most were Romans subjugated for debt. As in Mesopotamia or early Greece, Romans unable to satisfy their creditors had to sell themselves or their children to discharge their obligation. Slavery was not as harsh then as it would later become. The term of debt servitude was usually limited, with freedom guaranteed after a fixed period of years. After debt slavery was outlawed in the late fourth century BCE, foreign captives took the place of Romans. Conditions worsened because the captives did not share the culture of their owners, but the fact that most slaves continued to live under their master's roof and shared his table partially limited their dehumaniza-

tion. **Marcus Porcius Cato** (Kay'-toh, 234–149 BCE), the author, general, and statesman who wrote extensively on rural society under the Republic, reported that his wife sometimes nursed the children of slaves. Nevertheless, slaves remained property and could be sold, beaten, or killed without recourse to law.

Women and Children. By this legal status, the slaves differed little from the other members of the familia. Theoretically and legally, the father, or *paterfamilias* (pah'-ter-fah-mill'ee-us), had absolute power over the life and death of his children and slaves. His wife, too, was subject to his will, but he could neither kill nor sell her. In practice, affection and the need for domestic tranquility diluted the brutality of the law. By the second century BCE, women had, through court decisions

FIGURE 4.3 *A Wedding Ceremony.* This Roman fresco, from the time of Augustus (c. 27 BCE and 14 CE), shows a mythic version of a wedding ceremony. The bride-to-be, dressed in white, sits on the edge of the bed and waits for the bridegroom to lead her, as was the custom, from her father's house to his own. Venus, goddess of love, comforts and encourages her while a companion of the goddess pours perfumed oil into a shell. At the right, a draped female figure, probably the mother, stands at a basin preparing a bath for the bride. The groom lounges at center, and on the left, musicians play.

and senatorial decrees, gained a much larger measure of control over their persons and dowries than they had enjoyed in the early years of the Republic. In much the same way, the sale or execution of a child rarely took place without the approval of the entire family, and public opinion had to be considered as well. Rome, like ancient Greece, was a "shame" society that exercised social control primarily through community pressure. Reputation was vitally important, and Romans regarded the mistreatment of women and children as shameful.

Women managed the day-to-day life of the household. They, too, guarded their reputations, and, like men, were expected to exhibit physical and moral courage of the highest order and to conform to the ideals of *dignitas* (dig'-ni-tahs), *fides* (fee'-days), and *pietas* (pi'-eh-tas) (dignity, faithfulness, and piety). Custom demanded that women rebuke their menfolk if they failed to honor the same ancient virtues. In many ways, the Roman model of feminine behavior was more Spartan than Athenian.

Roman families formed part of larger social groups that influenced conduct. The importance of clans and tribes from an earlier time has been much debated, but **clientage,** the system of mutual dependency in which a powerful individual protects the interests of others in return for their political or economic support, was legally enforceable and even more highly developed than in Mesopotamia.

Roman Religion. Religion sanctioned all of these arrangements. The Roman pantheon of gods superficially resembled that of the Greeks, with Jupiter corresponding to Zeus, Juno to Hera, Venus to Aphrodite, and so on. However, in the early days at least, the gods do not seem to have had clearly defined human forms. No myths surrounded them, and no one suggested that they engaged in the kind of sexual antics common among the

Olympians. When Greek culture became fashionable in the second half of the third century BCE, such distinctions tended to vanish. The Romans adapted Greek myths to their own pantheon and began to portray Roman gods and goddesses according to the conventions of Greek art. The Romans also believed in a host of spirits that governed places and natural processes. They consulted the omens before virtually every act, public or private, and performed sacrifices to ensure its success. The sacrifices might involve the burnt offering of an animal, which was usually then eaten, or a libation (ritual pouring) of wine or oil. Gods and spirits alike had to be appeased. Priests of both sexes specialized in the care of temples or in foretelling the future. They never formed a separate caste. At home, the father presided over religious rites and was responsible for ensuring that the family did not offend the gods. The Romans appear to have had no concept of personal immortality, and their ethical concepts were largely unrelated to divine will.

GOVERNMENT IN THE ROMAN REPUBLIC (509–133 BCE)

As in most societies, some Romans were richer than others. The source or extent of their greater wealth is hard to determine, but at an early date the kings identified 100 men of substance and appointed them to an advisory body known as the **Senate.** The senators represented families that owned land, held slaves, and could afford to fight on horseback instead of on foot. They presided over elaborate networks of clientage in which mutual obligation was enforced by religious and legal sanctions. When the monarchy fell and two governing magistrates replaced them, the Senate remained to advise them. The magistrates eventually came to be known as **consuls,** and the senatorial families became the core of the patrician order.

The *patricians* (pa-trih'-shuns) were the hereditary aristocracy of the Roman Republic. Although ordinary citizens, or *plebeians* (pleh-bee'-ans), could vote, at least in theory, only patricians could hold office as magistrates or serve in the Senate. The plebeians resisted this situation from the start even though many of them were bound to individual patricians by ties of clientage. Some

ST. AUGUSTINE ON THE ROMAN RELIGION

St. Augustine (354–430 CE) was born Aurelius Augustinus in the Roman province of Numidia in North Africa, the son of a Christian mother and pagan father. Augustine moved to Rome, where he taught rhetoric and continued to accept traditional Roman religious practice. He converted to Christianity in his thirties and became a priest, returning to Africa, where he served as Bishop of Hippo. His writings, especially his autobiographical *Confessions* and *The City of God*, were extremely influential in shaping early Christianity. In an excerpt from *The City of God* describing the Roman religion of his and the Republic's youth, Augustine has begun by saying that the Romans had so many gods and goddesses that just naming them would take several volumes. Furthermore, Romans believed that the power of each deity was limited to a specific feature or function. To illustrate, he uses the gods and goddesses of agriculture from seed to harvest.

The Romans . . . did not even think that the care of their lands should be entrusted to any one god; but they entrusted their farms to the goddess Rumina, and the ridges of the mountains to the god Jugatinus; over the hills they placed the goddess Collatina, over the valleys, Vallonia. Nor could they even find one Segetia so potent that they could commend their cereal crops entirely to her care; but so long as their seed grain was still under the ground, they desired to have the goddess Seia watch over it; then, when it was already above

ground and formed standing grain, they set over it the goddess Segetia; and when the grain was collected and stored, they entrusted it to the goddess Tutilina, that it might be kept safe. Who would not have thought the goddess Segetia sufficient to protect the standing grain until it had passed from the first green blades to the dry ears? Yet she was not enough for men who loved a multitude of gods. . . . Therefore they set Proserpina over the germinating seeds; over the joints and knobs of the stems, the god Nodutus; over the sheaths enfolding the ears, the goddess Volutina; when the sheaths opened and the spikes emerged, it was ascribed to the goddess Patelana; when the stems were of the same height as new ears, because the ancients described this equalizing by the term hostire, *it was ascribed to the goddess Hostilina; when the grain was in flower, it was dedicated to the goddess Flora; when full of milk, to the god Lacturnus; when maturing, to the goddess Matuta; when the crop was "runcated"— that is, removed from the soil—to the goddess Runcina.*

From St. Augustine, *The City of God*, books 4 and 8, from *Roman Civilization*, 3rd ed., 2 vols. Naphtali Lewis and Meyer Rheinhold, eds. Copyright © 1990, Columbia University Press. By permission.

Question: Do you think these were all gods like Jupiter and Venus, or do you think they were personifications of natural processes to be enlisted as needed?

---

of them had grown rich during the years of expansion under the monarchy and resented being excluded from public life. Most had grown poorer. Their farms, which had never been large, had been divided and divided again by inheritance until many citizens were virtually landless. Roman law insisted on **partible inheritance,** the more-or-less equal division of property among heirs. The practice persists today wherever the Roman legal tradition remains and is a major obstacle to the preservation of a family's wealth. Apart from war or disease, only territorial growth could solve the problems partible inheritance created. When new lands were conquered, the Senate distributed some of it to Roman citizens, but those who had commanded the legions received the lion's share. The state held the rest as public land and rented it out to people with political connections (although some of it was inevitably taken over by squatters). Poor plebeians, faced with imminent bankruptcy, wanted a fairer division of this public land and an end to debt slavery.

Plebians rich and poor knew that their aims could be achieved by combining forces against the patricians. As a result, plebeian efforts to develop institutions and win

for themselves a place in government dominated Roman politics from the beginnings of the Republic until the early third century BCE. This **Struggle of the Orders** forged the basic institutions of the Roman State.

The Struggle of the Orders (494–287 BCE)

The power of the patricians was deeply rooted in law and custom, but even before the fall of the monarchy, their power had begun to diminish against the realities of warfare. Infantry formed the heart of the Roman army, and Roman survival depended on the swords and spears of plebeians, not the efforts of horse-mounted aristocrats. In Rome, as in the Greek polis, political rights would grow from military service.

The plebeians began their struggle in 494 BCE when they answered a senatorial call to arms by leaving the city and refusing to fight against the Volscians, a neighboring people who threatened to invade Roman territory. This dramatic gesture won them the right to elect **tribunes,** who could represent their interests and defend them against unjust decrees by the magistrates. In the following year, plebeians erected a temple on the Aventine hill to Ceres, the goddess of edible plants. Ceres, unlike the sky gods favored by the patricians, had long been associated with peasants and artisans. The temple, along with its *aediles* (eh′-dyels), or wardens, gave sacred status to the plebeian cause and placed its tribunes under divine protection. It also provided the physical site for a political organization. The Plebeian Council began to meet within its precincts and issue decrees or *plebiscites* (pleb′-ih-sites) in opposition to the patricians. Moreover, Romans, like the ancient Greeks and Hebrews, shared tribal affiliations whose full significance remains only partially understood. An assembly based on membership in these tribes appeared at roughly the same time and together with the *consilium plebis* (con-sil′-ee-um pleb′-iss) evolved into what plebeians regarded as a kind of alternative government.

The Twelve Tables (c. 451–450 BCE). Pressure from the plebeian and tribal assemblies bore fruit more than a generation later in the publication of the **Twelve Tables.** They formed the first body of written law in Roman history, and Livy called them, with some exaggeration, "the fountainhead of all public and private laws." The codified laws reinforced the privileges of the patricians, recognized the plebeians as a distinct order, and indirectly offered them a measure of legal protection. Patrician judges, who often acted out of self-interest or class prejudice, could not alter written laws at will. Furthermore, because these laws applied to patricians and plebeians alike, the tables also introduced the principle of equality before the law *(aequatio iuris)*. The Twelve Tables themselves were destroyed during the Gallic sack of Rome in 387 BCE, and their provisions are known today primarily through the commentaries of later jurists (see Document 4.3). Seen through the eyes of these commentators, the tables seem harsh and regressive. The principle of *patria potestas* (pah′-tree-a poh-tay′-stahss), for example, gave the husband the powers of "head of the family" and instructed him to kill a deformed baby. Another table stated that women were perpetual minors under the guardianship of their fathers or husbands, a legal principle that persisted in European law for more than 2,000 years. Although the Twelve Tables might seem conservative, they did mark an important step forward in establishing plebeian rights and the rule of law.

Among the more revolutionary features of the Twelve Tables was their recognition of wealth, in addition to birth, as a measure of social stratification. This may not seem like an advance, but it reflected an important part of the plebeian agenda. By 443 BCE, property qualifications ranked all citizens and determined not only their place in the army but also their right to participate in the centuriate assembly that elected the consuls and other important magistrates. A new official, the *censor,* was elected to determine the rankings on an ongoing basis, and the census became an important civic and religious ritual (see *The Roman Census*).

The Census. The census divided the entire body of male citizens into centuries that roughly corresponded to the size of a maniple, the military unit that, in its original form, had probably contained about 100 men. The centuries were in turn divided into classes ranging from the first class of heavily armed hoplites to a fifth class armed only with slings. The patrician *equites* (ek′-witayz), or cavalry, and the *proletarii* (pro-luh-tar′-ee-eye), who, as the saying went, "owned only their children" and could afford no weapons, were technically outside the class system, but this was little more than a convenient social fiction. The centuries voted in order of wealth. The voting stopped when a majority had been reached, thereby disenfranchising the poorer citizens. This protected the wealthy of both orders and, on property issues at least, made them allies. Wealth, rather than birth, was becoming the chief source of political power.

The Licinian-Sextian Laws (367 BCE). Property issues came to a head after the Gallic invasion of 387 BCE. Many poor Romans lost their property and were forced into debt slavery. Popular rebellions in 385 BCE and 375 BCE, although unsuccessful, led to a series of reforms. The **Licinian-Sextian Laws** (Lih-sin′-ee-un–Sex′-tee-un) of 367 BCE admitted plebeians to the highest offices of the state and allowed the popular assembly to pass laws subject to senatorial approval. This legislation produced a century of change. New laws abolished debt slavery and expanded the distribution of public land to poor citizens. Rapid territorial expansion after 350 BCE made implementation easier. The rich could no longer seize all of the gains. Shortly thereafter, the Senate admitted plebeians to membership for the first time, and in 287 BCE, the Senate lost its veto power over the plebiscites of the popular assembly. The Struggle of the Orders had ended.

The Reformed Government of the Roman Republic (287–133 BCE)

The government that emerged from this prolonged controversy was, in theory at least, carefully balanced to represent the interests of all Roman citizens and for this reason was of great interest to the theorists who framed the U.S. Constitution 2,000 years later. A measure of legislative authority rested in the centuriate, tribal, and plebeian assemblies, although the decrees of the latter may not have been binding for all citizens and most laws were actually made and imposed by magistrates.

The Magistrates. The most important function of the **centuriate** (sen-tour′-ee-ate) **assembly** was to elect the more important magistrates, including the consuls.

ULPIAN ON ROMAN LAW

The Roman jurist Ulpian was born at Tyre in Phoenicia and died in 225 CE. His writings on the law make up almost one-third of Justinian's *Digest of the Laws* (see Chapter 7). In this selection, Ulpian describes the moral and intellectual basis of Roman law and, in so doing, demonstrates its importance in Roman thought and practice. Note in particular Ulpian's understanding of natural law, which was to have a great influence on Western jurisprudence down to the present day.

When a man means to give his attention to law, he ought first to know whence the term law (ius) is derived. Now it is so called from justice (iustitita). In fact, as Celsus neatly defines it, ius is the art of the good and fair. Of this art we may deservedly be called the priests; we cherish justice and profess the knowledge of the good and the fair, separating the fair from the unfair, discriminating between the permitted and the forbidden, desiring to make men good, not only by the fear of penalties, but also by the incentives of rewards, affecting, if I mistake not, a true and not a simulated philosophy.

This subject comprises two categories, public law and private law. Public law is that which regards the constitution of the Roman state, private law that which looks to the interest of individuals; for some things are beneficial from the point of view of the state, and some with reference to private persons. Public law is concerned with sacred rites, with priests, with public officers. Private law is tripartite, being derived from the rules of natural law, or of the law of nations, or of civil law. Natural law is that which all animals are taught by nature; this law is not peculiar to the human race, but is common to animals which are produced on land or sea, and to the birds as well. From it comes the union of male and female, which we call matrimony, and the procreation and bearing of children; we find in fact that animals in general, even the wild beasts, are marked by acquaintance with this law. The law of nations is that which the various people of mankind observe. It is easy to see that it falls short of natural law, because the latter is common to all living creatures, whereas the former is common only to human beings in their mutual relations.

From Justinian, *Digest of the Laws*, I:3–4, from *Roman Civilization*, 3rd ed., 2 vols., Naphtali Lewis and Meyer Rheinhold, eds. Copyright © 1990, Columbia University Press. By permission.

Question: According to Ulpian, what is the purpose of private law and on what is that purpose based?

The two consuls led the state and commanded its armies. They served 1-year terms and could succeed themselves only after a 10-year interval. In theory, the consuls inherited the full *imperium* or authority of the old monarchy, and their edicts had the force of law. In practice, they consulted closely with the Senate and could veto each other's measures if necessary. In war, one consul normally commanded the legions while the other remained at home to govern, but it was not uncommon for both consuls to take the field and command the army on alternate days. In moments of extreme crisis, the consuls could also appoint a **dictator,** subject to senatorial approval. The dictator, who was always an experienced general, held absolute power for up to 6 months and could mobilize the full resources of the state without legal interference.

These arrangements met the defensive needs of a small community, but as Rome expanded, campaigns grew longer. Armies had to be maintained in distant areas for years at a time. In 325 BCE, the office of **proconsul** was created by extending a consul's field command for the duration of the campaign even though his term as consul had expired. This institution, even more than the office of dictator, became a threat to the survival of the Republic in later years, for it allowed the proconsul to develop an independent geographic and military base based upon the legions he commanded and the part of the empire they controlled.

Other magistrates called *praetors* (preh'-tors) administered justice, although they, too, might serve as generals in time of war. Upon taking office, they made a public declaration of the principles by which they would interpret the law, and these statements became landmarks as the body of Roman law developed. The most respected office in the Roman State was that of **censor.** There were two of them, and they registered citizens as well as supervised morals and guaranteed the validity of public contracts. They could also remove senators from office on financial or ethical grounds. Other offices included the *quaestors* (kwess'-tors), who assisted the consuls, especially on financial matters, and four *aediles* (eh'-dyels), who supervised markets and other public services. All were subject to interference from the tribunes, whose persons remained sacrosanct (protected by religious law) and who served as spokesmen for those who felt oppressed by the magistrates.

The Senate. More than an advisory body, the Senate remained the most powerful institution of the Roman State (see Document 4.4). The consuls originally appointed its members; after 312 BCE that right was given to the censors. Some senators were former consuls, and

The Roman Census

A Census. Every 5 years, Rome conducted a census to facilitate recruitment into the army ranks and to ensure that citizens were properly assigned to their classes. In this stone relief from around 115 to 97 BCE, citizens (on the left) make their declarations to a scribe and an assessor in the presence of soldiers. On the right, a bull, a ram, and a pig are offered in sacrifice to the god Mars. Like most civic rituals in the Republic, a religious ritual accompanied the census.

TABLE 4.1 THE FIRST CENSUS, 444 BCE

This classification of male citizens into numbers of troops provides a measure of Roman wealth and population in the early Republic. The assignment of wealth in terms of asses—a coin introduced in the third century BCE when about 33 asses purchased a bushel of wheat—is approximate, but scholars believe that it provides a fair estimate of the citizen population and its relative poverty.

Question: Assuming that most of these men had families with at least two children, estimate the total population of Rome in 444 BCE exclusive of slaves and foreigners.

CLASS RANK	NUMBER OF CENTURIES	NUMBER OF MEN	PROPERTY QUALIFICATION (IN ASSES)
Cavalry	18	1,800	
I	80	8,000	100,000
II	20	2,000	75,000
III	20	2,000	50,000
IV	20	2,000	25,000
V	30	3,000	12,500
Engineers	2	200	Ranked with class I
Musicians, proletarians, and others	3	300	None
Total	193	19,300	

Adapted from T. Frank, ed., *An Economic Survey of Ancient Rome*, vol. 1 (Paterson, NJ: Pageant Books, 1959, p. 20).

most were men of great wealth and experience—the leading citizens of Rome. Few consuls dared to ignore their advice, and the quaestors, who were mostly young men ambitious for higher office, followed them without hesitation. Because the quaestors administered public expenditures, this gave the Senate de facto control over finance.

The Senate was also responsible for provincial affairs, including the distribution of newly acquired public lands and of income derived from provincial sources. This enormous source of patronage supplemented the vast resources already available to the rich and power-ful. Whether patrician or plebeian, the senators were all *nobiles* (no-bih'-lays) and patrons who could count on the support of clients in the assemblies and at every level of the administration. They could therefore influence legislation in a dozen ways and affect its implementation by the magistrates when it passed.

Senatorial Factions. The tendency of such networks to combine within the Senate greatly augmented their power. There were no political parties as such, but the senators grouped themselves into factions or cliques associated with five great historic clans—the Fabii (Fab'-

FIGURE 4.4 *A Lictor (Magistrate's Attendant).* This bronze figurine from about 20 BCE portrays a *lictor,* one of the officials who accompanied consuls and other high magistrates on ceremonial occasions. In his left hand he carries **fasces,** the Roman symbol of power. The fasces consists of an axe bound in the center of a bundle of rods and symbolizes the power of the magistrates to impose punishment. The lictor is dressed in a toga, the formal wear for all Roman citizens. He wears a wreath on his head and carries laurel leaves in his right hand, a religious symbol to both Greeks and Romans.

ee-eye), Claudii (Claw'-dee-eye), Cornelii (Cor-nell'-ee-eye), Aemelii (Eh-mee'-lee-eye), and Valerii (Vuh-leer'-ee-eye). Clientage and friendship, as well as agreement on policy, provided political cohesion and a measure of class solidarity. Able men of relatively humble parentage—Cato provides an excellent example—might also attach themselves to a senatorial clan and be carried by this form of clientage to the highest levels of the state. In other words, the organization of senatorial cliques mirrored that of society as a whole.

Factions of this sort could wield enormous power at every level of society. When they could agree on a policy, which was not unusual because they all came from the same social and economic group, their combined influence was overwhelming. The Senate's constitutional role as a mere advisory body was therefore something of a fiction. By controlling the informal mechanisms through which business was done, the Senate remained the heart of the Roman State.

THE GROWTH OF A ROMAN EMPIRE UNDER THE REPUBLIC (201–133 BCE)

The new constitutional order was put to the test in less than a generation. In 264 BCE, Rome embarked on a mortal struggle with Carthage—a struggle that threatened Rome's existence and ended only after more than a century of bitter warfare. Rome's eventual success in

this conflict brought it control of the western Mediterranean and involved Romans for the first time in the governance of peoples outside the Italian peninsula. With success came a change of attitude on the part of Rome's governing classes. They embarked on an active campaign of expansion in Greece, Spain, and North Africa that brought Rome a vast Mediterranean empire.

The Wars with Carthage (264–201 BCE)

By the middle of the third century BCE, the former Phoenician colony of Carthage had become the dominant naval power in the western Mediterranean. Like their ancestors, the Carthaginians were great merchants and colonizers. Unlike their ancestors, they gradually assumed direct control of the colonies they had planted in western Sicily, Spain, Sardinia, Corsica, and the Balearic Islands. Theirs was a true empire, financed by trade with three continents and defended by a magnificent fleet (see Document 4.5). Because Rome was still an agrarian state with few commercial interests, the Carthaginians did not regard it as a threat. For centuries the two powers had enjoyed a cordial, if somewhat distant, relationship.

The First Punic War with Carthage (264–241 BCE). The conflict known as the First Punic (Pew'-nik) War (*punic* is the Roman adjectival form of Phoenician, Phoenicia having founded Carthage as a colony) started in Sicily. A nest of pirates and mercenaries, the Mamertines (Mam'-er-teens), had established themselves at Messana (Messina), a port that controlled the strait between Sicily and the Italian mainland. The city of Syracuse on Sicily sent an army to root them out, whereupon one faction among the Mamertines appealed to Carthage, the traditional enemy of the Sicilian Greeks. When the Carthaginians gained control of Messana, the other faction among the Mamertines appealed to Rome. After long debate, the Senate agreed to help, for if Carthage conquered Sicily, it could threaten the basis of Roman power in the south. No real evidence existed of Carthaginian interest in the mainland, however.

Rome Becomes a Naval Power. The resulting war was a long, drawn-out affair in which the Romans tried to besiege the Carthaginian towns in western Sicily. Although the Roman army won consistently in the field, it could do nothing to prevent the Carthaginians from reinforcing their Sicilian garrisons by sea. The Romans soon realized that only sea power could defeat Carthage and, for the first time in their history, constructed a navy. After some remarkable victories and one catastrophic defeat, they destroyed the main Carthaginian fleet in an epic battle off Drepanum (Trapani) in March 241 BCE. Knowing that it could no longer hold Sicily, Carthage sued for peace.

POLYBIUS ON ROMAN GOVERNMENT

Polybius (c. 200–118 BCE) was a Greek who wrote the history of Rome's wars with Carthage and Macedon. He was also fascinated by the Roman system of government. The following excerpt from *The Histories* describes it as a mixed constitution with monarchic, aristocratic, and democratic elements.

The consuls, before leading out the legions, remain in Rome and are supreme masters of the administration. All other magistrates, except the Tribunes, are under them and take their orders. They [the consuls] introduce foreign ambassadors to the Senate; bring matters requiring deliberation before it; and see to the execution of its decrees. If, again, there are any matters of state which require the authorization of the people, it is their [the consul's] business to see to them, to summon the popular meetings, to bring the proposals before them, and to carry out the decrees of the majority.

The Senate has control of the treasury and regulates receipts and disbursements alike. . . . Similarly, all crimes committed in Italy requiring a public investigation such as treason, conspiracy, poisoning, or willful murder, are in the hands of the Senate. Besides, if any individual or state among the Italian allies requires a controversy to be settled, a penalty to be assessed, help or protection to be afforded,—all this is the province of the Senate. Or again, outside Italy, if it is necessary to send an embassy to reconcile warring communities, or to remind them of their duty, or sometimes to impose requisitions upon them, or to receive their submission, or finally to proclaim war upon them, this too is the business of the Senate.

After this, one would naturally be inclined to ask what part is left for the people. . . . Again, it is the people who bestow offices upon the deserving, which are the most honorable rewards of virtue. It also has the absolute power of passing laws; and, most important of all, it is the people who deliberate on the question of peace and war.

From Polybius, "The Histories," in *The Histories of Polybius*, vol. 1, trans. Evelyn S. Shuckburgh (London: Macmillan, 1889).

Question: How do the powers of the Roman Senate differ from those of the U.S. Senate?

Rome was now a major naval power and the ruler of Sicily, but peace did not last, for the attitude of Rome's political elite began to change. After the First Punic War, Rome's intentions became more openly aggressive and expansionist when the possibility of achieving vast wealth through conquest began to dawn on even the most honorable of men. Sicily became the first Roman province. The Romans granted most of its people neither citizenship nor allied status, although they treated some of the cities, including Syracuse and Messana, as exceptions. Roman governors exercised full powers limited neither by local custom nor by interference from Rome. They levied heavy taxes and distributed large tracts of land to wealthy Romans who worked them with slaves captured in the war. Another sign of Rome's changing policy came when the mercenaries who constituted most of the Carthaginian army mutinied in 238 BCE. Rome took advantage of the situation and annexed the islands of Corsica and Sardinia. The Carthaginian leaders concluded from this that the Romans were bent on acquiring an empire and must be stopped.

The Second Punic War (218–201 BCE).
Fortunately for Carthage, a new war with the Gauls distracted Rome for several years. Hamilcar Barca, a prominent Carthaginian who had waged guerrilla warfare against the Roman army in Sicily, used this respite to consolidate the Carthaginian hold on Spain. A variety of Celtiberian (Selt-eye-beer'-ee-un) tribes, whose common characteristics included an aptitude for war, inhabited the Spanish interior. Hamilcar and his son-in-law and successor, Hasdrubal, bound them to Carthage by force or negotiation, creating in the process the nucleus of a formidable army. The Second Punic War grew out of Roman attempts to interfere with this process and nearly ended in the destruction of Rome. Rome demanded a treaty limiting Carthaginian expansion to the region south of the river Ebro in Spain but then formed an alliance with Saguntum, a Spanish city within the Carthaginian sphere of influence. The new Carthaginian commander, Hamilcar's son **Hannibal** (247–c. 183 BCE), had long dreamed of avenging his country's defeat in the First Punic War. Knowing that the Romans would retaliate, he took Saguntum by siege. Then, while the Romans raised an army to invade Spain, he took the war to Italy, threatening Rome and forcing the Romans to divide their forces.

Hannibal Invades Italy.
With his Spanish army, his African mercenaries, and a famous contingent of war elephants, Hannibal crossed the Alps and allied himself with the Gauls, whose hatred for Rome had in no way diminished. He knew that Rome was too large and well fortified to be conquered, but he hoped a show of force would disengage the allegiance of their Italian allies. Despite tireless diplomacy and exquisite care for the

POLYBIUS COMPARES ROME WITH CARTHAGE

The Carthaginian or Punic Wars (264–201 BCE) marked the emergence of Rome as a world power. The struggle, however, was evenly matched and the outcome in doubt for many years. In an excerpt from his history, Polybius provides a contemporary description of the strengths and weaknesses of two societies that had little in common. This comparison of the rivals is influenced by the author's suspicion of democracy, but it remains a useful measure of their strengths and weaknesses.

The constitution of Carthage seems to me to have been originally well contrived as regards its most distinctive points. For there were kings [sic] [the chief officials were annually elected shofetim, or judges] and the house of elders was an aristocratic force, and the people were supreme in matters appropriate to them, the entire frame of the state much resembling that of Rome or Sparta. But at the time when they entered on the Hannibalic War, the Carthaginian constitution had degenerated, and that of Rome was better. . . . The multitude of Carthage had already acquired the chief voice in deliberations; while at Rome the senate still retained this, as in the one case the masses deliberated and in the other the most eminent men, the Roman decisions on public affairs were superior. . . .

But to pass to differences of detail...the Carthaginians are naturally superior at sea, both in efficiency and equipment, because seamanship has long been their natural craft, and they busy themselves with the sea more than any other people; but as regards infantry services, the Romans are much more efficient. They indeed devote their whole energies to this matter, whereas the Carthaginians wholly neglect their infantry, though they do pay some slight attention to their cavalry. The reason for this is that the troops they employ are foreign and mercenary, whereas those of the Romans are natives of the soil and citizens. So that in this respect we must pronounce the political system of Rome superior to that of Carthage, the Carthaginians continuing to depend for the maintenance of their freedom on the courage of a mercenary force, but the Romans on their own valor and that of their allies.

Adapted from Polybius, *Histories,* book 4:2–3, trans. W. R. Patton, Loeb Classical Library (Cambridge, MA: Harvard University Press, 1960–1968).

Question: According to this excerpt, which state was more democratic, Rome or Carthage?

---

lives and property of the Italians, this effort was largely a failure.

Success in battle proved easier to achieve. Hannibal defeated the Romans on the banks of the river Trebbia and then crossed the Apennines to defeat them again at Lake Trasimeno. The Romans adopted a mobile defense under the leadership of the dictator Quintus Fabius Maximus (known as "the delayer"). Realizing that he could not defeat the Carthaginians in the field, Fabius drew them into southern Italy, maintaining contact with the enemy but avoiding a battle. Many Romans believed that this strategy was suitable only for cowards, but when the successors of Fabius reversed his policies and sought a battle at **Cannae** (Kahn'-ee) 216 BCE, the Roman legions were virtually annihilated. Hannibal had uncovered the tactical weakness of the Roman legions: trained only to move forward, the legions were vulnerable to cavalry attacks from the sides and rear. Hannibal's Spanish and African infantry fell back before the Roman assault but did not break its formations. The Carthaginian cavalry then surrounded the Romans. As many as 48,000 Romans and their allies were slain on the spot.

Cannae was the worst defeat in the history of the Roman Republic and one of the great military disasters of all time. It led to the defection of Capua, the largest city in Campania, and, indirectly, to a revolt in Syracuse that threatened Roman control over Sicily. The Romans were forced to besiege both cities while reverting to Fabian tactics in Apulia where Hannibal remained at large. With nearly 200,000 men under arms in Spain, Italy, and Sicily, Rome was approaching the end of its agricultural and financial resources. Italian agriculture had been devastated by the campaigns, and Rome was increasingly dependent upon imports of grain from Sicily and Sardinia. The Carthaginians, who understood the economic dimensions of war better than most, attacked the latter in 215 BCE while forming an alliance with Philip V of Macedon, who harassed Rome's allies on the eastern shore of the Adriatic. Rome was engaged on no fewer than five fronts.

Carthaginian Defeat. The turning point came in 207 BCE, when Hannibal's younger brother, who commanded the Carthaginian garrisons in Spain, decided to reinforce Hannibal's army. A second Carthaginian army crossed the Alps, but the Romans, who had remedied the tactical deficiencies that had plagued them at Cannae, destroyed it before it could join forces with Hannibal. They killed Hannibal's brother, leaving Spain helpless in the face of a

FIGURE 4.5 *Hannibal and His Elephants Cross the Rhone River.* A modern etching showing how Hannibal may have crossed the Rhone River (in southern France) with his elephants. Historians believe that the military value of elephants was more psychological than tactical, but they impressed the Romans. As this and many other modern pictures attest, Hannibal's elephants also captured the imagination of a later age.

Rome's victory over Carthage remained in doubt almost until the end. It had been purchased with enormous expenditures of wealth and manpower, but the ink on the treaty had scarcely dried when the Senate called for yet another war, this time in Greece. Roman motives for intervening in that troubled region are not entirely clear. Macedonian power had waned during the third century BCE, and two loose and turbulent federations now dominated Greek politics: the more aggressive Aetolian (Eh-tol'-ee-un) League in central Greece, and the Achaean (Uh-kee'-un) League in the south. Warfare was constant. This suited the purposes of three neighboring states with vested interests in the area. Rhodes, a commercial center with a fine navy, and Pergamum, a growing kingdom in western Asia Minor, feared the revival of Macedonian power and saw Rome as a potential ally. The third state, Ptolemaic Egypt, had attempted since its founding to undermine both Macedon and the Seleucid kingdom in Syria (see Chapter 3). By 202 BCE, the accession of a child to the throne of the Ptolemies had weakened Egypt and upset the balance of power among the three Hellenistic monarchies. Freed from the restraining influence of the Ptolemies, Philip V of Macedon (238–238 BCE) concluded a secret pact with the Seleucid monarch Antiochus III in the hope of regaining control over Greece. Antiochus was not interested in Europe. He sought only to annex Phoenicia, Philistia, and those parts of Asia Minor that remained under Ptolemaic Egypt's rule. Although the situation was unstable, it did not appear to endanger Rome.

Publius Cornelius Scipio

new Roman offensive. The Roman commander **Publius Cornelius Scipio** (Sip'-ee-o, 236–c. 183 BCE) was only 25 years old when he assumed the proconsular imperium, but he proved to be Hannibal's equal and the greatest Roman general of the age. By the end of 206 BCE, he had driven the Carthaginians from Spain.

The loss of Spain meant that Carthage was deprived of its chief source of wealth and manpower. In 204 BCE, Scipio landed in Africa with a powerful army. Hannibal was recalled from Italy, and in 202 BCE, he fought his last battle against the Romans at Zama (Zah'-mah). Hannibal's North African allies deserted him, and Scipio won the title *Africanus* by defeating Hannibal with tactics similar to those used by Hannibal at Cannae. With their army destroyed, the Carthaginians agreed to peace terms that included the surrender of Spain and the islands and the dismantling of their war fleet. Rome was the undisputed master of the western Mediterranean.

The Macedonian War (201–197 BCE). When they discovered the existence of the treaty, many senators pretended to feel otherwise. On the eve of the Second Punic War, Rome had sent a naval expedition to suppress piracy along the eastern shore of the Adriatic. Philip V felt threatened by the navy's presence and, in the dark days after the battle of Cannae, declared war against Rome in alliance with Carthage. His action had little effect on the outcome of the war, but Rome remembered. At the same time, many prominent Romans had grown enamored of Greek culture. Rome was still in many ways a crude place. It had yet to develop an art or literature of its own, and wealthy families relied on Greek tutors to educate their sons. Some of these boys, including Scipio Africanus and most of his extended family, grew up to become ardent Grecophiles. Even hard-bitten traditionalists such as Cato spoke Greek and were familiar with Greek literature. The appeals to Rome from Rhodes and other Greek communities for protection against Philip therefore fell upon sympathetic ears.

In the war that followed, sea power gave Rome a decisive advantage, while the Roman maniples outmaneuvered the Macedonian phalanx at the battle of Cynoscephalae (Sin-uh-sef'-uh-lee, 197 BCE). Philip retreated within his borders. He became a staunch ally of Rome and for the remainder of his reign concentrated on rebuilding the shattered Macedonian economy. The Greek leagues remained intact.

The War against the Seleucids (191–189 BCE).
The Romans then turned their attention to Antiochus III. The Seleucid monarch had by this time achieved his goals in Palestine and Asia Minor. Egged on by Hannibal, who had taken refuge at his court, and by the Greek Aetolian League, which had turned against Rome as soon as it was delivered from Philip, Antiochus took advantage of Macedonian weakness to cross the Dardanelles and annex Thrace. This time, the Senate was less eager for war. Efforts to remove Antiochus from Europe by negotiation failed. A Roman army routed him in 191 BCE at the historic site of Thermopylae. In the winter of 190–189 BCE, a second Roman army marched into Asia to defeat Antiochus again near Sardis. The Seleucid king abandoned all thought of Europe and surrendered most of his lands in Asia Minor to Rome's ally, Pergamum. The Romans kept nothing, but in 133 BCE the childless Attalus (At-tah'-lus) III of Pergamum bequeathed the entire kingdom to Rome in his will.

The Settlement of Greece (168–146 BCE).
The defeat of the two Hellenistic kingdoms proved that Rome was now the dominant power in the Mediterranean world. Greece, meanwhile, remained unstable. Rome was forced to intervene repeatedly in Greek affairs, and with each new intervention, the Senate's impatience grew. Two main factions emerged in the Senate. The Grecophile Scipios and their allies still hoped to achieve a settlement based on friendship with the Greek leagues. Their views have been preserved by **Polybius** (Po-lib'-ee-us, c. 200–c. 118 BCE), an Achaean Greek who wrote the history of Rome's wars in Greece and with Carthage and who was himself an important example of Greek influence on Roman thinking. Cato headed the opposing faction. He was immune to any form of sentimentality and wanted an end to adventures in the east. He thought that contact with Greeks was corroding the traditional Roman values that he had extolled in his writings, and although he had no desire to annex Greek territory, he was prepared to end their mischief-making by any means possible.

Cato's views gradually prevailed. Perseus, the son of Philip V of Macedon, allowed Pergamum to maneuver him into another disastrous war with Rome. The Romans defeated him at Pydna in 168 BCE and divided Macedon into four parts, but their patience was wearing thin. They destroyed seventy towns in Epirus, which had supported Macedon, and sold 150,000 of its inhabitants into slavery. They then

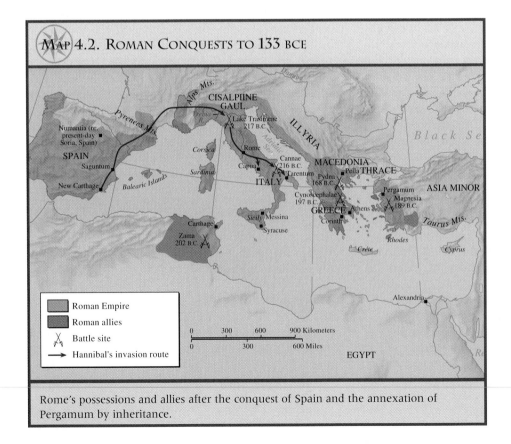

MAP 4.2. ROMAN CONQUESTS TO 133 BCE

Rome's possessions and allies after the conquest of Spain and the annexation of Pergamum by inheritance.

A SOLDIER'S TALE FROM LIVY'S "HISTORY OF ROME"

In this famous passage, an old soldier speaks out against his comrades' demands to be discharged from the army. He supports his appeal by recording his own experiences—that of a common citizen who became an exceptional soldier—and acknowledges the fairness of his comrades' desires. Still, his evident pride in his own service—an attitude which was widespread in the armies of the Republic—leads him to advocate continued service and helps to explain how Roman armies conquered much of the known world. He addresses his speech to the Consul, Publius Licinus, to whom he has already offered four men in addition to himself.

"I, Spurius Ligustinus of the Crustuminian tribe, am of Sabine origin. My father left me a iugerum of land and a small cottage in which I was born and bred, and I am living there today. As soon as I came of age, my father gave me to wife his brother's daughter, who brought nothing with her but her free birth and chastity, and together with these a fruitfulness which would have been enough even for a wealthy house. We have six sons and two daughters, both of them already married . . . I became a soldier in the consulship of Publius Sulpicius and Gaius Aurelius [200 BCE]. For two years I served as a common soldier in the army, which was taken over to Macedonia, fighting against Philip; in the third year Titus Quinctius Flaminius made me, for my bravery, centurion of the tenth maniple of the hastati. After Philip and the Macedonians were defeated and we were brought back to Italy and discharged, I at once volunteered to go with the consul Marcus Porcius [Cato] to Spain . . . It was this commander who thought me worthy of being appointed centurion of the first century of the hastati. Again I served, for the third time, as a volunteer in the army which was sent against the Aetolians and King Antiochus. I was made first centurion of the principes by Manius Acilius . . .Then I served in Spain twice . . . I joined Tiberius Gracchus in the province at his request. Four times within a few years, I held the rank of chief centurion, thirty-four times I have been rewarded for bravery by my commanders. I have received six civic crowns [for saving the life of a citizen]. I have served twenty-two years in the army and am more than fifty years old. But even if I had not served my full time and my age did not yet give me an exemption, still, Publicius Licinus, as I was able to give you four soldiers to replace me, it would have been right that I should be discharged. But I want you to take what I have said simply as a statement of my case. For my part, as long as anyone who is enrolling soldiers judges me fit for service, I will never plead excuses. What rank the military tribunes think I deserve is for them to decide; I will see to it that no man in the army surpasses me in bravery. And as for you, fellow soldiers, though you are within your rights in making this appeal, it is proper that, as in your youth you never did anything against the authority of the magistrates and the senate, so now, too, you should place yourself at the disposal of the consuls and senate, and consider any position in which you will be defending your country as an honorable one."

From Livy, "History of Rome," book 34, from Roman Civilization, 2 vols., Naphtali Lewis and Meyer Rheinhold, eds. (New York: Columbia University Press, 1990). Reprinted by permission.

Question: Based on the discussion of Roman military practices in the text, how was it possible for a poor man like Spurius Ligustinus to support a family while serving almost continually in the army?

sent troops to strengthen the pro-Roman party in the Aetolian League, and took 1,000 hostages from Achaea even though the Achaeans had supported Rome. One of the hostages was Polybius, who used his exile to form a connection with the Scipios. The others were not so fortunate. Most were dispersed among the Italian provincial towns. Those who survived were returned in 151 BCE after 17 years in exile.

Meanwhile, a revolt had broken out in Macedonia under the leadership of a man who claimed to be Perseus's son. The Romans easily suppressed it and annexed Macedon as a Roman province, but the Achaeans, still angry over the hostage issue, decided to challenge Roman authority on several fronts. The response was devastating. In 146 BCE, the Achaean League suffered its last defeat on the battlefield. The Romans, thoroughly exasperated, destroyed the an-cient city of Corinth in reprisal. They killed the men, enslaved the women and children, and carried away the city's priceless art treasures. They then abolished the Greek leagues and replaced democratic governments in several cities with oligarchies responsive to Rome. Years later the Romans loosened the terms of settlement, but Greece remained a Roman protectorate with no independent policy of its own.

The Conquest of Spain and North Africa (197–146 BCE)

It is a measure of Rome's enormous power that, while annexing Macedon, defeating Antiochus, and reordering the affairs of Greece, the Republic abandoned none of its ambitions in the west. Between 201 BCE and 183 BCE, the

FIGURE 4.6 *A Roman Ship of the Late Republic.* This mosaic in the Sousse Museum, Tunisia, shows a galley with a single bank of oars and two masts, each of which carries a square sail. An eye is painted on the prow, which is carved in the shape of a dragon with a fish in its mouth.

Destruction of Carthage. Meanwhile, Carthage had been observing the terms of the peace treaty. Its military power and much of its wealth were gone, but the Roman faction headed by Cato wanted nothing less than the total destruction of its old rival. For years Cato had ended every speech in the Senate, regardless of the subject, by saying *"Ceterum censeo delendam esse Carthaginem"* ("Moreover, I think Carthage must be destroyed"). In 151 BCE, he and his followers saw their chance.

Since joining the Romans at the battle of Zama, the able and ambitious Masinissa, king of Numidia, had built a powerful North African state at Carthage's expense. When the Carthaginians tried to stop him, his Roman allies saw their action as a breach of the treaty. In a series of cunning diplomatic moves, the Romans demanded ever-greater concessions, ending with a demand for the destruction of the city and the removal of its population. Not surprisingly, the Carthaginians refused even though they had been deprived of most of their weapons. After a long and bitter siege, the city fell in 146 BCE. Carthage was destroyed as promised, and a furrow plowed through it that was then sown with salt to indicate that the land would never be occupied again.

Romans annexed Liguria, the area around modern Genoa, and settled their old score with the Gauls. They defeated the Gallic tribes that lived south of the Po River. When many of the Gauls then fled beyond the Alps into what would later become France, Rome replaced them with Italian colonists.

At the same time, the Romans embarked on a bitter struggle for the Iberian (Eye-beer'-ee-un) Peninsula. After Carthage surrendered, Roman magistrates seized its Spanish colonies and extracted a fortune in tribute that came ultimately from mines in the interior. The towns, supported by a number of Celtiberian tribes, rebelled in 197 BCE, and Cato was sent to suppress them. Cato believed that "war supports itself." He insisted that his troops live off the country, and although modestly successful in military terms, his campaign of atrocity and confiscation ensured that the war would continue.

The Celtiberians resorted to guerrilla warfare. Other communities became involved, and it was not until 133 BCE that Numantia (Noo-man'-tee-uh), the last center of Spanish resistance, fell to the Romans after a lengthy siege. Scipio Aemilianus, the Roman commander and adopted grandson of Africanus, ordered it burned to the ground without waiting to consult the Senate. The siege of Numantia, like the war itself, had been conducted with unparalleled savagery on both sides. The Romans massacred whole tribes even when they surrendered on terms guaranteeing their safety, but Spain, too, was now Roman territory.

Provincial Government under the Republic

By 133 BCE, Rome had acquired seven overseas provinces. They incorporated Carthaginian territory into a new province of Africa and protected it by an alliance with the Numidians. Spain, although technically a single province, had been divided in two by Scipio Africanus: Nearer Spain (Hispania Citerior), comprising the east coast from the Ebro valley to Cartagena, and Further Spain (Hispania Ulterior), which was to the south and west, in what is now Andalusia. Macedon, too, became a Roman province, and Rome protected it by making alliances with the Illyrians, who inhabited the east coast of the Adriatic, and by ensuring the utter dependency of the Greeks on Roman favor. Roman Sicily, Corsica, and Sardinia were islands in a sea commanded by the Roman fleet. Pergamum became the Roman province of Asia Minor with the bequest of Attalus III in 133 BCE.

CICERO ON THE CRIMES OF A PROVINCIAL GOVERNOR, FROM *AGAINST VERRES*

Cicero (Marcus Tullius Cicero, 106–43 BCE) was the greatest lawyer and orator of his time (see Chapter 5). Verres was a governor of Sicily whom Cicero prosecuted in the Senate for corruption. The following excerpt from Cicero's *Against Verres* is a kind of summation. Elsewhere in his address Cicero specifically describes many examples of bribery and extortion as well as some highly imaginative accounting frauds. This kind of behavior was all too common among provincial governors in the later Republic.

For the space of three years, the law awarded nothing to anybody unless Verres chose to agree; and nothing was so undoubtedly inherited from a man's father or grandfather that the courts would not cancel his right to it, if Verres asked them to do so. Countless sums of money, under a new and unprincipled regulation, were wrung from the purses of the farmers; our most loyal allies were tortured and executed like slaves; the guiltiest criminals bought their legal acquittal, while the most honorable and honest men would be prosecuted in [their] absence, and condemned, and banished unheard; strongly fortified harbors, mighty and well-defended cities, were left open to the assaults of pirates and buccaneers; Sicilian soldiers and sailors, our allies and our friends, were starved to death; fine fleets, splendidly equipped, were to the disgrace of our nation destroyed and lost to us. Famous and ancient works of art, some of them the gifts of wealthy kings, who intended them to adorn the cities where they stood, others the gifts of Roman generals, who gave or restored them to the communities of Sicily in the hour of victory—this same governor stripped and despoiled every one of them. Nor was it only the civic statues and works of art that he treated thus; he also pillaged the holiest and most venerated sanctuaries . . .

From Cicero, *Against Verres*, trans. L. H. Greenwood (Cambridge, MA: Harvard University Press, 1959).

Question: What made it possible for men like Verres to commit these crimes without interference?

The Romans had not planned to create a world empire and were at first unprepared to govern it. Their political institutions, although sophisticated, were those of a city-state. Financial structures remained primitive. The Senate would not extend ally status to the newly conquered regions and was at first reluctant to organize them into provinces or to maintain armies for their defense. Among other things, the senators feared that the creation of new magistrates and proconsuls might dilute their own membership and weaken their power as individuals.

Provincial government under the Republic was neither as efficient nor as capable as it would eventually become. Provincial charters varied widely. Different provinces were taxed at different rates, and certain towns paid no taxes at all. In some places, overtaxation caused widespread poverty, but whatever the rates, collection was almost always inefficient. Private contractors, called *publicans* in the Bible, extracted cash, bullion, or agricultural commodities from taxpayers and kept a portion of the yield for themselves, a system that bred corruption and led to interminable complaints. The governors were at first admired for their honesty, but Roman virtue soon crumbled in the face of older, more cynical traditions. Bribes and extortion could make a magistrate rich beyond imagination. No imperial bureaucracy provided effective oversight, and for many, the temptation proved irresistible (see Document 4.7). Provincial government could be brutal and even extortionate, but for most of those who found themselves under Roman rule, it was probably no worse than the governments to which they had long been accustomed. Most offered no resistance to the new order and in time accepted it as preferable to any conceivable alternative.

CONCLUSION

In the years when Greek civilization was at its height, Rome was still a modest settlement in central Italy. Poor and surrounded by powerful enemies, it survived by developing a superb army and a political system that, although authoritarian enough to be efficient in times of crisis, was based on the active participation of its citizens and the rule of law. From these humble beginnings, Rome first conquered Italy and then acquired an empire. The Romans did not set out, like Alexander, to conquer new worlds, but neither did they gain their empire in a fit of absentmindedness. They understood from the beginning that security depended on controlling the activities of their neighbors. Gradually, "fear of the enemy," as Polybius put it, gave way to larger ambitions. Rome's elite seems to have adopted the goal of imposing order on the world as they knew it. The Second Punic War was the turning point. After that narrow brush with catastrophe, a combination of greed and impatience led the Romans onward. By the midsecond century BCE, they had politically united the Mediterranean world for the first time. Roman provinces stretched from the Atlantic to southwest Asia (Asia Minor), and those peoples who were not under Roman rule were Roman allies or dependents. But if the Senate was willing to shoulder massive new responsibilities, it refused to follow that willingness to its logical conclusion. Many years would pass before Rome learned to govern its new possessions effectively. In the meantime, Rome itself had changed almost beyond recognition.

Review Questions

- What was the Roman policy toward its defeated neighbors in Italy, and how did it help them secure hegemony over the peninsula?
- How did Roman government work after the Struggle of the Orders?
- How did Rome differ from Carthage, both as a society and as a political system?
- How did Roman attitudes about Greece affect its policies in the region?
- How did Roman policy in conquered territories change after the Carthaginian Wars?

For Further Study

Readings

Cornell, Tim, *Beginnings of Rome: Italy and Rome from the Bronze Age to the Punic Wars* (London: Routledge, 1995). A good recent study of early Italy.

Errington, Robert M., *The Dawn of Empire: Rome's Rise to World Power* (Ithaca: Cornell, 1971). A standard work on the growth of Rome's empire under the Republic.

Gardner, Jane F., *Being a Roman Citizen* (London: Routledge, 1993). Deals with the status of women, children, the disabled, and other members of Roman society.

Lazenby, J. F., *The First Punic War: A Military History* (Stanford, CA: Stanford University Press, 1996). Along with Lazenby's *Hannibal's War* (Warminster, UK: Aris & Phillips, 1978), the best treatment of the Punic Wars.

Sherwin-White, A. N., *Roman Citizenship*, 2nd ed. (Oxford: Clarendon Press, 1973). The classic treatment of citizenship and how the Romans extended it to others.

InfoTrac College Edition

Visit the source collections at *http://infotrac.thomson learning.com* and use the search function with the following key terms.

Using Key Terms, enter the search terms:
Roman History   *Roman Republic*
Archimedes

Using the Subject Guide, enter:
Roman Mythology   *Roman Law*

Web Site

http://www.roman-empire.net

The Illustrated History of the Roman Empire. A large site with good information under the headings *The Founding, The Kings, Early Republic, Religion,* and *The Army.*

THE RISE OF THE ROMAN REPUBLIC

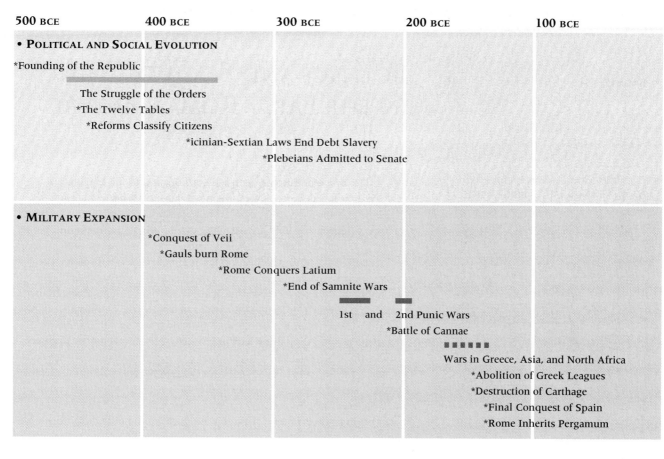

500 BCE	400 BCE	300 BCE	200 BCE	100 BCE

• POLITICAL AND SOCIAL EVOLUTION

*Founding of the Republic

The Struggle of the Orders
*The Twelve Tables
*Reforms Classify Citizens
*icinian-Sextian Laws End Debt Slavery
*Plebeians Admitted to Senate

• MILITARY EXPANSION

*Conquest of Veii
*Gauls burn Rome
*Rome Conquers Latium
*End of Samnite Wars

1st and 2nd Punic Wars
*Battle of Cannae

Wars in Greece, Asia, and North Africa
*Abolition of Greek Leagues
*Destruction of Carthage
*Final Conquest of Spain
*Rome Inherits Pergamum

Visit the Western Civilization Companion Web Site for resources specific to this textbook:
http://history.wadsworth.com/hause02/

The CD in the back of this book and the Western Civilization Resource Center at *http://history. wadsworth.com/western/* offer a variety of tools to help you succeed in this course, including access to quizzes; images; documents; interactive simulations, maps, and timelines; movie explorations; and a wealth of other sources.

FOCUS QUESTIONS

- How did the social problems created by the growth of the empire eventually lead to the collapse of republican government?
- How did Augustus come to power, and what changes did he make in the government of Rome?
- How did the Augustan principate evolve into a truly imperial system ruled by a semidivine emperor?
- What were the major reasons for slow economic growth and a general decline in population under the empire?

Chapter 5

POLITICS AND SOCIETY IN THE EARLY ROMAN EMPIRE

In 133 BCE, when Rome acquired both Spain and the kingdom of Pergamum in western Asia, the newly elected tribune Tiberius Gracchus (Tie-beer'-ee-us Grak'-kus) reportedly said: "The men who risked their lives fighting for Italy are granted only air and light: house and home are denied them and they are left to wander with their wives and children in the open air. . . . They die for foreign luxury and riches, in name the masters of the world, in fact not even masters of their own plot of land." It was only a slight exaggeration. The acquisition of an empire changed the basic fabric of Roman society and created tensions that, as Tiberius Gracchus knew, could not be resolved with the existing political system. Civil strife produced by these tensions, and by the emergence of a professional army whose members had no stake in the preservation of traditional society, led eventually to the breakdown of republican institutions. Rival commanders struggled for control of the state until, in 31 BCE, Octavian (Ahk-tay'-vee-un), known as Augustus, emerged supreme and imposed a new system of government. Although he retained the outward forms of republicanism, Augustus was an autocrat. During the first century CE, his successors gradually abandoned republican pretense and adopted the ceremonial trappings of the Hellenistic monarchies. The Roman world, now governed by a semidivine emperor, was far larger than it had been under the Republic. The civil wars of the first century BCE involved Egypt, Syria, Gaul, and Britain, regions that were incorporated into the Roman Empire. Rome now stretched from the moors of Northumberland to the borders of Persia.

Chapter 5 describes how social tensions arising from the acquisition of an empire led to the fall of the Roman Republic and how Octavian emerged from the resulting civil wars to lay the foundation of a new system of imperial government. After a brief history of the first emperors, this chapter analyzes trade and the imperial economy. The chapter concludes by examining how people, both enslaved and free, actually lived in the city of Rome and in the provinces during the early empire.

THE FALL OF THE REPUBLIC (133–31 BCE)

Ordinary Romans gained little from the acquisition of an empire. Thousands found only an unmarked grave in some remote corner of Spain or the Balkans. Those who returned often discovered that their ancestral farms had been devastated by neglect or—after the Second Punic War—by the passage of armies. All faced a burden of wartime taxation that would have made economic survival difficult in any circumstances. Meanwhile, the great senatorial families profited enormously. Roman military commanders came almost exclusively from this class, and they took most of the loot from captured provinces. This included not only gold, silver, and commodities of every sort but also tens of thousands of slaves. In addition, the Senate granted vast provincial estates to those whose leadership it regarded as outstanding.

The Development of Great Estates. The recipients of this new wealth invested much of it in Italy. Small farmers, impoverished by war and taxes, sold their plots to former officers who incorporated them into large, slave-worked plantations. Whenever possible, investors purchased land in different parts of the peninsula so that each property could be devoted to a specialized crop. This allowed owners to take maximum advantage of soil and climate while minimizing the risks of a bad harvest, for it was unlikely that every part of Italy would be hit simultaneously by drought or other catastrophes. Specialization also permitted economies of scale. Owners devoted careful thought to the optimum size for a vineyard, an olive plantation, or a ranch. Slaves may have been cheap in the aftermath of the wars, but feeding more of them than necessary was pointless.

Ideally, in addition to its cash crop, an estate produced just enough to support its labor force. Self-sufficiency reduced costs and was relatively easy to achieve, in part because slaves were no longer regarded as part of the family. In the past, most slaves had been Italian. Now they were foreign captives and less likely to fit into the fabric of Roman life. Conditions on some of the estates were appalling. In the Sicilian grain lands, slaves worked on chain gangs and were locked up at night. To be sold to the Spanish mines was a death sentence. Elsewhere, conditions were better, but even the most enlightened owners viewed slaves as an investment, and slave revolts were common (see Document 5.1).

Rise in Landlessness. In this way, wealthy families developed networks of specialized properties that brought in huge profits and, through diversification, ensured them against risk. Ordinary farmers could not compete. Their small plots were inherently inefficient, and they lacked the capital either to expand or to make improvements. If they tried to do so, they had to borrow from their wealthier neighbors, and although debt slavery had long been abolished, many lost their land through foreclosures. Others were forced out of business by unfair competition. Someone with a half-dozen great estates could easily sell below cost if by so doing he or she could drive out a competitor and pick up his or her land at distress-sale prices.

Citizens by the thousands gave up their land and migrated to the cities, but opportunities were limited. Imperialism had concentrated wealth in the hands of a few while doing little to increase the overall rate of economic activity. The rich developed habits of conspicuous consumption that horrified traditionalists such as Cato, but their most extravagant wants could be met by a handful of artisans, many of whom were skilled slaves from the east. Slaves, whether in town or country, consumed little, and citizens who had been driven from the land consumed less. Most of the latter were destitute. After 213 BCE, senatorial factions began to distribute charity among them in return for votes.

The *Equestrians*. Aside from the senatorial elite, only one other group appears to have benefited from the wars—the merchants, purveyors, and military contractors who organized the logistics of imperial expansion.

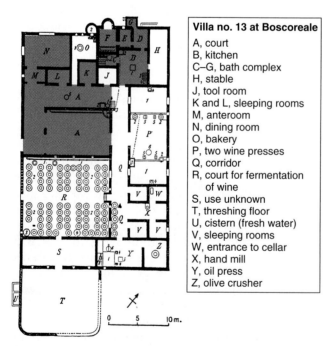

Villa no. 13 at Boscoreale

A, court
B, kitchen
C–G, bath complex
H, stable
J, tool room
K and L, sleeping rooms
M, anteroom
N, dining room
O, bakery
P, two wine presses
Q, corridor
R, court for fermentation of wine
S, use unknown
T, threshing floor
U, cistern (fresh water)
V, sleeping rooms
W, entrance to cellar
X, hand mill
Y, oil press
Z, olive crusher

FIGURE 5.1 *Estate Plan of a Typical Villa in the Late Republic.* This villa at Boscoreale near Pompeii was the headquarters of a typical working estate. Wealthy Romans spread their financial risks by investing in several such properties during the later Republic. Worked by slaves, this one produced wine. The existence of a threshing floor (T) indicates that it was more diversified in its products than some other farms. Although its living quarters were comfortable enough by the standards of the time, the primary emphasis was on efficiency and practicality.

DIODORUS DESCRIBES A SLAVE REVOLT IN SICILY

The habitual mistreatment of slaves under the late Republic provoked a series of terrifying slave revolts. The one described here by Diodorus (Dee-o'-dor-us) of Sicily lasted from 134 to 131 BCE and involved an army of more than 70,000 slaves. Another great uprising occurred in Sicily from 104 to 100 BCE, and yet another in Italy under the gladiator Spartacus (73–71 BCE) in which 100,000 slaves were said to have been killed.

The Servile War broke out from the following cause. The Sicilians, being grown very rich and elegant in their manner of living, bought up large numbers of slaves . . . and immediately branded them with marks on their bodies. Oppressed by the grinding toil and beatings, maltreated for the most part beyond all reason, the slaves could endure it no longer.

The whole revolt began in the following manner. There was a man in Enna named Damophilus, magnanimous in his wealth but arrogant in disposition. This man was exceedingly cruel to his slaves, and his wife Megallis strove to outdo her husband in torture and general inhumanity toward them. As a result, those who were thus cruelly abused were enraged like wild beasts and plotted together to rise *in arms and kill their masters. They applied to Eunus [a slave from Syria who was also a well known magician] and asked whether the gods would speed them in their design. Performing some of his usual mumbo-jumbo, he concluded that the gods granted it, and urged them to begin at once. Thereupon they forthwith collected 400 of their fellow slaves and, when the opportunity presented itself, they burst fully armed into the city of Enna with Eunus leading them and performing tricks with flames of fire for them. They stole into the houses and wrought great slaughter. They spared not even the suckling babes, but tore them from the breast and dashed them to the ground. It cannot be expressed with what wanton outrage they treated wives before the very eyes of their husbands. They were joined by a large throng of the slaves in the city, who first visited the extreme penalty upon their masters and then turned to murdering others.*

Diodorus of Sicily, from L. Naphtali and M. Rheinold, eds, *Roman Civilization: Third Edition*, 2 Vol. Set (New York: Columbia University Press, 1990). Reprinted with permission of the publisher.

Question: Why did the treatment of slaves deteriorate in the later years of the Roman Republic?

Most were men of humble origin, often manumitted slaves who used knowledge and connections gained from their former masters to win contracts. They amassed great wealth in shipbuilding, arms manufacture, and commodity speculation and made an effort to acquire estates because land remained the most secure and prestigious source of income. Others followed the lead of certain senators and invested their surplus capital in urban real estate—ramshackle five-story tenements built to house the growing masses of urban poor. In later years these people would be known as *equestrians* (eh-kwes'-tree-uns), a separate class that worked steadily to increase its power in government.

Roman society had changed completely in little more than a century. Although pockets of traditional life remained, most of the small-acreage independent farmers who had been the backbone of the Republic had been reduced to dependency. Slaves produced most of the goods and services while a few families lived in luxury that seemed more Oriental than Roman. The situation could lead only to civil strife.

The Reforms of the Gracchi (133–121 BCE)

In 133 BCE, a newly elected tribune, **Tiberius Sempronius Gracchus** (163–133 BCE), initiated reform legislation. A member of the aristocracy and a descendant of Scipio Africanus, he hoped to improve the condition of landless Romans by redistributing public lands acquired through conquest. Such properties were to have been allocated among the citizens as a whole, but families like his own often had seized them illegally through the use of political influence. His motives included both moral outrage and personal ambition; his most persuasive argument, however, was practical. From the beginning of the Republic, land ownership was a prerequisite for military service. An absolute decline in the number of free citizens caused by their death in the wars, coupled with a loss of property by thousands of others, threatened the security of the state by shrinking its base of recruitment. Only by restoring land to Roman citizens could the legions be preserved.

A number of powerful senators agreed. The dislocations of the past century threatened to undermine recruitment as well as the moral fiber of society. Moreover, Tiberius tried to couch the proposal in terms acceptable to the landowners. Up to 1,000 *iugera* (you-gair'-a; about 600 acres) of land per family could be excluded from the distribution, even if it had been taken illegally, and only Romans would receive the proceeds of the confiscations.

This was not enough. Some senators balked at giving up land held by their families for three or four generations. They were backed by a tremendous outcry from the

Italian allies. Wealthy Italians, too, had received public lands. They would be forced to surrender them, not to other Italians, but to Romans. To them, the reform was clearly discriminatory.

Faced with an uncertain outcome in the Senate, Tiberius decided to bypass it altogether. He went to the plebeian assembly, which rapidly authorized the necessary legislation. When another tribune vetoed the bill, he convinced the plebeians to vote the man out of office. Ignoring the Senate was bad politics, but deposing a tribune was unconstitutional. To make matters worse, Tiberius left himself open to charges of corruption by entrusting the redistribution of lands to a committee composed of himself, his brother Gaius (Gay'-us), and his father-in-law.

Murder of Tiberius Gracchus (133 BCE). The Senate began to close ranks against Tiberius. While allowing the committee to proceed with its work, the senators refused to appropriate money for its support. This was critical, because land reform proved more difficult than Tiberius had expected. Establishing clear title to many public lands was nearly impossible, and virtually every decision aroused protest. Desperate for funds, he asked that revenues from the newly acquired kingdom of Pergamum be devoted to the task. The Senate saw this as an assault on its traditional dominance in the areas of finance and provincial policy. In its view, Tiberius and his reforms had become a threat to the constitution.

Knowing that if he left the tribuneship, he would lose judicial immunity and be charged with treason by his enemies, Tiberius decided to run for a second term. This, too, was unprecedented, if not unconstitutional, and a group of senators claimed that he was trying to establish himself as a tyrant. They started riots during which they and their clients killed Tiberius and 300 of his followers. It was the first outbreak of civil violence in the history of the Roman Republic, but it would not be the last. The divisions in Roman society were too great to be resolved without constitutional change, and ambitious politicians had learned from Tiberius that they could ride to power on the shoulders of the multitude. Such people were called *populares* (pop-you'-lar-es). Their opponents, who supported the traditional role of the Senate, were known as *optimates* (op'-tim-a-tes).

Reforms of Gaius Gracchus (123–121 BCE). Among the populares was **Gaius Gracchus** (153–121 BCE), the younger brother of Tiberius. When elected tribune in 123 BCE, he prepared to implement reforms more far-reaching than those favored by his brother (see Document 5.2). Gaius realized that the agrarian problem was only one of many created by the transformation of Roman society. First he reenacted his brother's agrarian law, which had been repealed in 129

BCE. Then, knowing that not everyone could receive land in Italy, he guaranteed annual grain rations to every poor Roman at a fixed price and tried to set up overseas colonies for those willing to emigrate in return for land. The first of the new settlements was to be established on the site of Carthage.

To prevent the reversal of these policies, Gaius allied himself with the equestrians to weaken the power of the Senate. The assemblies were given the sole right to establish capital courts, and he replaced senators with equestrians as jurors in cases of extortion. A more important attack on senatorial prerogatives came in the area of provincial administration. The Senate had for years influenced the behavior of consuls by waiting until after their election to designate which provinces they would control. By forcing them to make their appointments before the election, Gaius deprived the senators of an important source of political leverage. From the senatorial point of view this was even worse than another new policy by which he allowed syndicates of rich equestrians or *publicani* (the publicans of the Bible) to bid at auction for the right to collect provincial taxes. In later years this practice became a fertile source of corruption.

The Problem of the Italian Allies. The issue of whether a tribune could succeed himself had apparently been resolved since Tiberius's death, and Gaius was reelected tribune in 122 BCE. Having addressed the grievances of the poor and satisfied the equestrians in his first term, he turned to the problem of the Italian allies, who remained angry over agrarian reform and a host of other slights. His proposal, although not original, was straightforward: admit them to Roman citizenship. Had this been done, Rome might have been spared a bloody war, but the plebeian assembly had no desire to share its privileges. A conservative reaction set in, and Gaius was defeated for reelection in 121 BCE. When the assembly began to repeal its earlier reforms, rioting began. Gaius and a band of followers fortified themselves on the Aventine hill. The Senate declared martial law for the first time in its history, and the reformers were slaughtered. The violence was committed by Roman troops, not by members of the senatorial opposition and their clients.

The Transformation of the Army and the Beginning of the Civil Wars (107–44 BCE)

The Gracchi (Grak'-kee) had tried to address Rome's fundamental problems and failed. Although the Senate's view of the constitution triumphed, that failure ultimately led to the collapse of the Republic. Equestrians and Italian allies felt excluded from their rightful place in the political system, and far too many citizens remained landless and dependent on what amounted to

PLUTARCH ON THE REFORM PROGRAM OF GAIUS GRACCHUS

Here Plutarch summarizes Gaius Gracchus's plan for reforming Roman society as he presented it 123–121 BCE. Aside from an expansion of the jury system, its provisions are largely economic.

Of the laws which he now proposed with the object of gratifying the people and destroying the power of the senate, the first concerned public lands, which were to be divided among the poor citizens; another provided that the common soldiers should be clothed at public expense without any reduction in pay, and that no one under seventeen years of age should be conscripted for military service; another concerned the allies, giving the Italians equal suffrage rights with the citizens of Rome; a fourth related to grain, lowering the market price for the poor; a fifth, dealing with the courts of justice, was the greatest blow to the power of the senators, for hitherto they alone could sit on the juries, and they were therefore much dreaded by the plebs and equites. But Gaius joined 300 citizens of equestrian rank with the senators, who were also 300

in number, and made jury service the common prerogative of the 600. . . .When the people not only ratified this law but gave him power to select those of the equites who were to serve as jurors, he was invested with almost kingly power, and even the senate submitted to receiving his counsel. . . .

He also proposed measures for sending out colonies, for constructing roads, and for building public granaries. He himself undertook the management and superintendence of these works and was never too busy to attend to the execution of all these different and great undertakings.

From Plutarch, "Life of Gaius Gracchus," from L. Naphtali and M. Rheinold, eds, *Roman Civilization: Third Edition*, 2 Vol. Set (New York: Columbia University Press, 1990). Reprinted with permission of the publisher.

Question: Why did these proposals convince the Senate that Gaius had to be killed?

---

welfare. The army, deprived of an adequate number of recruits, grew steadily weaker. Although this was not the time for foreign adventures, the Senate reluctantly declared war on Numidia (Noo-mid'-ee-a) in 111 BCE. The African kingdom had been engulfed by a succession struggle during which the Romans backed the losing candidate. The winner, Jugurtha, celebrated his victory by murdering a number of Roman businessmen. Because most of the victims were equestrians, a tremendous outcry arose in the plebeian assembly, and the Senate was forced to give way.

For nearly 4 years the war went badly. The plebeian assembly and its equestrian allies knew that the senators disliked the war and began to suspect that some of them were taking Numidian bribes. In 107 BCE, they elected Gaius Marius (Mar'-ee-us, c. 157–86 BCE) consul. Like Cato before him, **Marius** was a "new man," not of the aristocracy but a member of the equestrian order who came to politics with the support of an old senatorial family. To gain the votes of the assembly, he turned against his patrons. If his ethics were questionable, his military abilities were not. He defeated Jugurtha without capturing him and then turned his attention to the north, where two Germanic tribes, the Cimbri and the Teutones, threatened the Roman settlements in Gaul. His lieutenant, the quaestor Lucius Cornelius Sulla (Suh'-la, 138–78 BCE), was left to track down the Numidian and destroy him in a hard-fought guerrilla campaign that made his reputation and infuri-

ated Marius, who thought that the younger man had taken too much credit for the victory.

The Marian Land and Military Reforms (107–88 BCE).
War on two fronts at a time when social dislocation had reduced the pool of eligible recruits made keeping the legions up to strength virtually impossible. Marius believed that he had no choice but to reform the army by admitting volunteers, even if they owned no land. Recruits were to be paid in cash as they had always been. Marius also promised them a plot of land in Gaul or Africa when they retired.

To thousands of slum dwellers and landless peasants, the Marian reforms offered an escape from grinding poverty, but the recruitment of proletarians created a new danger for the state. Lacking property of their own, the men became wholly dependent on their commander for pay and, more important, for the security of their old age. Although land and money came ultimately from the Senate, neither could be obtained without the influence of the consul or proconsul who requested them. The troops, in short, became the clients of their general, who could then use military force to threaten the government. Rome was at the mercy of its own armies.

The implications of this change became evident after the Italian wars of 90–88 BCE. For decades the Italian allies had sought Roman citizenship to no avail (see Table 5.1). Their patience exhausted, they abandoned Rome

TABLE 5.1 CITIZENSHIP IN THE ROMAN REPUBLIC, 264–270 BCE

These census estimates refer only to adult male citizens and are taken primarily from Livy. The lower figure for 208 BCE seems to reflect the defection of Capua and other allies after the defeat at Cannae as well as war losses. The major increases after 204 BCE and 115 BCE reflect the extension of citizenship rights to non-Romans rather than a change in underlying demographics.

Source: Data from Tenney, Frank, ed, *An Economic Survey of Ancient Rome*, vol. 1 (New York: Pageant Books, 1959, pp. 56, 216–217).

YEAR	CENSUS TOTAL
264 BCE	292,234
251 BCE	297,797
246 BCE	241,212
240 BCE	260,000
233 BCE	270,713
208 BCE	137,108
204 BCE	214,000
154 BCE	324,000
147 BCE	322,000
142 BCE	328,442
136 BCE	317,933
131 BCE	318,823
125 BCE	394,736
115 BCE	394,436
86 BCE	463,000
70 BCE	910,000

Question: How would the extension of citizenship rights help Rome in its imperial wars?

Silver Denarius from the Italian Wars (91–89 BCE). The design of coins often carries a political message. This silver denarius was minted by Rome's Italian allies when they rebelled against Rome in 91 BCE. The Italians, who had long served in Rome's armies, wanted Roman citizenship and a fair distribution of conquered lands, but the Romans had refused. The coin shows eight men holding their swords out toward a kneeling figure holding a pig. They are taking an oath to fight together against the Romans. The writing on the reverse of this coin is not in Latin, but in a native Italian language and alphabet called Oscan. The Italian Wars lasted 3 years. The Romans won, but they granted citizenship to the Italians to avoid further conflict.

and decided to form an independent confederation. Belatedly, the Romans extended citizenship to all who returned to their allegiance, but 2 years of fighting were required to reach a final settlement.

Sulla, whose reputation as a soldier grew even greater during the Italian wars, was elected consul in 88 BCE with the support of the Senate. His services were needed in the east, where Mithradates (Mith-rah-day'-teez), King of Pontus (a kingdom on the southeast shore of the Black Sea), had annexed parts of southwest Asia and invaded Greece. At this point the aged Marius came out of retirement and convinced the plebeian assembly to appoint him commander instead. His action, based in part on personal resentment of Sulla, provoked a lengthy crisis. Sulla, ostensibly to defend the Senate, marched on Rome and drove out Marius. When Sulla left for Asia, Marius returned with his own army and conducted a bloody purge of his opponent's senatorial friends before dying of a stroke in 86 BCE. Finally, in 83 BCE Sulla returned and established a dictatorship. To do so he had to conclude a compromise peace with Mithradates and fight a civil war on Italian soil against the remaining supporters of Marius and his faction.

Dictatorship of Sulla (83–79 BCE). Sulla's dictatorship was unlike any that had yet been declared. It lasted 4 years and was intended to reform the state from within, not to protect the state from outside enemies. To do this, Sulla launched a reign of terror by proscribing or outlawing his opponents, his personal enemies, and the rich, whose only crime was that their property was needed to pay his troops. He then passed a series of laws intended to strengthen senatorial power and improve the criminal justice system. Some of these changes survived his retirement in 79 BCE. Sulla was in theory a conservative who sought only to preserve the traditional system, but his career marked the end of constitutional government. For almost a decade Roman soldiers had been used repeatedly against Roman citizens and against one another. Power now rested with the legions and those who commanded them, not with the Senate or the assemblies.

Sulla's departure created a political vacuum. Generals, including his former lieutenants **Pompey** (Pom'-pee, 106–48 BCE) and **Crassus** (Crass'-us, 112–53 BCE), vied for preeminence using the wealth and power generated by their proconsular commands. (You will recall that a proconsul commanded an army in the field, beyond Rome's or the Senate's control, and this command allowed him to develop an independent geographical, economic, and military base.) Such commands proliferated in the first century BCE, mainly because the perception of disorder at home encouraged Rome's enemies, including slaves and conquered peoples who wished to regain their independence. Roman politicians welcomed proconsular appointments because they needed armies of their own as protection against their domestic rivals and because military campaigns made it possible to acquire great wealth through booty and confiscations. Spain rebelled under a former ally of Marius and had to be suppressed by Pompey. At the same time, Italy was threatened by a massive slave rebellion led by **Spartacus,** a Thracian gladiator. A direct result of the brutality and greed of the slave owners, it was put down with great difficulty by Crassus, who crucified 6,000 of the rebels along the Appian Way between Rome and Capua. To the east, Mithradates of Pontus resumed his aggression, while in the Mediterranean as a whole, widespread piracy threatened trade and communications throughout the empire.

The First Triumvirate (60 BCE). The Senate unwisely responded to each crisis by granting extraordinary proconsular appointments, often in violation of the constitution, and then refusing full honors to the victors when they returned. The Senate was especially stingy in denying these men the great ceremonial processions known as *triumphs.* Grants to veterans were also delayed. The senators thought that in this way they could weaken the authority of successful commanders, but their policy served only to irritate them. Although Pompey and Crassus feared and disliked each other, in 60 BCE they made common cause with another popular politician, **Gaius Julius Caesar** (See'-zer, c. 100–44 BCE), to dominate the elections and create a kind of governing committee known as the **First Triumvirate.**

The Rise of Julius Caesar. Pompey and Crassus had disbanded their legions when they returned to Rome.

Either they were loyal to republican institutions or failed to understand that Marius and Sulla had changed the political rules. Caesar's vision was clearer. He knew that talent alone was useless without an army, and he used the power of the triumvirate to grant him proconsular authority over Cisalpine Gaul. From 58 to 50 BCE he used that power as a base to conquer Transalpine Gaul, an area roughly equivalent to modern France, Belgium, and the Netherlands. A master of public relations, he offered a selective account of these exploits in the *Commentaries,* a classic that remains the first book read by most students of Latin.

The Gallic campaign brought Caesar enormous wealth, an army of hardened veterans, and a reputation. The other triumvirs were less fortunate. Fearing Caesar's ambition, the Senate appointed Crassus and Pompey as consuls in 55 BCE. Crassus became commander of Rome's armies in Syria while Pompey received his former post in Spain. In 53 BCE, Crassus died fighting in Asia. Pompey and Caesar—with their armies—were now in direct competition for control of Rome. To the Senate, Caesar seemed the greater threat. When it became apparent that neither man would disband his forces, the Senate made yet another mistake by ordering Caesar to return home as a private citizen. Knowing that to do so would end his career and perhaps his life, Caesar crossed the Rubicon, the small river that divided Cisalpine Gaul from Italy, and marched on Rome in 49 BCE. His only choice now was victory or death, hence the expression "to cross the Rubicon," describing an irreversible action.

Civil War (49–46 BCE). The civil war that followed lasted 3 years. Because legions loyal to either Pompey or Caesar could be found from Spain to Syria, it involved almost every part of the empire. Pompey was murdered at Alexandria in 48 BCE, but his friends continued the struggle until 46 BCE, when Caesar returned to Rome in triumph as sole consul. Caesar's power, like Sulla's before him, was based on control of a professional army whose ties to the political order had been broken by the Marian land reforms. Unlike Sulla, Caesar did not intend to retire. Although Caesar's rule was destined to be brief, the Roman Republic had fallen, never to be revived.

THE ORIGINS OF IMPERIAL GOVERNMENT (44 BCE–68 CE)

The Assassination of Julius Caesar (44 BCE). Caesar's government was generally benign and devoted to reform, including the proclamation of a new "Julian" calendar that remained standard in Europe until the sixteenth century, but it was autocratic and clearly unconstitutional. On the ides of March (March 15) in 44 BCE, he was assassinated as he entered the Senate house. The conspiracy involved sixty senators under the leadership of Gaius Cassius (Cas'-shus) Longinus and Marcus Junius Brutus (Broo'-tus), who believed that his death would restore the powers of the senatorial class. The murder led to 13 more years of war and the establishment of an autocratic state that became in time a system ruled by semidivine emperors. The violent and dramatic events of this period have fired the imagination of writers and artists down to the present day and have been analyzed by a host of political theorists.

The Rise of Augustus and the Augustan Principate (44 BCE–14 CE)

Alliance between Mark Antony and Octavius. Caesar's heirs were his close associate Marcus Antonius **(Mark Antony)** and his grandnephew Gaius **Octavius** (63 BCE–14 CE), then a boy of 18. Antony, in a famous funeral oration, turned the mob against Caesar's assassins and forced them to flee the city. Those senators who were not assassins but who favored the restoration of the Republic feared that Antony, or Antony in combination with Octavius, would seize control of the state. Their leader was Marcus Tullius Cicero (Siss'-er-oh, 106–43 BCE), the brilliant lawyer, writer, and philosopher whose works are among the finest monuments of Latin literature (see Chapter 4). Cicero's political career had been blocked only by his failure to achieve military command. He was the finest orator of the age. He easily persuaded the Senate that Antony was unprincipled and a potential tyrant and that a consular army should be sent against him. He then tried to drive a wedge between Octavius and Antony, who resented that most of Caesar's enormous wealth had been left to the younger man.

Caesar's heirs disliked one another, but the policy misfired. When the consuls of 43 BCE died fighting against Antony in Cisalpine Gaul, the Senate, on Cicero's advice, gave Octavius command of the armies but refused him the consulship because he was still only 19 years old. The future Augustus, who now called himself Julius Caesar Octavianus, or Octavian, went to Rome with his legions and took the office by force.

The Second Triumvirate (43–36 BCE). Octavian, although young, understood the need for overwhelming military power. He made peace with those who commanded the remaining legions—Antony and a former Caesarian governor named Lepidus (Lep'-i-dus)—and together they formed the Second Triumvirate. To consolidate their position and, above all, to pay their legions, they outlawed and killed more than 300 senators, including Cicero, and 2,000 equestrians who had, by definition, no part in politics. Octavian then turned his army against Brutus, who had taken refuge in Macedon, while Antony defeated Cassius in Syria. In the course of these actions, both of Caesar's assassins were killed in battle.

Antony and Cleopatra. Octavian and Antony were the dominant figures of the triumvirate. With the removal of Lepidus in 36 BCE, they divided the empire between them. Octavian took the west; Antony, the east. Realizing that conflict with Octavian was inevitable, Antony turned for assistance to the Egyptian queen **Cleopatra VII** (69–30 BCE). A woman of great charm and intelligence, Cleopatra was determined not only to revive the power of the Ptolemies but also to play a part in Roman affairs. To that end, she had become Julius Caesar's mistress when he visited Egypt in 48–47 BCE and traveled to Rome where she bore him a son. When Caesar died, she returned to Alexandria and arranged for the murder of her brother, who was also her husband and coruler according to the Egyptian custom. Now sole ruler of Egypt, she hoped that through

FIGURE 5.2 *Bronze Coin with Portrait of Cleopatra.* Cleopatra VII, the last of the Ptolemaic dynasty, failed to preserve Egypt's independence from Rome despite her involvement with both Julius Caesar and Mark Antony. Her defeat at the battle of Actium in 31 BCE and subsequent suicide paved the way for Octavian's triumph. Portraits of Cleopatra are exceedingly rare. The only examples that date from her own lifetime, and thus with a reasonable claim to authenticity, occur on her coinage. The front of this bronze coin shows a portrait of the queen engraved in her lifetime at the mint of Alexandria.

FIGURE 5.3 *Portrait Head of Mark Antony.* This intaglio ring in red jasper dates from 40–30 BCE and may have been used as a seal by one of Mark Antony's supporters. The exceptionally clear profile portrait, with long tousled hair, hooked nose, and prominent chin resembles Antony's coin portraits and agrees with contemporary descriptions of his appearance.

THE FACES OF AUGUSTUS

Octavian, or Augustus as he came to be called, had the rare ability to combine personal force and dignity with a relaxed, friendly, nonthreatening style. Both attributes tended to neutralize what might have become significant opposition to his ever-increasing power.

Suetonius Describes the Political Style of Augustus

The following passage from *Lives of the Caesars* by Suetonius (c. 69–after 122 CE) describes the ruler's political style. Suetonius supported the senatorial tradition and opposed the Julio-Claudian emperors, but his admiration for Augustus, although grudging, was real. Here he provides a brief word portrait of the perfect politician.

He always shrank from the title dominus *["master," a title that became obligatory under Caligula and his successors] . . . He did not if he could help it leave or enter the city or town except in the evening or at night, to avoid disturbing anyone by the obligations of ceremony. In his consulship he commonly went through the streets on foot, and when he was not consul, generally in a closed litter. His morning receptions were open to all, including even the commons, and he met the requests of those who approached him with great affability, jocosely reproving one man because he presented a petition*

Augustus as Princeps. This statue shows Augustus as the resolute military leader of the empire—a man to be trusted and followed. His features, although probably idealized, are identical to those in other portraits and probably represent his actual appearance. The fingers on his right arm have been wrongly restored: he was originally holding a lance *(hasta)* in his right hand and a sword, rather than a scepter (a restoration) in his left. The breastplate marks the emperor as an army leader.

Antony she could preserve the empire of the Ptolemies for herself and her children.

For his part, Antony needed the immense wealth of the Ptolemies to defeat Octavian. The alliance of Antony and Cleopatra resulted in the birth of twins as well as a formidable combination of military and financial power. Octavian, in a skillful propaganda campaign, portrayed himself as the champion of Rome and the west against the decadent east as symbolized by the Egyptian queen. In 31 BCE, he defeated Antony and Cleopatra at the naval battle of Actium and followed them to Alexandria, where, in the summer of 30 BCE, they both committed suicide.

The Principate of Augustus (27–14 BCE). Octavian became the undisputed ruler of the Western world. With characteristic subtlety, he asked only that he be called *princeps* (prin'-sepps), or first citizen, and over the next 7 years, he moved to consolidate his influence in ways that would not offend the Senate or other traditionalists. He treated the senators with courtesy and expanded their numbers. The Senate retained its control over disbursements and its function as chief appellate court for

the empire, while gaining the right to legislate for the first time in its history. The princeps, however, insisted on reviewing all legislation before it was proposed. This was possible because Octavian was named consul in every year before 23 BCE, but the real basis of his power was his proconsular authority over Spain, Gaul, and Syria, the border provinces that contained a majority of the legions. After 23 BCE, this proconsular *imperium* (authority) was extended to Rome, making his annual appointment as consul unnecessary. In that year he was also awarded the powers of a tribune, to be renewed annually for the remainder of his life. This enabled him to participate in the plebeian and tribal assemblies and gave him veto power over their legislation. As tribune, his person was sacrosanct, although the Senate, in 27 BCE, had already granted him the semidivine title *Augustus*. His religious functions expanded when he had himself appointed *pontifex maximus*, or head of the state religion, in 12 BCE. Under Augustus, the title of *imperator* (impair'-uh-tor), or emperor, used to describe his successors, normally referred only to his proconsular imperium.

In person, the new Augustus tried to appear modest and unassuming. As an administrator, he was without to him with as much hesitation "as he would a penny to an ele-phant." On the day of a meeting in the Senate he always greeted the members in the House and in their seats, calling each man by name without a prompter; and when he left the House, he used to take leave of them in the same manner, while they remained seated. He exchanged social calls with many, and did not cease to attend all their anniversaries until he was well on in years.

From *Suetonius*, vol. 1, trans. R. C. Rolfe. Loeb Classical Library (Cambridge: Harvard University Press, 1913).

Augustus on His Own Accomplishments

This passage from the *Res Gestae Divi Augusti* (The Deeds of the Divine Augustus) reveals that Augustus, if modest in person, was not unwilling to remind Romans of his greatness in other ways. He wrote this as part of a much longer inscription that was to be placed on bronze pillars in front of his mausoleum.

Twice I celebrated ovations, three times curule triumphs, and I was proclaimed imperator twenty-one times. When the senate de-creed additional triumphs to me, I declined them on four occa-sions. I deposited in the Capitol laurel wreaths adorning my fasces [the bundle of bound sticks surrounding an axe that sym-bolized unity and military authority], after fulfilling the vows which I had made in each war. For successes achieved on land and on sea by me or through my legates under my auspices the senate decreed fifty-five times that thanksgivings be offered to the immortal gods. Moreover, the number of days on which, by decree of the senate, such thanksgiving was offered, was 890. In my tri-umphs there were led before my chariot nine kings or children of kings. At the time I wrote this document, I had been consul thir-teen times, and I was in the thirty-seventh year of my tribunician power [14 CE].

From Augustus, *Res Gestae Divi Augusti*, from L. Naphtali and M. Rheinold, eds, *Roman Civilization: Third Edition*, 2 Vol. Set (New York: Columbia University Press, 1990). Reprinted with permission of the publisher.

Question: How would you describe the political style and tactics of Augustus?

equal. By controlling the electoral apparatus, Augustus made certain that magistracies went to men of ability with little regard for their origins. Provincial adminis-tration, a disgrace under the later Republic, was greatly improved. He placed some of the provinces under his direct rule as princeps and appointed legates to rule them as his personal representatives. In the senatorial provinces, his expanded proconsular authority gave him the right to overrule the policies of governors and develop policies for the empire as a whole. Legates and governors now received salaries, which tended to re-duce corruption.

Expansion of the Empire. The improvement of provincial government was essential in part because the empire continued to expand. The defeat of Antony and Cleopatra resulted in the annexation of Egypt, which Augustus regarded as his personal possession and ruled although an appointed prefect. He also added several provinces in Asia, including Judaea, and extended the northern borders of the empire to the Danube and the Rhine. As he grew older, he came to believe that the em-pire had grown enough, but his successors would add Britain and Mauretania (Morocco), Armenia, Assyria, Dacia (Romania), and Mesopotamia.

Urban Renewal at Rome. In Rome, Augustus em-barked on an ambitious program that replaced many of the city's old wooden tenements, established rudimen-tary fire and police services, and improved the city's water supply. Much of this was accomplished by using the vast resources of Egypt, which he had appropriated, not by taxing the Romans. When Augustus died in 14 CE, he had established a legacy of sound administration and what has been called the ***pax romana*** (pox ro-mah'-na), an era of peace and prosperity that later ages would look upon with envy (see Document 5.3).

The First Emperors

Augustus's successors, the Julio-Claudian emperors, at first continued his administrative policies, although none of them was his equal as statesmen. His adopted son, the capable Tiberius, succeeded him by inheri-tance; Tiberius ruled 14–37 CE. Caligula, Claudius, and Nero (Ca-lig'-you-la, Claw'-dee-us, Neer'-oh) increas-

PLUTARCH ON THE PAX ROMANA

The *pax romana* referred to the peace within the empire that had been established by Augustus. Although it did not preclude a number of regional revolts, it was a remarkable achievement. As this sensible, if unheroic, passage from *Precepts of Statecraft* makes clear, the pax romana became the primary justification for Roman rule.

The greatest blessings that cities can enjoy are peace, prosperity, populousness, and concord. As far as peace is concerned, the people have no need of political activity, for all war, both Greek and foreign, has been banished and has disappeared from among us. Of liberty the people enjoy as much as our rulers allot them, and perhaps more would not be better. A bounteous productiveness of soil; a mild, temperate climate; wives bearing "children like their sires" [a quotation from the Greek poet Hesiod] and security for their offspring—these are the things that a wise man will ask for his fellow citizens in his prayers to the gods.

From Plutarch, *"Precepts of Statecraft,"* 32, from L. Naphtali and M. Rheinold, eds, *Roman Civilization: Third Edition*, 2 Vol. Set (New York: Columbia University Press, 1990). Reprinted with permission of the publisher.

Question: If Plutarch's arguments are correct, why were provincial revolts common?

ingly abandoned republican formalities and sometimes treated the Senate with open contempt. The eccentric Caligula (37–41 CE) so scorned the republican tradition that he is said to have designated his horse, Incitatus, as his co-consul. His brief reign revealed the fundamental weakness of the Augustan system: an erratic or incompetent ruler could be removed only by military force. After 4 years, the Praetorian (Pree-tor'-ee-un) Guard, an elite army unit established by Augustus for the protection of the princeps, assassinated Caligula and replaced him with Claudius, thought by the Senate to be an incompetent figurehead. Despite a speech defect and physical disabilities, Claudius astonished everyone by ruling capably and conscientiously. He took the first steps toward establishing a regular imperial civil service staffed by members of the equestrian order.

The Julio-Claudian dynasty came to an end with Nero (ruled 54–68 CE), who ascended the throne at the age of 16. Guided at first by his tutor, the stoic philosopher **Seneca** (Senn'-a-ca), Nero began well but grew increasingly brutal and erratic. He was not responsible for the great fire at Rome in 67 CE, nor did he fiddle while the city burned, but his frequent appearances as an actor and singer and the murder of his own mother aroused universal contempt. Nero committed suicide when the Spanish legions under Galba (Gal'-ba) rebelled in 68 CE and proclaimed him Nero's successor. By this time it had become evident that the immediate successors of Augustus had institutionalized the pow-

FIGURE 5.4 *Base of the Column of Antoninus Pius.* This scene shows the *apotheosis* of the emperor Antoninus (reigned 138–161 CE) and his wife, Faustina; that is, both members of this imperial pair are in the process of becoming gods after their death. Based on the symbolism of the eagles, they are about to become the new Jupiter and Juno. It is an indication of how the imperial office had become deified after the death of Augustus.

MAP 5.1. THE ROMAN EMPIRE AT THE DEATH OF AUGUSTUS (14 CE)

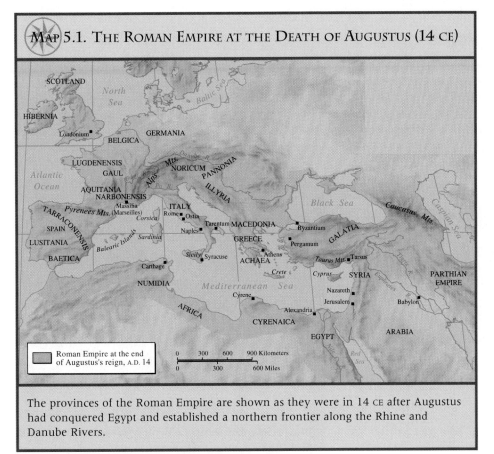

Roman Empire at the end of Augustus's reign, A.D. 14	

0   300   600   900 Kilometers
0   300   600 Miles

The provinces of the Roman Empire are shown as they were in 14 CE after Augustus had conquered Egypt and established a northern frontier along the Rhine and Danube Rivers.

ers that had been granted personally to him as princeps and rendered the Senate ineffectual. The Roman Empire was becoming a hereditary monarchy, although as always, real power rested with the army, which could, if dissatisfied, overthrow dynasties.

The Year of the Four Emperors (68 CE). After Nero's death, the legions began a series of revolts that created no fewer than four emperors in 1 year. Each of Rome's armies had come to believe that it could secure its own retirements only if their commander seized power. The last of these emperors, Vespasian (Vess-pay'-zhun, ruled 69–79 CE), established the Flavian dynasty, which lasted until 96 CE. He restored the empire's finances and was the first to adopt formally the title *imperator*. When his descendant, Domitian (Doe-mish'-an), left no successor, the Senate revived sufficiently to appoint another general in his place named Nerva, who ushered in the age of the "five good emperors."

The Five "Good" Emperors (96–180 CE). The age of the five good emperors—Nerva, Trajan, Hadrian, Antoninus Pius, and Marcus Aurelius (Ner'-va, Tray'-jun, Hay'-dree-un, An-to-nee'-nus Pie'-us, Mar'-kus Oh-ree'-lee-us)—was later remembered as one of exceptional happiness. The pax romana described by Plutarch (Ploo'-tark)

seemed to be a permanent condition, and trade flourished. Trajan and Hadrian sponsored lavish building programs, and Trajan introduced the *alimenta* (al-i-men'-ta), a subsidy to help poor parents in raising their children. All five emperors refined and strengthened imperial administration, but the possibility of military intervention remained. Nerva, Trajan, Hadrian, and Antoninus Pius were childless. Each appointed his successor on the basis of merit, although each of them claimed an increasing measure of divinity to strengthen the authority of their office.

Marcus Aurelius (ruled 161–180 CE) broke this tradition, not only by having a son but also by having the poor judgment to leave him the throne. The reign of Commodus (Cohm'-oh-dus), from 180 to 192 CE, was a disaster that ended in yet another military revolt. But by this time the empire was experiencing difficulties that had little to do with the personality of its rulers.

ART, LITERATURE, AND THOUGHT IN IMPERIAL ROME (31 BCE–180 CE)

Painting and Sculpture. Throughout the late Republic and early empire, the culture of Rome's elite remained heavily dependent on Greek models. Painting and sculpture were an integral part of most public places and adorned the luxurious palaces of the rich. Reliefs on public buildings featured mythological subjects or idealized versions of historic events. Private collectors bought reproductions of famous Greek statues from Roman workshops, and a thriving trade existed in bronzes from Greece. In some cases these skillful copies provide the only access to lost originals. Only in portrait statuary did the Romans break with established tradition. Ignoring the Greek tendency to idealize the human form, they produced busts whose photographic realism is a monument to individual men and women.

Architecture. Architecture, too, abandoned Greek precedent. Temples and theaters recalled Hellenistic

ROMAN ARCHITECTURE

Roman architecture borrowed heavily from the Greeks. It continued to use the Doric, Ionic, and Corinthian orders illustrated in Chapter 3, but the Romans also used the arch and the dome, neither of which was known to the Greeks. They probably learned the techniques of arch construction from the Etruscans. The dome appears primarily in temples, where it may have been intended to suggest the dome of the heavens. The Romans used stone, especially in columns, but most of their major buildings are of brick or concrete faced in travertine (a kind of smooth limestone) or stucco.

The Temple of Hercules, Rome. This round temple, sometimes called the Temple of Vesta, dates from the first century BCE and is one of the few buildings to survive from the Roman Republic. Built at a time when Greek cultural influence was at its height in Rome, it uses Corinthian columns in the Greek mode, but its round design and tile roof is purely Roman.

The Pantheon, Rome. The Pantheon was built between 118 and 125 CE by the Emperor Hadrian as a temple to all the gods. The portico at the front was originally part of an earlier building begun by Agrippa in 27 CE. The combination of the domed structure with a post-and-lintel portico on the Greek model shows how Greek and Roman ideas could be combined. The basic structure, however, is round, because the Romans did not know how to construct a dome on a square base.

Interior of the Pantheon. The huge dome is 142 feet in diameter and constructed of brick laid over a supporting system of brick arches hidden under the stucco surface of the dome's interior. The *oculus*, or eye, at the top of the dome is open to the sky. The dome, although heavy, has survived nearly 2,000 years of weather, earthquakes, and the vibrations from modern Roman traffic.

models, while other public buildings used the arch and vault construction favored by the Etruscans. Augustus and his successors built baths, aqueducts, warehouses, and stadia for games and chariot races whose scale virtually precluded the post-and-lintel construction of the Greeks. Some structures, such as the Mausoleum built by Augustus for his family and the Pantheon constructed by Hadrian, featured domes that spanned enormous spaces. Increasingly, columns, friezes, and pediments evolved into decorative elements without structural purpose. Engineering and an imperial taste for grandeur triumphed over the aesthetics of simplicity.

Philosophy. In philosophy as in art, the Romans tended to borrow Greek conventions and adapt them to their own purposes. The dominant current in Roman thought was Stoicism. Cicero, Seneca (4 BCE?–65 CE), and the emperor Marcus Aurelius wrote extensively on Stoic themes, in part because, as men of affairs, they appreciated the philosophy's moral activism and the comfort it offered a politician in difficult times (see Document 5.4). Their emphasis, however, was on the practical application of Stoic principles, and their writings added little or nothing to the speculative tradition.

Science. The same might be said of Roman writings on science. Alexandria remained the center of scientific and philosophical inquiry and Greek the primary language of scientific publication. The most important scientific work in Latin, the *Natural History* of **Pliny the Elder** (Plinn'-ee, 23–79 CE), was little more than a vast compendium of information, much of it false, gleaned by the author from nearly 500 sources—327 of them Greek. The work is important primarily because it summarized ancient knowledge and transmitted it to a later age.

Literature. Roman literature was more original than Roman thought. By ancient standards, literacy was widespread in the late Republic and early empire (perhaps 15 percent of the population), and the Romans produced books in large numbers. As many as thirty copies at a time could be made by having a reader dictate to slaves who wrote the words on papyrus scrolls. A more modern form of the book, the **codex,** made its appearance in the first century BCE. Written on vellum or parchment (the skin of a sheep or goat tanned and prepared for writing) and bound in leather, it was preferred by lawyers and, later, by Christian scholars who needed to compare several texts at a time and found codices more convenient to handle than scrolls.

The Romans favored practical treatises on agriculture, the mechanical arts, law, and rhetoric. **Cicero,** as the most successful litigator of his day, was especially valued for his writings on oratory and his attempt to reconcile traditional jurisprudence with the Stoic idea of natural law. His work, together with that of **Quintilian** (Kwin-till'-ee-un, c. 35–100 CE), elevated rhetoric (the art of using language to persuade others) to a science and had a profound impact on educational theory. Another literary form unique to Rome was the publication of personal correspondence, with Cicero and Pliny the Younger providing the best and most interesting examples. History, too, was popular, although it was rarely studied in a spirit of objective inquiry. Caesar wrote to advance his political career, whereas Livy (see Chapter 4) sought to revive republican virtue.

DOCUMENT 5.4

SENECA ON THE STOIC IDEAL

Seneca was tutor to the emperor Nero and the dominant political figure of the early part of his reign. Although Seneca enriched himself in dubious ways and was involved in the murder of Nero's mother, his writings on Stoic themes reflect a different, more attractive side of his character. He committed suicide on Nero's orders in 65 CE. Here he describes the Stoic equanimity that comes from an understanding of divine providence.

What is the principal thing in human life? . . . To raise the soul above threats and promises of fortune; to consider nothing as worth hoping for. For what does fortune possess worth setting your heart upon? What is the principle thing? To be able to enjoy adversity with a joyful heart; to bear whatever betide just as if it were the very thing you desired . . . For you would have felt it your duty to desire it, had you known that all things happened by divine decree. Tears, complaints, lamentations are rebellion.

From Seneca, *Natural Questions,* trans. J. Clarke (London, 1910).

Question: Why was this philosophy so popular with men who were active in public life?

Tacitus (Tass'-ih-tus, c. 56–120 CE) produced a history of the early emperors from a point of view similar to Livy's and a remarkable study of the Germanic tribes who lived beyond the northern borders of the empire. His younger contemporary, **Suetonius** (Sweh-tone'-ee-us), provided a background of scandalous personal gossip in his *Lives of the Caesars,* but the vices he attributes to the Julio-Claudian emperors transcend normal human capacities. **Plutarch** (c. 46–after 119 CE), a Greek whose popular *Lives* included famous Romans as well as Greeks, pursued a less sensational approach to biography and wrote extensively on ethics.

Poetry. These contributions, however great, pale by comparison with the poetry that made the Augustan age synonymous with Rome's highest literary achievement. The greatest of the Augustan poets, **Virgil** (Ver'-jil, 70–19 BCE), was responsible for the *Eclogues* (Ek'-logs), a series of pastoral poems based loosely on Hesiod, and for his masterpiece, *The Aeneid* (En-ee'-ud), the national epic about the founding of Rome. Both were gratefully received by Augustus as expressions of the civic virtue he was trying to encourage. The odes and satires of **Horace** (65–8 BCE) were equally acceptable, but the works of **Ovid** (Ah'-vid, 43 BCE–17 CE) were not. Augustus was sufficiently offended by his *Ars Amatoria,* a poetic manual of seduction, to exile the poet to a remote town on the Black Sea.

Drama. Surprisingly, drama, the most public and political of all art forms, never achieved great importance in Rome. Greek tragedies aroused enthusiasm among Roman intellectuals, but the public preferred comedy. **Plautus** (Plot´-us), in the late third century BCE, and Terence in the second century BCE, produced works that, although based heavily on the Greek New Comedy, had a ribald vigor. In later years, public taste turned toward mime and simple-minded farce, while theater attendance declined as gladiatorial combats and similar entertainments became more popular. The nine tragedies of Seneca, so inspiring to the great dramatists of the late Renaissance, were apparently written to be read, not performed.

ECONOMIC AND SOCIAL LIFE IN THE EARLY EMPIRE (31 BCE–180 CE)

The age of Augustus and the century that followed were a time of relative prosperity. Italy and the regions affected by the civil wars recovered quickly, and neither Augustus nor his successors afflicted their subjects with excessive taxation. Their policies were conducive to economic growth, because the pax romana, by uniting the Western world under a single government, limited warfare to the periphery of the empire and created a market of unprecedented size. Tariffs on the transfer of goods between provinces generated revenue but were too low to inhibit trade. For the first time in its history, the west had uniform coinage and systems of banking and credit that transcended national boundaries.

Changes in Land Ownership. The policy of settling veterans on land of their own, although it sometimes dispossessed existing farmers, may also have temporarily improved the well-being of the peasant class. The initial effect of these resettlements was to reduce the number of **latifundia** (lat-i-fun´-dee-a), or great slave-worked estates. Many regions saw a resurgence of the small independent farm, while middling properties of the kind described by Cato prospered. The number of slaves declined, in part because the annexations of Augustus did not involve the large-scale enslavement of new subjects and in part because manumission was common. On the estates that remained, the treatment of slaves appears to have improved. Slaves grew more valuable as the supply dwindled, and owners found that they could best be replaced by encouraging them to reproduce. The Augustan age did not see a resumption of slave rebellions like the one led by the gladiator Spartacus during the last century of the Republic.

In time, however, the economies of scale that had doomed the small-acreage farmers of the Republic re-asserted themselves. Not every veteran understood agriculture; those who did could not always compete with their larger neighbors. Eventually, these men or their descendants sold their farms and returned to the city, or they became tenants (coloni; coh-loh´-nee) of the great estates. In the early empire, coloni remained technically free, leasing their land and returning a portion of the yield to the estate owner. This was thought to be less efficient than slavery, but it became increasingly common as slaves grew scarcer. Once again the average size of properties began to grow and peasant income resumed its decline. By the end of the first century CE, half of the land in the province of Africa was owned by six men.

The Distribution of Wealth. Changes in the distribution of wealth were therefore both temporary and relative. If veterans benefited from the distribution of land and from cash payments derived from booty, the wealthy gained even more from imperial gifts. Townspeople, too, received payments from the emperors as a kind of bribe for good behavior and sometimes found work on the construction projects funded by Augustus from the spoils of Egypt. Another burst of prosperity seems to have followed the great fire of 67 CE, which destroyed much of Rome; Nero financed a massive reconstruction that gave work to thousands. Temporary benefits of this kind may have improved the lives of ordinary people, especially in Italy, but the amounts involved were too small to expand significantly their role as consumers or to change the basic distribution of wealth.

Trade and the Imperial Economy

The economic polarization that had characterized Roman society from the second century BCE continued to influence the development of trade (see Table 5.2). Although Julius Caesar had attempted to limit the number of Romans eligible for the grain dole, it remained available to all Roman citizens under Augustus. This, together with the policy of encouraging people in the provinces to move into cities, ensured the continuation of a massive trade in bulk agricultural commodities. Spain, Africa, Sicily, and, above all, Egypt exported vast quantities of grain to the growing cities of the empire. Italy produced wine and oil, but it had many competitors and probably declined in its relative economic importance as the first century BCE progressed.

Manufacturing. Meanwhile, the lack of an adequate consumer base limited manufacturing. Too few people possessed the means to buy manufactured products on a large scale. Something like a mass market existed for metal tools and weapons, and several Italian towns produced red-glazed pottery for export to every corner of the empire. Some potteries may have employed

TABLE 5.2 ROMAN WAGES AND PRICES IN THE LATE REPUBLIC

These figures regarding wages and prices are estimates for central Italy c. 150 BCE. Prices of wheat in particular fluctuated wildly during the civil wars, but the numbers listed here are a fair estimate of those in the early years of Augustus. Prices were lower in the Po valley and in other areas remote from Rome. There were sixteen copper asses, or four *sesterces* in a silver denarius. The difference in wages between a slave hired for the day and a free laborer demonstrates why so many of the latter were unemployed.

Three Copper Asses c. 90 BCE. Although most Romans were far from rich, the sheer size of the population created an immense demand for small coins. Ancient mints found it difficult to produce enough low-value bronze coins like these *asses* because they had to strike each coin with the blow of a hammer. To speed up the process, they sometimes cast coin blanks in strips before separating them into individual coins. This was an ancient attempt at mass production for an economy that had become huge even before the fall of the Republic.

SERVICE OR PRODUCT	AVERAGE COST
Unskilled slave laborer	2 sesterces per day
Free laborer	3 sesterces per day
Soldier	120 denarii per year
Wheat	3 sesterces per *modius* (a unit of measure sufficient to make 20 pounds of bread)
Barley	2 sesterces per modius
Wine (average grade Italian)	3–4 asses per liter
Wine (best imported)	1–4 denarii per liter
Olive oil	6–8 asses per liter
Beef	4–5 asses per pound
Pork	2–3 asses per pound
Clothing (Cato's toga, tunic, and shoes)	100 denarii
A farm slave (purchase price)	500 denarii
An ox for plowing	60–80 denarii
A sheep	6–8 denarii
A cavalry horse	500 denarii

Source: Data from Tenney, Frank, ed., *An Economic Survey of Ancient Rome,* vol. 1 (New York: Pageant Books, 1959, p. 200).

Question: Try to calculate how much bread, oil, wine, and meat a free worker could purchase with his daily wage. How large a family could he feed?

more than fifty workers, most of them slaves. Woolen cloth, once processed in the home, was more commonly manufactured for sale. The size of this trade is difficult to estimate, and it, too, probably employed mostly slaves. Generally speaking, the availability of slave labor, although declining, continued to hold down the wages of free workers and to restrict the development of technology. Perhaps the greatest innovation of the period was the development of glassblowing at Sidon in Phoenicia.

Long-Distance Trade. Most commodities were more limited in their distribution. Egypt retained its monopoly on papyrus, and the cities of what had once been Phoenicia produced glass and the expensive dyes and textiles for which they had long been famous. Linens, drugs, perfumes, precious stones, and such delicacies as dried fruit and pickled fish came from various sources within the empire. Other luxuries came from far away. The Silk Road across central Asia connected Syria with China. More than 100 ships sailed annually from the Red Sea ports to India for cargoes of spice, and

Africa continued as it had for centuries to provide the Mediterranean world with gold, ivory, palm oil, frankincense, and rhinoceros horn.

Almost without exception, these were low-volume, high-profit trades that entailed a substantial element of risk. They made a few people, mostly equestrians or freedmen who eventually merged with the equestrian class, enormously rich, but the prosperity they generated was not widely shared. Aristocrats, too, sometimes invested in such ventures or speculated on the commodities market. They usually did so through agents, because the old prejudice against trade died hard. Overall, the economy of the empire remained agrarian, and mercantile activities were restricted to a few.

Upper-Class Life in Imperial Rome

In the first century CE, 1 million people may have lived in the city of Rome, a nearly incredible total given the limits of ancient technology and systems of distribution. As in any community, their lives were constrained by

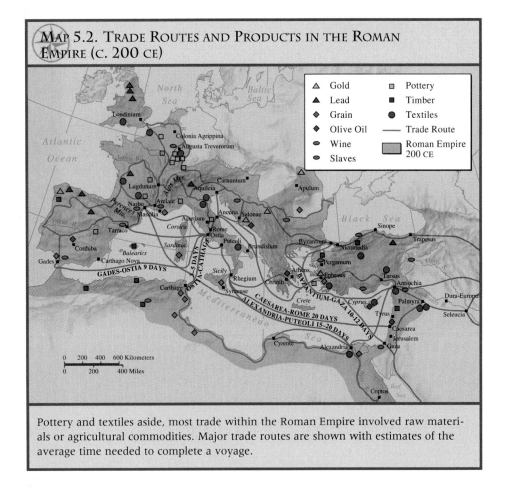

Map 5.2. Trade Routes and Products in the Roman Empire (c. 200 CE)

Pottery and textiles aside, most trade within the Roman Empire involved raw materials or agricultural commodities. Major trade routes are shown with estimates of the average time needed to complete a voyage.

the day to politics, business, or the law courts, but like Romans of every class, the rich found time for physical exercise and an elaborate bath before the main meal of the day. In imperial times, this was usually taken in the evening and might involve a banquet of epic proportions. Women sat upright while the male guests reclined on couches around a central table and consumed delicacies brought from specialized farms in the area around the city. Songbirds, exotic fruits, and fish grown in special ponds were extremely popular, as were vintage wines such as the famous Falernian. Excess was common. Afterward, the guests would return home, sometimes in coaches or litters (covered couches carried on the shoulders of slaves by means of poles), but always accompanied by a small army of bodyguards. After dark, the Roman streets were dangerous.

Moralists seeking a return to the more restrained attitudes of an earlier time objected to this behavior. Their

an elaborate social structure. Although most were desperately poor, few would have chosen to live anywhere else. Rome was, to the Romans, the center of the world.

The palaces of the rich occupied about one-third of the city's land area. The most spectacular clustered on the Palatine Hill. Some of these structures, with their courtyards, galleries, baths, and gardens, covered several acres and employed hundreds of domestic slaves. Because Romans believed, or pretended to believe, that the pursuit of wealth and luxury for their own sake was dishonorable, such homes were meant to fulfill a public function. They devoted the atrium, or courtyard, and the rooms that surrounded it to entertaining and conducting business. The rear of the house with its garden or gardens provided a retreat for the family.

The senatorial or equestrian families that lived within derived their wealth primarily from land, although virtually all engaged in some form of trade or speculation as well. Most therefore owned country villas in addition to their city property. Cicero, who was not particularly wealthy, owned eight such residences in various parts of Italy and visited them according to the season.

The life of such a man began at dawn, when his clients arrived at his home to show their respect, request favors, or receive his instructions. He devoted most of

FIGURE 5.5 *Central Courtyard of an Urban Roman Villa (First Century CE)*. The homes of wealthy Romans were normally one story in height and built around a series of courtyards. This one, from the House of the Amorini Dorati in Pompeii, was preserved in 79 CE, when the volcano Mt. Vesuvius buried Pompeii in volcanic ash, killing most of the city's 20,000 inhabitants while preserving the city almost intact. Its excavation in modern times provided a unique glimpse of ancient urban life.

complaints had little effect until Augustus began to support reform as a matter of official policy. Romans of the late Republic and early empire believed in physical fitness, but they had long since lost Cato's taste for simplicity, and their attitude toward sex had become remarkably casual. Homosexuality and bisexuality, although perhaps not as common as among the Greeks, were mocked but tolerated, even in public figures such as Julius Caesar. Casual sex of every kind was encouraged by the institution of slavery.

Upper-Class Women. Roman women, too, had achieved a level of sexual and personal freedom that has rarely been equaled before or since. In the first century BCE, they acquired the legal right to own and manage their property apart from that of their husbands. The women of the upper classes therefore owned slaves and managed estates of their own. Many were successful businesswomen, and not a few involved themselves in politics.

Economic independence freed such women from marital tyranny and in some cases encouraged both sexes to seek divorce for political or financial advantage. Among the more prominent families, four or five marriages in succession were not uncommon, and extramarital affairs were frequent. No real penalty was meted out for such behavior, because the laws of the Republic regarded divorce as a private matter that could be concluded by simple agreement. Wives in such cases retained their dowries. Tradition held that adultery could be punishable by death, but the law in question was confusing and had not been enforced for generations.

New Marriage Laws under Augustus. Augustus believed that this situation undermined traditional Roman virtues and deterred men from marrying, at least in part, because they could not control their wives. But the precipitous decline in marriage rates among the Roman upper class had other causes as well. An increasing number of both sexes regarded children as an expensive nuisance and preferred to remain single, believing that they could guarantee a far more pleasant life by surrounding themselves with legacy hunters who hoped to be included in their wills. Beginning in 18 BCE, Augustus tried to legislate against these abuses by demanding seven witnesses to a divorce and making it possible for a man—although not a woman—to sue for adultery thereafter. Legacy hunters were restrained by limiting the bequests that could be received by widowed or unmarried persons. Augustus's efforts aroused intense opposition and seem to have had little immediate effect beyond enriching the treasury with the estates of those whose heirs had been disqualified, but they mark a turning point of sorts in the history of Roman morals (see Document 5.5). Others shared his distaste for sexual license and their attitudes, later reflected in Christianity, gained ground with the passage of time.

DOCUMENT 5.5

AUGUSTUS PUBLISHES HIS JULIAN LAW ON ADULTERY

In 18 BCE, Augustus promulgated the *Lex Julia de adulteriis coercendus* to correct what he saw as growing immorality. The following provisions sound harsh but were probably milder than earlier legislation that had proved unenforceable. Note that the rights of fathers remain unlimited while those of husbands do not. If the adulterous couple included two Roman citizens and the husband could not get his father-in-law to kill them, he was obligated to charge them in open court.

[This law] punishes not only the defilers of marriages of others . . . but also the crime of debauchery when anyone without the use of force violates either a virgin or a widow of respectable character.

By the second section a father, if he catches an adulterer of his daughter . . . in his own house or that of his son-in-law, or if the latter summons him in such an affair, is permitted to kill the adulterer with impunity, just as he may forthwith kill his daughter.

A husband is also permitted to kill an adulterer of his wife [but only if the adulterer is a procurer, actor, gladiator, convicted criminal, freedman, or slave] . . . in his own home. And it [the law] directs a husband who has killed any one of these to divorce his wife without delay . . .

The law punishes as a procurer a husband who retains his wife and lets the adulterer go. In such a case the husband should be punished because he cannot claim the excuse of ignorance on the pretext of not believing it.

It was enacted that women convicted of adultery be punished by confiscation of half of their dowry and a third of their property and by relegation to an island, and that male adulterers be punished by like relegation to an island and by confiscation of half of their property, with the proviso that they be relegated to different islands.

From "*Acti Divi August,*" from L. Naphtali and M. Rheinold, eds, *Roman Civilization: Third Edition*, 2 Vol. Set (New York: Columbia University Press, 1990). Reprinted with permission of the publisher.

Question: How could this law achieve results even if it were not fully enforceable?

Augustus may have been right in thinking that divorce and sexual misconduct led to social instability, but their prevalence did not imply that all of the men and women of the Roman upper class were irresponsible pleasure seekers. A high level of education, secured largely by private tutors, was common to both sexes, and magnificent private libraries were a status symbol. Moreover, a measure of debauchery did not seem to interfere with the effective management of complex enterprises. In the Roman system of values, the ability when necessary to control the passions, not the vice, mattered.

Slavery under the Empire

Slaves were the constant companions of the rich, and even poor households might own one or two. They may at various times have numbered as much as a third of the city's population, but their role in Roman society defies easy categorization. The influx of new slaves declined as the rate of imperial conquest slowed. By the first century CE, most had become Roman in culture and were therefore less likely to be abused than their predecessors. Conditions in the countryside could still be bad, but the lot of urban slaves was in some ways preferable to that of the poor citizen.

Domestic slaves lived as part of their master's household and were sometimes friends or lovers. Others were highly skilled professionals: teachers, physicians, librarians, or entertainers who might have homes of their own in the city and earn additional fees by offering their services to the general public. Craftsmen and industrial workers generally lived apart and returned a portion of their earnings to their owners, keeping the rest for themselves. Although slaves, their daily lives were similar to those of ordinary citizens.

Roman slavery was a legal and personal relationship that had little to do with lifestyle. Simply put, slaves were not persons under the law. The only virtue required of them was loyalty to their master, and they could neither serve in the army nor participate in public life. Although slaves could testify in court, it was customary to torture them first on the theory that this released them from their obligation of loyalty. Owners sometimes inflicted corporal punishment as well, but the emperors introduced legislation against the worst excesses. Claudius forbade the exposure of slaves who were old or sick. Domitian prohibited their castration, and Hadrian abolished private executions, even for criminal behavior.

As is often the case with legislation, these acts lagged far behind practice. Most owners knew that the system worked only if the loyalty of the slaves was genuine. No one would want to be shaved by a malcontent or protected by untrustworthy bodyguards. Slaves who rebelled might expect the fate of Spartacus. Urban slaves who were merely difficult might be threatened with being sent to the farm, a fate that to most of them must have seemed worse than death.

Manumission. Although kindness was important, the prospect of manumission was a better guarantor of personal and public safety. Urban slaves of either sex could look forward to being freed, usually by the time they reached age 30. This was about the average life expectancy in ancient Rome, but many lived far longer, and as in all preindustrial societies, the percentage of very old people in the population was probably not much less than it is today. To know with reasonable certainty that one would be freed mitigated despair, and it also made economic sense for the owners.

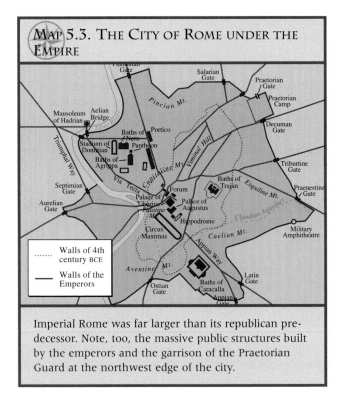

MAP 5.3. THE CITY OF ROME UNDER THE EMPIRE

Imperial Rome was far larger than its republican predecessor. Note, too, the massive public structures built by the emperors and the garrison of the Praetorian Guard at the northwest edge of the city.

The Roman system allowed slaves to purchase their freedom as soon as they could accumulate their purchase price. Those who worked outside the household could do this easily. Domestics, too, were often encouraged to develop private sources of income. The owner could then use the most productive years of a slave's life and recover his or her purchase price before sickness and old age diminished the total profit. As an added incentive to manumission, the freed slave became the owner's client, a relationship that might work to the advantage of both.

The Slave Population. After the third century BCE, nearly all slaves were foreigners, with Gauls, Syrians, and Africans being perhaps the most numerous. Rome was therefore a multihued city of immigrants in which people from every corner of the known world mingled without apparent racial tension. Consciously or not, slavery was the means by which they were turned into Romans. The owner purchased them, introduced them to Roman ways, and in many cases provided them with the training and education needed to survive. Once free, their lives were often more prosperous than those of citizens who had nothing but a monthly allotment of grain (see Document 5.6).

The Daily Life of Poor Citizens

Most of Rome's free citizens were officially categorized as poor. Some found work, often in jobs so hazardous or unhealthy that they could not be given to valuable slaves. Those who ran small shops faced intense competition from slaves and freedmen who were better connected than themselves, whereas a few managed, for a time at least, to hang on to whatever money they had realized from the sale of their country farms. Most lived in near destitution, kept alive only by occasional labor, the grain dole, and contributions from the rich. Nearly everyone, however, belonged to mutual aid societies that helped their members in times of need and guaranteed them a decent burial.

Housing. Like most of the urban slaves and freedmen, the poor inhabited a room or two in one of the innumerable *insulae,* or tenements, that packed the lower regions of the city. After the rebuilding projects of Augustus and the fire of 64 CE, these structures were usually of brick with concrete grills instead of windows. Although an improvement over the makeshift buildings of the Republic, the new insulae were not safe. Wooden floors, stairs, and roofs kept the fire companies busy, and excessive height and cheap construction sometimes caused them to collapse and kill their inhabitants (see Document 5.7). Individual apartments must have been dark and smoky with poor ventilation and no heat beyond that provided by a charcoal brazier for cooking.

Public Entertainments. Fortunately, Romans spent little time at home. They met their friends in the street or in the Forum, where they would gather to pick up gossip and make their views known by rowdy demonstrations. Wealthy Romans affected to despise the mob, but no politician, not even the emperor, could afford to ignore it. Great efforts were made to distract and amuse the citizenry, for the stability of the state depended on "bread and circuses." Those with political ambitions funded theatrical presentations, circuses, gladiatorial combats, chariot races, and huge public feasts in which the entire body of Roman citizens ate and drank itself into oblivion. Only the enormous cost of such entertainments could justify the wealth amassed by the Roman aristocracy.

Whatever their political function, such spectacles did little to elevate public taste. Circuses involved the slaughter of exotic animals by men, or of men by animals. The Romans enjoyed seeing convicted criminals mauled by bears or lions almost as much as the gladiatorial contests in which specially trained slaves fought to the death. Chariot racing, too, was a blood sport in which fatal accidents were common. Various teams represented political factions, and betting was heavy.

Public Health. After the games—or a hard day's work—Romans headed for the public baths. These massive facilities, which could be enjoyed by anyone, provided exercise rooms, steam baths, and hot and cold pools for bathing. Separate areas were reserved for men and women, although the women were given no place to exercise. Because the Romans had no soap, the

bathing ritual began with a steam bath. They then scraped their bodies with an instrument called a *strigil* and immersed themselves successively in hot and cold water. The whole process was lengthy enough to provide further opportunity for socializing.

Amenities provided at little or no cost made life in the city tolerable, even for the poor. The streets were

JUVENAL ON CITY LIFE IN THE ROMAN EMPIRE

Satire was a highly developed genre in Latin literature, and the poet Juvenal (c. 60–after 128 CE) was among the greatest of Roman satirists. In his *Third Satire*, he congratulates a friend on the decision to leave Rome for a small country town by cataloging the hazards of urban life. He exaggerates, but other authors provide similar accounts.

> Who, on Tivoli's heights, or a small town like Gabii, say,
> Fears the collapse of his house? But Rome is supported on
>   pipestems,
> Matchsticks; it's cheaper, so, for the landlord to shore up his ruins,
> Patch up the old cracked walls, and notify all the tenants

An Apartment House, or Insula. This architectural model of an apartment complex at Ostia (Rome's port of the mouth of the Tiber River) portrays luxury urban housing during the early empire. Shops occupied the lower floors. Poorer Romans did not live this well. Many of them inhabited buildings that were little better than tenements.

> They can sleep secure, though the beams are in ruins above them.
> No, the place to live is out there, where no cry of
> Fire!
> Sounds the alarm of the night, with a neighbor yelling for water,
> Moving his chattels and goods, and the whole third story is
>   smoking.
> This you'll never know: for if the ground floor is scared first,
> You are the first to burn, up where the eaves of the attic
> Keep off the rain, and the doves are brooding over their nest eggs.
> Look at the other things, the various
>   dangers of nighttime. . . .
> You are a thoughtless fool, unmindful of sudden disaster,
>   If you don't make your will before
>   you go out to have dinner.
>   There are as many deaths in the
>   night as there are open windows
>   Where you pass by; if you're wise,
>   you will pray in your wretched
>   devotions,
>   People may be content with no more
>   than emptying slop jars.

From *The Satires of Juvenal*, trans. R. Humphries (Bloomington, IN: Indiana University Press, 1958, pp. 40, 43). Used by permission.

Question: If life in the city was so difficult and dangerous, why did most Romans prefer to live there?

noisy—even at night—and the crime rate was relatively high, but those who had neither jobs nor possessions could ignore such problems. The city was clean by all but twentieth-century standards. Massive aqueducts brought pure water into every neighborhood where it bubbled up in innumerable fountains, and even the meanest apartment had a terrace garden or a few potted plants, for the Romans, although thoroughly urbanized, never lost their taste for growing things.

Yet by modern standards, the lives of ordinary Romans must have been largely without root or purpose. Few married, and people tended to contract casual relationships with little regard for the social standing of their partners. The birthrate remained correspondingly low, and children born to these unions were often left in public places to die or be found by slave traders. The population of the city would have declined had it not been for the steady influx of slaves and of refugees fleeing from the hard life of the countryside.

Life in the Provinces

The Romans made little effort to impose their culture on the peoples of the empire, asking only that taxes be paid and peace maintained. Areas such as Egypt or Judaea, whose cultures were long established and fundamentally alien to Greco-Roman values, therefore remained unassimilated. Tribal societies, or those in which the ideal of civic life had native roots, were more likely to imitate Roman models. By the end of the prin-

FIGURE 5.6 *Gladiators*. This relief shows one of the many forms of gladiatorial contest popular with Romans. These are *bestiarii* who specialized in fighting animals in the arena. Lions and what appears to be a bear are shown. Other gladiatorial contests involved combat between men using various combinations of weapons, such as sword and shield versus a trident and net.

cipate, Italy, Spain, Africa, and much of Gaul had been thoroughly Romanized, whereas Greece, Syria, and the Greek-speaking communities of Asia Minor, although they retained their native cultures, were drawing closer to the Roman orbit.

Cities. Cities provided the common element. The empire had more than 1,000 of them, and Roman policy encouraged them to govern themselves. Like Rome, most ancient cities had long been governed by magistrates and city councils, although the process by which these governments were elected varied widely. The Romans honored those eligible for such offices by granting them Roman citizenship and enrolling them in a separate social order, the *decurions* (deh-cure'-ee-ons). The financial requirements for membership were lower than those for Roman senators or equestrians, but a decurion had to be wealthy enough to make gifts, or *liturgies*, to his city. These might include anything from the production of a play to the building of an aqueduct. In the beginning, at least, they were voluntary.

Because wealth was inherited, the decurionate became for all practical purposes hereditary in the course of the first and second centuries CE, and the decurions became a permanent provincial aristocracy. When the emperors extended equestrian and even senatorial status to provincials, they integrated these local aristocrats with those of Rome. Provincial loyalty was further solidified, at least on occasion, by granting Roman citizenship to other townsmen as well. On the frontiers where urban life had not fully developed, citizenship was sometimes extended on a tribal basis, often with considerable success.

In general, the social structure and daily life of western cities resembled that of Rome. Eastern towns were different. Slavery was much less widespread, and the bulk of the artisans and laborers were citizens. Most of the latter, although poor, appear to have been self-supporting. Craft production in the eastern cities was far more important than that in the more agrarian west, and their average size was probably greater. Alexandria, still more Greek than Egyptian, was almost as large as Rome, whereas places such as Pergamum and Antioch probably had close to a half million inhabitants.

Rural Life. Country life also differed. In the west, large farms and latifundia, worked either by slaves or the coloni, were common. In the east, wealthy townsmen and city governments owned tracts that they rented to tenant farmers in return for cash payments or a portion of the yield. In both regions, independent farmers worked freehold plots with varying degrees of success. Egypt remained as it had been under the Ptolemies—a world of impoverished peasants laboring for the state under an appalling burden of taxation.

CONCLUSION

The age of Augustus and the early emperors has been called the peak of Roman civilization. Its achievements were great, but beneath the surface, social polarization continued to limit economic growth and lay the foundation for future crises. The pax romana was something of an illusion. Roman rule masked, but did not resolve, underlying political and economic tensions in many parts of the empire. Riots and revolts were common and became more so with the passage of time. The empire, in short, could barely sustain itself even in the absence of external threats, and it had become obvious even in the reign of Augustus that a threat of monumental proportions was developing in the north. Masses of Germanic tribesmen had begun to press against the Rhine and Danube frontiers. Unprecedented efforts would be needed to contain them, and, as time would tell, the social and economic structures of the empire proved unequal to the task.

Review Questions

- Why did the Gracchi fail in their efforts to reform the Roman Republic?
- How did the Marian reform of the army help create a situation in which men like Pompey, Caesar, and Octavian could threaten the integrity of the state?
- What were the basic policies of Augustus?
- What were the major causes of political instability under the early emperors?
- What was the relationship between slave and free labor in the cities of the empire?

For Further Study

Readings

Gelzer, Matthias, *Caesar, Statesman and Politician,* trans. P. Needham (Cambridge: Harvard, 1968).

Goodman, Martin, *The Roman World, 44 BC to AD 180* (London: Routledge, 1997). A concise, up-to-date survey.

MacMullen, Ramsay, *Roman Social Relations, 50 BC to AD 284* (New Haven, CT: Yale, 1981). Brief and readable.

Stockton, David, *The Gracchi* (New York: Oxford University Press, 1979). A good study of the Gracchi and their reforms.

Syme, Richard, *The Roman Revolution,* rev. ed. (London: Oxford University Press, 1967). The classic study of the transition from Republic to Empire.

InfoTrac College Edition

Visit the source collections at *http://infotrac.thomson learning.com* and use the search function with the following key terms.

Using Key Terms, enter the search terms:
Roman History   *Roman Empire*

Web Site

http://www.fordham.edu/halsall/ancient/asbook.html

The Internet Ancient History Sourcebook. The section on Rome contains a large number of sources, plus information on various aspects of imperial history, including the provinces.

ROME: FROM REPUBLIC TO EMPIRE

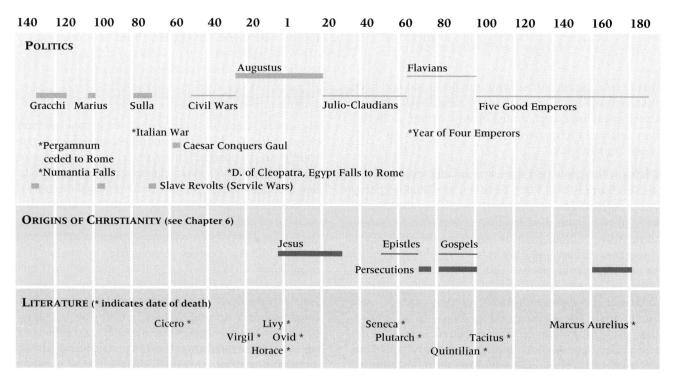

Visit the Western Civilization Companion Web Site for resources specific to this textbook:
http://history.wadsworth.com/hause02/

The CD in the back of this book and the Western Civilization Resource Center at *http://history. wadsworth.com/western/* offer a variety of tools to help you succeed in this course, including access to quizzes; images; documents; interactive simulations, maps, and timelines; movie explorations; and a wealth of other sources.

Chapter 6

THE ORIGINS OF CHRISTIANITY AND THE DECLINE OF THE ROMAN EMPIRE

FOCUS QUESTIONS

- How did Christianity begin, and how did it spread throughout the early empire?
- What was the military situation of the Roman Empire after 180 CE, and why did the emperors find it difficult to meet its strategic needs?
- Why did Christianity become the dominant religion of the late empire?
- Why was the empire divided, and how was its eastern half able to survive while the west gradually collapsed as a political entity?

*I*n the summer of 410 CE, the Visigothic chieftain Alaric besieged Rome. On August 24, his allies within the city opened the gates, and for 3 days his troops plundered at will. Alaric generally treated the inhabitants well and burned only a few buildings, but the event shocked the world. It was the first time in 800 years that Rome had fallen even briefly to an enemy, and the city's vulnerability showed what the Roman Empire had become. By 410 it had been divided into two unequal halves, with the real center of power located hundreds of miles to the east in Constantinople. Rome was no longer even the capital of the west. The emperor Honorius had transferred his government to the more secure city of Ravenna in 402. By 476, the western empire itself had ceased to exist. Romans and Germanic tribesmen had begun to form a new society that combined the institutions and culture of both peoples with a single religion: Christianity. It was the beginning of what modern historians call the Middle Ages.

Chapter 6 begins with an examination of how Christianity emerged from the religious ferment of early imperial Rome to become the empire's dominant faith. As Christianity grew, the empire fell into a prolonged decline, apparent by the end of the second century and generated by an expansion beyond its economic resources. The emperors of the third and fourth centuries tried to reverse the process of economic and social decay, but gradually, the western and eastern halves of the empire grew further apart. The west, pressured by Germanic invaders and weakened by a stagnant economy, disintegrated. The Greek-speaking east, richer and untroubled by Germans, survived until 1453. This chapter concludes with the fall of the Roman Empire in the west and with the evolution of the Western church as a unifying institution during the fourth and fifth centuries CE.

RELIGION IN THE ROMAN EMPIRE (C. 100 BCE–C. 200 CE)

Roman *Pietas*. The traditional religion of Rome as described in Chapter 4 provided a framework for civic patriotism. Its rites and sacrifices expressed in ritual form what it meant to be Roman, and *pietas* (pee'-et-as), or piety, was defined by their timely performance. As in Greece, ethics had become the province of philosophy, although not even the widespread acceptance of Stoicism could erase an earlier, unwritten code of behavior. That code was not grounded on precepts handed down from the gods but rather on honor and other traditional values whose origins were ultimately tribal. The gods demanded pietas and patriotism and offered only their conditional blessing in return. Roman visions of the afterlife were murky or nonexistent, and the concept of personal salvation was unknown.

FIGURE 6.1 *The Cult of Dionysus.* This detail from a much larger wall painting comes from the so-called Villa of the Mysteries in Pompeii and dates from the first century BCE. It shows what appears to be part of an elaborate initiation rite, but its significance is unknown. Dionysus was the Greek god of wine (*Bacchus* in Latin) and, among other things, was supposed to have died and then returned to Earth. The Dionysiac mysteries were popular among Roman women, but the authorities (and husbands) regarded them with suspicion because of their supposedly orgiastic character.

Divination and Magic. For help in dealing with the troubles and anxieties of everyday life, most Romans relied on divination, the attempt to foretell the future through a careful examination of portents and omens. Portents were natural signs, including thunderstorms or the flight of birds, whose meaning was read by a college of priests known as *augurs*. The term *inaugurate* comes from the Roman practice of beginning any enterprise only after consulting augurs. Omens were words overheard out of context or uttered unintentionally that struck the listener as meaningful. They had to be interpreted without professional help.

To supplement the information gained from portents and omens, a Roman could fall back on the ancient Mesopotamian art of astrology, which tried to read the future in the stars. These efforts to foretell the future bred a sense of helplessness that amounted to fatalism. Only magic seemed to give the Romans a measure of control over their lives, and they supported a legion of sorcerers whose spells and potions could help reverse an evil portent or influence someone else to do their bidding.

The Mystery Religions. As Roman communal values eroded during the late Republic and early empire, superstition flourished and traditional observance declined. For many Romans, the state religion, with its emphasis on communal life, was superceded by cults—most of them imported from the east—that offered immortality in the hereafter and a more intimate relationship with the divine. These **mystery religions,** as they are called, had certain features in common. In most of them, immortality was made possible by a divine sacrifice in which the god comes to Earth in human form and suffers a terrible death on behalf of his followers. He is then resurrected as a promise of eternal life. Certain aspects of the event were frequently commemorated by a symbolic meal.

Although the mystery religions achieved great popularity in the Roman world, few of them were universal in their appeal. The Orphic cult, for example, attracted women. The government disliked it because celebrations of the death and resurrection of Orpheus were thought to involve orgies. The cult of Cybele (Sib'-el-ee), a mother-goddess also called the *Magna Mater* (Great Mother) whose rich pageantry and terrifying rituals were described by the poet Catullus, demanded that its priests castrate themselves. This requirement alone limited its popularity among men, but for women who could afford to participate in her lavish ceremonies, Cybele offered a powerful religious experience. Mithraism, based on the worship of the Persian sun god, was restricted to men. Popular with the army and the imperial bureaucracy, it demanded high ethical standards and enough wealth to support its expensive rituals. The beliefs and rituals of Mithraism—such as the miraculous birth of

APULEIUS DESCRIBES A PROCESSION OF THE CULT OF ISIS

Apuleius (Ah-pu-lee´-yus) is the only Latin novelist whose work has survived to modern times. He was born c. 124 CE in North Africa and was educated at Carthage, Athens, and Rome. His marriage to a rich widow provoked charges that he had used witchcraft to win her, and his successful defense helped establish his literary reputation. His surviving masterwork, *The Golden Ass*, is chiefly remembered as a ribald classic, but it contains fascinating descriptions of contemporary life. This excerpt describes a procession dedicated to Isis, when her cult was the most popular religion in the empire.

Now the special procession of the savior goddess was moving by. Women resplendent in white garments, rejoicing in varied ornaments and wearing wreaths of spring flowers, strewed with blossoms from their bosoms the path along which the sacred procession was passing. Others turned shining mirrors, held behind their backs, toward the goddess as she came, to demonstrate their reverence on the way. Others, carrying ivory combs, with the gestures of their arms and the movements of their fingers went through the motions of combing and adorning the queenly hair. Others sprinkled the streets with various ointments, including delightful balsam scattered drop by drop. In addition, there came a great number, of both sexes, with lamps, torches, wax tapers, and other lights, propitiating with light the offspring of the celestial stars. Then pleasant harmonies sounded, pipes and flutes in the sweetest tones. These were followed by a delightful chorus of very select

young men, resplendent in white garments and festal array, repeating a charming song . . .

There came, too, trumpeters devoted to the great Serapis [the husband of Isis, associated with the Greek god Dionysius] who with slanting reeds stretched to the right ear repeated the familiar melody of the temple and god. And there were many who called for free room for the sacred rites. Then poured in masses of initiates in the divine rites, men and women of every rank and age, who glistened in their white linen garb. The women had their hair anointed and decked with a bright covering, but the men, their hair completely shaven, had glistening pates.

When we came to the temple itself, the high priest, those who carried the divine images, and especially those who had long been initiated in the venerable secrets went from the chamber of the goddess . . . From a raised platform, [the priest] read forth from a book, offering propitious vows for the great emperor, the senate, the entire Roman . . . then, gleaming with joy, the populace, carrying leafy boughs, twigs, and garlands, kissed the places on the steps where the silver statue of the goddess had rested, and departed to their homes.

From Apuleius, *The Golden Ass*, book 11, trans. Robert Graves (New York: Pocket Books, 1951).

Question: What elements of this procession would have been unacceptable to Christians or Jews?

---

the son of god, baptism of the faithful, and ritual consumption of bread and wine in memory of the savior—bore a superficial similarity to Christianity.

The Cult of Isis. Only the cult of Isis (Eye´-siss), with its unfathomable mysteries and almost Christian ethics, appealed to people of every class and gender. It had reached Rome in the third century BCE, and its adherents were persecuted until Caligula granted the religion public recognition. It then grew rapidly and was the most popular religion in the Roman Empire until the beginning of the fourth century CE (see Document 6.1).

The general enthusiasm for mystery religions revealed a new and widespread yearning for personal immortality. Scholars have seen in this a sign of increased individualism, a turning inward reminiscent of the Hellenistic withdrawal from public life in the face of conditions similar to those in the later empire. It certainly marked a diminished confidence in human capacities. In the world of the mysteries, the only thing that could save a human soul was the miraculous sacrifice and resurrection of a god. Human efforts, no matter how sincere, were not

enough. In a sense, the mystery religions paved the way for the acceptance of Christianity.

Rome and the Jews. The breakup of the Hasmonaean dynasty, as the descendants of the Maccabees were known, resulted in a protracted, messy civil war in which outside forces supported the various contenders. Rome, in the person of Pompey, intervened in 66–64 BCE as part of the effort to defeat Mithridates and capitalize on the collapse of the Seleucid Empire. The consequent spread of Roman influence in the Middle East alarmed Parthia, the successor of the Persian Empire, and aroused the interest of Cleopatra, who opposed Roman policy in the region even as she seduced Caesar and Antony. The religious struggle between Jewish Sadducees and Pharisees (see Chapter 3) further complicated the situation.

Eventually, a Roman client, Herod "the Great" (73–4 BCE), emerged supreme and imposed an interval of much-needed peace. Although Arab by birth, Herod practiced Judaism and generally favored the more numerous Pharisees over their opponents. His

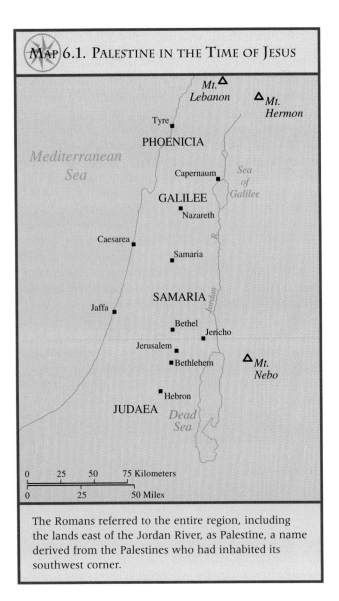

MAP 6.1. PALESTINE IN THE TIME OF JESUS

Mt.
Lebanon

Mt.
Hermon

Tyre

PHOENICIA

Mediterranean Sea

Capernaum

Sea of Galilee

GALILEE

Nazareth

Caesarea

Samaria

SAMARIA

Jordan R.

Jaffa

Bethel

Jericho

Jerusalem

Bethlehem

Mt.
Nebo

Hebron

JUDAEA   *Dead Sea*

| 0 | 25 | 50 | 75 Kilometers |
| 0 | 25 | | 50 Miles |

The Romans referred to the entire region, including the lands east of the Jordan River, as Palestine, a name derived from the Palestines who had inhabited its southwest corner.

realms extended north to the borders of Syria and east into Transjordan and provided the revenues for an extensive building campaign, the jewel of which was the reconstruction of the Temple at Jerusalem. Some of its huge stones are still visible at the base of the Western Wall. None of this endeared him to the more observant Jews, but they accepted his rule.

When Herod died, he divided his kingdom into three tetrarchies, each ruled by a son. Archelaus (Ark'-ah-lay-us), the Tetrarch of Judaea, so offended his Jewish subjects that they asked Augustus to replace him with a Roman prefect. Augustus agreed to do so, but the experiment failed. In theory, the prefects were supposed to look out for Roman interests while leaving internal matters to the Jewish court known as the Sanhedrin, but if the Jewish historian Josephus (c. 37–100 CE) may be believed, each prefect found new ways of insulting Jewish religious and political sensibilities. By 7 CE, a

group known as the Zealots had dedicated themselves to the overthrow of Roman rule.

After this, the turmoil in Jerusalem was broken only by the short reign of Herod Agrippa, a Jewish prince who governed Judaea from 41 to 44 CE under Roman protection. Riots and protests accompanied a growing belief in the coming of the Messiah, who would deliver the Jews from their enemies and restore the world. False messiahs appeared with predictable regularity and caused great concern among the Romans, who feared that one of them might organize a general revolt. Finally, in 66 CE, the emperor Nero dispatched an army under Vespasian and Titus to restore order. Both men later became emperors. The Zealots and most of the population resisted, and Jerusalem fell to the Romans after a long and terrible siege.

The Jewish Diaspora (70 CE). Exasperated by his inability to come to terms with the Jews even after their defeat, Vespasian, who had by this time become emperor, ordered the Temple destroyed and the Jews scattered to the far corners of the empire in 70 CE. They retained their freedom to worship and the exemption from sacrificing to the state cult that had been granted them by Julius Caesar, but the new exile, or **diaspora,** changed the character of Judaism. The destruction of the Temple forced the abandonment of sacrifices and other temple rites, for it was thought that the Temple could be restored only by the coming of the Messiah. The role of the priesthood diminished. Instead, rabbis, or teachers who interpreted the law to far-flung congregations, provided religious guidance. The more distinguished of their opinions formed the **Talmud,** the vast collection of scriptural commentaries that is, together with scripture, the basis of Jewish learning and of modern Judaism. Only a handful of Jews remained in Judaea. A band of perhaps 900 Zealots held out in the great desert fortress of Masada until 73 CE, when they committed mass suicide rather than surrender to the Romans. Sixty years later, another small group of Jews launched a futile rebellion under Bar Kochva, but nearly 2,000 years would pass before the establishment of another Jewish state.

THE ORIGINS AND SPREAD OF CHRISTIANITY (1–324 CE)

Jesus of Nazareth. The founder of Christianity lived in the midst of this chronic turbulence. He was probably born at Bethlehem in Judaea, between 7 and 4 BCE, and grew up in Nazareth. Both the year and date of his birth are now regarded as the products of later calculation, but the year assigned to his birth (1 CE) marks the start of the Common Era in Western history. Western, but not Eastern, Christians celebrate December 25 as the day of his birth. A precise chronol-

FIGURE 6.2 *Relief from the Arch of Titus, Rome.* Roman emperors erected triumphal arches to commemorate their military victories. This relief from the arch of Titus shows the spoils taken from the capture of Jerusalem. The arch was erected after Titus's death, probably about 81 CE, and commemorates the dual triumph celebrated by Vespasian and Titus in 71 CE after their victory over the Jews and the destruction of the Temple. Note the menorah on left. The seven-branched candelabra, used in celebrating the festival of Hanukkah, first became a symbol of the Jewish people during this era.

Death and Resurrection of Jesus (trad. 33 CE). This message enraged the Pharisees but attracted many, especially among the poor. When he entered Jerusalem at Passover accompanied by symbols attributed to the Messiah by prophetic tradition, Jesus provoked a crisis. The Sanhedrin demanded his arrest. The Roman prefect, Pontius Pilate (Pont'-ee-us Pie'-lat), agreed, fearing that Christ's presence would provoke further disorder when virtually the entire country had come to town for the festival. Jesus was tried by the Sanhedrin for blasphemy and by Pilate for treason, although both trials as described by the Gospels were of dubious legality. Jesus was crucified with uncommon haste to avoid the possibility of demonstrations; everyone responsible seems to have been motivated by political expediency. After his execution, his followers reported that he had returned from the dead and ascended into Heaven after promising to return on the Day of Judgment.

ogy of Jesus's life is impossible because the four **Gospels**—the most important sources dealing with his life and ministry—provide no dates. Although written by different authors more than a generation after his death (Mark, the earliest, was written about 70 CE; John, the latest, shortly before 100 CE), their accounts generally agree but differ in important ways.

They describe the circumstances of Jesus's birth and of an appearance at the Temple when he was about 12 but remain silent about his activities until the age of 30, the point at which he began to attract a following as an itinerant rabbi. Accompanied by twelve close associates, or disciples, he preached throughout the Judaean countryside to ever-increasing crowds. He directed his message primarily against the Pharisees. Jesus believed that their rigid observance of the Law was an obstacle to faith and that the simple commandment to "love thy neighbor as thyself" superseded regulations. At the same time, his preaching left no doubt that he regarded himself as the Messiah (the Greek word for which is *christos,* or Christ). By this he did not mean the traditional messiah who would lead the Jews to earthly glory, but the Son of God who brought them eternal salvation in an afterlife. His kingdom, he said, was "not of this world," and those who believed in him "would not perish but have eternal life."

The Spread of Christianity. The story of Jesus's death and resurrection solidified his followers into a new Jewish sect, but Saul of Tarsus (c. 5–67 CE), who had never heard him preach, spread his teachings throughout the Roman world. Saul was a Pharisee who had originally persecuted the followers of Jesus. After a dramatic conversion to the faith of his opponents, he began to use his Roman name, **Paul,** and devoted the rest of his life to the task of converting Jews and non-Jews alike. Although a Pharisee, Paul's early education had been cosmopolitan and strongly influenced by Hellenism. To him, the teachings of Jesus were universal. With some difficulty, he persuaded the more conservative disciples to accept converts without forcing them to observe the Jewish dietary laws or be circumcised. Had he not done so, Christianity probably would never have become a universal church. By emphasizing faith over the minute observance of the law, Paul influenced the theology of the growing church as well.

In his letters, Paul portrayed himself as small of stature and physically weak, but he made heroic efforts

FIGURE 6.3 *Crucifixion.* Crucifixion was the most common form of execution in Roman times. Courts applied this penalty to thieves, murderers, rebellious slaves, and enemies of the Roman state. The detail in this seventeenth-century engraving shows the various methods of crucifixion used until their abolition by Constantine early in the fourth century. Normally, the victim was tied to the cross. The weight of the body dislocated the shoulders and he died after about 3 days of agony. The Gospels say that Jesus was nailed to the cross, an unusual procedure that hastened his death. The Romans probably wanted a speedy execution to reduce the possibility of riots by Jesus's followers. The cross remains the primary symbol of the Christian faith.

on behalf of the faith. After Jesus died, his teachings had begun to spread through the Jewish communities of the Roman Empire. Opposition from the Jewish leadership could not prevent the formation of small, often secret, congregations that became the organizational basis of Paul's efforts. Traveling incessantly, he and others, including several of the disciples, moved from one to the other, prevailing upon them to accept non-Jews as converts, preaching to the gentiles, and helping individual churches with matters of belief and practice. By so doing, he not only gained converts but provided stability and a vital link between isolated communities that might otherwise have lost contact with one another and drifted into confusion.

The Pauline Epistles. When he could not visit the churches in person, Paul and his associates communicated with them by letters that seem to have been composed in answer to specific questions. These **Epistles,** written in Greek and popularly attributed to Paul (although several were written by others), form an important part of the New Testament. Some of them deal with theological questions; others deal with morality, ethics, and church organization. For issues not addressed by Jesus, the Epistles—persuasive, fervent, and rooted solidly in Scripture—became the basis of later church doctrine. Through Paul's efforts and those of the other disciples, the Christian church grew rapidly.

In the beginning, Christianity appealed largely to women, slaves, and other people of modest social standing, for it was universal in the sense that it accepted converts regardless of gender or background. Salvation was open to all, although Paul objected strongly to women preaching. Its high ethical standards appealed to a generation that seems to have been increasingly repelled by pagan vice, and its ceremonies were neither as terrifying nor expensive as those of the mystery religions. The most important were baptism with water—not bull's blood, as in the rites of Mithras—and a love feast or *agape* (ah-gah'-pay) in which the entire congregation joined. After a common meal, the Christians celebrated communion in bread and wine. By 153 CE, the love feast had been abandoned in favor of communion alone, which was preceded by a service that included preaching and the singing of hymns.

Organization of the Early Church. Although humble, the early church was remarkably well organized. Originally, a committee of *presbyters,* or elders, governed each congregation under the guidance of an "overseer," or bishop. Deacons, readers, and exorcists assisted them. Most of these officials were men, but some women served as deacons and sometimes as presbyters, especially in the Greek churches. This situation did not survive the first century. Bishops, elected by their congregations, replaced the committee structure of the apostolic churches. The presbyters became priests. The extent of a bishop's power in earliest times has been the subject of much debate, but the doctrine of **apostolic succession** clearly assisted its expansion. This teaching, which holds that the authority of bishops derives from powers given by Jesus to his disciples, was generally accepted by the end of the second century.

The Persecutions. Organization helped the young church survive persecution, for the Christians were hated. Persecution came from two sources. Many Jews believed that Christianity divided and weakened their communities and were quick to denounce Christians to the authorities. The authorities, whether Roman or provincial, had other motives. Like the Jews, Christians refused to sacrifice to the Roman gods. The Jews were exempt from this requirement by their status as a separate nation whose customs were honored by Roman law, but Christianity was not. Many Romans feared that Christian exclusiveness masked a certain hostility to the state. Their suspicions were fed by the low social status of the Christians and, ironically, by the secrecy they had adopted for their protection. To avoid detection, Christians met in private houses or in the underground burial places known as **catacombs.** Rumors of cannibalism, based on a misunderstanding of communion, only made matters worse.

Christians, in short, were unpopular and lacked the protection of powerful individuals who might otherwise have intervened on their behalf. They made ideal scapegoats. Nero, for example, blamed them for the great fire at Rome and launched the first wave of executions that claimed the life of Paul in 64 CE (see Document 6.2). Persecutions by later emperors caused great loss of life until well into the third century. Eusebius of Caesarea (You-see'-bee-us of Sez-a-ree'-a, c. 260–340) chronicled them in horrific detail in his history of the Church, but to the annoyance of the pagans, "the blood of martyrs" became, as the Christian writer Tertullian put it, "the seed of the church." Too many Christians died bravely. Their cheerful heroism, even as they were torn apart by wild beasts, impressed spectators and powerfully endorsed the concept of eternal life. Many pagans converted despite the obvious danger. Admittedly, had the persecutions been consistent they might have succeeded, but not all emperors were anti-Christian. Each persecution was followed by a generation or more in which the numbers of the faithful could be replaced and even grow.

The Church Fathers. Although persecution backfired, Christianity needed to explain itself to the educated elite to gain general acceptance. Moreover, as the movement spread, differences of opinion began to develop within it. During the second and third centuries, a growing number of writers addressed themselves both to the task of defining Christian doctrine and explaining it in terms acceptable to those who had received a Greco-Roman philosophical education. These men, who eventually became known as the Fathers of the Church, included the apologist Justin Martyr and theologians such as Tertullian, Origen (Or'-i-jen), and Clement of Alexandria. Together, they began the process of forging a new intellectual tradition based on reason as well as faith.

By the end of the third century, perhaps 10 percent of the empire was Christian. Most of the followers were

FIGURE 6.4 *Catacomb of Saint Sebastian, Rome.* Unlike pagans, who generally cremated their dead, Christians insisted on burial, often in underground vaults known as *catacombs*. In times of persecution, they held religious services in these tombs to avoid detection. The walls of catacombs were usually covered with paintings and inscriptions.

concentrated in the east or in Africa. More significant, the Fathers had done their work: converts came increasingly from the upper classes. In the cities of Syria and Asia Minor, Christians had become a majority, and even the leading families had accepted the faith. The last, and one of the most terrible, of the persecutions occurred under Diocletian (Die-oh-clee'-shan) in 303 CE, but by then the church was too strong to be destroyed (see Table 6.1).

THE CRISIS OF THE LATE ROMAN EMPIRE (180–337 CE)

In 1776, Edward Gibbon described the fall of Rome as "the triumph of Christianity and barbarism." Although his *History of the Decline and Fall of the Roman Empire* is one of the great masterworks of history, he was at best only half right. Neither Christianity nor pagan immorality contributed to the catastrophe that befell the western empire in the fifth century. The "barbarians" clearly played a major role, but they were little more barbaric than some of the emperors they replaced.

TACITUS ON NERO'S PERSECUTION OF CHRISTIANS

Tacitus (c. 56–120 CE) is among the greatest of the ancient Roman historians. He was born to a patrician family in Gaul, educated at Rome, rose to the Senate, and became consul under Nerva in 97 CE. Tacitus produced two long histories, *The Annals* (covering 14–68 CE) and *The Histories* (covering 68–96 CE). Together they provide the best record of the early Principate. *The Annals*, from which the following excerpt is taken, is one of the few contemporary sources to mention Jesus of Nazareth.

A disaster followed, whether accidental or treacherously contrived by the Emperor is uncertain, as authors have given both accounts; a fire—worse, and more dreadful than any which have ever happened to this city—broke out amid the shops containing inflammable wares, and instantly became fierce and rapid from the wind. . . . It devastated every place below the hills, outstripping all preventive measures; the city, with the narrow winding passages and irregular streets that characterized old Rome, was at its mercy. . . .

All human efforts, all the lavish gifts of the Emperor, all attempts to placate the Gods, did not dispel the infamous suspicion the fire had been started at someone's command. To quiet the rumor, Nero blamed and ingeniously tortured a people popularly called Christians, hated for their abominations [including their prediction that the world would soon end in a conflagration marking the second coming]. Christus, from whom the cult had its origin, suffered the extreme penalty during the reign of Tiberius, at the hands of one of our procurators, Pontius Pilate, but this noxious superstition [Christianity], suppressed for a moment, broke out again not only in Judaea, where it began, but in Rome itself, where all things hideous and shameful from every part of the world become popular.

Nero first arrested all who confessed [to being Christians]; then, upon their testimony, a vast multitude was convicted not so much of arson as of hatred of the human race. Mockery of every sort was added to their deaths. They were sewn in the skins of beasts and torn to pieces by dogs. Many died nailed on crosses or burned at the stake to illuminate the night. Nero gave his gardens for the spectacle and put on a circus, mingling with the crowd in the costume of a charioteer. . . . Thus, even though the victims deserved the severest penalty, a feeling of compassion arose on the ground that they suffered not for the public good but to glut the cruelty of one man.

From Tacitus, *The Annals*, book 15, chaps. 38, 44, trans. A. J. Church and W. J. Brodribb (New York: Macmillan, 1906).

Question: Based on this document, why did Nero decide to persecute the Christians, and what effect did the persecution have on the development of the new faith?

Population Pressure. The true cause of imperial decline was instead a generalized crisis whose basic outlines had become apparent as early as the second century. When Marcus Aurelius died in 180, an army of more than a half million men patrolled a border of several thousand miles. Within that border, only occasional riots disrupted the *pax romana*, but beyond it, powerful forces were gathering. Germanic tribes—Franks, Alemanni, Burgundians, and others in the west and Visigoths and Ostrogoths to the east—pressed against the Rhine and Danube frontiers. For reasons that remain unclear, their populations had grown beyond the available food supply in central Europe. Behind them, on the eastern steppes, other peoples with similar problems pushed westward into the German tribal lands. Population movements on this scale created intolerable pressure when they came up against settled borders. The Germans did not hate Rome. They sought only to settle within it. They were hard, determined fighters whose grasp of strategy was anything but primitive. In fighting them, Marcus Aurelius faced unpredictable attacks in force delivered along a perimeter too extensive to be manned completely by the legions. His bitter struggle with the tribes was an inkling of things to come.

The Eastern Frontier. To the east, the Romans faced a more conventional foe. The Parthian Empire was a sophisticated territorial state, based, like Rome, on taxes and tribute. It fought until it exhausted its resources and then made peace until its economy could recover. The pressure it exerted on the eastern borders was therefore sporadic rather than constant, but it was nevertheless severe. Rome defeated the Parthians in 198 and briefly annexed Mesopotamia. A change of dynasty in the eastern kingdom followed. An Iranian prince, Ardashir I, overthrew the Parthians and established the Sassanid (Sa-san'-id) dynasty, which lasted until the Arab conquests of the seventh century. Determined to recapture Mesopotamia, he and his successors launched a series of wars that further depleted the Roman treasury, weakened the eastern provinces, and ended in 260 with the capture of the emperor Valerian.

Economic Decline. The Roman economy could not sustain this level of military commitment on two fronts,

TABLE 6.1	THE MORE IMPORTANT ROMAN EMPERORS AND THEIR YEARS OF REIGN

Emperors whose names are highlighted launched major persecutions of the Christians. The gaps between persecutions, often amounting to several generations, help explain why they were ineffective.

27 BCE–14 CE Augustus	
14–37 Tiberius	218–222 Elagabalus
37–41 Caligula	222–235 Severus
41–54 Claudius	Alexander
54–68 Nero	249–251 Decius
68–69 The year of	253–260 Valerian
the four emperors	253–268 Gallienus
69–79 Vespasian	268–270 Claudius II
79–81 Titus	Gothicus
81–96 Domitian	270–275 Aurelian
96–98 Nerva	284–305 Diocletian
98–117 Trajan	306–337 Constantine
117–138 Hadrian	337–361 Constantius II
138–161 Antoninus Pius	361–363 Julian the
161–180 Marcus Aurelius	Apostate
180–192 Commodus	364–375 Valentinian
193–211 Septimius	364–378 Valens
Severus	379–395 Theodosius
211–217 Caracalla	

Economic decline, although general, did not affect all regions of the empire equally. Those provinces closest to the front suffered the most because they were subject to requisitions of food, draft animals, and equipment and because governors could extract forced loans from citizens who found themselves in harm's way. Both east and west suffered, but the strain was greater in the west because the Germans exerted a steady, unrelenting pressure, whereas the cyclical nature of the struggle with Persia allowed time for the eastern provinces to recover between wars. Africa and Egypt, far from the battlefields, suffered only from the same ruinous taxes that afflicted everyone.

The crisis fed upon itself in an unending spiral of decline. The imperial government became more brutal and authoritarian in its efforts to extract resources from an ever-narrowing economic base, and with each exaction, poverty increased. The social consequences were appalling. A steady decline in population is evident from the midsecond century onward, which inhibited recruitment for the army and reduced the tax base even further (see Table 6.2). Growing poverty and political helplessness blurred social distinctions and encouraged resistance that, in turn, forced the government to adopt even sterner measures.

Imperial Efforts at Reform from Septimius Severus to Diocletian (193–305 CE)

Much of this new authoritarianism was the legacy of **Septimius Severus** (Se-veer'-us), emperor from 193 to 211 CE. Having commanded legions on the Danube, he believed that the full human and economic resources of the state had to be mobilized to meet the German threat. He introduced laws that imposed forced labor on the poor and trapped the decurions who controlled city governments in an inescapable web of obligations. The army, meanwhile, was showered with favors. Severus doubled the soldier's pay—the first increase in more than 200 years—and allowed officers to wear the gold ring that signified membership in the equestrian order. Such measures improved morale, but they were not enough. Hard terms of service and the declining population of the interior provinces continued to make recruitment difficult. To compensate, Severus opened even the highest ranks to men from the border provinces and, for the first time since the days of Marius, allowed soldiers to marry.

These reforms, although rational and probably necessary, widened the gap between soldiers and civilians. The post-Severan army, composed largely of men with only the slightest exposure to Roman culture, was privileged as well as self-perpetuating. Children raised in the camps usually followed their father's profession. When they did not, they remained part of a garrison

and the third century was one of almost unrelieved crisis. The prosperity of Augustan times had been in some respects artificial. Much of it was based on the exploitation of new wealth derived from imperial expansion. When the expansion stopped, that wealth was not replaced. Beneath the glittering surface of the early empire, the economy remained stagnant. The mass of slaves, tenant farmers, and unemployed citizens consumed little. Their productivity was low, and they had no incentive to improve efficiency to encourage growth. Without growth, the number of rich could not increase, and in the Roman system, it was only they who could provide a market for luxuries and craft goods.

Arguably, had the Roman economy been able to expand, the empire might have been able to meet its military obligations. Instead, the imperial government tried to extract more and more resources from an economy that may already have been shrinking. Taxes and forced requisitions to support the army consumed capital, reduced the expenditures of the rich, and drove ordinary people to destitution. Basic industries such as the trade in earthenware vanished, and food shortages became common as harvests were diverted to feed the troops. Trade languished.

MAP 6.2. THE ROMAN EMPIRE AT ITS HEIGHT (117 CE)

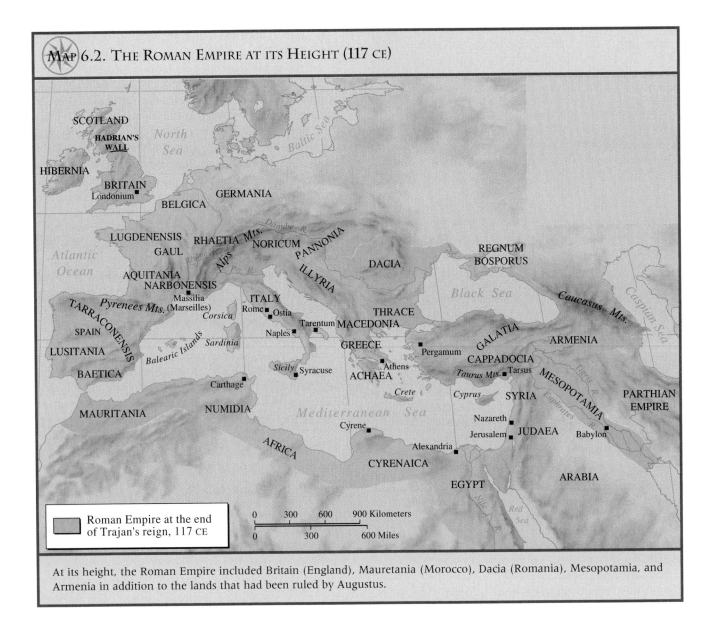

At its height, the Roman Empire included Britain (England), Mauretania (Morocco), Dacia (Romania), Mesopotamia, and Armenia in addition to the lands that had been ruled by Augustus.

community whose political and economic interests conflicted with those of the society it protected.

Because the soldiers, now half-barbarian themselves, continued to create emperors, the implications of this change were potentially disastrous. Severus was an African whose family members had long been senators and were thoroughly Romanized. His wife, Julia Domna, was a gifted administrator and a patron of Greek and Latin intellectuals who worked tirelessly for cultural unity. The emperors who followed were of a different sort. The tyrannical son of Severus and Julia, Caracalla, was followed by men whose only common characteristic was that they enjoyed the support of a faction within the army. Most were poorly educated provincials who seemed like foreigners to a majority of their subjects. A few were eccentrics or even children, and their average tenure in office was short. All, however, tried to follow

the deathbed advice of Severus: "Stay on good terms, enrich the soldiers, and don't take much notice of anything else." He had been nothing if not a realist.

Continued Economic and Demographic Decline. As the third century progressed, "enriching the soldiers" grew more difficult. Both the economy and the population continued to decline. The rate of conception slowed, in part because people believed that they could no longer afford to raise families. Furthermore, malnutrition and disease contributed to the population loss. The first great epidemic struck in the reign of Marcus Aurelius (161–180 CE). It was followed by others whose exact nature is unknown.

Defense costs could not be reduced. The middle years of the third century saw a renewal of the Persian Wars and the invasion of the Goths, a Germanic people

TABLE 6.2 THE POPULATION OF THE ROMAN EMPIRE (1–600 CE)

These estimates of the population of the Roman Empire are necessarily imprecise, but they show dramatic population declines in every region of the empire after about 200 CE. The Balkan figures include Illyria, Pannonia, Dacia, Macedonia, and Thrace. The dramatic decline around 400 CE marks the loss of Dacia in Eastern Europe. Note that, even at its peak, the population of the empire remained small relative to the size of the army it was forced to maintain. In 200 CE, the army and its auxiliaries (reserves) numbered about 400,000 men (0.9 percent of the population). It may have been twice that in Diocletian's day (2 percent). Armies of that size were not seen again in the West until the beginning of the nineteenth century, and even today, the armed forces of the United States number only about 0.48 percent of its far wealthier population.

Question: What were the major causes of population decline in the empire after the year 200?

REGION	Population in Millions			
	1 CE	200 CE	400 CE	600 CE
Africa	3.75	4.0	3.5	2.75
Asia Minor	6.0	7.0	6.0	5.0
Balkans	2.8	3.25	1.75	1.25
Britain	*	1.75	*	*
Egypt	4.75	4.75	4.0	3.25
Gaul	5.75	7.5	5.75	4.75
Greece	2.0	2.0	1.5	0.8
Italy	7.0	7.0	5.0	3.5
Spain	4.5	5.0	4.5	3.5
Syria and Palestine	2.25	2.25	1.75	1.5
Total	38.8	44.5	33.75	26.3

*Britain was not part of the empire during these years.

Source: Figures derived from McEvedy, C., and Jones, R., *Atlas of World Population History* (Harmondsworth: Penguin Books, 1978).

---

who forced the Romans to abandon their provinces north of the Danube (the area now known as Romania) and threatened the interior as well. Imperial politics alone demanded enormous expenditures as regional commanders struggled against one another for the throne. Of the twenty-six emperors who ruled between 235 and 283, only one died of natural causes. All had to bribe the legions for their support; some even bribed the enemy. They also spent large sums to buy peace from both the Sassanids and the Goths, but such efforts predictably failed.

Emperors beginning with Caracalla tried to deal with these problems by reducing the precious metal content of their coinage, a practice that did little more than add inflation to the empire's list of economic woes. Taxation and forced requisitions had long since reached the limits of productivity. Decurions and tenant farmers, impoverished by an insatiable bureaucracy, abandoned their properties in favor of begging, banditry, and piracy. The emperors, distracted by war and by the requirements of personal survival, could do little about it. Whole regions fell under the control of men who were, in effect, warlords. In the east, Zenobia, queen of the caravan city of Palmyra, managed briefly to gain control of Syria, Egypt, and much of Asia Minor.

Diocletian Decentralizes the Empire. The emperors Claudius II Gothicus and Aurelian brought the military situation under control between 268 and 275. However, major reforms were necessary. **Diocletian,** who came to the throne in 284, embarked on a reorganization of the entire empire. To enlarge the army without increasing its potential for anarchy, he divided the empire into two halves, each ruled by an **augustus.** Each augustus then adopted a **caesar** to serve as his subordinate and successor. Because each caesar had primary responsibility for a region of his own, Diocletian in effect created four emperors. He named his colleague Maximian as augustus for the west, with Constantius serving as caesar in Gaul and Britain. Diocletian took the east for himself, in recognition of its greater wealth and importance, and established his headquarters at Nicomedia in Asia Minor. His trusted lieutenant Galerius became caesar with special responsibility for Syria and Egypt.

Decentralization worked well as long as the authority of Diocletian remained intact. He was probably right in assuming that no one man could effectively govern so vast and beleaguered an empire. If Maximian and the two caesars remained loyal, they could respond more quickly to crises without losing control of an army that numbered more than 650,000 men. To ensure even quicker response, the army was divided into permanent garrisons and mobile expeditionary forces. The latter, reinforced with heavily armored cavalry (*cataphracti*) on an unprecedented scale, were capable of moving rapidly to threatened sectors of the frontier.

To separate military from civilian authority, Diocletian assigned each augustus and caesar a **praetorian prefect** with broad judicial and administrative powers. He then

The Reign of Diocletian (284–305)

Diocletian's scheme for dividing the empire did not long survive him. His persecution of Christians, although fierce, proved futile, but his reform of provincial administration became the institutional basis of the eastern, or Byzantine, empire for centuries to come. By all accounts a powerful, if unpleasant, personality, he made a strong impression on his age.

Portrait Bust of Diocletian. This head, found at the emperor's capital city of Nicomedia, just east of Byzantium in what is now Asiatic Turkey, avoids the abstraction of other imperial statues of the day. It is probably a recognizable likeness.

The Tetrarchs, St. Mark's Venice. The sculpture shows Diocletian and his colleagues as an inseparable unit for purposes of propaganda. In reality they were frequently at odds.

subdivided the existing provinces, increased the civil powers of their governors, and grouped the new, smaller units into **dioceses** supervised by imperial **vicars.** The vicars reported to the praetorian prefects.

Economic Reforms of Diocletian. The new administrative system would be the model for the later empire—and for the Christian church when it eventually achieved official status. Diocletian used it primarily to implement economic reforms. To him, and to his successors, only a command economy in which the government regulated nearly every aspect of economic life could provide the resources needed to maintain both the army and a newly expanded bureaucracy. All pretense of a free market was abandoned. Diocletian attempted to solve the labor shortage by forbidding workers to leave their trades and by binding tenants to the great estates for life. In later years, these provisions be-

TABLE 6.3 DIOCLETIAN'S EDICT OF MAXIMUM PRICES (301)

Among his reforms, the emperor Diocletian made an important effort to control high prices and stabilize the currency. Limiting the maximum permissible wage in many jobs and the maximum prices of commodities and transportation, his edict provides a vivid picture of economic life in the late empire. But like most such attempts to regulate the economy, his edict proved unenforceable. Even vigorous applications of the death penalty failed to prevent the development of a thriving black market.

Diocletian therefore failed to stabilize the currency, but by reforming the collection of revenues and ending Italy's exemption from taxation, he placed the government on a sound financial basis for the first time.

Transactions of the American Philological Association, 71 (1940), 157.

Question: Why did this edict fail to stabilize wages and prices even though violations were punishable by death?

COMMODITY WEIGHING ONE *MODIUS* (C. 2 GALLONS)	COST IN *DENARII*
Millet	50
Rye	60
Beans	60
Wheat	100
Rice	200
Salt	100

COMMODITY WEIGHING ONE *SEXTARIUS* (C. 16 OUNCES)	COST IN *DENARII*
Wine	30
Ordinary wine	8
Beer	4
Egyptian beer	2
Honey	40
Olive oil	40
12 oz. pork	12
10 sparrows	16
12 oz. fish	24
2 chickens	60
100 oysters	100
1 pheasant	250

LABOR	DAILY WAGE IN *DENARII*
Shepherd	20
Farm laborer	25
Camel driver	25
Sewer cleaner	25
Carpenter	50
Baker	50
Shipwright	60
Painter	75

SKILLED LABOR TASK	WAGE IN *DENARII*
Scribe, per 100 lines	25
Notary, per document	10
Tailor, cutting one cloak	60
Tailor, breeches	20
Lawyer, simple case	1,000

TEACHERS	MONTHLY WAGE PER PUPIL IN *DENARII*
Elementary	50
Arithmetic	75
Greek language	200
Rhetoric	250

came hereditary, but they did nothing to retard economic stagnation. In the long run, restricting the free movement of labor probably made matters worse, as did continued tax increases and a new, more efficient system of forced requisitions that he introduced early in his reign. The army could now seize food and equipment directly from the farmers in a systematic way.

The long-term effect of these changes was obscured by peace, which enabled the economy to recover some-what in spite of them, but Diocletian's effort to control inflation failed quickly and visibly (see Table 6.3). He restored the metal content of silver and gold coins, devalued under his predecessors, but could not issue enough of them to meet demand. Silver-washed copper coins known as *nummi* remained the most common money in circulation and depreciated even faster in relation to the new coinage. Prices continued to rise. In 301, Diocletian responded by placing a ceiling on wages

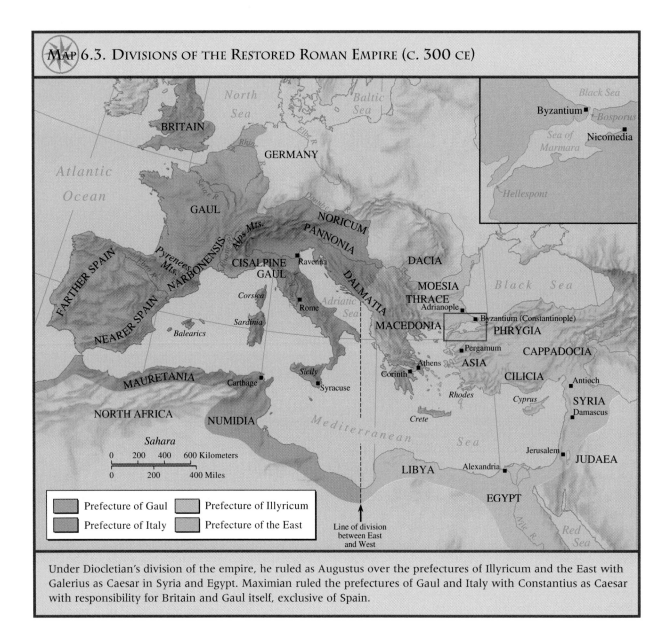

MAP 6.3. DIVISIONS OF THE RESTORED ROMAN EMPIRE (C. 300 CE)

Under Diocletian's division of the empire, he ruled as Augustus over the prefectures of Illyricum and the East with Galerius as Caesar in Syria and Egypt. Maximian ruled the prefectures of Gaul and Italy with Constantius as Caesar with responsibility for Britain and Gaul itself, exclusive of Spain.

and prices. Like all such measures, the edict proved impossible to enforce. Riots and black marketeering greeted its introduction in the more commercial east, and the agricultural west seems to have ignored it altogether. He abandoned the program after a year.

Whatever their shortcomings, the reforms of Diocletian were perhaps the best answer that administrative genius alone could apply to the problems of the later empire. Little else could have been done within the constraints imposed by Rome's defensive needs. To preserve his achievements, Diocletian abdicated in 305 and retired to the magnificent fortified palace he constructed on the shores of the Adriatic. Although many of his reforms endured, all plans for an orderly succession collapsed long before he died in 313.

The Age of Constantine (312–337 CE)

Even if had Diocletian's colleagues been fully willing to accept his settlement, their sons were not. Maximian, the western augustus, abdicated in favor of his caesar, Constantius, but when the latter died in 306, his son **Constantine** (Con'-stun-teen, c. 280–337) was proclaimed augustus by the troops, and Maximian's son, Maxentius, rebelled against him. In 312, Constantine defeated Maxentius at the battle of the Milvian Bridge and became undisputed augustus of the west. In the east, Licinius (Li-sin'-ee-us), who governed the dioceses on the Danube frontier, eventually succeeded Galerius and made an uneasy alliance with Constantine that ended, after much maneuvering, with the defeat

FIGURE 6.5 *The Emperor Constantine.* This monumental head, more than 8 feet tall, came originally from a much larger statue that adorned the Basilica of Maxentius and Constantine in Rome. It now stands, together with a hand and other surviving parts, in Rome's Palazzo dei Conservatori. It showed the emperor seated on his throne and was meant to convey a godlike impression. Constantine had many such heads made to official specifications and dispatched throughout the empire as propaganda.

and execution of Licinius in 324. Constantine, known thereafter as "the Great," had reunited the empire under his personal rule.

Adoption of Eastern Court Rituals. Constantine, like Diocletian and the rest of his imperial colleagues, came from the provinces along the lower Danube and had only an approximate acquaintance with traditional Roman culture. In administrative matters, he continued the policies of his predecessor and surpassed him in ritualizing the imperial office. All traces of republican values were abandoned. Under Constantine, the emperor became a godlike figure surrounded by eastern rituals who spoke to all but the most privileged of his subjects from behind a screen.

Transfer of the Capital from Rome to Byzantium. Eastern ritual was appropriate because the empire's center of gravity had long since shifted to the east. The constant military pressure exerted by the Germans had drained the west of much of its wealth. What little remained tended to flow eastward, as westerners continued to purchase craft and luxury items from the more advanced cities of Syria and southwest Asia. More than ever, the west had become a land of vast, self-sufficient estates, worked by tenants and isolated from the shrinking towns whose chief remaining function was to house a bloated imperial administration. Constantine, who had spent most of his adult life in the west, knew this all too well. That was why, in 324, he established a new capital at Byzantium on the shores of the Bosporus. Rome, the city, had declined in importance. Most of the emperors since Marcus Aurelius had passed their reigns closer to the military

frontiers, and some had never visited the ancient capital. Constantine's move was therefore an acknowledgment of existing realities. Byzantium, renamed Constantinople in honor of himself, was at the strategic and economic center of the empire. Rome, although still a great city, was becoming a museum.

Constantine Accepts Christianity. Moving the imperial capital from Rome to Constantinople hastened the decline of the west, but it was only one of several steps taken by Constantine that revealed the shape of the future. The most important was his personal acceptance of the Christian religion. His reasons for doing so are not entirely clear. Constantine's mother, Helen, was a Christian, but he grew up a virtual hostage at the pagan court of Diocletian. It was not until the battle of the Milvian Bridge in 312 that he had his troops paint Christian symbols on their shields. Afterward, he claimed that a flaming cross in the sky had led them to victory. Constantine's grasp of Christian principles remained weak to the end, and he may have converted simply because he thought that the magic of the Christians was stronger. An element of political calculation probably also entered into his decision.

In the course of the third century, the Christians had become a political force in the eastern half of the empire. No longer a church of the weak and helpless, it included people of great influence in Diocletian's administration, some of whom were thought capable of fraud and violence. In 303, Diocletian became convinced that they were plotting against him and launched the last and most savage of the persecutions. He was encouraged in this by Galerius, whose tenure in the east had convinced him that the Christians were a menace to imperial government as a whole. When Diocletian abdicated, Galerius continued to pursue anti-Christian policies until his own death in 311 and bequeathed them to his successor, Maximin Daia (Die'-ya). Constantine perhaps adopted Christianity because he and his then-ally Licinius needed Christian support in their successful struggle with Maximin Daia. However, no direct evidence of this is available, and little reason exists to suppose that Christian support affected the final outcome of these imperial struggles.

Christianity Becomes an Accepted Religion. In any case, Constantine's adoption of Christianity changed the basic character of the church. Although paganism continued to be tolerated, Christianity now had many of the characteristics of an official religion. Christians abandoned homes and catacombs as centers of worship in favor of the basilica, an oblong structure of the sort used for Roman public assemblies. Imperial money funded the new construction and paid the clergy. Membership in the Christian church became both a mark of status and a necessity

FIGURE 6.6 *The Basilica of San Apollinare in Classe, Ravenna, Italy.* The church of San Apollinare in Classe is an excellent example of an early Christian basilica. The *nave,* or central aisle, of the church is supported by arches and topped by a simple pitched roof supported by crossbeams. Clerestory windows above the side aisles let in the light. The apse behind the altar at the east end of the church is built in a half dome. The Romans used this form of construction for all sorts of judicial, commercial, and governmental buildings. Italian churches were built in this way until late in the Middle Ages.

for those who wished to reach the highest levels of the imperial service.

Christian Legal Reforms. Converts poured in, and Christian principles became the basis for a mass of legislation. Even before his final victory in 324, Constantine moved to limit the brutality of official punishments and to expand poor relief. Crucifixion was banned. To provide poor women with an alternative to infanticide, the most common and effective method of birth control in ancient times, the government made arrangements for the care of foundlings. Most measures were benign, but new and savage penalties for adultery, prostitution, and premarital sex reflected the sterner side of Christian morality.

Theological Controversy. Constantine may not have understood the intricacies of Christian theology; however, as a practical ruler he knew that doctrinal disputes could lead to political disorder. He sought from the beginning of his reign to end the heresies that disturbed the church. The most important of these involved the doctrine of the Trinity. By 260, a majority of Christians believed that there was one God, but that God had three persons—the Father, the Son (Christ), and the Holy Spirit. In the reign of Constantine, an Alexandrian priest named Arius advanced the view that Christ was a created being, neither fully God nor fully man. Some time later, another Alexandrian advanced the **Monophysite** idea that Christ possessed only one divine nature "of the Word incarnate." Both views called the nature of Christ's sacrifice into question, for, if he were not both fully man and fully God, how could his suffering on the cross have atoned for the sins of humankind?

The Council of Nicaea (325). The popular interest aroused by these arguments is hard to imagine today, but Trinitarian disputes became a fruitful source of riots and other violence in the cities of the empire. **Arianism,** as the views of Arius were called, spread widely among the Germanic Vandals, Goths, and Lombards by Arian missionaries. The Monophysites achieved wide acceptance in the towns of Syria, Palestine, and Egypt. The controversies may therefore have masked political and regional grievances that owed little to religion. In any case, Constantine was forced to call the first ecumenical (universal) meeting of the bishops. In 325, the **Council of Nicaea** (Nye-see'-a) decreed that Christ was both fully man and fully God. This formula was defined even more carefully by the Council of Constantinople in 381 and again by the Council of Chalcedon (Kal-see'-don) in 451 (see Document 6.3). It eventually became the orthodox position in both the eastern and the western churches, but Arian, Monophysite, and other views remained popular in some regions for years to come.

THE FINAL DIVISION OF THE EMPIRE AND THE DECLINE OF THE WEST (337–476 CE)

In retrospect, the reign of Constantine seemed to many a golden age. People saw the reunification of the empire, the establishment of a new capital, and the acceptance of Christianity as extraordinary achievements whose luster was enhanced by the godlike ritual that surrounded the emperor and by the overall competence of his administration. Yet for all his apparent brilliance, Constantine failed to solve the basic problems that were tearing apart the empire. He did nothing to limit the political influence of the army or to develop an orderly process of imperial succession. Although he was lucky enough to escape a major crisis along his northern and western borders, the underlying military and economic weakness of the west remained. By shifting the center of government from west to east, he may have accelerated the west's decline.

Constantine's death in 337 was followed by a bitter struggle between his sons that ended with the victory of the Arian Constantius II (d. 361). Constantius's successor, Julian, known as the Apostate, rejected Christianity altogether. His effort to restore paganism died with him in 363 on a remote Mesopotamian battlefield. Imperial unity died as well. To western Germans such as the Franks and Alemanni, Julian's ill-fated attempt to destroy the Sassanid Empire in the east provided them with an opportunity for renewed attacks along the Rhine and upper Danube. Realizing that the German threat would require all of his attention, the new emperor, Valentinian (reigned 364–375), established himself at Milan in northern Italy and left the eastern half of the empire to his brother Valens (Vay'-lens, reigned 364–378). The brothers maintained separate courts and administrations—the one Latin-speaking, the other Greek. The division between east and west, which had slowed at least outwardly under Constantine, accelerated.

Valentinian neutralized the Germans on the Rhine. Upon his death in 375, he left the western half of the empire to his son, Gratian (Gray'-she-an). The next year a more serious crisis developed in the Balkans. The Huns, an Asiatic people of uncertain origin, conquered the Ostrogothic kingdom north of the Black Sea and pressed westward against the Visigoths who inhabited the lower Danube. The Visigoths asked and received permission to seek refuge within the empire. They repaid Valen's generosity by looting the Balkan provinces. The emperor was forced to break off yet another war with the Persians to confront them. The result was disaster. In 378, the Visigothic cavalry destroyed Valens and his army at Adrianople (now Edirne in European Turkey), a strategic site that controls the land approaches to Constantinople. Gratian, as the surviving augustus, appointed the Spanish general **Theodosius** (Thee-a-doh'-shee-us) to succeed his uncle as emperor in the east.

Theodosius (347–395) Makes Christianity the Official Religion. Theodosius was in many respects a remarkable character. He restored order in the Balkans by allowing the Visigoths to set up an independent, although allied, Germanic state on imperial soil. Believing that the battle of Adrianople had demonstrated the superiority of cavalry, he reduced the role of the legions and made heavily armored cataphracti the dominant element in a reorganized Roman army. It was a major step in the development of medieval warfare, but the importance of cavalry had been growing steadily since the military reforms of Diocletian.

His religious policies were equally important. Theodosius made Christianity the official religion of the empire and actively suppressed not only paganism but also Arianism. Paganism remained more firmly entrenched in the west than in the east, especially among the educated upper classes. When Gratian's successor,

---

DOCUMENT 6.3

THE COUNCIL OF CHALCEDON DEFINES THE NATURE OF CHRIST

The nature of Christ was the most important issue in early debates over the Trinity. The official view in both eastern and western churches was that He was fully human and fully divine, in part because only then would His suffering on the cross be capable of saving people's souls. In 451, the Council of Chalcedon confirmed the dual nature of Christ as both God and human in opposition to the Monophysites, who argued that Christ possessed a single nature. Using precise and legalistic language, the definition leaves no room for Arian, Monophysite, or other interpretations.

Following the holy fathers we teach with one voice that the Son [of God] and our Lord Jesus Christ is to be confessed as one and the same [Person], that he is perfect in manhood, very God and very man, of a reasonable soul and [human] body consisting consubstantial with the Father as touching his Godhead, and with us as touching his manhood; made in all things like unto us, sin only excepted; begotten of his Father before the world's beginning according to his Godhead; but in these last days for us men and for our salvation born of the Virgin Mary, the Mother of God according to his manhood. This one and the same Jesus Christ, the only begotten Son [of God] must be confessed to be in two natures, unconfusedly, immutably, indivisibly, inseparably, and that without the distinction of natures being taken away by such union, but rather the peculiar property of each nature being preserved and being united in one Person and subsistence, not separated or divided into two persons, but one and the same Son and only-begotten, God the Word, our Lord Jesus Christ.

From Chalcedon, in P. Schaff and H. Wace, eds., *A Select Library of Nicene and Post-Nicene Fathers of the Christian Church*, vol. 14, 2nd series (New York: William B. Eerdmans Publishing Company, 1899–1900).

Question: Why was defining the nature of the Trinity important to early Christians?

Valentinian II, died in 392, Theodosius became sole emperor after suppressing a revolt in the west that had been inspired at least partially by paganism. Nicaean Christianity was imposed upon the west, and for 2 brief years the empire was once again united.

The Final Division of the Empire. The final division came in 395, when the dying Theodosius left the empire to his two sons. The eastern half went on as before, an empire in its own right which, although using the Greek language, continued to evolve according to Roman legal and administrative precedents. The west,

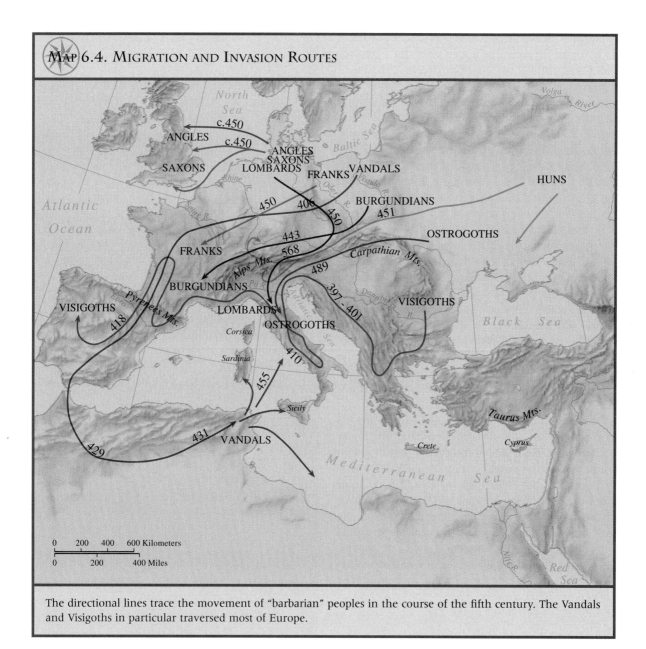

MAP 6.4. MIGRATION AND INVASION ROUTES

The directional lines trace the movement of "barbarian" peoples in the course of the fifth century. The Vandals and Visigoths in particular traversed most of Europe.

as a political entity, ceased to exist within three generations. Long before the reign of Theodosius it had begun to exhibit the economic, political, and religious decentralization that is thought of today as medieval. As trade and the circulation of money decreased, the great estates grew larger and more self-sufficient. Their powerful owners, anxious to protect their workforce, prevented their tenants from joining the army. This, together with a slow but persistent decline in population, forced the emperors to recruit barbarians by offering them land within the empire. Barbarian chiefs or commanders sometimes acquired great estates as a reward for their services, and by the end of the fourth century,

the line between Roman and barbarian had become blurred, especially in Gaul.

Few of these men understood or accepted Roman ideas of law and culture. The persistence of old tribal or personal allegiances, in addition to conflict between Romans and barbarians, led to internal violence that the imperial government could rarely control. Faced with increasing disorder in the countryside, the landed estates developed small armies of their own, while peasants—both Roman and barbarian—were forced to seek protection by becoming their tenants. Those whose situation was truly desperate were accepted only under the harshest of terms and became little more than serfs.

The Fall of the Empire in the West: Two Contrasting Views

For those deeply attached to the traditions of ancient Rome, the collapse of the western empire in the fifth century was an unmitigated tragedy. For those long burdened by its taxes, its official corruption, and its stagnant economy, barbarian rule may have come as a relief.

St. Jerome on Barbarian Conquest of the Roman Empire's Cities

St. Jerome (c. 347–420) is best known as the translator of the Bible into Latin. He was also deeply attached to Roman culture. This fragment from his letters is dramatic evidence of his dismay at the condition of the empire as well as of his skill as a rhetorician.

Nations innumerable and most savage have invaded all Gaul. The whole region between the Alps and the Pyrenees, the Ocean and the Rhine, has been devastated by the Quadi, the Vandals, the Sarmati, the Alani, the Gepidae, the hostile Heruli, the Saxons, the Burgundians, the Alemanni, and the Pannonians. O wretched Empire. Mayence, formerly so noble a city, has been taken and ruined, and in the church many thousands of men have been massacred. [The city of] Worms has been destroyed after a long siege. Rheims, that powerful city, Amiens, Arras, Speyer, Strasbourg—all have seen their citizens led away captive into Germany. Aquitaine and the provinces of Lyon and Narbonne, all save a few towns, have been depopulated; and these the sword threatens from without, while hunger ravages within. I cannot speak without tears of Toulouse, which the merits of the holy Bishop Exuperius have prevailed so far to preserve from destruction. Spain, even, is in daily terror lest it perish, remembering the invasion of the Cimbri; and whatsoever the other provinces have suffered once, they continue to suffer in their fear.

I will keep silence concerning the rest, lest I seem to despair of the mercy of God. For a long time, from the Black Sea to the Julian Alps, those things which are ours have not been ours; and for thirty years, since the Danube boundary was broken, war has been waged in the very midst of the Roman Empire. Our tears are dried by old age. Except for a few old men, all were born in captivity and siege, and do not desire the liberty they never knew. Who could believe this? How could the whole tale be worthily told?

From Robinson, James Harvey, ed, *Readings in European History*, vol. 1 (Boston: Ginn, 1904).

Salvianus on Roman Acceptance of Barbarian Rule

Salvianus ("Salvian the Presbyter" c. 400–480) saw the fall of Rome as God's judgment on those who had oppressed the poor. His view is a valuable correction to that of St. Jerome and explains clearly why most Romans accepted barbarian rule without serious protest.

But what else can these wretched people wish for, they who suffer the incessant and even continuous destruction of public tax levies. To them there is always imminent a heavy and relentless proscription. They desert their homes, lest they be tortured in their very homes. They seek exile, lest they suffer torture. The enemy is more lenient to them than the tax collectors. This is proved by this very fact, that they flee to the enemy in order to avoid the full force of the heavy tax levy. This very tax levying, although hard and inhuman, would nevertheless be less heavy and harsh if all would bear it equally and in common. Taxation is made more shameful and burdensome because all do not bear the burden of all. They extort tribute from the poor man for the taxes of the rich, and the weaker carry the load for the stronger. There is no other reason that they cannot bear all the taxation except that the burden imposed on the wretched is greater than their resources.

From *The Writing of Salvian the Presbyter*, trans. J. F. O'Sullivan (Washington, DC: Catholic University of America Press, 1947).

Question: What accounts for the differing views of these two churchmen?

Even the church did little to promote unity. It remained essentially an urban institution. The term *pagani*, or *pagans*, was originally Latin slang for rustics, and Christianity had long found penetrating the rural world difficult. That world was dominated by the estate owners, some of whom still embraced the values of ancient Rome. Others, especially those of German origin, were Christian but remained Arians until well into the seventh century.

The church was more powerful in the western towns. It maintained a degree of independence that contrasted sharply with attitudes prevalent in the east. There, the imperial office retained some of the religious character it had inherited from paganism. The emperor normally appointed the eastern bishops and sometimes tried to influence dogma, especially when Monophysite or other theologies created a political problem. Western bishops, meanwhile, were elected, sometimes by public acclamation. They often controlled their city governments and had begun to formulate the idea of separation between church and state. **St. Ambrose** (c. 339–397), as bishop of Milan, once imposed a public penance on Theodosius for ordering the massacre of rebels and told him on another occasion, "Do not burden your conscience with the thought that you have any right as Emperor over sacred things."

The Fall of the Western Empire.

A society so burdened by poverty and fragmented by decentralization could not defend itself against the renewed onslaughts of the barbarians. In 402, the emperor Honorius moved the capital from Rome to Ravenna, a more defensible city on the Adriatic coast. Between 406 and 429, the Germanic people known as the Vandals moved through Gaul and Spain to establish themselves in Africa. In 410, an army of Visigoths sacked Rome. Attila the Hun invaded Italy between 451 and his death in 453. In 455, Rome was sacked again, this time by Vandals. The emperors had long been forced to rely on barbarian armies for protection. As the barbarians soon realized, the emperor had become largely irrelevant.

The wars of the fifth century were in fact struggles between various barbarian armies for control over the remains of the western empire. In 475, Orestes, the overall commander of imperial troops in the west, deposed the existing emperor and placed his own young son, Romulus Augustulus, on the throne. **Odoacer** (O-doh-ah'-ser, c. 433–493), one of Orestes's officers, became incensed when Orestes denied his tribesmen the land he had promised them as a reward for service. In August 476, he led a mutiny that ended in the execution of Orestes and the deposition of Romulus Augustulus, the last emperor of the west. Zeno, the emperor at Constantinople, recognized the change by making Odoacer his patrician, although Odoacer preferred to style himself king. This event is known conventionally as "the fall of Rome," but the western empire had long since ceased to exist. Vandals ruled Africa; Visigoths governed Spain; and Gaul was now divided into a variety of jurisdictions ruled by Franks, Burgundians, and other tribes. Italy was given over to the Ostrogoths, but their rule was not destined to last.

The Survival of the Eastern Empire.

Sixty years later, in a final effort to reunite the empire, the eastern emperor **Justinian** "the Great" (reigned 527–565) conquered North Africa from the Vandals and mounted a campaign for the recovery of Italy under the command of Belisarius, the greatest general of the age. Assisted by his wife, **Theodora** (c. 497–548), a former actress and prostitute who was his equal in political skill and his superior in courage, Justinian sought to rebuild the empire of Constantine. He accomplished much, including the building of the great church of St. Sophia at Constantinople and the long overdue codification of Roman law, but his attempts at reunification failed. He was the first of the **Byzantine** emperors, a term devised by historians to distinguish the empire centered on Constantinople from its western counterpart.

In 552, after 17 years of warfare, an army under Justinian's eunuch general Narses defeated the Ostrogoths. The resources of the peninsula were by now depleted. Byzantine war taxes, together with forced requisitions and looting by both sides, destroyed the basis of subsistence, while terrible plagues, spread by the passage of armies, killed tens of thousands who

FIGURE 6.7 *Mosaic of Justinian and Attendants.* In this mosaic from the Church of San Vitale in Ravenna, Italy, the emperor is shown with his soldiers on the left and a priest, or perhaps a bishop, on the right. Note the halo that surrounds his crown and indicates the semidivine nature of his office. The mosaic is one of a pair. The other shows Justinian's wife, the Empress Theodora, with her own entourage.

had survived the war. Some parts of Italy shrunk to a mere seventh of their former population.

Devastated by war and by years of economic decline, the country became easy prey for yet another wave of Germanic invaders, the Lombards. These fierce people quickly seized most of northern Italy. Unlike the Ostrogoths, they preferred to kill the remaining Roman landholders and confiscate their estates. The successors of Justinian, impoverished by his ambitious policies, could do little to stop them. By the end of the seventh century, Byzantine control was limited to the coastal regions along the Adriatic. The *exarch,* or military governor, who ruled this territory did so from Ravenna, a city built on a sandbar and protected from the armies of the mainland by a broad lagoon.

THE EVOLUTION OF THE WESTERN CHURCH (306–529 CE)

In the midst of political turmoil, the church in the west continued to expand. As **St. Augustine** (354–430) pointed out in his book **The City of God,** no essential connection existed between the kingdom of Heaven and any earthly power. Moreover, Christians should leave politics alone if they valued their souls. Augustine was bishop of Hippo, near Carthage, and his view grew naturally from the suspicion of political authority that had been characteristic of the African church. He was also the friend and convert of St. Ambrose. *The City of God,* completed in 426, was written in response to the first sack of Rome. In it, Augustine argued that "two cities have been formed by two loves: the earthly by love of self, even to the contempt of God; the heavenly by the love of God, even to the contempt of self." The earthly city must inevitably pass away as the city of God grows. In practical terms, this implied that the authority of the church must eventually supersede that of the state, although ideally church and state should cooperate for the greater protection of the faithful.

The Issue of Papal Authority. Augustine's work lies at the root of medieval political thought and reflects the growing gap between western and eastern concepts of the church's role. That gap widened further as the papacy evolved. The church recognized five patriarchs—bishops whose authority exceeded that of the others. They ruled the dioceses (ecclesiastical districts) of Rome, Constantinople, Alexandria, Jerusalem, and Antioch. Of these, the bishop of Rome was most venerated, although veneration did not necessarily imply obedience. The erosion of political authority in the west and the removal of the capital to Constantinople caused the popes, notably Innocent I (served 402–417) and Leo I

DOCUMENT 6.4

POPE LEO I DEFINES THE PETRINE THEORY

Pope Leo I ("the Great") delivered one of the clearest expositions of the Petrine theory. As bishop of Rome and successor to St. Peter, Leo I claimed universal authority over the Christian church because in Matthew 16:18 Jesus had said: "Thou art Peter, and upon this rock I will build my church; and the gates of hell shall not prevail against it."

Our Lord Jesus Christ, the Saviour of the world, caused his truth to be promulgated through the apostles. And while this duty was placed on all of the apostles, the Lord made St. Peter the head of them all, that from him as from their head his gifts should flow out into all the body. So that if anyone separates himself from St. Peter he should know that he has no share in the Divine blessing. . . . Constantinople has its own glory and by the mercy of God has become the seat of the empire. But secular matters are based on one thing, ecclesiastical matters on another. For nothing will stand which is not built on the rock [Peter] which the Lord laid in the foundation [Matt. 16:18]. . . . Your city is royal, but you cannot make it apostolic.

From Thatcher, O. J., and McNeal, E. H., eds., *A Source Book of Medieval History* (New York: Scribner's, 1905).

Question: Which of the Latin Church's institutional claims does the Petrine theory support?

(served 440–461), to claim universal jurisdiction over the church and to base their claims more firmly on the Petrine theory (see Document 6.4). The title "pope" is derived from the Latin (and Italian) word *papa,* meaning "father." The eastern church contested these claims, and the Council of Chalcedon (451) greatly annoyed Leo by granting the patriarch of Constantinople primacy in the east, but papal claims rested to some extent on political reality. Throughout the dark years of the fifth century, the popes often provided leadership when the imperial office failed.

Augustine (354–430). Intellectually, too, the western church continued to flourish. In addition to *The City of God,* Augustine elaborated on Paul's concept of sin and grace in a way that was to have a long-lasting impact on Western thought. He was moved to write on this subject by the teachings of Pelagius, a Briton who believed in unlimited free will. Pelagius argued that a Christian could achieve salvation simply by choosing to live a godly life. Augustine, whose early struggles with sin are chronicled in his **Confessions,** claimed that human nature was so corrupted by its fall in the Garden

SELECTIONS FROM THE RULE OF ST. BENEDICT

St. Benedict Hands over the Rule of the New Order to the Monks of Monte Cassino, Turino Vanni (fl. 1390–1415).

All religious orders follow a rule, or set of regulations handed down by their founder. The Rule of St. Benedict orders the lives of Benedictine monks, the largest cloistered order in the West, and is the basis of many other rules as well. The following sections capture St. Benedict's view that monks should live a disciplined life dedicated to apostolic poverty. The Romans reckoned the hours of the day as beginning at dawn, not midnight. Hence nones, or the devotions held at the ninth hour of the day, customarily took place at about 3:00 PM.

Chapter 33—The sin of owning private property should be entirely eradicated from the monastery. No one shall presume to give or receive anything except by order of the abbot; no one shall pos-

sess anything of his own, books, paper, pens, or anything else, for monks are not to own even their own bodies and wills to be used at their own desire, but are to look to the father of the monastery for everything.

Chapter 48—Idleness is the great enemy of the soul, therefore monks should always be occupied, either in manual labor or in holy reading. The hours for these occupations should be arranged according to the seasons, as follows: From Easter to the first of October, the monks shall go to work at the first hour and labor until the fourth hour, and the time from the fourth to the sixth hour shall be spent in reading. After dinner, which comes at the sixth hour, they shall lie down and rest in silence; but anyone who wishes may read, if he does it so as not to disturb anyone else. Nones shall be observed a little earlier, about the middle of the eighth hour, and the monks shall go back to work, laboring until vespers. But if the conditions of the locality or the needs of the monastery, such as may occur at harvest time, should make it necessary to labor longer hours, they shall not feel themselves ill-used, for true monks should live by the labor of their own hands, as did the apostles and the holy fathers.

From *"Regula Monchorum,"* in O. J. Thatcher and E. H. McNeal, eds., *A Source Book of Medieval History* (New York: Scribner's, 1905).

Question: How does this segment of the rule support Benedict's concept of a sound mind in a sound body?

---

of Eden that salvation was impossible without God's grace and that grace is given selectively. God, in other words, **predestines** some to salvation and some to punishment. In 529, long after both men were dead, the Synod of Orange rejected Pelagianism but did not officially endorse the Augustinian view, which remained an undercurrent in medieval theology, only to surface again with renewed vigor in the Protestant Reformation of the sixteenth century. The rest of Augustine's

thought was less controversial. His concept of the church, its sacraments, and even his view of history were widely accepted in the Middle Ages and remain influential among Christians today.

Jerome (c. 347–420). Although not an original theologian, Augustine's older contemporary **St. Jerome** was an outstanding scholar and Latin stylist who supported Augustine in the Pelagian controversy and continued the history of the church begun by Eusebius. His most important contribution, however, was the Latin translation of the Bible known as **the Vulgate,** which remained the standard for Western Christendom until the sixteenth century.

The Beginnings of Monasticism (291–547). Perhaps the most striking feature of Christian life in the late Roman Empire was the spread of monasticism. Most of the world's great religions have produced, at one time or another, men and women who dedicate themselves to a life of religious devotion away from the distractions of the secular world. In Christianity, this impulse first surfaced when the church began to change from a persecuted congregation of believers to a universal faith. In 291, a young Egyptian named Anthony took to heart the words of Jesus: "If you will be perfect, go sell all thou hast and give to the poor, and come, follow me." He retired to a cave in the desert. When other hermits followed his example and settled in the vicinity, he provided them with a rule that stands as the foundation of **anchorite** (noncommunal) monasticism.

Within only a few years, another Egyptian, **Pachomius** (Pa-ko'-me-us, c. 290–346), realized that the isolated life of the hermit placed demands on the mind and body that only the strongest could survive. Ordinary mortals, however devout, need the support and discipline of a community that shares their goals. He therefore organized eleven formal congregations of hermits and gave them a rule that became the basis of all subsequent monastic institutions in the west. The monks were to live in common and divide their time between work and prayer. Like most early Christians, Pachomius assumed that poverty and chastity were essential to a life lived in imitation of Christ and that obedience was a natural part of communal living. Poverty, chastity, and obedience became the three basic vows taken by monks and by their female counterparts, the nuns.

During the age of Constantine, monasteries, some of them with congregations numbering in the thousands, sprang up throughout the Middle East. Women were as attracted to the movement as men. Athanasius (c. 293–373), bishop of Alexandria and energetic opponent of the Arians, spread the gospel of monasticism during his travels in the west, and by the end of the fourth century, the institution was solidly established in every part of Europe. Augustine practiced communal living as a matter of course, and Jerome established a convent of saintly women at Jerusalem.

The chaos of the fifth century may have enhanced the attractions of monastic life, but monasteries were not as isolated from the world as their inmates might have wished. Many, if not most, houses were established in rural areas whose populations were imperfectly Christianized. The Gospels demand that Christians attempt to convert their neighbors. Monks surrounded by pagans therefore had to attempt their conversion, and the monasteries became centers for the spreading of the faith. Each community, moreover, had to be supported economically. Peasants attached themselves to nearby convents and monasteries in much the same way that they became tenants of the great secular estates—and for many of the same reasons. The larger foundations became huge properties worked by *coloni* like their secular counterparts. Abbots and abbesses mastered the art of administration and exerted a substantial influence on regional politics. But monasticism made its greatest contributions in the intellectual realm. In a world of declining literacy, monasteries remained the chief purveyors of education and the heart of whatever intellectual life remained. Their libraries preserved the Latin classics for a later, more appreciative age.

The Benedictine Rule of Monastic Life. The heart of monastic life was the rule that governed the lives of monks or nuns. In the west, the rule of **St. Benedict of Nursia** (c. 480–547) was universally accepted for nearly six centuries and remains the basis of daily life in many religious orders today (see Document 6.5). Benedict was abbot of the great monastery at Monte Cassino, north of Naples. His rule, although not wholly original, was brief, moderate, and wise in its understanding of human nature. He based it on the ideal of *mens sana in corpore sano,* "a healthy mind in a healthy body." He stressed work, prayer, and study equally in an atmosphere governed by loving discipline. The Benedictine rule prescribes an ordered, pious life well suited to the development of one of medieval Europe's most powerful institutions.

Conclusion

The growing importance of monasticism was only one of the ways in which late Roman society began to foreshadow that of the Middle Ages. It was above all increasingly Christian, although the western church had long since begun to diverge in organization and practice from its eastern counterpart. It was also agrarian and generally poor. Although small freeholds continued to exist in Italy, Frankish Gaul, and elsewhere, much of the countryside was dominated by self-sufficient estates worked by tenants and defended by bands of armed retainers. An increasing number of these estates supported monasteries. For reasons that are as yet poorly understood, crop yields rarely rose above the subsistence level. Western cities, reduced to a fraction of their former size, were often little more than large agricultural villages whose inhabitants tilled their fields by day and retreated within the walls at night. Ruled in many cases by their bishops, they retained something of their Roman character, but lack of specie and the violence endemic in the countryside limited trade and communications. Contacts with the eastern empire, although never entirely abandoned, became rare. By the end of the fifth century, the Mediterranean unity forged by Rome had ceased to exist. A distinctively European society, formed of Roman, Celtic, and Germanic elements, was beginning to emerge.

Review Questions

- Why were the so-called mystery religions popular in the late Republic and early empire?
- What was Rome's policy toward the Jews?
- How was the early Christian church organized, and how did that organization change over time?
- Describe the reforms instituted by Diocletian.
- What was the role of monasticism in the later empire?

For Further Study

Readings

Ferrill, A., *The Fall of the Roman Empire: The Military Explanation* (London: Thames & Hudson, 1986). A military analysis.

Frend, W., *The Rise of Christianity* (Philadelphia: Fortress Press, 1984). A massive but useful study of Christian origins and the early church.

Hopkins, Keith, *A World Full of Gods: The Strange Triumph of Christianity* (New York: Free Press, 2000). Places Christianity in the context of contemporary Jewish and pagan religion.

MacMullen, Ramsay, *Constantine* (New York: Dial, 1969). Brief, readable, and full of insights.

Walbank, F. W., *The Awful Revolution. The Decline of the Roman Empire in the West* (Toronto: Toronto University Press, 1969). A concise analysis of the empire's decline.

InfoTrac College Edition

Visit the source collections at *http://infotrac.thomson learning.com* and use the search function with the following key terms.

Using Key Terms, enter the search terms:
Roman Empire   *Augustine*

Using the Subject Guide, enter the search term:
Early Christianity   *Roman Law*
Constantine

Web Sites

http://www.fordham.edu/halsall/ancient/asbook.html
The Internet Ancient History Sourcebook has two outstanding sections on this period. Look at *Late Antiquity* and *Christian Origins*.

http://www.pbs.org/wnet/heritage/index.html
The PBS Heritage series *Civilization and the Jews* offers an excellent Web site on all periods of Jewish history.

http://www.pbs.org/wgbh/pages/frontline/shows/religion
The PBS Frontline series *From Jesus to Christ: The First Christians* is also useful.

THE DECLINE OF THE ROMAN EMPIRE IN THE WEST

160	180	200	220	240	260	280	300	320	340	360	380	400	420	440	460	480

IMPERIAL POLITICS

S. Severus

Diocletian

Theodosius

Romulus Augustulus
Deposed 476–*

Marcus
Aurelius

Military Anarachy

Constantine

MAJOR BARBARIAN INCURSIONS (Lesser Raids Continuous)

Alaric Sacks Rome*

Vandals Sack Rome*

PARTHIAN/-PERSIAN WARS

*-256 Valens Captured

THE CHRISTIAN CHURCH

Persecutions

*-Conversion of
Constantine

*-Christianity Becomes
Religion of the Empire

*-Council of Nicaea

*-Council of
Chalcedon

Age of the Fathers
(Patristic Era-)

*-d. of Tertullian

*-d. of Jerome

*-d. of Augustine

Visit the Western Civilization Companion Web Site for resources specific to this textbook:
http://history.wadsworth.com/hause02/

The CD in the back of this book and the Western Civilization Resource Center at *http://history. wadsworth.com/western/* offer a variety of tools to help you succeed in this course, including access to quizzes; images; documents; interactive simulations, maps, and timelines; movie explorations; and a wealth of other sources.

The West in the World

THE ANCIENT EURASIAN CIVILIZATIONS

The Neolithic Revolution occurred simultaneously at many places in the world, and Egypt and Mesopotamia were not the only centers of ancient civilization. Advanced cultures developed in other river valleys. The Indus and its tributaries became the heart of an Indian civilization. Another distinctive culture developed in northern and central China. All four cultures emerged at approximately the same time and achieved similar levels of technological progress and social organization.

India

The Indus culture may have been related to that of ancient Sumer. By 3000 BCE or shortly thereafter, it had discovered the wheel and created systems of writing and mathematics. By 2500 BCE, the region had become fully urbanized. Scholars believe that some form of centralized government united the Indus cities, but because neither their language nor their system of writing has been deciphered, this remains uncertain. Art forms and the presence of elaborate bathing facilities reflect the concerns of later Indian cultures.

By 1800 BCE, the Indus civilization began to decline, perhaps because of an extended drought. At about the same time, an Indo-European people known conventionally as the **Aryans** began migrating into the area. They spoke and wrote **Sanskrit,** a language readable to moderns because it is related to those of Persia and western Europe. We know little about Aryan political institutions, but urban life revived and, after 1000 BCE, spread to the valley of the Ganges. The first written historical records and the **Vedas,** a body of texts that forms the basis of modern Hinduism, appeared during this period. The Vedic texts reflect a polytheistic faith based on rituals, most of which had to be performed by a priestly class known as the Brahmins. They also established the caste system that persists in India today. A reaction against the Vedas' religious formalism may have influenced the thinking of **Guatama Buddha,** who taught at Benares on the Ganges around 500 BCE. **Buddhism** became one of the world's great religions, although it had a greater impact on the Far East than in its own homeland.

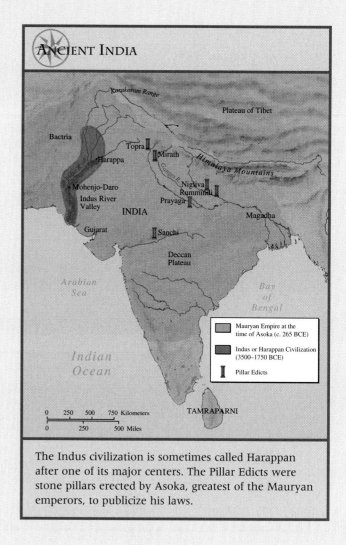

The Indus civilization is sometimes called Harappan after one of its major centers. The Pillar Edicts were stone pillars erected by Asoka, greatest of the Mauryan emperors, to publicize his laws.

Politically, northern India achieved a brief measure of unity under the Mauryan Dynasty before reverting to a society of smaller kingdoms after 185 BCE. The best known of the Mauryans, **Asoka,** ruled over an empire of some 50 million people. His edicts, based in part on Buddhism, defined the sense of social order known as *dharma,* a set of teachings based on nonviolence, tolerance, and generosity.

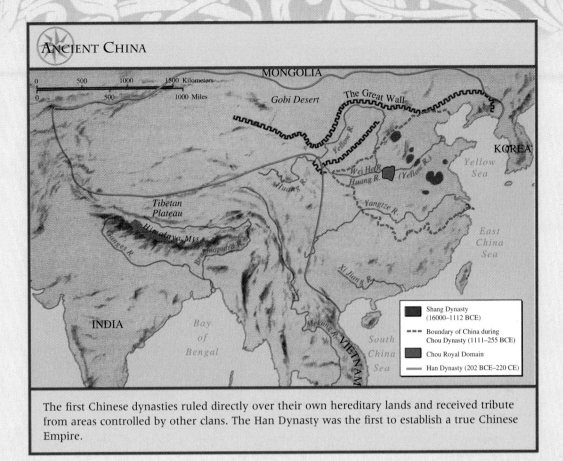

ANCIENT CHINA

MONGOLIA

Gobi Desert

The Great Wall

KOREA

Yellow Sea

Yellow R.

Wei He R.

Huang R. (Yellow R.)

Huang He

Tibetan Plateau

Himalaya Mts.

Ganges R.

Brahmaputra R.

Yangtze R.

East China Sea

INDIA

Bay of Bengal

Xi Jiang R.

Mekong R.

VIETNAM

South China Sea

Shang Dynasty (16000–1112 BCE)

Boundary of China during Chou Dynasty (1111–255 BCE)

Chou Royal Domain

Han Dynasty (202 BCE–220 CE)

0   500   1000   1500 Kilometers
0   500   1000 Miles

The first Chinese dynasties ruled directly over their own hereditary lands and received tribute from areas controlled by other clans. The Han Dynasty was the first to establish a true Chinese Empire.

China

China evolved from a group of cultures that inhabited the Hwang Ho (Yellow) and Yangtze River valleys. Writing, jade implements, the wheel, and ancestor-worship had all appeared by 3000 BCE. Political unity came later. The first imperial dynasty, the Shang (c. 1700–1112 BCE) ruled over a patrimonial state based on an elaborate network of kinship ties. Everyone was bound by multiple levels of obligation that allowed the Shang to build massive palaces and fortifications using what might be called conscript labor. Religious beliefs of great antiquity relied upon the worshipper's ancestors to intercede with Ti, a deity so remote that he was never worshipped in his own right.

Almost from the start, "barbarians" from the north created much the same kind of military problems that would trouble the Roman Empire. Like the Germans, the northerners sought to enter the empire rather than to destroy it. War with the barbarians weakened the Shang. The Chou Dynasty that succeeded them (1111–255 BCE) was really a confederation of states, each of which had its own army and bureaucracy. The basic principles of Chinese administration developed in these years, as did the classics of Chinese thought and

literature that would form the basis of the administrators' education until the early twentieth century. The writings of Confucius (551–479 BCE), Mencius, Sun Tzu's *Art of War* and the Classics of History and Poetry all appeared during the last troubled centuries of the Chou Dynasty. This was China's classical age, comparable to the classical age of contemporary Greece.

After a brief interval in which the reforming emperor Shih Huang-ti (221–209 BCE) completed the Great Wall, simplified the system of writing, codified the laws, and provoked a civil war, the Han Dynasty (202 BCE–220 CE) created the pattern of Chinese government that would last until the twentieth century. Dividing the empire into multiple administrative units, they established a land register and a conscript army. The first census counted 59,595,000 people in 2 CE. Much of the Han bureaucratic infrastructure collapsed during the era of the Six Dynasties but revived under the T'ang after 618.

Western contact with both of these civilizations was limited. India traded with Persia, the Seleucid monarchy, and to a lesser extent, Rome. Alexander the Great reached the Indus but is not mentioned in Indian history. The Silk Road across central Asia brought a limited number of Chinese products to the west beginning in

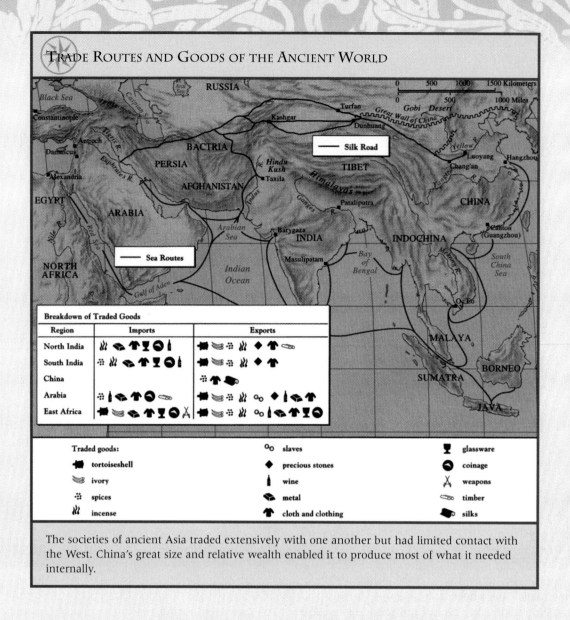

Trade Routes and Goods of the Ancient World

Breakdown of Traded Goods

Region	Imports	Exports
North India		
South India		
China		
Arabia		
East Africa		

Traded goods:

- tortoiseshell
- ivory
- spices
- incense
- slaves
- precious stones
- wine
- metal
- cloth and clothing
- glassware
- coinage
- weapons
- timber
- silks

The societies of ancient Asia traded extensively with one another but had limited contact with the West. China's great size and relative wealth enabled it to produce most of what it needed internally.

the first century BCE, and a Roman mission reached China in 166 CE to little effect. Of course, none of the great Eurasian cultures knew anything of the American continent, or of the great civilizations that were beginning to develop there after 1000 BCE.

Question: Based on what you have learned about the development of the ancient west, what might account for the almost simultaneous technological and cultural achievements of societies that had little or no contact with one another?

ANCIENT EURASIAN CIVILIZATIONS

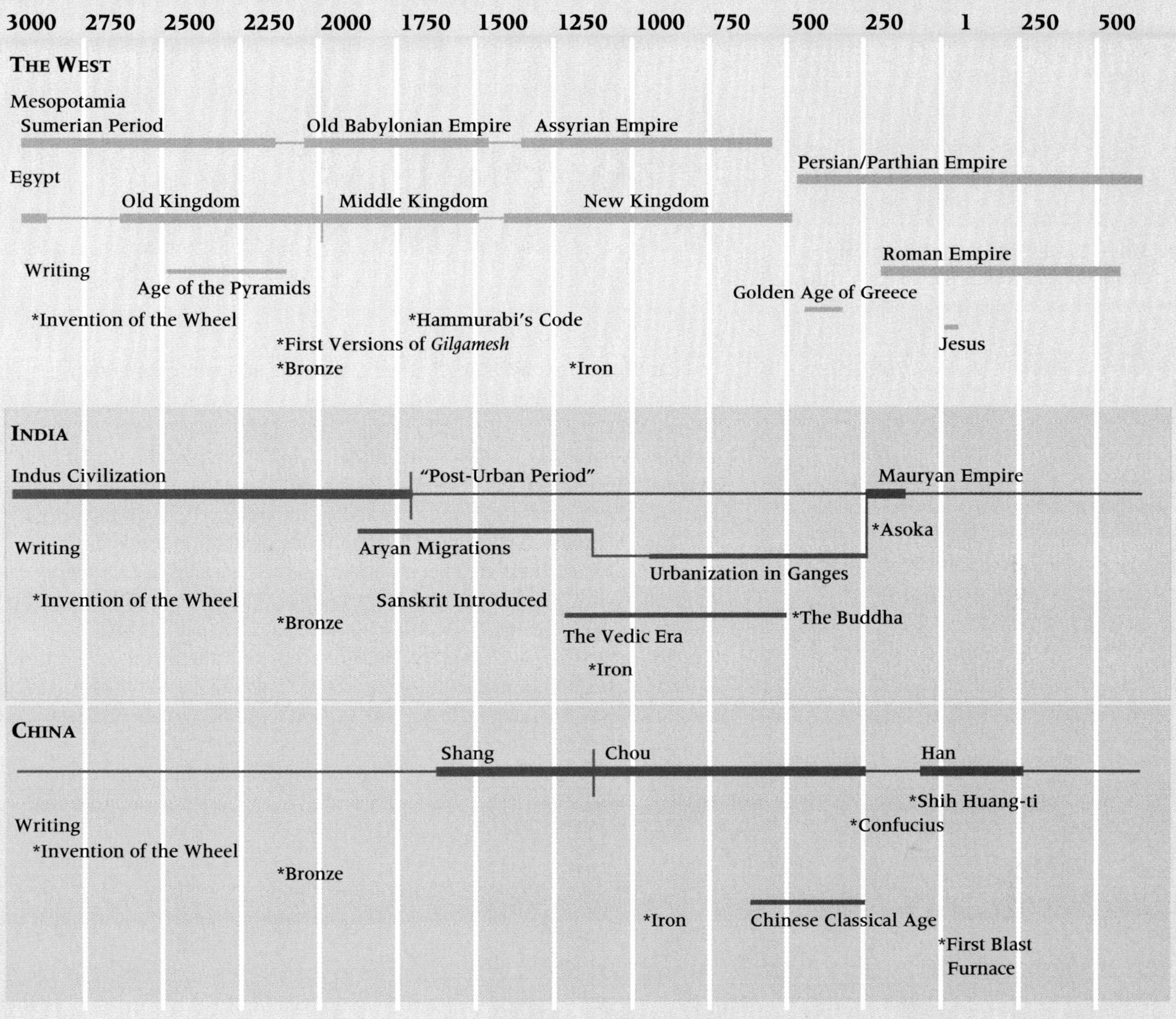

3000	2750	2500	2250	2000	1750	1500	1250	1000	750	500	250	1	250	500

THE WEST

Mesopotamia
Sumerian Period   Old Babylonian Empire   Assyrian Empire

Persian/Parthian Empire

Egypt
Old Kingdom   Middle Kingdom   New Kingdom

Roman Empire

Writing
Age of the Pyramids   Golden Age of Greece

*Invention of the Wheel   *Hammurabi's Code

*First Versions of *Gilgamesh*   Jesus

*Bronze   *Iron

INDIA

Indus Civilization   "Post-Urban Period"   Mauryan Empire

Writing   *Asoka

Aryan Migrations

Urbanization in Ganges

*Invention of the Wheel   Sanskrit Introduced

*Bronze   *The Buddha

The Vedic Era

*Iron

CHINA

Shang   Chou   Han

*Shih Huang-ti

*Confucius

Writing
*Invention of the Wheel

*Bronze

*Iron   Chinese Classical Age

*First Blast Furnace

FOCUS QUESTIONS

- How did the social and political structures of Byzantine society differ from those of the early medieval west?

- How, in the course of a single century, did Islam become the dominant faith in the entire region from Spain to India?

- How were early Germanic societies organized, and what were the basic concepts behind their legal system?

- What ideas and institutions did the empire of Charlemagne contribute to the later development of European society?

Chapter 7

ROME'S SUCCESSORS: BYZANTIUM, ISLAM, AND THE GERMANIC WEST

On Christmas Day, 800, Charlemagne (Shar'-le-main), the Frankish king who had already conquered much of Europe, attended church in Rome. After Mass, Pope Leo III unexpectedly crowned him emperor of the Romans. Charlemagne later claimed that if he had known, he would have avoided church even on Christmas. Some, believing that the king had engineered the coronation himself, remained unconvinced by his modesty. The truth remains unclear, but Charlemagne's coronation marked the revival of a dream. There had been no Roman emperor in the west for almost 400 years. The "fall of Rome" in the fifth century had symbolized the breakup of Mediterranean civilization and the emergence of three new—and very different—societies: Byzantium, Islam, and the medieval west. All three were heirs to Roman culture, but the west was by far the poorest and most politically fragmented. It was also far less sophisticated intellectually and technologically. The crowning of Charlemagne therefore offered a ray of hope after years of disorder, but as events would show, his revival of the western empire would be temporary at best.

The first half of Chapter 7 describes the two medieval civilizations that lived in close proximity to Europe and influenced the west in many ways. The Byzantine (Biz'-an-teen) Empire, Greek in language and Roman in its institutions, survived until 1453. The rise of Islam as a religion and as a civilization challenged both Byzantine and western Christendom and created a society that was for many centuries wealthier and more sophisticated than either. The west, on the other hand, developed slowly as a fusion of Roman, Germanic, and Celtic cultures with a religious and intellectual tradition of its own. After describing the world of the early medieval west, this chapter ends with the establishment of a European empire by Charlemagne. That empire did not survive its founder, but its memory and the institutions it created had a powerful influence on the subsequent history of Europe.

THE BYZANTINE EMPIRE AND ITS GOVERNMENT (527–1453)

The reforms of Diocletian and Constantine established the institutional framework of the Byzantine Empire long before the separation of east and west. The system they created evolved without interruption until 1453, although the empire had been reduced in size by the conquests of Islam in the seventh century and weakened after 1100 by the impact of the Crusades.

The Emperor. The heart of that system remained the person of the emperor. Although he was usually the designated heir of his predecessor, he had to be acclaimed by the Senate, the army, and the people of Constantinople before he could be crowned. The empress, who might be the emperor's wife, sister, mother, or aunt, often exerted substantial power of her own and could rule independently if the emperor were incapacitated or a minor. Once in office, the emperor's power was theoretically absolute. As the vicar of God on Earth, he held the lives and property of every subject in his hands and could punish or confiscate without appeal. In practice, law and common sense limited the exercise of this arbitrary power. Any of the electoral groups—usually the army—could proclaim a successor if an emperor proved unsatisfactory. The choice then had to be confirmed by the Senate and the people before the usurpation was complete. The voice of the people was normally expressed by the crowd at the Hippodrome, the great racetrack that lay next to the imperial palace at the heart of the city. Chariot racing remained a dominant passion in Byzantine life, and as many as 100,000 spectators would gather to cheer on the Blues or the Greens, racing teams that were also political factions (see Document 7.1). The possibility of being deposed and blinded by rival generals—or perhaps dismembered by the mob—preserved a measure of imperial accountability. Only about half of the Byzantine emperors died a natural death in office.

Justinian's Code. The Roman legal tradition acted as a further restraint on arbitrary behavior. The emperor **Justinian,** who came to the throne in 527 and reigned for nearly 40 years before dying at age 83, saved the body of Roman law that has reached modern times. He and his advisers compiled the distillation of Roman laws and legal commentaries known as the *Corpus Iuris Civilis (Body of the Civil Law)* and published it at Constantinople in 533 (see Document 7.2). Its three large volumes became one of the most influential law books ever written. Ironically, the *Codex, Digest,* and *Institutes* produced under Justinian may have been more important in the west than in the east. In the west, Roman law was largely replaced by Germanic traditions and had to be revived in the twelfth century, a process that would have been impossible without access to Justinian's Code. In contrast, eastern courts maintained Roman law without interruption, modifying it on occasion to reflect Christian values. Respect for the tradition was universal, and although the emperor had the power to appoint and remove judges, he rarely if ever ignored their opinions.

The Imperial Bureaucracy. A massive bureaucracy, established originally by Diocletian and greatly expanded in the centuries after his death, carried out the imperial commands. It regulated every aspect of

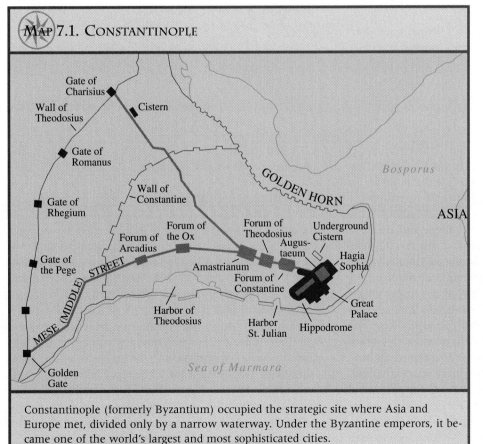

MAP 7.1. CONSTANTINOPLE

Gate of Charisius
Wall of Theodosius
Cistern
Gate of Romanus
Wall of Constantine
Gate of Rhegium
GOLDEN HORN
Bosporus
ASIA
Forum of the Ox
Forum of Arcadius
Forum of Theodosius
Underground Cistern
Augustaeum
Hagia Sophia
Gate of the Pege
Amastrianum
Forum of Constantine
Great Palace
MESE (MIDDLE) STREET
Harbor of Theodosius
Harbor St. Julian
Hippodrome
Golden Gate
Sea of Marmara

Constantinople (formerly Byzantium) occupied the strategic site where Asia and Europe met, divided only by a narrow waterway. Under the Byzantine emperors, it became one of the world's largest and most sophisticated cities.

THE EMPRESS THEODORA AND THE NIKA REVOLT

The *Nika* (Victory) Riots of 532 nearly put an end to the reign of Justinian and were in some ways typical of Byzantine revolts. They began when the government tried to suppress rioting between the Blues and the Greens, supporters of two chariot racing teams that were also political factions. This selection from the fifth-century Byzantine historian Procopius credits the empress Theodora (see Chapter 6) with saving the day. It demonstrates that although Byzantine institutions endured, the life of an emperor was always perilous. In his *Secret History*, written toward the end of his life, Procopius presents a far less favorable view of the royal couple, and especially of Theodora, whom he accuses of immorality and corruption.

At this time the officers of the city administration in Byzantium were leading away to death some of the rioters. But the members of the two factions, conspiring together and declaring a truce with each other, seized the prisoners and then straightway entered the prison and released all who those who were in confinement there, whether they had been condemned on a charge of stirring up sedition or for any other unlawful act. And all of the attendants in the service of the government were killed indiscriminately; meanwhile, all of the citizens who were sane-minded were fleeing to the opposite mainland, and fire was applied to the city as if it had fallen under the hand of an enemy.

Now the emperor Justinian and his court were deliberating as to whether it would be better for them if they remained or if they took flight in the ships . . . And the empress Theodora also spoke to the following effect: "As to the belief that a woman ought not to be daring among men or assert herself boldly among those who are holding back from fear, I consider that the present crisis certainly [demands that we] settle the issue immediately . . . My opinion is that the present time, above all others, is inopportune for flight, even though it brings safety . . . for one who has been an emperor, it is unendurable to be a fugitive. May I never be separated from this purple, and may I not live to see the day on which those who meet me shall not address me as empress. If now it is your wish to save yourself, O Emperor, there is no difficulty. For we have much money, and there is the sea, here the boats. However, consider whether it will come about after you have been saved that you would gladly change that safety for death. As for myself, I approve an ancient saying that royalty is a good burial shroud." When the queen had spoken this, all were filled with boldness, and turning their thoughts to resistance, they began to consider how they might be able to defend themselves if any hostile force should come against them.

From Procopius, *History of the Wars*, trans. H. B. Dewing. Loeb Classical Library (Cambridge: Harvard University Press, 1913, pp. 219–239).

Question: What does this passage tell us about the role of the public—and of women—in Byzantine government?

---

economic, political, and religious life. Prices and wages were fixed by law, and a system of internal passports designed to prevent people from leaving their homes or hereditary occupations controlled movement within the empire. An effective police system unlike anything in the medieval west maintained order in town and countryside, while a fleet of galleys patrolled the seas to keep them free of pirates. Other officials managed state-owned factories, the mines, and the distribution of water.

Many of these people, especially at the higher levels of the bureaucracy, were eunuchs—men who had been castrated in youth. The law excluded eunuchs from the imperial office, and their inability to produce heirs prevented the establishment of administrative dynasties, much less the kind of hereditary aristocracy that encouraged political decentralization in the medieval west. Emperors therefore trusted them, and their employment made a substantial contribution to Byzantine stability. Ambitious parents sometimes had their sons castrated to advance their careers, not only in the church or civil service but also in the army.

The Byzantine Military. The Byzantine military, like the civil service, evolved from Roman precedents modified by experience in the east. The army was composed of heavy armored cavalry (*cataphracti*) supported by archers and by a heavy infantry armed with shields and swords or axes. **Greek fire,** a kind of napalm whose composition remains secret to this day, was used on both land and sea. Siege craft was a highly developed art. Although the Byzantines prided themselves on their superior grasp of military strategy, they preferred whenever possible to rely on negotiation. Their diplomacy was known for its subtlety as well as for its lavishness. They believed that even massive subsidies were cheaper than a war. They gave magnificent gifts to prospective enemies, and if such people chose to call it tribute, what else could one expect from barbarians?

EMPEROR JUSTINIAN ON JUSTICE AND THE LAW FROM *THE INSTITUTES*

The Institutes is the shortest of the four parts of the *Corpus Iuris Civilis* and provides a framework for the entire *Corpus.* The first section of the first book of the Institutes opens with a preamble on the nature of justice and law, and the best means of teaching it to students. The discussion then moves to general categories in the law, ranging from the law of persons to penalties for overeager litigants who bring frivolous suits. The section on disinheriting children reflects partibility as the basis of inheritance in Roman law; that is, children must normally inherit equally.

1.1 JUSTICE AND LAW. Justice is an unswerving and perpetual determination to acknowledge all men's rights. 1. Learning in the law entails knowledge of God and man, and mastery of the difference between justice and injustice. 2. As we embark on the exposition of Roman law after these general statements, the best plan will be to give brief, straightforward accounts of each topics. The denser detail must be kept till later. Any other approach would mean making students take in a huge number of distinctions right at the start while their minds were still untrained and short of stamina. Half of them would give up. Or else they would lose their self-confidence—a frequent source of discouragement for the young—and at the cost of toil and tears would in the end reach the very standard they could have attained earlier and without overwork or self-doubt if they had been taken along an easier road. 3. The commandments of the law are these: live honorably; harm nobody; give everyone his due.

1.3 THE LAW OF PERSONS. The main classification in the law of persons is this: all men are either free or slaves. 1.

Liberty—the Latin libertas gives us liberi, free men—denotes a man's natural ability to do what he wants as long as the law or some other force does not prevent him. 2. Slavery, on the other hand, is an institution of the law of all peoples; it makes a man the property of another, contrary to the law of nature.

2.13 DISINHERITING CHILDREN. Someone with a son within his authority must be sure to appoint him heir or to disinherit him specifically. If he passes over him in silence, his will becomes a nullity. . . . However, the old rules did not apply with the same rigor to daughters or to other male or female members of the family descended through the male line. If they were neither appointed heirs nor disinherited the will was not wholly invalidated. Instead they had a right to come in for their proper shares. The head of the family was also not obliged to disinherit them by name but could do it by a general clause.

4.16 PENALTIES FOR OVER-EAGER LITIGANTS. We should notice what pains the guardians of the law have taken to see that people do not turn lightly to litigation. This is our concern as well. The main checks on the eagerness of plaintiffs and defendants are money penalties, oaths to bind the conscience, and the fear of disgrace.

From *Justinian's Institutes,* ed. and trans. Peter Birks and Grant MacLeod (Ithaca, NY: Cornell University Press, 1987, pp. 37–39).

Questions: If slavery is against the law of nature, why is it tolerated in Roman law? How does Section 2.13 ensure partible inheritance (the division of property among all heirs)?

Taxation and Social Services. The Byzantines paid heavily for all of this security and regulation. A land tax fell upon every property in the empire, including monasteries and the imperial estates. Reassessment took place every 15 years. If a farmer could not pay, his neighbors had to assume his obligation under a system known as *epiboli* (eh-pib'-oh-lee). The government also collected a head tax on each individual, regardless of property. Levies on farm animals, business inventories, imports, and exports were supplemented by surtaxes in times of special need.

Few governments have been more efficient in their extraction of surplus wealth, but some of the proceeds were spent on alleviating poverty. Although regular distributions of grain to the poor stopped at the beginning of the seventh century, officials still tried to provide food in times of scarcity and administered a host of orphanages and other charities. The heavy taxes permitted only a few to rise above the poverty level, but fewer still were destitute.

Byzantine Society

In time, the autocratic and intrusive character of the Byzantine state produced a social structure that had few parallels in the medieval world. Asia Minor and the Balkan Peninsula formed the heartland of the Byzantine Empire, even before the Muslims took Syria, Egypt, and North Africa in the seventh century. Both are rugged lands whose narrow valleys and small plateaus are cut off from one another because of geography and because their inhabitants come from different ethnic groups with long histories of mutual conflict. It would be hard to imagine a site less likely to encourage social equality and weak kinship ties, but that is what happened.

BYZANTINE ART AND ARCHITECTURE

Byzantine taste in art and architecture tended toward the formal and symmetrical. It normally portrayed human figures in full frontal view with rigid draperies. Facial expressions reflect the status of the subject rather than his or her personality, and the portrayal of nudity was unknown.

Hagia Sophia, the Church of the Divine Wisdom. Constantinople (present-day Istanbul) Turkey. The church was built between 532 and 537 at the direction of the emperor Justinian. Although it became a mosque after the Turkish conquest of 1453, it remains the greatest masterpiece of Byzantine architecture. The domed construction and rounded arches are purely Roman in inspiration. There is no remnant of the post-and-lintel construction used by the ancient Greeks.

In the face of overwhelming imperial power, social distinctions receded. Below the throne, everyone was equal. Wealth varied, but Byzantine society had absorbed Christian teachings, so it did not regard money as a measure of virtue. Prestige depended primarily on bureaucratic rank, and rank depended on merit or on the bureaucrat's usefulness to the emperor. The widespread employment of eunuchs and the principle that all wealth could be appropriated to the service of the state inhibited the growth of those elaborate social hierarchies characteristic of the medieval west. As a result, social distinctions were fluid and relatively minor. The empress Theodora was not the only great personage to come from the lower levels of society. Justinian's family members were Latin-speaking peasants from what is now Serbia, and it was said that he never learned to speak Greek without an accent.

Even ethnic distinctions became largely irrelevant. The Byzantines were remarkably free of prejudice, although they sometimes persecuted Jews on religious grounds and may have, in the early years, looked down on the Germans who were found in disproportionate numbers among their slaves and household servants. The imperial court embraced Greeks, Serbs, Bulgars, Armenians, Cappadocians, and a score of other ethnic groups without distinction; the ordinary citizen could do no less.

The same conditions that promoted social equality may have discouraged the growth of extended families. A few great clans attached themselves to the imperial court, often for several generations, but the western development of **lineages**—extended families who took their names and social identities from their estates—had no parallel in the east until the tenth or eleventh century. Instead, the Byzantines lived overwhelmingly in tight-knit nuclear families, often maintaining a certain distance in their dealings with others. Some writers warned against friendship because it might arouse the suspicions of the state. Most people, encouraged perhaps by the epiboli, acknowledged the obligation to

Mosaic of Christ Pantocrator, Cefalu, Sicily. Mosaics, in which tiny pieces of colored glass or tile are assembled to form a picture, were the most common form of Byzantine art. This example portrays Jesus as Christ Almighty, who mediated between God and humankind, and covers the central dome of a church in Cefalu, Italy. It is typical of the images found on the domes or on the main apse (the east end of the church behind the main altar) of Eastern Orthodox churches. Mosaics, often with political as well as religious themes, also adorned the walls of churches and palaces.

help one's neighbors. However, Byzantine society, for all its outward regimentation, remained on the personal level individualistic, self-seeking, and often cynical in its relationships.

The Economy. Roman law reinforced these tendencies to some extent by ensuring the equal division of property among heirs and by favoring the preservation of freehold tenures. Most Byzantines were small-acreage farmers who owned their own land. Some were serfs or tenants on the estates of the emperor or his more important servants, and some were slaves, although the incidence of slavery declined throughout the Byzantine era and by the eleventh century had attracted the opposition of the church on moral grounds. Commerce centered in the great city of Constantinople, which, until the Crusades, dominated the trade between Asia and the west. With its population of more than 400,000, it dwarfed the other towns of the empire. Provincial cities declined steadily in importance throughout the Byzantine centuries as bureaucracy and centralization strangled the ancient Greek municipal tradition.

Religion and the Church

Christianity, not civic ideals, formed the moral and intellectual center of Byzantine life. Even the Byzantines sometimes complained that buying a piece of fruit in the market was impossible without becoming immersed in a discussion of the Trinity, but religion to them was more than a mental exercise; it was the conceptual framework of their lives. Religious disputes thus played an important role in Byzantine politics. The struggle between the orthodox and the **Monophysites,** who held that Christ's nature was fully human but that it had been transformed by the divine, convulsed the empire for nearly four centuries. The Iconoclastic Controversy over the use of religious images or icons generated revolts and persecutions from 726 to 843.

Differences between Eastern and Western Christianity. Although the Greek and Latin churches did not divide formally until 1054, they followed different lines of development almost from the first. In the east, church organization continued to parallel that of the imperial bureaucracy. Its higher officials—patriarchs, bishops, and metropolitans—were monks appointed by the emperor. The church expected them to be celibate, if not eunuchs. Village priests, however, normally married, in part because popular wisdom held that this would protect them from sexual temptation.

Like Byzantine society as a whole, eastern Christianity maintained a high degree of individualism within its rigidly hierarchical framework. It emphasized the inner transformation of the believer rather than sin and redemption. Its **icons,** or religious paintings, portray God as Pantocrator, or ruler of the universe, and virtually ignore Christ as the crucified redeemer until late in the empire's history. They show saints as abstract figures whose holiness is indicated by the golden aura of sanctity that surrounds them, not by individual features. Western legalism—the tendency to enumerate sins and prescribe penances—was almost wholly absent, and even monasteries often encouraged individual development at the expense of communal living. Saintly hermits remained the most revered figures in Byzantium, advising emperors from their caves or from the top of pillars where they lived exposed to the elements, often for decades.

Before the death of Constantine, this faith had transformed the Greek way of life. The preoccupation with personal salvation, as well as the vast weight of the imperial bureaucracy, rendered the old idea of community meaningless. The ancient preoccupation with the human body vanished. The Byzantines wore long brocaded robes and heavy makeup that disguised the body's natural outlines and, like westerners, gradually abandoned the practice of bathing because the church thought of it as self-indulgent. For medieval Christians, the "odor of sanctity" in both east and west was no mere figure of speech. In deportment, solemnity became the ideal, even for children, who, like their elders, were supposed to mimic the icons that gazed down serenely from the domes of churches.

Byzantium and the Slavs

At the height of its power, the Byzantine Empire exerted only a minor influence on the development of western Europe. It maintained contact with the west through the irregular correspondence of churchmen and through the remaining Byzantine possessions in southern Italy. Western poverty imposed severe limitations on trade as a medium of cultural exchange. The greatest impact of Byzantium on the west came later, through the Crusades and through cultural borrowings transmitted by Slavs (Slahvz) and Muslims.

Byzantine influence on eastern Europe was, however, profound.

The Slavs came originally from central Asia and, by 2000 BCE, had settled a broad arc of territory from the shores of the Black Sea northwestward into what is now Poland. They appear to have weathered the passage of Celts and Germans, but the collapse of the Hunnish Empire after 455 CE started another cycle of population movements in eastern Europe. Slavic peoples from the valley of the Dnieper (Nee'-per) moved northward into Russia, while those from the Vistula and Oder valleys moved westward as far as the Elbe (El'-buh) River in eastern Germany and south into Bohemia, Moravia, and what is now Hungary. By the middle of the sixth century, they had penetrated deep into the Balkan Peninsula. The Serbs, Bulgars, and Vlachs then became involved in a long and fruitful interaction with the Byzantine Empire. The northern shores of the Black Sea, long the granary of Greece and Asia Minor, remained a vital focus of Byzantine diplomacy as well, and here, too, relations were quickly established.

Contacts were not always peaceful, but the ties between Slavs and Byzantines were ultimately those of economic self-interest. War, trade, and diplomacy brought the Slavs within the larger orbit of Byzantium. With their usual indifference to ethnicity, the Byzantines accepted many of these people into the empire. By the ninth century, a number of emperors had been of Slavic origin, and Slavs of many sorts were firmly entrenched in the bureaucracy.

Conversion of the Slavs. The churches, both eastern and western, made every effort to convert those Slavs who lived outside imperial territory. A bitter competition broke out between the Greeks and the Germans over whether the Greek or Latin rites should triumph. Saints Cyril and Methodius converted the Serbs and Bulgars to the eastern church in the middle of the ninth century. The Croats, Slovenes, Poles, and Czechs, among others, accepted the Latin Church. In each case, the acceptance of Christianity appears to have been part of a movement toward political consolidation. During the ninth and tenth centuries, Bohemia, Serbia, and Croatia emerged as independent states, and Bulgaria, which had existed in rudimentary form since the seventh century, evolved into an empire that became a serious threat to Byzantine power until the Byzantines destroyed it in 1014.

Kievan Rüs. Finally, at the end of the tenth century, Byzantine missionaries converted Vladimir "the Saint," ruler of Kiev (Key-ev). Located on the Dnieper River in what is now the Ukraine (You-krayn'), Kiev was the center of a trading network that connected the Baltic and Black Seas and drew furs, amber, and wood from the forests of central Russia. Scandinavian adventurers

MAP 7.2. BYZANTIUM AND THE EXPANSION OF ISLAM

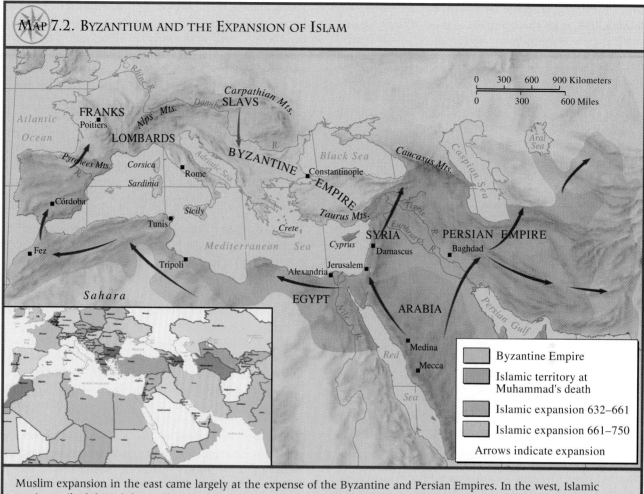

Byzantine Empire

Islamic territory at Muhammad's death

Islamic expansion 632–661

Islamic expansion 661–750

Arrows indicate expansion

Muslim expansion in the east came largely at the expense of the Byzantine and Persian Empires. In the west, Islamic armies easily defeated the weak rule of the Vandals in North Africa and the Visigoths in Spain.

FIGURE 7.1 *Plaque with the Virgin.* Made in Kievan Rüs during the twelfth century, this cloisonné plaque formed part of a princely crown. Cloissoné work is created by setting enamel in metal or metal wire, in this case, gold. Crowns of this kind consisted of several plaques attached to each other; traditionally, they bore representations of Christ (the principal figure), the Evangelists, saints, and various ornamentation. The early date of this piece shows not only the skill of Russian craftsmen but how quickly the Russians adopted Byzantine religion and its attendant art forms.

had gained control of the city a century before. *Rüs* (Russ), the Slavic term for these Scandinavians, is the root of the name Russia. By Vladimir's time, Kiev was again thoroughly Slavic in language and culture and the center of the first great Russian state. The conversion of Kievan Rüs ensured that the eastern Slavs would adopt not only Greek Christianity but also the Greek alphabet and many elements of Byzantine culture. The connections forged in these centuries between the Byzantine Greeks and the Serbs, Bulgars, and Russians remain a powerful cultural bond to this day.

THE RISE OF ISLAM (622–1097)

Islam is the other great society whose interaction with both Byzantium and the west would have profound consequences. **Islam** is a religion, a civilization, and a way of life. The word means submission, in this case to the will of Allah, and the followers of Islam are known as **Muslims.** Both the religion and the civilization based upon it grew from the revelation granted to one man.

Muhammad the Prophet. Muhammad, the founder of Islam, was born about 570 in the Arabian caravan town of Mecca. He married a wealthy widow named Khadija and became a merchant. As he entered middle age he formed the habit of going into the mountains to meditate and pray. There, in about the year 610, the first of the teachings that make up the Koran were revealed to him. Three years later, with his wife's encouragement, he began to preach, but Mecca was the center of an important pagan cult, and the townspeople saw his activities as a threat to their livelihood. In 622, he and his followers fled to the nearby city of Medina. This *hejira* (heh-jeer'-uh), or immigration, marks the beginning date of the Muslim calendar. After a series of battles and negotiations, the Prophet and his followers returned and Mecca became once again the spiritual center of the movement.

The **Koran** is the scriptural basis of Islam, which, to Muslims, supersedes the earlier revelations found in the Jewish and Christian Bibles. It is supplemented by the *sunna* (soon'-ah), or tradition of the prophet, a collection of sayings attributed to Muhammad that are not thought to be divinely revealed. The distinction is important, because Islam is uncompromisingly monotheistic. As the *shahada* or profession of faith says: "There is no God but God, and Mohammad is his prophet." That is to say, Muslims do not regard Muhammad as divine but only as the man through whom God's will was revealed. That revelation, embodied in the Koran, provides the Muslim with a comprehensive guide to life and thought that has the force of divine law.

Elements of Islamic Faith. Islam, like every other great world religion, eventually developed elaborate theologies, heresies, and schisms, but its essence is straightforward. Its creed demands belief in the one God, the angels, the revealed books, the prophets, and the Day of Judgment. The Five Pillars, or obligatory duties, are to recite the profession of faith; pray five times daily; pay the *zakat* or purification tax for the benefit of the poor; fast during the month of Ramadan, which commemorates the time in which the Koran was "sent down"; and make a pilgrimage to Mecca, if wealth and family duties permit.

These are the basic requirements of Islam, but the goal of pious Muslims is to live according to *shari'a,* a way of life totally commanded by God. The guides to that life are the Koran, the tradition, and reason; no mysteries are required. Islam, like Judaism, is essentially a religion of the law. Based firmly on the Arabic of the Koran, which in theory should not be translated, Islam has always been committed to the conversion of all peoples. This universality, together with the clarity of its ethical and theolog-ical demands, made the Muslim faith attractive to millions. By the time Muhammad died in 632, Islam had conquered most of the Arabian Peninsula. Within the space of another generation, it had spread throughout the Middle East.

The Expansion of Islam

From the beginning, Islam spread largely through military conquest. Muhammad had been a capable commander, and his *caliphs* (kah'-leefs), or successors, followed in his footsteps. The first Muslim attack on the Byzantine Empire occurred in 629, while Muhammad was still alive. In 635, Arab armies seized Damascus for the first time. Recently converted Syrians took Mesopotamia in 638–639, and Egypt fell to an Arab army in 640. The motives behind this expansion were not entirely religious. Some Muslims regarded the conquests as a *jihad,* or holy war, and believed that they could attain paradise through death on the battlefield. Not all of the conquerors were religious, however, and some were not even Muslim. For such men, the Arabic tradition of raiding and the hope of booty would have been reason enough. Because Islam prohibits war against fellow Muslims, the raiding impulse tended to be directed outward, at least in the early years when the memory of the Prophet was still fresh.

The terrifying speed of the Arab conquests was, in part, a measure of Byzantine weakness. The emperor Heraclius (c. 575–641) had been engaged from 603 to 628 in a bitter struggle with the Persian Empire during which parts of Syria and Palestine had been ruined or occupied. At the same time, he was forced to deal with Lombard attacks on Byzantine Italy, increased activity among the Slavs on the Danube border, and incursions by Berber tribesmen against the settlements in North Africa. Heraclius was an able general—the first emperor to take the field in person since the days of Theodosius—but a war on four fronts was more than the resources of his empire could bear.

Without adequate manpower in Syria and Palestine, the Byzantines resorted to a mobile defense-in-depth conducted in part by Arab mercenaries. That is, they tried to draw the enemy into the interior, disrupting his communications and defeating his smaller contingents in detail. The size and speed of the Muslim attack coupled with an almost complete lack of intelligence about Arab intentions rendered this strategy futile. The Muslims overwhelmed their Byzantine opponents and then consolidated their victory with mass conversions in the conquered territories. By 640, they had seized Syria, Palestine, Mesopotamia, and Egypt, often without encountering significant local resistance. Many of the empire's subjects disliked both its taxes and its insistence on religious orthodoxy and were unprepared to exert themselves in its defense.

The Sassanid Empire of Persia proved a more difficult target, but it, too, had been weakened by its long
war with Byzantium. Attacked by several Arab contingents from Mesopotamia, the Persians maintained a
heroic struggle until their last armies were overwhelmed in 651. In only 20 years, Islam had conquered
everything from the Nile to Afghanistan.

The Sunni/Shi'ite Schism. The death of the Caliph
Omar in 644 marked the beginning of disputes over
who should succeed him, and for another 20 years the
newborn world of Islam was convulsed by civil wars.
The eventual triumph of Mu'awia (ruled 661–680),
founder of the Omayyad Dynasty, led to Islam's first
and greatest schism. His rival, Muhammad's son-in-
law Ali, was murdered in 661, but his supporters refused to recognize Mu'awia and became the first
Shi'ites (Shee'-ites). Most of these people were
Persians who may have resented Arab dominance even
after their conversion to Islam. In the centuries to
come, they would develop their own system of law;
their own version of the *Hadith*, or tradition; and a
number of ideas borrowed from Zoroastrian and other
sources. Although a minority among Muslims as a
whole, Shi'ites became the dominant Islamic sect in
Iran and what is now Pakistan. The majority of western Muslims remained loyal to the sunna and are
called **Sunni** Muslims to this day. In 681, a Sunni army
marched from Egypt to the Atlantic Ocean and added
North Africa to the house of Islam. From there, a
mixed army of Berbers and Arabs crossed the Strait of
Gibraltar in 711, defeated the Visigothic king Rodrigo,
and by 713 had seized all of Spain with the exception
of a handful of Christian principalities that continued
to survive on its northern coast and in the foothills of
the Pyrenees.

Islamic Policy toward Conquered Peoples.
Islam may have been spread by conquest, but it does
not sanction forced conversions. The attractive qualities of the faith aside, Islamic triumphs in the Middle
East appear to have resulted in part from anti-
Byzantine sentiment among populations long persecuted for Monophysite and other heresies and from the
shrewd policy of offering tax breaks and other preferred treatment to converts. In areas such as Spain
and North Africa, the invaders may have seemed less
alien to the Romanized population than their
Germanic rulers. Their faith was different, but the
Muslims generally shared the broader cultural values
of the Mediterranean world. Nowhere was an attempt
made to persecute Christians or Jews, the other "peoples of the book." Christian and Jewish communities
lived peacefully within the Islamic world until Muslim
intolerance arose in the twentieth century as a response to European colonialism.

FIGURE 7.2 *Caliph Omar the Great Entering the Captured
Jerusalem (637 CE).* This nineteenth-century engraving by
O. Fikentsher recreates the capture of Jerusalem by the Caliph
Omar (d. 640), the greatest soldier among Muhammed's immediate successors. Omar is said to have stated, "Four things never
return: the spoken word, the sped arrow, the past life, and the
neglected opportunity." Before battle, his general Khaled, who
had captured Damascus (Syria) on their way to Jerusalem,
urged his men forward with, "Paradise is before you, the devil
and hell behind. Fight bravely, and you secure the one; fly, and
you will fall into the other." The leadership of such men helps
to explain the success of the Arab conquests.

Islamic Society

The Arab warriors who conquered the world from the
Indus to the Pyrenees came from a society that was still
largely tribal in its organization. Lacking governmental
institutions, they retained those of the Byzantines or
Persians, modifying them when necessary to conform
with Islamic law. Roman law was abandoned.

Government. In theory, the **caliphs** ruled the entire
Islamic world as the executors of God's law, which they
interpreted with the assistance of a body of religious
scholars known as the *ulama* (oo-lahm'-uh). The
Abbasid Dynasty, which claimed descent from the
Prophet's uncle Abbas, displaced the Omayyads in 749
after a bitter struggle and occupied the office with declining effectiveness until 1538. After the reign of al-
Mansur from 754 to 775, they made their capital in the
magnificent, newly founded city of Baghdad and administered their decrees through bureaucratic departments or *diwans* supervised by a *vizier,* or prime minister.
In practice, local governors enjoyed the independent
powers conferred by distance. By the middle of the
ninth century, political decentralization was far advanced, and by 1200, the power of the Abbasids had become largely honorific. Local dynasties, which pursued

their own policies while nominally acknowledging the authority of the caliph, ruled the Muslim world. Spain, which had never accepted the Abbasids, retained an Omayyad caliphate of its own. Although the caliph at Baghdad might call himself "the shadow of God on Earth," the dream of a politically united Islam proved as elusive as that of reviving the Roman Empire in the west.

The world of Islam was immense. Its geographic extent and its many different ethnic and religious groups ensured that it would be no more monolithic, politically or socially, than Catholic Europe. What unity it possessed derived from the fact that although Jews and Christians continued to make valuable contributions to its culture, a majority of its peoples accepted the teachings of the Koran.

Society. Generalizing about social structure in the Muslim world is difficult because of this diversity. In theory, Islam is wholly indifferent to race or class. However, the first Arab conquerors inevitably became a kind of urban aristocracy that superimposed itself on the older societies of the countryside without changing their economic structures. Systems of land tenure varied widely.

Slavery was common in all parts of the Muslim world but was rarely the basis of anything except narrowly defined regional economies. It provided domestic servants and, in a development almost unique to Islam, soldiers. In the days of the great conquests, every male had the duty to defend the faith in battle. The Abbasid caliphs soon introduced the practice of purchasing slaves on the central Asian frontier, converting them to Islam, and training them in the martial arts. These **Mamluks** (Mam'-lukes) were mainly of Turkic origin and became the backbone of Islamic armies until well into the nineteenth century. When they enjoyed a local monopoly of military force, they sometimes usurped political power and established regional governments of their own.

Clerics. Muslim clerics have never become a privileged class like their Christian counterparts in the west. The scholars of the ulama are revered on the basis of their piety and wisdom, and some engage in preaching; however, no Muslim equivalent exists of the Christian sacraments, and any male Muslim can participate equally in prayers. The mosque, or Muslim place of worship, admits no hierarchies, and monasticism is unknown. Consequently, institutionalized religion based on the Christian model did not develop, although pious Muslims often established *waqfs*, or religious endowments, for charitable and other purposes.

Women in the Islamic World. Another unusual feature of Islamic society, at least by Western stan-dards, was its treatment of women. The Koran permits Muslims to have as many as four wives, provided they are treated justly. In the Muslim past, practical considerations restricted polygyny largely to the rich; in modern times it has vanished almost entirely. Although shocking to Western sensibilities, this limited form of polygyny was a major improvement over the customs of pagan Arabia, which seems to have permitted unlimited numbers of wives and unlimited freedom in divorcing them. However, under Islamic law, divorce remained far easier than in contemporary Christian codes. The Prophet's clear distaste for what he called "repudiation" has influenced subsequent legislation and made divorce more difficult in modern times. Another improvement was the Koranic injunction that permitted daughters to inherit property, albeit at half of the amount allotted to their brothers.

As in all such matters, the intent of the Koran was to protect women and encourage domestic morality, but men retained the ultimate responsibility for their welfare (see Document 7.3). Moreover, a number of customs that are regarded as typically Muslim have no Koranic basis. For example, the common practice of having women wear a veil in public was not based directly on the Koran, which says only that "women should not make an exhibition of their beauty." The custom seems to have arisen in the eighth century, when Muslim conquerors found themselves among people whose behavior seemed dangerously immoral. They covered the faces of their wives to protect their virtue in what they perceived to be an alien and dangerous environment.

Islamic Culture, Science, and the Arts

Intellectually, the first few centuries after the Muslim conquests were a kind of golden age. Drawing from Greek, Persian, and Indian sources, Muslim thinkers made broad advances in mathematics, astronomy, and medicine that would eventually be adopted by the west (see Document 7.4). The use of Arabic numerals and the Arabic names of the stars are examples of this influence. Western medicine, too, was based largely on the translation of Arabic texts until the "anatomical" revolution of the sixteenth century.

Philosophy reached its highest development later, between the ninth and the twelfth centuries. Muslim thinkers had better access to Greek sources than their western counterparts, and the works of such men as al-Kindi or Ibn Sina (Avicenna) were rooted firmly in the Aristotelian tradition. When they were translated into Latin in the twelfth century, their impact forced a major transformation in western thought (see Chapter 9).

Art and Architecture. The arts also flourished. The Arab elite cultivated an image of sophisticated refinement

THE KORAN ON WIVES AND ORPHANS

Sûrah 4, *An-Nisâ* (Women), is one of the longest sections in the Koran and is thought to have been revealed shortly after the battle of Uhud in which many Muslims were killed. This brief extract is the basis of the Islamic toleration of polygyny, but its overall message concerns broader issues.

In the Name of Allah, the Compassionate, the Merciful

Men, have fear of your Lord, who created you from a single soul. From that soul He created its mate, and through them He bestrewed the earth with countless men and women.

Fear Allah, in whose name you plead with one another, and honor the mothers who bore you. Allah is ever watching over you.

Give orphans the property which belongs to them. Do not exchange their valuables for worthless things or cheat them of their possession; for this would surely be a great sin. If you fear that you cannot treat orphans [girls] with fairness, then you may marry other women who seem good to you: two, three, or four of them. But if you fear that you cannot maintain equality among them, marry one only or any slave-girls you may own. This will make it easier for you to avoid injustice.

Give women their dowry as a free gift; but if they choose to make over to you a part of it, you may regard it as lawfully yours.

Do not give the feeble-minded the property with which Allah has entrusted you for their support; but maintain and clothe them with its proceeds, and give them good advice.

Take care of orphans until they reach a marriageable age. If you find them capable of sound judgement, hand over to them their property, and do not deprive them of it by squandering it before they come of age.

Let the rich guardian not touch the property of his orphan ward; and let him who is poor use no more than a fair portion of it for his own advantage.

When you hand over to them their property; Allah takes sufficient account of all your actions.

From *The Koran*, trans. N. J. Dawood (Penguin Classics 1956, 5th rev. ed. 1990). Copyright © N. J. Dawood, 1956, 1959, 1966, 1968, 1974, 1990, 1993, 1997, 1990, 2003. Reprinted by permission of Penguin Books Ltd.

Question: What is the basic ethical purpose of this passage?

---

that is reflected in their poetry and in the elegant calligraphy that dominated the visual arts. The Koran forbids the representation of human or animal figures. Muslim artists excelled in calligraphic, geometrical, and floral decorations that were an integral part of both architecture and illuminated manuscripts. Muslim architecture, based ultimately on late Roman and Byzantine technology but with a character all its own, influenced builders in Spain, Italy, the Balkans, and Central Europe. The pointed arch favored by Muslim builders became a standard feature of Gothic architecture in places as far away as England.

FIGURE 7.3 *An Illuminated Koran.* This Turkish manuscript Koran from the fourteenth century is folio size (30 × 20.4 inches) and bound in brown Morocco leather. The headings of the *Sûrahs,* or chapters, are illuminated. The creation of magnificent Korans by skilled calligraphers was, and is, among the highest forms of Islamic art.

ISLAMIC ART AND ARCHITECTURE

Islamic art has always been influenced by the belief that the Koran forbids the making of human or animal images. Architectural decoration and manuscript illumination therefore featured floral and geometric patterns or calligraphy (elegant writing) in Arabic. The exceptions to this rule are found largely in Persia, Turkey, and Muslim India, where the art of painting beautiful miniatures of human and animal subjects flourished. Muslim architecture drew heavily on late Roman and Byzantine precedent but developed a distinctive style of its own.

The Dome of the Rock, Jerusalem. Caliph Abd al-Malik began the construction of this superb example of early Islamic architecture on the site of Solomon's temple around 690 CE. Although Byzantine influence is clear, the structure is a new departure. It encloses the rock formation from which Muhammed ascended into heaven. The site remains a fertile source of controversy between Muslims and Israelis to this day. Note the Arabic calligraphy that encircles the entire cornice.

The Great Mosque of Córdoba, Spain. The Main Prayer Hall. Built in the tenth century when Córdoba was the capital of a united Muslim Spain, this enormous structure has an undistinguished exterior largely obscured by the buildings that surround it, but its interior is one of the finest examples of Islamic architecture in western Europe, if not the world. It has since been appropriated to Christian purposes and now serves as the Cathedral of Córdoba. This picture shows the main prayer hall, where thousands gathered for daily prayers.

Islam and the West. Throughout most of the Middle Ages, the Islamic world was richer and more sophisticated than the Christian west; its technology, military and otherwise, was generally superior. Although not escaping the limitations imposed by epidemic disease, marginal food supplies, and the other miseries of life before the Industrial Revolution, it probably offered a more comfortable standard of living as well. Yet westerners perceived that world as implacably hostile and tended to define themselves in opposition to its religious and cultural values. They knew little or nothing about either, whereas Muslims, if they thought about westerners at all, regarded them as ignorant barbarians useful primarily as slaves.

From the eleventh century onward, the economic and military balance between the two cultures began to shift slowly in favor of the west. The advent of the Crusades and the revival of western trade increased contact between the two civilizations at every level, but the hostility remained. Europeans borrowed Muslim ideas, Muslim technologies, and Muslim tastes while waging war against Islam on land and sea. They rarely acknowledged these borrowings even when they became important components of western culture.

POLITICS AND SOCIETY IN THE POST-ROMAN WEST (C. 450–771)

The Peoples of Continental Europe. After the fifth century, the Germanic peoples whose migrations had brought about the fall of Rome dominated Europe. Visigoths (West Goths) ruled Spain, and Vandals controlled the ancient province of Africa until Muslims supplanted both groups in the eighth century. In Italy, Lombards superseded the Ostrogoths (East Goths) and maintained a violent and precarious frontier with the Byzantine Greeks. Gaul was divided among Visigoths in the southwest, Burgundians in the east, and Franks in the north. Most of these groups were themselves divided into subtribes with chieftains of their own.

Beyond the Rhine were the Alemanni, the Bavarians, and the Saxons. Slower to accept Christianity than their western cousins, they served as a barrier between the lands of what had once been the empire and the non-Germanic peoples to the east. Of these, the most important were the Slavs and the Avars, an Asiatic tribe related to the Huns who had seized control of the middle Danube valley.

Britain. Most of Britain fell to Germanic conquerors in the course of the sixth century. Small bands of Angles, Saxons, Jutes, and Frisians obtained a foothold on the eastern coast of England before the year 500. Culturally related to one another, they came from Scandinavia and northern Germany and seem to have made few efforts to preserve their tribal identities once they had arrived in their new home. English historians refer to them collectively as Anglo-Saxons. The large-scale migration that followed during the sixth century resulted in the establishment of seven small kingdoms: Kent, Mercia, East Anglia, Northumbria, Essex, Sussex, and Wessex. They covered virtually the entire island, from the English Channel to the Firth of Forth. Wales and West Wales (Cornwall) remained Celtic strongholds, as did western Scotland and the Highlands.

Those Britons who had accepted Roman culture took refuge in Wales, where their efforts to fight the invaders inspired the legend of King Arthur and his knights. Tales of their exploits recorded in the ninth century by the Welsh writer Nennius became, with substantial modification, the basis of the Arthurian cycle of romances that helped define chivalric behavior in the later Middle Ages. England, however, had become Anglo-Saxon. The great epic *Beowulf* (see Document 7.5) is part of a sizeable body of Anglo-Saxon poetry that was written down for the first time around the year 1000. Although monastic scribes added Christian elements to a basically pagan literature, the works still reflect the values of an earlier Scandinavian world.

Christianity came to England in 597, when Pope Gregory I dispatched a Roman monk named Augustine and several of his fellows to convert the Anglo-Saxons. Augustine baptized Ethelbert, King of Kent, and became the first Bishop of Canterbury. The other kingdoms followed suit in the course of the seventh century. Bede (Beed; d. 735), the English monk who, among other things, devised the system of dating events as BC or AD, chronicled these conversions in his *Ecclesiastical History of the English People.*

Social Organization of the Germanic Tribes. Although politically fragmented, the Germanic world was unified by its social and cultural similarities. War chiefs provided leadership in battle and divided the spoils among the ***comites*** (ko-mit'-ace), or warriors sworn to their personal support. The more prominent leaders acquired landed estates through conquest or through intermarriage with older, non-Germanic families. In time, they formed the nucleus of an ethnically

THE SUTTON HOO TREASURE

The Germanic peoples who lived around the shores of the North Sea sometimes buried chieftains in their ships with their weapons, jewelry, and other material goods. One of the greatest of ship-burials, dating from the seventh-century CE, was unearthed at Sutton Hoo in Suffolk, England. The artifacts discovered there are Anglo-Saxon, but they closely resemble similar items from Scandinavia and northwest Germany. They show that, artistically and technologically, the inhabitants of the northern world were far from barbaric.

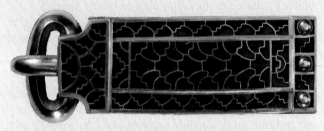

A Gold and Garnet Cloisonné Buckle from a Sword Belt. This buckle, found crushed beneath the sword, fastened the belt from which the sword hung. It is the only gold object in the Sutton Hoo burial that is damaged. The buckle has a small oval loop, cut-away shoulders, and long rectangular front and back plates. The end of the belt ran between these two plates and was held securely in place by three gold rivets at the end of the buckle and two hidden rivets in the shoulders. The front of the buckle is decorated with panels of cloisonné garnets that are deliberately set at different levels, as though to emphasize the raised central panel. All the garnets are set over gold foils that reflect light back through the stones to make them sparkle.

An Iron Helmet Covered with Decorative Panels of Tinned Bronze. This extraordinary helmet has been reconstructed after being badly damaged in the collapse of the burial chamber. Its panels are decorated with heroic scenes. The face mask has eye-sockets, eyebrows, and a nose (which has two small holes cut in it to allow the wearer to breathe freely). The bronze eyebrows are inlaid with silver wire and garnets. Each ends in a gilt-bronze boars head—a symbol of strength and courage. Placed against the top of the nose, between the eyebrows, is a gilded dragon head that lies nose to nose with a similar dragon head placed at the end of the low crest that runs over the cap. The nose, eyebrows, and dragon make up a great bird with outstretched wings that flies on the helmet rather like the bird of prey on the shield.

mixed aristocracy. The estates continued to be farmed by *coloni,* or tenants, almost all of whom were drawn from the original, preinvasion, populations.

Poorer tribesmen held small *allods,* or freehold properties, which they worked with their nuclear families and perhaps a slave or two. During the summer fighting season, the women typically managed the farms. This gave them a measure of independence unknown to their Byzantine or Muslim sisters, but marriage laws were loose and concubinage common. Kings and tribal chieftains often remained openly polygamous even while claiming to be Christian. The church devoted some of its best efforts to modifying these customs but had only modest success until the great religious revivals of the eleventh and twelfth centuries.

Law. Clerical attempts to restrain violence were even less successful. Endemic warfare among the tribes and subtribes reflected a society based firmly on the vendetta or feud. As a result, Germanic legal codes developed an elaborate system of fines as punishment for acts of violence. Their purpose had nothing to do with justice but was intended to prevent feuds by compensating the families of those who were killed or injured (see Document 7.6). Although this worked often enough within the framework of the tribe, it was almost useless when applied to outsiders. Each of the Germanic peoples "lived its own law," even when on foreign territory. That is, a crime committed by a Frank against a Burgundian on Burgundian land could be resolved only by a duel—if the parties could agree upon

Beowulf is the oldest surviving heroic poem in English literature. Little is known about its authorship or the era it describes. A single manuscript version of the poem has survived in the British Library. It is written in Old English (or Anglo-Saxon), the language of the Germanic peoples who invaded England during the fifth century and the remote ancestor of modern English. The first sentence is from the opening of the poem. It is repeated in the original Old English to show how the language has changed. The rest is from a later segment of the poem and describes Beowulf's struggle with Grendel, a monster who has been killing and eating Danish warriors as they slept in the great hall.

Listen! We have heard the glory of the Spear-Danes, in the old days, the kings of tribes—how noble princes showed great courage! [Hwæt! Wē Gār-Dena in geār-dagum, pēod-cyninga, prym gefrūnon, hū ða æpelingas ellen fremedon!].

The evil warrior, deprived of joys, came up to the building; the door burst open, though bound with iron, as soon as he touched it, huge in his blood lust; enraged, he ripped open the mouth of the hall; quickly rushed in—the monster stepped on the bright paved floor, crazed with evil anger; from his strange eyes an ugly light shone like fire. There in the hall he saw many men—the band of kinsmen all sleeping together, a troop of young warriors. Then his heart laughed, the evil monster, he thought he would take the life from each body, eat them all before the day came; the gluttonous thought of a full-bellied beast was hot upon him . . . He stepped further in, and caught in his claws the strong-minded man [Beowulf] . . . the shepherd of sins then instantly knew that he had never encountered, in any region of this middle earth, in any other man, a stronger hand-grip; at heart he feared for his life, but he could not move . . . It was hateful to each that the other lived. The terrible creature took a body-wound there; a gaping tear opened in his shoulder; tendons popped, muscle slipped the bone. Glory in battle was given to Beowulf; Grendel fled, wounded, death-sick, under marshy hills to his joyless den; with that huge wound he knew for certain that his life had ended, the sum of his days. The desire of all Danes had come to pass in that deadly fight. Beowulf's deed was praised aloud; many kept saying that north or south, between the two seas, across the whole earth, no other man under heaven's vault, of all shield-holders could be more worthy of kingdoms.

From *Beowulf: A Dual Language Edition,* trans. Howell D. Chickering, Jr. (Garden City, NY: Doubleday, 1977).

Question: How does the poem justify Beowulf's kingship over the Danes?

---

terms—or by war. The only common feature of these Germanic codes, apart from their reliance upon fines, was that they were customary: judges based their decisions upon the resolution of similar cases in the past. Precedent was supposed to reflect the accumulated wisdom of the people, or "folk," and formed the basis of "common" as opposed to Roman law.

Taking their cue from the Romans, historians have characterized these people as barbarians and the period from the fifth to the eighth century as the Dark Ages. It is, like most such characterizations, exaggerated, but material life in these years reached a level far lower than it had been or than it was later to become. Intellectually and artistically, the glories of antiquity dimmed and for a time almost vanished, whereas those of the Middle Ages were as yet only beginning to emerge.

Ireland. Learning flourished primarily in far-off Ireland, a Celtic society that had been spared the turbulence of the continent. Although tribal and decentralized in its social and political organization, the Christianization of the island in the early fifth century released extraordinary energies. St. Patrick, who is generally credited with converting the Irish, was active primarily in the north and west.

There were in fact a number of missionaries, most of whom were monks. By the seventh century, a rich monastic culture had evolved that stressed knowledge of the Latin classics—religious and secular—as well as a strict personal discipline. Many of the monks were hermits who practiced the discipline of exile: self-isolation from family and community. In setting sail for distant places—Scotland, the north of England, and even the Baltic and North Sea coasts of the continent, they encountered pagans and, in obedience to the Gospels, sought to convert them. In this way, Irish monks transmitted Christianity to many parts of northern Europe, often at great personal risk. Other monks sought to preserve Latin learning, ornamenting it with manuscript illuminations based on a rich artistic heritage. The eighth-century *Book of Kells* is a superb example of their work.

Frankish Society and Politics

Origins of the Frankish Kingdom. The development of a Frankish kingdom that would, by the eighth century, impose political unity on much of continental Europe began with the reign of **Clovis** (c. 466–511),

MAP 7.3. THE NEW KINGDOMS OF THE OLD WESTERN EMPIRE

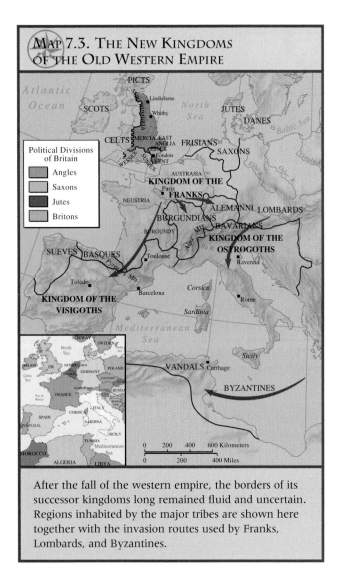

After the fall of the western empire, the borders of its successor kingdoms long remained fluid and uncertain. Regions inhabited by the major tribes are shown here together with the invasion routes used by Franks, Lombards, and Byzantines.

MAP 7.4. THE SPREAD OF CHRISTIANITY, 400–800

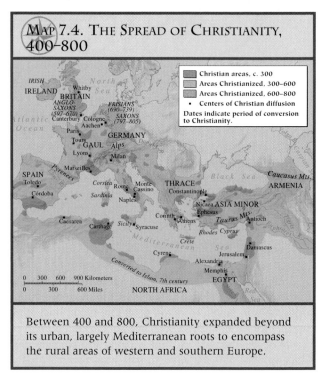

Between 400 and 800, Christianity expanded beyond its urban, largely Mediterranean roots to encompass the rural areas of western and southern Europe.

Visigoths. To traditional historians, Clovis was the first king of France and founder of the **Merovingian** Dynasty.

Merovingian Government. The Frankish kings regarded the monarchy as their private possession. They divided its lands and privileges equally among their sons, when they died and seemed to have no sense of obligation toward their subjects. Personal interest dictated policy. Their subjects in turn felt no special loyalty to the king and served him only in return for benefices or gifts. These might take the form of land, grants of revenue, or other valuables. Unlike the benefices of later—feudal—times, such gifts implied no long-term obligation or relationship. Each new service demanded a new favor. This absence of institutional sanctions ensured chronic instability. Frankish kings were frequently deposed or murdered by disgruntled followers, family members, or wives.

The king's revenues came from his own estates, war booty, fines, and confiscations. After the seventh century, the Roman land tax no longer applied to ethnic Franks. Kings depended on their comites to collect revenues and enforce the law in the regions assigned to them, but in an age of poor communication, comites often proved independent, if not openly disloyal. Legislation took the form of royal *capitularies*, or edicts that reflect Roman legal principles, even although the legal system as a whole remained rooted in customary law.

All of this was typical Germanic practice. The major difference between the Frankish idea of kingship and that of the other Germanic peoples was that the church

a chief of the Salian or "salty" Franks whose center was at Tournai in what is now Belgium. With skill and ferocity, he consolidated his power over other branches of the Franks and seized all of Gaul north of the Loire River. He then routed an invasion by the Alemanni, conquered the Burgundians, and drove the Visigoths out of Aquitaine (Ahk-ee-ten) in what is now southwest France. When he died, at what was for a Frank the ripe old age of 45, Clovis ruled everything from the North Sea coast to the borders of Septimania, the province that extended along the Mediterranean coast from Provence to the Pyrenees. In time, the entire region came to be called Francia, or France. To his biographer, the Gallo-Roman bishop **Gregory of Tours** (c. 539–595), Clovis was a new Constantine because he converted to Catholic Christianity under the influence of his wife, Clotilda, probably in the year 506. His subjects therefore became Catholics, unlike the Arian Burgundians and

RAPE AND MURDER IN FRANKISH LAW

These excerpts from the law of the Salian Franks show how the assessment of fines was based not only on the presumed seriousness of the crime but also on the status of the victim. Note that while rape was taken more lightly than murder, the murder of a pregnant woman was regarded as far more serious than that of a free man. The value of a woman was related almost solely to her fertility. The higher fines for concealment may reflect a presumption of premeditation.

Title XIII. Concerning Rape Committed by Freemen

1. If three men carry off a free born girl, they shall be compelled to pay 30 shillings.

2. If there are more than three, each shall pay 5 shillings. . . .

4. But those who commit rape shall be compelled to pay 2500 denars, which makes 63 shillings.

Title XXIV. Concerning the Killing of Little Children and Women

1. If any have slain a boy under 10 years . . . and it shall have been proved on him, he shall be sentenced to 24,000 denars, which is 600 shillings. . . .

3. If any one have hit a free woman who is pregnant, and she dies, he shall be sentenced to 28,000 denars, which make 700 shillings. . . .

6. If any one shall have killed a free woman after she has begun bearing children, he shall be sentenced to 24,000 denars, which make 600 shillings.

7. After she can have no more children, he who kills her shall be sentenced to 8,000 denars, which make 200 shillings.

Title XLI. Concerning the Murder of Freemen

1. If any one shall have killed a free Frank, or a barbarian living under the Salic Law, and it have been proved on him, he shall be sentenced to 8000 denars.

2. But if he shall have thrown him into a well or into the water, or shall have covered him with branches or anything else to conceal him, he shall be sentenced to 24,000 denars, which make 600 shillings.

3. But if any one has slain a man who is in the service of the king, he shall be sentenced to 24,000 denars, which make 600 shillings.

4. But if he have put him in the water or in a well, and covered him with anything to conceal him, he shall be sentenced to 72,000 denars, which make 1,800 shillings.

5. If any one have slain a Roman who eats at the king's palace, and it be proved on him, he shall be sentenced to 12,000 denars, which make 300 shillings.

6. But if the Roman shall not have been a landed proprietor and table companion of the king, he who killed him shall be sentenced to 4,000 denars, which make 100 shillings.

From Henderson, E. F., *Select Historical Documents of the Middle Ages* (London: G. Bell & Sons, 1892, pp. 176–189).

Question: Based on the penalties listed, how did the Franks define legal and social status?

---

invested Frankish kings from the time of Clovis onward with a sacred quality that other chieftains lacked. A bishop anointed the king with oil at his coronation to indicate that he ruled by God's grace. Such an endorsement could not always save the life or throne of an individual ruler, but it helped stabilize the position of the dynasty as a whole.

The Economy of Frankish Gaul. Economically, Francia or Frankish Gaul had changed little since the days of the Roman Empire. Most of its people were non-Frankish tenants on estates owned either by members of the old Gallo-Roman aristocracy or by Frankish warriors. The poorer Franks and a few Gallo-Romans owned smaller farms, but life even for the freeholder remained a struggle. Yields were far lower than in Roman times—one-and-a-half grains for each grain planted seems to have been the rule. Coins were rarely

seen by any but the rich, who tended to hoard them or convert them into jewelry, which became one of the dominant art forms of the day.

In any case, little was available to buy. Every landowner, great or small, tried to be self-sufficient. When necessary, farmers could barter for necessities at a town fair, but towns were few and poor and often far away. A handful of Jews and Syrians managed the remnants of the long-distance trade in which metalwork was the chief Frankish export. The superbly crafted iron tools and weapons of the Franks found a market in nearly every part of Europe.

Frankish Warfare. Better weapons may have given the Franks a small advantage over their neighbors, for their military organization remained no better than that of any other Germanic tribe. Every male Frank, as opposed to the Gallo-Romans and other non-Frankish

FRANKISH ART AND CRAFTSMANSHIP

Although Frankish society remained in many ways poorer and less sophisticated than its Byzantine and Muslim counterparts, the Franks were skilled metalworkers and jewellers who built upon the Roman and early Germanic artistic traditions.

A Glass Drinking Horn. Made of olive-green glass with a trailed decoration, this Merovingian drinking horn comes from fifth century. Large horns such as this would have been passed between guests at feasts and drinking sessions. The shape of the horn is derived from late provincial Roman models, which in turn imitated vessels made from cattle horns adapted for drinking with metal mounts. The color of this horn is typical of post-Roman glass and is probably due to natural salts in the composition.

Ivory Plaque with Scenes of the Annunciation, Nativity, and Adoration of the Magi. This panel is believed to have been produced at Aachen, the primary seat of Charlemagne, between 800 and 814. It was either half of a diptych or the outer wing of a five-part hinged carving that formed the cover for an illuminated gospel. The blue and red paint and traces of gilding visible on the panel are not original; they indicate that ivory, like marble sculpture in the ancient world, was traditionally painted. The lively postures and fluttering drapery of the figures bear little resemblance to the conventions of Byzantine art.

inhabitants of the realm, was expected to answer the king's call to arms and to support himself for the duration of the campaign. Most Franks fought on foot, armed with a short sword and the small throwing axe that served as an emblem of their tribe. Unlike their ancestors who fought the legions of Rome, they seem to have been wholly innocent of strategy or of tactics that went much beyond the straightforward brawl, but this impression may reflect only the inadequacy of historical sources. Literacy had declined during the years of imperial collapse, and written records in this period are few and incomplete.

Merovingian Decline. The Merovingian Dynasty began to decline almost immediately after the death of its founder. The Frankish custom of dividing even a kingdom equally among heirs ensured that each generation would be involved in bitter feuds that often ended in murder if not civil war. Many of the kings appeared to suffer from physical or mental problems and left the political direction of their realms to their queens. The chronicler Fredegar claimed that one queen, Brunhilda (d. 613), encouraged this tendency by murdering no fewer than thirteen kings in the course of her career. His claim was exaggerated, but she was the most forceful political figure of the age. For other royal women, reality could be very different. Their value depended upon their usefulness as a bargaining chip in diplomatic negotiations. When the king needed a new alliance, he might discard his wife and marry another, or simply have her murdered. Brunhilda's sister, Galsuenda, was strangled in her bed on the orders of her husband, King Chilperic, when he decided on a new wife.

After the death of Dagobert I in 639, the dynasty sank into utter incompetence. War leadership as well as the administration of the royal properties fell into the hands of **the mayor of the palace.** This official was usually one of the Arnulfings, a powerful clan whose wealth derived from estates in the same region from which Clovis had sprung. Originally no more than the major-domo or manager of the royal household, the mayor had, by the end of the seventh century, become the de facto ruler of Francia. Only the sacred character of Merovingian kingship, derived ultimately from the sanctions of the church, prevented the Arnulfings from claiming the throne for themselves.

Rise of the Carolingians. Eventually, they did just that. The Arnulfing mayors of the palace were capable men whose military exploits brought them respect. One of them, **Charles Martel** (Charles "the Hammer"), united the Frankish realms that had long been divided among various Merovingian heirs and won special glory in 732 by defeating a Muslim raiding party near Poitiers in central France. Although not perhaps as decisive an encounter as was sometimes claimed, this battle marked the farthest penetration of Islam in Europe and caught the imagination of the Franks. Finally, Charles's son, Pepin the Short, used the growing prestige of his family and his close relations with the church to depose the last Merovingian. With the full support of Rome he had himself crowned king of the Franks in the winter of 751–752.

THE EMPIRE OF CHARLEMAGNE (771–814)

The dynasty founded by Pepin is called **Carolingian** after its greatest member: Charles the Great, or **Charlemagne** (c. 742–814). In 47 years he brought most of what is now France, Germany, and northern Italy under his rule, had himself crowned Roman emperor, and either reformed or created a host of institutions, both secular and religious. To the historians of a generation ago he stood at the beginning of European history. To **Einhard** (Ine'-hard), his biographer and a contemporary (see Document 7.7), Charlemagne held out the promise of a new Roman empire. But few of the emperor's achievements survived his death, and even fewer were the product of a grand and systematic historical vision.

Conquest of Northern Italy. The great king was above all a warlord who, like his father, allied himself with the church to further his interests. Pepin had left him western and northern France and the Frankish territories along the lower Rhine. A brother, Carloman, took the rest of France and parts of southwest Germany, including the western Alps. When Carloman died in 771, Charlemagne annexed his brother's kingdom, forcing his wife and children to take refuge among the Lombards of northern Italy who had for some time been hostile to Charlemagne. Realizing that the Lombards threatened papal territories, and perhaps Rome itself, Pope Adrian I allied himself with Charlemagne. After 2

DOCUMENT 7.7

EINHARD'S DESCRIPTION OF CHARLEMAGNE

This brief passage from Einhard's biography of Charlemagne is both vivid and unusual in that it provides personal details often omitted by the authors of the day.

Charles had a big and powerful body and was tall but well-proportioned. That his height was seven times the length of his own feet is well known. [He seems to have been about 6'3'', or more than a foot taller than the average man of his day.] He had a round head, his eyes were unusually large and lively, his nose a little longer than average, his gray hair attractive, and his face cheerful and friendly. Whether he was standing or sitting his appearance was always impressive and dignified. His neck was somewhat short and thick and his stomach protruded a little, but this was rendered inconspicuous by the good proportions of the rest of his body. He walked firmly and his carriage was manly, yet his voice, though clear, was not as strong as one might have expected from someone his size. His health was always excellent, except during the last four years of his life, when he frequently suffered from attacks of fever. And at the end he also limped with one foot. All the same, he continued to rely on his own judgment more than on that of his physicians, whom he almost hated because they ordered him to give up his customary roast meat and eat only boiled meat instead.

From Einhard, *The Life of Charlemagne*, trans. Evelyn Scherabon Firchow and Edwin H. Zeydel (Coral Gables, FL: University of Miami Press, 1972, p. 87).

Question: What does the inclusion of these personal details tell us about Einhard's purpose in writing his biography?

FIGURE 7.4 *Gold Solidus of Charlemagne.* Cash remained scarce in Charlemagne's empire, but a number of coins that he issued have survived. This one was minted in Dorestad, the Netherlands, at some point between 774, when Charlemagne conquered the Lombards, and 812, when the Byzantine emperor recognized him as emperor in the west. The inscription describes him as king of the Franks and the Lombards, not as emperor. In form and weight, the coin recalls the gold *solidus* of Roman times.

MAP 7.5. THE CAROLINGIAN EMPIRE

Frankish kingdom: 768

Territories gained by Charlemagne

NORTHUMBRIA
IRELAND
York
North Sea
DANISH MARCH
Baltic Sea
WALES
MERCIA
EAST ANGLIA
ESSEX
FRISIA
WESSEX
WEST WALES
KENT
SUSSEX
SAXONY
Aachen
Atlantic Ocean
Verdun
Mainz
TRIBUTARY
BRITTANY
Paris
AUSTRASIA
NEUSTRIA
ALEMANNI
SLAVIC
Bordeaux
BURGUNDY
Lyons
Alps Mts.
BAVARIA
PEOPLES
AQUITAINE
Milan
VENETIA
Pyrenees Mts.
UMAYYAD KINGDOM OF SPAIN
SPANISH MARCH
PAPAL STATES
Toledo
Barcelona
Corsica
Rome
DUCHY OF BENEVENTO
Córdoba
Sardinia
Mediterranean Sea
BYZANTINE EMPIRE
Sicily

NORWAY
SWEDEN
North Sea
Baltic Sea
IRELAND
UK
NETHERLANDS
POLAND
Celtic Sea
BELGIUM
GERMANY
CZECH REP.
SLOVAKIA
Bay of Biscay
FRANCE
SWITZERLAND
AUSTRIA
HUNG.
SLOVENIA
CROATIA
BOSNIA HER.
ITALY
SPAIN
CORSICA
PORTUGAL
SARDINA
SICILY
ALGERIA
Mediterranean Sea

0 200 400 600 Kilometers
0 200 400 Miles

Charlemagne expanded a Frankish empire that had already grown significantly under his predecessors. His greatest additions were Northern Italy, Saxony, and Catalonia (the Spanish Marches).

years of hard fighting, Charlemagne defeated the Lombards in 774 and annexed their kingdom.

Conquest of Germany.

North Germany, too, required attention. The region between the Rhine and the Elbe was inhabited mainly by pagan Saxons, who raided Frankish settlements in the Rhineland and killed the missionaries sent to convert them. Treaties and agreements were useless because the Saxons acknowledged no political authority beyond that of the individual war band, and each chieftain felt free to act on his own.

Characteristically, Charlemagne's strategy focused on religion. In 772, he raided deep into Saxon territory and destroyed the *Irminsul* (Er'-min-sul), the great tree that formed the heart of one of their most sacred shrines. He apparently thought that by doing so he would demonstrate the stronger magic of the Christian God, but the outrage marked the beginning of a long and bloody struggle. The Saxons destroyed Christian settlements and monasteries. The Franks resorted to wholesale massacre and deportations until they at last converted the Saxons and incorporated them into the empire in 797. Charlemagne did not shrink from converting people at sword's point.

The rest of Germany fell into his hands when he deposed the ruler of Bavaria, who was not only a Christian but also a nominal tributary of the Franks. Then, to secure his borders, he defeated the Avars in 791 and 803, pressing into Croatia, which he partially resettled with Slavic and German immigrants. In the west, he repelled a Muslim raid on Narbonne and seized Catalonia, which after 811 became a Christian enclave in Muslim Spain. When he died 3 years later, Charlemagne ruled everything from Catalonia to the Baltic, and from the Netherlands to the middle Danube.

Charlemagne's Government.

To govern this vast territory, Charlemagne relied on counts (whose office evolved from the earlier *comites*), dukes, and bishops who supposedly acted on his behalf in their own regions and who transmitted his decrees to their subjects. He bound these men to him by personal allegiance fortified with powerful oaths, but distance, poverty, and primitive communications left them with a great deal of independence. Although imperial administration remained fragmentary, the king maintained communication through ***missi dominici*** (mis'-see doe-min'-i-see), royal officials who traveled constantly from place to place on the ruler's business (see Document 7.8). Charlemagne did, however, establish the principle that law would be administered on a territorial instead of a tribal basis. That is, if a Frank committed a crime in Burgundian territory, he was to be tried under Burgundian, not Frankish, law. This change represented a greater advance than it seems, for, in most instances, jurisdictional disputes no longer paralyzed the resolution of cases.

Charlemagne and the Church.

Everywhere, Charlemagne relied heavily on the church to support his policies. In return, he strengthened its financial and institutional base. Monasteries established by royal grants on the fringes of the empire converted, and in some cases civilized, new subjects. Many of these foundations were unparalleled in their size and magnificence. He extended the parish system, long established among the Franks to provide spiritual care in rural areas, throughout Europe, and firmly subordinated parish priests to their bishops. Bishops, in turn, were forced to obey the pope. To further secure the work of conversion, Charlemagne established new dioceses, reformed old ones, and introduced a compulsory **tithe** for their support. In theory, the tithe represented ten percent of a householder's harvest; in practice, it was often negotiated at a lower rate. Charlemagne's efforts, although not always popular, laid the institutional foundations of the medieval church.

Coronation as Emperor. None of these measures could have been imposed by religious authority alone. They required the threat of military force wielded by a ruthless and dedicated monarch. Charlemagne had become the chief supporter of the papacy and the mainstay of its efforts to convert the Slavs and Germans. His assumption of the imperial title at the hands of Pope Leo III on Christmas Day in 800 reflected only what had become obvious to many: Charlemagne, not the pope, was the true leader of western Christendom. Despite this, the motives and conduct of everyone involved in the coronation have been the subject of controversy. Even its practical consequences remain unclear. It seems to have meant little to the governing of Charlemagne's empire or to his relations with other princes, although the Byzantine emperor, after initial protests, acknowledged the title in 811.

Charlemagne established the count and county system and created a basis for the resolution of legal disputes throughout Europe. His empire, however, rested in the last analysis on the personal authority of its ruler. The Frankish custom of divided or partible inheritance ensured that his arrangements would not long survive him. Even had his son and grandsons been willing to ignore the ancient Salic law (the law of the Salian Franks), the difficulties they faced would have been insurmountable. The empire's weak subsistence economy and poor communications could not sustain the development of institutions that might have saved it. For all its Roman and ecclesiastical trappings, the Carolingian Empire remained a Germanic chieftainship, different from its predecessors primarily in scale.

The Carolingian Renaissance. Charlemagne's interest in the church went beyond mere political calculation. Although he used the church—and the papacy—to further his interests, his personal piety and dedication to the conversion of pagans cannot be questioned. In addition to the essentially administrative reforms instituted, he took a lively interest in matters that might in other circumstances have been left to the pope. Charlemagne tried, with some success, to reintroduce the Gregorian chant, a form of plainsong developed for church services by the papal choir and codified under Pope Gregory I (d. 604). He also encouraged the practice of auricular confession in which the laity confess their sins to a priest rather than to one another.

A major obstacle to the adoption of these reforms was the ignorance of the clergy. To correct their deficiencies, he established a school at his palace in Aachen (Ahk'-en) and staffed it largely with Irish and English scholars, the most famous of whom was **Alcuin** (Al'-kwin) **of York** (c. 732–804). Charlemagne intended these men to raise the intellectual level of his court and to educate his sons. Under the king's patronage, his scholars began the task of recovering the classics, especially the religious ones, and copying them accurately in the beautiful, standardized hand known today as **Carolingian minuscule.** It is the basis of all modern systems of handwriting.

The major purpose of this activity was to provide a body of texts that could serve the needs of clerical education. Gathering the best minds of Europe together in a common enterprise paid other dividends as well. The courts of Charlemagne and his son, Louis the Pious, served as an intellectual beacon in the dark days to come. To be sure, the achievements of this **Carolingian Renaissance,** as it has been called by modern scholars, were in some cases forgotten, if not obliterated, in the chaos of the ninth century. Moreover, it was at best a partial renaissance, which is French for rebirth, because the Carolingians limited themselves almost entirely to

FIGURE 7.5 *Carolingian Minuscule.* This sample is from Bede's *Expositio in Lucam* (Commentary on Luke), copied at Tours c. 820. Note how closely the letters resemble those used today. The *minuscule* script introduced by Alcuin of York is so called because the letters are lowercase. They do not, however, fit within parallel lines. Letters such as *b* and *d* rise above the line of script, whereas those like *p* or *q* fall below it. Capitals are used to indicate the beginning of sentences. Carolingian minuscule replaced the earlier *uncial* script based on large letters of the same height and is the basis of modern handwriting.

the study of religious classics. At no time did the volume or importance of their work equal that of later classical revivals, but Charlemagne's scholars laid the foundations of medieval learning nevertheless.

CONCLUSION

The fall of Rome conventionally marks the beginning of European history, but Europe did not develop in isolation. It was one of three great societies that emerged after the breakup of Mediterranean civilization. The Byzantine Empire inherited and expanded upon the Roman political and legal tradition while developing a literary culture based on Greek and a church whose practices differed in important ways from those of the Latin west. It pursued few contacts with western Europe but had an enormous influence on the Slavic world. The rise of Islam in the seventh century marked the beginning of a new and vital society that continues to dominate North Africa and the Middle East. The Muslim world inherited Greco-Roman thought and science and put that tradition to good use within the broader context of Islamic religion. For centuries it surpassed the west in wealth and sophistication while confronting both halves of Christendom politically and militarily.

By comparison, western Europe in the early Middle Ages was a poor relation of these two dominant cultures. Although it, too, inherited much of the Roman tradition, poverty and political fragmentation forced it to look inward. Trade and learning stagnated, although its monks preserved the ancient texts and made successful efforts to convert pagans on the northern and eastern frontiers. Gradually, a more stable polity evolved on

the continent. The empire of Charlemagne, born of a close, self-conscious cooperation between church and monarchy, brought new achievements in politics and learning. His empire did not last, but it stands at the beginning of a recognizable European history.

Review Questions

- In what ways did Byzantium and Islam influence the society of western Europe?
- In what ways may Islamic society be regarded as an heir to the culture of ancient Greece and Rome?
- How did the Frankish kings, and Charlemagne in particular, use the church to further their political goals?

For Further Study

Readings

Jenkins, Romilly, *Byzantium: The Imperial Centuries* (Toronto: University of Toronto Press, 1985). A good general survey.

Kennedy, Hugh, *The Prophet and the Age of the Caliphates: The Islamic Near East from the Sixth to the Eleventh Century* (New York: Longman, 1986).

Wood, Ian, *The Merovingian Kingdoms, 450–751* (New York: Longman, 1994).

McKitterick, Rosamund, *The Frankish Kingdoms under the Carolingians, 751–987* (New York: Longman, 1985). Wood's and McKitterick's texts represent the most recent scholarship on the Frankish kingdoms.

Wemple, Suzanne Fonay, *Women in Frankish Society: Marriage and the Cloister* (Philadelphia: University of Pennsylvania, 1981).

InfoTrac College Edition

For additional reading. go to your online research library at *http://infotrac.thomsonlearning.com.*

Using Key Terms, enter the search terms:

Carolingian   Charlemagne

Using the Subject Guide, enter the search term:

Byzantium   *Middle Ages*

Web Sites

http://www.fordham.edu/halsall/sbook.html

The Internet Medieval Source Book. Look under: Byzantium, Islam, Early Germans (including Franks and Anglo-Saxons), Celtic World, Carolingian.

http://sunsite.berkeley.edu/OMACL/

The Online Medieval and Classic Library. Complete texts and sources.

ROME'S SUCCESSORS

Timeline: "Rome's Successors"

Time axis: 480, 520, 560, 600, 640, 680, 720, 760, 800, 840, 880, 920, 960, 1000

THE BYZANTINE EMPIRE
- Justinian
- Heraclius
- Iconoclastic Controversy
- *Justinian's Code
- *Hagia Sophia
- Conversion of Bulgarians and Serbs
- *Conversion of Vladimir (Kiev)

MEDIEVAL ISLAM
- Muhammad
- Koran*
- The Conquests
- The Hejira
- Omayyads
- Abbasids
- (Increasing Decentralization)
- Shi'ite Schism
- Omayyads in Spain

WESTERN EUROPE
- Frankish Monarchy
- Carolingians
- Clovis
- Merovingians
- Charlemagne
- *Charles Martel
- Conversion of Ireland
- Age of the Great Raids (Viking, Muslim, Magyar)
- Anglo-Saxon Conquest of England

Visit the Western Civilization Companion Web Site for resources specific to this textbook:
http://history.wadsworth.com/hause02/

The CD in the back of this book and the Western Civilization Resource Center at *http://history.wadsworth.com/western/* offer a variety of tools to help you succeed in this course, including access to quizzes; images; documents; interactive simulations, maps, and timelines; movie explorations; and a wealth of other sources.

FOCUS QUESTIONS

- What was the military response to the great raids of the ninth and tenth centuries, and what major changes in European society did the new form of warfare require?
- What do we mean by *feudalism*, and how did it become a self-perpetuating social and political system in much of medieval Europe?
- What is *manorialism*, and why did it become more prevalent in the wake of the great raids?
- How did the growth of feudal institutions affect the development of European monarchies?

Chapter 8

THE BEGINNING OF THE FEUDAL AGE

On Thursday, April 7, 1127, a group of knights came before Count William of Flanders to give homage in return for **fiefs,** or grants of land, that they had been promised in return for military service. The count asked the first of them if he wished to become "his man." The knight responded, "I do wish it," and placed both of his hands between those of the count. The two kissed, whereupon the new vassal promised on the relics of the saints to observe the homage owed to Count William against all men, "in good faith and without deceit." When all of them had performed this act of homage, the count struck each of them on the shoulder with a rod, thereby completing the act of investiture. It was an act performed thousands of times during the Middle Ages. A prolonged military crisis that began with devastating raids by Vikings, Magyars, and North African Muslims had forced Europeans to develop new military tactics and new ties of dependency. Some, like those between Count William and his knights, were feudal. Others were not, but in much of Europe, men and women of all classes found themselves involved in new social and economic relationships.

Chapter 8 begins by describing the great raids of the ninth and tenth centuries and the military tactics developed to contain those raids. The need to pay for these innovations led to the emergence of feudal institutions and to an expansion of manorialism even in some of those places untouched by feudalism. After analyzing feudalism, manorialism, and the social and economic structures of nonfeudal Europe, this chapter concludes with a brief description of politics in the following feudal monarchies of the high Middle Ages: France, Norman England, and the German Empire.

176

THE GREAT RAIDS OF THE NINTH AND TENTH CENTURIES

Even before Charlemagne's death, reports reached him of trouble along the borders of his empire. Muslim raiders, sailing out of their North African ports in search of slaves and booty, had begun to harry the Mediterranean coasts. In the north, the dragon prows of Viking longboats made an unwelcome appearance sea coast villages. The Northmen came to trade, if a village was well defended, and to loot, if it was not. By the middle of the ninth century, these first tentative incursions had become massive raiding expeditions that threatened the survival of European life. Some years later, the Magyars, a nation of horsemen whose origins lay in the steppes of central Asia, pastured their herds on the rich grasses of the Danube valley and began to plunder their neighbors to the west.

The North African Muslims. The motives behind this activity varied. For many Muslims, the Christian west represented a backward society that could be pillaged at will. A wealthier, more technologically advanced society usually attempts to exploit a poorer one, especially if it is nearby. In fast sailing vessels using the triangular lateen rig of the Arab *dhow,* a vessel originally developed for the Indian Ocean trade, the North Africans raided extensively along the coasts of southern Europe. Because European communities were poor, they sought mainly to acquire slaves. Soon, the North Africans established an advanced base in the Balearic Islands. By 842, they had infested the Camargue, a marshy region on the European mainland, and raided in the valley of the Rhône as far as Arles. A half-century later they established themselves in an impregnable position at Freinet near the present site of Saint-Tropez. From these European bases they could devastate the countryside in a systematic way. By the middle of the tenth century, detachments of Muslims had raided villages and monasteries as far afield as St. Gall in the Swiss Alps.

In Italy, the Muslim conquest of Sicily simplified the raiders' task. Palermo fell to the North Africans in 831, but it required more than 70 years of warfare, enlivened by native revolts against both the Greeks and the Muslims, for the raiders to gain control of the island. The Muslims did not expel the last Byzantine garrison until 965. Long before this, western Sicily had become a staging point for raids on the Italian mainland. Muslim slavers were still encountered as far north as the environs of Rome at the beginning of the eleventh century.

The Magyars. The Magyars, a nomadic people from central Asia who spoke a non–Indo-European language, had been driven westward across the Carpathians by another of those population movements characteristic of the Asian heartland. Organized into seven hordes, they probably numbered no

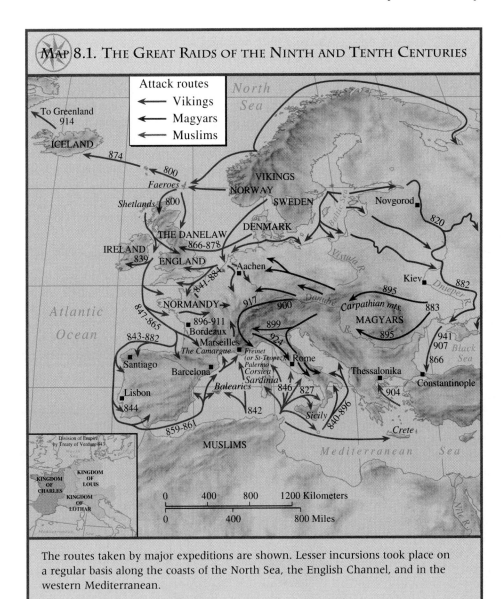

MAP 8.1. THE GREAT RAIDS OF THE NINTH AND TENTH CENTURIES

Attack routes
- Vikings
- Magyars
- Muslims

The routes taken by major expeditions are shown. Lesser incursions took place on a regular basis along the coasts of the North Sea, the English Channel, and in the western Mediterranean.

more than 25,000 people, but they were formidable warriors and had little trouble moving into the power vacuum created in what is now Hungary by Charlemagne's defeat of the Avars in 796. Their raids, which penetrated as far as the Meuse River in northeastern France, continued their nomadic tradition. The Magyars traveled rapidly in fairly large numbers and, initially, were willing to meet western armies on equal terms. Later, they became more cautious and relied upon speed and evasion to make good their escapes.

The Vikings

The Vikings were perhaps the most formidable raiders of all. The name is generic and refers to all of those Scandinavians—Danish, Norwegian, and Swedish—who terrorized the coasts of Europe between 800 and 1050. Their society bore a marked resemblance to that of the early Germanic tribes. Scandinavia was a world of small-acreage farmers and fishermen who lived in widely scattered communities connected primarily by the sea. The heart of such communities was their market and their *Thing,* the assembly of free men that met, usually on market days, to discuss matters of public concern. These gatherings also ratified the selection of kings, who were in the beginning little more than regional warlords. Drawn mostly from the ranks of a hereditary aristocracy, these chieftains relied on personal loyalties, the fellowship of the chief's great hall where warriors drank and celebrated, and the distribution of loot to organize war parties of free farmers and craftsmen. A large population of slaves, or *thralls,* provided the leisure for such pursuits. Even the smallest farms might have at least three, and the need to replenish their numbers provided an important incentive for the raids. In the summers while the men raided, the women managed the farms, the slaves, and the continued production of craft goods and services. Following the pattern of other maritime communities before and since, Scandinavian women tended to be far more independent and economically active than their inland sisters.

Scandinavian Culture. Warfare and raiding had been endemic in the region long before the dawn of the Viking age, as was an extensive trading network that helps explain the cultural similarities of the Scandinavian peoples. Danes, Swedes, and Norwegians spoke related languages, shared the system of formal writing known as *runes,* and enjoyed a common tradition of oral literature that they finally committed to writing in the thirteenth century. The literature's characteristic form was the saga, a mixture of historical fact and legend that reached its highest development in Iceland. Scandinavian religion was polytheistic and bore a close resemblance to those of other Germanic peoples.

Viking burial customs reveal much about Scandinavian art and technology. Dead chiefs were sometimes buried in their boats together with their possessions, a practice that left behind rich hordes of artifacts, including exquisite carvings and jewelry. The boats were an extraordinary technical achievement. The typical Viking longship was about 65 feet in length, open-decked, and double ended (see *Viking Artifacts*). It could be propelled by oars at speeds up to 10 knots or by a single square sail, and it was strongly built of overlapping planks that carried the structural load of the hull. Such vessels could cross oceans. Because their draft was rarely more than 3 feet, they could also be beached without damage or rowed far into the interior in the shallowest of rivers. With a crew of forty to sixty men and no decks for shelter, they cannot have been comfortable, but they provided the ultimate in operational flexibility.

The reasons for the Viking incursions are unclear. The Scandinavian population presumably had begun to exceed the available supply of food, perhaps because the cold, wet weather that troubled the rest of Europe in this period reduced northern harvests to an untenable level. Charlemagne's conquest of the Saxons also may have roused the suspicions of their Danish neighbors. In any case, the Northmen grew more aggressive with the passage of time. In the early years of the ninth century, they contented themselves with lightning raids on coastal settlements, stealing what they could and putting out to sea before the inhabitants could call for reinforcements. Within a generation, they had adopted the Muslim tactic of establishing bases from which they could loot the surrounding countryside. By

FIGURE **8.1** *Portable Bronze Scales Used by Viking Traders.* The Vikings were merchants as well as raiders, and they often combined both activities in a single voyage. Portable bronze scales that folded into a bronze container no larger than a man's palm were indispensable to Viking merchants, who traded their wares for precisely measured amounts of silver and gold. Traders exchanged coins by the weight of precious metal, not denomination, and kept a supply of chopped-up coins on hand to put the scales into perfect balance.

VIKING ARTIFACTS

Technical skill and first-rate equipment contributed more to Viking success than mere ferocity. The objects shown here were part of a chieftain's burial horde, and therefore more elaborate than those used by ordinary Vikings, but they reveal the craftsmanship and aesthetic sense of medieval Scandinavians.

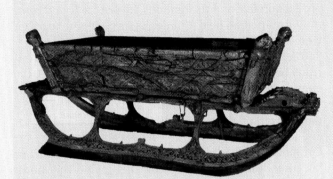

The Sheteligs Sledge, Oseberg. In snowy Scandinavia, horse-drawn wooden sledges served as winter transportation for people and trade goods. This example is carved elaborately, as befits the property of a king. The head posts held the ties that secured the box to its runners. In summer, the detachable body was set on a wheeled frame and became a carriage.

The Oseberg Ship (ninth century). Part of the burial horde of a wealthy Viking chief, this vessel has the elegant and sea-worthy lines typical of Viking longships. The swan-necked prow rises 16 feet above the deck. The general impression is one of both beauty and menace. Note the shallow draft and the overlapping plank construction. The racks mounted at either gunwale hold the 30 oars that were deployed through the oar holes cut in both sides of the ship. Clinker-built vessels, as this type of construction is called, continued to be built into the twentieth century. The Vikings had no saws, however, and shaped the timbers with the axe and the adze.

midcentury, they had established permanent colonies on the European mainland.

Their range was enormous. In 844, Vikings raided the Atlantic ports of Spain. In the following year, they sacked Paris, and in 859–860, they reached Italy, penetrating the Val d'Arno almost to the outskirts of Florence. Fortunately for the Italians, they did not return. In the north, the Vikings soon learned how to extend their range by traveling on stolen horses when their ships reached the limits of navigation. Nothing seemed beyond their reach.

Viking Settlement in England and Normandy.
The establishment of permanent settlements grew from the habit of wintering in England or on the Continent in preparation for the next raiding season. Given the fear inspired by the raids, the dangers of this practice were minimal and many Vikings brought their wives and families. In the decades after 851, they occupied all of northeastern England from Essex to the further limits of Yorkshire. The region came to be known as **the Danelaw** because the legal autonomy granted to the Danes by Saxon kings survived until the thirteenth century. From 1014 to 1042, a Danish dynasty ruled all of England. Around 900, other Vikings established a large state in northern France around the mouth of the Seine. It was called Normandy, or the land of the Norsemen (see Document 8.1). In 1066, these Normans conquered England and displaced its Danish kings.

The Vikings in Russia. At the opposite end of Europe, Viking traders penetrated the Russian heartland by following the great rivers. From the western branch of the Dvina, which flows into the Baltic at Riga, they were able to reach the headwaters of both the Dnieper and the Volga and to float from there to the

THE VIKING SETTLEMENT OF NORMANDY

This version of the settlement of Normandy comes from the *Saga of Harald the Fairhaired* (c. 860–940). One of the so-called king sagas collected by the Icelandic poet Snorre Sturlason in his *Helmskringla* (Orb of the World), it tells how one of the losers in a Scandinavian struggle for political consolidation established a permanent Viking community on Frankish soil. The story begins shortly after Harald, after many struggles, has established himself as king of Norway.

Rolf became a great Viking, and was of so stout a growth that no horse could carry him, and wherever he went, he must go on foot; and therefore he was called Gange-Rolf [Rolf the Walker]. He plundered much in the East sea. One summer, as he was coming from the eastward on a viking's expedition to the coast of Viken, he landed there and made a strandhug [raid]. As King Harald happened, just at that time, to be in Viken, he heard of it, and was in a great rage; for he had forbidden by the greatest punishment, any plundering within the bounds of the country. The king assembled a Thing and had Rolf declared an outlaw over all Norway . . .

Gange-Rolf went afterwards over sea to the West to the Hebrides or Sudreyar, and at last further west to Valland [France] where he plundered and subdued for himself a great earldom which he peopled with Northmen, from which the land is called Normandy. Gange-Rolf's son was William, father of Richard, and grandfather to of Robert Longspear, and grandfather of William the Bastard [William the Conqueror] from whom all the succeeding English kings are descended.

From Snorre Sturlason, *Helmskringla*, in *The Norse King Sagas by Snorre Sturlason*, trans. S. Lang (London and New York: Dent, 1930).

Question: Why did Rolf establish a permanent Viking settlement on what had been Frankish soil?

gates of Constantinople. In the process, they founded Novgorod and established themselves as the ruling aristocracy at Kiev, but they had little impact upon what was to remain a thoroughly Slavic culture. Somewhat ironically, they gave Russia its name: *Rüs* or *Rhos* was the Slavic word for Viking.

The establishment of these Viking enclaves, like the contemporary colonization of Iceland and Greenland and the exploration of the North American coast by Bjarni Herjolfsson (c. 986) and Leif Ericsson (c. 1000), indicates that hunger for arable land was an important reason for the great raids. In the two centuries between 850 and 1050, the North Sea became the center of a cosmopolitan society in which interaction between Scandinavian and non-Scandinavian cultures grew increasingly complex. As the medieval kingdoms of France and England evolved, they eventually assimilated the Norsemen, but in the meantime Viking incursions had helped provoke a reorganization of European society.

MILITARY CRISIS AND SOCIAL REORGANIZATION (814–1050)

The great raids, Muslim, Magyar, and Viking, brought something like anarchy to most of Europe. An orgy of violence submerged the normal bonds of social interaction. No one's person or property was safe. Agricultural production fell, and the tenuous lines of trade and communication that held Charlemagne's empire together were virtually severed (see Document 8.2).

The attacks fell upon a political order that was already beginning to disintegrate. Impressive as it was, the empire of Charlemagne had been doomed from the start by poverty, partible inheritance, and the problem of distance. It lacked the surplus wealth to support either war or governance. Harvests, never abundant in the Carolingian age, may have declined even before Europe felt the destructive effects of the raids. The north European climate had entered one of its cold, damp cycles. Yields of one-and-a-half grains for every seed planted were apparently normal, and people grew barely enough for their own use. The problem of distance would afflict society for centuries to come, but it was especially severe in the early Middle Ages. In Charlemagne's empire, major population centers were far apart and connected only by primitive tracks that became nearly impassable in bad weather. Local magnates and local loyalties began to assert themselves while Charlemagne was still alive. Neither his lines of communication nor his military resources could hold them fully in check. After his death the division of the empire among his three grandsons only made matters worse.

The Division of Charlemagne's Empire. Charlemagne's son Louis the Pious (reigned 814–840) had hoped to pass on the empire intact, even though the Salic law required that it be split equally among his heirs. He had three sons by his first marriage: Lothair, Pepin, and Louis "the German." A fourth son, Charles "the Bald," was born to his second wife, Judith of Bavaria, in 823. Pepin died before his father in 838. Lothair was Louis's intended heir, but Judith instigated a civil war among the brothers in the hope of securing a kingdom for her son. After the emperor's death in 840, the surviving sons divided his lands by the Treaty of Verdun (843). Lothair took the central portion including Italy, the Rhineland, and the Low Countries. Charles (d. 877) held most of what is now France, and Louis (d. 875) gained Bavaria, Austria, and the eastern part of Germany. When Lothair died in 855, the middle kingdom was divided again among his three sons and

FIGURE 8.2 *The Murder of King Edmund.* This illustration from an eleventh-century English religious history shows how Viking chieftains tried to gain victory without fighting. In 866, the Danish Viking Ivar led about 1,000 warriors in an attack on the Anglo-Saxon kingdom of East Anglia. Ivar towers over his troops as he instructs a messenger to demand the surrender of the East Anglian King Edmund. In the end, Edmund refused the offer and was defeated. Ivar had him tied to a tree and shot full of arrows until, in the words of a later chronicler, he resembled "a sea urchin whose skin is closely set with quills."

DOCUMENT 8.2

THE GREAT RAIDS

The following is extracted from the *Annals of Xanten* (Zan'ten), a chronicle thought to have been written in the archdiocese of Cologne at about the time of the events it describes. The year is 846, with the final sentence coming from the entry for 847. Frisia includes most of the northern Netherlands and the coastal region of northwest Germany. Lothair was the grandson of Charlemagne who ruled the middle part of his empire known as Lotharingia. The passage reveals the sense of helplessness and isolation induced by disasters on every front.

According to their custom the Northmen plundered Eastern and Western Frisia and burned the town of Dordrecht with two other villages, before the eyes of Lothaire, who was then in the castle of Nimwegen, but could not punish the crime. The Northmen, with their boats filled with immense booty, including both men and goods, returned to their own country.

At the same time, as no one can mention or hear without great sadness, the mother of all churches, the basilica of the apostle Peter, was taken and plundered by the Moors or Saracens, who had already occupied the region of Beneventum. The Saracens, moreover, slaughtered all the Christians whom they found outside the walls of Rome, either within or without this church. They also carried men and women away prisoners. They tore down, among many others, the altar of the blessed Peter, and their crimes from day to day bring sorrow to Christians. Pope Sergius departed life this year.

After the death of Sergius no mention of the apostolic see has come in any way to our ears.

From Robinson, James Harvey, ed., *Readings in European History,* vol. 1 (Boston: Ginn, 1904).

Question: What does this passage imply about the continuity of political and religious authority in the time of the great raids?

quickly ceased to be a major factor in European politics. By 870, all that remained of Charlemagne's empire was a West Frankish kingdom (France) under Charles and an East Frankish kingdom (Germany) under Louis. Northern Italy became the playground of regional factions and Byzantine generals.

Knights and Castles: The Military Response to the Raids

None of these states possessed the resources to mount a credible defense against the raiders. Cash remained scarce, and the kings that followed Charles the Bald and Louis the German were not always inspiring leaders. Militarily, the problem resembled that faced by the Roman emperors in the second and third centuries, but its scale was far greater and complicated by the decentralization of political power within the Carolingian empire. Each of the successor kingdoms faced attacks along borders that extended for thousands of miles. The attacks might come by land or by sea. The defenders could predict neither their objective nor the size of the forces involved. Because Carolingian Europe was poor and sparsely settled, peasant communities could not defend themselves against such formidable enemies as the Vikings. The old Frankish system of levies had always been slow and cumbersome. By the time infantry mobilized and marched to the point of contact, the enemy frequently was gone. Fortunately for the Europeans, Scandinavians and North Africans tended to fight on

FIGURE 8.3 *A Knight and His Equipment.* This manuscript illumination shows a knight wearing the conical helmet and long coat of chain mail or birney typical of the early feudal period. He is shown at the charge with lance in hand. The high saddle made him difficult to unhorse, while the stirrups allowed him to stand up for greater impact.

foot during earlier raids without benefit of the massed infantry tactics known to antiquity. The Magyars were a typical nomadic light cavalry. If they could be intercepted, all of these raiders were vulnerable to attack by heavily armed and armored horsemen—the prototypes of the medieval knight.

Technologically, two innovations enhanced the value of knights and their way of fighting: the iron horseshoe and the stirrup. Neither were in common use before the ninth century. The iron shoe permitted a horse to carry heavy weights over bad ground without splitting its hooves. The stirrup allowed an armored man to brace himself and even to stand in the saddle. This made it easier to wield a heavy lance, shield, and double-edged sword on horseback. The new system produced an increase in offensive power over that available to ancient or nomadic cavalry, and a heavy chain mail coat offered an effective defense against most edged weapons. The Franks, with their traditional skill in ironwork, easily fashioned the necessary equipment.

A defensive system evolved that was based on mobile detachments of heavy cavalry garrisoned in scattered strongholds or castles and supported economically by the people they were intended to protect. In theory, a band of horsemen could reach the site of a raid within hours or, at worst, a day or two. As hundreds of smoking villages continued to attest, this solution was not perfect, but it forced the marauders to pay a higher cost in blood than they might otherwise have done. With time and practice, the knights became a reasonably effective deterrent.

The new system was equally useful in struggles that had nothing to do with the raids. The division of the empire encouraged territorial disputes that continued even in the face of external threats. Armored knights could be used to harry the lands of a hostile neighbor. Other knights could be sent out to oppose them, but castles provided the more effective defense. The presence of a castle filled with armed men posed a serious threat to any invading force, and operations had to be suspended until that threat could be eliminated. For this reason, sieges were more common in medieval warfare than pitched battles between mounted knights. Knights directed the sieges and played a prominent role in the fighting. The hard work of digging, undermining the walls, and manning the rams or catapults fell to peasants levied for the occasion.

A major defect of this kind of warfare was its expense. The cost of a horse and armor amounted to the rough equivalent of two dozen cattle. Few could afford it. Before his death, Charlemagne had begun to encourage the development of heavy cavalry, but the tiny elite that served him had to be supplemented under his successors by the enlistment of nearly everyone who was rich enough and strong enough to fight on horseback. Moreover, the kind of warfare in which medieval knights engaged demanded constant readiness and a high level of skill. Training was difficult to acquire and could be maintained only through constant practice. The construction and maintenance of castles required vast reserves of labor and materials. Even those able to afford the initial outlay could not be expected to support themselves indefinitely. In an age when people were chronically short of cash, the most practical, and perhaps the only, solution was to provide these men with grants of land that could be set aside for their use in return for military service.

The Emergence of Feudal Institutions

Feudalism as a Historical Term. Feudalism refers to the social and political institutions that arose from this exchange of land for military service. The term itself was not used in medieval times. It became common during the eighteenth-century Enlightenment and has been used in a pejorative sense by writers from Voltaire to the present. Scholars who study the medieval period therefore tend to dislike it. They also point out that much of Europe never adopted feudal institutions; many areas developed other forms of political and economic dependency at approximately the same time. Despite these reservations, no other generally agreed-upon term has emerged to describe the system that arose in France and Germany in response to the great raids and spread to England and southern Italy during the Norman conquests. *Feudalism* is used here only in deference to common usage.

The Origin of Feudal Ties. In its simplest form, a feudal bond was created when a fighting man placed his hands between those of his lord or liege and vowed to support him on the battlefield in return for a grant of land known as a **benefice** or **fief** (feef). By doing so, he became the lord's man, or **vassal**. The terms of such contracts varied widely and were the subject of much negotiation, but the basic principle of mutual obligation remained constant. A vassal promised to support his lord and to do nothing contrary to his interest; the lord promised to provide his vassal with personal and legal protection as well as material support. "Money fiefs," which paid cash for military service, existed, but in a virtually cashless society, they were rare.

The precedents for such arrangements were ancient. In principle, feudalism is a form of clientage that has been given sanction in law. In practice, the idea probably dates back to the oaths taken by members of a Germanic *comitatus,* or war band. The great men of Visigothic Spain and Merovingian Gaul had maintained bodies of armed companions who were pledged to them by oath. Some of these men were free, but others were *vassi* who had entered into contractual relationships of dependency. Under the early Carolingians, vassalage began to lose its humble connotations. Charles Martel and his successors

FIGURE 8.5 *The Act of Homage.* In this manuscript illumination, the lord, who is seated among his other knights, takes the new vassal's hands between his own. The vassal's extra hands are symbolic. With two of them, he points to the stalks of grain, which symbolize the fief for which he does homage. With the other, he points to himself.

sometimes granted land to their retainers, who often became great lords in their own right. Charlemagne tried to make such arrangements legally binding, but the legal union of vassalage and benefice was achieved only in the reign of his son, Louis the Pious. By this time, the term *vassal* had lost all taint of servility.

In the dark years after the death of Louis, feudalism spread throughout the Frankish kingdoms. Kings extended vassal homage not only to household companions but also to regional magnates whose military assistance they valued. Bishops and abbots became vassals as well, even though they were not supposed to shed blood, because in most respects there was little difference between secular and ecclesiastical lordships. Monasteries and Episcopal sees had long been endowed with temporalities, grants of land that in difficult times required the protection of armed men. A prominent churchman might therefore command a substantial force. In some cases, including most of those that involved the church, a prospective vassal surrendered land to the liege in return for his protection, and the liege returned it after the oath of fealty had been taken. In most cases, the vassal received a new estate ranging in size from a few acres to an entire county. It might or might not contain a castle. The vassal was expected to make some provision for the security of his fief as part of the agreement. When a fief was very large, this could be done only through **subinfeudation.** The vassal would recruit his own contingent of fighting men by offering them portions of his fief in return for their oaths of fealty. In this way, the number of feudal jurisdictions increased rapidly within a few short years.

The Military Effectiveness of Feudalism. This decentralization of military force worked as well as could

FIGURE 8.4 *Escomb Church.* An Anglo-Saxon Church, built in what was then the kingdom of Northumbria (now County Durham, England), Escomb probably dates from the eighth century. Its builders reused Roman masonry to construct its high stone nave and low entrance portal. Archaeologists have found that it was once surrounded by a wall. Churches of this kind were easy to fortify and often served as refuges in time of war or invasion.

be expected. Its chief virtue was flexibility. Units of heavy cavalry based in fortified strongholds could usually break up minor raids or at least impose unacceptable casualties on the raiders. The building of castles, many of which were little more than halls surrounded by wooden palisades, might deter a weak attacker. Greater threats could be met by a general levy, which gathered the war bands of many vassals into a great host. Such an army, organized by **Otto the Great** (912–973), met and defeated the Magyars at the battle of the Lechfeld (Leck'-feld) in 955. Otto's victory ended the last major incursion from the east. His reign as king of the East Franks—he was crowned Holy Roman Emperor in 962—marked the turning of the tide. Christian forces drove the Muslims from Freinet in 972, and the number of Viking raids began to decline even in the west. They ceased entirely after about 1030.

How much of this resulted from the new military organization and how much from other factors is hard to determine. Otto the Great clearly discouraged the Magyars, but they had already begun to turn away from raiding as they discovered the rich agricultural possibilities of the Hungarian plain. After 950, a series of civil wars in North Africa distracted the Muslims. For the most part, it was not feudal levies but naval forces based in the Italian towns that undertook the hard work of dislodging them from their bases in Spain and the Balearics. The western Mediterranean achieved relative security only by the end of the eleventh century.

Like the Muslims, the Vikings may have returned home for reasons of their own. Even as they raided, the Scandinavian chiefs fought for hegemony among themselves. They used much of the treasure they seized to buy influence and hire mercenaries for their dynastic quarrels. By the beginning of the eleventh century, this process had created the kingdoms of Denmark, Norway, and Sweden. The new rulers sought divine sanction by adopting Christianity and did everything in their power to monopolize the use of military force. They actively discouraged freebooting because it led to the creation of alternative centers of power, while the church condemned raiding because it was directed against Christians. In the meantime, agricultural productivity seems to have improved, allowing reformed Vikings to accept the new policy without too much hardship.

Subinfeudation. Feudalism did not guarantee the salvation of Europe, but in much of the subcontinent it altered the structure of society. An expedient adopted in a time of poverty and dire peril evolved into a complex of social and economic relationships that survived for half a millennium. The process began with **subinfeudation,** which increased political decentralization and weakened the power of kings (see Document 8.3). The bonds of homage and fealty were entirely personal. A vassal who held his benefice from a count owed nothing to the king who had granted the land to the count in the first place. If a **tenant-in-chief** (a lord who held land directly from the sovereign) chose not to honor his obligations under the feudal contract, all of his subtenants could be expected to follow suit. Moreover, vassals commonly accumulated fiefs from more than one lord. Conflicts of loyalty were therefore inevitable, and some of the greater vassals used them to build a power base of their own. The counts of Flanders, for example, held lands from the kings of both East Francia and West Francia. They played one against the other to create what amounted to an independent state by the end of the ninth century.

Because feudal tenures were theoretically based on service and good only for the lifetime of the vassal, depriving a disloyal tenant of his benefice should have been easy, but this was not the case. By granting their lands in fief, kings reduced their military force to a household guard that might be no more numerous than the companions of any major tenant-in-chief. Deprivation of one important vassal therefore required the assistance of others, and most were reluctant to participate in an action that could one day be applied to them.

Inheritance of Fiefs. Political pressures moved strongly in the opposite direction. As the decentralization of military force increased, kings had to offer better terms in return for support. Fiefs inevitably became inheritable. Vassals wished to provide for the security of their families, and with increasing frequency, they demanded the right to pass lands on to their children when negotiating feudal contracts. Rulers knew that impoverishing the widows and orphans of their vassals encouraged disloyalty. The inheritance of fiefs therefore became common in France and Italy by the end of the ninth century and became universal in the eleventh century. In Germany, heritability at first applied solely to the more important benefices. By the end of the twelfth century, fiefs held for life had become a rarity even there.

Inheritance by Women. The original grantor of a fief expected the heirs to renew their father's oaths and be capable of fulfilling them. They therefore denied the right of succession to women because women could not, in theory, provide military service. Neither of these rules survived the first feudal age. Heirs frequently failed to appear before their liege but nevertheless retained possession of their benefices. Women inherited fiefs in southern France before the end of the tenth century, and this practice spread quickly throughout the feudal world. Lords tried to ensure that in these cases a representative, usually the woman's husband, fulfilled the service aspects of the contract. This gave them an excuse to intervene in the marriage plans of their female vassals. Women who possessed great estates often defied such claims. Others, like Matilda of Tuscany (c. 1046–1115) simply refused to remarry af-

SUBINFEUDATION

This declaration of homage indicates some of the problems caused by subinfeudation as well as the kind of compromise that might, in theory, alleviate them.

I, John of Toul, make known that I am the liege man of the lady Beatrice, countess of Troyes, and of her son, Theobald, count of Champagne, against every creature, living or dead, saving my allegiance to Enjourand of Coucy, lord John of Arcis, and the count of Grandpré. If it should happen that the count of Grandpré should be at war with the countess and count of Champagne on his own quarrel, I will aid the count of Grandpré in my own person, and will send to the count and countess of Champagne the knights whose service I owe to them for the fief which I hold of them. But if the count of Grandpré shall make war on the countess and the count of Champagne on behalf of his friends and not by his own quarrel, I will aid in my own person the countess and count of Champagne, and will send one knight to the count of Grandpré for the service which I owe him for the fief which I hold of him, but I will not go myself into the territory of the count of Grandpré to make war on him.

From Thatcher, O. J., and McNeal, E. H., eds., *A Source Book of Medieval History* (New York: Scribner's, 1905).

Questions: How does this document undermine the basic principles of feudal loyalty? How do you think an arrangement like this would work in practice?

Subinfeudation. This illumination from the same manuscript as Figure 8.5 appears to represent the process of subinfeudation. The hand of one of the vassals in the center rest on the shoulder of another man in the group on the left.

ter the death of her husband. Ruling on her own and deploying a powerful army, she became a dominant figure in Italian politics for almost 40 years.

"Alienation" of Fiefs. The alienation, or sale, of fiefs for cash or other considerations was far more difficult to achieve than heritability, but it became common by the twelfth century. The lord's permission remained necessary if a fief changed hands, but the increasing frequency of such transactions indicates that the long process of transition to private property and a cash-based economy had already begun.

Private Jurisdiction. Private jurisdiction, or the establishment by vassals of feudal and manorial courts, was another matter. The practice of allowing great men to maintain their own courts of law dates back to the latter days of the Roman Empire. Feudalism extended this benefit to nearly every vassal with subjects of his or her own. Prospective vassals commonly demanded the right to preside over their own court. Princes and tenants-in-chief accepted this because their own courts

could not cope with the proliferation of local disputes. A distinction was maintained between minor and major causes, the latter being reserved for royal or county jurisdictions, but the proliferation of feudal and manorial courts inevitably weakened what threads of central authority remained.

Within a few short generations, feudalism had created a political system based on decentralization and hereditary privilege. Although at first confined within the limits of the old Carolingian Empire, the Norman expansion brought feudal institutions to England in 1066 and after 1072 to Sicily and southern Italy. In all of these regions, a tangled web of legal contracts and the diffusion of military power, among what had become a warrior caste, ensured the permanence of the system.

The Origins of Chivalry. The values and attitudes of that caste were increasingly defined by adherence to the ideals of **chivalry.** The term comes from the French word for horse and reflects the self-conscious superiority of the mounted warrior. In subsequent centuries, the chivalric code grew increasingly elaborate as its rituals became fixed by a vast literature. Ceremonial initiations, designed to set the warrior apart from society as a whole, marked the creation of knights from the beginning of feudalism. They are not to be confused with the ceremony of vassalage but were the culmination of a long period of training and preparation. Boys of 10 or 12 were usually sent by their fathers to serve as pages in the household of another lord. There they learned the arts of war, including horsemanship and the use of a lance, shield, and sword. Intense physical training consumed much of their time, but pages also learned fortification and enough physics to construct siege engines and other military devices.

Their first exposure to warfare was as squires, who attended a knight on the battlefield, tended his horses and weapons, and protected him if he fell. When and if he successfully completed this apprenticeship, the squire was dubbed a knight. In the early days, the ceremony could be performed by any other knight and was usually concluded with a blow to the head or shoulders. Touching with the flat of a sword came later. In the Germanic world, the new knight was girded with his sword, a practice that probably dates from the knighting of Louis the Pious by his father, Charlemagne. Religious elements began to creep into these initiations by the middle of the tenth century and symbolized the growing sense that knights, like priests, had a divinely established vocation.

Manorialism and Dependency in Medieval Europe (850–1250)

A fief could support a fighting man only if someone else were available to work it. As a general rule, knights did not till the soil even in the days before their status became too great to permit physical labor. They were on call whenever danger threatened, and their training normally required several hours of practice and exercise each day. Even hunting, their primary recreation, which they always pursued on horseback, was a form of military exercise. The provision of labor therefore created problems from the start, and the manorial system that lords and knights adapted to provide for it grew hand in hand with the feudal institutions of the new aristocracy.

Manorial Agreements. Manorialism as a means of securing scarce labor had existed since ancient times and would survive in eastern Europe until the nineteenth century. The basis of the medieval system was the manorial tenure, which in some respects paralleled the feudal tenures of the knights. In its simplest form, a peasant surrendered his allod, or freehold, to a lord in return for the lord's protection. The lord would then grant it back to him as a **tenement** with stipulations that made the tenant the legal subject of the lord. Those who possessed little or no land could also request protection, but their poverty placed them at a disadvantage in negotiating the terms.

The nature of manorial tenures varied widely. Although a tenant could remain technically free, in most cases tenancy involved a descent into serfdom. Serfs resembled slaves, but unlike slaves they could not be sold as individuals and were entitled to hold property. They could also, within certain limits, negotiate contracts, undertake obligations, and testify in court. Both their land and their personal rights, however, were contractually encumbered. Once they had placed themselves under a lord's protection, they bound themselves to their tenement for life and were often forbidden to marry anyone other than a subject of the same lord. Because they were legally subject to another person, they lost all political rights including the right to sue a free man in court.

Economically, these agreements obliged the tenant to return a portion of his annual crop to the lord or provide labor on the lord's lands for a fixed number of days per year. Most contracts required both (see Document 8.4). Labor services might also involve maintenance work on the lord's castle or on the infrastructure of the manor, including roads, ditches, and other facilities. Some agreements required military service, usually for a maximum of 40 days per year between planting and harvest. Untrained peasant troops were ineffective in a military environment dominated by heavy cavalry, but they could provide logistical support, dig trenches, and guard the baggage.

Another feature of these agreements involved services purchased exclusively from the lord. The tenant accepted the jurisdiction of the lord's court and agreed to use only the lord's mill or the lord's animals at stud in return for payments in kind. Other stipulations might involve access to the lord's orchards, woodlands, or streams. The right of tenants to hunt, fish, or gather fallen wood for fuel was strictly regulated. In return, the lord agreed to protect the tenant and his property both physically and in the event of legal proceedings. Although manorial tenures usually could be inherited, the lord commonly required an investiture fee from the peasant's heirs when a tenement changed hands.

Women as Tenants. Women rarely had the right to make such contracts in the first instance. If they were married, their legal rights were largely subsumed under those of their husbands, and their testimony in a peasant court was accepted only in limited circumstances. They could, however, inherit tenements. In such cases, substitutes, who were usually paid in goods and services instead of cash, fulfilled the woman's military and labor obligations.

MANORIAL OBLIGATIONS

John Cayworth was one of the larger tenants on the English manor of Bernholme in 1307. His obligations were correspondingly great and may be compared with the data in Tables 11.1 and 11.2. This excerpt from the Custumals (customs of the manor) of Battle Abbey provides a good example of how manorial tenures worked. Such agreements were almost never written down before the end of the thirteenth century, and it is doubtful if the monetary value of the obligations would have been calculated in this way before the widespread commutation of services for cash.

They say, moreover, that John Cayworth holds a house and 30 acres of land, and owes yearly 2s. at Easter and Michaelmas; and he owes a cock and two hens at Christmas, of the value of 4d.

And he ought to harrow for two days at the Lenten sowing with one man and his own horse and his own harrow, the value of the work being 4d.; and he is to receive from the lord on each day 3 meals, of the value of 5d.; and then the lord will be at a loss of 1d. . . .

And he ought to carry the manure of the lord for 2 days with 1 cart, with his own 2 oxen, the value of the work being 8d.; and he is to receive from the lord each day 3 meals of the price as above, and thus the service is worth 3d. clear.

And he shall find 1 man for two days for mowing on the meadow of the lord, who can mow, by estimation 1 acre and a half, the value of the mowing of an acre being 6d.; the sum is therefore 9d.; and he is to receive each day 3 meals of the value given above; and thus the mowing is worth 4d. clear. And he ought to gather and carry that same hay which he has cut, the price of the work being 3d. . . .

And he ought to carry wood from the woods of the lord as far as the manor [house] for two days in summer with a cart and 3 animals of his own, the value of the work being 9d. And he shall receive from the lord each day 3 meals of the price given above; and thus the work is worth 4d. clear.

And he ought to find a man for 2 days to cut heath, the value of the work being 4d., and he shall have 3 meals each day of the value given above; and thus the lord will lose, if he receives the service, 3d.

And he ought to carry the heath which he has cut, the value of the work being 5d., and he shall receive from the lord 3 meals at the price of 2½d., and thus the work will be worth 2½d. clear.

The Gatehouse of Battle Abbey. One of Engand's greatest monasteries, Battle Abbey was built on the site of the Battle of Hastings as a penance imposed by the papal authorities in 1070 for the bloodshed caused by the Norman invasion. The building shown here replaced the original structure in the late middle ages.

And he ought to carry to Battle twice in the summer season, each time half a load of grain, the value of the service being 4d. And he shall receive in the manor each time 1 meal of the value of 2d. And thus the work is worth 2d. clear.

The total of the rents with the value of the hens is 2s. 4d.

The total of the value of the works is 2s., 3 1/2d., owed from the said John yearly.

From "Custumals of Battle Abbey," in Edward P. Cheyney, ed., *Pennsylvania Translations and Reprints*, vol. 3, no. 5 (Philadelphia: University of Pennsylvania Press, 1902, p. 30).

Questions: How did the lord offset the costs involved in providing labor service? Why do you think the tenant not simply offer a cash payment or its equivalent in goods?

The Burden of Rents and Services. The sum of these manorial burdens could be great or relatively small and might be compounded by tithes or other obligations owed to the church. Peasants preferred rents calculated as a portion of the total harvest to those expressed in fixed amounts because fixed rents could bring starvation in a year of bad harvests. Miller's fees and similar charges would have to have been paid in any case and involved only a theoretical loss of freedom. Most people could not afford to transport grain or livestock to distant villages for milling or stud services. Labor services, however, could be onerous and deeply resented.

FIGURE 8.6 *Harvesting Apples on the Manor.* An idealized picture of life on the manor from the late 1400s. The manorial systems introduced in the tenth and eleventh centuries persisted in some cases until the 1700s. (From: Petrus de Crescentiis, *Des profits ruraux des champs.* France, late 1400s.)

the mercy of all sorts of armed marauders, including neighboring lords whose behavior was often no better than that of the Vikings. Faced with the prospect of unending, uncontrolled violence, most people accepted their loss of freedom as a necessity. Instances of coercion by prospective lords were apparently rare and sometimes subtle. The manorial system was, like its feudal counterpart, a necessary adaptation to a world gone mad.

Manorial Organization. A manor can best be defined as an estate whose tenants are the subjects of their lords. It was therefore a legal and economic, rather than geographical, concept. This meant that, in physical terms, no two manors were exactly alike. Their character differed widely according to topography, agricultural practices, and local custom. Some might contain an entire village or group of villages. Others might be composed of a group of tenements scattered among several villages, with each village inhabited by the subjects of different lords. The latter situation arose in Germany and parts of France because, in the beginning at least, peasants could sometimes commend themselves to the lord of their choice. In Italy and southern France, the survival of allodial holdings in the midst of feudal and manorial tenures complicated matters even further. A peasant might own some of his land outright and hold the rest as a tenement from his lord. Only in England was the village manor almost universal.

Even the lands of an individual tenement were not necessarily contiguous. A peasant family could rarely cultivate more than the equivalent of 30 or 40 acres without assistance. Many plots were far smaller. With the passage of time and the vagaries of inheritance, farmers could find themselves holding fragments of land scattered over several square miles. Parcels of arable land might also be set aside for the lord and for the priest if there was one. Most communities also possessed common land that was available for allocation by the village elders.

Management. Few manors boasted a lord in residence and few lords managed their properties directly. An appointed steward typically collected the lord's dues and saw to the maintenance of his property. The steward (reeve, *maire*, or *Bauermeister*) was originally a capable peasant who received lands, exemptions, or special privileges for his work on the lord's behalf. Such men almost invariably became wealthy, and in the later

In a society that was still largely illiterate, these contracts were not written down and the precise terms of each tenure were submerged in an oral tradition called "the custom of the manor." In later years, the margin of survival for a peasant family often depended on the negotiating skills of their ancestors.

The bargains struck between lords and peasants were unequal, but the harshness of the system was softened to some extent by the ideal of mutual obligation. In feudal Europe, land—the basis of nearly all wealth—was no longer regarded as private property. Peasants held their tenements from lords, who held their fiefs from the king, who held his kingdom ultimately from God. The terms by which land was occupied were spelled out in law and custom, and they could rarely be changed or abrogated without difficulty. Fiefs could not be sold at will, and tenants could not be dispossessed without cause. Moreover, lords were obligated to protect their subjects' property as well as their persons. Some were wise enough to take a paternalistic interest in the welfare of those who inhabited their estates. Whether a lord was good or bad, tenants enjoyed a measure of security that the wage laborers of a later day would never know. If the lot of a medieval peasant was hard, it was in part because the margin of subsistence was small. Most people grew little more than enough to feed their families and could scarcely afford to contribute anything.

It should also be remembered that, in the beginning, most peasants had voluntarily accepted their manorial tenures. A peasant without protection was at

FIGURE 8.7 *A Steward Overseeing the Reaping of Grain.* The steward served as the lord of the manor's representative, collecting his rents and supervising work on the manor's infrastructure. In rare cases, he might supervise the harvest as well, although most peasants knew perfectly well how to reap their crops. (From the Queen Mary Psalter, an English manuscript of the early 1300s.)

Middle Ages, some of them transcended the limitations of peasant status and acquired knightly status and a coat of arms, usually by serving their lord in a military action. Along with the *ministeriales,* the household officials who served the immediate needs of the lord and his castle or residence, the stewards constituted an intermediate social class of some importance. Few, however, were popular. Some were petty tyrants who extorted goods and favors from the peasants while embezzling from their lord. Even the best stewards were powerful figures who had to be placated at every turn. In some regions, they not only collected rents and dues but also served as judges in peasant courts and determined the boundaries of tenements in cases of dispute. In other, happier places, the villagers themselves assumed these functions.

Manorialism could and did exist without feudalism. Where manorialism and feudalism combined, they produced a social and political system that was highly resistant to change. The knights had achieved a monopoly of both economic and military power and thus could impose the values of their class on society as a whole.

NONFEUDAL EUROPE (850–1250)

By the middle of the tenth century, feudal institutions dominated what had been the Carolingian Empire. Another, nonfeudal part of Europe successfully resisted the new social order. Scandinavia, untroubled by raids or invasions, preserved the main features of its social structure and system of land tenure until well into the early modern period. Individual farmsteads, often located at a distance from the nearest village and worked by the owner's family and servants, continued to be common. Slavery declined and eventually disappeared under the influence of Christianity. Houses, built of logs and connected to their outbuildings for protection against the winter, retained the sturdy simplicity of those in Viking days.

Anglo-Saxon England. Until the Norman invasion of 1066, the Anglo-Saxons, too, were able to function within the limits of their traditional social order, although the basis of land tenure changed dramatically. The Anglo-Saxon *ceorl* (churl), or peasant, was typically a freeholder who paid taxes for the support of his king's household and served in the *fyrd,* a kind of militia whose tactics resembled those of the Frankish hosts. As in other Germanic cultures, the kings were further served by a *comitatus* of fighting men, known as *gesiths. Gesiths* sometimes received land as a reward when they retired. They were usually supported during their fighting careers by the bounty of the king's hall and by the sharing of treasure.

Before the Viking invasions, England had been divided into seven kingdoms: East Anglia, Essex, Kent, Mercia, Northumberland, Sussex, and Wessex. Their small size made a decentralized mobile defense unnecessary, and feudal institutions did not develop; however, the chaos of the midninth century forced large numbers of hitherto independent ceorls to seek the protection of manorial relationships. Manorialism was firmly established and may have been the dominant form of English economic organization when **Alfred the Great** of Wessex (reigned 871–899) began the process of uniting England into a single kingdom.

In Alfred's view, the achievement of political unity depended in part on the revival of learning and a sense of common cultural identity. He arranged for the translation of religious classics into Old English and commissioned the *Anglo-Saxon Chronicle,* one version of which was updated continuously until 1154. His policies bore fruit in the reign of Edgar, from 959 to 974, when England finally achieved political unity and scholars compiled the rich body of Anglo-Saxon poetry into four great books, the most important of which was the epic *Beowulf.* The political failure of the succeeding years should not obscure the vibrant, functional society that fell to the Normans in 1066.

Ireland. The Celtic world, although also subject to the full fury of the Norsemen, resisted the temptation to exchange land for military service until forced to do so in the twelfth and thirteenth centuries. Even then, the penetration of feudalism was far from complete. The Vikings ravaged Ireland from end to end and established nonfeudal enclaves in the vicinity of Dublin and elsewhere. In the rest of the country, the old system of clans and kings survived. A large number of chieftains, each ruling a limited area and surrounded by his own band of fierce warriors, provided a relatively effective mobile defense without resorting to heavy cavalry. It was not until 1171–1172 that feuding among the Irish chiefs gave Henry II of England an excuse to invade the country. The Anglo-Normans established feudalism in Meath, Leinster, and other areas that submitted to their rule. When English control weakened during the fourteenth century, an Irish political and cultural revival inspired the abandonment of feudalism in some of these regions. A feudal enclave remained, but much of Ireland preserved its nonfeudal way of life into early modern times.

Wales. The experience of Wales was similar. At the height of the raids, traditional chieftains had established a kind of manorialism in the more exposed coastal areas. The rugged and inaccessible upland areas remained free. After 1093, Norman adventurers tried to impose feudal tenures on certain parts of South Wales and Pembrokeshire. These efforts were partial and usually contested. Even in the areas of greatest Norman penetration, traditional institutions stood side by side with new ones until well into the modern age.

The Welsh owed much of their independence to the ruggedness of their native land. In general, upland areas even in the heart of continental Europe stood a good chance of escaping feudal domination. Peasant communities in the Alps and the Pyrenees were remote as well as poor. Like many of the Welsh, the inhabitants of these peasant communities lived by herding and subsistence agriculture supplemented by hunting and gathering. Because they produced little or no surplus and were prohibited by geography from engaging in large-scale agriculture, they tempted neither the raiders nor the lords. They also found it easy to defend themselves. Mounted knights fought at a disadvantage in a largely vertical landscape, and narrow gorges provided ideal sites for ambushes. Peasants of the high valleys usually retained their ancient freedoms, although they were never as completely isolated from the larger body of society as their mountaineer counterparts in Southeast Asia.

The Spanish Kingdoms. A rugged landscape also protected the remnants of Christian Spain. In other ways, the situation on the Cantabrian coast and the southern slopes of the Pyrenees was unique. Catalonia had been a county of the Frankish Empire, and feudalism appeared there at an early date. Asturias, León (Lay-own'), and Castile were poor but independent kingdoms composed largely of small-acreage farmers who held their land in freehold. By the ninth century, the shortage of good land had forced them to take the offensive against Islam, drawing back if the opposition became too intense, moving forward when a target of opportunity arose. In the beginning, much of the campaigning was done on a free enterprise basis. *Caudillos* (Cow-dee'-lyos), or war chiefs, commanding bands of free peasant warriors, organized the conquests. The kings encouraged this by allowing the chiefs to keep most, but not all, of the land they won. Kings often granted caudillos titles of nobility as well. The caudillos then parceled out much of the conquered land to their followers, who usually farmed it themselves. Although freeholders, these men now lived on a violent frontier. To protect themselves, they placed themselves in *encomienda,* or "commended" themselves to a lord, who protected them in return for dues and services. This created a *de facto* manor, but with peasants who retained full personal and property rights. Feudal tenures were unknown, private jurisdiction was strictly limited, and the king reserved the right to revoke both land and titles at will. The *señorios* (sen-yor'-ee-os), or lordships, created by these arrangements were often vast, but they were based upon a legal and political system unlike that of feudal Europe.

To hold and defend the conquered lands, kings and nobles also created municipalities to attract new settlers. Spanish towns played an important role in territorial expansion. They established urban militias in the early ninth century that soon became important components of the Christian military effort. Whether the militias fought on their own behalf or under the direct orders of the king, towns gained booty and royal grants, whose provisions resembled those of the señorios. Large tracts of land and many villages came under their control as peasants commended themselves to towns instead of to secular or ecclesiastical lords. The landholders who did so typically became citizens of the town and thus doubly immune to feudal institutions.

Northern Italy. In northern Italy, towns served as a barrier to feudal institutions for different reasons. Larger and richer than their Spanish counterparts, they had offered credible protection to their neighbors long before the beginnings of a feudal age. They continued to do so in the face of Muslim raids, and Italians had few incentives to develop a new political and military system. Northern Italy, however, was part of the Holy Roman Empire (see following discussion). In the tenth and eleventh centuries, the emperors established a number of important fiefs, primarily to reward supporters in an area far from their German power base. Those who held them became, at least temporarily, important influences in Italian politics, but feudalism itself never became a dominant institution. Instead, a patchwork of tenures developed in which allods, feudal manors, and urban jurisdictions existed side by side in a relatively restricted space. In contrast, southern Italy had been a region of large estates since Roman times. When Norman conquerors imposed feudalism at the end of the eleventh century (see Chapter 9), they substituted one set of lords for another while changing the legal basis of their holdings.

THE FEUDAL MONARCHIES (C. 950–1250)

This rapid survey of nonfeudal Europe reveals that although feudalism never became universal, the disorders of the ninth and tenth centuries led to the growth of manorialism—or other systems of collective security—in all but the most isolated sections of Europe. A majority of Europeans renounced personal and economic freedom as the price of survival. Peasants who had formerly been free, slave, or *coloni* now shared a common servility.

The Social Consequences of Dependency. The impact of this change on everyday life should not be exaggerated. The correlation between personal freedom and political or social influence has always been inexact. The free Anglo-Saxon or Frankish peasant had often been subordinated as effectively by debt and by the threat of personal force as his descendants were by the custom of the manor, and he was subjected to taxes and demands for military service that could be as onerous as the feudal dues of a later period. Women had never been free in the sense that they remained the legal subjects of their fathers or husbands.

Moreover, the world that emerged from the aftermath of the great raids retained many distinctions of wealth and status, even among peasants. Servility was not incompatible with a secure and even comfortable life, while freedom could mean a hardscrabble existence on marginal lands. Those who remained free often did so because they inhabited malarial swamps or mountain crags unwanted by either knights or Vikings.

The conversion to feudal and manorial tenures seems more dramatic when seen in relation to its effect on social institutions and attitudes—the ties that bound society together. After the great raids, the gap between the vast majority of the population and the aristocracy that ruled them widened perceptibly. Social mobility was not only difficult to achieve but also generally condemned. The writers of the day maintained that people should not attempt to rise above their class. A society that had just emerged from two centuries of near-anarchy valued permanence and security, but the longevity of

feudal institutions was based only in part on the natural conservatism of those who had suffered much.

Political Decentralization. The apparent success of heavy cavalry in dealing with the crises of the ninth and tenth centuries had created a powerful myth of class superiority. The medieval knight believed in this myth and made it the basis of an entire way of life. His education, leisure activities, and ultimately, the moral and aesthetic values of his class were grounded in the perception of himself as the armed and mounted protector of society—a perception that also gave him his chief claim to social privilege. By the end of the tenth century, the conditions that created the knights had largely disappeared, but the knights now possessed the bulk of society's resources and could neither be displaced nor effectively controlled. Class divisions henceforth widened and acquired a more elaborate ideological basis than they had formerly possessed. A system of military tactics that was by no means suitable for all occasions would be preserved until long after it had outlived its usefulness. Above all, the creation of a dominant social class whose power was based on widely scattered estates would perpetuate the decentralization of political authority for centuries to come.

An immediate consequence of this decentralization was feudal warfare, disruptive and endemic, but not as devastating as the great raids. The warrior's sense of vocation, the development of chivalry, a code of conduct based on the ideals of honor and courage, and the emphasis on individual and corporate rights characteristic of feudal law all encouraged the lords to fight one another in defense of what they considered their honor and their right. The church sought to restrain these tendencies by encouraging the "Peace of God" movement. Councils or bishops issued decrees against wanton violence and tried to limit the fighting to certain days of the week (see Document 8.5). Such measures achieved little. The political history of the age became in large measure an attempt by kings to control the centrifugal tendencies of feudalism in the interests of public order.

France and Norman England

The Norman Conquest of England. Nowhere was this more evident than in northwestern Europe, where the legacy of Norman expansion caused a protracted struggle between the kings of France and England. Anglo-Saxon England fell to the Normans when its last king, Edward the Confessor, died without heirs. There were three claimants to the throne: Edward's first cousin, William, duke of Normandy (c. 1028–1087); Harald Hardrada, king of Norway; and the Saxon Harold Godwinsson. When the English Witan, or council, chose Harold Godwinsson, the other claimants attacked him

THE PEACE AND TRUCE OF GOD

The following decrees were proclaimed by a council held at Toulouges in the far south of France. They are typical of such decrees from other regions of Europe and reveal a world of bandits, fortified churches, and armed monks, to say nothing of unrelieved violence against the peasantry.

1. This peace has been confirmed by the bishops, by the abbots, by the counts and viscounts and the other God-fearing nobles in this bishopric, to the effect that in the future, beginning with this day, no man may commit an act of violence in a church, or in the space which surrounds it and which is covered by its privileges, or in the burying ground around, or in the dwelling houses which are, or may be, within thirty paces of it.

2. We do not include in this measure those which have been, or which shall be, fortified as châteaux, or those in which plunderers or thieves are accustomed to store their ill-gotten booty, or which give them a place of refuge. Nevertheless we desire that such churches be under this protection until complaint of them should be made to the bishop or to the chapter.

3. Furthermore, it is forbidden that anyone attack the clergy who do not bear arms. . . .

5. Let no one burn or destroy the dwellings of the peasants and the clergy, the dove-cotes or the granaries. Let no man dare to kill, beat, or wound a peasant or serf or the wife of either, or to seize them and carry them off . . . but it is not forbidden to lay hold of them to bring them to justice.

6. The bishops of whom we have spoken have solemnly confirmed the Truce of God, which has been enjoined upon all Christians, from the setting of the sun on the fourth day of the week, that is to say, Wednesday, until the rising of the sun on Monday . . . If anyone during this truce shall violate it, let him pay a double composition and subsequently undergo the ordeal of cold water.

From *A Source Book of Medieval History*, ed. F. A. Ogg (New York and Cincinnati: American Book Co., 1935, pp. 229–230).

Question: Aside from trying to limit fighting to 3 days a week, what is the primary purpose of this document?

---

simultaneously on two fronts. Harold defeated a Norwegian invasion at Stamford Bridge on September 23, 1066, and rushed south to meet William, who had landed near Hastings on the same day. Exhausted by the battle and by a march of almost 300 miles, the Saxon army was crushed on October 14. William, now known as "the Conqueror" became king of England.

The Government of William the Conqueror. William imposed feudalism but tried to limit political decentralization. The fiefs he granted to his Norman followers in England consisted of manors scattered throughout the country. In theory, this would prevent them from consolidating their power over a geographical region. He also retained the Saxon office of **sheriff,** or shire reeve. The shire is the English equivalent of a county. The sheriff collected taxes, administered the royal domains, and presided over the shire courts, thereby maintaining a parallel structure of royal authority in the countryside. Then, in 1086, William's officials produced a comprehensive survey of all English properties known as the **Domesday** (Dooms'-day) **Book** (see Document 8.6). William, alone among the European monarchs of his day, knew the holder of every piece of land in his realm and its value. Norman England was in other words the most tightly administered monarchy of the central Middle Ages. But William's conquest gave birth to a political anomaly: the king of England was still duke of Normandy, and

therefore vassal to the king of France for one of the richest provinces on the Continent.

The Growth of France. The situation became critical in the reign of Henry II (1154–1189). The development of the French monarchy had been slow and painful. When Louis V, the last of the Carolingians, died in 987, the great French feudatories elected Hugh Capet (Cah-pey) king, primarily because his small holdings in the region of Paris made it unlikely that he would ever pose a threat to their interests. No one expected him to found a dynasty that would last until 1328. The Ile de France, as the area is called to this day, was a hotbed of feudal anarchy. The Capetian kings took more than a century to establish control. When Louis VI "the Fat" died in 1137 after a series of successful campaigns, he left a small but powerful state centered on Paris to his son Louis VII. Guided by his chief adviser, Suger (Soo-jey), abbot of St. Denis, Louis VII tried to double his holdings by marrying **Eleanor of Aquitaine** (Ak-wi-tain-ye, c. 1122–1204), heiress to vast estates in southwestern France. The marriage was a disaster. Louis was pious and ascetic; Eleanor was attractive, witty, and a patron of troubadours, the poet-musicians who served as guardians of chivalric culture. She apparently took the adulterous conventions of chivalric love too seriously, and Louis had the marriage annulled in 1152 amid charges of infidelity with one of her cousins. The couple had two daughters

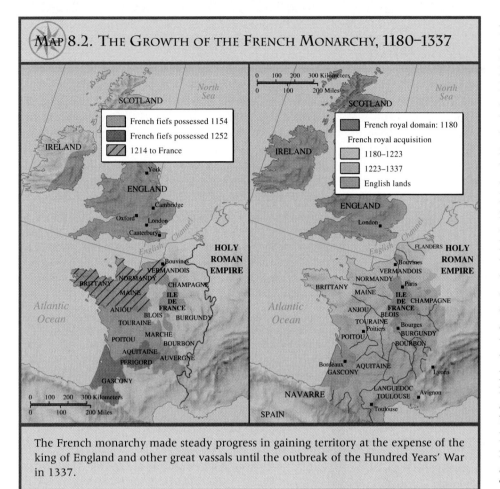

MAP 8.2. THE GROWTH OF THE FRENCH MONARCHY, 1180–1337

French fiefs possessed 1154
French fiefs possessed 1252
1214 to France

French royal domain: 1180
French royal acquisition
1180–1223
1223–1337
English lands

The French monarchy made steady progress in gaining territory at the expense of the king of England and other great vassals until the outbreak of the Hundred Years' War in 1337.

but no son. Eleanor soon married **Henry II of England,** her junior by 10 years.

Henry II of England. Henry was a king of boundless energy and ambition. Among other things, he reformed the royal courts and created a system of itinerant judges (the "justices in eyre") who offered sworn inquests and juries as alternatives to the duels and ordeals of baronial courts. Their decisions became the basis of English common law. Henry also strengthened the Exchequer, or treasury, so called because calculations were made by moving counters on a checkered tabletop. As part of his legal reforms, the king tried to assume royal jurisdiction over priests who committed crimes. **Thomas à Becket,** the king's own appointee as Archbishop of Canterbury, opposed him. After years of dispute, Henry lost patience and said something that may have been misunderstood by his followers. Four of them went to Canterbury and murdered the archbishop in front of his altar. It was one of the great scandals of the Middle Ages and made Becket a saint, but it did little to weaken Henry's power. He left England far stronger than he had found it.

Anglo-French Conflict. Unfortunately, his marriage to Eleanor of Aquitaine left Henry in possession of half of France. For Louis VII, this was a personal affront as well as a threat to his sovereignty. For the next 300 years, the primary goal of French policy was to secure either the obedience or the expulsion of the English. It was not an ethnic issue initially, for the English court remained culturally and linguistically French. Instead, the situation raised questions that went to the heart of feudal relationships: Could a sovereign prince be the vassal of another? What happened to ties of dependence when the vassal was richer and more powerful than his lord? The issue had been brought up in a somewhat different form by the powerful counts of Flanders who held lands from both the king of France and the Holy Roman Emperor. The issue would be revived in later years by the growth of the duchy of Burgundy. The dispute between France and England, however, remained the central issue of west European politics until the fifteenth century.

The establishment of Henry II's Angevin (An'-je-vin) Empire inspired a reorganization of the French monarchy. Begun by Louis VII, the work was completed by his son, **Philip II Augustus** (reigned 1179–1223). Louis created an effective royal army and, on the diplomatic front, concluded an improbable alliance with his ex-wife, Eleanor of Aquitaine. After 16 years of marriage and eight children, Eleanor decided that she would no longer tolerate Henry's infidelity or increasingly abusive behavior. She retired to Poitiers (Pwa-tyay) in France with her daughter, Mary, countess of Champagne, and established a court that was to become a veritable school of chivalry. In 1173, she and Louis encouraged her sons in an unsuccessful rebellion against their father. Two of these sons, **Richard I Lion-Heart** (reigned 1189–1199) and **John** (reigned 1199–1216), would, as kings of England, bring ruin to Henry's cause.

King John, Magna Carta, and the Loss of Normandy. Richard spent most of his reign crusading in the Holy Land at ruinous expense. On his return he

THE NORMAN CONQUEST, 1066

The Norman conquest transformed the history of England. Although the Normans were of Viking ancestry, they had adopted French language and culture. For many generations they ruled as a foreign aristocracy, but their associations with France and their introduction of feudal institutions tied England for the first time to the life of the continent. Eventually, the culture of the Norman French merged with that of their subjects to produce the English language and culture of modern times.

Description of a Manor from the Domesday Book

This description of the manor of Hecham, Essex, in 1086 illustrates the care with which William the Conqueror's administrators catalogued the wealth of England. It also provides a sense of what a medium-sized manor was like and of the dramatic changes brought by the conquest. A *hide* is a measure of land that varied between 80 and 100 modern acres. A *bordar* was the lowest rank of villein, who performed menial service in return for a cottage.

Peter de Valence holds in domain Hecham, which Haldane a freeman held in the time of King Edward, as a manor, and as 5 hides. There have always been 2 ploughs in the demesne, 4 ploughs of the men. At that time there were 8 villeins, now 10; then there were 2 bordars, now 3; at both times 4 servi, woods for 300 swine, 18 acres of meadow. Then there were 2 fish ponds and a half, now there are none. At that time there was 1 ox, now there are 15 cattle and 1 small horse and 18 swine and 2 hives of bees. At that time it was worth 69s., now 4£10s. When he received this manor he found only 1 ox and 1 acre planted. Of those 5 hides spoken of above, one was held in the time of King Edward by 2 freemen, and it was added to the manor in the time of King William. It was worth in the time of King Edward 10s., now 22s., and William holds this from Peter de Valence.

From "Domesday Book," II, 78b, in *Translations and Reprints from the Original Sources of European History*, vol. 3, no. 5 (Philadelphia: University of Pennsylvania, 1896, pp. 3–4).

Question: Assuming that Hecham was fairly typical, what does this passage tell us about changes in the English economy during the eleventh century?

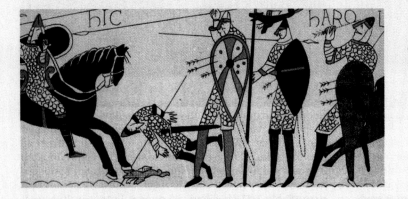

◀ *Detail from the Bayeaux Tapestry.* The Bayeux Tapestry commemorates the Norman invasion of England in narrative form. It was designed to run clockwise around the entire nave of the Cathedral of Bayeux (consecrated 1077) and was originally 230 feet long and 20 inches high. It is an embroidery, not a true, woven tapestry. The work was probably done by the women of the court, who seem to have known a great deal about war and seafaring. This segment shows the death of King Harold in the center.

was captured by the Emperor Henry VI and forced to pay an enormous ransom that pushed England to the brink of revolt. His brother John, who succeeded him, compounded this folly with a series of catastrophic mistakes. In 1200, he married a woman who was already engaged to a vassal of Philip Augustus. The vassal appealed to his lord, and Philip called upon John, as duke of Normandy, to present himself so that the case could be judged. This was the normal way of dealing with disputes between vassals of the same lord, but John, acting in his capacity as king of England, refused to submit to the justice of another sovereign. Philip responded by confiscating Normandy in 1204.

John's attempts to recover his lost duchy forced him to extreme financial measures that further alienated his subjects and brought him into conflict with the church. Pope Innocent III excommunicated him in 1209 and placed England under an interdict, a papal decree that forbade the administration of the sacraments. To lift it, John had to declare England a papal fief and renounce the royal appointment of bishops. The final blow occurred at the battle of Bouvines (Boo-veen) in 1214, when Philip Augustus defeated John's Anglo-Flemish-Imperial coalition in battle. Disgusted, a coalition of English barons rebelled and forced John to accept the **Magna Carta** (Great Charter). Although the Magna

The Keep, Rochester Castle. The Normans built massive castles, including Rochester and the Tower of London, to overawe their new subjects and forestall a potential revolt. The Tower of London has been extensively altered, but the ruins of Rochester provide a sense of how Norman castles actually looked. The view shown here is of the square keep, or central tower of the castle where the lord and his retainers lived. In the event of an attack, the keep would be the last stronghold to fall.

William the Conqueror. Detail from the Bayeaux Tapestry showing an idealized and uncharacteristically benign William the Conqueror.

Carta (see Document 8.6) is widely regarded as a landmark in the development of Anglo-Saxon constitutional thought, it was primarily an affirmation of feudal privileges. It did nothing for ordinary men and women and John's successors largely ignored it. A later age would see it as a bulwark of individual rights against the claims of the state.

The Reign of Philip Augustus. The failures of King John left Philip Augustus the most powerful figure in western Europe. By 1204, he had already added Artois (Ar-twah) and the Vermandois (Ver-man-dwa) to his realms. The struggle with John brought him

Normandy, Maine, Anjou (Ahn-zhoo), and Touraine (Too-rain'). Bouvines brought him Flanders. To govern his new estates, he appointed royal officials known as *baillis,* or seneschals (sen'-es-shals). Their function resembled that of an English sheriff, but they were usually lawyers with no prior connection to the territories in which they served. They therefore depended entirely on the king's favor and had little opportunity to build a power base of their own. Philip's policy established the pattern of French administration until 1789: provinces retained their own historic institutions, but officers of the crown administered them. By the end of the thirteenth century, Philip's successors had acquired

MAGNA CARTA

The following sections from the Magna Carta show that it was primarily intended to confirm and extend the privileges of the barons, but some of the provisions, such as number thirty-nine, had broader implications. Taken as a whole, the Great Charter set clear limits on the authority of the crown, and it is easy to understand why English revolutionaries of the seventeenth century regarded the document as one of the foundations of English liberty. Sections two and three restrict the crown's ability to extort fees from its vassals when a fief is inherited. *Scutage* (Skyou'-tidge) in number twelve was a fee paid by a tenant in lieu of military service. John and some of his predecessors had begun to levy it for other purposes.

1. In the first place we have granted to God, and by this our present charter confirmed, for us and our heirs forever, that the English church shall be free, and shall hold its rights entire and its liberties uninjured.

2. If any of our earls or barons, or others holding from us in chief by military service shall have died, and when he had died his heir shall be of full age and owe relief, he shall have his inheritance by the ancient relief; that is to say, the heir or heirs of an earl for the whole barony of an earl a hundred pounds; the heir or heirs of a baron for a whole barony a hundred pounds; the heir or heirs of a knight, for a whole knight's fee, a hundred shillings at most; and who owes less let him give less according to the ancient custom of fiefs.

3. If, moreover, the heir of any one of such shall be under age, and shall be in wardship, when he comes of age he shall have his inheritance without relief and without a fine. . . .

12. No scutage or aid shall be imposed in our kingdom except by the common council of our kingdom, except for the ransoming of our own body, for the making of our oldest son a knight, and for the once marrying of our oldest daughter, and for these purposes it shall be only a reasonable aid.

13. And the city of London shall have all its ancient liberties and free customs, as well by land as by water. Moreover, we will and grant that all other cities and boroughs and villages and ports shall have all their liberties and free customs. . . .

39. No free man shall be taken or imprisoned or dispossessed, or outlawed, or banished, or in any way destroyed, nor will we go

The Magna Carta. The charter of 1215 is not the version with which we are familiar today. It was reissued in 1216 with some of the clauses removed, and it reissued again in 1217 with more revisions. The final version, and the one that has been cited ever since, was accepted by Henry III in 1225.

upon him, nor send upon him, except by the legal judgments of his peers or by the law of the land.

From "Magna Carta," in *Pennsylvania Translations and Reprints,* trans. Edward P. Cheyney (Philadelphia: University of Pennsylvania Press, 1897, pp. 6–16).

Question: Based on sections 2 and 3, what had John been doing that was especially threatening to his barons?

Languedoc (Lahng-dok), Toulouse (Too-looz), Poitou (Pwa-too), and Champagne. Only English Aquitaine and Gascony remained outside their grasp.

The Ottonian Empire

France and England would remain the archetypal feudal monarchies. In the German-speaking lands to the east, an effort to revive the empire along feudal lines was begun by **Otto I the Great** (reigned 936–973), the victor at the Lechfeld. Otto self-consciously imitated Charlemagne, although he never sought to extend his rule over West Francia. Like Charlemagne, he enlisted the church on his behalf, drawing both his administrators and many of his feudal levies from the great ecclesiastical estates. In 962, Pope John XII crowned him emperor at Aachen in return for his help against an Italian enemy, Berengar of Friuli, and Otto agreed to protect the territorial integrity of the papal states. The price for all this was imperial control over ecclesiastical appointments. When John objected, Otto deposed him and forced his successor to swear allegiance to himself as emperor.

These events were recorded in detail because Otto, like Charlemagne, knew the value of a good biographer. **Hroswitha of Gandersheim** (c. 935–1000) was one of the great literary figures of the Middle Ages and part of a broader flowering of literary culture and manuscript illumination in the Ottonian Empire. Most of this activity was the work of women in religious orders. In addition to the *Deeds of Otto,* Hroswitha wrote a history of her convent, some religious poems, and six comedies based on the works of Terence. They are thought to be the first dramas written in medieval times. Abbesses of great convents such as Uta of Niedermünster (Oo'-ta of Nee'-der-min-ster) seem to have been even more powerful in Germany than elsewhere and patronized woman writers and illuminators. One of the extraordinary figures to emerge from this convent tradition was **Hildegard of Bingen** (1098–1179). The *Scivias* (Siv'-ee-us), a powerful record of her mystical visions, remains a classic of devotional and apocalyptic literature. She also wrote a treatise on medicine, at least one play, and the *Physica,* a categorical description of the natural world.

Although strong and culturally vital, the empire built by Otto and his successors, Otto II and Otto III, did not re-create the empire of Charlemagne. It claimed only the German lands of what had been East Francia and northern Italy as far south as Rome. Otto's involvement with the papacy drew him and his successors more deeply into the quagmire of Italian politics. Their efforts to limit the growing power of the north Italian towns and their bitter struggle with the papacy over the issue of lay investiture (the imperial appointment of bishops) were among the most important political conflicts of the Middle Ages (see Chapter 9). The issues were intertwined, and both required massive investments of political and military capital. Emperors could easily neglect German affairs or subordinate them to the needs of their Italian policy. Moreover, Germany had become thoroughly feudalized. The German nobles—and eventually German towns—found it easy to preserve their autonomy and to resist the development of a feudal monarchy on the French or English model. Germany, with its hundreds

FIGURE **8.8** *Holy Roman Emperor Otto III (980–1002).* The grandson of Otto the Great, Otto III inherited the throne at the age of 3. This illustration shows him on his throne holding an orb, the symbol of empire, and surrounded by knights and churchmen. It was apparently intended to enhance the prestige of the young monarch after he became emperor.

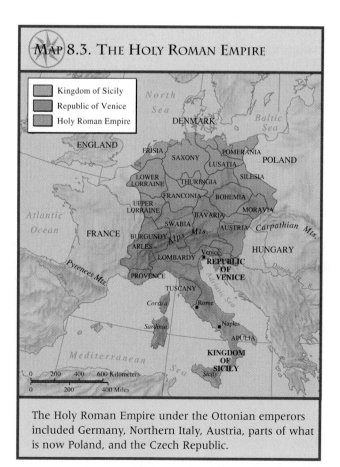

The Holy Roman Empire under the Ottonian emperors included Germany, Northern Italy, Austria, parts of what is now Poland, and the Czech Republic.

of small states, remained a stronghold of feudal particularism until the beginning of the modern age.

At their strongest, feudal monarchies such as England and France could command impressive resources. Their power was nevertheless limited. As long as fighting men were supported with land or by payments in kind, feudal lords could raise private armies and threaten the integrity of the realm. Kings had prestige and the legal advantages of sovereignty—their courts took theoretical precedence over all others, they could declare war, and they could coin money—but feudal kingdoms were inherently unstable because the crown held no monopoly on the use of force. Such a monopoly could be achieved only by eroding the foundations of feudalism itself. Until that occurred, good governance was largely a matter of personal character and good luck. For most of the Middle Ages, Europe would remain politically fragmented while retaining a social structure that conserved feudal privilege long after its original justification had passed.

CONCLUSION

The empire of Charlemagne did not long survive his death. As his grandsons divided their vast inheritance, Europe was attacked from all sides by ferocious warriors. Political decentralization aggravated by devastating raids threatened to destroy the fabric of society. New forms of military and social organization arose to combat the threat and gradually hardened into the system known as feudalism, in which fighting men received grants of land in return for military service. Economically, feudalism rested upon the far older social and economic system known as manorialism. Forms of manorialism had existed in Roman times, but a system based on tenants who were the legal subjects of their lord adapted easily to feudal circumstances and expanded enormously during the dark years of the ninth and tenth centuries. Together, feudalism and manorialism became the dominant institutions of medieval Europe and profoundly influenced the development of politics and social attitudes until well into modern times. By placing a near-monopoly of economic and military power in the hands of a military elite, the feudal system guaranteed that political power would remain decentralized for years to come.

Although feudalism pervaded most of what had been the Carolingian Empire and spread eventually to England and southern Italy, many parts of the subcontinent escaped its grasp. Freehold tenures remained common in Scandinavia, Spain, northern Italy, and wherever poverty or topography permitted a certain freedom, but even in these regions, nonfeudal ties of dependency sometimes developed in response to military or economic pressures.

Review Questions

- What technological and strategic advantages made the Vikings effective raiders?
- Why was the Carolingian empire at first unable to respond militarily or politically to the great raids?
- Which areas of Europe escaped "feudalism," and why?
- How did the quarrel between the kings of France and England arise out of the basic institutions of feudalism?

For Further Study

Readings

Bartlett, Robert, *England under the Norman and Angevin Kings, 1075–1225* (New York: Oxford, 2000). The latest scholarship in a readable account.

Bloch, Marc, *Feudal Society* (Chicago: University of Chicago, 1961). A classic essay.

Jones, Gwyn, *A History of the Vikings,* 2nd ed. (Oxford: Oxford University, 2001). A good, readable survey.

Reynolds, Susan, *Fiefs and Vassals: The Medieval Evidence Reinterpreted* (New York: Oxford, 1994). An important revisionist interpretation.

Strickland, Matthew, *War and Chivalry: The Conduct and Perception of War in England and Normandy, 1066–1217* (New York: Cambridge, 1996). Concentrates on the values and mentality of the knightly class.

InfoTrac College Edition

Visit the source collections at *http://infotrac.thomson learning.com* and use the search function with the following key terms.

Using Key Terms, enter the search terms:
Vikings not Minnesota   *Medieval England*
Medieval Germany

Using the Subject Guide, enter the search term:
feudalism   *feudal*
Middle Ages

Web Sites

http://www.fordham.edu/halsal/sbook.html
   The Internet Medieval Source Book. Look under:
   10th c. Collapse, England and France.
http://sunsite.berkeley.edu/OMACL/
   Texts and bibliography.

THE AGE OF THE GREAT RAIDS

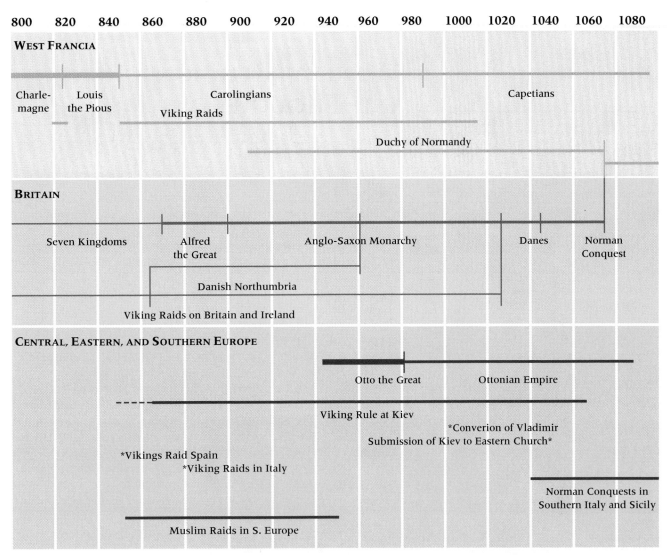

	800	820	840	860	880	900	920	940	960	980	1000	1020	1040	1060	1080

WEST FRANCIA

Charle-magne   Louis the Pious   Carolingians   Capetians

Viking Raids

Duchy of Normandy

BRITAIN

Seven Kingdoms   Alfred the Great   Anglo-Saxon Monarchy   Danes   Norman Conquest

Danish Northumbria

Viking Raids on Britain and Ireland

CENTRAL, EASTERN, AND SOUTHERN EUROPE

Otto the Great   Ottonian Empire

Viking Rule at Kiev

*Converion of Vladimir
Submission of Kiev to Eastern Church*

*Vikings Raid Spain
*Viking Raids in Italy

Norman Conquests in
Southern Italy and Sicily

Muslim Raids in S. Europe

Visit the Western Civilization Companion Web Site for resources specific to this textbook:
http://history.wadsworth.com/hause02/

The CD in the back of this book and the Western Civilization Resource Center at *http://history. wadsworth.com/western/* offer a variety of tools to help you succeed in this course, including access to quizzes; images; documents; interactive simulations, maps, and timelines; movie explorations; and a wealth of other sources.

Chapter 9

MEDIEVAL RELIGION AND THOUGHT

*I*n 1209, King John of England refused to accept the pope's appointment of Stephen Langton as Archbishop of Canterbury. He thought he was acting in accord with his traditional rights, but Pope Innocent III excommunicated him and placed all of England under an interdict during which priests could not administer the sacraments. To end the dispute, John believed that he had to grant "the whole kingdom of England and the whole kingdom of Ireland to our lord Pope Innocent III and his Catholic successors." In his letter of acceptance, the pope wrote: "He [Christ] has set one whom He has appointed [the pope] as his Vicar on earth . . . so all men should obey His Vicar and strive that there be one fold and one shepherd. All secular kings for the sake of God so venerate this Vicar, that unless they seek to serve him devotedly they doubt if they are reigning properly." Innocent then granted the kingdoms back to John as a fief in return for an annual payment of 1,000 marks. In little more than two centuries, the papacy had emerged from isolation and dependence on the secular rulers of central Italy to claim full authority over clergy and kings alike with varying degrees of success.

Chapter 9 describes how the church evolved from the dark days of the tenth century to the glories of the twelfth and thirteenth centuries—the great age of cathedrals and crusades, of the founding of universities, and of scholasticism, a system of thought that retains its influence today.

MONASTIC REVIVAL AND PAPAL REFORM (910–1261)

The disorder created by the great raids profoundly weakened the western church. Cut off from contact with each other and from Rome, bishoprics and monasteries fell under the control of secular rulers who could protect them. These lords then appointed political henchmen or their own younger sons to episcopal rank with little regard for spiritual qualities. Monasteries suffered the same fate. Even when a monastery retained its independence, isolation and the absence of supervision often led to relaxations of the rule. Lay people, who in this age tended to believe that their chances of salvation depended on the prayers of those holier than themselves, were scandalized and frightened.

The papacy shared in the general decline. As bishop of Rome, the pope was both spiritual and secular ruler of the city. From the deposition of Pope Nicholas the Great in 867 to the appointment of Clement II in 1046, a generalized state of anarchy permitted the great Roman families to vie for control of the office with only an occasional nod to religious priorities or to the wishes of the emperors. To the laity and to pious churchmen alike, the situation was intolerable.

The Cluniac Movement for Reform.

A reform movement that would transform both the papacy and the medieval church began in the Burgundian monastery of **Cluny.** Founded in 910 by William the Pious, duke of Aquitaine, its community followed a strict version of the Benedictine rule that emphasized liturgy and vocal prayer. In the decades that followed its establishment, the Cluniac ideal attracted those who sought a more spiritual and disciplined religious life. The original foundation became the mother house to nearly 1,500 affiliated monasteries.

The agenda of the Cluniac monks included more than prayer. They saw themselves as the vanguard of a broader reform that would enhance the spirituality of the church and free it forever from secular control. To achieve this, they sought to create an independent, reformed papacy and to restore episcopal subordination as a first step to rooting out corruption among parish priests and monks.

Imperial Support.

The reformer's first step was to gain the support of the Emperor Henry III (1017–1056), who agreed with many of their ideas and saw in them an opportunity to expand his own political influence. Henry entered Italy in 1046, deposed the three existing popes, and suppressed the Roman political factions that had supported them. He then used his authority to appoint a series of popes, the most important of whom was the Cluniac reformer Leo IX (served 1049–1054). Leo condemned simony, or the sale of church offices, called for the enforcement of clerical celibacy, and brought with him to Rome a number of young men who shared his convictions.

Henry's actions brought improvement, but to the monks, a papacy under imperial control was only slightly better than one controlled by Roman politicians. In the confusion that followed Henry's death, the reformers achieved something like full independence for the papacy. Taking advantage of the minority of Henry's young son, **Henry IV** (1050–1106), Pope Nicholas II placed the election of all future popes in the hands of the **College of Cardinals,** an advisory body comprised of the most important, or cardinal, priests of the Roman diocese. The first such election took place in 1061, and the basic procedure used on that occasion has remained more or less intact to this day.

The Investiture Controversy.

The next step was to achieve papal control over the appointment of bishops. With the establishment of feudalism, bishops came to hold fiefs over which they exercised civil as well as ecclesiastical authority. The secular rulers whose vassals they became usurped the right to invest, or formally install, them as bishops. When Hildebrand of Soana (So-ah'-na), one of the men who had come to Rome with Leo IX, was elected **Pope Gregory VII** in 1073 he made the abolition of lay investiture his chief priority. The emperor, like all other secular authorities, was forbidden to invest bishops with ring and crozier, the symbols of their office, on pain of excommunication. To Henry IV, this edict was a serious threat, not only because it seemed to question the religious basis of imperial power but also because bishops were the temporal as well as spiritual lords over much of Germany. All hope of imperial consolidation, to say nothing of good governance, would be thwarted if such men were appointed by an outsider. To the pope, lay investiture prevented him from exercising full control over the church and seemed to guarantee that its highest offices would be occupied by political hacks incapable of furthering the work of reform. At a more fundamental level, the quarrel was about the nature of political power itself (see the box *The Investiture Controversy*). Pope and emperor agreed that all authority derived from God's grace, but was that grace transmitted directly to the ruler or through the agency of the church?

The political crisis that resulted was known as the **Investiture Controversy,** and it set the stage for generations of conflict between the emperors and the popes. Henry called on his bishops to reject Gregory VII (see the box *The Investiture Controversy*). Gregory responded by excommunicating him and absolving his subjects of their allegiance. Excommunication meant that he was no longer regarded as a member of the church. The entire empire chose sides. Because most of the imperial princes and many of the growing towns

THE INVESTITURE CONTROVERSY

These two documents illustrate the ideas and claims that lay behind the dispute over the investiture of bishops. The so-called *Dictatus Papae* claim full dominion over all Christendom. Clearly, Pope Gregory VII has gone far beyond an ecclesiastical declaration of independence. Henry IV's letter reveals the theory common in imperial circles: The emperor is God's Vicar on Earth and cannot be deposed by anyone.

Gregory VII's Dictatus Papae *(c. 1073)*

The *Dictatus Papae*, or Dictates of the Pope, appears to be an internal memorandum produced by the circle of churchmen around Gregory VII. Although he did not in all probability write it himself, it sets forth his concept of papal rights and prerogatives under twenty-seven headings, the most important of which are listed here.

1. *That the Roman church was established by God alone.*
2. *That the Roman pontiff alone is rightly called universal.*
3. *That he alone has the power to depose and reinstate bishops. . . .*
8. *That he alone may use the imperial insignia.*
9. *That all princes shall kiss the foot of the pope alone.*
10. *That his name alone is to be recited in the churches. . . .*
12. *That he has the power to depose emperors. . . .*
16. *That no general synod may be called without his order.*
17. *That no action of a synod and no book shall be regarded as canonical without his authority.*
18. *That his decree can be annulled by no one, and that he can annul the decrees of anyone.*
19. *That he can be judged by no one.*
20. *That no one shall dare to condemn a person who has appealed to the apostolic seat. . . .*
22. *That the Roman church has never erred and will never err to all eternity, according to the testimony of the holy scriptures. . . .*
24. *That by his command or permission subjects may accuse their rulers.*
25. *That he can depose and reinstate bishops without calling a synod.*
26. *That no one can be regarded as Catholic who does not agree with the Roman church.*
27. *That he has the power to absolve subjects from their oath of fidelity to wicked rulers.*

From *"Ordericus Vitalis"* (1119), trans. T. Forester. In *Ecclesiastical History* (London: Bohn, 1853–1856). Reprinted in James Bruce Ross and Mary Martin McLaughlin, eds., *The Portable Medieval Reader* (New York: Viking, 1949).

Henry IV to Gregory VII

This excerpt is from a letter sent by the Emperor Henry IV to Pope Gregory VII in 1076. It sets out the basis of Henry's case and, in its mastery of invective, shows something of the heat generated by the argument over papal authority.

Henry, king not through usurpation but through the holy ordination of God, to Hildebrand, at present not pope but false monk. Such greeting as this hast thou merited through thy disturbances, inasmuch as there is no grade in the church which thou hast omitted to make a partaker not of honor but of confusion, not of benediction, but of malediction. For, to mention few and special cases out of many, not only hast thou not feared to lay hands upon the rulers of the holy church, the anointed of the Lord—the archbishops, namely bishops and priests—but thou hast trodden them underfoot like slaves ignorant of what their master is doing. . . . As if we had received our kingdom from thee! As if the kingdom and the empire were in thine and not in God's hands! And this although our Lord Jesus Christ did call us to this kingdom, did not, however, call thee to the priesthood. For thou has ascended by the following steps. By wiles, namely, which the profession of monk abhors, thou hast achieved money; by money, favor; by the sword, the throne of peace. And from the throne of peace thou hast disturbed peace. . . . Let another ascend the throne of St. Peter, who shall not practice violence under the cloak of religion, but shall teach the sound doctrine of St. Peter. I Henry, king by the grace of God, do say unto thee, together with all our bishops: Descend, descend, to be damned throughout all the ages.

From Thatcher, O. J., and McNeal, E. H., eds., *A Source Book of Medieval History* (New York: Scribner's, 1905, pp. 136–137).

Question: Insults aside, what is the basis of Henry's case in law and political theory?

---

believed that they would profit from a weakening of imperial authority, a revolt led by the dukes of Saxony placed the emperor in dire peril. In a clever move, Henry decided to ask absolution of the pope. As a priest, Gregory could not deny absolution (a decree of forgiveness) to someone who legitimately repented of his or her sins. At the castle of Canossa in the Italian Alps, Gregory supposedly forced the emperor to stand barefoot in the snow for 3 days before readmitting him to the fellowship of the church. Whatever satisfaction Gregory may have found in humiliating his rival did not compensate for being outmaneuvered. The revolt, deprived of its legitimacy by Henry's absolution, was over. Henry quickly reestablished his authority over the princes and in 1084 drove Gregory into exile.

The Concordat of Worms. The dispute over investiture was finally resolved in 1122 by **the Concordat of Worms.** Henry V (1086–1125) and Calixtus II (served 1119–1124) reached a compromise by which Henry renounced his right to appoint bishops but retained the power to grant them fiefs and other temporal benefits. In theory, the freedom of the church from secular interference was now securely established. In practice, the emperor still influenced episcopal appointments by withholding the income of a bishop who displeased him.

Whatever its importance for the evolution of church-state relationships, the investiture struggle marked the birth of a more assertive papacy that would one day claim *dominium* over the secular state. Gregory VII thought of the church as a body capable of giving law to all of Christendom and carefully fostered a growing interest in the study of canon or church law. This movement, which sparked a parallel revival of Roman civil law, reached its peak with the publication of **Gratian's** (Gray'-she-an) *Decretals* (c. 1140), an authoritative collection of papal and conciliar rulings supplemented by thirty-six *causae,* or sample cases. Subsequent popes and councils legislated so profusely that five new compilations were added in less than a century.

FIGURE 9.1 *Detail from a Legal Manuscript.* Like civil law, canon (church law) seeks to resolve conflicts. This detail of an illuminated A is from a manuscript of church law made at the cathedral priory of Christ Church, Canterbury, about 1125. It shows a man and a dragon fighting for possession of a fish and was intended as a wry commentary on the whole legal enterprise.

The Papacy under Innocent III. By the pontificate of Innocent III (served 1198–1216), the papacy had established itself as the legal arbiter of all matters, a speculator or overseer working in the best interests of the entire Christian commonwealth. The church had developed a legal bureaucracy that was the envy of secular princes. Appeals from both secular and ecclesiastical authorities were referred to the Papal Tribunal, which included the Penitentiary (for matters of faith and morals) and the Court of the Sacred Palace. A corps of Auditors prepared the cases. In 1322, they were organized into a court called the *Rota Romana,* which had appellate jurisdiction of its own. Difficult or important issues were referred to the pope, who might choose to decide them in consultation with the cardinals. The role of the cardinals, of course, was purely advisory, for no earthly power exceeded that of the pope. Papal decisions were handed down as decretals that formed the evolving basis of canon (church) law. In theory, popes could overrule legal precedent, although they rarely did so.

The claims of the papacy had reached their peak. Innocent, like his predecessors, believed that all earthly power was based on God's grace and that grace was administered by the church. When he argued that a pope could dethrone those who were ruling improperly, he did no more than carry the ideas of Gregory VII to their logical conclusion. Such theories were often difficult to implement, but in the case of King John of England, he showed that he was fully prepared to intervene in the affairs of a sovereign kingdom.

Clerical Celibacy. Although dramatic and politically controversial, the exalted notion of papal authority did not define the Cluniac program or the Hildebrandine or Gregorian reformation that arose from it. At the heart of the movement was a profound attachment to the monastic ideal and the belief that celibacy, or total abstention from sexual relations, was essential to a truly Christian life. Until the eleventh century, priests who had not joined a monastic order were permitted to marry and fathered families. Leo IX, one of the earlier Cluniac popes, ordered all of them to take vows of celibacy like monks. Predictably, many clergymen resisted (see Document 9.1). Later popes reinforced the order, but implementation was gradual because it left wives and children without support and because the laity was often suspicious of priests who lacked women of their own. In many areas of Europe, clerical celibacy remained a poorly enforced ideal until the modern era.

New Monastic Orders. The distinction between the "secular" clergy who serve bishops and parishes and the "regular" or monastic clergy dates from this period, with the regulars quickly gaining an advantage in the pursuit of high ecclesiastical office. This inevitably

THE CLUNIAC REFORMERS AND CLERICAL CELIBACY

The reforms of Pope Leo IX spread slowly in Western Christendom, and 50 years later, archbishops were still trying to impose a celibate life on priests. The following document is an account by Ordericus Vitalis in 1119 of how one French archbishop tried to enforce Leo's reforms.

Geoffrey, the archbishop, having returned to Rouen from attending the church council at Reims, held a synod of priests in the third week in November. Stirred up by the late papal decrees, he dealt sharply and rigorously with the priests of his diocese. Among other canons of the council which he promulgated was that which interdicted them from commerce with females of any description, and against such transgressors he launched the terrible sentence of excommunication. As the priests shrunk from submitting to this grievous burden, and in loud mutterings among themselves vented their complaints of the struggle between the flesh and the spirit to which they were subjected, the archbishop ordered one Albert, a man of free speech, who had used some offensive words, I know not what, to be arrested on the spot, and he was presently thrust into the common prison.

This prelate was a Breton and guilty of many indiscretions, warm and obstinate in temper, and severe in his aspect and manner, harsh in his censures, and withal, indiscreet and a great talker. The other priests, witnessing this extraordinary proceeding, were utterly confounded; and when they saw that, without being charged with any crime or undergoing any legal examination, a priest was dragged, like a thief, from a church to a dungeon, they became so exceedingly terrified that they knew not how to act, doubting whether they had best defend themselves or take flight.

From William of Malmesbury. *Chronicle*, trans. J. A. Giles (London: Bohn, 1847). Reprinted in James Bruce Ross and Mary Martin McLaughlin, eds. *The Portable Medieval Reader* (New York: Viking, 1949, pp. 57–58).

Question: Based on this passage, what proportion of the priesthood opposed the imposition of celibacy?

caused resentment among the seculars, but the monastic ideal continued to spread. Several new orders of both men and women were created, including the Carthusians in 1084 and the Premonstratensians in 1134. The Cistercians, founded in 1119, expanded under the leadership of St. Bernard of Clairvaux (Clarevo, 1090–1153) to include 338 monasteries at the time of his death.

The Age of the Great Cathedrals. The reformers were, in other words, triumphalists who believed that their monastic ideals should dominate the church and that the church should be the dominant institution in a Christian society. The visible symbols of that dominance were the great churches constructed during the eleventh and twelfth centuries in what has become known as the Romanesque style (see *Romanesque and Gothic Cathedrals*). Abandoning the basilica with its wooden roof, the builders covered the nave, or central isle of the church, with a massive barrel vault that rested on a clerestory. The clerestory, with its arched windows, rested on round arches reinforced by side aisles that served as buttresses. The new style consumed vast quantities of cut stone, producing an overwhelming impression of power and serenity.

In the course of the twelfth century, a new style evolved based on ribbed groin vaults and pointed arches. Flying buttresses were developed to support the weight of the vaulting, and the size of windows was increased until, in the High Gothic style of the thirteenth and fourteenth centuries, interiors were illuminated by vast sheets of stained glass that portrayed episodes from the Scriptures so that even the illiterate might absorb the teachings of the church.

The construction of cathedrals required enormous commitments of time and money. Some required centuries to build, and most were embellished with painting, sculpture, and stained glass on a grand scale. The improved collection of tithes and the more efficient management of church estates made such aesthetic achievements possible. Medieval society was prepared to invest much of its meager economic surplus in religious buildings. However, not everyone viewed this development with enthusiasm. The glories of Durham or Palermo, Chartres (Shar-tr) or Amiens, were ultimately paid for by the labor of peasants. Some complained that such magnificence was inappropriate for the worship of a simple carpenter from Galilee, but the reformers were inspired by a vision of divine grandeur that demanded tangible expression on Earth.

Unfortunately, this vision could not comprehend dissent. The faith born originally of the Cluniac revival would inspire intellectual and artistic achievement for years to come. It would also provoke the Crusades and the virtual expulsion of the Jews from western Europe.

THE CRUSADES (C. 1030–1291)

The Crusades were both an expression of religious militancy and the first of several European attempts to expand geographically at the expense of non-Christians. For the inhabitants of northern Europe, the Crusades provided their first sustained encounter with Islam, a society that was still in many ways more advanced than their own.

Christian Conquests in Europe

Spain and Portugal. The beginnings of the Spanish *reconquista,* or reconquest, provided the model for Christian expansionism. In 1031, the caliph of Córdoba was deposed during a prolonged civil war and Muslim Spain disintegrated into petty principalities based on the major towns. Their number soon reached as high as twenty-three. These small states, wealthy but militarily weak, offered a tempting opportunity to the Christian kingdoms. Taking advantage of Muslim disunity, the kings of Léon and Castile began extending their realms southward and received special privileges and plenary indulgences (remissions of the punishment for sins committed on behalf of the faith) from the papacy as an encouragement. The reconquest was not, however, a continuous or unified movement.

In 1086, the Almoravides, a religious reform movement originating in North Africa, reunited Muslim Spain. The Almoravid state disintegrated when the movement lost its original inspiration. Some years later, in 1172, the Almohades, an even more puritanical group from North Africa, restored unity only to see their own state collapse after 1212. In general, Christian advances came only in the intervals between periods of Muslim strength. In the meantime, the Christian princes continued to fight among themselves. One of these disputes led to the creation of the kingdom of Portugal in 1143. The age is best symbolized by the career of Rodrigo Díaz de Vivar, known as **"El Cid"** (El Sid, c. 1043–1099). El Cid fought for both Christian and Muslim potentates, changing sides as his interest required, until he acquired the kingdom of Valencia in 1092. His ruthless cynicism did not prevent him from becoming the hero of later chivalric romances.

During these years, Spain was a multicultural society in which Muslims, Christians, and Jews lived in uneasy balance. Both Muslim and Christian states practiced religious tolerance out of necessity, and the interaction between the three cultures gave birth to a rich philosophical and scientific tradition that flourished despite war and occasional outbreaks of religious violence. The balance tipped in 1212, when Alfonso VIII of Castile defeated the Almohades at the battle of Las Navas de Tolosa. The Muslim towns fell one by one until in 1248 Sevilla (Se-vee'-lya) surrendered to the Christians. The kingdom of Granada in far southern Spain was now the only Muslim enclave in Christian Europe.

Sicily. Christendom also advanced in Sicily. One problem with feudalism was that increases in the population of the knightly class produced more men trained in the profession of arms than could be supported by existing fiefs. In the highly stratified society of medieval Europe, these men neither could nor would seek other careers. Some found an outlet for their energies in baronial

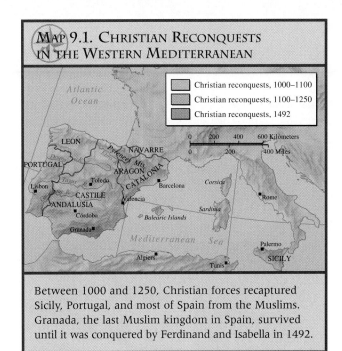

MAP 9.1. CHRISTIAN RECONQUESTS IN THE WESTERN MEDITERRANEAN

Christian reconquests, 1000–1100
Christian reconquests, 1100–1250
Christian reconquests, 1492

Between 1000 and 1250, Christian forces recaptured Sicily, Portugal, and most of Spain from the Muslims. Granada, the last Muslim kingdom in Spain, survived until it was conquered by Ferdinand and Isabella in 1492.

wars and in the Norman conquest of England, but by the mideleventh century, northern Europe's population of landless knights had become a threat to social peace. A group of Norman adventurers, including the twelve sons of the minor feudatory Tancred of Hauteville, took advantage of Byzantine weakness and established themselves in southern Italy by 1050. Pope Leo IX regarded them as a threat. Later popes, realizing that the Normans could be useful allies in the investiture crisis, supported one of Tancred's sons, Robert Guiscard (Gees-kar, d. 1085), in his attempt to seize control of the Italian south. Robert drove the Byzantine Greeks from Calabria but left the conquest of Muslim Sicily to his brother Roger (d. 1101). Roger completed the process in 1092. His son, Roger II, used his inheritance to create a powerful feudal kingdom on the Anglo-Norman model. Its superior resources and his qualities as a general enabled Roger to turn on his cousins and conquer all of southern Italy before his death in 1154.

The Struggle for the Holy Land

Christian successes in Spain and Sicily were greeted with enthusiasm throughout Europe. When added to the great wave of piety unleashed by the Cluniac reforms, they raised the prospect of a general offensive against the Muslim infidel. In 1095, Pope Urban II proclaimed a crusade to free Jerusalem and the Holy Land from Muslim control. The privileges and indulgences were similar to those granted earlier in Spain (see Document 9.2), but Urban based his decision to launch a crusade on the growing danger and complexity of Middle Eastern politics.

ROMANESQUE AND GOTHIC CATHEDRALS

Critics who favored the classical architecture of the Renaissance coined the terms *Romanesque* and *Gothic* to describe the architecture of the Middle Ages. They believed that medieval art was barbaric, but the cathedrals of the Middle Ages are now regarded as among the world's greatest architectural achievements. Vaulted roofs supported by massive piers and buttresses are characteristic of both styles. In the age of Viking raids, churchmen wanted to replace the wooden roofs of their basilicas with fireproof stone vaulting. Over time, the relatively simple barrel vaults of early Romanesque churches gave way to elaborate groin vaults based on pointed, rather than round arches. Decoration, too, became more elaborate, but the carved figures and stained glass of Gothic cathedrals nearly always conveyed a religious message.

The Abbey Church of Lessay, France. Located in Normandy, the church of Lessay is a classic example of Romanesque architecture. This view from the east shows the square towers and round arches on the windows typical of the style.

Durham Cathedral: A Romanesque Interior. The city of Durham (northeastern England) was founded by William the Conqueror as an outpost against the Scots. The cathedral, begun in 1093, is an excellent example of Norman Romanesque architecture. The nave, or central part of the church, shown here has the round arches, massive piers, and clerestory typical of the style. The pointed rib vaulting, constructed in 1104, is the first example of its kind in England and replaces the wooden roofs found in the earliest Norman churches.

Turkish tribes, most of them converts to Islam, had begun their long migration from the steppes of central Asia into the lands of the Greek empire. One such group, called the Seljuks after the name of their ruling family, defeated the armies of Byzantium and seized control of eastern Anatolia (now Asiatic Turkey) at the battle of Manzikert in 1071. Alarmed, the Byzantine emperors hinted delicately at the reunification of the eastern and western churches if only the west would come to their aid.

Twenty years later, the death of the Abbasid sultan of Baghdad, Malek Shah, inaugurated a civil war among his or governors in Syria and Palestine. The disorder was such that Christian pilgrims could no longer visit the Holy Land in safety. The pope found this intolerable, especially when Islam seemed elsewhere in retreat. The disintegration of

Salisbury Cathedral. One of the finest examples of English Gothic, Salisbury was begun in 1220. It is unusual because the tower was built over the crossing of the nave and transept, which had not been designed to support it. The stone piers began to buckle, and supports had to be built to prevent collapse. The spire measured 404 feet in height when completed in 1362. The competition to build towers higher reached the peak of absurdity at Beauvais in France, where the 512-foot tower collapsed in 1572. It was not rebuilt.

Gothic Interior: The Cathedral of Bourges. The nave of the Cathedral of Bourges, France, shows the elaborate vaulting and pointed arches characteristic of Gothic architecture. The cathedral was begun on a hill above the city in the late 1100s and finished in only 50 years. The stained glass at Bourges is especially beautiful.

the Caliphate of Córdoba, the expulsion of Muslims from the Balearic Islands in 1087, and the chaos in Syria could only encourage the dream of liberating Jerusalem and perhaps of uniting all Christendom under papal rule.

Urban II's proclamation of the First Crusade aroused greater enthusiasm than he had anticipated. Thousands of European men and women prepared to leave their homes and travel to fight in an unknown and hostile land. Their motives were in large part pious, but they had other reasons as well. The social pressures that had produced the Norman expansion continued to simmer throughout the feudal world. Younger sons hoped to claim Middle Eastern lands as their own, and an increasing number of landless peasants were happy to accompany them. Princes in turn were happy to see them go. The martial enthusiasm of the

FIGURE 9.2 *Pope Urban II Proclaims the First Crusade.* The pope, speaking from the pulpit of the cathedral in Clermont, France (November 1095), calls on the assembled clergy to support his plan to rescue the Holy Land from the Turks. By linking noblemen to the common cause of a Crusade, Urban II hoped to halt their habitual quarreling. Jean Fouquet provided this illustration for *Les Grandes Croniques de France* about 1460.

feudal classes had produced an alarming number of local wars and revolts. As we have seen, the church tried to restrain them by proclaiming the Truce of God, which attempted to restrict fighting to certain days of the week, but this effort failed. The Crusades promised to free the holy places from Muslim rule while providing an acceptable outlet for growing social tension in Europe. In a broader sense, they justified the continuing privileges of a feudal class that no longer had an external threat to combat.

The First Crusade. Although the Christian command was deeply divided by jealousies and infighting, Jerusalem fell to the Christians on July 15, 1099. The victors massacred the Muslim and Jewish population of the city and then divided the region as a whole into the county of Tripoli and three kingdoms organized on the feudal model: Jerusalem, Edessa, and Antioch. They organized all four as papal fiefs that provided new lands for ambitious knights and churchmen. In reality, they were fragile enclaves surrounded by a population that despised the Christians as barbarians. To protect them, the Christians constructed fortifications based on the more sophisticated engineering techniques of the Muslims and established two military orders: the Knights of the Hospital of St. John of Jerusalem (1113) and the Knights Templars (1119). Religious orders of fighting men, sworn to celibacy and dedicated to the

protection of the holy places, the Knights became a model for later orders that sought to expand the frontiers of Christendom in Spain and Germany.

Later Crusades. Despite these efforts, Edessa fell to the Muslims in 1144 and a Second Crusade was launched in retaliation. It accomplished little. In 1187, the Kurdish general Saladin (c. 1137–1193) took Jerusalem. He is revered as a great Muslim hero to this day. The Third Crusade (1189–1192) was a fiasco. Emperor Frederick Barbarossa (c. 1123–1190) drowned in a stream, weighed down by his body armor. Richard I Lion-Heart, king of England, quarreled with the French king Philip Augustus, who abandoned the siege of Jerusalem and returned to confiscate Richard's fiefs in France. Richard, trying to return home, was captured and held for ransom by Emperor Henry VI in Germany.

Subsequent crusades proved even less edifying. The Fourth Crusade (1202–1204) foundered when the crusaders failed to provide for the cost of their passage in Venetian ships. The Venetians demanded that they seize Zara in payment and then inveigled them into attacking Constantinople. Constantinople fell in July 1203. The Venetians eventually abandoned their conquest after extorting more favorable trade privileges from the Greeks in return for the city. In 1228, Emperor Frederick II was excommunicated for abandoning the Sixth Crusade, ostensibly because of seasickness. Frederick acquired Jerusalem by negotiation in the following year. The pope, who thought that he should have taken the city by force, was not pleased. The Muslims recovered it in 1244. Two more crusades by St. Louis IX of France accomplished nothing, and by 1291 the last Christian strongholds in the eastern Mediterranean had fallen to the Muslims.

The Impact of the Crusades on Europe

The first attempt at European expansion had mixed results. Only in Spain and Portugal was new territory added to Christendom, but a precedent was set for the more sustained efforts of the fifteenth and sixteenth centuries. In the meantime, the effort to convert non-Christian populations by the sword—a notion hardly envisioned by the fathers of the church—poisoned relations with the Islamic world and probably strengthened the forces of intolerance and rigidity within Islam. For the Byzantine Empire, the Crusades marked the beginning of the end. Fatally weakened by the Fourth Crusade, the Greeks continued to lose ground until they were at last overwhelmed by Turkish expansion in 1453.

THE PRIVILEGES OF THE CRUSADERS

These privileges, granted to prospective crusaders by Pope Eugenius III in 1146, demonstrate some of the spiritual and material advantages that induced men to go to the Holy Land.

Moreover, by the authority vested by God in us, we who with paternal care provide for your safety and the needs of the church, have promised and granted to those who from a spirit of devotion have decided to enter upon and accomplish such a holy and necessary undertaking and task, that remission of sins which our predecessor Pope Urban instituted. We have also commanded that their wives and children, their property and possessions, shall be under the protection of the holy church, of ourselves, of the archbishops, bishops and other prelates of the church of God. Moreover, we ordain by our apostolic authority that until their return or death is full proven, no law suit shall be instituted hereafter in regard to any property of which they were in peaceful possession when they took the cross.

Those who with pure hearts enter upon such a sacred journey and who are in debt shall pay no interest. And if they or others for them are bound by oath or promise to pay interest, we free them by our apostolic authority. And after they have sought aid of their relatives or lords of whom they hold their fiefs, and the latter are unable or unwilling to advance them money, we allow them freely to mortgage their lands and other possessions to churches, ecclesiastics, or other Christians, and their lords shall have no redress.

Knight Kneeling in Prayer. The crusading ideal portrayed the knight as a pious defender of the faith, but most of those who went to the Holy Land had practical as well as religious motives. From the *Westminster Psalter* (English, twelfth century).

From Otto of Freising, *Gesta Federici*, 1, 35. *Pennsylvania Translations and Reprints*, trans. Edward P. Cheyney (Philadelphia: University of Pennsylvania Press, 1897, p. 13).

Questions: What financial incentives are offered here to the crusaders? How important do you think they might have been?

The Venetians, as the architect of Greek misfortunes, benefited for a time by establishing a series of colonies on Greek soil. In the end these, too, were lost to the Turks.

Persecution of the Jews. European Jews suffered as well. The militant attitude fostered by a reformed papacy led indirectly to persecutions, most of which were based on the blood libel that Jews sacrificed Christian children as part of their rituals (see Document 9.3). Several popes specifically rejected this slander, but an aroused laity seemed unwilling to tolerate the existence of non-Christians at any level. It was no accident that such crusading princes as Richard I Lion-Heart of England and St. Louis IX of France supported the expulsion of Jews from their lands in the twelfth and thirteenth centuries. Most of the refugees moved eastward into Germany, where, for a time at least, they were relatively safe.

Prosecution of Homosexuals. The general climate of intolerance may also have affected the treatment of homosexuals. Although formally condemned by church doctrine, homosexuality appears to have been tolerated until the midthirteenth century. A substantial literature praising homosexual love had been created by clerical writers at the time of the Hildebrandine reform. After 1250, for reasons that are unclear, virtually every region of Europe passed laws making homosexual activity a crime punishable by death. These laws, and the sentiments they reflected, remained in effect until well into modern times.

Effect of the Crusades on Women. In personal terms, few of the crusaders gained the wealth and status they sought, but western women of the upper classes probably benefited from the Crusades. Many accompanied their husbands to the Middle East, where they astonished the Muslims with their free-spoken manners. Those who stayed home often assumed the role of managers and defenders of the family's estates. In either case, the absence of husbands enhanced their independence and economic value.

Economic and Cultural Impact. Of more permanent value was the increase of trade in Eastern luxury goods. The Crusades, by bringing western Europeans

Medieval Religion and Thought 209

POPE GREGORY X DENOUNCES THE BLOOD LIBEL

A Jewish Family Burned at the Stake. Jews were persecuted throughout the Middle Ages for imagined attacks on Christians or their sacred symbols. This painting by Paolo da Ucello (1397–1475) shows a Jewish pawnbroker and his family being burned at the stake for profanation of the host or communion wafer. They had been accused of roasting it.

Persecution of the Jews was often based on the "blood libel" that accused Jews of killing Christian children in order to use their blood in religious ceremonies. A succession of popes inveighed against the blood libel with varying degrees of success. This letter by Gregory X (served 1271–1276) is similar in tone to earlier letters by Innocent III and Innocent IV. The subsequent expulsions of Jews reveal that papal good sense had little impact on some of Europe's monarchs and their subjects.

Since it happens occasionally that some Christians lose their Christian children, the Jews are accused by their enemies of secretly carrying off and killing these same Christian children and of making sacrifices of the heart and blood of these very children. It happens, too, that parents of these children or some other Christian enemies of these Jews, secretly hide these very children in order that they may be able to injure these Jews, and in order that they may be able to extort from them a certain amount of money by redeeming them from their straits.

And most falsely do these Christians claim that the Jews have secretly and furtively carried away these children and killed them,

and that the Jews offer sacrifice from the heart and blood of these children, since their law in this matter precisely and expressly forbids Jews to sacrifice, eat, or drink the blood, or to eat the flesh of animals having claws. This has been demonstrated many times at our court by Jews converted to the Christian faith; nevertheless very many Jews are often seized and detained unjustly because of this.

We decree, therefore, that Christians need not be obeyed against Jews in a case or situation of this type, and we order that Jews seized under such a silly pretext be freed from imprisonment, and that they shall not be arrested henceforth on such a miserable pretext, unless—which we do not believe—they be caught in the commission of the crime. We decree that no Christian shall stir up anything new against them, but that they should be maintained in that status and position in which they were in the time of our predecessors, from antiquity till now.

From Marcus, Jacob R., *The Jew in the Medieval World*, (New York: Atheneum, 1972, p. 154).

Question: How does Pope Gregory demonstrate that the blood libel was malicious nonsense?

into contact with a more technologically advanced civilization, fueled their growing taste for spices, silks, Damascus cutlery, and similar items. The Eastern trade not only broadened cultural perspectives, at least in a material sense, but also encouraged capital accumulation, especially in the Italian towns. A related benefit was the improved knowledge of engineering, stonemasonry, and fortification that Europeans acquired by observing Arab models.

Unfortunately, the nature of the crusading enterprise severely limited exchanges at the intellectual level. The average crusader viewed the glories of Arab philosophy, mathematics, astronomy, and medicine with deep suspicion. When they were eventually introduced to Europe—not by crusaders but by scholars working in the free atmosphere of multicultural Spain—the church reacted defensively. Arab poetry, mysticism, and religious thought were ignored.

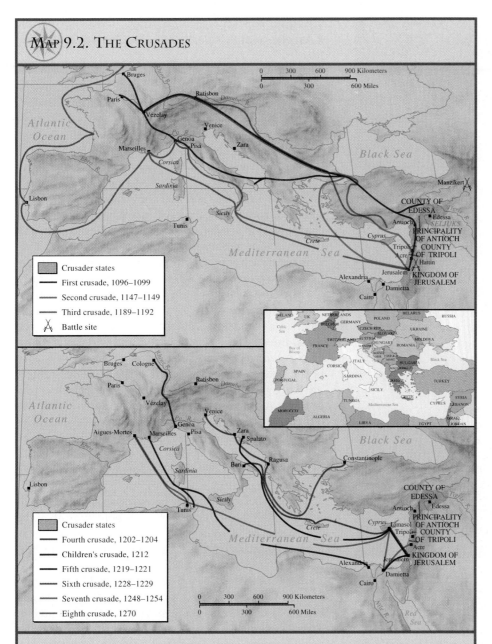

MAP 9.2. THE CRUSADES

Crusader states
— First crusade, 1096–1099
— Second crusade, 1147–1149
— Third crusade, 1189–1192
⚔ Battle site

Crusader states
— Fourth crusade, 1202–1204
— Children's crusade, 1212
— Fifth crusade, 1219–1221
— Sixth crusade, 1228–1229
— Seventh crusade, 1248–1254
— Eighth crusade, 1270

The first three crusades (top) recaptured the Holy Land from the Muslims and established the "Crusader States" of Edessa, Antioch, Tripoli, and Jerusalem. All of them collapsed by 1300. The Fourth Crusade (bottom) resulted only in the sack of Constantinople by the Venetians. The last four crusades accomplished little or nothing. As time passed, the crusaders increasingly preferred the faster and safer sea routes to travelling over land through the Balkans.

THE INTELLECTUAL CRISIS OF THE TWELFTH CENTURY

By the beginning of the twelfth century, the Latin church was the dominant institution and chief unifying force of western and central Europe. Although feudal monarchies did not always acknowledge its political pretensions, they usually acknowledged its spiritual direction and sometimes heeded its calls for crusades or other actions on behalf of the faith. Religiously and intellectually, it had no rivals. As a result, neither theology nor speculative philosophy was highly developed. Creative thought rarely evolves in an atmosphere of unanimity, and the teachings of the church had not been seriously challenged since the Patristic era. The monastic and cathedral schools, which educated the priesthood, avoided major controversies until the middle of the eleventh century. After that, whatever intellectual complacency Christians may have felt began to erode, and by 1200 it was entirely shattered.

Faith or Reason. Around 1050, a heated controversy developed over the ideas of Berengar of Tours (Bear'-en-gur of Toor, d. 1080). Arguing from logic, he rejected the doctrine of **transubstantiation,** which explained how, in the miracle of the mass, the bread and wine were transformed into the body and blood of Jesus Christ. Transubstantiation was not yet a dogma of the church in that it had not been proclaimed as such by a council, but it had long been generally accepted. His writings created a furor. The dispute opened up two issues that were to perplex the church for centuries. The first was over the use of reason itself. St. Peter Damian espoused Tertullian's argument that faith required no support from logic; revelation was enough. Others, including St. Anselm of Canterbury (1033–1109),

FIGURE 9.3 *The Elevation of the Host.* In 1215, the Fourth Lateran Council defined *transubstantiation* as a central doctrine of the Catholic Church. It states that in the sacrament of communion, the *substance* of the bread and wine is changed, or *transubstantiated,* into the body and blood of Christ. In this Italian painting from the fourteenth century, a priest elevates the host or communion wafer, consecrating it before offering it to the communicants.

ern historians thought that they foreshadowed the Renaissance of the fourteenth and fifteenth centuries.

The Question of Universals. The second issue was that of universals, which had first been raised by the sixth-century Christian philosopher Boethius (Bo-ee'-thee-us) and was implicit in the arguments of Berengar of Tours. The question, central to virtually all medieval thought, is: Are ideas or qualities objectively real? Does such a thing as "redness," for example, exist apart from any physical object that is "red"? Realists held that such universals were real and that they constituted the substance of things. The physical manifestation of a substance was its accident. Nominalists believed that universals are merely *nomina,* or names that reflect little more than arbitrary linguistic convention. No distinction could be made between substance and accident.

Christian doctrines such as the Trinity and transubstantiation were usually explained in language that implied the reality of universals. In the miracle of the mass, the substance of the bread and wine in communion is changed or transubstantiated into the substance of the body and blood of Christ; the accidents remain unchanged. If, like Berengar, one did not believe in the distinction between substance and accident, this was difficult to accept. A partial solution to the problem was proposed by **Pierre Abelard** (Ab-e-lard, 1079–1142), who argued that a universal was a logical term related to both things and concepts. The controversy, however, was only beginning.

While Abelard avoided the extremes of either realism or nominalism, his career as a whole intensified the growing spirit of contention. He is best known outside theological circles for his affair with Heloise, the brilliant niece of Canon Fulbert of Chartres. Their relationship produced a child and some memorable letters before her relatives had him castrated. He thereupon became a monk and she a nun, but his penchant for making enemies was not yet satisfied. Abelard was determined to provide a rational basis for Christian doctrine, and his provocative writings—including *Sic et Non,* a list of apparently contradictory passages from the Fathers—set the agenda for much of what would one day be called *scholasticism.*

To Abelard, Anselm, and the other philosophers of the cathedral schools, reason meant the logic of Aristotle as embodied in those parts of the *Organon* that had been translated into Latin by Boethius. They had no direct access to Aristotle's works, and their knowledge of his thought was derived largely from the commentaries of his translator; however, they were convinced that God's world must necessarily operate on logical principles. They also believed that Aristotle and other virtuous pagans would have accepted Christianity had they not been born before the time of Christ. It was in many ways an age of innocence.

argued that reason could only illuminate faith and improve understanding.

Although the advocates of formal logic would triumph, at least in the schools, a third group distrusted them for other reasons. Led by **John of Salisbury** (d. 1180) and centered at the cathedral school of Chartres, these scholars feared that an excessive concentration on reason might narrow the scope of learned inquiry. They developed an interest in the secular literature of ancient Rome. Their efforts have been called the "Renaissance of the Twelfth Century" because mod-

The Discovery of Arabic and Jewish Thought.
That innocence was shattered after the midtwelfth century by the discovery that Aristotle was far better known in Baghdad and Cairo than he was in the west and that his logic had been employed for centuries by thinkers who were not Christian, but Muslim or Jewish. A group of scholars established themselves in the Spanish frontier city of Toledo and began to translate the works of Aristotle, Galen, Ptolemy, and other Greeks from Arabic into Latin. They then produced Latin editions of Arabic writers. Many of these works were on science or medicine. The medical treatises revolutionized the thinking of Western physicians, but works on logic and speculative philosophy were received with greater caution.

The translations revealed a new world of philosophical sophistication, and it was not a reassuring place. Al-Kindi (d. c. 870) and Ibn Sina (Avicenna, 980–1037) were more or less orthodox Muslims. Abu Bakr al-Razi (c. 865–923) was an enemy of all religion, and Maimonides (My-mahn'-uh-dees, 1135–1204) was a pious Jew. Ibn-Rushd (Averroës, 1126–1198) was perhaps the most influential. The greatest of the commentators on Aristotle, he believed as firmly as Anselm or Abelard that the logic of the Philosopher could be used to uphold revelation, but in his case, the revelation was that of the Koran. For the first time since antiquity, the church was faced with an intellectual challenge of threatening proportions.

The Rise of Heresies. Before a counterattack could be fully mounted, an even more serious challenge to orthodoxy appeared. Formal heresies attracting thousands of adherents surfaced, not in the newly converted regions of the north and west, but in the earliest established centers of Western Christendom: northern Italy and the south of France. To some extent these movements were a reaction against what was perceived as the greed and arrogance of a triumphant clergy. The newly exalted claims of the papacy, the cost of church buildings, and the more rigorous collection of the tithe led to demands for a return to apostolic poverty. This was the primary concern of the **Waldensians,** named after their apparent founder Waldes of Lyon, later known as Peter Waldo (flourished 1170–1179). Their condemnation by the orthodox eventually led them to reject papal authority. Like the Protestants of the sixteenth century, the Waldensians regarded Scripture as the sole source of religious truth and translated the Bible into the vernacular. They also rejected several of the church's sacraments.

A far larger movement, the **Cathars** (sometimes known as **Albigensians** (Al-bi-jen'-si-ans) after the southern French town of Albi that served as one of their centers), went further. They embraced a dualistic system reminiscent of Zoroastrianism or the ancient

FIGURE **9.4** *St. Dominic and the Albigensians.* St. Dominic preached to the Albigensians, but like other churchmen of the day, he also believed in burning their books. From an altarpiece by Pedro Berruguete (c. 1450–1504) in the cloister of Santo Tomás, Avila.

Manicheans. The physical world and the God of the Old Testament who had created it were evil. Spirit, as exemplified in Christ, whose own physical body was an illusion, was good. They had no clergy. *Parfaits* (Parfays), or "perfects," of both sexes administered the rite of *consolamentum* that guaranteed passage into Heaven. After consolation, one became a parfait. It was then forbidden to own property, to have sex, or to eat anything that was the product of a sexual union: meat, fish, eggs, or cheese. The parfait acquired the meager necessities that remained by begging. Some new converts deliberately starved themselves to death, but for the ordinary believer, Albigensianism held few terrors. Those who died without receiving the consolamentum would merely be reincarnated into a new life on Earth. The church, its hierarchy, its sacraments, and its monetary levies were categorically rejected. By the year 1200, the Cathar faith had attracted tens of thousands of adherents in southern France. It enjoyed the support of powerful political figures and even of priests, who retained their ecclesiastical rank while openly assisting the heretics. Once again, the church was on the defensive.

REPRESSION AND RENEWAL (1215–1292)

The Albigensian Crusade. Innocent III, who was not one to shrink from repressive measures, largely crafted the official response to these challenges. The church's first reaction to the heretics had been gentle. Preachers, including **Bernard of Clairvaux,** were sent to reconvert the Albigensians, but their eloquence had little effect. In 1209, Innocent, infuriated by the murder of a papal legate, proclaimed a crusade. Under the leadership of Simon de Montfort, an army comprised largely of knights from northern France embarked on a campaign of massacre and atrocity. Like their compatriots who went to the Holy Land, the crusaders were inspired by the hope of acquiring new lands as well as salvation. The worst slaughter of the Albigensian Crusade happened near the Pyrenees Mountains in the town of Béziers (Bay'-zyay). The people of Béziers refused to surrender some 200 Cathars living there, so the crusaders decided to follow the famous exhortation of the abbot of Cîteau: "Kill them all; God will know his own." They stormed the town and killed 20,000 of its inhabitants, Cathars and Catholics alike.

By 1212, most of Languedoc (the old name for Southern France) was in their hands, but the Cathars and the southern lords who supported them took refuge in remote castles and waged guerrilla warfare until 1226. Louis VIII of France then launched a decisive campaign. He saw the crusade as an opportunity to expand his royal domain and forced the southerners to surrender in 1229. The last great Cathar stronghold, a mountain-top castle known as Montségur, finally fell in 1244. More than 200 Cathars refused to abjure their faith and were burned together on a huge pyre. The church built great cathedrals at Albi and Narbonne to proclaim the triumph of the faith, but Cathar communities flourished in secret until after 1300.

The Papal Inquisition. Innocent III established the papal Inquisition to ferret them out. An *inquisition* is basically a court established to investigate and root out heresy. Bishops had begun organizing inquisitions at the diocesan level in the midtwelfth century. These episcopal inquisitions proved ineffective in the Albigensian heartland, where heresy permeated entire communities. Even bishops who were themselves untainted by error might be reluctant to proceed against prominent indi-

FIGURE 9.5 *The Cathedral at Albi.* The cathedral at Albi, France, was begun in 1277 to overawe the population of a city that had given the Albigensian heresy its name. Unlike most cathedrals of the age, it was built of brick and lacked flying buttresses. This view of the tower captures the building's militant character.

viduals or members of their own families. By placing the Inquisition under papal control, Innocent III secured a measure of impartiality. He dispatched legates responsible only to him as needed, making it more difficult for heretics to take refuge behind local privilege. To believers, heresy was a terrible crime because it brought about the eternal damnation of those who accepted it. Inquisitors therefore felt justified in using every means available, including torture, to secure a confession. If a confession was not forthcoming or if the heretic confessed but would not repent, he or she would be turned over to the secular authorities and burned alive, the standard penalty for heresy in both canon and civil law.

After 1233, Pope Gregory IX introduced the tribunal to the south of France on a systematic basis. It burned as many as 5,000 heretics there by the end of the century. The Inquisition had other interests as well. Anyone, including academic theorists, who overstepped the bounds of theological propriety was subject to its jurisdiction. If the church of the early Middle Ages had been absorbed in its missionary role and relatively indifferent to the definition of orthodoxy, those days were gone.

The Fourth Lateran Council. The Fourth Lateran Council solidified the new order. Called by Innocent III in 1215, it was designed to resemble the great councils of the early church. Not only bishops, abbots, and the heads of religious and military orders but also princes and municipal authorities from all over the Latin west were invited to consider a carefully prepared agenda. In only 3 days of formal meetings, the delegates adopted a confession of faith that specifically rejected Albigensian beliefs, defined the seven sacraments, and enshrined transubstantiation as dogma. The delegates ordered all

PRIVILEGES OF THE STUDENTS AT PARIS

King Philip Augustus in 1200 granted the following privilege to the students at Paris. It seeks to protect academic freedom by ensuring that students accused of crimes are tried only by ecclesiastical courts.

Neither our provost nor our judges shall lay hands on a student for any offense whatever; nor shall they place him in our prison, unless such a crime has been committed by the student that he ought to be arrested. And in that case, our judge shall arrest him on the spot, without striking him at all, unless he resists, and shall hand him over to the ecclesiastical judge, who ought to guard him in order to satisfy us and the one suffering the injury. . . . But if the students are arrested by our count at such an hour that the ecclesiastical judge cannot be found and be present at once, our provost shall cause the culprits to be guarded in some student's house without any ill-treatment as is said above, until they are delivered to the ecclesiastical judge. . . . In order, moreover, that these decrees may be kept more carefully and be established by a fixed law, we have decided that our present provost and the people of Paris shall affirm by an oath, in the presence of the scholars, that they will carry out in good faith all the abovementioned points.

From Augustus, Philip, "Privileges of the Students at Paris," in *Pennsylvania Translations and Reprints*, vol. 2, trans. Edward P. Cheyney (Philadelphia: University of Pennsylvania Press, 1897, pp. 5–7).

Question: What is the purpose of these provisions, and how are they related to the larger issue of ecclesiastical privilege?

Manuscript Detail. This detail of a manuscript initial shows a master in a disputation with his students. It marks the opening of Aristotle's *De Interpretatione,* an anthology of grammatical and scholastic texts illuminated in the early 1300s.

Christians to confess and receive communion at least once a year and adopted a variety of reforms aimed at the purification of ecclesiastical life. In terms of its influence on both doctrine and practice, it was the most important council of the Middle Ages.

The Mendicant Orders. The organization of mendicant orders, the Dominicans and the Franciscans, must also be seen as a response to the crisis of the twelfth century. Among those who had hoped to convert the Albigensians by peaceful means was the Castilian preacher Domingo de Guzmán, or **St. Dominic** (c. 1170–1221). After several years among the heretics, he came to believe that if the teachings of the church were presented by competent preachers who lived a life of apostolic poverty, heresy could not survive. In 1207, he organized a convent of women who had recently converted. In 1216, he secured papal confirmation of an order of men dedicated to preaching and living a life of austerity equal to that of the parfaits. Popularly known

as the **Dominicans,** they stressed the intellectual formation of their members and lived by begging. Within a generation, they had taken their place among the intellectual leaders of the church.

A second order, founded by Dominic's contemporary **St. Francis of Assisi** (Uh-see'-see, c. 1181–1226), did not directly concern itself with the problem of heresy but embraced the idea of evangelical poverty with even greater fervor. The son of a wealthy merchant, Francis was inspired by a series of visions to abandon his family and retire to the town of Assisi, where he began to preach, although still a layman. He had no intention of forming a religious order in the conventional sense, but his preaching and the holiness of his life attracted disciples. In 1209, he went to Rome with eleven others and secured Innocent III's approval of a new rule dedicated to the imitation of Christ.

The **Franciscans,** as they were called, met a contemporary need. Their dedication to absolute poverty and the attractive spirit of their founder endeared them to the laity, and they soon became the largest of the mendicant orders. The Second Order of St. Francis, sometimes known as the Poor Clares, was created for women. Soon after their founding, the Franciscans split over the issue of property. The **Observant, or Spiritual, Franciscans** insisted on following the rule of St. Francis to the letter and refused to own property of any kind. The **Conventual Franciscans** argued that it was necessary to live in convents owned by the Order if they were to fulfill their mission and maintain discipline. Pope John XXII condemned the Observant view in 1322, but they remained a powerful underground movement in the late medieval church. Two smaller mendicant orders, the Carmelites and the Augustinians, were created in the same period. The friars, as the mendicants were called, emerged as the leaders of the great intellectual revival already under way in response to the challenges of the twelfth century.

The Founding of the Universities. The locus of that revival was a new institution: the university. Although copied by other cultures in modern times, the idea of the university is uniquely Western. It is, or was, a corporation of masters, so called because they had been certified as masters of their academic discipline and therefore competent to teach. Ideally, it is independent from political or religious influence and therefore open to freedom of inquiry. In practice, powerful interests have always sought to control universities, but despite interference, the Western university has remained committed, at least in theory, to independent thought.

Ironically, the first universities emerged from the same regularizing impulses that inspired the consolidation of feudal states and the reforms of Innocent III. The twelfth-century revival of learning led to a proliferation of competing schools in centers such as Paris and Bologna. Church and municipal authorities became alarmed at the potential for disorder, and the masters soon recognized the need for an organization that could both protect their interests and ensure that new masters were properly trained. By about 1150, rudimentary guilds or associations of masters had begun to evolve.

Paris, the First University. Sometime between 1150 and 1170, the chancellor of the Cathedral of Notre Dame organized a number of small schools into the University of Paris. In 1211, Innocent III formally recognized it as a legal corporation. The scholars, however, soon found themselves in conflict with the cathedral chapter of Notre Dame, which tried to control them, and with the townspeople who sought mainly to protect their lives and property against the students (see Document 9.4). The students, although theoretically studying for the priesthood, were for the most part adolescent males who lived without supervision. They sometimes committed rape, theft, and murder. The stu-

dents in turn complained of gouging by landlords and tavern keepers. Parisian authorities tended to ignore student grievances while their attempts to arrest student criminals often led to bloody riots. Each new outrage brought a flood of appeals to the pope or the king. Between 1215 and 1231, a series of statutes and charters was issued that established the privileges of the university in both civil and canon law.

Oxford and Cambridge. The situation at Oxford was not much different. In 1167–1168, the conflict between Henry II and Louis VII forced English scholars to leave Paris. They gathered in Oxford, a market town that had no cathedral or other ecclesiastical organization against which to rebel. Their relations with the townsfolk, however, soon became as envenomed as those at Paris. In 1209, after a violent riot, classes had to be temporarily suspended and many of the scholars departed for Cambridge to found a separate university. Only the papal humiliation of King John in 1213 saved Oxford's privileges. The king had supported the interests of the town against what he perceived as clerical privilege. Innocent III not only sided with the masters but forced the municipality to provide an annual subsidy for impoverished students.

Bologna. The University of Bologna was the north Italian counterpart of Paris and Oxford. If its origins were less violent, it was because its faculty emphasized the study of law instead of theology or the liberal arts. The students tended to be older men of considerable influence who found it easy to secure imperial and papal privileges without knifeplay. They also refused to be ruled by their teachers. The students, who hired the faculty and determined the curriculum, dominated Bologna and the other Italian universities based on its model.

Medical Schools. Medical schools were at first unrelated to the universities and, in at least two cases, predated them. Salerno, in the kingdom of Sicily, became a center of medical studies in the eleventh century, well before the introduction of Arabic learning. The interference of the state in the person of Emperor Frederick II reduced its vitality, and Montpellier largely superseded it after 1231. Montpellier (Mone-pel-lyay), in southern France, had been founded before 1140 and was a center of Arabic learning from the start. It gradually evolved during the thirteenth century into the major university that it is today. Other medical faculties were incorporated into universities at an early date, with Bologna (Bo-lo'-nya) and Paris achieving particular renown.

Organization and Curriculum. Organizationally, the heart of Paris, Oxford, and Cambridge was the faculty of liberal arts. The masters of arts had secured the independence of the universities. The theologians, although important, had been compromised by their obedience to ecclesiastical authority. The arts curriculum included the *trivium* (grammar, dialectic, and rhetoric) and the *quadrivium* (geometry, arithmetic, astronomy, and music). Dialectic meant the logic of Aristotle; rhetoric was largely the science by which one could unravel figures of speech. Those who received the master of arts were licensed to teach these subjects.

A course of the liberal arts had to be completed before a student could enter the schools of theology. By midcentury, the mendicant friars dominated the theology faculties. Their curriculum was based heavily on the *Sentences* of Peter Lombard (c. 1100–1160), a collection of theological arguments and propositions first published about 1150. Gratian's *Decretals* formed the basis of legal education. Because books were handwritten and expensive, teaching methods were simple: the master read the text and explained its meaning. Formal disputations between masters made a welcome alternative to these lectures and often drew large and sometimes violent crowds.

Masters controlled the academic lives of their students. Personally, they were on their own, although some lived in houses maintained by their religious orders or in colleges, which began to appear in the thirteenth century. The latter were foundations established for the support of students and contained living facilities that were more or less supervised. Masters and students alike enjoyed full clerical immunity as part of their university charters. They could be tried only in ecclesiastical courts, even if they committed civil crimes. A rector, elected for a term of no more than 3 months, governed the university as a whole and acted as its public spokesman. The only administrator in the modern sense was the beadle, or common servant of the scholars, who collected their fees and tried to enforce the regulations.

Gradually, universities became a source of prestige for those who founded them. By 1500, nearly every major region of Europe boasted a university of its own. Most of them were princely foundations, but some, like Erfurt and Cologne, were established by clerics with the help of city governments. Long before then, universities had become powerful corporations whose independence guaranteed them a certain freedom of thought. That freedom, although not unconditional, brought a breadth and vigor to Western culture that it would otherwise have lacked.

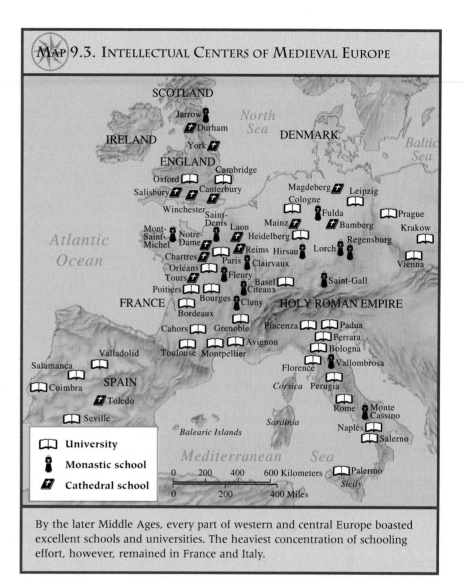

MAP 9.3. INTELLECTUAL CENTERS OF MEDIEVAL EUROPE

By the later Middle Ages, every part of western and central Europe boasted excellent schools and universities. The heaviest concentration of schooling effort, however, remained in France and Italy.

Scholastic Thought

Scholastic Method. The term *scholasticism* is generally used to describe the thought of the medieval universities. It was not an "ism" in the modern sense—that is, an ideology or system of belief—but a method for dealing with a wide range of questions in theology, philosophy, ethics, and the natural sciences. It relied almost exclusively on the system of linguistic logic adopted from Aristotle and, by the midthirteenth century, had evolved into a standard form of argumentation. The master proposed a question, suggested an answer (thesis) and analyzed all possible objections to that answer before coming to a final conclusion. Earlier authorities were cited in support of theses and objections alike. Reason determined the answer unless a clear statement on the issue could be drawn from Scripture or the authority of the church. Even then, some of the more radical thinkers ventured forward on the basis of logic alone. It was a method of extraordinary power, and in the universities of thirteenth-century Europe, it created an unparalleled flowering of creative thought.

Aquinas. Much of this effort was initially based on the need to confute the followers of Averroës (A-ver-ro'-eez). Some of them, such as Siger (Si-jair) of Brabant (d. c. 1281), held that faith could not be supported by reason and adopted a view that was essentially skeptical. Others developed ideas that could be described as pantheistic. Early attempts to suppress the Arabic commentators and their followers failed, although the University of Paris finally condemned the teachings of the Averroists in 1269–1270. In the meantime, two Dominicans, Albertus Magnus (c. 1200–1280) and his pupil **St. Thomas Aquinas** (Uh-kwine'-us, c. 1225–1274) developed an effective synthesis of Aristotelianism and Christian doctrine. Aquinas is generally regarded as one of the world's greatest thinkers. His approach to philosophy and theology, known as **Thomism,** has had a profound influence on Western thought and underlies much of Roman Catholic theology to this day. At the same time, he was a man of his times. His condemnation of Jews and homosexuals and his belief in the natural inferiority of women, although commonplace in the thirteenth century, had a disproportionate effect on Western attitudes as well.

Born to a noble family in the border marches between Naples and Rome, Thomas spent most of his life at the University of Paris and at Rome, where he was theological adviser to the papal curia. In his student days, his massive physique and natural reticence caused him to be nicknamed "the dumb ox," but his gentleness and courtesy, unique among the cantankerous academics of his day, endeared him even to opponents. His best-known works, the *Summa Contra Gentiles* and the unfinished *Summa Theologica*, reveal his purpose. They are comprehensive summations on practically every subject of contemporary theological and philosophical interest, and for all his insistence that learning is done even from errors, their intent is polemical.

An Aristotelian to his fingertips, Aquinas believed that God's universe was both rational and intelligible. On the question of universals, he was a moderate realist whose views were reminiscent of Abelard's. Knowledge must be based on the experience of the senses; thought enables the universal to be isolated in the particular. Both substance and accident are real, but substance provides the limits within which accidents may exist. This position was the basis of equally moderate conclusions on subjects ranging from the nature of the soul to the origins of evil and the problem of time, and it sets Aquinas firmly in the tradition of Aristotelian humanism. The intellect, although sustained by God, is a part of every human being. The soul is the form or essence of the body, of sensation, and of thought. In thinking, the soul transcends this form and becomes independent of matter.

Scotism. A majority of Aquinas's fellow Dominicans eventually adopted these ideas. The Franciscans, including his friend St. Bonaventura (c. 1217–1274), disputed them. Franciscan thought generally followed the tradition of St. Augustine and emphasized the importance of love and will as opposed to intellect. They believed that the gulf that separates human beings from God cannot be minimized or forgotten, and the intellect should not be identified too closely with the soul. Several aspects of this Franciscan approach crystallized in the work of **Duns Scotus** (1265–1308). A Scot who studied and taught at Paris, Oxford, Cambridge, and Cologne, he sought to preserve the concerns of St. Bonaventura without doing violence to Aristotle. To Scotus, everything had a reality of its own that existed independently of any universal. Universals existed only in the mind. This view enabled him to emphasize the uniqueness both of God and of individuals, but by denying the connection between human and divine intellect, he opened a gulf so vast that it could be bridged only by extraordinary means.

To Scotus and many of his contemporaries, the majesty and isolation of God were so great that special intercession was required. It could be provided only by the Virgin Mary, whose veneration became a central feature of their piety. The **Marian devotion** that emerged around the beginning of the fourteenth century would have a profound influence on Catholic spirituality. Scotus was its early

FIGURE 9.6 *Thomas Aquinas.* This painted panel by Zanobi di Benedetto Strozzi (1412–1468) shows the great philosopher lecturing to his students.

advocate and one of the first to formulate the doctrine of the Immaculate Conception, which holds that Mary was preserved from all taint of original sin when she was conceived.

Ockhamism. Scotus never saw himself as an opponent of Aquinas. He did not question the usefulness of reason in illuminating faith. That task was left to another Franciscan, **William of Ockham** (c. 1285–1349). Ockham carried the ideas of Scotus a step further and declared that only individuals are real and that the object of the senses and of the intellect are the same. Universals are no more than mental patterns created by recurring similarities of experience. Although a subtle difference, it meant that God was unknowable, at least to the intellect.

Ockham was an Observant Franciscan who opposed the papacy after the condemnation of 1322. He was not a heretic. When the Inquisition questioned his conclusions, he insisted that the doctrines of the church must be accepted in their entirety as revealed truth. His followers became known as **nominalists** because they supposedly believed that universals were only nomina, or names. The "Three Ways," Thomism, Scotism, and Ockhamism, were the three dominant strains of thought in the later Middle Ages. By the fifteenth century, however, the Occamists had become a majority on most university faculties. Some of them, such as Nicholas of Autrecourt (Oh-tre-koor, flourished 1340), went further than their master and declared that not even the existence of the material world could be demonstrated by rational means. Each person knows only his or her own soul. Although Thomism and Scotism continued to attract adherents and Thomism was revived in the sixteenth century at the time of the Counter-Reformation, the Ockhamist critique of reason proved highly corrosive. It presumed a dichotomy with faith that made formal thought virtually irrelevant. When such views became widespread, the creative age of scholasticism was over.

CONCLUSION

The Latin Church had survived the fall of the Roman Empire in the west to become the major unifying element in European society. It provided western Europeans with a common set of values and, through its universality and the reservation of the Latin language, with a measure of diplomatic and intellectual communication. With the passing of the great raids, the church gradually evolved into something more: a vast, institutionalized bureaucracy headed by popes who claimed full authority over a subordinate clergy as well as secular rulers. The emperor and other princes vehemently contested that authority, but all agreed that Europe was a Christian commonwealth ruled in theory by divine law.

The church of the High Middle Ages possessed great wealth, political influence, and a virtual monopoly of thought and education, but its importance cannot be understood in purely institutional terms. Although medieval people were neither excessively good nor moral, their personal identities and habits of thought were formed by near total immersion in Christian practices and ideas. The sacraments, from baptism to extreme unction, defined the stages of people's lives. The people measured time by the canonical hours and holidays of the church. They bound themselves by religious oaths that, to their minds, carried with them the real threat of eternal damnation, and explained everything from politics to natural phenomena as the expression of God's will. In more concrete terms, the church building was both the physical and social center of their communities and the most visible expression of communal civic pride. Priests, monks, and nuns organized the distribution of charity, cared for the sick, and provided lodging for travelers in the great monasteries that dotted the countryside. The church at all times claimed divine inspiration, but it had also become a human institution whose importance to the life of medieval people is scarcely conceivable today.

Review Questions

- What was the Investiture Controversy, and how was it resolved?
- What was the basis of papal claims of dominium over the secular states?
- What major consequences did the Crusades produce in Europe?
- How were medieval universities organized, and why did they develop?
- What was scholasticism, and what impact did it have on European thought?

For Further Study

Readings

Cobban, Alan B., *The Medieval Universities: Their Development and Organization* (London: Methuen, 1975). Brief, but comprehensive.

Cohen, Jeremy, *The Friars and the Jews. The Evolution of Medieval Anti-Judaism* (Ithaca: Cornell, 1982). An important essay on an often-misunderstood topic.

Colish, Marcia L., *The Medieval Foundations of the Western Intellectual Tradition, 400–1400* (New Haven: Yale, 1997). A good survey from Augustine through the scholastics.

Mayer, Hans Eberhard, *The Crusades*, trans. J. Gillingham, 2nd ed. (New York: Oxford, 1988). One of the best works to cover the Crusades as a whole.

Tellenbach, Gerd, *The Church in Western Europe from the Tenth to the Twelfth Century*, trans. T. Reuter (Cambridge: Cambridge University Press, 1993). A comprehensive survey.

InfoTrac College Edition

For additional reading, go to your online research library at *http://infotrac.thomsonlearning.com.*

Using Key Terms, enter the search terms:
Saint Francis

Using the Subject Guide, enter the search term:
Middle Ages   *Crusades*

Web Sites

http://www.fordham.edu/halsall/sbook.html
The Medieval History Sourcebook. Look under: Roman Church; Crusades; Europe and the Papacy; Iberia.

http://www.netserf.org   Netserf, The Internet Connection for Medieval Resources. Look under: Cathedrals and Churches; Abbies and Monasteries; St. Thomas Aquinas, Philosophy.

MEDIEVAL RELIGION AND THOUGHT

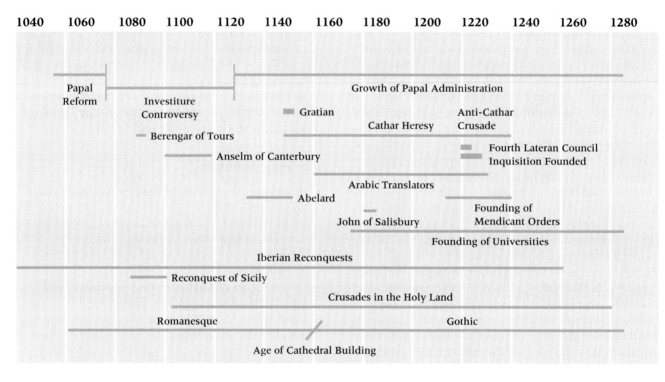

Chapter 10

ECONOMIC DEVELOPMENT AND URBAN GROWTH IN THE HIGH MIDDLE AGES

FOCUS QUESTIONS

- What were the major reasons for the increases in agricultural productivity after about 1000?
- What caused the extensive revival of trade, banking, and manufacturing between 1000 and 1250?
- What caused the rapid growth of European towns in the same period, and how did they achieve a measure of self-government that sometimes amounted to full political independence?
- What role did the medieval towns play in the development of Western civilization?

On February 23, 1250, in the Church of Santa Maria delle Vigne in Genoa, the five owners of the ship *Great Paradise* agreed to charter their vessel to a consortium of twelve merchants headed by Ido Lercari. In a Latin document several pages long, the ship owners agreed to provide the ship (with every sail, anchor, and coil of rope enumerated), a crew, and twenty-two crossbowmen (as protection from pirates) for a voyage from Genoa to Acre in Syria. The document specifies the quantity of goods to be shipped, the charter rates, and penalty clauses for nonperformance, together with precise statements as to which exchange rates and which weights and measures are to be used in the calculations. Three witnesses, including a judge, concluded the agreement by fixing their signatures. There was nothing unusual in this. Similar scenes had been enacted for years in all the ports of western Europe. They reveal that in the two centuries since the great raids, a sophisticated commercial culture based on the towns had evolved to manage a large-scale trade in both agricultural commodities and manufactured goods. That trade was based in turn on a broad growth in agricultural productivity. Greater productivity between 1000 and 1250 led to an agricultural surplus, which increased prosperity and encouraged population growth.

Chapter 10 begins by analyzing the technological basis of medieval society. It then shows how and why agricultural production increased between 1000 and 1250 and how this growth in productivity increased real wealth and allowed the population of Europe to double during the same period. Improved productivity also encouraged agricultural specialization, which led to the growth of a trade in agricultural products. Eventually, new wealth and the influence of the Crusades created a long-distance trade in luxury goods as well. The chief beneficiaries of this new commercial activity were the towns. This chapter concludes with a description of town life in the High Middle Ages and of how European towns established a substantial measure of political freedom.

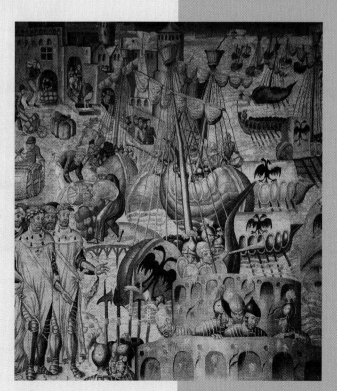

MEDIEVAL TECHNOLOGY: ENERGY, TOOLS, AND TRANSPORT (C. 500–1450)

Medieval technology, like that of the Romans, was based on two primary materials: wood and iron. The demand for both always exceeded the available supply. Even in ancient times, wood had been scarce in the Mediterranean basin. By the end of the Middle Ages, its availability was limited in northwest Europe as well. Only in the Baltic regions and in eastern Europe was timber plentiful, and even there prices increased steadily throughout the Middle Ages in response to increased demand from other regions. Given that wood was a primary building material as well as the major source of fuel, this is hardly surprising.

Fuel. Medieval households burned wood for cooking and to heat the home, although western Europeans normally used only the residual heat from cooking except in the coldest weather. Charcoal, an expensive commodity made by charring wood, was used primarily in the smelting and forging of metals, whereas coal, first mentioned in European sources around the year 1200, did not come into general use for another 400 years. This was largely because mining techniques remained primitive. In the absence of effective pumps, the pits could not be kept dry, and the development of effective pumps depended on metallurgical techniques that were as yet unknown. Alloy steels capable of surviving the friction in a constantly worked pump would not be invented until the nineteenth century. The continuous working of pumps also requires a cheap, reliable source of power. Pumping by hand involved high labor costs. Windmills, used from the fifteenth century onward to drain the tidal wetlands of Holland, suggested a possible solution, but they proved ineffective where hills masked the breeze or in regions where wind strength was inconstant. These problems remained largely unsolved until the age of steam. In the meantime, coal and ores could be mined only from shallow pits, and transportation costs ensured that coal would be used only in the immediate vicinity of the mines. The scarcity of metals made ore worth transporting, but it was always best if deposits could be found near abundant sources of charcoal so that smelting might occur on the spot.

Construction Materials. Reliance on wood for most forms of construction further increased its cost. Ships had to be built almost entirely of wood and consumed vast quantities of the best timber. Their keels and frames demanded rare, naturally curved compass timbers, and their masts required tall, straight trees with few branches. Planking was almost invariably of the best available oak. However high the quality of planking, constant immersion in water and the ravages of marine organisms ensured a maximum life of 7 or 8 years before a ship's timbers had to be replaced. Given the hazards of navigation, many ships went to the bottom of the ocean long before such repairs could be made, with even higher replacement costs as a result.

On land, most buildings were at least framed in wood. Fully wooden structures had once been common in northern Europe, but by the twelfth century they had already become rare outside of Scandinavia and the Baltic. The growing cost of lumber forced builders to construct walls out of cob, wattle and daub, or some other combination of earth mixed with straw. Homes usually had thatched roofs and floors of earth or clay. Only public buildings and the houses of the very rich were built of stone and roofed with slate or tile. Masonry construction was more common in the Mediterranean basin, although precious wood was still used for joists and roof beams.

FIGURE 10.1 *Registering the Sale of Wood at Paris.* The importance of wood in shipbuilding, construction, and tool-making made it expensive and therefore of great interest to the political authorities. In this illustration from the early 1400s, a cargo of wood offered at Paris is graded and recorded for purposes of quality control and taxation by an official known as a *mouleur.* From the *Ordinnances Royaux de la Jurisdiction de la Prevot des Marchands de la Ville de Paris* (1428).

THE TIMBER PROBLEM IN MEDIEVAL EUROPE

In 1140, Suger, abbot of Saint-Denis (near Paris), decided to construct a new church that would require twelve 35-foot beams. His experience in a landscape virtually denuded of large trees indicates how serious the problem of adequate timber supplies had become.

On a certain night, when I had returned from Matins, I began to think in bed that I myself should go through all the forests of these parts. . . . Quickly disposing of all duties and hurrying up in the early morning, we hastened with our carpenters, and with the measurements of the beams, to the forest called Ivelines. When we traversed our possession in the Valley of Chevreuse we summoned . . . the keepers of our own forests as well as men who know about the other woods, and questioned them under oath whether we would find there, no matter with how much trouble, any timbers of that measure. At this they smiled, or rather would have laughed at us if they had dared; they wondered whether we were quite igno-

rant of the fact that nothing of the kind could be found in the entire region, especially since Milon, the Castellan of Chevreuse . . . had left nothing unimpaired or untouched that could be used for palisades and bulwarks while he was long subjected to wars both by our Lord the King and Amaury de Montfort. We however—scorning what they might say—began with the courage of our faith as it were, to search the woods; and toward the first hour we found one timber adequate to our measure. Why say more? By the ninth hour or sooner, we had, through the thickets, the depths of the forest and the dense, thorny tangles, marked down twelve timbers (for so many were necessary) to the astonishment of all.

From Panovsky, Erwin, trans. and ed. *Abbot Suger, on the Abbey Church of St. Denis* (Princeton, NJ: Princeton University Press, 1973).

Question: According to this, what was the major cause of the timber shortage in the region around Saint-Denis?

Tools. Tools tended to be made of wood or of wood tipped with iron. Alloy steel was as yet unknown, and the handwrought carbon steel used in knives and edged weapons was expensive. The process required great skill and enormous quantities of fuel. Even implements made from lower grades of iron represented a major capital outlay for farmers and artisans. The high cost of iron resulted in part from the limitations of mining technology, but skilled ironworkers were few in number, and the making of charcoal for use in the forges consumed large quantities of wood.

Energy. The primary energy source in medieval Europe remained the muscle power of humans or animals, although by the eleventh century, water mills were universally employed for the grinding of grain. The water wheel had been used in western Asia as early as the first century, but it was apparently unknown in the west until brewers in northern France adopted it around 820 to grind their grain. By the midthirteenth century, waterpower was also used in the fulling of cloth and to drive the hammers and bellows of forges. Fulling thickened a piece of cloth either by treading on it in a trough or by pounding it with wooden mallets. Like the hammers of a forge, mallets could be driven by a revolving drum attached to the mill shaft. Wind provided assistance for ships at sea, but windmills, a Persian invention introduced to Europe at the end of the twelfth century, did not become common until the fifteenth century.

FIGURE 10.2 *A Watermill.* Water, harnessed by mill wheels like the one shown here, provided an important source of power throughout the Middle Ages and well into modern times. Gears on the water wheel were connected to a shaft that turned the millstones and ground the grain. In other mills, the millshaft worked hammers for fulling cloth or forging iron. From *L'Instruction Dung Josne Prince* (1400s).

Land Transport. The high cost of iron and wood resulted not only from scarcity but from the problem of distance. Both materials were heavy and expensive to ship. Owing to political fragmentation and the decay of the Roman highway system, land transportation in the

FIGURE 10.3 *A Delivery of Wine Barrels at Paris.* Most medieval trade involved bulk agricultural commodities such as wine or grain. When possible, goods were transported by boat, which was far cheaper than shipping them over the poor-quality roads of the time. Paris was located in the midst of a grain-growing area and imported most of its wine from other parts of France. This miniature from the *Life and Miracles of Saint Denis* (1317) shows three boats loaded with wine barrels moored to a quay on the Seine. A client on the middle boat tastes the wine to confirm its quality, while the buyer and merchant on the first boat have already reached agreement. A carriage drawn by two horses rolls from the left through the gate into the city. On the right, a doctor (seated) examines a urine bottle while his patient pays him for the treatment.

Middle Ages was more arduous and expensive than it had been in antiquity. Besides raising shipping costs in general, this made it difficult to compensate for local shortages or crop failures by importing goods from other regions. Shipping grain overland for 200 miles might raise its price by a factor of 7, making it unaffordable to the poor, even if they were starving.

Land transport was generally conducted over roads that were little more than tracks, choked with dust in dry weather and axle-deep in mud when it rained. If the mud froze, ruts made the highways impassable for wheeled vehicles. For this reason, people traveled on foot or on horseback and generally preferred pack animals to ox-driven carts except in optimum conditions.

Boats and Shipping. Water transport, if available, was far more efficient. Many European rivers are navigable for much of their length. Boats, rafts, and barges became increasingly important with the passage of time. The sea remained the greatest highway of all, uniting the peoples who lived along its shores. The Baltic, the North Sea, and the Atlantic coasts were served by a variety of ship types whose chief common feature was the use of a square sail set amidships. This rig handled easily and provided excellent performance downwind. It

was virtually useless for sailing into the wind or in confined waters. Many of the smaller craft therefore carried oars or sweeps and could penetrate coastal estuaries as had the Viking longships on which they were often modeled.

In the Mediterranean, many ships carried the triangular lateen sail, invented by Arab sailors in the Indian Ocean and introduced to Europe by the Byzantine Greeks. It permitted a ship to sail close to the wind and could be used on both galleys and the larger round ships that were propelled by sails alone. The round ship, broad-beamed and steered by long oars slung from the stern quarters, was sturdy, capacious, and very slow. It was the bulk carrier of the Middle Ages. Perishable cargos or those with a high value-to-weight ratio required galleys. Fast and maneuverable, they were as dependent on the land as their ancient counterparts and too fragile for extensive use in the open Atlantic.

The Rate of Technological Change. These generalizations, referring as they do to a period of more than 1,000 years, imply that little technological change was evident in the Middle Ages. This is not true, but by modern standards the rate of change was relatively slow. The medieval economy remained basically agricultural, with more than 90 percent of the population directly engaged in the production of food. By modern standards, cash remained scarce and the surplus of goods and services beyond those needed for mere subsistence small. Even at the height of the commercial revolution, most people had little discretionary income. This made the accumulation of capital for investment in new technologies difficult and retarded the demand for innovations.

AGRICULTURAL IMPROVEMENTS IN THE ELEVENTH AND TWELFTH CENTURIES

The rate of technological change, although slow by modern standards, did not prevent Europe from doubling its agricultural productivity between the years of 1000 and 1250. Population doubled as well. Climatological evidence suggests that a general warming trend extended the growing season and permitted the extension of cultivation to more northern regions and to higher elevations. No major famines occurred during this period, and crises of subsistence tended to be local and of short duration. But changes in the climate alone cannot account for such an unprecedented expansion.

The Return of Settled Conditions. The return of more or less settled conditions after the great raids of the ninth and tenth centuries was certainly a factor in economic expansion. The annual loss of food, tools, livestock, and seed grain to the marauders had been substantial. When augmented by forced requisitions and by the depredations of local feudatories, its impact on subsistence must have been great. A number of technical innovations also increased productivity, although some were dependent on a preexistent improvement in conditions for their success. The exten-sion of the three-field system through much of north-west Europe is an example.

The Expansion of the Three-Field System. In the early Middle Ages, most of Europe had cultivated the land using a two-field system. Each year, farmers left half of their land fallow (uncultivated) while planting the rest. This allowed the unplanted soil to recover at least some of its nutrients. The three-field system that became common after the tenth century permitted more intensive cultivation by leaving only one third of the land fallow in a given year. Winter grains like wheat or rye were planted on another third while the remaining third grew such spring crops as oats, barley, peas, or beans. By leaving only one-third of the land fallow in any given year, as opposed to half under the earlier system, peasants increased both their yields and the diversity of their crops without seriously diminishing the fertility of their land.

The success of this scheme depended on the quality of the soil and the availability of adequate rainfall. Northwestern Europe, although at the same latitude as Newfoundland or Labrador, is mild and moist. Its weather is moderated by the Atlantic Ocean and, in particular, by the Gulf Stream, a warm water current that rises in the Caribbean and washes the shores of England and France. Pleasant summers with temperatures that usually do not exceed 80° Fahrenheit follow long, wet winters in which prolonged freezes are rare. The prevailing winds are westerly, bringing abundant rainfall even in the summer months, as Atlantic squalls, forced northward by high pressure over the Iberian Peninsula, drop their moisture on the land. In much of the Mediterranean basin, where little or no rain falls to support summer crops, the two-field system remained dominant; in the harsh, dry tablelands of Castile, seven-field systems in which only one-seventh of the land was cultivated at a time were common.

The Iron Plow. The introduction of the heavy iron plow, or *carruca* (car-roo'-ca), and the complex technology that surrounded it further increased production. This device was apparently of Slavic origin. Mounted on wheels, it consisted of a horizontal plowshare and an angled mould board that turned the sliced earth aside. Cutting a deeper furrow than its Roman predecessor (see *Architectural Technology*), the iron plow made the seed less vulnerable to late frosts and to the depredations of birds and rodents. This increased yields and extended the limits of cultivation by allowing the seed to survive in colder climates. Heavy clay soils impervious to the scratchings of ancient plowmen could now be used for the first time, and the clearing of virgin land was greatly simplified.

Horse Plowing. Iron plows, however, were expensive. They also required the increased use of draft animals if

---

TABLE 10.1 POPULATION CHANGES IN MEDIEVAL EUROPE

The first column (500 CE) shows the European population shortly after the fall of the Roman Empire in the west. The numbers were still falling in 600 CE, but they had begun to increase dramatically by 1000 CE. The increase continued until the Black Death of 1347–1350 (see Chapter 12), when perhaps one-third of Europe's population died. The year 1340 marks a peak that was not reached again until the late 1500s. The figures for 1450 remain close to the levels of 1350. Estimates are in millions.

Question: What caused the population to increase between 1000 and 1340?

	Population in Millions				
REGION	500 CE	600 CE	1000 CE	1340 CE	1450 CE
British Isles	0.5	0.5	2.0	5.0	3.0
France–Low Countries	5.0	3.0	6.0	19.0	12.0
Germany–Scandinavia	3.5	2.0	4.0	11.5	7.5
Greece and the Balkans	5.0	3.0	5.0	6.0	4.5
Hungary	0.5	0.5	1.5	2.0	1.5
Iberia	4.0	3.5	7.0	9.0	7.0
Italy	4.0	2.5	5.0	10.0	7.5
Slavic lands	5.0	3.0			
Poland–Lithuania			2.0	3.0	2.0
Russia			6.0	8.0	6.0
TOTAL	27.5	18.0	38.5	73.5	51.0

Adapted from Cipolla, Carlo, *The Middle Ages, Fontana Economic History of Europe* (London: Colliers, 1973, p. 36). Reprinted by permission of HarperCollins Publishers Ltd.

Agricultural Technology

The Mediterranean "Scratch" Plow. The Mediterranean scratch plow preceded the heavy wheeled plow and had been used throughout the Roman Empire. It remained popular in dry regions and in regions with light, easily cultivated soils until modern times because it did not turn over the furrows and therefore helped preserve moisture in the soil. Note the harness and yoke on the oxen. From the *Latin/Luttrell Psalter* (1300s).

Removing Weeds or Thistles. The wheeled plow, first introduced to Western Europe in the ninth and tenth centuries, helped farmers clear land and cultivate heavier soils with greater efficiency.

their full potential was to be realized. The old Roman plow required, at the most, a single team of oxen, and in light soils, it could often be pulled by a pair of human beings. The heavy plow might require as many as eight beasts. The increasing use of three- and four-yoke teams from the ninth century onward was responsible for a reorganization of labor on more cooperative lines. It was also an indication of greater prosperity, as was the innovation of plowing with horses. Horses are not as strong in absolute terms as draft oxen, but they are much faster. Horse plowing increases the amount of land that can be cultivated in a day by more than 30 percent. This represented a great increase in efficiency. However, horses are more inclined to sickness and injury than oxen, and their diet must be supplemented by feed grains. Oxen, for the most part, need only to graze. The introduction of horse plowing was therefore limited to regions that already enjoyed a considerable surplus of grain. It also required the

development of a new type of harness. Horses cannot be yoked like oxen without constricting their windpipes, and attaching the plow to their withers or tail is not only cruel but woefully ineffective. The modern harness, without which a draft horse is virtually useless, appears to have been developed in Asia and introduced to Europe around the year 800.

Manure. A fringe benefit associated with the increased use of draft animals was the greater availability of manure. Medieval peasants knew that manure greatly increased the fertility of soils, just as they knew that marl could be used to reduce soil acidity and that soils could be mixed to improve workability or drainage. All of these techniques were labor intensive. Substantial quantities of manure were required to fertilize even a moderately sized field, and although draft animals were numerous after 1100, livestock produc-

226 *Chapter 10*

The Sickle and the Scythe. On the left, a reaper harvests grain with a short-handled sickle of the kind used since antiquity. Its short cutting blade and even shorter handle limited the amount that could be cut in one sweep and forced its user to work while bending over in a back-breaking posture. The two-handed scythe was introduced in Frankish times and immediately increased the amount of grain that could be harvested by a single farmer. It was also much easier on the farmer's back. With both tools, harvesting was often conducted by several men working the field in a diagonal line to prevent them from being cut by their neighbor's implement.

tion for meat remained modest until the second half of the fourteenth century.

Stall-Feeding of Cattle. Perhaps the most important advance in this area was the Frankish invention of the scythe, a two-handed mowing instrument with a long, curved blade. The scythe largely replaced the short, one-handed sickle and permitted large-scale haying and the stall-feeding of cattle. Stall-feeding allowed farmers to keep animals through the winter and encouraged weight gain through greater feed efficiency. They kept cattle for meat and dairy products and carefully collected their manure for spreading on the fields. However, stock-raising is a fundamentally inefficient use of land. Vegetable crops suited for direct human consumption fed more people from the same acreage. On marginal lands where even intensive cultivation provides modest yields, stock-raising is uneconomic and animal protein a luxury.

Supplies of manure, although improved, were therefore limited and were probably applied most frequently to household gardens and other small plots. The use of human waste as fertilizer, although common in Asia, was apparently rare in the West.

Average Crop Yields. Larger fields could retain their productivity only by being left fallow or through crop rotation. Even at the height of the so-called agricultural revolution, yields by modern standards remained poor, but they were a great improvement over those of Charlemagne's time. Whereas harvesting one-and-a-half grains for every grain planted was once common, harvesting four or five became possible. Theoretically, the maximum yield of wheat from an unfertilized field is about 12 bushels per acre. Peasants in the thirteenth century probably averaged about half this amount from fields that today produce 60 bushels

TABLE 10.2 MEDIEVAL GRAIN YIELDS

The following range of grain yields is taken from harvest records on the estates of the bishops of Winchester (England) between 1209 and 1349, a relatively fertile area that enjoyed good management. The figures are therefore probably higher than those for medieval Europe as a whole but far below what can be achieved with modern technology. Yields of wheat on similar lands today have been known to reach 70 to 80 bushels per acre. The difference goes far to explain the insufficiency of medieval diets.

	Yield in Grains per Grain Planted		Yield in Bushels per Acre	
GRAIN	MAXIMUM	MINIMUM	MAXIMUM	MINIMUM
Barley	5.6	2.8	27.6	11.0
Oats	3.4	1.8	16.0	7.5
Wheat	5.3	2.6	13.6	5.8

Titow, J. Z., *Winchester Yields* (Cambridge: Cambridge University Press, 1972, p. 14).

Question: Why were grain yields so much lower in medieval times than they are today?

per acre or more, but 5 to 7 bushels per acre was a substantial improvement over times past (see Table 10.2).

Agricultural Specialization. The improvement of yields, the extension of cultivation into new areas, and the reduction in the amount of labor required to produce a given quantity of food produced consistent surpluses of crops in those areas where they grew best. This in turn led to agricultural specialization. The regions around Beauvais (Bo-vay) or the Ile de France, for example, were ideal for the cultivation of wheat but produced only small quantities of inferior wine. Parts of Burgundy produced excellent wine but relatively meager stands of wheat. Landholders found that they could improve their revenues as well as their standard of living by selling off surpluses and using the profits to purchase commodities that grew poorly, if at all, on their own manors. In time, whole regions were devoted to the cultivation of grains while others specialized in wine, olives, or other commodities. The great wine-growing areas were planted for the most part in the twelfth century, usually along navigable rivers such as the Loire (Lwar), the Rhône, or the Rhine to facilitate transport. Corking and bottling had not yet been invented, so wine was shipped in casks that were too heavy to transport easily on land.

For peasants, specialization was a mixed blessing. Monoculture left them more vulnerable to crop failures than the subsistence farmers who grew a little bit of everything. Some evidence is available that diets deteriorated as more and more land was devoted to the cash crop. But from the standpoint of the European economy as a whole, specialization improved efficiency. It increased the overall production of commodities because land was not wasted on unsuitable crops, and it probably improved their quality as well. It also, by definition, created the basis for a trade in bulk agricultural commodities that grew into a full-blown commercial revolution.

THE COMMERCIAL REVOLUTION (1000–1250)

Trade in the Early Middle Ages. In the early Middle Ages, most trading was local and conducted through barter. With the growth of agricultural specialization, this form of commerce expanded without changing its essential principles. Villagers brought their surplus goods to weekly markets held in a nearby town and exchanged them for clothing, tools, or agricultural products that they could not produce efficiently themselves. Larger transactions were conducted at great annual fairs, such as the one at Champagne that attracted merchants from all over Europe until well into modern times.

At first, long-distance commerce was largely in the hands of Jews. Although Jews were not invariably barred from holding land, Christian hostility kept them socially peripheral and reinforced the natural cosmopolitanism of a people in exile. Their wide-ranging contacts, reinforced by strong kinship ties, gave them a powerful advantage when virtually everyone else was bound by interest and circumstance to the locality of their birth. This situation began to change in the eleventh century. The increased volume, safety, and profitability of trade began to make it more attractive to Christian entrepreneurs, who were able to squeeze out their Jewish competitors by securing favored treatment from Christian authorities. The anti-Semitic persecutions that began in the twelfth century arose primarily from the crusading impulse, but they coincided with a perceived decline in the economic usefulness of the Jews.

The Growth of Trade in Italy. The most aggressive of the new traders were the inhabitants of the Italian coastal towns. By the beginning of the eleventh century, a number of Italian cities had outgrown their local food supplies and emerged as net importers of agricultural commodities. Grain, oil, and other commodities had to be purchased abroad, usually in Spain or Sicily. Ports such as Pisa, Amalfi, and Genoa possessed the maritime skills necessary for this trade and were often forced to engage in it for their own survival. Only the threat of Muslim piracy stood in their way. By combining their fleets and taking advantage of political disorder in North Africa, the three cities were able to drive the Muslims from their bases in Sardinia, Corsica, and the Balearic Islands by 1088.

Venice, the greatest trading city of them all, had no *contado* (the term literally means "county," but it refers to rural areas controlled directly by the town) or agricultural land of its own. It produced little more than glass and sea salt, but being located at the head of the Adriatic, it was the perfect center for trade between the eastern Mediterranean and central Europe. Dependent on commerce almost from its beginnings, Venice, like other Italian ports, owed its eventual success to sheer necessity, maritime skill, and location. By the beginning of the twelfth century, the Italians were dominant in the Mediterranean carrying trade and were beginning to extend their routes northward.

The Crusades and the Development of Long-Distance Trade.

The Crusades expanded Italian trade and greatly increased its value. Crusaders who wished to go to the Holy Land by sea went for the most part in Italian ships and paid dearly for the privilege. When they arrived, they found a civilization that was in many ways more sophisticated than their own. They quickly developed a taste for silks, spices from India, and the superior cutlery of Damascus, to name a few of the items that by 1250 had become the components of an immense commerce. Those who returned to Europe brought their new tastes with them and created a fashion for Eastern luxuries that the Italians were well positioned to fill. Each shipload of crusaders offered its master the opportunity to make commercial contacts along the route, and elaborate trading networks soon developed between the Italians and their merchant counterparts in Greece, the Aegean, Turkish Anatolia, and the Levant.

Demand for Eastern luxuries became possible only because the real wealth of the west had increased since Carolingian times. The agricultural revolution was primarily responsible for this phenomenon. The return of settled conditions also permitted gold and silver that had been hoarded during the bad old days to be released into circulation. This, together with the slow but steady increase in European mining during the eleventh and twelfth centuries, increased the amount of specie available for trade. Copper coinage remained the standard in everyday transactions, but silver became more common, and in the midthirteenth century gold coinage was introduced for the first time on a large scale.

From the Italian point of view, the Eastern trade was ideal. Luxuries from the East possessed a far higher ratio of value to weight than did agricultural products and could generate greater profits. The risks were correspondingly high, but as in the case of the spice trade, a single voyage could make a trader's fortune. Spices, the most important of which were black pepper, nutmeg, and cinnamon, originated in India or in what is now Indonesia and were transported across the Indian Ocean in the dhows of Arab merchants. They were then transhipped by caravan to the Mediterranean ports, where Italian traders purchased them and carried them home by ship. Other merchants then took the spices overland to consumers beyond the Alps. At each stage of this journey except the last, profits might amount to several hundred percent on

FIGURE 10.4 *The Venetian Harbor.* Venice was the greatest trading city of medieval Europe. This miniature from an edition of Marco Polo was done by an English illuminator who seems to have known the city well. It shows Polo as he embarks on his great expedition to the court of Kublai Khan. The small boat (near the pier) takes him to a ship anchored in the deeper waters of the Venetian Lagoon. The church of San Marco, with its four bronze horses, is in the upper left, with the Palace of the Doges beside it. The column on the waterfront is topped with the Lion of St. Mark, a symbol of the city.

A COMMENDA FROM VENICE, 1073

This is a fairly standard example of a commenda contract from the early period of the commercial revolution.

In the name of the Lord God and of our Savior, Jesus Christ. In the year of the Incarnation of the same Redeemer 1073, in the month of August, eleventh indiction, at Rialto, I, Giovanni Lissado of Luprio, together with my heirs, have received in partnership from you, Sevasto Orefice, son of Ser Trudimondo, and from your heirs, this amount: 200 Lira Venetian. And I myself have invested 100 Lira in it. And with this capital we have acquired two shares of the ship in which Gosmiro da Molina is captain. And I am under obligation to bring all of this with me on a commercial voyage to Thebes in the ship which the aforesaid Gosmiro da Molino sails as captain. Indeed, by this agreement and understanding of ours I promise to put to work this entire capital and to strive the best way I can. Then if the capital is saved, we are to divide whatever profit the Lord may grant us from it by exact halves, without fraud and evil device. And whatever I can gain with these goods from any source, I am under obligation to invest all of it in the partnership. And if all these goods are lost because of the sea or of hostile people, and this is proved—may this be averted—neither party ought to ask any of them from the other; if, however, some of them remain, in proportion as we invested, so shall we share. Let this partnership exist between us so long as our wills are fully agreed.

But if I do not observe everything just as is stated above, I, together with my heirs, then promise to give and to return to you and your heirs everything in the double, both capital and profit, out of my land and my house or out of anything that I am known to have in this world.

From Lopez, Robert S., and Raymond, Irving W., *Medieval Trade in the Mediterranean World* (New York: Columbia University Press, 1955).

Questions: What is Giovanni Lissado actually promising to do with the borrowed money? What is his collateral?

invested capital. However, ships were frequently lost to pirates, bad weather, or the unpredictable fortunes of war and politics.

Finance and Banking. Risky ventures of this kind were often supported by a *commenda* contract (see Document 10.2). An investor, usually an older man or a woman, would finance the voyage of a younger merchant in return for half of the total profits. After two or three such voyages, the younger man could then retire and become an investor in his own right. The Eastern trade never equaled bulk commodities either in volume or in total value, but as a means of capital accumulation it was unsurpassed. Many Italians became enormously rich. They reinvested much of this wealth in banking, which soon became international in scope. Banking began when traders sought to deposit their cash with goldsmiths or moneychangers who had the facilities for storing it safely. A fee was normally charged for this service. As the number of customers grew, the likelihood that they would try to redeem their deposits at the same time decreased. As long as the banker maintained an adequate reserve, a portion of his deposits could be loaned out to other businessmen at a profit.

Aware that a trading community needed a stable coinage, Venice and Florence established the *ducat* (duck'-at) and the *florin*, respectively, at fixed values that made them the currency of choice throughout Europe and much of the Middle East. The rulers of other countries often reduced the precious metal content of their coins to pay off their debts in depreciated money. Investors preferred currencies that protected them from this inflationary practice and, wherever possible, deposited their money with the Italians. To facilitate this, and to take advantage of the need for capital in other, less developed parts of Europe, Florentine, Venetian, and Milanese bankers established branches in leading centers of trade throughout the subcontinent.

By the thirteenth century, Italian bankers were the dominant force in international moneylending. Although in theory Christians could not loan money at interest, the Italians used their branch banks and the natural variations in exchange rates at different locations to avoid the church's ban. Bills of exchange would be issued at the Venetian rate, for example, and redeemed after a fixed period or usance at the higher London rate (see Document 10.3). The difference between the two exchange rates would reflect the cost of the loan. Most churchmen were not fooled by this, but bills of exchange satisfied the technical requirements of theology.

Manufacturing in Italy. Additional Italian wealth was invested in manufacturing. A major problem with the Eastern trade was that at first the East had little or no interest in Western merchandise and tended to demand payment for its goods in cash. A real chance existed that the trade would be destroyed by balance of payment problems similar to those that had beset the later Roman Empire. Many of the wiser merchants began to invest in the creation of products that would attract Eastern consumers. Among them were fine finished cloths based on merino wool from Spain, which were dyed and woven according to specialized techniques in Italy. Florence took an early lead in this trade, as it did in the production of fine leather goods. Silk, too, became an important Italian export when it was discovered that the mulberry trees on which silk worms grew could survive in southern Italy. Italians soon mastered the technique of spinning and weaving silk, and although the primary market for this

A BILL OF EXCHANGE

Genoese Bankers at Work. This late fourteenth-century illumination shows a Genoese banker and his assistant at their bench. Banking had by this time become an important industry in its own right, and the prominence of Genoese bankers would last until well into the seventeenth century.

This sample bill of exchange demonstrates how the system worked. Barna, in Avignon, orders his correspondents, the Bartoli of Pisa, to pay off a loan of 4.5 percent from Tancredi Bonagiunta and partners. Landuccio Busdraghi and com-

pagni (partners) were Bonagiunta's correspondents in Lucca, which is only a few miles from Pisa. Several copies of such documents were usually sent to avoid accidental loss in transit. This one is marked "First" as the original.

Avignon, October 5, 1339

In the name of God, amen. To Bartolo and partners [compagni], Barna of Lucca and partners [send] greetings from Avignon.

You shall pay by this letter on November 20 [1]339, to Landuccio Busdraghi and partners of Lucca, gold florins three hundred twelve and three fourths for the exchange [per cambio] of gold florins three hundred, because I have received such money today from Tancredi Bonagiunta and partners at the rate [raxione] of 4 1/2 per 100 to their advantage. And charge [it] to our account. Done on October 5 [1]339.

Francesco Falconetti has ordered us to pay in your behalf 230 gold scudi to the Acciaiuoli compagnia.

[Address on outside:]

To Bartolo Casini and Partners, in Pisa First.

From Lopez, Robert S., and Raymond, Irving W., *Medieval Trade in the Mediterranean World* (New York: Columbia University Press, 1955).

Question: Why did Barna not simply send the payment directly to his creditor in Lucca, which was, after all, his own hometown?

---

commodity remained European, the new industry helped them reduce imports while developing a highly profitable sideline.

Other European Centers of Trade and Industry.

As a result of these activities, Italy was perhaps 50 years ahead of the rest of Europe in economic development, but other areas enjoyed remarkable growth as well. The Catalans were formidable competitors in the Mediterranean trade. In the Baltic, German traders achieved a commanding position after the decline of their Scandinavian rivals in the tenth and eleventh centuries. The north German towns, of which Lübeck (Lue'-bek) was the most important, dealt in salt herring, furs, amber, wax, timber, pitch, tar, iron, and all the other products of the northern world. Organized into **Hansas** (Hahn'-sas), or city leagues, they prospered greatly throughout the High Middle Ages.

Ghent, Bruges (Broozh), Ypres (Ee'-per), and the other Flemish cities concentrated primarily on the manufacture of cloth. Their position near the mouths of the Meuse (Muse) and the Rhine made them natural ports that connected the European interior with the sea

routes to England, Scandinavia, and northern Spain. Some of them also rivaled the Hanse in the salt trade, which was vital because salt was the primary means of preserving food. By the end of the thirteenth century, the Low Countries had become a highly urbanized center of wealth that rivaled Italy in commercial importance. Other, smaller centers of trade and manufacturing developed along the main trade routes or wherever a local product achieved some level of renown.

Guilds and the Organization of Manufacturing.

Manufacturing in the Middle Ages did not normally employ elaborate machinery or the techniques of mass production and cannot, therefore, be described as truly industrial, although some of the larger wool shops in Italy or Flanders employed as many as 150 workers. Goods were produced by artisans who, after the tenth century, were typically organized into guilds or associations that attempted to regulate price and quality in a particular trade. Because they included the masters who owned the shops, journeymen who worked for them, and apprentices who would one day be admitted to full membership, the guilds combined a variety of functions.

THE GUILDS AND SOCIAL WELFARE

This excerpt is from the "customs" of the Guild of the Holy Trinity at Lynn, England, dating from the late fourteenth century. It illustrates the degree to which guilds provided for the security and social welfare of member families. The church required payment for funeral masses and masses for the dead.

If any of the aforesaid brethren shall die in the said town or elsewhere, as soon as the knowledge thereof shall come to the alderman, the said alderman shall order solemn mass to be celebrated for him, at which every brother of the said guild that is in town shall make his offering; and further, the alderman shall cause every chaplain of the said guild, immediately on the death of any brother, to say thirty masses for the deceased.

The aldermen and skevins [from the French echevin—*essentially the same as an* alderman; *in this case both terms refer to the guild's governing board] of the said guild are by duty obliged to visit four times a year all the infirm, all that are in want, need, or poverty, and to minister to and relieve all such out of the alms of the said guild.*

If any brother shall become poor and needy, he shall be supported in food and clothing, according to his exigency, out of the profits of the lands and tenements, goods and chattels of the said guild.

From *Pennsylvania Translations and Reprints*, vol 2. trans. Edward P. Cheyney (Philadelphia: University of Pennsylvania Press, 1897).

Question: What institutions provide these benefits in the modern world?

Banner of the
Guild of Tinmen

Banner of the Guild of
Pin and Needle Makers

Banner of the Douai
Guild of Shoemakers

Banner of the St. Lô
Blacksmiths Guild

They set wages and prices as far as market forces would permit. They supervised the training of apprentices and tried to guarantee a quality product through inspections and the use of such devices as the masterpiece, a work whose acknowledged excellence permitted its creator to be enrolled as a master in the guild. Because mechanisms for social support were few, guilds often attempted to provide for the welfare of widows, orphans, and those members who could no longer work (see Document 10.4). They sponsored banquets and drinking parties, and they inevitably became the vehicle through which their members exerted political influence in the community. For the town-dwelling artisan family, the guild was the center of social, political, and economic life.

Effects of the Commercial Revolution. The commercial revolution of the Middle Ages marked a turning point in the history of the West. The years of relative isolation were over. By the midthirteenth century, an economy that spanned the known world touched even the most remote European villages. Trading connections gave Europeans access to the gold and ivory of Africa, the furs and amber of Russia, and the spices of the Far East. Even China, at the end of the long Silk Road across central Asia, was within reach, and a few Europeans, among whom the Venetian Marco Polo (1254–1324) is the most famous, traveled there. Few rural communities had in any sense become dependent on long-distance trade, but their horizons had been broadened immeasurably. Those communities located at the hub of trade routes had begun to transform themselves into great cities.

THE GROWTH OF TOWNS (1000–1450)

The commercial revolution brought a revival of the urban life that had been largely dormant since the fall of Rome. Trade inevitably centered on the towns. As trade increased, towns grew into cities and some of those cities became sovereign states. Many of the more important medieval towns, including Paris, London, Florence, Milan,

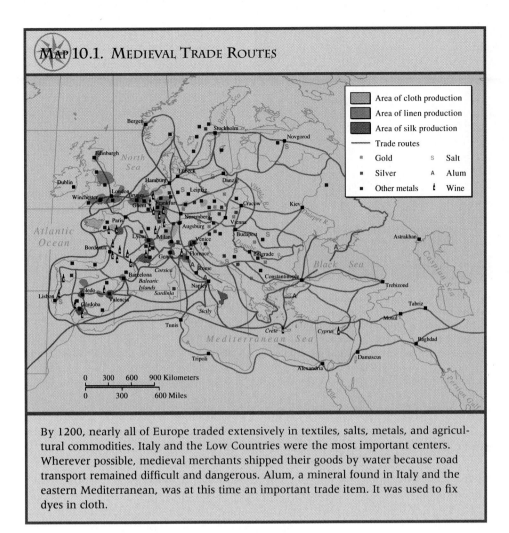

MAP 10.1. MEDIEVAL TRADE ROUTES

Area of cloth production
Area of linen production
Area of silk production
Trade routes
Gold   S Salt
Silver A Alum
Other metals   Wine

By 1200, nearly all of Europe traded extensively in textiles, salts, metals, and agricultural commodities. Italy and the Low Countries were the most important centers. Wherever possible, medieval merchants shipped their goods by water because road transport remained difficult and dangerous. Alum, a mineral found in Italy and the eastern Mediterranean, was at this time an important trade item. It was used to fix dyes in cloth.

cated with an eye to commercial development.

Immigration and Mortality. Whatever their origins, towns soon became a magnet for the unemployed, the ambitious, and the malcontent. The rapid increase in population after the tenth century coupled with more efficient agricultural methods tended to displace villagers whose labor was redundant and for whom no new land was available. These workers were "freed from the soil," an economist's euphemism for becoming unemployed, and moved to the towns in the hope of finding work as laborers. Some succeeded. If they survived, their descendants eventually became citizens and, in a few cases, grew rich. The Medici (Meh'-di-chee), arguably the greatest of Renaissance families, were descended from humble immigrants who came from a remote rural district known as the Mugello to work as laborers in the wool shops of Florence during the thirteenth century.

Most immigrants, however, simply died. The rapid growth of medieval and early modern towns was almost purely a function of inward migration, for urban death rates greatly exceeded live births until the eighteenth century. Yet for some cities, including Venice, Florence, and Milan, populations reached 100,000 or more by the midthirteenth century, and several others topped 50,000.

The Rise of the Communes. Rapid increases in population and commercial activity mandated sweeping changes in town government. The old system of rule by a bishop or secular lord assisted only by a handful of administrators was no longer effective. Town life was not just becoming more complex. An increasingly wealthy and educated class of merchants, rentiers, and artisans was growing more assertive and less willing to have its affairs controlled by traditional authorities whose knowledge of commerce was deficient and whose interests were not always those of the business community. From an early date, these people began or-

and Naples, had existed in Roman times, but others were relatively new or had grown from humble beginnings. Venice was founded by refugees fleeing from the Lombard invasion. Other communities grew up around the castles of bishops or secular lords. Still others grew up at river crossings or heads of navigation, or near natural harbors.

The pattern of urban growth in frontier areas was different. Dozens of Spanish towns in New Castile and Extremadura were built on lands captured from the Muslims during the twelfth and thirteenth centuries. Laid out geometrically around a central plaza, their builders modeled them on the Roman military *colonia,* or colony, whose function had been much the same. Along the Baltic coasts, in Silesia, and eastward into Poland and the Ukraine, German towns were founded throughout this period, often by princely fiat, to secure newly acquired regions or to protect existing borders. Because Germany remained politically decentralized and because territories changed hands frequently owing to the vagaries of partible inheritance, princely foundations of this kind were common there as well. Although most were intended to be garrisons, market towns, or princely residences, a few were lo-

Figure 10.5 *Medieval Italian Tower Houses.* This view of San Gimignano, Tuscany, shows a cluster of typical medieval tower houses designed to protect the inhabitants from their neighbors in times of civil unrest. Most towers were built in the eleventh or twelfth centuries. Clusters of such towers owned by relatives or friends sometimes formed tower associations, which served as a basis for local government. Ironically, the survival of these towers is a tribute to San Gimignano's relative isolation from the troubles of the thirteenth century, when towers in other cities were destroyed.

government. In regions such as Italy or north Germany, where conflicting ecclesiastical or feudal authorities created a power vacuum, many cities evolved into sovereign states.

The Emergence of City-States in Italy

In Italy, the movement toward independence was set in motion by the Investiture Controversy. Communes apparently arose as a response to military threats posed by the struggle between pope and emperor. Once established, both parties courted them in the hope of securing their material support. The townsmen were happy to oblige in return for privileges that escalated as the crisis became more dire, and something like a bidding war developed between political authorities who supported the pope and those who supported the emperor. By the time the investiture issue was settled by the Concordat of Worms (1122), most Italian cities had achieved full sovereignty as a result of charters granted by one side or the other. They now had the right to coin money, declare war, and govern their own affairs without limitations of any kind. They immediately used these powers to secure control over the surrounding countryside, or contado, and to pursue policies of aggression against neighboring towns. Control over the contado was essential to stabilizing inadequate food supplies. Towns offered neighboring landholders the opportunity to become citizens of the commune. If they refused, the city militia annexed their estates and drove them into exile, whereupon they typically complained to their liege lord, the emperor, who was obliged by feudal agreement to support them.

ganizing themselves into what became **communes,** or elected town governments.

The basis of the communes varied widely. The more substantial townspeople had long been members of occupational organizations such as the guilds or of neighborhood organizations that dealt with problems too minor to concern the bishop or lord. These neighborhood organizations might be based on the parish, the gate company (a volunteer organization created to maintain and defend one of the city's gates or a portion of its walls) or, as in Italy, the tower association, a group of citizens whose tower homes stood in close proximity to one another, usually around a single piazza, and whose members were usually related to one another by blood or clientage.

In times of crisis, such as an attack on the city, representatives of these groups would gather together to concert a common policy. As the meetings of these ad hoc committees became more frequent they gradually evolved into permanent councils, which increasingly challenged the political and judicial authority of their nominal lords. They succeeded in this primarily because the nascent communes represented wealth and manpower that the lords desperately needed. Negotiations between lords and communes were rarely high-minded. A lord or bishop would request money to meet a crisis, and the commune would grant it on condition that he surrender a coveted right (see Document 10.6). In time, even cities such as London that were located in powerful kingdoms achieved a substantial measure of self-

Bloodshed and disorder attended the entire process. The violent conflicts between cities were worse. In Italy, trade rivalries and disputes over the control of scarce agricultural land intensified an engrained localism. This tendency had been evident even in the throes of the investiture crisis. Because Florence supported the pope and had received its charter from his ally Matilda of Tuscany, neighboring towns such as Siena or Pisa supported the emperor and received their charters from Henry IV. Once free of political constraints, they pursued vendettas against their neighbors with enthusiasm. The resulting wars were unnecessarily bloody and accompanied by the wholesale destruction of vines, crops, and olive groves. Pressured by dispossessed vassals and

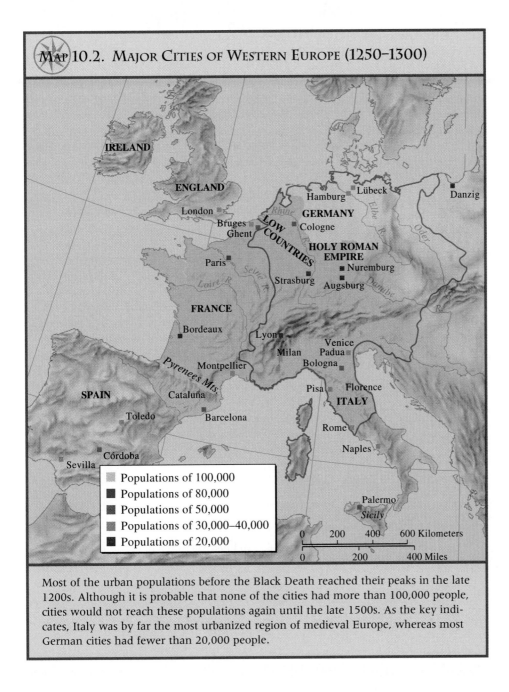

MAP 10.2. MAJOR CITIES OF WESTERN EUROPE (1250–1300)

IRELAND

ENGLAND

London

Bruges
Ghent

Paris

FRANCE

Bordeaux

Montpellier

Pyrenees Mts.

SPAIN

Cataluña

Toledo

Barcelona

Córdoba

Sevilla

Hamburg   Lübeck   Danzig

GERMANY
Cologne

LOW COUNTRIES

HOLY ROMAN EMPIRE

Nuremburg

Strasburg   Augsburg

Rhine   Elbe R.   Oder   Danube

Seine R.   Loire R.

Lyon

Milan   Venice
         Padua
         Bologna

Pisa   Florence

ITALY

Rome

Naples

Palermo
Sicily

Populations of 100,000
Populations of 80,000
Populations of 50,000
Populations of 30,000–40,000
Populations of 20,000

0   200   400   600 Kilometers

0   200   400 Miles

Most of the urban populations before the Black Death reached their peaks in the late 1200s. Although it is probable that none of the cities had more than 100,000 people, cities would not reach these populations again until the late 1500s. As the key indicates, Italy was by far the most urbanized region of medieval Europe, whereas most German cities had fewer than 20,000 people.

Frederick therefore installed an imperial *podestà*, or governor, at San Miniato, a town on the road between Florence and Pisa, and went on to be drowned on the Third Crusade. The place was known thereafter as San Miniato del Tedesco (San Miniato of the German), and the Tuscans leveled it when they regained their freedom in 1197 after the premature death of Barbarossa's son, Henry VII.

Clientage, Factionalism, and Urban Strife.

Internally, the Italian cities were beset from the start by factionalism. Clientage and kinship ties often proved stronger than allegiance to the commune, and by the beginning of the thirteenth century, civil strife was universal. Constitutional remedies such as elections by lot or the institution of the podestà, an administrative judge who was by law a foreigner, proved relatively ineffective. Emperor **Frederick II** (1194–1250) tried to use this situation to restore imperial authority in northern Italy, but the papacy proved as effective an obstacle to his designs as it had to those of his grandfather. Frederick, the son of Henry VI and Constance,

hoping to profit from Italian disunity, the **Emperor Frederick Barbarossa** (*Barbarossa* means "Red-beard" in Italian) decided to intervene.

The Lombard League. Pope Alexander III, who had no desire to strengthen imperial authority in Italy, responded by organizing the **Lombard League,** which defeated Frederick and his German knights at the battle of Legnano (Leh-nyan'-o) in 1176. At the peace of Constance in 1183, Frederick confirmed the sovereign rights of the Lombard towns. The Tuscans had refused to join the league out of hatred for their northern neighbors and were specifically excluded from the settlement.

daughter of Roger II of Sicily, inherited a powerful, well-organized kingdom in southern Italy that, together with his imperial election, made him a genuine threat both to the freedom of the Italian towns and to papal autonomy. When a political faction, hard-pressed by its rivals, sought his support, its enemies invariably turned to the pope. In this way two great "parties," the **Guelfs** (Gwelfs) and the **Ghibellines** (Gib'-e-lins), were born (see Document 10.6). In theory, Guelfs supported the pope and Ghibellines the emperor, but ideological and even class differences were minimal. The real issue was which faction among the richer citizens would control the city.

GUELFS AND GHIBELLINES IN FLORENCE

This passage is from an anonymous Florentine chronicler known as the pseudo-Brunetto Latini. It describes the incident that marked the beginning of the Guelf–Ghibelline conflict and, in the process, provides a fascinating glimpse of social behavior and values in the early thirteenth century.

In the year 1216 . . . Messer Mazzingo Tegrimi . . . had himself struck knight at a place called Campi, about six miles from Florence, and invited thither all the best people of the town. And when all the knights had sat down to meat, a buffoon snatched away the full plate set before Messer Uberto dell' Infangati, who was paired at table with Messer Buondelmonti de' Buondelmonti. That angered Messer Uberto greatly, and Messer Oddo Arrighi de' Fifanti, a man of valor, roughly reproved him on this account. In reply, Messer Uberto told him he lied in his throat, at which Messer Oddo Arrighi tossed a plate full into his face. And the whole assembly was in an uproar. When the tables had been removed, Messer Buondelmonti struck at Messer Oddo Arrighi with a knife and wounded him severely.

As soon as all the company had returned to their homes, Messer Oddo Arrighi took counsel with his friends and relatives . . . and their advice was that peace should be concluded over the issue and that Messer Buondelmonti should take for wife the daughter of Messer Lambertuccio de' Amidei who lived at the head of the bridge. The bride-to-be was the niece of Messer Oddo Arrighi. Accordingly the marriage contract was drawn up and the peace arranged and on the following day the wedding was to be celebrated. Thereupon Madonna Gualdrada, the wife of Messer Forese Donati, sent secretly for Messer Buondelmonte and when he came spoke to him as follows: "knight, you are forever disgraced by taking a wife out of fear of the Uberti and the Fifanti; leave her you

have taken and take this other [Madonna Gualdrada's daughter] and your honor as a knight will be restored." As soon as he had heard, he resolved to do as he was told without taking counsel with any of his kin. And when on the following day . . . the guests of both parties had assembled, Messer Buondelmonte went . . . to pledge troth with the girl of the Donati family; and her of the Amidei he left waiting at the church door.

This insult enraged Messer Oddo Arrighi greatly and he held a meeting with all his relatives . . . Some counseled that Buondelmonte be given a cudgeling, others that he be wounded in the face. At this spoke up Messer Mosca de' Lamberti: Whoever beats or wounds him let him first see to it that his own grave is dug; what this case requires is not half measures but clean work. Thereupon they decided that the vendetta was to be carried out . . . when the parties had gathered for the exchange of the marriage vows. And thus it came about that when on Easter morning Messer Buondelmonte [with his bride] . . . came riding over the bridge . . . Messer Sciata degli Uberti rushed upon him and striking him on the crown with his mace, brought him to earth. At once Messer Oddo Arrighi was on top of him and opened his veins with a knife. And having killed him they fled.

Immediately there was a tremendous tumult . . . On this day . . . for the first time new names were heard, to wit, Guelf and Ghibelline party.

From *Pseudo-Brunetto Latini*, in F. Schevill, *Medieval and Renaissance Florence*, vol I (Harper and Row, 1961, pp. 106–107). Copyright © James Schevill, 1961.)

Question: How did ties of kinship and clientage contribute to the situation described?

The Rise of the Despots. The Guelf–Ghibelline struggles led to the breakdown of civil government in many Italian cities. Fearful of their own citizens, governments began the practice of hiring *condottiere* (kone-dot-ti-air'-ay), or mercenaries, to defend them against their neighbors. In so doing, they created another mortal danger to their independence. Victorious captains proved capable of seizing the town when the danger had passed. By the end of the thirteenth century, an exhausted citizenry was prepared to accept almost any remedy, and nearly all of the towns fell under the rule of despots. In some cases, as in Milan, the despot was the leader of a faction that finally triumphed over its rivals. In others, desperate citizens sought or accepted the rule of a prominent local family, a mercenary captain, or a popular *podestà*. They abandoned their cherished republican constitutions in return for the right to pursue business and personal in-

terests in relative peace. It was not always a good bargain. Whatever their titles, despots were absolute rulers whose survival demanded a certain ruthlessness. Some were competent and relatively benign. A few were bloodthirsty psychopaths. But none was prepared to encourage the rich culture of civic participation that would one day produce the Renaissance.

The Florentine Republic. That task was left to Florence and Venice, two cities that escaped the soft trap of despotism. In Florence, the Guelf triumph of 1266 paved the way for a guild-based democracy that survived, in theory at least, until the end of the fifteenth century. Social and economic tensions were expressed in the long struggle over whether the major guilds, which were dominated by the great bankers, should control the electoral process and therefore the *signoria* (si-nyor'-ee-a), or city council. The issue was revolved in favor of the major guilds in 1382, but in 1434, a clientage group headed by the banker-statesman **Cosimo de' Medici** gained control of the machinery of government. Although they outwardly maintained republican institutions, the Medicis and their friends manipulated the constitution for their own purposes until 1494.

The Venetian Republic. Venice, settled only in 568 and located among the desolate islands at the head of the Adriatic, had never been part of the Holy Roman Empire. Its development was therefore unlike that of any other Italian town. Several small refugee settlements coalesced during the ninth century into a single city ruled by an elective *doge* (dozh), or duke. Isolated from the imperial struggles on the mainland and interested primarily in the development of trade and an overseas empire, the Venetians evolved a system of government that has been called both a model republic and a class despotism.

Like other cities, Venice was troubled by clientage groups headed by prominent merchant families. To prevent any one family from gaining control of the state, the Venetians eliminated the monarchical powers of the doge between 1140 and 1160 and vested legislative power in an elected Great Council with forty-five members. A Minor Council was established to assist the doge in his new role as administrator. The system achieved its final form between 1290 and 1310, when a series of mishaps and scandals raised the specter of social revolution. A reform movement headed by the great merchant families expanded the Great Council and then closed its membership to anyone who did not have an ancestor sitting on it in 1297. A genealogical registry established pedigrees, and the membership hovered thereafter between 1,200 and 1,400 certifiable members of the Venetian aristocracy. The Great Council elected the doge, whose role became largely ceremonial; his counselors; and the Senate, a 160-man body that controlled the state. The Great Council was thus both the electorate and the pool from which officeholders were drawn. Only a revolution could alter this closed system, and the chances of a revolution succeeding were greatly diminished by the Council of Ten. This was a committee on state security, elected by the Great Council for one-year, nonrenewable terms, and granted almost unlimited power to deal with threats to the Venetian state at home or abroad. The constitution remained in effect until 1798.

Civic Life and Cultural Vitality. Broad-based participation in public affairs, at least among the upper classes, is thought to have produced a civic culture of unusual vitality in both Florence and Venice. Although the government of the Medici has been called a family despotism, Cosimo made every effort to draw everyone

of importance into his web of clientage. In Venice, a fairly numerous aristocracy had no alternative to participation in civic life, whereas in true despotism, participation was restricted to the ruler and his immediate entourage. This level of civic activity contributed to the cultural and intellectual movement known as the Renaissance, but from the standpoint of social history, the Renaissance as a historical period has little meaning. The underlying realities of daily life in the Italian towns changed little between 1200 and 1500, and most generalizations that can be made about urban society, whether in Italy or elsewhere, are good for the Middle Ages as well as much of the early modern period.

The Cities of Northern Europe

Beyond the Alps only a relative handful of cities achieved anything like full sovereignty. Most were in Germany. In the period of imperial disintegration that followed the death of Frederick II, free cities and those that owed their allegiance to the emperor were generally able to expand their privileges. The larger, richer communities, such as Nürnberg (Nuern'-berg) or Lübeck, became virtual city-states, although they retained their nominal allegiance to the empire. Others were less secure, as emperors had been known to pledge them to neighboring princes in return for support or in the settlement of disputes.

The German Leagues. Although almost all German towns, including those that had been founded by princes, enjoyed a wide measure of freedom guaran-

FIGURE 10.6 *Trading Ships on the Baltic Coast at Lübeck.* Lübeck was the most important city of the Hanseatic League and was a center of the rich trade in furs, amber, grain, and forest products from Russia, Poland, and Lithuania. This undated German woodcut (the design of the ships indicates that is probably from the fourteenth or fifteenth century) shows ships moored in the city's harbor. Note the iron mooring rings fixed to the rocks. Early German woodcut (anonymous).

THE LIBERTIES OF TOULOUSE, 1147

The following is a typical, if somewhat abbreviated, example of the liberties granted by princes and noblemen to towns in the High Middle Ages.

Let it be known to all men living and to be born that I, Alphonse, Count of Toulouse, proclaim, recognize, and grant that in no way do I have tallage or tolls in the city of Toulouse, nor in the suburb of St. Sernin, nor against the men and women living there or who will live there, nor shall I have in the city the right to summon the militia to campaign unless war be waged against me in Toulouse, nor shall I make any loan there unless it should be the lender's wish. Wherefore I confirm and commend to all citizens of Toulouse and its suburb, present and future, all their good customs and privileges, those they now enjoy and which I may give and allow to them. All this, as it is written above, Raymond of St. Gilles, son of the said count, approves and grants.

From Mundy, John H., and Riesenberg, Peter, eds., *The Medieval Town* (Princeton: Van Nostrand, 1958).

Question: In addition to confirming the town's existing privileges, what specific new exemptions does the Count offer in this document?

teed by charter, the threat of noble encroachment and the uncertainties of imperial politics favored the formation of leagues. The various Hansas of north Germany had political and economic purposes. The Rhenish League (1254) and the Swabian League (1376) provide further examples, and the Swiss Confederation, founded in 1291, evolved with relatively minor changes into the Switzerland of today. The original nucleus of three small forest cantons—Uri (Oo'-ree), Schwyz (Shveets), and Unterwalden—was joined by larger communities when it demonstrated its ability to defend itself against the Hapsburgs at Morgarten (1315). The process of confederation culminated only with the admission of Basel in 1501 and Geneva in 1536. Each canton governed itself as an independent unit and sent representatives to the Swiss Diet when presenting a united front became necessary. Although in many ways typical of late medieval leagues, the Swiss survived through sheer military prowess and the democratic character of their cantonal governments, which tended to limit social strife.

Towns and the Monarchies of Western Europe. In areas that possessed a strong monarchy, urban development took a somewhat different form. In Spain, France, and England, the king retained a large measure of control over the towns. Royal officials or bailiffs col-

lected taxes, interfered in elections, and served as personal representatives of the king. London, however, achieved substantial autonomy in the chaotic reigns of Richard I and John. Urban privileges, when they were granted, were usually the fruit of royal weakness. In the Low Countries, cities enjoyed more independence than their French or English counterparts because the counts of Flanders and Holland and the dukes of Brabant could rarely bring them to full obedience. The consolidation of a powerful Burgundian state in the fifteenth century curtailed some of their freedoms, but they still retained more independence than royal towns whose government was influenced at every stage by the presence of a royal bailiff.

But even in France or England, the towns enjoyed a freedom unknown in the countryside. In matters of taxation, public works, social policy, sanitation, and regulation of trades, the elected town councils were remarkably autonomous. Kings normally honored the decisions of city courts except when they came into conflict with royal justice. In France, the towns were represented both in the provincial estates and the Estates-General, advisory bodies that had the right to approve or reject new taxes. City officials collected royal taxes, negotiated with the crown over the specific amounts, and then made the assessments themselves. Citizens, in other words, had the opportunity to participate in their own governance and were exempt from feudal dues and obligations. Although royal authority might be strong, the German saying held true: *Stadtluft macht frei* (city air makes one free). Personal freedom and the demands of civic responsibility made medieval cities, although they held less than 10 percent of Europe's population, its primary agents of cultural and intellectual change.

Town Life in the Middle Ages

The freedom of a medieval town was a matter of personal and legal status; the life lived within it was by most modern standards highly regulated and even claustrophobic. The town walls defined a world of perpetual shade—a constricted maze of narrow, winding streets broken only occasionally by the open spaces of a churchyard or market. Because space within the walls was scarce and expensive, houses tended to be narrow, deep, and high, with upper stories that often overhung the street below until they nearly touched their neighbors. Light and ventilation were usually poor and privacy nonexistent. Much of the intensity of town life came from everyone knowing everyone else's business.

Health and Sanitation. Crowding, together with the virtual absence of sanitary facilities, accounted for the extreme susceptibility of urban populations to epidemic disease. Town councils issued regulations against dumping human waste into the streets, but piling it in

FIGURE 10.7 *A Street Scene in Fourteenth-Century Siena.* This detail from *The Effects of Good Government*, a fresco done between 1337 and 1340 by Ambrogio Lorenzetti (d. 1348), is a vivid portrayal of medieval Siena, an important city in Italy that retains much of its medieval appearance even today. The image shows the crowded narrow streets, towers, and overhanging second stories. In the foreground, men, women, and pack animals transport produce while one man drives his flock of sheep to market.

courtyards, sometimes in close proximity to wells, was common. Travelers could smell a town long before it came into view. Officials made valiant, if usually futile, efforts to keep the streets clean and to ensure the purity of the water supply. In the absence of a germ theory, this usually meant prohibitions on washing wool in the public fountains or orders restricting tanneries to locations downstream, if not necessarily downwind. Death rates predictably exceeded birth rates in almost every European city.

Regulation of Business. Both public health and civic peace depended on the regulation of business practices. Virtually every occupation had to be licensed. City governments set business hours and ensured the accuracy of weights and measures. They also tried to enforce standards of quality for the cloth industry and the victualing trades. City inspectors checked the age and condition of meat or fish, the often-dubious contents of sausages, and the conditions under which perishables of all kinds were prepared and sold. They regularly examined sacks of grain or flour to determine whether sand or other substances had been added to increase its weight. A constant problem involved market women who tried to sell products in competition with the official guild monopolies and who reacted violently if interrupted. Surviving city ordinances and court records provide a rich catalog of ingenious frauds and entrepreneurial excess. As in modern cities, every aspect of the operation of taverns, inns, wine shops, and bathhouses was minutely regulated to prevent them from becoming criminal hangouts.

The Threat of Fire. After disease, the other great curse of medieval towns was fire. Even small market towns organized volunteer fire companies and proposed regulations to prevent the most hazardous practices, but the combination of wood or wood-frame construction and gross overcrowding could still turn ordinary kitchen mishaps into holocausts that threatened the entire community.

Citizenship and the Fear of Strangers. The city's walls not only defined the space in which townspeople lived but also symbolized their attitude toward the outside world. For all their far-flung interests, medieval towns were intensely parochial. Carnival plays and masks are a useful key to a people's deepest fears. In cities such as late medieval Nürnberg, the citizens' nightmares seem to have revolved around nobles, Jews, peasants, and Turks. The fear of Jews and Turks was the fear of infidels, and the nobles were everywhere a threat to the freedoms of the town. Townspeople saw peasants as deceitful, sexually promiscuous, and violent. In even the largest cities, the countryside was never more than a few minutes' walk away, and the urban economy could not have existed without its rural suppliers. However, mutual distrust was universal. Watchmen locked the city's gates every evening, and all visitors had to secure permission to enter even in broad daylight. Jews and foreigners were commonly forced to live in **ghettos,** often for their own protection. The word *ghetto* is of Venetian origin and refers to the section of the city reserved for Jews, but London had its Steelyard, where the Hansa merchants locked themselves up at night, and a Lombard Street, where Italian merchants lived and operated their businesses. City-dwellers of the Middle Ages perceived the outside world as threatening; only a fellow-citizen could be fully trusted.

Citizenship was a coveted honor and often difficult to achieve. With the exception of certain Swiss towns where the franchise was unusually broad, only a minority of the male residents in most cities enjoyed the right to participate in public affairs. For the most part that right was hereditary. Citizenship could be earned by those who performed extraordinary services for the commune or who had achieved substantial wealth in a respectable trade. Town councils tended to be stingy in granting citizenship, which carried with it status and responsibility. They relied on citizens to vote, hold office, perform public service without pay, and contribute to special assessments in time of need. Full participation in the life of the commune could be expensive and required a certain stability and firmness of character.

The Urban Upper Class. The distinction between a citizen and a noncitizen was the primary social division in the medieval town, but there were others. In most cities, economic and political power rested in the hands of the richest citizens: bankers, long-distance traders, or their descendants who lived off of rents and investments. Their wealth and leisure enabled them to dominate political life. Inevitably, they guarded their prerogatives and resisted the claims of other social groups. Serving the patricians, and sometimes related to them by blood, was a professional class composed of lawyers, notaries, and the higher ranks of the local clergy.

The men of this class frequently enjoyed close relations with princes and nobles and served as representatives of their cities to the outside world. In the later Middle Ages, their contribution to the world of literature and scholarship would be disproportionate to their numbers. The women of the urban patriciate, however, were probably more isolated from society and more economically dependent than the women of any other social class. As wives, their economic role was negligible. Even housework and the care of children were usually entrusted to servants. As widows, however, they could inherit property, enter into contracts, and in some cities, sue on their own behalf in court. These rights allowed patrician widows to become investors, although, unlike the women of the artisan class, their direct involvement in management was rare.

The Artisan Class. Compared with the patricians and rentiers, artisans were a large and varied group, in which not all were created equal. The social gap between a goldsmith and a tanner was vast, but their lives bore certain similarities. Artisans were skilled workers who processed or manufactured goods and who belonged to the guild appropriate to their trade. Patricians were rarely guild members except in such towns as Florence, where guild membership was a prerequisite for public office. The masters of a given trade owned their own workshops, which doubled as retail salesrooms and typically occupied the ground floor of their homes. They sometimes worked alone but more often employed journeymen to assist them. These skilled workers had served their apprenticeships but did not own their own shops and usually lived in rented quarters elsewhere. Because the master had demonstrated his competence with a masterpiece that had been accepted by the other masters of his guild, he was also expected to train apprentices. These young men, often the sons of other guild members, learned the trade by working in the master's shop and living in his household. Apprenticeships typically began around the age of 12 and continued for 7 years in northern Europe and 3 or 4 years in Italy.

Women and Work. Artisan households were often large, complex units. The master's wife usually managed the family's business. While her husband concentrated on production and training the apprentices, she dealt with marketing, purchasing, and finance. If the artisan died, she often continued the enterprise, using hired journeymen in his place or doing the work herself, for many women had learned their father's trade as children. Some cities admitted widows to guilds, although not without restrictions.

Women's work was therefore crucial to the medieval town economy. According to the *Livre des Métiers* (Book of Trades), written by Etienne Boileau in the thirteenth century, women were active in 86 of the 100 occupations listed for contemporary Paris. Six *métiers,* or trades, all of which would today be called part of the fashion industry, were exclusively female (see Document 10.7). In addition, women everywhere played an important part in the victualing trades (brewing, butchering, selling fish, and so on) and in the manufacture of small

WOMEN IN THE PARIS SILK INDUSTRY

Silk spinning in thirteenth-century Paris was a woman's trade. The women owned their own spindles and could take apprentices. Paris, however, lacked the freedom of the Italian and German towns. Like other métiers, or trades, in this era, the spinsters had no true guild organization. Craft ordinances were proclaimed and enforced in the king's name by the provost of Paris, and the spun silk was purchased by merchants operating on the "putting-out" system. They took raw silk to the spinster's home and collected it when it was spun. Those ordinances listed below were compiled between 1254 and 1271 and offer a glimpse of the conditions under which medieval tradeswomen worked.

Any woman who wishes to be a silk spinster on large spindles in the city of Paris—i.e. reeling, spinning, doubling, and retwisting— may freely do so, provided she observe the following usages and customs of the craft:

No spinster on large spindles may have more than three apprentices, unless they be her own or her husband's children born in true wedlock; nor may she contract with them for an apprenticeship of less than seven years or for a fee of less than 20 Parisian sols to be paid to her, their mistress. The apprenticeship shall be for eight years if there is no fee, but she may accept more years and money if she can get them. . . .

No woman of the said craft may hire an apprentice or workgirl who has not completed her years of service with the mistress to whom she was apprenticed. If a spinster has assumed an apprentice, she may not take on another before the first has completed her seven years unless the apprentice die or foreswear the craft forever. If an apprentice spinster buy her freedom before serving the said seven years, she may not herself take an apprentice until she has practiced the craft seven years. . . .

If a working woman comes from outside Paris and wishes to practice the said craft in the city, she must swear before two guardians of the craft that she will practice it well and loyally and conform to its customs and usages.

If anyone give a woman of the said craft silk to be spun and the woman pawn it, and the owner complains, the fine shall be 5 sols.

No workwoman shall farm out another's silk to be worked upon outside her own house.

The said craft has as guardians two men of integrity sworn in the king's name but appointed and charged at the will of the provost of Paris. Taking an oath in the provost's presence, they shall swear to guard the craft truly, loyally, and to their utmost, and to inform him or his agents of all malpractices discovered therein.

From Boileau, Etienne, "Livres de Métiers," in Julia O'Faolain and Lauro Martines, *Not in God's Image: Women in History from the Greeks to the Victorians* (New York: HarperCollins, 1973).

Question: In what ways do these regulations protect the merchants rather than the spinsters themselves?

---

metal objects, including needles, pins, buckles, knives, and jewelry.

Women also played an important role as street peddlers. Operating from makeshift booths or simply spreading their goods on the ground, the market women sold everything from trinkets to used clothing, household implements, and food. After the expulsion of the Jews, many women became pawnbrokers. Their central role in retail distribution, aggressive sales techniques, and propensity to engage (like their male counterparts) in monopolies and restrictive trading practices brought them into frequent conflict with the guilds and with the authorities who tried, often in vain, to regulate their activities.

Many market women were the wives or daughters of journeymen; most probably came from a lower echelon of urban society—the semiskilled or unskilled laborers who served as porters, construction helpers, wool carders, or any one of a hundred menial occupations. Such people were rarely guild members or citizens, and their existence was often precarious.

Employment tended to be sporadic. A laborer's wage was sometimes capable of supporting a bachelor but rarely a family, and everyone had to work to survive. In cloth towns, women often worked in the wool shops along with the men. For the aggressive and quick-witted, the street market was a viable alternative. Domestic service was another and provided employment for a substantial number of both men and women.

Poverty and Crime. These respectable, if disenfranchised, workers formed a probable majority in every city, but there was also a sizeable underclass of beggars, prostitutes, criminals, and people who for one reason or another depended on charity for their survival. In theory, the poor were the responsibility of the church or of pious individuals who contributed to their welfare. In practice, town governments tended to see poverty, like criminality, as a question of social control. Begging in many places was licensed, as was prostitution. The latter could be an important source of revenue, and most towns, such as Nürnberg, preferred to localize the trade

FIGURE 10.8 *Women in the Silk Industry.* This engraving from *Vermis Sericus* (the Silkworm) by Philip Galle (1537–1612) shows women engaged in the manufacture of silk. After the eggs have hatched into worms, the women cover them with mulberry leaves and put them on branches, where they weave their cocoons. The silk from the cocoons is then woven into cloth.

in official brothels whose profits could be taxed. In the later Middle Ages, some communities began to follow the lead of Venice in establishing hospitals, orphanages, and regular distributions of food to the needy. Even when governments established such institutions with their own funds, they normally relied on members of the religious orders for staffing and management.

Crime was more difficult to control. The intimacy of town life encouraged theft, and the labyrinth of streets and alleys provided robbers with multiple escape routes. No police force existed. Most towns had watchmen for night patrols and a militia that could intervene in riots and other disturbances, but competent thieves were rarely caught and interpersonal violence, which was fairly common, aroused little concern. If an encounter stopped short of murder or serious disfigurement, the authorities usually looked the other way. They were far more concerned with maintaining the social and economic order and with public health. Politically, even this was by no means easy.

Social Strife. The close proximity between rich and poor and the exclusivity of most town governments made social tension inevitable. Laborers, the urban poor, and even some of the journeymen lived in grinding poverty. Entire families often occupied a single, unheated room and subsisted on inadequate diets while the urban rich lived with an ostentation that even the feudal aristocracy could rarely equal. The contrast was a fertile source of discontent. Although riots and revolts were usually led not by the poor but by prosperous malcontents who had been excluded from leadership in

the commune, such people found it easy to play on the bitter resentments of those who had nothing to lose but their lives.

Civil disturbances would reach a peak in the years after the Black Death, but urban patriciates had long been fearful of popular revolts. Disgruntled weavers and other cloth workers in the towns of thirteenth-century Flanders launched revolts based openly on class warfare. Everywhere the apprentices, who shared the violent impulses of most adolescent males, reinforced the social and economic demands of the artisans. Riots were common even though city governments suppressed them with extreme brutality.

In southern Europe, social tensions were muted, although not eliminated, by clientage. The factions that dominated city politics had tentacles that reached down to the artisan and the laboring classes. Mutual obligation, although unequal in its benefits, tended to moderate class feeling and reduce the social isolation of the patriciate, which, in Flemish and German towns, was far more extreme. Despite this, Venice faced the specter of revolution in the late thirteenth century, and a struggle between the so-called major and minor guilds dominated the political life of fourteenth-century Florence and revealed deep social divisions. In France, England, and Castile, where a strong monarchy backed the city governments, discontent proved easier to control.

The Role of Towns in Medieval Civilization. Medieval towns, themselves the products of trade, connected the agrarian hinterland in which most Europeans lived and the great world outside. They also served as the cultural and intellectual catalysts for society as a whole. The requirements of business and of participation in government demanded literacy of the urban upper class. The intensity of urban life encouraged vigorous debate. Some measure of intellectual life therefore flourished within the city walls. At the same time, the tendency of surplus wealth to concentrate in cities permitted an investment in culture that was far beyond the capacity of even the greatest agricultural estates. Civic pride inspired much of that investment. If they could find the money, city councils supported the building and decoration of churches or other public buildings and paid out substantial sums for festivals and celebrations whose chief purpose was to demonstrate the superiority of their town over its neighbors. The absurd competition over the height of church towers may have been unproductive and at times hazardous, but it symbolized a spirit that produced much of medieval art and architecture.

Even the strife endemic to medieval towns had its positive side. Resistance to social injustice reflected the vitality of ancient ideals. Ordinary people continued to believe that the town was, or should be, a refuge for those seeking personal freedom and economic opportunity. They demonstrated by their actions that the Greco-Roman ideal of civic participation was far from dead. Medieval cities may often have been deficient and even brutal in their social arrangements, but they preserved important values that had no place in the feudal countryside. As the institutional matrix for creating, preserving, and disseminating the Western cultural tradition, the town had, by the thirteenth century, replaced the monastery.

CONCLUSION

When the great raids ended, agricultural production began to increase. The gradual return of settled conditions, an apparent improvement in the European climate, and a series of innovations in farming technology increased productivity and encouraged population growth. It also permitted large-scale agricultural specialization, which in turn led to the development of a trade in bulk agricultural commodities. Greater prosperity and the impact of the Crusades enabled merchants to expand their markets. In the Mediterranean and the Baltic, the long-distance trade in low-volume, high-value goods accumulated wealth that could be invested in banking and manufacturing. The result was a true commercial revolution. Commerce in turn revived old towns and created new ones. From about 1000 to 1250, the cities of Europe experienced rapid growth—in size, wealth, and power. As popes and princes grew more dependent on their resources, the towns used their wealth to free themselves from feudal or ecclesiastical rule and to negotiate new privileges that made them bastions of civic freedom in the midst of feudal Europe. Some became sovereign states. Rich, free, and self-confident, the towns of medieval Europe began the great tradition of urban culture that would eventually leaven the whole of Western society.

Review Questions

- What was the basis of medieval technology in terms of materials and sources of power?
- What new technologies contributed to the improvement in agricultural production?
- How did the first long-distance trades develop, and how did they contribute to the growth of banking and manufacturing?
- Why did the cities in Italy and Germany achieve greater independence than those in France, Spain, and England?

For Further Study

Readings

Duby, Georges, *The Early Growth of the European Economy: Warriors and Peasants from the 7th to the 12th Centuries.* trans, H. B. Clarke (Ithaca: Cornell, 1978).

Ennen, Edith, *The Medieval Town.* trans. N. Fryde (Amsterdam: North Holland Publishing, 1978). A good introduction to the subject.

Lopez, Robert S., *The Commercial Revolution of the Middle Ages: 950–1350* (Englewood Cliffs, NJ: Prentice Hall, 1971). A classic.

Tabacco, Giovanni, *The Struggle for Power in Medieval Italy.* trans. R. B. Jensen (New York: Cambridge University Press, 1989). Looks at medieval Italian politics with special reference to the cities.

White, Lynn, *Medieval Technology and Social Change* (Oxford: Clarendon Press, 1962). The pioneering work on medieval technology.

Web Site

http://www.fordham.edu/halsall/sbook.html
Internet Medieval Sourcebook. The section on Economic Life contains an enormous range of documents dealing with agriculture, trade, banking, manufacturing, and the towns.

Visit the Western Civilization Companion Web Site for resources specific to this textbook:
http://history.wadsworth.com/hause02/

The CD in the back of this book and the Western Civilization Resource Center at *http://history.wadsworth.com/western/* offer a variety of tools to help you succeed in this course, including access to quizzes; images; documents; interactive simulations, maps, and timelines; movie explorations; and a wealth of other sources.

ECONOMIC DEVELOPMENT AND URBAN GROWTH

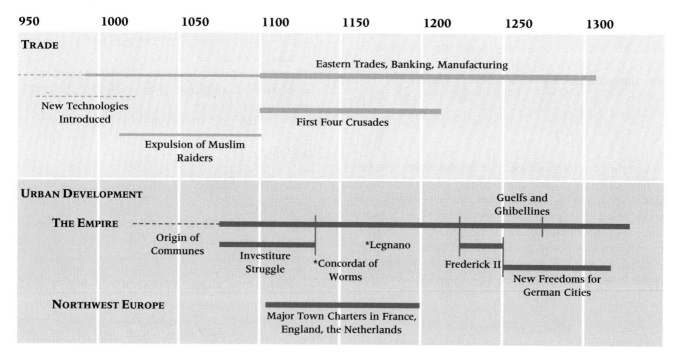

Chapter 11

MATERIAL AND SOCIAL LIFE IN THE MIDDLE AGES

FOCUS QUESTIONS

- How did medieval diets differ from those in the industrialized countries of today?
- In terms of birthrates, mortality, and age distribution, how did medieval populations differ from those of today?
- What role did the chivalric idea play in the life of medieval nobles?
- How were medieval villages organized in terms of work, wealth, power, and social control?

round 1300, a Milanese moralist named Galvano Flamma complained about the increase of luxury in his own time and contrasted it unfavorably with a simpler past. "Life and customs were hard in Lombardy at the time of Frederick II (d. 1250)," he said. "[Men's] clothes were cloaks of leather without any adornments, or clothes of wool with no lining. With a few pennies, people felt rich. There were no fireplaces. Expenses were kept to a minimum because in the summer people drank little wine and wine cellars were not kept. At the table knives were not used; husband and wife ate off the same plate, and there was one cup or two for the whole family. One ate cooked turnips, and ate meat only three times a week." The life described in this paraphrase of a longer document was not that of the poor, but of rich peasants and the urban middle class. The poor had less meat and often no plate on which to eat it. By modern standards, medieval life lacked comforts, but it was by no means simple. Daily life required skills that have long since been lost. Social relationships were almost certainly more complicated than those of our own time.

Chapter 11 describes how people lived in the Middle Ages. It begins with a discussion of diet, disease, and the demographic consequences of living in a world where malnutrition was common and the germ theory unknown. Then, because the life of the feudal nobility bore almost no similarity to that of ordinary people, it examines the world of the castle, the tournament, and chivalric values before turning to the humble villagers who supported everything. After analyzing the social and material basis of village life, it concludes with a discussion of medieval attitudes toward childhood, old age, and death.

245

THE MEDIEVAL DIET

The material life of medieval Europe resembled that of antiquity in several important respects and remained substantially the same until the Industrial Revolution. The biological regime established by the Neolithic revolution had not changed. Most people continued to subsist largely on grains. They preferred wheat, but millet, spelt, barley, oats, and rye were also staples, especially among the poor. Ground into flour and then baked as bread or served in the form of gruels and porridges, grains were literally "the staff of life" and provided most of the calories in the average person's diet.

Bread. Bread was commonly baked outside the home because medieval ovens were large brick affairs that consumed great quantities of fuel. It required several hours to heat them to the proper temperature, and economies of scale demanded that many loaves be baked at the same time. Only the households of the very rich, with their dozens of servants and retainers, needed ovens of their own—or could afford to dispense with the services of the village baker. Many different kinds of bread existed, ranging from the fine white loaves and cakes prized by the nobles and high-ranking clergy to coarse breads made of rye or of oats and mixed grains. Bakers graded bread according to the grains used and the proportion of bran left in the flour. (Bran is the broken husks of the grains and has to be sifted out of the flour after it is milled.) This created a strange paradox: the lower grades of bread consumed by the poor often had more nutritional value than the bread of the rich, which was made with bleached, highly refined, wheaten flour. Another oddity of the baker's trade was that, in many countries, law or custom fixed the price of a loaf of bread but not its size. A "ha'penny loaf" in England always cost ½d. (d. was the English abbreviation for *pence*, the plural of *penny*), but its weight varied radically according to the price of grain. Local preference determined the shape and appearance of loaves, which differed widely from region to region. Whatever its form or content, baked bread was often too expensive for the very poor, especially on a regular basis. Unbaked bread, or gruel, could be cooked at home, and all classes ate it for its economy and ease of preparation.

Baked or unbaked, bread accounted for at least 50 percent of a rich family's diet and for more than 80 percent of the calories consumed by poor people. The price and availability of grain therefore provides a valid measure of living standards because there were few substitutes for it and a bad harvest brought widespread misery. Rice was expensive and little known outside parts of Spain and the Middle East until the fifteenth century. It seems to have been consumed largely by wealthy invalids. In some upland areas, peasants ground chestnuts and baked them into a coarse, yet nutritious,

FIGURE **11.1** *Baking Bread.* Only the largest and wealthiest private homes could afford a large brick or stone oven. Most people went to professional bakers like this one, who is shown putting bread in his oven with a wooden paddle. This illumination is from a French book of hours produced in the 1400s.

bread. In most areas, the best insurance against hunger was to grow several kinds of grain at different seasons.

Proteins. A diet of bread was monotonous and lacked virtually every nutritional element except carbohydrates. Whenever possible, people tried to supplement it with other foods, but their choices were limited. Protein came largely from dried peas, beans, lentils, or chickpeas cooked in a variety of soups and stews. Meat was rare except on the tables of the feudal aristocracy. Their chief leisure pastime was hunting, and they tended to consume vast quantities of game, which, after the twelfth century, was seasoned with powerful spices from the East and washed down with great drafts of wine or beer. Many peasants could not afford to keep animals at all, although some raised ducks and chickens for their eggs and then stewed them or made them into soup when they had passed their prime. Those with capital or excess land might have some hogs or a cow. Even for them, meat was likely a seasonal delicacy. The cost of feeding livestock over the winter was high, and even the wealthier peasants slaughtered their animals in the fall, eating some meat and preserving the rest by smoking or salting it. By Lent (the 6 weeks of fasting before Easter), these preserved meats had been consumed, which probably meant that the church's prohibition against eating flesh in the holy season caused little additional hardship.

Hunting and fishing provided other dietary supplements, even though in many areas, both fish and game belonged to the lord and ferocious penalties discouraged poaching. Even the gathering of nuts in the forest might be prohibited. Milk and cheese offered an additional source of protein to those who could afford them, and salted herring became increasingly important as an item of commerce in the thirteenth century. Owing to the widespread use of salt as a preservative and to the general monotony of diets, scholars believe that medieval people consumed many times the quantity of salt that Westerners eat today.

Fruits and Vegetables. Fresh fruits and vegetables were both rare and seasonal. Those who possessed a kitchen garden might have a fruit tree or a cabbage patch, but many of today's most common vegetables were either unknown or, like lettuce, raised for medicinal purposes. Onions and garlic, however, were common, as were indigenous spices such as thyme, rosemary, basil, and marjoram. Honey provided sweetening. Sugar, an import from the east, remained prohibitively expensive until the seventeenth century, when it could be imported in quantity from the New World.

Drinks. A variety of fermented beverages completed the medieval diet. Wine grapes did not normally grow north of the forty-ninth parallel (roughly the latitude of Paris), but wine was the preferred beverage of the rich everywhere. In southern Europe, even peasants drank it occasionally. North of the wine districts, the popularity of mead, a drink made from fermented honey, declined during the Middle Ages, whereas that of cider appears to have increased. Beer, or "liquid bread," provided an important food supplement throughout all of central and northern Europe. Properly speaking, medieval beer was a form of ale. They brewed it from malted grain, yeast, and water using the top fermentation process in which the yeast rises to the top of the brewing vat after fermentation and produces a thick foam. Hops were sometimes used on the continent to provide a hint of bitterness, but never in the British Isles. Without hops, the result was a dark, rather heavy beverage that resembled the stouts and Scotch ales of today. In the fifteenth century, the Germans invented bottom fermentation to produce lager or pilsner beers. Until then, brewing normally took place in the home and, like other aspects of the beverage trade, was controlled by women. A skilled woman otherwise housebound by small children could manage the process and provide an important economic sideline for a family who could afford the vats and other equipment. Tea, coffee, and tobacco were yet unknown in the West, and alcohol, distilled in alembics (small retorts) on a small scale, was used primarily for medicinal purposes. Physicians and laymen alike regarded water with suspicion because it was thought to cause illness, an impression undoubtedly created by the effects of drinking from polluted sources.

The Nutritional Value of Medieval Diets. The nutritional value of medieval diets is difficult to determine. It varied widely according to region and social class and tended to fluctuate with the seasons. Autumn, when trees bore their fruit and animals were killed for the winter, usually meant a time of relative abundance, whereas spring, for all its promise of harvests to come, was the leanest of seasons. Considerations of price and availability often meant more than the change of seasons. The relative scarcity or abundance of different commodities caused dramatic and often terrifying fluctuations in price, especially for the poor, who had limited opportunities to store food. The failure of a single harvest could lead to hunger for the economically marginal.

Rich townsfolk and the inhabitants of pastoral villages probably enjoyed the best balance between protein, fats, and carbohydrates in their diets. Urban laborers and peasants on manors whose primary crop was grain suffered chronic deficiencies of everything except carbohydrates.

Everyone else fell somewhere in between, although the feudal aristocracy may be suspected of eating too much animal protein. The Middle Ages knew nothing of vitamins. The general scarcity of fresh fruits and vegetables ensured that minimum daily requirements would rarely have been met by anyone and deficiencies were probably common. The poor often suffered from deformities caused by rickets or goiter and were physically smaller than those with better access to protein in youth. The average height of an adult male may not have been much more than 5 feet, but this differed widely by class and region.

The general inadequacy of medieval diets arose in part from a paradox. Agricultural production increased dramatically between 1000 and about 1250, but because population increased proportionately, more food only supported more people at the same levels of subsistence. By 1250, yields had begun to decline, and new land was available for cultivation. Poverty and social unrest increased. In 1314–1315, events proved that when production and population became too closely balanced, a failed harvest could bring disaster.

DISEASE AND DEMOGRAPHY

Inadequate nutrition affected population rates in several ways. The rate of conception and the quality of maternal nutrition during pregnancy largely determine the number of live births in a given society. Both are related to diet. A third factor, obstetrical technique, is also important, but this changed little until the medical developments of the nineteenth and twentieth centuries.

Rates of Conception and Live Births. The total number of childbearing years available to women partially determines the rate of conception. In the Middle

PRICES AND EARNINGS IN THIRTEENTH-CENTURY ENGLAND

The relationship between earnings and prices is an important measure of living standards. Wages increased very little during the thirteenth century. After a dramatic increase between 1214 and 1228, prices rose more slowly on average until the Black Death of 1347–1350. It should be noted, however, that the prices of all commodities fluctuated widely according to each year's harvest.

TABLE 11.1 WAGES AND EARNINGS IN THIRTEENTH-CENTURY ENGLAND

This table provides estimated average earnings for several occupations in medieval England. Women, then as now, earned less than men for the same work. The annual wage of a mason reflects the fact that bad weather shortened the number of days he could work. For the same reason, a carpenter doing outdoor work would make less than the amount noted here. The wages for skilled laborers increased by 40 to 50 percent after the Black Death.

| | Estimated Earnings | |
OCCUPATION	PER DAY	PER YEAR
Agricultural laborer		
Boy	½d.	
Female	1d.	£1.7s. 3d.
Male	2d.	£2.14s. 6d.
Carpenter	3d.–3½d.	£4.
Mason	5d.–6d.	£4.8s. 5d.
Peasant family with 20 acres		£4.
Royal huntsman	7½d.	
Rural priest		£5–£15
Sawyer	3½d.–4d.	£5.
Stonecutter	4d.	£5.8s.
Thatcher's assistant (female)	1d.	£1.7s. 3d.
Town priest		£75–100
Unskilled laborer	2d.	£2.14s. 6d.

12 pennies (d.) = 1 shilling (s.). 20 shillings = 1 pound (£).

TABLE 11.2 PRICES IN THIRTEENTH-CENTURY ENGLAND

PRODUCT	AVERAGE PRICE
Ale (per gallon)	¼d.–¾d.
Bread (per loaf, weight varied)	¼d.–½d.
Candle wax (per pound)	4d.–5d.
Capons (each, fully fattened)	2d.–3d.
Eggs (per 100)	4d.
Hens (each)	½d.
Pears (per 100)	3½d.
Pepper (per pound)	10d.2s.
Pike (each)	6s.8d.
Salt herrings (per 10)	1d.
Second-quality malt—2 quarters (1-year supply of ale for 4)	7s.7d.
Sugar (per pound)	1s.–2d.
Wine (per quart)	£1.3s. 6d.
Wheat—4 quarters (1-year supply for a family of 4)	4s.6d.–5s.10d.

12 pennies (d.) = 1 shilling (s.). 20 shillings = 1 pound (£).

Figures taken from John Burnett, *A History of the Cost of Living* (Harmondsworth: Pelican Books, 1969, pp. 17–54).

Question: Try to calculate an annual budget for a peasant family of four.

Ages, malnutrition, obstetrical accidents, and epidemic disease shortened life expectancy and dramatically reduced the number of childbearing years. Women started menstruating at an older age than is typical today, thus further limiting years of conception. Medieval women seem to have reached puberty at an average age of 17, as opposed to today's average of 12.4. Nutrition is usually blamed for the difference. Inadequate nutrition can also prevent ovulation in mature women, which reduces conception rates even further.

After conception, poor maternal diet led to a high rate of stillbirths and complications during pregnancy. If brought to term, the fetus then faced the hazards of childbirth. Midwives normally delivered babies at home

FIGURE 11.2 *Trotula.* Dame Trotula is said to have taught at the University of Salerno (Italy) and to have written the best-known work on obstetrics in the Middle Ages. She was hailed as an "empress among midwives" and is seen here holding the orb, an imperial symbol.

in unsanitary conditions. The midwives were usually experienced but knew nothing of sterilization and lacked the most elementary equipment. Forceps, for example, were not invented until the middle of the eighteenth century. Although **Trotula,** a woman physician, taught at the University of Salerno in the thirteenth century and published a treatise on obstetrics, most medieval physicians were men and knew no more about childbirth than a competent midwife. Their services, in any case, were available only to the rich.

Infant Mortality. Infants who survived the obstetrical techniques of the day then faced the possibility that their mothers would be unable to nurse. Malnutrition interferes with lactation, as does the stress of poverty, exposure to war, and other forms of physical and mental insecurity. Turning the infant over to a wet nurse could solve the problem, but this was not always a satisfactory solution. The wet nurse was typically another woman who had milk to spare because she had recently lost her own baby. She had to be paid—a serious problem for a new mother who was poor—and did not always care for the child as she might have cared for her own. Babies put out for nursing had a much higher mortality rate than those who remained at home. Either way, the children of poorly nourished mothers were often weak and susceptible to disease. The birthrate therefore remained low by modern standards and the rate of infant mortality high. Valid statistics are unavailable for medieval times, but deaths presumably ranged from 30 to 70 percent in the first 2 years of life, depending on such variables as current food supply and the presence or absence of epidemics.

Unwanted Children. In hard times, personal decisions hindered population growth as well. Those whose own survival was in doubt abstained from sex, used the primitive means of contraception then available (notably *coitus interruptus*), or when all else failed, resorted to infanticide. Although abortion existed, it was extremely dangerous, and most women preferred to carry a fetus to term even if they could not afford to keep the baby. Infanticide may have been emotionally devastating to the mother and murder in the eyes of the law, but it could easily be concealed in a world where infant mortality was common and doctors were scarce. Its incidence in the Middle Ages has therefore become a matter of scholarly controversy. Medieval religious and civil authorities thought it was common, and many an old folk tale recalls its horrors.

Abandonment, the most common alternative to infanticide, appears to have declined sharply in the prosperous years of the eleventh and twelfth centuries. It became more frequent as population pressures increased during the thirteenth century and revived between the famines of 1315–1317 and the Black Death. As in ancient times, estimating how many of these abandoned children survived is impossible. If hard times persisted, less dramatic forms of birth control came into play. People simply refused to marry and remained celibate, sometimes for life. The marriage rate almost invariably declined during periods of economic stress.

Hygiene. Those who survived infancy still faced heavy odds. Crowding and a widespread indifference to personal hygiene encouraged the spread of disease. In the absence of a germ theory, personal cleanliness was a matter of aesthetics, and Christian thinkers, who associated it with pagan luxury or with Jewish and Muslim rituals, regarded it with suspicion. The rich bathed as a matter of status; the poor could not. By the twelfth century, firewood, like timber, had become scarce and expensive everywhere in western and central Europe. No one wanted to bathe in cold water in an unheated room, and most people had better uses for their limited supplies of precious firewood. Rashes and skin infections were therefore common. Crowding, often for warmth, and the custom of keeping livestock and pets in the home added to the problem by ensuring that many Europeans would play host to a variety of insect pests. This encouraged the spread of epidemics because lice and fleas carried infectious diseases, including typhus and, later, plague.

Disease and Injury. Contaminated drinking water accounted for another group of deadly ailments, and airborne viruses and bacteria were as numerous as they are today. Here, too, the absence of a germ theory rendered public health measures ineffective. Water that looked clean was thought to be safe, and indoor air was purified by scenting it with perfumes and herbs. Medieval doctors thought that breathing miasmas, or foul air, caused malaria, a disease endemic in much of Europe. It is actually spread by mosquitoes. The offending parasite remains in the bloodstream for life, causing recurring attacks of chills and fever even if it fails to kill its victim outright. Those weakened by malnutrition or other ailments were the most likely to succumb.

Some medieval diseases appear to have no modern counterparts, a tribute to the rapidity with which viruses and bacteria can evolve. Others, such as measles and chicken pox, the great killers of late antiquity, were now restricted largely to children. The medieval population had acquired a hereditary immunity, but even childhood diseases could carry off the weak or poorly nourished. In general, malnutrition weakened resistance to every ailment and, like crowding, acted as a silent partner in the high rate of mortality. Towns may have been more dangerous than the countryside, but poverty, wherever its location, often proved fatal.

Death by injury or misadventure was also common. Upper-class males destroyed themselves in battle or in hunting accidents. Villagers encountered the inevitable hazards of agricultural life. Infants fell into fires, crawled into the path of carts, or were mauled by hogs. Adults fell out of trees while picking fruit or gathering firewood or toppled into wells while drawing water. They severed limbs and arteries with their scythes or accidentally brained each other with their flails. Drink and the absence of illumination by night took its toll. Happy harvesters fell off their carts and were run over, and people returning from late-night drinking bouts drowned in ditches or passed out and froze to death in the road.

Medical Practice. Against this formidable array of human ills, doctors remained as helpless as they had been in antiquity. Their theories and the remedies available to them had changed little. By the thirteenth century, many physicians had been trained at a university, but they tended to concentrate on diagnosis and the prescription of drugs, most of which were of dubious value (see Document 11.1). Many treatments were based on natural magic, a then-legitimate science that relied on the supernatural or on hidden forces thought to be found in nature. The surgeons who, unlike physicians, performed medical procedures, learned their trade through apprenticeship. They operated without sterilization and without anesthetics. Broken bones could sometimes be set, but wounds often became infected with fatal results. In any case, most people had no access to either physicians or surgeons and relied on folk remedies, about which little is known. These remedies were probably as effective as the nostrums advocated by learned doctors. Survival still depended on good luck, heredity, and the recuperative powers of the patient.

Population Distribution. All of these things affected the distribution of population. Medieval life expectancy was probably in the low thirties at birth (see Table 11.3). Averages, however, can be deceiving. Many people lived into their fifties, and the proportionate

TABLE 11.3 LIFE EXPECTANCY IN THE MIDDLE AGES

The figures below represent the estimated life expectancy of male landholders in medieval England. They are arranged according to the average number of years a man might expect to live at a given age (from birth to 80) and demonstrate the substantial changes in mortality that occurred over time. The drop in life expectancy after 1348 is due to recurring episodes of the Black Death (see Chapter 12). Life expectancy for women was probably somewhat shorter owing to the dangers of childbirth.

Question: What might account for the variations in life expectancy over time?

AGE	1200–1276	1276–1301	1301–1326	1326–1348	1348–1376	1376–1401	1401–1425	1425–1450
0	35.3	31.3	29.8	27.2	17.3	20.5	23.8	32.8
10	36.3	32.2	31.0	28.1	25.1	24.5	29.7	34.5
20	28.7	25.2	23.8	22.1	23.9	21.4	29.4	27.7
30	22.8	21.8	20.0	21.1	22.0	22.3	25.0	24.1
40	17.8	16.6	15.7	17.7	18.1	19.2	19.3	20.4
60	9.4	8.3	9.3	10.8	10.9	10.0	10.5	13.7
80	5.2	3.8	4.5	6.0	4.7	3.1	4.8	7.9

Cipolla, Carlo, *The Middle Ages, Fontana Economic History of Europe* (London: Colliers, 1973, p. 47). Reprinted by permission of HarperCollins Publishers Ltd.

JOHN OF GADDESDEN ON THE TREATMENT OF DISEASE

The following remedies are taken from a standard medical text, *Rosa Anglica practica medicine a capite ad pedes (The Rose of England, the Practice of Medicine from the Head to the Feet)*, by John of Gaddesden (1280–1361), a graduate of Oxford and of the medical school at Montpellier. The treatments he prescribes are a typical mixture of common sense and magic.

For smallpox: In the case of the noble son of the English king, when he was infected with this disease . . . I made everything around the bed to be red.

 For tuberculosis: 1). Keep in check the catarrh and the rheumata; 2). cleanse the body; 3). divert and draw away the matter [of the disease] to a different part; 4). strengthen the chest and head so that they do not take up the matter, and that it there multiply; 5). cleanse and dry up the ulcers and expel the matter from them; 6). consolidate them; 7). restrain and cure the cough by using demulcent drinks with ointments and stupes; 8). assist the patient to sleep; 9). strengthen and bring back the appetite; 10). keep in check the spitting of blood; 11). do what can be done to make the breathing more easy and to remove the asthma and the hoarseness; 12). regulate the way of life so far as the six nonnaturals; 13). cure the putrid or hectic fever which goes with the

disease. As to food, the best is the milk of a young brunette with her first child, which should be a boy; the young woman should be well-favored and should eat and drink in moderation.

 For toothache: Again, write these words on the jaw of the patient: In the name of the Father, the Son, and the Holy Ghost, Amen. +Rex+Pax+Nax+in Christo Filio, and the pain will cease at once as I have often seen. . . . Again, some say that the beak of a magpie hung from the neck cures pain in the teeth and the uvula and the quinsy. Again, when the gospel for Sunday is read in the mass, let the man hearing mass sign his tooth and head with the sign of the holy Cross and say a pater noster and an ave for the souls of the father and mother of St. Philip, and this without stopping; it will keep them from pain in the future and will cure that which may be present, so say trustworthy authorities.

Clendening, L., ed., *A Source Book of Medical History* (New York: Dover, 1960, pp. 83–85).

Questions: Which of these procedures is likely to have helped the patient? Why do you suppose that a learned man like John of Gaddesden would have given equal credence to the magical cures?

►FIGURE **11.3** *Surgeons at Work.* University-trained physicians did not normally perform surgical operations. Surgery was performed by surgeons who learned their trade as apprentices, and they were often barbers as well. This English illumination from the 1100s shows the excision of hemorrhoids, the removal of cataracts, and the extirpation of nasal polyps. Unsterilized instruments and the lack of anesthetics limited the success of such operations.

number of individuals over the age of 85 may not have been much smaller than it is today. Nevertheless, medieval people were on average far younger and had shorter working lives than their modern counterparts in industrialized countries. Because they matured later and died younger, their reproductive lifetimes were also shorter. For people of mature years (aged 30 to 50), men may have outnumbered women, primarily because many women died in childbirth.

These conclusions are based on estimated averages for the entire population. The wealthy were too few to alter the statistics in any significant way, but for them, demographic realities differed. They enjoyed lower infant mortality and higher life expectancy than the poor. They also tended to have more children, but even the rich suffered from mortality rates far greater than those common today.

THE LIFE OF THE NOBILITY

The nobility made up only a small part of Europe's population. They constituted a hereditary caste that possessed titles, coats of arms, and specific legal privileges, including virtual freedom from prosecution under the

CASTLES AND MANOR HOUSES

The military aristocracy of medieval Europe lived originally in castles whose purpose was to defend its inhabitants against attack. From the tenth to the midtwelfth century, the strength and complexity of their defensive arrangements increased, as did the luxury of their accommodations, but they were always expected to withstand a siege. By 1200, unfortified manor houses began to replace castles in areas that were not under military threat. A century later, social unrest encouraged nobles to fortify once again, this time as protection against their own tenants.

The Castle of Falaise. The castle of Falaise in Normandy was begun in the 1100s as the primary seat of the Dukes of Normandy. The square keep dominates the town from the top of a rocky crag, and it served not only to provide protection for the duke's family and its retainers but to intimidate the surrounding countryside. The English constructed the round tower at the right in the early 1400s to strengthen the fortifications in the later stages of the Hundred Years' War. William the Conqueror was born at Falaise before the current structure was built.

law. Free in person and property, their only real obligation was loyalty and military service to the king or tenant-in-chief who had granted them their status. As we have seen, even this was not always enforceable. Although few in number, the nobility and their families dominated the world outside the free, chartered cities. They held most of the land and had a virtual monopoly of military force. In theory, they protected their tenants and provided a measure of justice in their manorial courts, but these obligations could not legally be enforced. In practice, they answered only to social pressure from other members of their class.

Not all nobles, however, were created equal. Kings and those who shared their royal blood occupied the top of the social hierarchy. Royal relatives, especially the younger sons of kings, monopolized such titles as prince and duke and held vast properties (*appanages* in French) that were virtual kingdoms in their own right. An intermediate group, mostly counts and barons, did not normally have royal blood but held many manors and great influence in the countryside. Simple knights descended from the younger sons of this secondary nobility and often possessed only a single manor. In some

cases, they had nothing but their horse, sword, and armor and lived as mercenaries or as bodyguards and military retainers of a powerful lord. Rich or poor, they retained their legal privileges and a measure of access to even the highest level of society. The lives led by noblemen and noblewomen bore almost no resemblance to those of ordinary people.

Castles and Manor Houses. In the bloody days of the tenth and early eleventh centuries, most nobles lived in castles built for defense rather than comfort. Castles consisted of a central tower or keep surrounded by a wall that was protected by an outer ditch or moat. Within the keep, the inhabitants slept and ate together in a great hall with little or no provision for privacy. Castles occupied by kings, princes of the blood, and the more important members of the secondary nobility were often surrounded by a sizable town that served their needs and those of their retainers.

The symbol of feudal authority, the castle underwent an architectural metamorphosis during the eleventh and twelfth centuries. Kings and the greater vassals had always tried to build in stone. As their wealth and se-

The Manor House at Boothby Pagnell, England. Boothby Pagnell was built around 1200 in a time of relative peace and security. The second story is occupied by a great hall; the ground floor contained storage and service areas. The structure is sturdy, but it would have been difficult to defend against a mob of peasants, much less an invading army.

Bodiam, a Decorative Castle. Sir Edward Dallingridge built Bodiam Castle, Sussex, England, in 1385. Although it looks formidable, it is in fact a decorative exercise in chivalric nostalgia typical of the later Middle Ages. By building it, Sir Edward apparently hoped to improve his prestige in the neighborhood. It could have protected him from an attack by his own peasants, but it would have been useless against a professional force. Moats of this kind were usually created by a dam or by diverting water from a stream. By destroying the dam or diversion, a real army with a few hundred pioneers, as military ditch diggers were called, could drain a water defense like this one in an afternoon.

curity increased, they extended the practice to relatively modest structures. Wooden palisades gave way to stone curtain walls with towers spaced at regular intervals on the Roman model. The keep, or central stronghold, became more livable, if not luxurious. Windows, side aisles, and even fireplaces were added to the hall. Separate kitchens and chapels became commonplace, and private chambers were built for the use of the lord and his immediate family. This tended to remove them from the life of the hall and introduced the revolutionary idea of personal privacy. In politically secure areas, the lesser nobility built stone manor houses on the same model without troubling about walls. Setting the hall above a raised ground floor and entering it by a staircase was thought to be protection enough.

These developments reflected a basic change, not only in the function of the castle but also in the character of the noble class as a whole. With the passing of the great raids, society no longer needed the protection of the knights and the purely military importance of the castles declined.

Castle building almost ceased by the end of the twelfth century. Its revival in the thirteenth century was primarily a response to growing social unrest. The largest structures, such as the great Welsh castles of Edward I (1272–1307; see Chapter 12), were intended to hold territory that was newly annexed by an expanding monarchy. Smaller castles protected nobles from their tenants in a time of growing poverty and frustration. Both purposes involved an element of political theater. The castles built to protect country gentlemen against their tenants, like those built to overawe the Welsh, were stronger and more sophisticated than any attack that was likely to be made against them.

The Evolution of the Chivalric Ideal. The knights, too, became more decorative and theatrical with the passage of time. As the importance of their original function began to diminish, the concept of nobility began to evolve in its place. Originally, the code of chivalry had focused on the personal qualities of courage, loyalty, strength, and courtesy. These attributes soon came to be regarded as hereditary. The process began with the introduction of dubbing to knighthood in the late eleventh century. By this time, knights had become, in the language of the church, an *ordo,* or order in

FIGURE 11.4 *Heraldry.* Heraldry evolved from the practice of decorating a knight's shield with his coat of arms so that he could be more easily recognized in the heat of battle. By 1300, it had become a complex science that defined an individual—and a family's—place in upper-class society. Here, the king at arms, who served as the official arbiter of social and heraldic matters, shows the Duc de Bourbon the armorial bearings of knights who are to take part in a tournament. Miniature from the *Tournois du roy René* (1400s).

FIGURE 11.5 *A Troubadour.* By traveling from one castle to another and reciting romances of chivalry, troubadours played an important part in preserving and extending chivalric values. Here, Adenez, known in his day as The King of the Minstrels, recites the *Roman de Cleomadès* to the Countess d'Artois, Mathilde de Brabant, and Blanche of Castile, Queen of France.

their own right—a social institution, rather than a mere body of fighting men. Before long, a priest customarily blessed the knight's weapons and invested him with them in a rite reminiscent of ordination. This was perhaps inevitable when crusades were becoming the last legitimate outlet for military virtues. Finally, in the century after 1130, knighthood was transformed into a hereditary privilege. In 1140, Roger II of Sicily declared that only the descendants of knights would be admitted to knighthood. By 1187, new laws made it illegal to knight a peasant in the Holy Roman Empire and prohibited peasants from carrying a sword or lance. Similar provisions appeared in almost every European kingdom by the second half of the twelfth century.

Such prohibitions were not airtight. Members of the urban patriciate could sometimes achieve knightly rank, but their elevation was neither cheap nor easy. Knights could also be created on the battlefield by a grateful superior. To forestall the proliferation of titles, kings achieved a statutory monopoly over the granting of knighthood and forbade the ancient custom whereby any knight could make another. At the same time, kings created a profusion of counts and barons to distinguish between their greater and lesser vassals. **Heralds** and "kings of arms" achieved unprecedented importance. From their original role as knights who announced war and peace and carried messages between commanders on the battlefield, heralds became arbiters of chivalric behavior, genealogists, and experts on the coats of arms that identified knightly families. This process reached a peak in England and in the Holy Roman Empire, where colleges of heralds graded the status of noble families in exquisite detail. When the military changes of the fourteenth century (see Chapter 12) brought commoners back to the battlefield in great numbers, such policies had to be reversed. Kings retained the sole right to grant titles but bestowed them once again on people of humble origin. The feudal nobility, whose importance in war was by this time greatly diminished, regarded such creations as an outrageous betrayal of chivalry.

Chivalric Values and Behavior. Legal developments went hand in hand with an expansion of the chivalric ideal. What had once been little more than a prescription for courage and loyalty evolved into an all-encompassing moral and esthetic code. The church, in its drive to influence all European institutions, bore partial responsibility for the change. Courtesy, clemency to a fallen enemy, and respectful treatment of women became hallmarks of the knight, although such behavior was extended only to members of the noble class. Peasants could still be raped and murdered with impunity under the laws of war.

Along with these presumed virtues went a style of speech and personal carriage that clearly set the knight and his lady apart from the rest of society. It could not be easily imitated because peasants no longer associated with the nobility on a regular basis and had few opportunities to observe them. The speech, movements, and gestures of ordinary men and women were eventually stigmatized as uncouth and boorish.

Chivalric Literature.

Troubadours disseminated chivalric values. Heralds and kings of arms presided over the conventions of heraldry and acted to some extent as arbiters of taste. As literacy spread, the oral tradition of the troubadours was written down and circulated in manuscript form as the **romance**. Although intended primarily as entertainment, the romance exalted and, to some extent, defined chivalric values. Perhaps the most important were the five works based on the legendary court of King Arthur that Chrétien de Troyes (Shre'-tyen de Trwah) composed sometime after 1164. They formed the basis of an entire literary genre. Many others of similar importance also existed. A body of lyric poetry that exalted chivalric love served as further reinforcement for the new values. The language of this literature was French, and French, which the Normans had helped spread from England to Sicily, became the language of the chivalric class. Social separation was now virtually complete. In some regions, knights could no longer speak the language of their tenants.

The Tournament.

Theoretically, war remained the center of noble life and the justification for its privileges. Males were still expected to master the profession of arms in youth and practice it until age, wounds, or ill health permitted a dignified retirement. In practice, the development of hereditary knighthood gravely weakened this ideal. In the first feudal age, men who lacked the requisite ability commonly remained squires for life. In the twelfth and thirteenth centuries, they could expect to be knighted regardless of their achievements.

Relative peace was an even greater threat to the knightly ethos. In the absence of Vikings or Magyars, the Crusades became a useful outlet for martial talents. As the interval between crusades grew longer, tournaments gradually took the place of war as the central preoccupation of the feudal class. **Tournaments** were stylized forms of combat in which two mounted knights, generally separated by a barrier, attempted to unhorse one another with their lances. They might then attempt to fight on foot with swords or other weapons. The rules were elaborate and varied widely according to the occasion. It was, in other words, a sport. The bouts were refereed; murder was not the primary object, but serious injuries and fatal mishaps were unavoidable. Women, who participated only as spectators, were a powerful symbolic presence. A knight entered the lists as champion of a particular lady and wore her scarf or some more intimate garment as a token of her favor.

FIGURE 11.6 *Tournament.* This French painting, done in 1812, shows the kind of tournament commonly conducted in the Middle Ages. The knight at center right has unhorsed his opponent, who thrusts at him from the ground with his lance. The king at arms, serving as a kind of referee, blows his horn to stop the engagement. The spectators watch from specially constructed boxes: ladies on the left, men on the right, and the sponsor of the tournament in the center. Print of oil on canvas by Pierre-Henri Révoil (French, 1776–1824).

Because the conventions of chivalric love encouraged adulterous flirtations, the lady was not ordinarily expected to be his wife.

For all its frivolity, the importance of the tournament as a social ritual should not be underestimated. Those who were good at it could expect great rewards. A penniless younger son such as William the Marshall (d. 1219) was able to parlay his athletic talent into an advantageous marriage, an estate, and a remarkable political career that ended with his appointment as regent for the King of England.

Kinship and Marriage. This was the point of the whole system. Beneath the veneer of chivalry, most nobles devoted their lives to the advancement of personal and family interests through the accumulation of estates. A sense of lineage, strengthened immeasurably by the concept of nobility itself, developed early in the great families. For them, kinship ties were stronger than ties in other segments of society. The need to acquire and preserve landed estates ensured that the extended family would be a relatively common form of household organization and that weddings would almost always be arranged, often at an early age. The disposition of great properties could not be entrusted to the vagaries of youthful lust. This may help account for the fascination with adultery that characterized chivalric literature. However, a surprising number of noble marriages appear to have been happy and mutually supportive. The women of the feudal class were often formidable personages, capable of managing an estate or defending their castle against a siege in their husbands' absence. Some, such as Matilda of Tuscany or Eleanor of Aquitaine, became major political figures in their own right. Virtually all were at home in the world of political intrigue. Their survival and that of their children often depended on it.

Clientage. Clientage, of which feudalism and other forms of dependency were in some respects a formalized expression, was also highly developed at this level of society. Almost everyone sought the favor and protection of those more powerful than themselves and tried wherever possible to develop clients and retainers of their own. People measured the importance of a family less by the grandeur of its castle than by the hospitality of its hall. The greater households often included not only the lord and his nuclear family but also a respectable number of collateral relatives, stewards, servants, knights, and other retainers who owed him their allegiance and lived at least partially from his bounty. This much, at least, had changed little since the early Middle Ages, and as always, the peasants bore the cost.

Ironically, noble ambitions seemed to increase as the economic fortunes of their class began to decline. The greater availability of specie in the twelfth century led to the widespread commutation of feudal obligations for cash. Landholders greeted this development with enthusiasm because it increased their liquidity, but they made the mistake of commuting payments hitherto made in labor or in kind for fixed sums of money. These sums, not the proportional values that had determined them, quickly became enshrined in law and precedent, and inflation slowly consumed their value (see Table 11.4). During the thirteenth century, a strong demand for land caused by population growth masked the consequent decline in the real value of rents. When harvest failures were followed by the demographic catastrophe of 1347–1350, property values collapsed and social tensions became insupportable.

THE LIFE OF MEDIEVAL PEASANTS

In the Middle Ages, 90 percent of all Europeans lived in the countryside and engaged directly in agriculture. They were not exclusively occupied with farming; many people had special skills that brought in supplementary income. Most communities could boast millers, carpenters, brewers, seamstresses, harness makers, blacksmiths, midwives, and other specialists, but these people also worked in the fields as needed and frequently held land of their own. Wealthier peasants were more likely to have a trade than were their poorer neighbors, for a trade required skills as well as a substantial investment in tools or equipment.

The Physical Environment of the Village. Freestanding peasant farmsteads existed in the Alps, the Pyrenees, and parts of Scandinavia, but most medieval Europeans lived in villages that, on average, probably numbered about 250 inhabitants. The physical environment of these villages varied widely. The heart of a larger village was the parish church, which by the twelfth century was almost always of masonry construction. Timber churches continued to survive in northwest England, in parts of Germany, and in Scandinavia, but their numbers were declining. Lords frequently built or improved village churches as an act of piety and to increase their family's prestige. Some of them were, and are, architectural gems. The peasants ultimately paid for them in the form of dues and tithes, but the church was at least a form of expenditure that the villagers could enjoy. It was usually the only substantial building in the community unless the lord maintained a residence there in the form of a castle or manor house. If a village lacked a church, priests from nearby communities tried to serve its spiritual needs, most often on an infrequent basis.

Smaller villages might lack a church or manor, but each contained a cluster of peasant houses or cottages built around a central plaza or constructed at narrow

TABLE 11.4 THE EXPENSES OF THE RICH

An earl's income in thirteenth-century England might range from £1,000 per year to more than £5,000. From this, a nobleman or noblewoman was expected to maintain a large household of servants and spend huge sums on food, building, travel, and recreation. A single household, for example, might require 40 horses and more than 100 servants; spices were consumed in large quantities. A fowler killed wild game birds for the table. Wealthy women often wore an elaborate girdle like a belt around their waists as an article of adornment. Some of the costs, few of which would ever have been incurred by a peasant, are given to the right.

Question: Based on the figures given here and in Table 11.1, how many years of a peasant family's income would be required to purchase a war horse or a fur coverlet?

HOUSEHOLD ITEM	COST
Bonnet	16d.
Candlewax	5d. per pound
Cloth cloak	3s. 4d.
Fowler	3s. 4d. per week
Fur coverlet	£20
Hunting bow	2s. 4d.
Hunting falcon	£5–10
Huntsman	7½d. per day
Lady's gold girdle	£37. 12s.
Minstrel	12d. per day
Pack of hounds	£100 per year
Saddle horse	£5–27
Stockings	4s. the pair
War horse	£40–80

SPICES AND DELICACIES (PER POUND)	
Almonds (5 pounds)	1s.
Anise	3d.
Black pepper	10d.–2s.
Cloves	3d.
Cumin	2d.–10d.
Ginger	10d.–2s.6d.
Horseradish	3d.
Nutmeg	3d.
Pomegranates	6d. each
Rice	1½d.
Saffron	10s.–14s.
Sugar	1s.–2s.

12 pennies (d.) = 1 shilling (s.). 20 shillings = 1 pound (£).

Figures abstracted from John Burnett, *A History of the Cost of Living* (Harmondsworth: Pelican Books, 1969, pp. 31, 34–35, 37).

intervals along a single street. Medieval peasants preferred to build their homes in close proximity to their neighbors for added safety and to leave more land for planting. The lands of the village fell into several categories. A peasant's tenement normally included a house, a kitchen garden, and the fields on which the family grew their primary crops. In some villages, tenants cultivated their fields as individuals and separated them from their neighbors' with balks of turf that served as pathways. Their plots might be widely scattered or far from the village proper, making it necessary to spend valuable time traveling from one to another. Other villages, especially in areas that used the heavy wheeled plow, followed **the open-field system.** Each tenant held several strips of land, but few could afford a plow of their own or the four-to-six animal team necessary to pull it. The entire village therefore shared plows and draft animals and worked the fields in common. After the harvest, they divided the proceeds according to the size of their individual tenements. Most villages also possessed a **commons,** or common land that belonged to the entire village. Different villagers might cultivate portions of it in rotation or use it for grazing. More rarely, the community maintained it as a woodlot to provide firewood and small game for everyone. Some villages also set aside land for the lord or priest and cultivated them communally in lieu of individual tithes or dues.

Housing. The availability of building materials and the structure of families determined the character of domestic architecture. In southern Europe, where timber had been scarce since biblical times, brick or stone construction was the rule. Peasant houses were sometimes large, having been expanded at various times to accommodate an increase in family size. If the family grew smaller, the permanence of the building materials often precluded the demolition of all or part of the house. This helps explain why Mediterranean villages often appear larger today than their census figures indicate. It

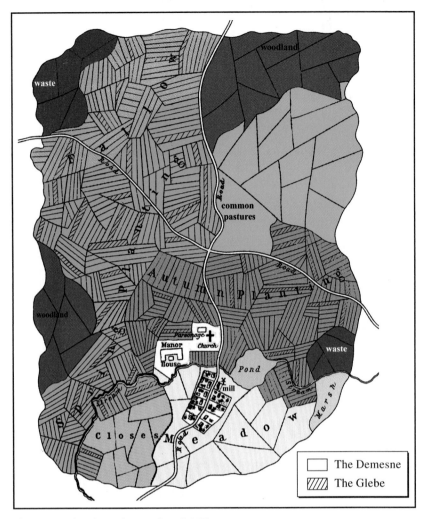

FIGURE 11.7 *Plan of a Medieval Village.* This drawing shows an English village containing both a manor house and a church. The grouping of dozens of small fields into larger sections for spring and fall plantings as well as fallow indicates that it used the open-field system. *Demesne* refers to land held directly by the lord. Note that much of it is in larger fields called closes. The glebe partially supported the church and its priest. Note how it is scattered throughout the lands of the village. The fields of the tenants would have been scattered in the same way. In this village, the meadow and the common pasture belonged to the village, but the woodlands were held by the lord.

location for reasons of health or economic advantage, leaving nothing behind but rubble and the outlines of their foundations.

In the days of Charlemagne, many houses were made of solid wood or logs, a practice that became prohibitively expensive as wood became scarcer. By the end of the eleventh century, a house in a northern village was typically framed in wood and composed of bays or sections added together, usually in a linear pattern. Bays could be built or torn down as needed because the walls were so flimsy that thieves sometimes broke through them rather than bothering with the door. Such homes were inexpensive. Newlyweds had little difficulty in setting up a place of their own, and people often had cottages built for them in their old age to separate them from their grown children. Although some houses had lofts or attics, few possessed a true second story. Windows, if there were any, tended to be small and covered with wooden shutters. Chimneys were not introduced until the end of the Middle Ages. Instead, builders placed a raised hearth at the center of the house and made a hole above it in the thatched roof to let the smoke out. Most people went to bed at nightfall and rose at dawn. Candles provided interior lighting if a family could afford them. Because floors were of swept earth covered with straw or rushes, the danger of fire was ever-present.

Cleanliness. In these circumstances, cleanliness was as hard to achieve as safety. The interior of a peasant home was inevitably dark and smoky. Although the marks of vigorously wielded medieval brooms are still visible in archeological digs, housekeeping inevitably fell below modern standards. This was in part because people lived in close proximity with their livestock. Most peasant homes, north or south, possessed a yard or garden and even outbuildings. The yard, croft, or close was an integral part of the family's living space. It was basically a walled or fenced-in working area in which children and animals wandered at will, and peasants made great efforts to prevent its disorder from invading the sleeping quarters. Drainage ditches and thresholds provided the best defense, but

may also have encouraged the formation of extended families by making free space available to newly married couples.

Thanks to their sturdy construction, many communities in Spain, Italy, and southern France have changed little since the Middle Ages. Existing knowledge of northern villages is the product of painstaking archeological reconstruction. The use of wattle and daub (interwoven twigs or rushes covered by mud) or other impermanent materials meant that peasant housing in England, northern France, the Low Countries, and north Germany often lasted only for a generation or two. Entire villages sometimes moved to a different

FIGURE 11.8 *A Prosperous Peasant's Cottage in Winter.* This depiction of a peasant cottage is from the *Tres riches heures,* an illuminated prayer book commissioned by the Duc de Berry and painted by Paul, Herman, and Jean Limbourg in 1413–1416. The beehives, the number of animals in the close, and even the dresses of the women indicate that this was a wealthy household. The magnificent book from which this illustration comes was intended to provide an idealized view of rural life.

muddy feet and wandering livestock were an inevitable part of the farmer's world. Moreover, in cold weather, it sometimes became necessary to house animals in a separate bay or in an unused room of the house. In one-room cottages, livestock might share the living space with humans.

Furnishings. Most homes contained no furniture beyond the straw pallets on which people slept; their blankets, which were sometimes used as outer wear in winter; and their cooking utensils. The latter might consist of no more than a pot and two or three spoons. Castles and manor houses might contain a bedstead for the lord and cupboards for the storage of leftovers. Chairs were rare enough to be considered symbols of royalty. Much of medieval life was lived on the floor.

Personal Possessions. This material simplicity extended to purely personal possessions as well. Like the lord in his hall, the peasant ate with his fingers and a knife. Stews and gruels were served from a wooden bowl or straight from the pot and eaten with wooden spoons. Soups were often drunk. Among the rich, a piece of coarse bread served as a plate for meat and was ideally given to the poor after it had absorbed the juices of the meal. On special occasions, the wealthy might eat from wooden trenchers. Even at formal banquets, two people might be expected to share a plate, a custom that sometimes contributed violence to the day's entertainment.

Clothing. For the peasant, clothing consisted of little more than a homespun smock, leggings, and perhaps a hat for men and a simple smock or dress for women. Shoes were normally reserved for bad weather. Until the late fourteenth century, even peasants who could afford to do otherwise appear to have ignored the dictates of fashion. Most people seem to have owned only one set of working clothes and another outfit of better quality for church or festive occasions. They washed both when possible. Workday garments were worn until they fell apart. Children, once they were out of the swaddling clothes in which they were wrapped as infants, dressed like their parents.

Village Society. In village society, wealth rather than social class determined status. The richer peasants held tenements or other lands on secure contracts. Such properties were often larger than they could work themselves, and they either sublet portions of their property to others or hired laborers as needed. They were also more likely than poorer peasants to own draft animals and to graze livestock on the village common. If they had been careful in planning their marriages or had formed a business relationship with the lord or his steward they could become as wealthy as minor nobles. Their families tended to be larger than those of the poor and their houses more substantial.

Perhaps the largest group in every community was that of the smallholders, whose lands were insufficient to support their families, but who supplemented their earnings by leasing additional fields, practicing a trade, or engaging in occasional labor in return for food or wages. They usually had their own house and garden, and they might keep poultry or a hog. Below them on the economic scale were landless laborers, whose situation was often precarious. Accounting for perhaps one-fourth of the community, they depended on charity in hard times and sometimes resorted to petty theft, although small-scale pilfering provided a common income supplement for more fortunate groups as well. Slavery, although still common in the cities of southern Europe, disappeared in the north and in rural areas during the twelfth century.

Social Mobility. Social movement was extremely limited. The evolution of nobility as a social ideal opened an unbridgeable gap between the peasantry and those who bore arms. Wealthier peasants sometimes placed one of their children in the church, but even in this, the most egalitarian of medieval institutions, humble birth was a grave barrier to advancement. Within the narrow world of the village, wealth and social status could be increased through careful management, good marriage strategies, and luck. Over time, many families and a few individuals did so, but the pinnacle of ambition remained a place on the manorial court, control of a mill, or an appointment as one of the lord's stewards. Generally, the medieval villager had no choice other than to accept the status into which he or she had been born. To do otherwise not only would have been fruitless but also would have run counter to the most cherished prejudices of an age in which stability was a paramount social goal.

Cooperation. Although stratified by wealth, the medieval village was a powerful, tightly knit social organism whose survival into modern times testified to its adaptability. In size, it typically numbered between 250 and 500 inhabitants, with smaller villages being the more common.

Many of its inhabitants were interrelated. However, the ecclesiastical prohibition against marrying one's relatives worked steadily against the pressures of isolation and an endemic distrust of strangers. People identified strongly with their village and tended to see it for what it was: a community made up exclusively of peasants, which, after family, was their chief protection against a hostile world.

Cooperation was therefore an essential feature of village life, even though the relative wealth of individual peasants varied immensely. At the very least, villagers had to maintain a united front in negotiating with outside forces that might pose a threat to their prosperity, such as their lord, the church, a city, or a neighboring village whose inhabitants tried to encroach on their lands or rights. If peasants seemed wily, grasping, or suspicious to outsiders, it was because outsiders were often trying to detach the peasants from their meager wealth.

Within the village, some measure of cooperation was essential to the peasants' daily pursuits. In regions that followed the open-field system, agricultural operations from plowing to harvesting were undertaken in common for efficiency's sake. In grazing areas, the rounding up and shearing of sheep was, and for the most part still is, a cooperative effort involving the entire population of the village. If the village possessed common lands, their use had to be regulated to prevent overexploitation, either by individuals or by the community as a whole. Peasants tended to be keenly aware of the limits of their local ecology and took great care to limit the number of animals that could be grazed on a particular parcel or the quantity of wood, nuts, and other products that could be harvested from woodlots. If they planted the commons to additional row crops, the land had to be allocated fairly. Families took turns using the commons according to a rotation established by custom. In some places, including much of Spain, an annual lottery determined the allocation.

The community also maintained the village's infrastructure. Manorial obligations usually mandated the construction and repair of roads, bridges, and ditches. Teams of peasants typically did this work together. Villages also undertook public improvements on their own. On the private level, friends and relatives helped with projects such as the construction or modification of a house or the digging of a drainage ditch around the close. Such help was intended to be reciprocal. Labor exchanges of this kind were central to the peasant economy and are in themselves an extension of communal bonds.

Social Control. Peasant communities also tried to control the social behavior of their inhabitants. The more prosperous villagers often sat on manorial courts that judged minor disputes within the village. Where the influence of the lord was weak, such matters might be dealt with by a council of village elders. The selection of village leaders, including those who supervised communal labor and the allocation of common lands, remains something of a mystery. Some may have been elected. In most places, they seem to have been chosen through an informal process of consensus building that avoided the confrontation of a vote.

Crime, such as it was, normally involved petty theft or interpersonal violence that fell far short of murder. Most villages were relatively peaceful, in part because everyone knew everyone else's business. Privacy, as in the towns, would have been impossible to achieve. If an individual's behavior ran counter to prevailing local standards, he or she would be subjected to ridicule and abuse that in extreme cases might make life insupportable. In general, public opinion provided a more powerful instrument of social control than manorial courts or the lord's bailiff. If someone, especially a stranger, committed a serious crime, custom decreed that every able-bodied man in the village should give chase, help capture the criminal, and hold him for the bailiff. The English called this a "hue and cry." The practice could be dangerous for all concerned and was fortunately uncommon.

Peasant Families. The structure of medieval family life varied immensely according to location, social class, and individual preference. It also varied over time as individual households adjusted to economic change and to the life cycles of their members. As a general rule, wealthier households were larger and more complex than those of the poor.

In northern Europe, the nuclear family predominated, at least among peasants. A married couple and their children lived together, rarely sharing their space with other relatives. When children married, they left the home and established a household of their own.

Old people tried to maintain their independence as long as they could. The wasting diseases of old age were not prolonged as they are today by the miracles of modern medicine. If someone grew feeble or senile, they sometimes moved in with one of their grown children. That the elderly often preferred to board with an unrelated villager is a tribute to the relative weakness of kinship ties. Such an arrangement usually involved the transfer of land or other payments.

The nuclear family was also the most common form of household organization in Mediterranean Europe, but extended families in which adult siblings and grandparents lived under the same roof were not unusual. Many others lived as nuclear units in close proximity to their relatives and acted in common with them when necessary. Such behavior indicates that kinship obligations were more broadly defined than they were in the north. The phenomenon is probably related to the concept of the *domus* (dome'-us), or house, as a basic component of family identity.

Lineage Groups. The term *domus,* or **lineage group,** refers to a family descended from the holders of an estate from which they took their name. In northern Europe, the practice was largely restricted to the feudal aristocracy. In Spain, Italy, and southern France, the continuing presence of allodial land and the relative weakness of feudal ties extended the concept to relatively humble folk, although rarely to the very poor. In its extreme forms—the Catalan *masia* (mas'-ee-uh), for example—the name of the family, the stone house in which it lived, and the property upon which it was located all bore the same name. The prevalence of family names among peasants reveals the degree to which domus was associated with family in a given region. In Italy, family names had become well established in the twelfth century. Even those who did not own land sometimes adopted the custom in imitation of their social superiors, and with it the concept of familial obligation that it implies. In much of northern Europe, family names did not become common among ordinary folk until after the Black Death of 1347–1350 (see Chapter 12). Until then, people went by their first names, sometimes adding the name of their father, husband, or occupation to avoid confusion.

To southern Europeans with modest property and a name, the extended family was likely to be seen as a source of economic and social support. This created a sense of mutual obligation that many chose to ignore but that could be of great value in difficult times for those who did not. For them, the family provided a refuge and protection against a hostile world. Some, no doubt, went further and agreed with Peter Lombard that those outside the family were enemies. This notion, however, disturbed jurists and helps explain why the villages of Spain and Italy were as troubled by faction and vendetta as their cities.

The organization of all European families, nuclear or extended, was typically patriarchal. Households dominated by widows have been recorded, as have *phratries* (fra'-trees) in which two or more brothers with their own nuclear families inhabited the same house. Such variants probably developed as family strategies to meet specific conditions. Otherwise, the authority of the husband or father was universally recognized in law and custom. Unlike their Roman predecessors, medieval fathers did not possess life and death authority, and Christian writers from Augustine to Albertus Magnus hoped that their actions would always be tempered by familial love. In extended families, the problem of authority became more complex. Decisions might sometimes require consensus, but one individual, usually a mature male characterized by greater wealth or force of character than the others, was generally acknowledged as the family's leader. The same pattern of leadership appeared in the clientage groups that developed, as they had done in antiquity, from the economic or political success of prominent families.

Inheritance. The laws of inheritance had less to do with family organization than might be supposed. They, too, exhibited wide regional variations, but two main types emerged: partible and impartible. **Partible inheritance** provides equally for all heirs. It was a fundamental principle in Roman law and was far more common than its alternative, especially in continental Europe. Its chief disadvantage is that a multiplicity of holdings eventually results and each holding is too small to support a family. **Impartible inheritance** leaves everything to a single heir. This preserves a family's estate while reducing most of its members to penury. **Primogeniture,** or exclusive inheritance by the eldest son, is the best-known form of impartible inheritance, but some peasant societies left everything to the youngest son on the theory that the eldest might not long survive his parents.

Everyone knew that partibility could impoverish and eventually destroy a family and that impartibility was grossly unfair and tended to destroy the family's bonds of affection. Many people therefore adopted strategies to circumvent the law or regional custom. Much of England, Scandinavia, and northern France had adopted primogeniture by the twelfth century. Bequeathing the bulk of a family's land to a single heir and making other provisions for noninheriting children while the parents were still alive became customary. A couple could also make special legacies in their wills that partially subverted the law's intent.

Where the law demanded partibility, strategies varied. In Italy and southern France, siblings entered into a variety of arrangements (*consorterie* in Italian) that helped preserve the integrity of the estate. Some sold or leased their portion to an elder brother in return for monetary or other considerations. Others agreed not to marry and remained on the family property.

Such arrangements worked best when there was an extended family structure or, at the very least, a strong sense of family identity. In Castile, the practice of entailing parts of an estate on behalf of a single heir began as early as the thirteenth century. Places like Galicia in northwest Spain and parts of southwest Germany illustrated the grim alternatives. Where the law mandated strict partibility, the inexorable subdivision of the land caused widespread misery among the peasants. Their plots soon became too small to support them. Even

among the princely families of Germany, partibility led to a bewildering proliferation of petty states incapable of sustaining themselves against more powerful rivals.

Marriage. The proportion of married people in the medieval population was probably lower than it is today. Many joined the church and became celibate. Far more remained single because they were too poor to support families. A majority, however, eventually married. In the peasant societies of northern Europe, this normally happened in the early or midtwenties for both men and women, a pattern now regarded as the Western norm (see Table 11.5). In southern Europe and everywhere among the upper classes, the custom was different. In Italy, husbands were on average 7 to 10 years older than their wives, and women in their teens often married men already in their thirties or older. The most extreme disparities were found in royal and princely families where marriages were used to cement political alliances and might be arranged when the

TABLE 11.5 AVERAGE AGE OF WOMEN AT FIRST MARRIAGE

Most of the statistics in the following table are taken from sixteenth- and seventeenth-century sources because data were not compiled outside of Italy in the Middle Ages. They are probably a reasonable approximation of medieval figures because the age at which women married does not seem to have changed substantially in the preindustrial period. It did, however, fluctuate according to economic conditions, as the figures from Colyton, Elversele, and Amsterdam demonstrate.

Question: Based on the discussion in the text, why are the data from Florence so unlike those from northern Europe?

PLACE	TIME PERIOD	AGE
Amiens (France)	1674–1678	25
Amsterdam	1626–1627	25
	1676–1677	27
Elversele (Flanders)	1608–1649	25
	1650–1659	27
England	1575–1624	21
Titled nobility	1625–1675	22
Village of Colyton	1560–1646	27
	1647–1719	30
Florence	1351–1400	18
	1401–1450	17
	1451–1475	19

Adapted from Cipolla, Carlo, *Before the Industrial Revolution*, 2nd ed. (New York: W. W. Norton, 1980, p. 154).

bride was a mere child. Thankfully, such unions were not immediately consummated.

Freedom to choose one's mate was greatest at the lower end of the social scale. Arranged marriages were almost unknown among the landless poor, slightly more common among established peasants, and virtually obligatory among the rich. However, families did not invariably ignore the wishes of the couple, and even peasants did not marry as a general rule without seeking their parents' blessing. Like almost everything else connected with the institution of marriage, a wedding was usually the product of delicate and informal negotiations involving the couple, both families, and the village opinion makers. The degree to which the couple controlled the process was determined by local custom and family attitudes and varied enormously within the same village or social class.

When a couple publicly announced their intention to marry, village opinion generally permitted them to begin living together immediately. The church officially confirmed this custom at the beginning of the thirteenth century because in villages without a resident priest, or when the costs of a wedding could not immediately be met, there was no other choice. If the couple produced a child before the sacrament of marriage could be officially celebrated, that child was legitimate. Village gossips as well as the priest assumed that the couple would marry as soon as the opportunity arose. Townspeople, wealthy peasants, and the aristocracy could afford to be less relaxed about such matters. They lived separately until the wedding and tended to celebrate the occasion with as much ostentation as possible. Wedding feasts were as central to medieval social life and folklore as they are today.

The Medieval Wife. When a medieval woman married, she was expected to present her husband with a **dowry,** or wedding gift in the form of land, cash, or other property. The early medieval custom of giving the bride a husband's gift had largely disappeared by the end of the twelfth century. If the husband died before his wife, his family returned the dowry if it had not already been spent. While alive, the husband controlled both the dowry and all of the other resources owned by the couple. In some regions, the return of the dowry was all that a widow could legally expect from her husband's estate. In others, she was entitled to at least a portion of his property. As in all other aspects of inheritance law, many husbands found ways to subvert the system and provide other legacies for their widow's support.

The choice, though, was his. Married women had few legal rights. They could not hold property in their own name. Although they were not to be killed or permanently maimed, they could be beaten with impunity and domestic violence appears to have been more frequent than it is today. In some jurisdictions, women could not testify in court. Where they could, their testimony was not equal to that of a man. However, legal status did not always reflect the balance of power in everyday life. No two relationships were, or are, the same, and medieval marriages ranged from the abusive to the happy and companionate. Medieval people presumably did not enter into marriage with modern expectations. The idea of romantic love had not yet fully developed and, to the degree that it existed at all, was associated with the adulterous conventions of chivalry.

Practical considerations governed the selection of a mate. Property, strength, temperance, and in the case of wives, the ability to bear children were essential considerations. Of course, everyone hoped that, given these virtues, *caritas* (charity) would find a place in the household and a genuine affection would develop with time.

Marriage and the Church. Many of these ideas and practices differed from those of the early Middle Ages. The church had adopted the institution of marriage as its own in the days of the Cluniac and Hildebrandine reforms and, despite its own mysogynistic traditions, had greatly improved women's circumstances as a result. Concubinage was condemned, if not eradicated, as was feudal interference in the marriage of vassals and tenants. Divorce, a catastrophe for women who had no means of support, became virtually impossible for all except the very rich. Canon law, confirmed by the Fourth Lateran Council of 1215, defined the terms under which a wedding might take place and spelled out the impediments that might prevent it. Most of them involved prohibited degrees of relationship or consanguinity, including godparenthood. Parish priests strictly enforced these regulations, which posed a considerable hardship for the inhabitants of remote villages.

Widowhood. These efforts can be seen as a positive step toward the development of patrilineal descent and companionate marriages, but they did not ensure domestic bliss. Hostility between the sexes remained a common theme in medieval writings. Many women deeply resented their subordinate status. Beginning in the early thirteenth century, increasing numbers sought refuge in the convent and widows frequently chose not to remarry. A woman who had passed the age of childbearing and who could claim property of her own experienced an immediate change of status upon the death of her husband. With her legal and personal rights restored, she could become a powerful figure in the village community. Some, such as Chaucer's Wife of Bath, remarried, but they did so usually to a younger, poorer man who posed little threat to their independence. Companionship aside, only the poor suffered from widowhood. Without property, a woman might have to depend on the kindness of her surviving children or become a semioutcast living on the charity of her neighbors.

Childhood, Old Age, and Death

In the natural law theories favored by the scholastic philosophers, the birth of children justified marriage. A medieval child was brought into the world by the village midwife and baptized as quickly as possible, lest the terrible infant mortality of the day carry it into Limbo (a sort of never-land, cut off from God yet free of the pains of hell) before its salvation was ensured. So deep was this concern that the sacrament could be administered by a layman if a priest was not available. Parents designated godparents, usually family friends, to support the child if they died. In southern Europe, they sometimes gave this role to a powerful friend or patron of the father. The baby was typically named for one of the godparents, a favored relative, or a patron saint. This practice, together with the limited number of names in contemporary use, sometimes resulted in more than one sibling having the same name. In everyday life, such children were differentiated by the calling them major or minor or by giving them nicknames.

Child-rearing Practices. If possible, most women preferred to nurse their own babies. They typically swaddled them in tightly wrapped cloths during the day. At night, babies sometimes slept with their mothers, although medieval experts, like their modern counterparts, frowned on this, fearing the mother might roll over in her sleep and smother the child. By the end of the first year, children were permitted to crawl about on their own. Medieval parents did not sentimentalize childhood as a world of innocence, but they loved their children and suffered emotionally if they died. This might seem self-evident, but it has been the subject of controversy. Some scholars have argued that the high infant mortality rate prevented parents from making an "emotional investment" in their children.

Parents encouraged their children to develop in stages not unlike those of today. Young children spent most of their time playing. As they grew older and stronger, they took on responsibility for various tasks until, in their mid to late teens, they began to do the work of adults. For most children, this kind of informal apprenticeship was the only education they would receive. Few villages had a school, and lords often claimed a fee from the parents if they sent their children away. Fearing that workers would be lost to the manor, they also sought agreements that forbade children to enter the church.

The little that is known about child-rearing practices comes from the end of the Middle Ages and seems to indicate that discipline was very harsh. This may not be applicable to earlier times. The fourteenth and fifteenth centuries were characterized by a deep fear of social disintegration and the perceived decline of parental authority. Criminals were punished more savagely than they had been before. Children, too, may have been increasingly victimized by the frustrations of society as a whole.

Orphans and Wicked Stepmothers. As efforts to circumvent the laws of inheritance indicate, parents made every attempt to provide for a child's future. This included the possibility of orphanhood, which was common in a world of high mortality rates. Godparents were nominally responsible for the care of children whose parents had died. More often, aunts, uncles, or other relatives undertook the task. Stepparenting was also common because men, at least, tended to remarry upon the death of their wives. This created a form of extended family that has become common again today as a result of divorce. Legends about wicked stepmothers indicate that the new relationships were often difficult for all concerned. However, stepparents who loved their spouse's children as their own were common enough to be accepted as the ideal.

Wardship in any form created problems because guardians sometimes exploited children financially or sexually. A substantial body of case law developed around these issues. Orphanages as such were unknown until the fourteenth century, when several Italian towns established hospitals for foundlings (so called because people left their infants to be found by others). The work of these institutions is not to be confused with **oblation,** in which parents gave children to the church by placing them in monastic houses at an early age. Such placements required a substantial donation. For the rich, oblation provided a living for children without encumbering the family estate. The practice fell into disfavor during the twelfth and thirteenth centuries, when churchmen began to realize that those consigned to a monastery or convent at the age of 7 did not always have a secure vocation.

Attitudes toward Children. Available evidence seems to indicate that medieval attitudes toward children were not radically different from those of today. Controversy aside, ample evidence demonstrates that medieval people loved their children and mourned them if they died. Most parents did whatever they could to ensure their children's futures. Noble families sent their sons to learn courtesy and the profession of arms in the household of a powerful friend or patron. Townsmen sent their children to be apprenticed, and those who could afford to do so offered them to the church at an early age. None of these practices imply indifference. They were in some ways analogous to sending a child to boarding school, and the normal expectation was that contact with the family would be maintained or, at least, resumed at some point in the future.

Death. Medieval attitudes toward death are less familiar to moderns. They were conditioned by the realization that life was likely to be short and by the universal belief in a hereafter. Medieval Christians saw death as a transition. The preservation of life, although an important value, was not the all-consuming passion that it has since become, in part because the soul was thought to live eternally. Thus, most jurists thought heresy to be worse than murder. Heresy killed the soul, whereas murder killed the body, which would perish in any case.

People tried to live as long as possible, but they also hoped to make a "good death." They knew that they had limited means for preserving life in the face of disease or injury and worried deeply about the future of their souls. When the end drew near, they prepared themselves with prayer, pious reflections, and the last rites of the church. They regarded suffering as a trial sent by God, to be borne with patience and Christian fortitude. Above all, they hoped to die with dignity, because death, like so many other aspects of medieval life, was a public affair. Medieval people wanted to die in their own beds, surrounded by family, friends, and neighbors who could ease their passage to a better world. Most of them appear to have succeeded. Hospitals were few and were intended for travelers, the homeless, and other unfortunates. The injured, if possible, were carried to their homes, and a priest was called if one was available. Not everyone died well, but edifying deathbed scenes were by no means uncommon and few people reached adulthood without having been present at a number of them. In a sense, death was a part of everyday experience.

Burial. Burial was in the churchyard. It, too, was a communal experience because space was limited and medieval villagers did not want to use good agricultural land as cemeteries. Archeological digs reveal that bodies were often buried several layers deep. The dead slept as they had lived—in close proximity to their friends and relatives without a monument to mark their passing. The wealthy, as in so many other things, were the exception. Their graves were marked, increasingly decorated by their effigies, and located indoors, either within the parish church or in a separate crypt. Husband and wife typically had themselves portrayed together, he in his armor and she in court attire. In the later Middle Ages, humility of a sort set in and tombs were sometimes adorned with effigies of corpses or skeletons, but the idea of the grave as a memorial to the deceased remained.

FIGURE 11.9 *Preparation for Burial.* Two women sew the corpse of a man into his shroud before placing him in his coffin. The domestic interior indicates that like most medieval people, he died at home and his corpse was prepared for burial by the women of his family. Detail from the *Hours of the Duke of Burgundy* (1454–1455).

CONCLUSION

Medieval society differed in almost every respect from that of the modern industrial world. The basic conditions of material life had changed little since the Neolithic revolution and would remain relatively constant until the Industrial Revolution. Chivalric and Christian values, however, influenced social behavior in ways unknown to the ancients. Those values achieved gradual acceptance in the early Middle Ages but would, at least among the privileged, undergo substantial modification in the centuries after the Black Death. The breakdown of the feudal system and the intellectual upheavals of the sixteenth and seventeenth centuries profoundly altered the behavior and self-perception of the upper classes. The lives of peasants changed more slowly. Without mass communication to inform them of changes in learning or fashion, they remained immersed in the demands of an agricultural routine that was much the same in the eighteenth century as it had been 500 years earlier.

For some, conditions may have grown worse with the passage of time. The lives of most Europeans in the twelfth and thirteenth centuries were simple and, by modern standards, hard, but society was more secure than it had been for many centuries. Wars were either limited or far away, and famines were rare. The activities of ordinary men and women, like the great intellectual and architectural triumphs of the age, reveal a certain confidence in the world's predictability and a willingness to build for the future. Yet society in the late thirteenth century was beginning to show signs of stress. There seemed to be too many people. They still ate, but poverty and landlessness were increasing. Wealthy people began to build moats around their houses to protect them from poorer neighbors, while moralists lamented the passing of a golden age. The following century would show that the moralists were in a sense correct: The relative balance of social and economic forces that characterized the High Middle Ages was giving way to conditions that people of all classes would find profoundly troubling.

Review Questions

- How does diet influence the rates of conception, birth, and mortality?
- Why was medieval society more vulnerable to epidemic disease than we are today?
- How were patterns of marriage and family structure in southern Europe different from those in the north?
- What role did cooperation normally play in village life?
- What are the differences and similarities of medieval child-rearing practices compared with those of today?

For Further Study

Readings

Duby, Georges, *The Chivalrous Society.* trans. C. Postan (London: Arnold, 1977). A study of upper-class life in the medieval west.

Duby, Georges, *Rural Economy and Country Life in the Medieval West.* trans. C. Postan (Columbia: University of South Carolina, 1968). A classic survey.

Hanawalt, Barbara, *The Ties that Bound: Peasant Families in Medieval England* (New York: Oxford, 1986). A vivid picture of English peasant life.

Le Roy Ladurie, E., *Montaillou,* trans. B. Bray (New York: Braziller, 1978). A bestseller that describes everyday life in a southern French village c. 1300 from contemporary documents compiled by the Inquisition.

Russell, Josiah Cox, *The Control of Late Ancient and Medieval Populations* (Philadelphia: American Philosophical Society, 1985). A basic work covering diet, disease, and demography.

InfoTrac College Edition

For additional reading, go to your online reasearch library at *http://infotrac.thomsonlearning.com.*

Using Key Terms, enter the search term: *peasantry*

Web Site

http://www.fordham.edu/halsall/sbook.html The Internet Medieval Sourcebook. Under the heading *Economic Life,* see "Rural Life." See also *Social History* and the more developed section, *Sex and Gender.*

MATERIAL AND SOCIAL LIFE IN THE MIDDLE AGES

1050	1100	1150	1200	1250	1300	1350

Average Life Expectancy of 25–32 Years Remained Generally Constant in These Years

Villages of 250–500 People (a Constant Feature from Neolithic Times to the Present)

Growth in Trade and Population — Economic Stagnation

Open-Field System and Commons (until the eighteenth century)

Improved Nutrition — Famines

Manorial Courts (until the seventeenth and eighteenth centuries in some places)

Increased Social Unrest

Black Death

First Four Crusades

Knighthood Becomes Hereditary

Age of the Troubadours
*Arhurian Romances of Chrétien de Troyes
*Fourth Lateran Council Defines Marriage Laws

Visit the Western Civilization Companion Web Site for resources specific to this textbook:
http://history.wadsworth.com/hause02/

The CD in the back of this book and the Western Civilization Resource Center at *http://history. wadsworth.com/western/* offer a variety of tools to help you succeed in this course, including access to quizzes; images; documents; interactive simulations, maps, and timelines; movie explorations; and a wealth of other sources.

The West in the World

FROM 500-1400

Throughout the Middle Ages, Europe was largely isolated from the rest of the world. The West knew little or nothing of the great civilizations of India and China and nothing at all about the Americas. Its contacts with the Islamic world grew, but for the most part, it remained hostile. That isolation was about to end. By 1300, India, China, and the Islamic world had become more interconnected, and Europe was beginning to accumulate the wealth and technological expertise that would enable it to play a more aggressive role in world affairs. The West, however, was still poorer and in some ways less sophisticated than its Asian neighbors.

India

Although a wealthier and somewhat less violent society, India's political development from 510 to about 1100 resembled that of medieval Europe. With the collapse of the Gupta Dynasty in 510, the Indian subcontinent became a patchwork of regional kingdoms, some of which aspired briefly to imperial status. Village organizations, trade guilds, and the caste system provided the basic structure of society. Beginning in 1141, Muslims from Afghanistan, most of them of Turkish origin, moved into Hindu areas of what is now Pakistan, and by 1202, a Muslim sultan ruled most of northern India from his capital at Delhi (Del'-ee). The new rulers made few efforts to convert the population, nor did they interfere in local government. Northern India remained a traditional Hindu society while paying tribute and taxes to a small group of Muslim rulers. Those rulers, however, derived much of their elegant culture from Persia and en-

joyed close ties to the rest of the Muslim world. Southern India remained beyond their reach and ruled by a succession of Hindu dynasties. Throughout this period, Indian commerce with both China and the Muslim west grew. Indian textiles, in particular, benefited from the invention of a wooden cotton gin and the spinning wheel.

China

By most measures, the classical age of Chinese civilization reached its peak under the Tang (618–906) and Sung (960–1269) dynasties. The Tang developed the system of imperial administration that lasted until 1911. The Sung created the civil service exams upon which it was based, and both dynasties encouraged astronomy, mathematics, and the arts. Imperial policy favored contacts with the outside world. Chinese missionaries brought Taoism, Buddhism, and Confucianism to Japan and Korea, and

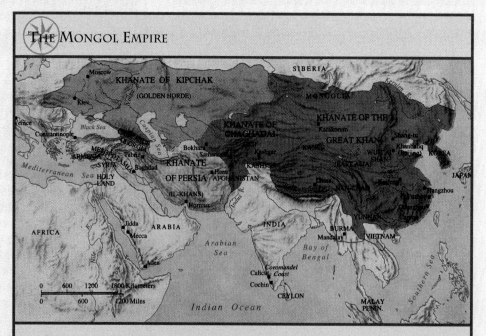

Within 50 years, the Mongols conquered most of the Eurasian landmass. Their empire was too large to rule as a single state, and they divided it into four segments, each ruled by a Khan. In Chinese history, the Khanate of the Great Khan is called the Yüan Dynasty.

Chinese merchants sailed regularly to Japan, Egypt, and the Persian Gulf. To protect this trade, the Sung emperors constructed a large navy. The financial system they developed was secure enough to permit the establishment of paper currency in 1204. By 1250, at least three Chinese cities had populations of more than 1 million.

The Islamic World

Medieval Europe's contact with Asia depended on its Muslim neighbors. After 861, the political unity of Islamic society diminished as the authority of the Caliph at Bagdad declined, but its cultural and economic vitality remained. The Muslims had long traded with India and China. The Crusades and the Christian reconquest of Spain, although deeply resented by Muslims, introduced Westerners to products of the East. Wealthier Europeans developed a taste for Indian spices and Chinese silks as well as the traditional products of the Middle East. Throughout the Middle Ages, the Western role in this trade remained marginal, small-scale, and largely indirect, but Europe was now taking its first steps into the world market. At the same time, a handful of western scholars discovered Muslim thought, which had preserved much of Greek philosophy and absorbed Chinese and Indian advances in mathematics and science. The ideas of Muslim thinkers helped spur the development of scholastic philosophy.

The Mongols

The Mongol invasions of the 1200s, although widely perceived as a disaster, facilitated even closer ties among the civilizations of the East. In 1280, Kublai Khan added China to the Muslim conquests in Russia, Persia, and Central Asia, thereby creating a sort of common market that embraced most of the Asian landmass. Kublai's Yüan Dynasty lasted less than a century in China, and Mongol rule in the rest of Asia was never centralized, although for a time the Mongol presence encouraged a higher level of communication and trade throughout Asia. Without it, the Venetian Marco Polo would not have been able to make his extraordinary journey to China.

The Americas

Most Europeans, of course, had little contact with Muslims or Mongols and no contact with the Indians and Chinese. Many who read the tales of Marco Polo did not believe them. Neither they nor the Asians knew much of Africa south of the Sahara, and no one had heard of the great civilizations then developing in the Americas. There was not even a rumor of the Mayans in Central America, of the Toltec civilization that emerged in the Valley of Mexico between 1000 and 1200, or of the complex societies that began to emerge in Peru as early as 200 BCE. Although progress had been made in commerce and in knowledge of the world, no one in 1400 could have predicted that in less than 100 years Europeans would be trading, fighting, and attempting to spread Christianity from America to Japan.

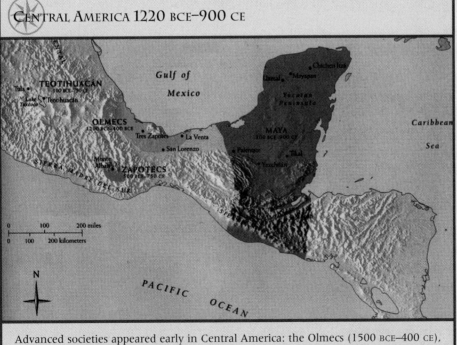

CENTRAL AMERICA 1220 BCE–900 CE

Advanced societies appeared early in Central America: the Olmecs (1500 BCE–400 CE), the Zapotecs in Oaxaca (500 BCE–800 CE), and Teotihuacán in the Valley of Mexico (1–750 CE). The Maya, in northern Guatemala and southern Yucatan after 300 CE, spread northward after 900.

FOCUS QUESTIONS

- What were the most important economic and social consequences of the Black Death?
- What caused the transformation of warfare in the fourteenth century?
- What were the causes of the Hundred Years' War?
- What were the major causes of conflict on Europe's eastern frontiers?

Chapter 12

PLAGUE, WAR, AND SOCIAL CHANGE IN THE LATE MIDDLE AGES

*I*n October 1347, a new and terrible disease appeared among Genoese sailors arriving in Sicily from the Black Sea ports. The victims displayed black swellings in the groin and armpits, followed by large black spots on the skin caused by internal bleeding. Most died after being in excruciating pain for 4 or 5 days. The disease spread silently from Sicily to the port towns of the Mediterranean and from there inland. Within 3 years, nearly one-third of Europe's population had died. In major cities such as Paris, the death toll was estimated at half the population. The *Black Death*, as it was called, followed a half-century of growing economic distress. Its psychological, religious, and economic impact was enormous, but the plague was only one of several disasters that befell Europe in the fourteenth century. The Hundred Years' War in the west and warfare on Europe's eastern frontiers accompanied a transformation in military affairs. Armies became larger, more complex, and above all, more expensive. Dynastic problems in France, England, and Spain threatened the monarchies. To many, the end of the world seemed at hand. In fact, the troubles of the fourteenth and fifteenth centuries marked not the end of the world but the beginning of a transition from medieval to early modern times. War, plague, and economic change weakened the bonds of feudal society and undermined its values. New institutions began to evolve, but few Europeans greeted them with hope or confidence.

Chapter 12 begins with the economic decline that reached a peak between 1315 and 1343. It then describes the Black Death of 1347–1351 and its consequences, including social unrest and the partial breakdown of feudal and manorial ties. The fourteenth-century transformation of warfare, however, had little to do with the Black Death. Its origins are found in financial and technological developments that profoundly affected monarchies already threatened with dynastic failure. The causes of military change are analyzed together with the centers of conflict in which they developed. The chapter concludes with a brief look at art and literature in an age of pessimism, if not despair.

FAMINE, ECONOMIC DECLINE, AND THE BLACK DEATH (1315–1350)

The fourteenth century was marked by a series of economic and demographic crises that had a profound effect on the social structure of Europe. Local crises of subsistence became common, and for the first time in two centuries, a large-scale famine struck northern Europe in 1315–1317 (Document 12.1). Southern Europe suffered a similar catastrophe in 1339–1340. Overpopulation was the underlying cause. By 1300, only the cultivation of marginal soils could feed the ever-growing populace. A succession of bad harvests brought on by unusually cold, wet weather made these lands virtually unusable and destroyed the ecological balance between the people and their food supply. The result was widespread misery and an end to population growth.

Scarcity pushed the price of bread to levels that only the rich could afford. Desperate peasants ate their seed grain, thereby destroying all hope for a harvest in the year to come. Others ate leaves, bark, and rats. Although adult deaths from malnutrition were probably rare, the demographic impact of the famine was seen in a declining rate of conception and increased infant mortality.

Decline of Trade. Predictably, trade declined. Defaults on loans increased, and the banking system came under stress. The great international banks still controlled their branches directly and had unlimited liability for their losses. If a branch failed, it created a domino effect that might bring down the entire structure. This happened in 1343, when the two leading Florentine banks—the Bardi (Bar'-dee) and the Peruzzi (Pair-ootz'-zee)—failed, setting off a widespread financial panic. The immediate cause of their failure was the repudiation of war debts by a major borrower, Edward III of England, but both banks had been gravely weakened before the final blow.

The Black Death

The Black Death struck in 1347–1351. Endemic in Asia since the eleventh century, the disease first entered Europe through the Mediterranean ports and spread with terrifying speed throughout the subcontinent. Following the trade routes, it reached Paris in the summer of 1348, Denmark and Norway in 1349, and Russia in 1351. Estimates are that within 4 years, one-third of the population of Europe died. It was the greatest demographic catastrophe in European history, and its ravages did not end with the first virulent outbreak. Subsequent epidemics occurred regularly in every decade until the beginning of the eighteenth century. Given that immunity apparently cannot be transmitted from generation to generation, the plague served as a long-term check on population growth, and most countries required more than two centuries to recover the population levels they had in 1300 (see Table 12.1).

Causes of the Plague. The relationship, if any, between the plague and poverty or malnutrition is unclear. In its most common form, bubonic plague is spread by fleas, which are carried by rats and other small mammals. A pneumonic form of the plague is

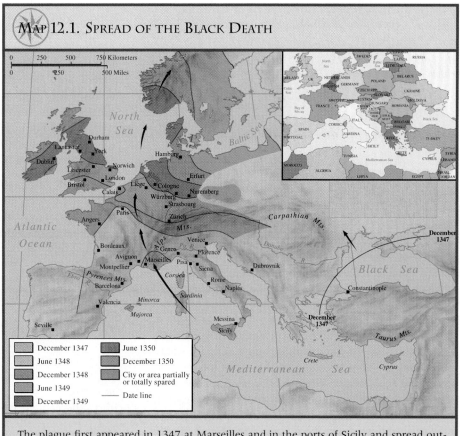

MAP 12.1. SPREAD OF THE BLACK DEATH

December 1347
June 1348
December 1348
June 1349
December 1349
June 1350
December 1350
City or area partially or totally spared
Date line

The plague first appeared in 1347 at Marseilles and in the ports of Sicily and spread outward from these original centers of contagion along the routes of trade and communication. The pattern shown by this map typifies the way in which epidemics progress.

THE FAMINE OF 1315 IN ENGLAND

This dramatic account of the famine is from the English chronicler Johannes de Trokelowe. The cause of the famine was a prolonged period of cold, wet weather that made it impossible for the crops to ripen. This is typical of famines in northern Europe. In the south, the usual cause of famine is drought and heat.

Meat and eggs began to run out, capons and fowl could hardly be found, animals died of pest, swine could not be fed because of the excessive price of fodder. A quarter of wheat or beans or peas sold for twenty shillings, barley for a mark, oats for ten shillings. A quarter of salt was commonly sold for thirty-five shillings, which in former times was quite unheard of. The land was so oppressed with want that when the king came to St. Albans on the feast of St. Lawrence [August 10] it was hardly possible to find bread on sale to supply his immediate household. . . .

The dearth began in the month of May and lasted until the nativity of the Virgin [September 8]. The summer rains were so heavy that grain could not ripen. It could hardly be gathered and used to make bread down to the said feast day unless it was first put in vessels to dry. Around the end of autumn the dearth was mitigated in part, but toward Christmas it became as bad as before. Bread did not have its usual nourishing power and strength because the grain was not nourished by the warmth of summer sunshine. Hence those who had it, even in large quantities, were hungry again after a little while. There can be no doubt that the poor wasted away when even the rich were constantly hungry. . . .

Four pennies worth of coarse bread was not enough to feed a common man for one day. The usual kinds of meat, suitable for eating, were too scarce; horse meat was precious; plump dogs were stolen. And according to many reports, men and women in many places secretly ate their own children.

From Trokelowe, Johannes, "Annales," in *Sources of Medieval History,* 4th ed, trans. and ed. Brian Tierney (New York: Knopf, 1983).

Question: How do these prices compare with those given for the preceding century in Chapter 11, Table 11.1?

spread by coughing. The onset of either form is rapid, and death usually comes within 3 days. The mortality rate seems to have been about the same for all who contracted the disease, so lowered resistance as a result of malnutrition likely did not play an important part in its spread. At the same time, death came most frequently to those who lived in crowded conditions. Soldiers, ships' crews, and the urban poor were at greatest risk, followed by those country folk whose poverty forced them to huddle together in their one-room cottages for warmth. The rich often escaped, either because they lived in more sanitary conditions or because, like the characters in Giovanni Boccaccio's (Joe-vahn'-ee Boe-kotch'-ee-oh) *The Decameron,* they had the means to flee from the centers of population.

No one knew what caused the plague. Most probably believed that it was a visitation from God and took refuge in prayer and religious ceremonies. Flagellants paraded from town to town, beating each other with metal-tipped scourges in the hope of averting God's wrath, while preachers demanded the reform of the church on the theory that its increasing interest in secular affairs had provoked divine retribution. Some have argued that the plague created a genuine and long-lasting demand for spiritual renewal. However, other, more sinister reactions occurred as well. In parts of Germany, whole communities of Jews were burned alive because they were thought to have spread the disease by poisoning wells.

The Economic Consequences of the Black Death

The psychological effects of the Black Death would have a profound impact on religious belief, but its material consequences were equally dramatic (see Table 12.1). Demographic collapse relieved pressure on the land. Food prices dropped immediately. Land values and rents followed close behind, declining by 30 to 40 percent in most parts of Europe between 1350 and 1400. For landholders, both lay and religious, this was a serious loss; for ordinary men and women, it was a windfall. Stunned by the horror they had experienced, the survivors found not only that food was cheaper and land more abundant but also that most of them had inherited varying amounts of property from their dead relatives.

Improved Nutrition. The delicate ecological balance of the thirteenth century improved. Acreage could be diverted to pursuits that were less efficient in purely nutritional terms but more profitable and less labor intensive. Fields were converted to pasture for grazing sheep and cattle. Marginal lands in Germany and elsewhere reverted to forest where hogs could root at will and where the next generation of peasants could presumably find cheap firewood and building material. A larger percentage of the grain crop was devoted to the brewing of beer, and in the south, vineyards spread over hillsides upon which in earlier times people had sought to grow food. If the prosperity of Europeans may be measured by their consumption of meat and alcohol, these were comfortable years. Some historians have referred to the period after the Black Death as the golden age of European peasantry. It did not last long.

Shortage of Labor. For most people, calorie and protein consumption undoubtedly improved. Wages, too,

THE SYMPTOMS OF THE PLAGUE

Monks with Plague Being Blessed by a Priest. Jacobus Omne Bonum, English, 1360–1380.

A description of the Black Death survives from one of the greatest of the late medieval writers. In 1348–1353, Giovanni Boccaccio, who would later become a founder of Renaissance humanism (see Chapter 13), wrote *The Decameron,* a series of stories told in a villa outside Florence, where a group of fashionable young people take refuge from the plague. The book begins with a description of the epidemic.

In the year of our Lord 1348, there happened at Florence, the finest city in all Italy, a most terrible plague; which, whether owing to the influence of the planets, or that it was sent from God as a just punishment for our sins, had broken out some years before in the Levant, and after passing from place to place, and making incredible havoc all the way, had now reached the west. There, in spite of all the means that art and human foresight could suggest, such as keeping the city free from filth, the exclusion of all suspected persons, and the publication of copious instructions for the preservation of health; and not withstanding manifold humble supplications offered to God in processions and otherwise; it began to show itself in the aforesaid year, and in a sad and wonderful manner. Unlike what had been seen in the east, where bleeding from the nose is the fatal prognostic, here there appeared certain tumors in the groin or under the armpits, some as big as a small apple, others as an egg; and afterwards purple spots in most parts of the body; in some cases large and but few in number, in others smaller and more numerous—both sorts the usual messengers of death. To the cure of this malady, neither medical knowledge nor the power of drugs was of any effect; whether because the disease was in its own nature mortal, or that the physicians (the number of whom, taking quacks and women pretenders into the account, was grown very great) could form no just idea of the cause, nor consequently devise a true method of cure; whichever was the reason, few escaped; but nearly all died the third day from the first appearance of the symptoms, some sooner, some later, without any fever or accessory symptoms.

From Boccaccio, Giovanni, "The Decameron," in *Stories of Boccaccio,* trans. John Payne (London: The Bibliophilist Society, 1903, p. 1).

Question: What public health measures did the city of Florence take to prevent the spread of plague?

---

increased, because the plague created a labor shortage of unprecedented severity. In Italy, employers tried to compensate by purchasing slaves from the Balkans or from dealers in the region of the Black Sea. This expedient was temporary and not successful. Before 1450, Turkish expansion brought an end to the trade, and although the Portuguese imported African slaves throughout the fifteenth century, they for the most part remained in Portugal. The handful of Africans who served the households of the very rich made no impact on the labor market. Wages remained high, and many people were able for the first time to leave their ancestral homes in search of better land or higher pay. Hundreds of communities were abandoned completely.

Such movements cannot be accurately traced, but the century after 1350 appears to have been a time of extraordinary mobility in which the traditional isolation of village life diminished greatly.

The Reaction of the Propertied Classes. These developments provoked a reaction from the propertied classes. Caught between rising wages and declining rents they faced a catastrophic reduction in their incomes. With the passage of time, some eased the situation by turning to such cash crops as wool or wine. Their initial response was to seek legislation that would freeze wages and restrict the movement of peasants. Between 1349 and 1351, virtually every European government

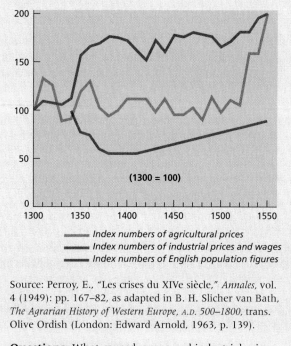
tried to fix wages and prices (see Document 12.3). For
the most part, their efforts produced only resistance.

The failure of such measures led to strategies based
on the selective modification of feudal agreements.
New restrictions were developed, and long-forgotten
obligations were revived. Southwest Germany provides
some instructive examples. Peasants subject to one lord
were often forbidden to marry the subject of another. If
they did so, their tenures would revert to the husband's
lord after the couple's death. Because population movements had created a situation in which few subjects of
the same lord inhabited the same village, this practically
guaranteed the wholesale confiscation of peasant estates. At the same time, landlords increasingly denied

peasants access to the forests, whose game, wood, nuts,
and berries they reserved for themselves or sold. These
new "forest laws" created enormous hardships and
were similar in their effects to the enclosure (legalized
confiscation) of common lands by the English gentry a
century later. Peasants who depended on these resources for firewood and for a supplement to their diet
might be driven from the land.

Sale and Privatization of Land. When such measures failed to raise enough money, landholders often
sold part of their holdings to investors. If the land in
question was held in fief, a sale usually required the
permission of the liege lord and could be secured by a
cash payment or in return for political favors. Some of
the buyers were merchants, lawyers, or servants of the
crown who wanted the status provided by a country estate. Others were simply landholders who sought to
consolidate their holdings at bargain rates. In either
case, the purchase of land tended to eliminate feudal
obligations in fact and sometimes in law. The new owners had no personal ties to the peasants on their newly
acquired estates and felt free to exploit their property as
efficiently as possible. The net effect was to accelerate
the shift toward private ownership of land that had begun with the commutation of feudal dues in the twelfth
and thirteenth centuries.

Princes, too, were affected by the drop in land values. Medieval rulers drew the bulk of their ordinary
revenues from exploiting their domains. Domain revenue came from a variety of dues, rights, and privileges,
as well as from rents, which were an important part of
the whole. Most princes were happy to make common
cause with the other great landholders or to compensate for their losses by levying new taxes.

SOCIAL DISORDER (1358–1382)

The Jacqueries. Attempts to reverse the economic
trends set in motion by the plague created widespread
discontent. In 1358, much of northern France rose in
bloody revolts called *Jacqueries* (Zhahk-er-ees; *Jacques
Bonhomme* being more or less the French equivalent of
John Doe). Peasants attacked the castles of their lords in
some of the worst outbreaks of social violence in centuries. There was no program, no plan—only violence
born of sheer desperation. In this case, peasant distress
was greatly aggravated by that portion of the Hundred
Years' War that had ended with the French defeat at
Poitiers (Pwah'-tyea) in 1356. The countryside was
devastated, and the peasants were taxed to pay the ran-
soms of the king and his aristocratic followers who had
been captured by the English on the battlefield.

Wat Tyler's Rebellion. Other revolts grew less from
poverty than from the frustration of rising expectations.

The English revolt of 1381, known as **Wat Tyler's Rebellion** in memory of one of its leaders, was triggered by the imposition of a poll or head tax on every individual. The rebels saw it as regressive, meaning it fell heavier on the poor than on the rich, and as a threat to the economic gains achieved since the plague.

The Bundschuh Revolts. In Germany, the exactions of princes and landholders, including the clergy, provoked a series of rebellions that flared periodically throughout the fifteenth century and culminated in the great Peasant Revolt of 1524–1525. These are generally referred to as the *bundschuh* (boont'-shoe) revolts after the laced boots that served as a symbol of peasant unity. Like the Jacqueries and Wat Tyler's Rebellion, these revolts were brutally suppressed by the princes.

Economic Change and Urban Unrest. Towns experienced great unrest as well, but the relationship of this violence to the plague and its aftermath is unclear. The overall volume of European trade declined after 1350, but this decline was offset to some extent by continuing strength in the market for manufactured and luxury items. A more equitable distribution of wealth broadened the demand for clothing, leather goods, and various furnishings, while the rich, in an apparent effort to maintain their status in the face of economic threats, indulged in luxuries on an unprecedented scale. The trade in manufactured articles, although smaller in total than it had been in the thirteenth century, was therefore larger in proportion to the trade in bulk agricultural commodities. It was also more profitable. Towns, now considerably smaller, seem to have enjoyed a certain measure of prosperity throughout the period.

Flanders and Germany. The new importance of manufacturing, however, changed the balance of politics. Craft guilds and the artisans they represented grew generally stronger at the expense of the urban patriciate, whose rents were greatly reduced in value. The process was not entirely new. The Flemish cloth towns of Ghent, Bruges, and Ypres had been the scene of periodic revolts for a century before 1350, and outbreaks continued for years thereafter. By 1345, the guilds had triumphed, at least in Flanders, but this in itself failed to create tranquility. The patriciate refused to accept exclusion from the government, and various factions among the guilds fought among themselves to achieve supremacy. Given the chronic discontent among the mass of laborers, most of whom were not guild members and were therefore disenfranchised, it was easy to incite riots almost regardless of the cause. The disturbances in the German towns of Braunschweig (1374) and Lübeck (1408) were apparently of similar origin. Political factions were able to mobilize popular discontent in the service of their own decidedly nonpopular interests.

DOCUMENT 12.3

"THE STATUTE OF LABORERS"

Issued by Edward III of England in 1351, this is a typical example of legislation designed to restrict the increase in labor costs created by the Black Death. Kent is a shire or county in the far southeast of England. The sheriff was the king's chief officer in the county and therefore the person normally designated to carry out his orders.

The King to the sheriff of Kent, greetings; Because a great part of the people, and especially of working men and servants, have lately died of the pestilence, many seeing the necessity of masters and great scarcity of servants, will not serve unless they may receive excessive wages, and others preferring to beg in idleness rather than by labor to get their living; we, considering the grievous incommodities which of the lack especially of ploughmen and such laborers may hereafter become, have upon deliberation and treaty with the prelates and the nobles and the learned men assisting us, with their unanimous counsel ordained: That every man and woman of our realm of England, of what condition he be, free or bond, able in body, and within the age of sixty years, not living in merchandise, nor exercising any craft, nor having of his own whereof he may live, nor land of his own about whose tillage he may occupy himself, and not serving any other; if he be required to serve in suitable service, his estate considered, he shall be bound to serve him which shall so require him; and take only the wages, livery, meed, or salary which were accustomed to be given in the places where he oweth to serve, the twentieth year of our reign of England [that is, in 1347], or five or six other common years next before.

From "The Statute of Laborers," from *Pennsylvania Translations and Reprints*, vol. 2, no. 5, trans. Edward P. Cheyney (Philadelphia: University of Pennsylvania Press, 1897).

Question: What does this statute reveal about upper-class attitudes toward the poor?

Rome. The revolts of 1382 in Paris and Rouen (Rooahn') appear to have been more spontaneous and closer in spirit to the rural uprisings of the same period, but the seizure of Rome by Cola di Rienzi (Ko'-la dee Ree-en'-zee) in May 1347 was unique and unrelated to the economic effects of the plague. Demanding a return to the ancient Roman form of government, he raised a great mob and held the city for 7 months under the title of tribune. The whole episode remains the subject of historical controversy. It was clearly related to the absence of the pope at Avignon (Ah'-veen-yon; see Chapter 14). The departure of the papal court in 1305 had wrecked the Roman economy and placed the city's

FIGURE 12.1 *Wat Tyler. 1381.* On June 15, Wat Tyler's peasant army (shown here, improbably, in full body armor) met King Richard II (then 14) at Smithfield, near the City of London. Wat Tyler (forefront in red), believing from Richard's earlier promises that he was sympathetic to the peasants, made further demands. Enraged, the Mayor of London (on the left) struck and killed him. Turning to the peasants, the king diffused the conflict by declaring himself their leader (upper right). Showing the king twice in the same painting was a common way of illustrating his different roles in the action.

government in the hands of such old aristocratic families as the Orsini and the Colonna. Popular dissatisfaction kept the city in turmoil for several years even after the great families forced Rienzi into exile.

The Ciompi Revolt. The revolt of the Florentine *Ciompi* (chom'-pee) in 1378 was the culmination of 30 years of civic strife. The depression of 1343 had led the *popolo grasso* (literally, "fat people") to betray their city's republican traditions by introducing a despot who would, they hoped, control the population. The subsequent revolt led to a government dominated by the minor, craft-oriented guilds and to the incorporation of the semiskilled wool carders (i.e., ciompi) into a guild of their own. In 1378, the Ciompi seized control of the city and introduced a popular and democratic form of government that lasted until the great merchants of the city hired a mercenary army to overthrow it in 1382.

Consequences of the Revolts. Few of these rebellions, urban or rural, had clearly developed aims, and none of them resulted in permanent institutional changes beneficial to the rebels. For the most part, the privileged classes found them easy to suppress. The wealthy still possessed a near monopoly of military force and had little difficulty in presenting a united

front. Their opponents, although numerous, were poor and usually disorganized. Communication among different groups of rebels was difficult, and outbreaks of violence tended to be as isolated as they were brief. These rebellions probably did not pose a fundamental threat to the existing social order, but they inspired fear. The chroniclers, who were by definition members of an educated elite, described appalling scenes of murder, rape, and cannibalism. They noted that women sometimes played a part in the agitation and regarded this as a monstrous perversion of nature. True or exaggerated, these accounts made it difficult for readers to sympathize with the rebels. Mass executions and new burdens on the poor usually followed the restoration of order.

The Behavior of the Nobility. In general, the social disorders of the fourteenth century weakened whatever sense of mutual obligation had been retained from the age of feudalism and probably hastened the trend toward private ownership of land. Moreover they increased the fear and insecurity of the elite, who reacted by developing an attitude of increased social exclusivity. The division between popular and elite culture became dramatic at about this time. The tendency was to ridicule and suppress customs that had once belonged to rich and poor alike but were now regarded as loutish or wicked.

Meanwhile, an impulse that must have been largely unconscious led the upper classes into new extravagance and the elaboration of an extreme form of chivalric excess. The tournaments and banquets described in the Chronicle of Jean Froissart (Zhan Frwa-sart, c. 1333–1400) surpassed anything that an earlier age could afford and were at least partially inspired by the flowering of chivalric romance as a literary form. Ironically, this "Indian summer" of chivalry occurred not only amid social and economic insecurity but at a time when the feudal aristocracy was losing the remnants of its military function.

THE TRANSFORMATION OF WARFARE (1295–1450)

Fourteenth-century Europe suffered not only from famine and plague but also from war. Although the age was probably no more violent than others before or since, the scale and complexity of warfare increased in

FIGURE 12.2 *Mercenary.* This woodcut by the Swiss military artist, Jost Amman (1539–1591) shows a mercenary being paid. He appears to be a member of one of the mercenary companies still being raised by Swiss cantonal governments in the early 1500s to fight for France or the pope. A mercenary is paid to fight for someone other than his own ruler. By 1400, rulers were also paying their own subjects to fight for them. These subject troops were not regarded as mercenaries.

highly visible ways. By 1500, it appeared that the preceding 200 years had witnessed a military revolution.

The Emergence of the Soldier.

Long before the Black Death, the feudal system of warfare had begun to break down. The warrior was becoming a soldier. The term *soldier* is used here in its original meaning: a fighting man who receives a cash payment, or *solde,* for his efforts as opposed to one who serves in return for land or for the discharge of some nonmonetary obligation. This was an important development, not only because it changed the way in which wars were fought but also because it altered the structure of western European society.

The increase in real wealth and in the circulation of money between 1000 and 1250 allowed princes to alter the basis of military service. The revival of trade augmented their revenues, which were based in part on import–export duties and occasional levies on moveable goods. Beyond that, the commutation of military and other services for cash helped create substantial war revenues exclusive of taxes. Scutage (a tax levied in commutation of military services), the payment of knight's fees, and similar arrangements by which even the feudal class could escape military service in return for cash payments are first noted in the midtwelfth century. By 1250, they had become commonplace. In 1227, Emperor Frederick II demanded 8 ounces of gold from every fief in his realms, but only one knight from

every eight fiefs. A quarter century later, the pope declared his preference for money over personal service from his vassals. They used the money to hire mercenaries or to pay knights to extend their service, often for an indefinite period.

The case of Edward I of England is typical. He spent much of his reign trying to subjugate the neighboring Welsh and Scots. If he abandoned these efforts every autumn when his feudal levies went home, his new subjects would simply reclaim the areas he had conquered. To create full-time garrisons, he therefore contracted with certain knights on a long-term basis, paying their wages from the proceeds of knight's fees and from the nine great taxes on moveable property he collected between 1297 and 1302.

The need for long-service troops and the superior professionalism of those who fought year in and year out for their livelihood made feudal levies increasingly obsolete. By 1340, unpaid feudal service had become rare in western Europe, although the crown was not yet the sole paymaster of its armies. Some lords continued to pay men from their own estates to fight for the king, and city governments paid their town militias if they accompanied the royal army. This changed by the midfifteenth century in England and France and by 1480 in Spain. Although towns and nobles might still be called on to provide equipment, most armies, whether comprised of the king's own subjects or of mercenaries provided by contractors, were now paid entirely by the crown.

The Polish Exception.

The major exception to this state of affairs was found in eastern Europe. In Poland, a numerous class of small and middling gentry continued to perform unpaid military service throughout the fifteenth century. Those who account for this by pointing to the frontier character of Polish society would be wrong. In Hungary, one of Europe's most exposed frontiers, even the *banderia,* a heavy cavalry unit comprised of noblemen, was paid in cash at an early date, and the armies of King János Hunyadi (Yah'-nosh Hun'-ya-dee, c. 1407–1456) and his son, Matthias I, were comprised largely of mercenaries.

The First Soldiers.

The first soldiers were probably poor knights or younger sons whose only inheritance was a sword, a horse, and a sound training in the profession of arms. They were soon joined by paid infantry, most of whom came from different social worlds. The fourteenth century also saw the evolution of infantry tactics that required either specialized skills or exceptional discipline and cohesion in battle. Given that those who possessed such training were rarely part of traditional feudal society, they, too, had to be paid in cash.

New Missile Weapons and Tactics.

The skills were largely associated with the development of new or

FIGURE 12.3 *The Crossbow and the Longbow.* The English soldier on the right holds a longbow. The French soldier on the left is pulling back the string of his crossbow using a small winch activated by a crank. Crossbows were accurate and powerful, but they were slow to rewind. The longbow was equally accurate and powerful, but it had a much faster rate of fire. A good longbowman could often fire six shots to the crossbow's one. The chief drawback of the longbow was that it required a lifetime of training and worked best in the hands of those who had used one since childhood.

improved missile weapons. Archery had always been a factor in medieval warfare, but its effectiveness had long ago been diminished by improvements in personal armor. The introduction of the crossbow therefore marked the beginning of a major change. This weapon offered great accuracy and powers of penetration, although at a relatively slow rate of fire. Originating in the Mediterranean, it was first used as a naval weapon and found special favor among the shipmasters of Genoa and Barcelona as a defense against pirates. Men selected and trained for this purpose had become numerous in the port cities of the western Mediterranean by 1300 and transferred their skills to land when the volume of maritime trade declined. The Genoese were especially noted for their service to France during the Hundred Years' War; natives of Barcelona and Marseilles were not far behind.

The advent of the crossbowmen marked an alien intrusion into the world of feudal warfare, and many knights resented it. Their world held little place for the urban poor. However, the involvement of marginal people with deviant forms of social organization was only beginning. The famous longbow was another case in point. Basically a poacher's weapon, it evolved beyond the edges of the feudal world in Wales and the English forests. Edward III introduced it in the Hundred Years' War with devastating effect. The longbow combined a high rate of fire with penetration and accuracy superior to that of early firearms. It required many years of training to be properly used. Because most of those who were expert in its use were marginal men in an economic and social sense, they were usually happy to serve as mercenaries.

Handguns followed a similar pattern. First seen in Italy during the 1390s, they achieved importance in Bohemia during the Hussite wars of the midfifteenth century. When peace returned, companies of handgun men found employment in Hungary and in the west.

Massed Infantry Formations. The emergence of the pike as a primary battle weapon in the fifteenth century overshadowed all of these weapons. The pike was a spear, 12 to 16 feet in length. Simple and cheap, it was used in a square formation similar to the Macedonian phalanx. If the pikemen stood their ground, it could stop a cavalry charge or clear the field of opposing infantry. Massed infantry formations of this kind had been neglected during most of the Middle Ages, because such tactics were incompatible with feudalism as a social system. Knights did not want peasants trained in the art of war, especially in a system meant to negate the advantages of heavy cavalry.

Pikemen had to be highly motivated and carefully trained to meet a cavalry charge without flinching. In medieval Europe, only two forms of social organization had the means or the motivation to create such a force: the city and the peasant league. Medieval towns were surrounded by enemies. In areas where princely authority was weak (Italy, the Low Countries, and parts of Germany), they developed effective armies at a relatively early date. Most towns lacked either extensive territory or a large native nobility trained in the profession of arms, so they had to rely on the creation of citizen militias supplemented on occasion by mercenaries. Townsmen who could afford to bought horse and armor and tried to fight like knights. Most served with pike or halberd (a long-handled battle-axe) and drilled on Sundays and holidays until they achieved a level of effectiveness far superior to that of peasant levies. The victory of the Flemish town militias over the chivalry of France at Courtrai (Koor-tray') in 1302 was a promise of things to come.

The Swiss. By 1422, pike tactics had been adopted by the Swiss Confederation, one of several peasant leagues

FIGURE 12.4 *Pikes in Action.* This illustration of the opening of a battle between formations of pikemen is a detail from *The Terrible Swiss War* by Albrecht Altdorfer, c. 1515. It commemorates an episode in 1499, when the Swiss achieved independence from the Holy Roman Empire after a fierce struggle with Emperor Maximilian I. The imperial forces are shown on the left; the Swiss, on the right. The painting shows the units coming into action with the "fall" of pikes as the pikemen "port their pikes" and level them at the throats of their opponents.

the feudal world had demanded little more than justice and military leadership from its kings, the new warfare demanded the collection and distribution of resources on an unprecedented scale.

The Development of New Military Technologies.

The monarchies of Europe were at first unprepared for such a task, and a contemporary revolution in military technology compounded the difficulties they faced. The development of Western technology is often seen as a sporadic affair in which periods of innovation were interspersed with longer intervals of slow, almost imperceptible change. This is an illusion that comes from thinking of the inventions themselves instead of the complex process that created them, but periods certainly existed during which breakthroughs occurred at an accelerated rate. One of these was the later Middle Ages. Few of the changes had an immediate impact on everyday life, but their effects on war, trade, and government were great.

formed in the later thirteenth century to preserve their independence from feudal demands. The successful defense of their liberties earned them a formidable military reputation, and after 1444, the Swiss were regularly employed as mercenaries by the French and by the pope. Other poor peasants in south Germany followed their example, emulated their system of training, and hired themselves out to the emperor and other princes. Pike squares remained a feature of European armies for 200 years, and mercenary contracting became an important element in the Swiss and south German economies.

The Decline of Cavalry.

The emergence of paid troops, new missile weapons, and massed infantry tactics changed the character of European warfare. By the end of the fourteenth century, armies had grown larger and cavalry was declining in importance. The social consequences of these changes were profound because they tended, among other things, to monetarize the costs of war. The simplest form of feudal warfare had required little cash. Men served without pay and normally provided their own food and equipment in the field. Feudal levies consumed resources in kind, but these costs rarely involved the state. This changed dramatically with the advent of the soldier, because only a sovereign state could coin money or raise taxes. Because feudal nobles could rarely do either, they gradually lost their preeminent role as the organizers of war while the eclipse of cavalry reduced their presence on the battlefield. During the fifteenth century, many great feudal families began to withdraw from the traditional function as protectors of society, leaving the field to men who served the sovereign for pay and privileges. In the process, the state, too, was transformed. Where

Artillery.

The development of artillery and portable firearms is a case in point. Evolution began with the invention of gunpowder. The black powder used until the late nineteenth century is composed of charcoal, saltpeter, and sulfur. In Europe, saltpeter was first identified in the twelfth century. How or why it was combined with charcoal and sulfur is unknown, but Roger Bacon mentioned the mixture in 1248. At that time, it seems to have been used chiefly for blasting in mines. The obstacles to its use in guns are fully documented. Saltpeter was scarce and expensive. Discovering the correct ratio of ingredients and powder grains of the proper consistency required years of experimentation. Mistakes were often fatal, for black powder is not totally safe or dependable in use and its chemistry has only recently been understood. Nevertheless, the invention of gunpowder presented fewer problems than the construction of the guns. Metallurgy, not powder milling, controlled the pace of artillery development.

The first guns, which appeared around the middle of the fourteenth century, were hand forged from wrought-iron bars and bound with iron hoops, a technique that made them heavy, expensive, and prone to bursting when fired. Despite these drawbacks, they re-

THE EVOLUTION OF ARTILLERY

Sieges were often more important than battles in determining the outcome of a medieval war, but the introduction of artillery between 1350 and 1450 changed the basic principles of siege warfare.

An Early Iron Gun. The trebuchet was accurate, but gunpowder artillery was more powerful. This piece from the 1400s is typical of the earliest guns. The barrel was hand-forged from iron, and the breach (at the rear, right in the picture) unscrewed for loading. The design of such guns made them prone to bursting from hairline cracks in the barrel, and they were slow to reload because the threading of the breach expanded from the heat of firing and had to cool before it could be removed. In practice, second shots were often loaded from the muzzle.

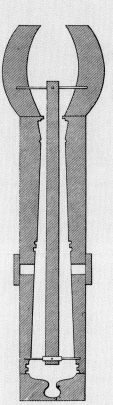

Gun-Casting Technique (after c. 1450). Guns cast from bronze (a mixture of copper and tin) were cheaper and more reliable than their iron predecessors. As this diagram shows, the gun was cast around a core that was lowered into the mold and centered by an iron "cross" that was left in the casting. The pouring head shown at the top of this drawing added weight to increase the density of metal at the bottom of the mold. This ensured that the mixture of tin and copper would not segregate during cooling and weaken the breach, which was, of course, where the greatest pressures occurred in firing. The pouring head was sawed off after the casting process was complete. Such guns were always loaded from the muzzle.

mained dominant until the middle of the fifteenth century, when guns cast from bronze superseded them. The bronze used was approximately 80 percent copper and 20 percent tin, and gun production required more of both metals than the market could supply. Finally, in 1450, German miners developed a process that extracted copper from ores in which copper and silver mingled. Large, previously unusable deposits in Saxony, Hungary, and Slovakia could now be exploited, and copper (as well as silver) production increased dramatically. The introduction of bronze cannons was further delayed by the lack of adequate furnaces and by an inability to deal with a physical property characteristic of bronze. Copper and tin tend to segregate as they cool, causing variations in the strength of the metal that might cause the guns to burst when fired.

Fortification. It required generations of experience to solve these problems, but by the 1460s, large numbers of bronze cannons began to appear in European armories. Within a half-century, every fortress in Europe

had become obsolete, for the high, relatively thin walls of medieval fortifications could withstand no more than a few hours of battering by the big guns. Towns and strongholds in militarily exposed areas had to rebuild if they were to survive. Between 1500 and 1530, Italian engineers developed a system of fortification that set the pattern for defensive works until the nineteenth century. Walls were lowered and thickened to widths of 40 feet or more. Bastions became wedge-shaped and were laid out geometrically so that every section of wall could be covered by the defender's guns. The works were then surrounded by a broad, steep-sided ditch that was usually faced with brick or stone.

The cost of all this was enormous. The guns themselves were expensive and required large numbers of skilled men and draft animals to maneuver. The new fortifications required less skill to construct than their medieval predecessors, but they were far larger in scale and therefore costly. The development of artillery had increased the already heavy burden of warfare on states and subjects alike.

THE EVOLUTION OF MEDIEVAL SHIP DESIGN

These three illustrations from contemporary sources show the evolution of medieval ship types described in the text. The most important developments were the adoption of the fixed, centerline rudder and the divided rig, in which different types of sails were carried for greater flexibility. The lateen sail, originally developed by the Arabs, enabled ships to sail closer to the wind.

A Venetian Merchantman, 1300. The ship's faintly Byzantine appearance reflects the strong links between Venice and Constantinople. Rising from the waterline, the stem is swept back, and the whole bow area is strengthened with double planking. The hull has a pronounced sheer, and the steerboards over both sides are protected by quarter-circular shields. Projecting out from the hull, the tops of these effectively formed side galleries. The ship had two decks, indicated by the rows of through-beams, and while some merchantmen had three lateen-rigged masts, most had only two, with the shrouds held taut by the Mediterranean-style block. In either case, the foremast had a noticeable forward rake, and access to the barrel-like lookout tops was by means of a "Jacob's ladder."

The Earl of Warwick's Cog, 1480–1485. The clinker-built hull and curved stem of this massive vessel are typical of northern European ship construction until about 1500. Like all cogs, it had a square stern and a rudder fixed to the hull on the centerline. It has four masts, with a single square sail on the fore, main, and mizzen masts, and a lateen sail on what was called the bonaventure mizzen. The yards and lookout tops are reached by "ratlines" fastened to the hull, and the running rigging (the elaborate network of lines used to set and furl the sails) is clearly shown. Warwick's coat of arms covers the entire mainsail. Note that guns have been mounted in the waist of the ship, projecting over the upper wale (later known as the gunwale). In 1501, French shipbuilders began to pierce the hull for gunports, which enabled them to carry the weight of the guns lower in the ship for greater stability.

Changes in Shipbuilding Technique. The development of navies, although not taking place in earnest until the sixteenth century, would have a similar effect. It rested upon changes in shipbuilding that by the fifteenth century had created vessels capable of crossing an ocean or using artillery in a ship-to-ship duel. The new ships resulted from a hybrid cross between two traditions of shipbuilding—the Mediterranean and the north European. The ships changed the world as few innovations have done before or since.

The dominant ship types in the medieval Mediterranean were the galley and the round ship. The galley was intended primarily for war. Long, narrow, and light, its chief virtues were speed and maneuverability independent of the wind. However, it was too fragile for use in the open Atlantic or for extended use in its home waters between October and May. It also lacked carrying capacity, and this, together with its high manpower requirements, limited its usefulness. Although galleys were sometimes used for commerce, especially by the

Venetians, the preeminent Mediterranean cargo carrier was the round ship. As its name implies, it was double-ended and broad of beam with a high freeboard. Steered like a galley by side rudders located near the stern, it normally carried a two-masted rig with triangular lateen sails (see *The Evolution of Medieval Ship Design*). The round ship was not fast or graceful, but it was safe, roomy, and thanks to its high freeboard, relatively easy to defend against boarders. Its caravel-type construction was typically Mediterranean. The hull planking was nailed or pegged edge on edge to a skeleton frame and then caulked to create a watertight hull in which the framing rather than the planks provided rigidity.

The ships of northern Europe were different. Most were clinker-built like the old Viking longships with overlapping planks fastened to each other by nails or rivets. Their variety was almost infinite. By the middle of the thirteenth century, the cog had emerged as the preferred choice for long voyages over open water. Of Baltic origin, the cog was as high and wide as the roundship. A long, straight keel and sternpost rudder made it different from and more controllable than its Mediterranean counterpart. The Genoese, in ships designed for their Atlantic trade, adapted caravel construction to this design to create a lighter, cheaper hull with greater carrying capacity.

The final step was the addition of multiple masts. Shipbuilders soon discovered that a divided rig reduced manning requirements because smaller sails were easier to handle. It also made possible the use of different sails, combined according to need, thereby increasing speed and maneuverability under a wider variety of conditions. With Portuguese, Dutch, and Basque innovators leading the way, a recognizably modern ship had evolved by 1500.

Given the military rivalry among states, a marriage between the new shipbuilding techniques and the cast bronze cannon was inevitable. The full tactical implications of this were not immediately apparent, but by the last quarter of the fifteenth century, the major states had begun to acquire ships capable of mounting heavy guns. The competition to control the seas was on, and no state with maritime interests could afford to ignore it.

Europe's Eastern Frontiers (1240–1453)

German Settlement in the East. For much of the later Middle Ages, the great North European Plain, where it made a borderless transition into Asia, was in turmoil. East of the Elbe River, two great movements were underway. The first was the eastward expansion of the German-speaking peoples. Population growth in the twelfth and thirteenth centuries led to the establishment of German settlements in Poland, Lithuania, and the Baltic regions, as well as in Transylvania and the Ukraine. The movement was not always peaceful, bringing the Germans into conflict with the Slavs who inhabited the region. Relations improved little with time, and the German "colonies" tended to remain isolated from their neighbors by linguistic barriers and mutual resentments. In its later phases, German expansion in the northeast was led by the **Teutonic Knights,** a military order on the crusading model. From the midthirteenth century, the Knights attempted the large-scale conquest of Slavic as well as unclaimed land on which they encouraged German peasants to settle.

The Mongol Invasions. On its eastern fringes (see Document 12.4), the Slavic world came under equal pressure from the Mongols. The Mongols were a nomadic people who pastured their sheep and horses on the high plains of central Asia. **Genghis Khan** (1162–1227; the name means "universal ruler") unified their many clans and tribes and set them on the path of world conquest. After 1230, their armies, comprised largely of light cavalry, moved westward, and by 1240–1242, they had conquered most of Russia and the Ukraine. In 1241, they defeated an army of Poles and Teutonic Knights in Silesia, but they advanced no further into Europe. Genghis Khan's grandson, Kublai Khan conquered China and in 1279 established his capital at what is now Beijing.

For the next 200 years, the Mongols retained at least nominal control over much of Russia and its neighbors to the south and east. They, and their descendants, are sometimes called *Tartars* or *Tatars*. The center of resistance to Mongol rule became the grand duchy of Moscow, founded by the son of the Russian hero, Alexander Nevsky. Nevsky had defeated a Swedish invasion in 1238 and the Teutonic Knights in 1240. His descendants had to concern themselves almost exclusively with Asia. Although continuing to pay tribute to the Mongol khans, the Muscovites engaged in sporadic warfare with them until 1480 when Ivan III refused payment and became, in effect, the first tsar. An early sign of the grand duchy's regional importance was the transfer of the Russian Orthodox patriarchate from Kiev to Moscow in 1299.

Formation of Poland-Lithuania. During the fourteenth century, Russian preoccupation with the Mongols encouraged the Teutonic Knights to step up their activities in the Baltic. The Catholic kingdom of Poland, established early in the eleventh century, and a rapidly expanding Lithuanian state whose rulers were still pagan provided resistance. In 1386, the two states merged for mutual defense. Under the leadership of the Lithuanian King Jagiello (Ya-gee-el'-lo), who converted to Catholicism and became king of Poland as well, the Knights were defeated at the battle of Tannenburg in 1410.

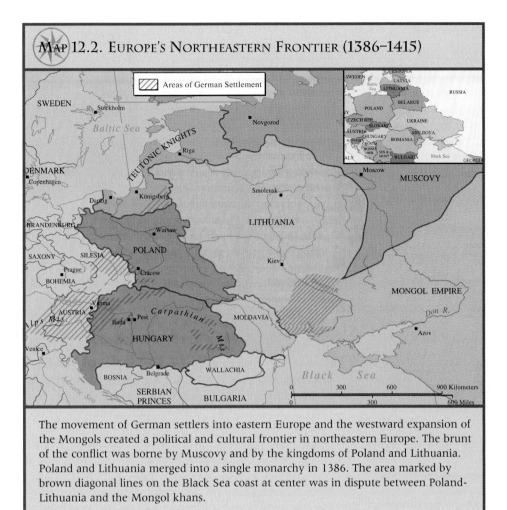

MAP 12.2. EUROPE'S NORTHEASTERN FRONTIER (1386–1415)

Areas of German Settlement

The movement of German settlers into eastern Europe and the westward expansion of the Mongols created a political and cultural frontier in northeastern Europe. The brunt of the conflict was borne by Muscovy and by the kingdoms of Poland and Lithuania. Poland and Lithuania merged into a single monarchy in 1386. The area marked by brown diagonal lines on the Black Sea coast at center was in dispute between Poland-Lithuania and the Mongol khans.

Jewish Settlement in Poland-Lithuania. The Knights no longer existed as an aggressive force, but conflict did not end. Poland-Lithuania did not evolve into a centralized territorial state. It remained an aristocratic commonwealth with an elected king and few natural defenses. However, it was at this time a remarkably open society in which people of many faiths and languages could coexist. It even became the place of refuge for thousands of Jews. Driven from western Europe by the persecutions that followed the Black Death, they found that their capital and financial skills were welcomed by the rulers of an underdeveloped frontier state. The parallels with the Iberian kingdoms are striking. By the midfifteenth century, Poland and Lithuania were the centers of a vigorous Jewish culture characterized by a powerful tradition of rabbinic learning and the use of Yiddish, a German dialect, as the language of everyday speech.

The Ottoman Advance in the Balkans. To the south, in the Balkan Peninsula, the fourteenth and fifteenth centuries marked the emergence of the **Ottoman Empire** as a threat to Christian Europe. By

1300, virtually all of the Byzantine lands in Anatolia had fallen under the control of *ghazi* (gah'-zee) principalities. The ghazis, of predominantly Turkish origin, were the Muslim equivalent of crusaders, pledged to the advancement of Islam. The last of the ghazi states to possess a common frontier with Byzantium centered on the city of Bursa in northwest Anatolia. Under the aggressive leadership of Osman (1258–1324), the first Ottoman state offered the opportunity for continued warfare to ambitious men from all over the Turkic world and a refuge to others who had fled from the Mongol advance in central Asia. With its population swelled by thousands of immigrants, the tiny emirate became the nucleus of the Ottoman Empire.

From the beginning, the Ottomans were a serious threat to the Byzantine state revived by Emperor Michael Paleologus after the Fourth Crusade. Deprived of his Anatolian heartland and caught between the Ottomans on one side and the Serbian Empire of Stephen Dushan (d. 1355) on the other, the Greek emperor was only one of many regional princes striving for preeminence in the tangled world of Balkan politics. Taking advantage of divisions among the Christians, Osman's son, Orkhan, ordered the first Turkish invasion of Europe in 1356. The best hope of expelling him lay in an alliance between the Serbians and the Bulgarians. A history of mutual distrust inhibited their cooperation, however, and the Serbian army was defeated in 1371. By 1389, the Turks had achieved military predominance in the peninsula.

The Fall of Constantinople. The threat to Constantinople was now imminent, and the Greeks sent missions to Rome in the hope of enlisting western support against the Turks. Negotiations broke down over theological and other issues. The pope was reluctant to compromise, and some Greeks came to believe that the Latin Church posed a greater threat to the survival of their religion than Islam. From the

Plague, War, and Social Change in the Late Middle Ages 283

THE NOVGOROD CHRONICLE

Novgorod was an important trading city north of Moscow. This excerpt from its city chronicle provides a vivid picture of conditions on Europe's eastern frontier in the year 1224. It provides a measure of the confusion caused by the first appearance of the Mongols in the midst of simultaneous attacks by the Germans and Lithuanians.

A.D.1224. Prince Vsevolod Gyurgevits came to Novgorod. The same year the Germans killed Prince Vyachko in Gyurgev and took the town. The same year, for our sins, this was not [all] the evil that happened: Posadnik [an elected official somewhat resembling a burgomaster or mayor] Fedor rode out with the men of Russia and fought with the Lithuanians; and they drove the men of Russia from their horses and took many horses, and killed Domazhir Torlinits and his son and of the men of Russa Boghsa and many others, and the rest they drove asunder into the forest. The same year, for our sins, unknown tribes came, whom no one exactly knows, who they are, nor whence they came out, nor what their language is, nor of what race they are, nor what their faith is, but they call them Tartars. . . . God alone knows who they are and whence they came out. Very wise men know them exactly, who understand books, but we do not know who they are, but have written of them here for the sake of the memory of the Russian princes and of the misfortune which came to them from them.

From *The Chronicle of Novgorod, 1016–1471*, trans. Robert Michell and Nevill Forbes, Camden Society, 3rd series, vol. 25 (London: Camden Society Publications, 1914).

Question: Why do you think that the chronicler knew nothing of the Tartars (Mongols) who attacked his city?

---

standpoint of Western intellectual development, this contact between Greek and Latin scholar-diplomats would have far-reaching consequences; politically it was a failure.

Meanwhile, southeastern Europe settled into a period of almost chronic warfare. The Serbs and Bulgarians were restless and unreliable tributaries of the Turks. The Byzantine emperor lacked a credible offensive force, but the Albanians remained a threat. In the northwest, the Hungarians were growing uneasy. Eventually, a crusade was organized by János Hunyadi, the *voivod* (prince) of Transylvania who would one day become king of Hungary. His defeat at Varna in 1444 and again on the plain of Kossovo in 1448 left the Turks in control of virtually everything south of the Danube. Only the Albanian mountains and Constantinople remained free.

In 1453, the great city, now seriously depopulated, fell to Mehmet "the Conqueror" after a long siege. The Byzantine Empire ceased to exist. The church of St. Sophia became a mosque, and the Greeks, together with the other Balkan peoples, became subjects of the Ottoman sultan. They preserved their faith and much of their culture, for the Turks did not believe in forced conversions, but the Greeks would not regain political independence until the nineteenth century.

Mehmet the Conqueror

THE HUNDRED YEARS' WAR AND ITS AFTERMATH (1337–C. 1470)

The Hundred Years' War, although centered on France and England, became a generalized west European conflict that also involved the Low Countries and the Iberian kingdoms of Castile, Aragon, and Portugal. Because its active phases were interspersed with periods of relative peace, the Hundred Years' War can be regarded not as one conflict but as several whose underlying causes were related. The most important of these causes, however, was the ongoing struggle over the status of English fiefs in France. With time, dynastic instability and the weakening of feudal institutions further complicated an already difficult situation.

The Conflict between France and England. Of all the problems created by feudalism, none was more exasperating than the ambivalent situation of the kings of England. For two centuries, they had struggled with their dual role as French vassals and as sovereign princes whose interests frequently conflicted with those of France (see Chapter 8). Every reign since that of Henry II had produced disputes over Guienne (Gwee-yen') and Gascony, the vast English holdings in southwest France.

Edward I of England and the Rise of Parliament. Among the more serious was the dispute between **Edward I** of England (1272–1307) and **Philip IV** (the Fair; 1285–1314). In addition to his invasions of Wales and Scotland, Edward fought several campaigns in France. To finance them, he relied on **Parliament,** which became for the first time an important factor in English politics. Parliament had originally been little more than a meeting of the Great

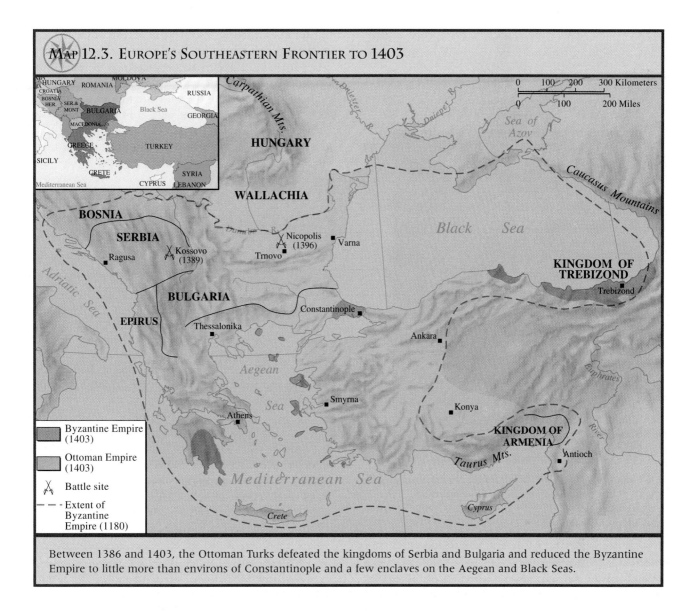

Map 12.3. Europe's Southeastern Frontier to 1403

Between 1386 and 1403, the Ottoman Turks defeated the kingdoms of Serbia and Bulgaria and reduced the Byzantine Empire to little more than environs of Constantinople and a few enclaves on the Aegean and Black Seas.

Council, in which the king's vassals provided him with advice. In 1295, Edward invited two knights from every county and two representatives from each chartered city to consider new taxes. They met with the lords, both secular and ecclesiastical, and eventually expanded their responsibilities to include legislation on other matters.

Philip IV and the Reform of French Government. In 1302, Philip created the first **Estates-General** for the same reason. The principle of "no taxation without representation" had long been universal in western Europe. Both kings needed the consent of their subjects if they were to finance their policies, and only a representative body could provide it. Philip also strengthened his administration by dividing it into

three parts: an advisory council; a *chambre de accounts*, or council of finance; and a *Parlement* that was actually the equivalent of a supreme court. By 1337, the two kingdoms had become far better organized and more representative than their purely feudal predecessors.

The Outbreak of War. The Hundred Years' War began in spring 1337, when Philip VI (1328–1360) ordered the confiscation of English fiefs in France. His action came at the end of a long diplomatic crisis. Nearly a decade earlier, Philip had been proclaimed king when his cousin, Charles IV, died without male heirs. England's **Edward III** (1327–1387) also claimed the throne as the son of Charles's sister, but the French Parlement denied his claim on the controversial premise that the Salic law forbade royal inheritance

FIGURE 12.5 *The English Parliament.* In this illustration, Edward I (reigned 1272–1307) presides over a session of parliament early in his reign. The justices and law officers (center) sit on woolsacks that symbolize the most important source of the kingdom's wealth. The lords are on the right, and the bishops and abbots are on the left. Two clerks seated on one of the woolsacks in the foreground record the proceedings.

through the female line. Edward, young and beset with internal enemies, chose not to press the point. Relations gradually deteriorated when Philip began to pursue more aggressive policies on several fronts. In the year of his coronation, he recaptured the county of Flanders from the urban rebels who had achieved independence from France at Courtrai in 1302. This represented a threat to the primary market for English wool, as Philip was now in a position to forbid its importation into the Low Countries. Worst of all, he began to support Edward's enemies in Scotland. By 1336, Edward was secure on his throne and began preparing for war. Papal attempts at mediation failed, and in May 1337, Philip ordered the confiscation of Gascony and Guienne, citing Edward's support for the Flemish rebels and other sins against feudal obligation as a pretext.

The First Phase of the War: Crécy and Poitiers. The first phase of the war went badly for France. This is at first sight surprising, as England was by far the smaller and poorer of the two countries with a population only one-third that of her rival. The difference lay in superior leadership. Edward quickly proved to be not only an able commander but also a

master at extracting resources from the English Parliament. By defeating the French in a naval battle off Sluys in 1340, Edward secured control of the English Channel. Subsequent cam- paigns were fought on French soil, including the ones that culminated in the victories of **Crécy** (Kray'-see, 1346) and **Poitiers** (1356). In both cases, French cavalry employing traditional tactics were defeated by the imaginative use of longbows in massed formations.

War in Spain. The treaty of Bretigny (Bret-in-yee, 1360) secured a breathing space of 7 years, during which time the locus of violence shifted to the Iberian Peninsula. Conflict there centered on the policies of Pedro of Castile, known to the Castilian aristocracy as "the Cruel" and to his other subjects as "the Just." Pedro's nicknames arose from his efforts to strengthen the crown against the landed nobility. When he became involved in a border war with Pedro "the Ceremonious" of Aragon, the latter encouraged an uprising of Castilian nobles under the leadership of Enrique (Enree'-kay) of Trastámara, Pedro the Cruel's half-brother. Enrique and his Aragonese ally then sought assistance from France.

They received it in part because of a phenomenon that surfaced for the first time after the peace of Bretigny. The practice of paying troops had created a class of men whose only trade was war and who, after a generation of fighting, had no place in civilian society. For them, peace was a catastrophe that forced them to become beggars or bandits. Most, understandably, chose the latter. Roaming the countryside, often in their original companies, they lived by systematic pillage and extortion reinforced by the threat of murder, arson, and rape.

The new French king, Charles V, was happy to dispatch a multinational contingent of these people to Spain under the command of Bertrand Du Guesclin (Du-Ge-klahn). Pedro of Castile responded by calling in the English under Edward of Woodstock, known as the Black Prince. The eldest son of Edward III and the winning commander at Poitiers, he repeated his triumph at Nájera (Na'-hair-a) in 1367. The Castilian war dragged on until 1398, when Enrique killed Pedro with his own hands and gained the throne. Because Enrique had won with the aid of the Castilian aristocracy, he was forced to confirm and extend their privileges, thereby guaranteeing that his successors would be faced with internal disorder. His victory was a defeat, not only for Pedro, but also for the state-building ideals he represented.

Revival of the War in France. An after-effect of the Spanish war was the pretext for reviving Anglo-French hostilities. To pay for his Castilian adventure, the Black Prince so taxed his subjects in Guienne that they appealed to Charles V for help. The war that followed was far less dramatic than the first. Charles adopted a strategy of attrition, avoiding battle whenever possible and using the tactical skills of Du Guesclin to harry and outmaneuver the English. By 1380, the English presence in France had been greatly reduced, but both kingdoms were at the limit of their resources. Fighting did not end completely. The next 35 years may be characterized as a period of military stalemate and internal disorder in both countries.

Agincourt. The last stage of the war began when Henry V of England invaded the continent in 1415. Ambitious and new to the throne, he sought to take advantage of the civil war then raging in France. The French king, Charles VI, had gone mad. His brother, the Duke of Orléans (Or-lay-ahn'), was named regent, thereby arousing the envy of John the Fearless, Duke of Burgundy. Burgundy was perhaps the most powerful of the king's relatives. His

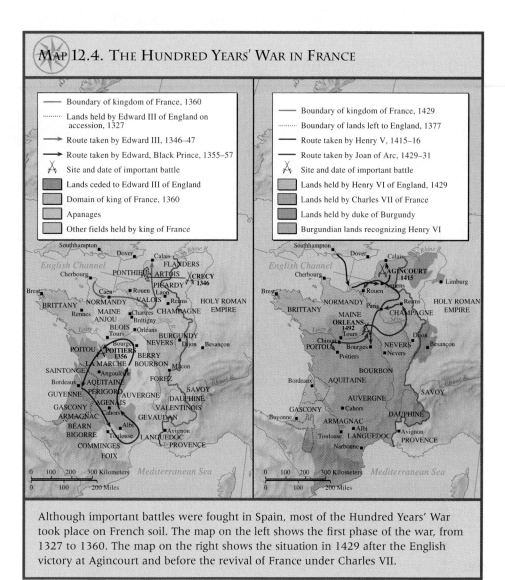

MAP 12.4. THE HUNDRED YEARS' WAR IN FRANCE

Boundary of kingdom of France, 1360
Lands held by Edward III of England on accession, 1327
Route taken by Edward III, 1346–47
Route taken by Edward, Black Prince, 1355–57
Site and date of important battle
Lands ceded to Edward III of England
Domain of king of France, 1360
Apanages
Other fields held by king of France

Boundary of kingdom of France, 1429
Boundary of lands left to England, 1377
Route taken by Henry V, 1415–16
Route taken by Joan of Arc, 1429–31
Site and date of important battle
Lands held by Henry VI of England, 1429
Lands held by Charles VII of France
Lands held by duke of Burgundy
Burgundian lands recognizing Henry VI

Although important battles were fought in Spain, most of the Hundred Years' War took place on French soil. The map on the left shows the first phase of the war, from 1327 to 1360. The map on the right shows the situation in 1429 after the English victory at Agincourt and before the revival of France under Charles VII.

appanage (estates granted to members of the ruling family) included the rich duchy of Burgundy and most of what is now Belgium and the Netherlands. He was probably wealthier than the king. John arranged the assassination of the Duke of Orléans in 1407 only to see another rival, Count Bertrand VII of Armagnac (Ar-man-yak), installed in his place. In the struggle that followed, Burgundy tried to ally himself with England, drawing back when he perceived the extent of Henry's ambitions. The English king saw that John would do nothing to defend Charles VI or his Armagnac supporters.

The English invasion was an immediate success. Using a variant of the tactics developed at Crécy and Poitiers, Henry and his longbow-men crushed the French at **Agincourt** (Ahj-in-koor) on October 25, 1415. Alarmed by the magnitude of the French defeat, Burgundy began to rethink his position, but he, too, was assassinated in 1419 by soldiers in the pay of the Armagnacs. His son, Philip, whose nickname "the

Good" belied a ferocious temper, sought revenge by allying Burgundy once again with England.

The French king was virtually isolated. In 1420, he was forced to ratify the treaty of Troyes, which disinherited his son, the future Charles VII, in favor of Henry V. When Charles VI and Henry both died in 1422, Henry's infant son, Henry VI of England, was proclaimed king of France with the English duke of Bedford as regent. The proclamation aroused great indignation in much of France where Charles of Valois (Val-wah) was accepted as the rightful king. Charles, unfortunately, was not an inspiring figure. Inarticulate, physically unimpressive, and only 19 years old, he retired with his supporters to Bourges (Boorzh), where he quickly developed a reputation for lethargy and indecision. The task of galvanizing public opinion fell to an extraordinary woman, **Joan of Arc.**

Joan of Arc. Joan was an illiterate peasant from the remote border village of Domrémy. When she came to

THE HUNDRED YEARS' WAR

Crécy (1346). The first great battle of the Hundred Years' War occurred in 1346 at Crécy, France, a few miles from the English Channel. The French, under Philip VI, lost more than 10,000 men; the English, only about 200. The English won largely because of their effective deployment of the longbow, a missile weapon hitherto unseen on the Continent. In this illustration, the English, with their longbows, are shown on the right; the French knights, covered by a few crossbowmen, are on the left.

Poitiers (1356). In 1356, the Black Prince, son of Edward III of England, defeated the French again at Poitiers with tactics similar to those used at Crécy.

Charles in March 1429 she was probably no older than 20 but had already achieved local fame for her religious visions. She told him that "voices" had instructed her to raise the English siege of Orléans, and Charles, who probably thought that he had little to lose, allowed her to go. The result was electrifying. By the time she arrived, the English had decided to give up, but the French did not know this. The apparently miraculous appearance of a young woman, dressed in armor and with her hair cut like a man's, was thought to have been the reason for the subsequent English retreat, and it created a sensation. The relief of Orléans, which preserved the south of France for Charles, was followed by a string of victories that led to the repudiation of the treaty of Troyes and his coronation at Rheims (Reemz) in July. All of this was popularly attributed to Joan, who was present throughout. She never commanded troops, but her inspiration gave them confidence, and even civilians, oppressed by a century of apparently pointless warfare, were roused to enthusiasm.

Unfortunately for Joan, Charles was not quite the fool he sometimes appeared to be. When she was captured by the English in 1430, he did nothing to secure her release or to prevent her from being tried at Rouen on charges of witchcraft and heresy. He no doubt preferred to take credit for his own victories and may have regarded her popularity as an embarrassment. The verdict was a foregone conclusion. Bedford discredited her as an agent of the devil and had her burned at the stake on May 30, 1431. Her habit of dressing as a man was taken as evidence of diabolical intent. Twenty-five years later, in a gesture of belated gratitude, Charles VII reopened the case and had her declared innocent. The church made her a saint in 1920.

Agincourt (1415). In October 1415, the English, under Henry V, defeated a far larger French army at Agincourt. The French are shown on the left retreating after charging over a plowed field at a prepared English position. The English archers, shown at right, killed hundreds of them before they reached the English knights. French casualties came to more than 6,000; the English lost fewer than 400.

Joan of Arc meets Charles VII of France at Chinon (1429). Charles VII's reversal of fortune began when he met Joan of Arc at Chinon in 1429. The Maid, as she was called, is shown here in armor and on horseback (center). Although she did not actually fight, her example helped inspire the French to raise the siege of Orléans, one of the first engagements in which artillery played an important part.

Joan's brief career offers a disquieting vision of fifteenth-century attitudes toward women, but it was a turning point for France. In 1435, Charles reconciled with Philip the Good of Burgundy, and by 1453, the English had been driven out of France in a series of successful campaigns that left them with only the port of Calais (Ka-lay) as a continental base.

Dynastic Collapse and Political Turbulence.

Dynastic failures played a major role in continuing and intensifying the Hundred Years' War. In a system based on heredity, the failure of a ruling dynasty to produce competent heirs in a timely manner meant either a disputed succession or a regency. The effect of a disputed succession may be seen in the origins of the war itself, in which the failure of all three of Philip IV's sons to produce heirs gave Edward III of England a pretext for

his quarrel with Philip of Valois, or in Castile, where a similar failure by Pedro the Cruel encouraged the pretensions of his half-brother Enrique.

Regencies occurred when the legitimate heir could not govern by reason of youth or mental incapacity. An individual regent or a regency council might be designated in the will of a dying monarch or by agreement within the royal family, but these appointments were almost always contested. The reason lay in the structure of European elites. Each branch of the royal family and each of the great landholding clans were a center of wealth, power, and patronage to which other elements of society were drawn by interest or by hereditary obligation. Rivalries were inevitable, and the king's duty was to serve as a kind of referee, using his superior rank to ensure that no one became an "overmighty subject." His subjects equated the king's failure to perform this role in an adequate manner with bad governance.

By these standards, no regency could be good. Regents were usually either princes of the blood or connected with a particular faction of the royal family. They were partial almost by definition. Once installed, they often used the wealth and power of the crown to advance their factional interests while threatening the estates and the lives of their rivals. Those excluded from a regency often believed that they had no alternative but to rebel, although their rebellions were usually directed not at the semisacred person of the king, but at his "evil counselors." This happened in the struggle between John the Fearless and the Armagnacs. The result was a civil war and renewed English intervention in France.

Castile. Other forms of dynastic failure had similar effects. In some cases, adult, presumably functional, rulers behaved so foolishly that their subjects rebelled. Castile in particular suffered from this ailment throughout much of the fifteenth century. Juan II (1405–1454) left the government in the hands of Alvaro de Luna (Ahl'-va-ro day Loo'-na), a powerful noble whose de facto regency factionalized the grandees, the highest rank of Spanish nobles who were not princes of the blood. Juan's son, Enrique IV "the Impotent" (1454–1479), was generally despised for his homosexuality, his tendency to promote his low-born lovers over the hereditary nobility, and his failure to maintain order. Faced with a monarchy they could neither support nor respect, the great landholding families raised private armies and kept the country in a state of near-anarchy until 1479.

England. In England, the regency appointed during the minority of Richard II (1377–1399) was accepted largely because the social unrest that culminated in the revolt of 1381 forced the aristocracy to close ranks. When he came of age, the favoritism and ineptitude of the young king aroused such opposition that he was deposed and murdered in 1399. The leader of the faction that deposed him, Henry of Lancaster, seized the throne as Henry IV (1399–1413). Reflecting contemporary attitudes, Richard II, like Enrique IV of Castile, was accused of homosexuality. The reign of Henry VI (1422–1461 and 1470–1471) was even more chaotic than that of Richard II. Coming to the throne as an infant, Henry remained under the control of others throughout his life. Although respected for his piety, he was wholly incapable of governing and suffered a complete mental breakdown in 1453. His incapacity led to the **War of the Roses,** a 9-year struggle between the Lancastrian and Yorkist branches of the royal family that ended with a Yorkist victory at Tewksbury in 1471

and the murder of yet another English king (see Chapter 13).

Whether the result of royal inbreeding or sheer bad luck, these dynastic failures retarded the development of western European states. The increasing cost of and sophistication of war were a powerful impetus to the growth of royal power, but these anarchic interludes tended to interfere with bureaucratic development and to strengthen local privilege, at least temporarily. Feudal nobles whose position was threatened by economic and military change often saw them as an opportunity to recover lost ground. Above all, they added to the sense of dislocation created by plague, war, and social change.

ART AND LITERATURE IN THE LATER MIDDLE AGES (1350–1450)

By the end of the fourteenth century, the accumulation of disasters was having an impact on the art and literature of Europe. The bonds of society seemed to be unraveling. Lords abandoned their ostensible func-

FIGURE 12.6 *The Triumph of Death.* In this fresco from about 1360, wealthy travelers fleeing from the plague find whole villages dying of pestilence and famine (livestock and poultry also died of the plague). The rider on the left is pointing to open coffins holding bloated corpses while another rider covers his nose. Paintings on this theme were common throughout much of Europe for decades after 1350 and were intended to remind the viewer that neither wealth nor youthful beauty could protect them against death. This one, attributed to Francesco Traini, dominated the Camposanto in Pisa, Italy.

tion as the military protectors of society and compensated for declining rents by preying upon their tenants. Peasants responded when they could by abandoning their tenures. The idea of mutual obligation that lay at the heart of feudalism could no longer be sustained, and many, including the fourteenth-century author of the English poem *Piers Plowman*, a section of which was quoted in Chapter 11, came to believe that greed and self-interest had triumphed everywhere. Moralists complained that the simpler manners of an earlier day had given way to extravagance and debauchery. War was endemic and all the more intolerable because it did not end for the common people when a truce was signed. They still had to pay for it through taxes while trying to defend themselves against unemployed soldiers who often did more damage than the war itself. Plague, the conquests by the Turk, and the rule of imbecile kings were seen by many as signs of God's wrath.

Upper-Class Nostalgia. The expression of these concerns varied. At one extreme was the upper-class tendency to take refuge in nostalgia for a largely fictional past. This took the form not only of chivalric fantasies but also of the idyllic visions offered in *Les très riches heures du Duc du Berry,* a magnificently illustrated prayer book in which happy peasants toil near palaces that seem to float on air.

The Fascination with Death. At the other extreme was a fascination with the physical aspects of death (see Document 12.5). The art of the period abounds with representations of skeletons and putrefying corpses. The Dance of Death, in which corpses lead the living in a frenzied round that ends with the grave, became a common motif in art and literature and was performed in costume on festive occasions. Popular sermons emphasized the brevity of life and the art of dying well, while series of popular woodcuts illustrated in horrifying detail how death would come to the knight, the scholar, the beauty, and a whole host of other human stereotypes. Not surprisingly, the word *macabre* seems to have entered the French language at about this time.

Flemish Painting: A Love of the Material World. Despair became fashionable, but it was not universal. In Brabant and Flanders, artists such as Rogier van der Weyden and the van Eycks developed techniques for portraying the beauties of the world with unprecedented mastery. Their paintings, intended for display in churches and hospitals, dwelled lovingly on fine costumes, the brilliance of jewels, and the richness of everyday objects while portraying the hard, worldly faces of their owners with unflinch-

---

THE VISION OF DEATH

Georges Chastellain (Shahs-te-lane, c. 1415–1475) was a Burgundian courtier best known for his *Chronicle*, but he also wrote poetry. The following excerpt is from a long poem entitled *Le Pas de la Mort* (The Dance of Death). It, like much of the art and literature of the age, was intended as a *memento mori*, or reminder of death.

> There is not a limb nor a form,
> Which does not smell of putrefaction.
> Before the soul is outside,
> The heart which wants to burst the body
> Raises and lifts the chest
> Which nearly touches the backbone
> —The face is discolored and pale,
> And the eyes veiled in the head.
> Speech fails him,
> For the tongue cleaves to the palate.
> The pulse trembles and he pants.
> The bones are disjointed on all sides;
> There is not a tendon which does not stretch as to burst.

From Chastellain, Georges, "Les Pas de la Mort," in Johan Huizinga, *The Waning of the Middle Ages* (New York: Doubleday Anchor Books, 1949, pp. 147–148). Copyright © Johan Huizinga. Reprinted by permission of Hodder Arnold.

Question: What spiritual purpose was the *memento mori* intended to serve?

---

ing honesty. Regarding their work as an affirmative answer to the emphasis on death is tempting. Some certainly believed that because life was grim and short its pleasures should be enjoyed to the fullest. However, more exists to these paintings than meets the eye. Many of the beautifully rendered objects they portray are also symbols of a moral or spiritual value whose meaning would have been clear at the time to all who saw them. The medieval fondness for allegory survived the fourteenth century and may even have grown stronger.

The people of the later Middle Ages still used religious language and religious imagery to express themselves. They still thought in religious, traditional, and hierarchic terms, but their faith in traditional assumptions and values had been shaken badly by events they barely understood. They looked with dismay upon what had happened, but the transformation of their world had just begun.

FIGURE 12.7 *The World of the Senses.* This detail from *Madonna with Canon George Van der Paele* (1436) by Jan Van Eyck (1390–1441) shows a different aspect of late medieval art. Van Eyck has painted St. Donatus in rich vestments decorated with precious stones. He has achieved an almost photographic realism, but the brilliance and intensity of the jewels exceeds anything found in nature. The work was commissioned by Canon Van der Paele, who demanded a lovingly accurate portrayal of the material world, as many patrons in the Netherlands of his day did.

CONCLUSION

To most historians, the fourteenth and fifteenth centuries mark the end of the Middle Ages. By 1300, economic conditions had begun to deteriorate, and in 1347–1350, the great epidemic known as the Black Death killed nearly one-third of Europe's population. Faced with these shocks, the bonds of feudal society began to unravel. Declining rents and the rising cost of labor impoverished the landholding classes while attempts to turn back the clock through legislation caused riot and social disorder. In the short term, peasants ben-

efited from inheritance and higher wage rates. But as ties of obligation weakened and lands were transformed from fiefs to capital investments, the face of European agriculture began to change. In many areas, stock raising began to replace row crops and peasants were dispossessed.

Warfare, too, changed. The commutation of feudal and manorial services for cash made it possible to pay men to fight. The monetarization of warfare further undermined the position of the nobility because they lacked the sovereign right to levy taxes or coin money. At the same time, new weapons systems greatly increased the size and cost of armies. The Hundred Years' War, complicated by intervals of political and dynastic collapse in each of the participating countries, was fought on a scale that had no precedent in feudal times. In eastern Europe, turmoil reigned from the Balkans to the shores of the Baltic Sea. To many, Europe seemed in danger of collapse, but as always, new institutions were beginning to emerge from the ruins of the old.

Review Questions

- What caused the economic decline at the beginning of the thirteenth century?
- How did the Black Death affect trade and the urban economy?
- What were the major causes of social disorder in both town and country after the Black Death?
- Why did paid soldiers replace feudal levies, and what economic developments made this change possible?
- What were the most important technological developments in the late medieval warfare?

For Further Study

Readings

Herlihy, David, *The Black Death and the Transformation of the West* (Cambridge: Harvard, 1997). A brief but valuable essay offering the most up-to-date scholarship.

Hilton, Rodney, *Bond Men Made Free: Medieval Peasant Risings and the English Rising of 1381* (London: Temple Smith, 1973). A comparative study of peasant revolts in the fourteenth century.

Huizinga, Johan, *The Autumn of the Middle Ages*, trans. R. J. Payton and U. Mammitzch (Chicago: Chicago University Press, 1996). A new translation of the classic treatment of late medieval culture, first published in English as *The Waning of the Middle Age*.

Perroy, Edouard, *The Hundred Years' War* (Bloomington: Indiana University Press, 1959). Still a classic study.

Tuchman, Barbara, *A Distant Mirror* (New York: Knopf, 1978). A best-selling popular history of the fourteenth century.

InfoTrac College Edition

For additional reading, go to your online research library at *http://infotrac.thomsonlearning.com.*

Using Key Terms, enter the search terms:
Black Death *Hundred Years' War*

Using the Subject Guide, enter the search term:
Middle Ages

Web Site

http://www.fordham.edu/halsall/sbook.html The Internet Medieval Sourcebook. Although not as strong in this section as on earlier periods, the site does contain a few documents in the section States and Society under the heading "The Calamitous Fourteenth Century."

Plague, War, and Social Change

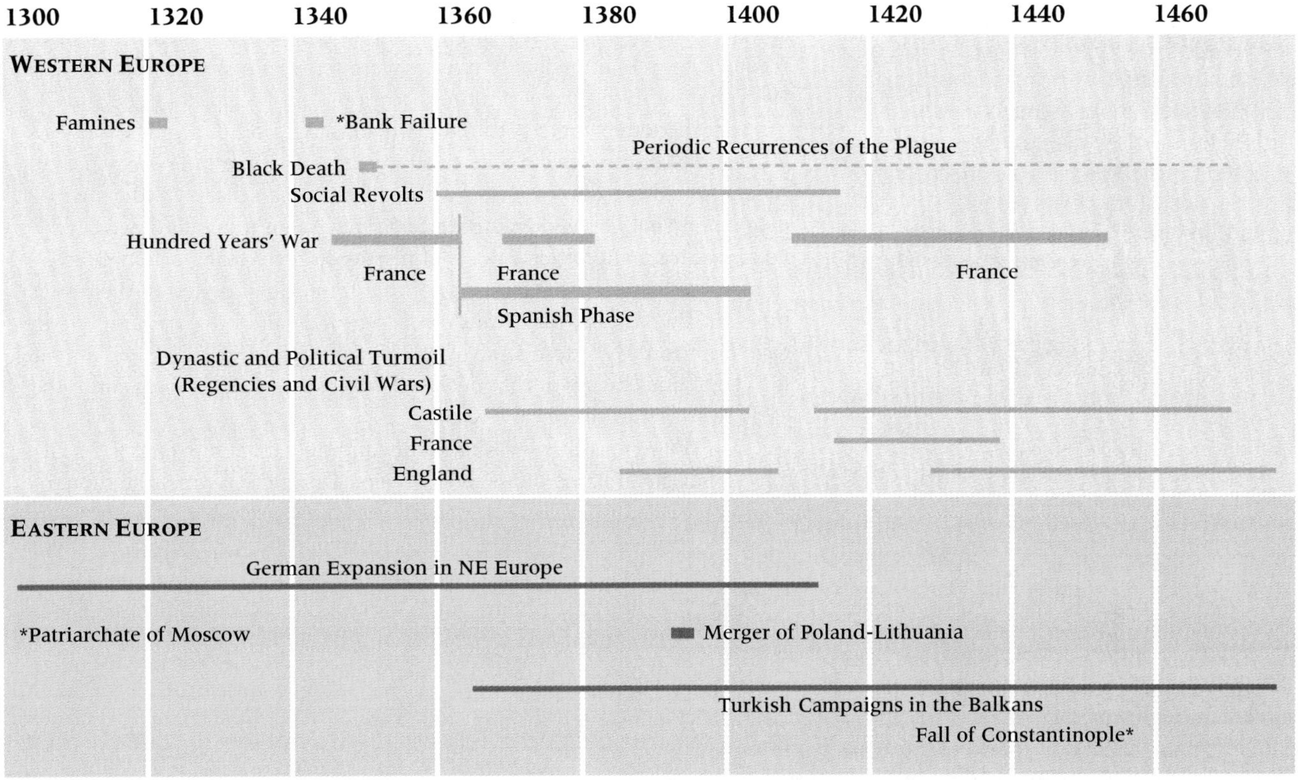

1300
1320
1340
1360
1380
1400
1420
1440
1460
Western Europe
Famines
*Bank Failure
Periodic Recurrences of the Plague
Black Death
Social Revolts
Hundred Years' War
France
France
France
Spanish Phase
Dynastic and Political Turmoil
(Regencies and Civil Wars)
Castile
France
England
Eastern Europe
German Expansion in NE Europe
*Patriarchate of Moscow
Merger of Poland-Lithuania
Turkish Campaigns in the Balkans
Fall of Constantinople*

Visit the Western Civilization Companion Web Site for resources specific to this textbook:
http://history.wadsworth.com/hause02/

The CD in the back of this book and the Western Civilization Resource Center at *http://history.wadsworth.com/western/* offer a variety of tools to help you succeed in this course, including access to quizzes; images; documents; interactive simulations, maps, and timelines; movie explorations; and a wealth of other sources.

Chapter 13

THE RENAISSANCE: POLITICAL AND INTELLECTUAL CHANGE

In 1345, a papal secretary known as Petrarch (a Romanized version of his real name, Francesco Petrarca) discovered a collection of letters at Verona. They had been written by the Roman orator Cicero, who died in 43 BCE. Petrarch immediately wrote Cicero to tell him about his discovery. He would write to Cicero on other occasions, but he did not expect an answer. The letters were Petrarch's way of making a literary point: he, a fourteenth-century Italian who lived much of the time in French-speaking Avignon, had more in common with a dead Roman than with his own neighbors. That perception, strange as it may seem to modern eyes, led Petrarch and many other Italians of his day to revive the ancient Greco-Roman past and apply the lessons of that reimagined period to their own times. In the process, they transformed virtually all of the arts and sciences, gave birth to the modern study of politics and history, and created a model for liberal arts education that persisted, with some modifications, into the early twentieth century.

The Renaissance was primarily an intellectual movement, but it has given its name to an entire era. During that time, the monarchies of western Europe reinvented themselves and began to create the early modern state. Chapter 13 begins with an analysis of why and how that transformation occurred. It then examines the origins of the Renaissance as an intellectual movement and concludes with the influence of the Renaissance on the arts and sciences.

THE CONSOLIDATION OF THE STATE (C. 1350–1500)

Medieval princes had worked, with varying degrees of success, to improve administration and strengthen royal authority, but most royal governments remained modest in size and centered firmly on the royal household until the later years of the thirteenth century. The transformation of warfare in the fourteenth and fifteenth centuries intensified the process of state building and gave it a new urgency. Under Henry III of England (1234–1272), for example, the royal budget hovered consistently in the range of £12,500 per annum. His son, Edward I, managed to spend more than £750,000 on war alone from 1297 to 1302, in part because he paid most of his fighting men in cash. Faced with a massive increase in the cost of war, sovereign states had to maximize their incomes from every conceivable source to survive.

Expansion of the Royal Domain. One way of increasing income was to expand the ruler's personal domain and to exploit it more efficiently. Domain revenues therefore fell into two main categories. The first was rents, fees, and other income that came from lands held directly by the prince. The simplest way to increase income from these sources was to expand the royal domain by keeping lands that had reverted to the sovereign through confiscation or in default of heirs. In the past, such lands had often been given to other subjects in return for military service almost as soon as they were received. By 1450, most states had reversed this practice, and some were actively seeking new pretexts for confiscation. The second source of domain revenues came from the exercise of traditional rights that might include anything from the collection of customs duties to monopolies on such vital commodities as salt. The yield from these sources was regarded as the personal property of the crown and, like profits from the land, could be increased primarily through better administration.

Prerogative Courts. Bureaucracies composed of "servants of the crown," paid in cash and serving at the pleasure of their ruler, were a legacy of the thirteenth century. They grew larger and more assertive with the passage of time. Given that the careers of the bureaucrats depended on producing new revenue, they sought not only to improve efficiency but also to discover new rights for which few precedents often existed. Their efforts brought the state into conflict with privileges that had long been claimed by towns, guilds, private individuals, and the church. Because such conflicts usually ended in the law courts, the state found it desirable to strengthen its control over the legal system. Royal officials began to attack manorial courts and other forms of

FIGURE 13.1 *The Court of King's Bench under Henry V of England.* The Court of King's Bench was a prerogative court, so called because it was established by the king's prerogative. The five red-robed judges shown here served at his pleasure. Prerogative courts sometimes permitted kings to enhance their power by overriding the provisions of the common law, but they were also favored by ordinary supplicants because they provided quicker, and therefore cheaper, justice.

private jurisdiction and to establish **prerogative courts,** so called because they served at the king's prerogative. A court whose judge was a servant of the king could be expected to deliver more favorable verdicts. Moreover, the fines and court costs levied by his court would go the royal government rather than to one of the king's subjects.

Introduction of Roman Law. The expansion of prerogative courts, although controversial, was eased by the growing acceptance of Roman or civil law. The extensive development of canon law by the church during the eleventh and twelfth centuries had sparked a revival of interest in Justinian's Code among laymen. By the thirteenth century, Roman legal principles had almost supplanted customary law in the empire and in Castile, where they formed the basis of the *Siete Partidas* (See-ey'-tay, Par-tee'-das), the great legal code adopted by Alfonso X (reigned 1252–1284). In France and England, the principles of civil law tended instead to modify common law practice, but Roman law gained ground steadily through the fifteenth century. Everywhere, rulers—and the prerogative courts they established—preferred Roman procedures because Roman law in the Middle Ages was based on the edicts of the ruler as opposed to legislative statutes and did not involve juries. The customary law, with its juries and its reliance on precedent, provided a stronger basis for resisting the claims of sovereignty. Unfortunately, juries and precedents that may never have been written down ensured that common law proceedings would be long and therefore costly. People often asked that their cases be transferred to prerogative or civil law courts in the hope of a speedier judgment.

Taxation. Taxation provided the second route by which the power of the state could be increased. Taxes, unlike domain revenues, could be raised only with the consent of representative bodies. Late medieval assemblies generally voted taxes for a single year, thereby forcing the princes to come back, hat in hand, to hear the complaints of their subjects on a regular basis. If the prince was popular, or if he needed the taxes to meet a genuine crisis, the sums involved might vastly exceed those generated from domain revenues, yet parliamentary bodies that held "the power of the purse" restricted the exercise of sovereignty. Most rulers no doubt preferred to "live of their own," as the saying went, but this was rarely possible in times of war.

Perpetual Taxes. The only solution to this dilemma was to convince hardheaded representatives of the landholding and merchant classes to grant at least some taxes on a perpetual basis on the theory that threats to the kingdom's integrity would never end. This was not easy, even in the interminable chaos of the Hundred Years' War, but the states that succeeded, notably France and Castile, became the great powers of the succeeding age. Not only did perpetual taxes make the revenues of these countries greater in real terms than those of their neighbors, but they also made them predictable. Budgeting for the long term became possible without the interference of elected bodies whose interests were not necessarily those of the prince. Above all, perpetual taxes made borrowing money easier because lenders could be guaranteed a return based on projected revenues.

The Basis of Medieval Taxation. Whether perpetual or temporary, late medieval and early modern taxes were usually levied on some form of moveable prop-

FIGURE **13.2**
A Sixteenth-Century Miner. Important changes in mining technology during the 1400s made vast sums of money for German bankers. The bankers in turn loaned money to rulers based on predictions of future revenue. The availability of credit made it much easier for the rulers to pay their soldiers on a regular basis and expand their domains. Engraving by Jost Amman.

erty. The governments of the day lacked the administrative technology to monitor personal incomes, and land, the principle form of wealth, was historically tax-exempt. The goods of merchants and artisans, however, were fair game, as were the commodities offered for sale by peasants. Taxes on moveable property were regressive in the sense that wealthy landholders and rentiers could usually avoid them, but their impact on other social groups is hard to measure. Collection was never uniform and rarely undertaken directly by the state. The most common practice was to negotiate the proposed yield from a tax with local authorities who would then be responsible for its collection. The rates collected were usually not those set by the legislation. Whatever their amount, late medieval taxes fell predominantly on the most economically active, if not the richest, segments of the population.

Encouragement of Trade and Stock Raising. Governments knew this and attempted to encourage the transfer of resources from tax-exempt to taxable activities. This is one reason for their almost universal efforts to foster trade, mining, and manufacturing. It also helps explain the policy, common to both England and Castile, of favoring sheepherders at the expense of those who cultivated the soil. Wool could be taxed; subsistence agriculture could not. Such policies clearly influenced economic development, but their overall impact on growth or on public well-being may have been negative. Taxes were ultimately paid by the consumer and were therefore a burden to be added to those already imposed by landholders in their efforts to compensate for falling rents.

Moreover, the maximization of tax yields often required changes in land use. Governments, through the decisions of their prerogative courts, tended to favor the extension of personal property rights over the claims of feudal privilege. An example was the English policy of encouraging landholders to "enclose" common lands for grazing. This practice, which reached a peak at the beginning of the sixteenth century, amounted to the confiscation of a village's common lands. It broke with feudal precedent and sometimes forced the expulsion of peasants who needed the marginal income provided by the commons for survival. As Sir Thomas More put it, "[I]n England, sheep eat men." This was perhaps an extreme case, and enclosures may not have been as common as More thought, but everywhere the extension of personal property rights to land had the effect of favoring governments and landholders at the expense of peasants. Thus, the most insistent demand of German peasant revolutionaries was for a return to the "old law" that protected their feudal status.

The Growth of Bureaucracy. If one part of state building was finding new revenues, the other was developing more efficient mechanisms by which they could be spent. Most late medieval states found this more difficult than locating the money in the first place. Bureaucracies whose purpose was to supply the needs of war grew like mushrooms but remained inefficient by modern standards until after the Industrial Revolution. They were inhibited in part by the same sense of corporate and personal privilege that resisted other aspects of state growth, but the underlying problem was structural. Communications were poor, and no precedent had been set for many basic administrative procedures. Archives, the basic tool of record keeping, were rare before the midsixteenth century. Censuses were unknown outside the Italian city-states, and it is hard to imagine how they might have been conducted in such kingdoms as France with their immense distances and isolated populations. To make matters worse, the costs of war continued to grow more rapidly than the sources of revenue. Neither taxation nor the development of public credit kept pace, and money was often in desperately short supply. Because soldiers and officials were often paid poorly and at irregular intervals, governments tolerated high levels of what would today be called corruption. Bribery, the sale of offices, and the misappropriation of funds troubled even those states that prided themselves on their high administrative standards. The situation would improve under the "absolutist" regimes of the eighteenth century, but even then the improvements were relative.

Opposition to the Crown. Although some individuals benefited from these efforts to increase the wealth and power of the state, most did not. In general, all attempts to increase revenue carried a high political cost. Only a strong, popular prince could overcome the entrenched resistance of powerful interests that sought to protect their privileges and opposed the increase of royal power. This is why the dynastic failures of the late fourteenth and early fifteenth centuries delayed the consolidation of the state, even if they could not stop it completely. No two states were, in any case, alike. Although all faced the need for consolidation and new revenues, they achieved their objectives in different ways according to their traditions and the personality of their rulers. Sovereign kingdoms and principalities must be examined individually or in regional groups if their late medieval development is to be understood.

The Iberian Kingdoms

The Iberian Peninsula was in some ways an unlikely birthplace for two of the most successful early modern states. Difficult terrain and an average annual rainfall of 20 inches or less produced little surplus wealth. Ethnic, political, and religious differences were great. In 1400, no fewer than five kingdoms shared this rugged land. Portugal was probably the most homogeneous, although it possessed significant Muslim and Jewish minorities. Castile, comprising the two ancient kingdoms of León and Castile, contained not only Jews and Muslims but also Basques and Galicians, who, although devoutly Christian, possessed their own languages and cultures. The kingdom of Aragon had three separate regions: Aragon, Catalonia, and Valencia. Each of them had its own language and traditions, but the Aragonese spoke Castilian and some linguists regard Valencian as a dialect of Catalan. Finally, there was the kingdom of Granada, the last but still vigorous remnant of the Islamic Empire on European soil, and the tiny mountain kingdom of Navarre straddling the Pyrenees between Castile and France.

Portugal. Portugal was the first European state to achieve consolidation, just as it would be the first to acquire an overseas empire. During most of the fourteenth century, it suffered like other monarchies from intrigue, dynastic failures, and ill-advised forays into the Hundred Years' War. In 1385, the Portuguese Cortes (parliament) solved a succession crisis by crowning the late king's illegitimate son as John I. In the same year, John defeated the Castilians in a decisive battle at Aljubarrota and suppressed most of the old feudal nobility, many of whom had supported the enemy. Under John's descendants, the house of Avis (Ah-vees'), Portugal avoided the revolts and dynastic failures that troubled other states and evolved virtually without interruption until 1580.

Spain under Ferdinand and Isabella.
Spain was another matter. Aragon and Castile had long been troubled by civil wars. Castile established a precedent for perpetual taxes in 1367, but the usurpation of Enrique of Trastámara left the crown dependent on the nobles who had supported him. His successors, especially Juan II and Enrique IV "the Impotent," were incapable of maintaining order, in part because their favorites aroused the jealousy of the grandees. The accession of Enrique's half-sister **Isabella of Castile** and her marriage to **Ferdinand of Aragon** brought an end to the period of anarchy and led to the eventual union of the two kingdoms. Isabella and Ferdinand inherited their respective thrones in 1479, a decade after their marriage. Each ruled independently, but they cooperated on the broad outlines of policy and agreed that their heirs would rule a united Spain by hereditary right.

The Problem of the Castilian Nobility.
The program of the Catholic kings, as they were called, was greatly assisted by the weariness brought on by decades of civil strife. The nobles of Castile were pacified by confirming their titles to all lands acquired by them, legally or illegally, before 1466 and by the judicious granting of *mayorazgos* (my-or-az'-gos), or entails permitting them to exclude younger children from their inheritances. This was important because Spanish law normally divided all property equally among the heirs, a practice that tended to deplete a family's wealth and influence over time. In return, the grandees agreed to give up all the land they had taken illegally after 1466 and to disband their private armies.

The Castilian Towns.
The towns, too, had suffered in the civil wars. Clientage and kinship ties were powerful in Castilian society, and many cities had fallen under the control of factions that persecuted their rivals mercilessly. At the Cortes of Toledo in 1480, the royal towns of Castile agreed to the appointment of *corregidores* (kor-regh'-i-dores), royal officials who 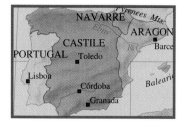 would reside in the city, protect the interests of the crown, and supervise elections. This ensured a high degree of royal authority over city governments and over those who were elected to represent them in the Cortes. The consequent willingness of this body to support new taxes and other royal initiatives was to become an important cornerstone of Spanish power.

Aragon.
None of these measures applied to Aragon. To ensure domestic peace, Ferdinand was forced to confirm a series of rights and privileges granted by his father in 1472 at the height of the civil wars. These concessions, however, were less important than they might appear. The kingdom of Aragon, with fewer than 1 million people, was about one-seventh the size of Castile, and its most vital region, Catalonia (the area around Barcelona), had been declining economically for more than a century. Castile was destined to be the dominant partner in this union of the crowns, and its dominance was only enhanced by its centralized institutions and higher level of taxation. In both kingdoms, administration was reformed and the crown's already extensive control over church appointments was strengthened.

The Search for Religious Uniformity.
With their realms at peace, the monarchs turned their attention to the kingdom of Granada. After 10 years of bitter warfare, they conquered the Muslim state in 1492, the same year in which Columbus sailed for the New World. It was also the year in which they expelled the

FIGURE 13.3 *Ferdinand and Isabella Enter Granada, 1492.* This wood relief was carved by Felipe Vigarny (c. 1480–1543) for the royal chapel built at Granada by Charles V. As heir to the Spanish kingdoms, Charles wanted to honor his grandparent's conquest of the Muslim kingdom in western Europe.

Jews from Spain, for the Catholic kings were committed to a policy of religious uniformity. Fanned by popular preachers, anti-Jewish sentiment had led to pogroms and a wave of forced conversions between 1390 and 1450. Many of these conversions were thought to be false, and the **Spanish Inquisition,** an organization wholly unrelated to the papal Inquisition, was founded early in Ferdinand and Isabella's reign to root out *conversos* (converts) who had presumably returned to the faith of their ancestors. It differed from the papal Inquisition not only in purpose but in the fact that it was organized and controlled by the crown, which appointed the inquisitors and kept most of their confiscations for itself. The Inquisition executed large numbers of converts or forced them to do penance during the 1480s and confiscated their property to help finance the Granadan War.

Expulsion of the Jews. The Inquisition, however, had jurisdiction over only those who had been baptized. The Jews who had escaped forced conversion were comparatively few and usually poor, but the crown saw even a small minority as a threat to the faith of the *conversos*. Those who still refused conversion were expelled in 1492. Some fled to Portugal, only to be expelled by the Portuguese in 1496. Others went to North Africa or found refuge within the Turkish Empire, whereas a few eventually settled in the growing commercial cities of the Low Countries.

The Italian Wars (1495–1513). The war for Granada and the supplies of money guaranteed by the perpetual taxes and cooperative legislature of Castile enabled Ferdinand to create a formidable army that was put to almost constant use in the last years of the reign. Through bluff, diplomacy, and hard fighting, he restored Roussillon (Roo-see-yone) to Catalonia and conquered the ancient kingdom of Navarre. In 1495, Charles VIII of France invaded Italy to make good on his dynastic claims to Milan and the kingdom of

Naples. Ferdinand used his actions as a pretext to intervene in Italian affairs. This first phase of the Italian wars lasted until 1513. Under the command of Gonsalvo de Córdoba, "the Great Captain," Spanish armies devised a new method of combining pikes with shot that defeated the French and their Swiss mercenaries and drove them from the peninsula. Spain added the kingdoms of Sicily and Naples to its growing empire and eventually became the dominant power in Italian affairs at the expense of Italy's independence.

Isabella died in 1504; Ferdinand, in 1516. So firm were the foundations they had built that the two crowns were able to survive the unpopular regency of **Cardinal Francisco Jiménez** (or Ximénez) **de Cisneros** (He-may'-nez de Siz-ner'-os) in Castile. The cardinal not only preserved the authority of the crown but also made substantial progress in reforming abuses in the Spanish church and in improving the education of the clergy. When the grandson of the Catholic kings, the emperor Charles V, ascended the two thrones and unified them in 1522, he inherited a realm that stretched from Italy to Mexico, the finest army in Europe, and a regular income from taxes that rested firmly on the shoulders of Castilian taxpayers.

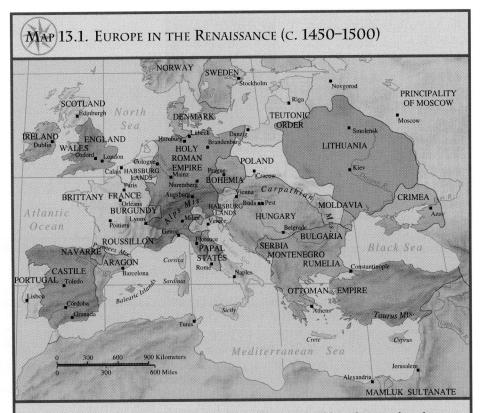

MAP 13.1. EUROPE IN THE RENAISSANCE (C. 1450–1500)

The consolidation of European states into something resembling their modern form became apparent by 1500. Monarchs engaged in state building by curbing the power of nobles and the church and by increasing domain and tax revenues to pay for larger, more efficient armies.

France: Charles VII and Louis XI

France, too, emerged from the Hundred Years' War with perpetual taxes that freed its monarchs from their dependence on representative institutions. The most important of these was the *taille* (tay), a poll or head tax of feudal origin that was in theory to be paid by every household. The Estates-General assigned it exclusively to the crown in 1439 at the height of the campaign to expel the English from France. In a series of ordinances passed between 1445 and 1459, Charles VII made it perpetual and extended it throughout his realm. The taille became the largest and most predictable source of crown revenue and virtually eliminated the need for the Estates-General. The meetings of the Estates-General at Tours in 1484 redoubled the royal desire to avoid future meetings by producing loud complaints about the impoverishment of the people by royal taxes (see Document 13.1). From 1484 to 1789 it met only once. Charles also laid the groundwork for a professional army, a national administration, and a diplomatic corps.

Territorial Consolidation. Charles's son, **Louis XI** (ruled 1461–1483), went further. Most of Louis's reign was consumed by a bitter feud with the dukes of Burgundy, who had established a formidable, multilingual state along his eastern borders. Including Burgundy, large parts of northern and eastern France and most of what is now Belgium and the Netherlands, it was almost certainly the wealthiest principality in Europe. Under Duke Philip "the Good" (d.

Louis XI of France

1467), it surpassed most kingdoms in courtly magnificence and in the richness of its musical and artistic life, but it was not a kingdom. Most of its territories were held in fief either from the Holy Roman Empire or from France. To enhance his independence, Philip had supported the English and some discontented elements of the French nobility against Louis in the League of the Common Weal, which Louis defeated in 1465. Philip's son, Charles (known to some as "the Bold" and to others as "the Rash"), hoped to weld his holdings into a single territorial state stretching from the Alps to the North Sea. His ambitions brought him into conflict with the Duke of Lorraine and with the Swiss, whose independence he seemed to threaten. These formidable opponents, richly subsidized by Louis, defeated and killed Charles at the battle of Nancy in 1477.

Charles died without male heirs. His daughter Mary was the wife of the Hapsburg archduke, Maximilian, who became emperor in 1486. Under Louis's interpretation of the Salic law, she could not, as a woman, inherit her father's French fiefs. Maximilian could not defend his wife's claims, and in 1482, Burgundy and her other French possessions reverted to the French crown.

The dismemberment of the Burgundian state marked the capstone of Louis's career. It was accompanied by acquisitions of equal value. Louis may have been clever and ruthless, but he was also lucky. In 1480, René, Duke of Anjou (Ahnzhoo), died without heirs, leaving Provence (the modern Riviera) and his vast estates in central France to Louis. Louis also purchased the rights of succession to Brittany when it became apparent that its duke, too, would die without producing male heirs. Charles VIII completed the annexation in 1488, when he married the duke of Brittany's daughter. When Louis died in 1483, he left a France whose borders were recognizably similar to those of today. Luck and a consistently antifemale interpretation of the laws of inheritance played their part, but he could not have done it without a superior army, fiscal independence, and great diplomatic skill. His immense resources permitted him to take advantage of the dynastic misfortunes of others.

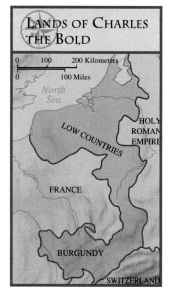

England: The Yorkists and Tudors

England was far smaller in land area and in population than either France or Spain. Its population was also

more homogeneous, although regional differences were still important until well into the sixteenth century. Perhaps because it dominated an island whose integrity was rarely threatened by foreign enemies, the English monarchy failed to develop perpetual taxes and its Parliament never lost "the power of the purse." England's development was therefore unlike that of the great continental powers and it remained a relatively minor player in international politics until late in the early modern period.

COMPLAINTS OF THE FRENCH ESTATES-GENERAL, 1484

The Devastation of the Farmer after the Warships Sail Away.

When the French Estates-General brought together representatives of the clergy, the nobility, and the commons (or third estate), these representatives produced pamphlets known as *cahiers*, describing their grievances. The following excerpt from a cahier of 1484 is a vivid complaint of the third estate against royal taxation and provides an example of popular resistance to the state-building activities of fifteenth-century kings.

One cannot imagine the persecution, poverty, and misery that the little people have suffered, and still suffer in many ways.

First of all, no region has been safe from the continual coming and going of armies, living off the poor. . . . One should note with pity the injustice, the iniquity, suffered by the poor: the armies are hired to defend them, yet these armies oppress them the most. The poor laborer must hire the soldiers who beat him, evict him from his house, make him sleep on the ground, and consume his substance. . . . When the poor laborer has worked long, weary, sweaty days, when he has harvested those fruits of his labor from which he expects to live, they come to take a share of it from him, to pay the armed men who may come to beat him soon. . . . If God did not speak to the poor and give them patience, they would succumb in despair.

For the intolerable burden of the taille, and the taxes—which the poor people of this kingdom have not carried alone, to be sure, because that is impossible—the burden under which they have died from hunger and poverty, the mere description of these taxes would cause infinite sadness and woe, tears of woe and pity, great sighs and groans from sorrowful hearts. And that is not mentioning the enormous evils that followed, the injustice, the violence, and the extortion whereby these taxes were imposed and seized.

From Bernier, A., ed., *Journal des états généraux de France tenus à Tours en 1484* (Paris: 1835). trans. Steven C. Hause.

Question: For what purpose were these taxes being collected?

The Wars of the Roses. Henry VI (reigned 1422–1461, 1470–1471) came to the throne as an infant and suffered from protracted bouts of mental illness as an adult. He was never competent to rule in his own right. For the first 30 years of the reign, his regency council fought bitterly among themselves, brought the kingdom to the edge of bankruptcy, and lost the remaining English possessions in France with the exception of Calais. Eventually, Richard, Duke of York, claimed the throne with the support of a powerful segment of the nobility. Richard was descended from Edmund of Langley, the fourth surviving son of Edward III, while the king was the great-grandson of Edward's third son, John of Gaunt, Duke of Lancaster. The civil war that followed is called the **War of the Roses** because the heraldic symbol of the Yorkists was a white rose; that of the Lancastrians, a red.

In the first phase of the war (1455–1461), the Lancastrians were led by Henry's formidable queen, Margaret of Anjou. She defeated the Yorkists at Wakefield and at St. Albans but failed to take London. Richard was killed at Wakefield. His son, an able commander, took advantage of her hesitation. He entered London and had himself proclaimed king as Edward IV. The struggle continued, but Edward retained the throne with one brief interruption until 1483. The last half of his reign was characterized by imaginative and energetic reforms in the administration of the royal domain. As customs duties were an important part of crown revenues, Edward used his extensive personal contacts in the London merchant community to encourage the growth of trade. He eventually became a major investor himself. The proceeds from these efforts, together with a pension extorted from Louis XI to prevent Edward from invading France, left him largely independent of Parliament. Some thought his methods unkingly, but when he died in 1483, he left behind an improved administration and an immense fortune.

Richard III. He also left two young sons under the guardianship of his brother. The brother quickly had himself proclaimed king as Richard III, and the two little princes disappeared from the Tower of London, never to be seen again. This usurpation caused several of the leading Yorkists to make common cause with the Lancastrians, and in 1485, Henry Tudor, the last remaining Lancastrian claimant to the throne, defeated and killed Richard at the battle of Bosworth.

The First Tudor. As **Henry VII** (reigned 1485–1509), Tudor followed the policies of Edward IV. A subtle diplomat, he avoided war, intensified the exploitation of his domain, and encouraged the development of trade. His Welsh connections—he had been born in Pembrokeshire and was partially of Welsh descent—secured him the cooperation of the principality and laid the groundwork for its eventual union with England in 1536.

Henry VII of England

The greatest threat to Henry's regime was the belligerence of the great nobles, many of whom continued to maintain private armies. He dealt with this menace through prerogative courts, including the Court of King's Bench and the Star Chamber, so called because it met in a room decorated with painted stars. Staffed by royal appointees, these bodies levied heavy fines for a variety of offenses against the crown that eventually destroyed the military power of the great families. Paradoxically, Henry may have been aided by several pretenders to the throne who claimed to be one or another of the missing princes and who enjoyed the support of disgruntled Yorkists or other "overmighty" subjects. The fines, confiscations, and executions imposed after each of these episodes added to the royal domain and further reduced the number of his enemies.

When Henry died in 1509, the treasury was full and the kingdom at peace. Many of the old feudal families were either impoverished or extinct, and a new elite composed largely of servants of the crown had begun to develop. The authority of the crown, in other words, was great, but the state as a whole remained dependent upon domain revenues. The later Tudors would find this dependence limiting. The Stuarts would be destroyed by it.

The Holy Roman Empire

The Holy Roman Empire of the later Middle Ages should be regarded as a confederation of cities and principalities instead of as a monarchy that failed. German

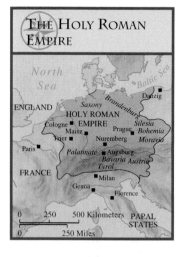

parallels to the growth of Spain, France, or England may be found in states such as Brandenburg, Saxony, and Bavaria, not at the imperial level. Their rulers sought, with varying degrees of success, to enhance domain revenues, control representative bodies, and impose new taxes. The imperial office was an unlikely vehicle for this type of development because it was elective and because it lacked several of the more important attributes of sovereignty.

Organization of the Empire. The century before the Black Death had been one of imperial paralysis and decentralization, caused in part by papal interference. The turning point came in 1355 when Charles IV renounced his Italian claims and turned his attention to reorganizing what would soon be called the Holy Roman Empire of the German Nation. **The Golden Bull of 1356** regularized imperial elections by placing them in the hands of seven permanent electors: the archbishops of Trier, Mainz, and Cologne; the Duke of Saxony; the Margrave of Brandenburg; the Count Palatine; and the King of Bohemia. It further declared that the territory of these princes would be indivisible and that inheritance in the secular electorates would be by primogeniture.

These measures strengthened the electors and made consolidation of their territories easier, but they did little to create a more viable imperial government. The electors had no incentive to increase the power of the emperor, and the lesser states feared the growing influence of the electors. Efforts to create an electoral union or *Kurfürstverein* (Kur-feerst'-fair-ine) with many of the powers of a central government were defeated in 1424, 1453, and 1500. The Common Penny, an imperial tax, was rejected by a majority of German states after it had been approved by their representatives in the Imperial Diet or Reichstag (Rike'-shtahg). The empire would remain an unstable grouping of 89 free imperial cities together with more than 200 independent principalities, most of which continued to divide and re-form according to the vagaries of partible inheritance. A few, such as Bavaria, achieved near-equality with the electoral states by introducing primogeniture. However, all sought to maximize their own power and to resist imperial and electoral encroachments.

"THE TWELVE ARTICLES OF THE GERMAN PEASANTS"

The Great Peasant War of 1524–1525 was the last in a long series of revolts against the claims of lords, princes, and the church. The Twelve Articles, half of which are abridged here, constituted a formal statement of peasant demands. Most of them expressed grievances that had been accumulating for centuries. Those noted below would have been as valid in 1424 as in 1524.

The Third Article. It has been the custom hitherto for men to hold us as their own property, which is pitiable enough considering that Christ has redeemed and purchased us without exception, by the shedding of His precious blood, the lowly as well as the great. Accordingly, it is consistent with Scripture that we should be free and wish to be so. . . .

The Fourth Article. [I]t has been the custom heretofore that no poor man was allowed to catch venison or wild fowl, or fish in flowing water, which seems to us quite unseemly and unbrotherly. . . . Accordingly, it is our desire if a man holds possession of waters that he should prove from satisfactory documents that his right has been wittingly acquired by purchase.

The Fifth Article. [W]e are aggrieved in the matter of wood-cutting, for our noble folk have appropriated all the woods to

themselves alone. . . . It should be free to every member of the community to help himself to such firewood as he needs in his home.

The Eighth Article. [W]e are greatly burdened by holdings that cannot support the rent exacted from them. We ask that the lords may appoint persons of honor to inspect these holdings and fix a rent in accordance with justice.

The Ninth Article. [W]e are burdened with the great evil in the constant making of new laws. In our opinion we should be judged according to the old written law, so that the case shall be decided according to its merits and not with favors.

The Eleventh Article. [W]e will entirely abolish the custom called Todfall [death dues], and will no longer allow it, nor allow widows and orphans to be thus shamefully robbed against God's will.

From "The Twelve Articles of the German Peasants," in Hans Hillerbrand, ed., *The Protestant Reformation* (New York: Harper Torchbooks, 1967, pp. 65–66).

Questions: When, according to the text, were most of these practices introduced? Do you think the peasant's movement was conservative or radical?

The Peasant's War. In the process, German states—and cities—imitated the western monarchies by trying to increase revenues at the expense of traditional rights and privileges. The peasants, already squeezed by landholders trying to reverse the economic effects of a declining population, added the actions of the princes to their list of grievances and rebelled. The last and most serious of the *bundschuh* revolts was the **Great Peasant War of 1524–1525** that ended with the defeat of the peasant armies and the imposition of **serfdom** in many parts of the empire (see Document 13.2). Serfs had no personal or legal rights and were usually transferred from one owner to another whenever the property on which they lived changed hands. Their status differed from that of slaves only in that they could not be sold as individuals. Serfdom was the final step in the destruction of peasant freedom.

Central and Eastern Europe

Serfdom as an institution was also established in eastern Europe. In Bohemia, Hungary, and Poland-Lithuania, the growing power of aristocratic landholders deprived peasants of their traditional freedoms and blocked the development of western-style states. If

western kings may be said to have tamed their nobles, in the east the nobles tamed their kings.

Bohemia and Hungary were in some ways politically similar, although Bohemia was part of the Holy Roman Empire and Hungary was not. Both were elective monarchies whose powerful Diets or representative assemblies were dominated by the landed aristocracy. Rich mineral deposits provided a source of revenues for both crowns. Once elected, a capable monarch could use this wealth as the basis for administrative and military reforms, but his achievements were unlikely to survive him. By the late fifteenth century, Diets customarily demanded concessions as the price of election, and as the great magnates dominated the Diets, their demands invariably tended to weaken the authority of the crown and threaten the rights of common people.

Bohemia. Bohemia, although wealthy and cultured, was convulsed throughout the fifteenth century by **the Hussite wars** and their aftermath. The Czechs, deeply resentful of a powerful German minority, launched what was probably the first national movement in European history. It was anti-German, antiempire, and under the leadership of **Jan Hus,** increasingly associated with

demands for religious reform. Hus was burned as a heretic in 1415. After many years of civil war, the Czechs succeeded in placing the Hussite noble George of Podebrady (ruled 1458–1471) on the throne. The king's ability and popularity were eventually seen as a threat to the great Bohemian landholders. When he died, the Diet elected Vladislav II (ruled 1471–1516), a member of the Polish Jagiello (Ya-gee-el'-lo) dynasty, on the promise that he would support their interests. Under Vladislav, the Bohemian nobles gained virtual control over the state, expelled the towns from the Diet, and introduced serfdom. The towns eventually achieved readmission, but the Bohemian peasantry did not recover its freedom until the eighteenth century.

Hungary. The policies of Vladislav could only recommend him to the Hungarian nobility. During the long and brilliant reign of **Matthias Corvinus** (Kor-veen'-us, ruled 1458–1490), the crown acquired unprecedented authority and supported a court that was admired even in Renaissance Italy. When Matthias died, the Hungarian Diet elected the more controllable

Vladislav to succeed him. Vladislav and his son, Louis II, who was in turn elected king of both Hungary and Bohemia, reversed the achievements of Matthias and left the Diet free to promote repressive legislation. Driven to desperation, the peasants rebelled in 1514 only to be soundly defeated. After bloody reprisals, the Diet imposed "real and perpetual servitude" on the entire Hungarian peasant class.

The Turkish Invasion. By this time, Hungary was on the edge of an abyss. The Turkish Empire, under the formidable **Süleyman the Magnificent** (Soo-lay-mahn', reigned 1520–1566), was preparing an invasion, and Louis was crippled by the aristocratic independence he had done so much to encourage. Although king of Bohemia as well as Hungary, he was unable to gain the support of the Bohemians. The Hungarians were divided not only by rivalries among the leading clans but also by an increasingly bitter feud between the magnates and the lesser nobility. Süleyman had little difficulty in annihilating a weak,

divided, and badly led Hungarian army at Mohács (Mo'-hahtch) in 1526. Louis, along with many great nobles and churchmen, was killed, and Hungary was partitioned into three sections. The center of the country would thereafter be ruled directly by the Turks. In the east, Transylvania became a Turkish client and tributary, while a narrow strip of territory in the west fell under Hapsburg rule.

Poland-Lithuania. After their union in 1386, Poland and Lithuania occupied an immense territory stretching from the borders of Baltic Prussia to the Black Sea. Despite its ethnic and religious diversity and a substantial number of prosperous towns, it was primarily a land of

great estates whose titled owners profited during this period from a rapidly expanding grain trade with the west. At the same time, the vast spaces of the north European plain and the Ukrainian steppe preserved the importance of cavalry and with it the military dominance of the knightly class.

The great magnates of both Poland and Lithuania negotiated their union after the death of Casimir the Great, and they continued to increase their power throughout the fifteenth century. The Jagiello dynasty survived mainly through capitulations. By 1500, Poland-Lithuania could be described as two aristocratic commonwealths joined by a largely ceremonial monarchy, not as a dynastic state. Serfdom was imposed in a series of edicts passed by the Polish Sejm (Same) or parliament between 1492 and 1501, and the crown, already elective in practice, became so in theory by 1572.

Russia. As in the case of Hungary, these aristocratic triumphs unfolded in the growing shadow of a menace to the east. Autocratic Russia, not the Polish-Lithuanian commonwealth, was destined to become the dominant power in eastern Europe, and by 1505, the borders of Lithuania were already shrinking. The process of transforming the grand duchy of Moscow into the Russian Empire began in earnest during the reign of **Ivan III** from 1462 to 1505. In the first 13 years of his reign, Ivan was able to annex most of the independent Russian principalities and the city-states of Vyatka and Novgorod. In 1480, he refused to pay tribute to the Mongol khans and began to style himself "tsar of all Russia." Finally, in 1492, he invaded Lithuania and, in two successive campaigns, annexed much of Belarus and the Ukraine.

Ivan was not a great field general. His son-in-law claimed rather sourly that "he increased his dominions

while sitting at home and sleeping," but Ivan built an effective army and introduced the first usable artillery to eastern Europe. As most of his troops were cavalry and therefore expensive to maintain, either he or his state secretary introduced the "service land" or *pomest'e* (po-mes'-tay) system, which granted land directly to cavalrymen instead of paying them in cash. It was an ideal way of supporting troops in a land that was still underpopulated and cash-poor. Pomest'e offered other dividends as well. It created an armed class that owed its prosperity directly to the tsar and permitted him to destroy local allegiances through the massive resettlement of populations. The annexation of Novgorod, for example, was followed by the removal of more than 7,000 citizens who were located elsewhere in Russia and replaced by Muscovites, many of whom were members of this service class.

Beginnings of Serfdom. The new service class cavalry came primarily from the middle ranks of society and depended for their economic survival on peasant cultivators who worked their land. To ensure the stability of the labor force, they secured an edict in 1497 that restricted peasant movement. Thereafter, peasants were allowed to change employers only during a brief period centered on the feast of St. George (April 23). It was the first step toward serfdom. True serfdom on the Hungarian or Polish model did not become general until the end of the sixteenth century.

The Russia of Ivan III had little in common with western states or with its immediate neighbors. The tsar was an autocrat who ruled with little regard for representative institutions. The Orthodox Church was implacably hostile to Latin Christendom. The pomest'e system, like many other Russian institutions, derived from Turkish, Persian, and Byzantine precedents, and even daily life had an oriental flavor. Men wore beards and skirtlike garments that touched the ground while women were secluded and often veiled.

Ivan the Terrible. In the reign of Ivan's grandson, **Ivan IV "the Terrible"** (1530–1584), the Russian state expanded eastward, adding Kazan and Astrakhan to its dominions. An effort to annex the areas now known as Latvia and Estonia was unsuccessful. Ivan attributed this failure to dissatisfaction among the boyars, or great nobles, and pretended to abdicate, returning only on the condition that he be allowed to establish an *oprich-*

FIGURE 13.4 *Tsar Ivan IV Vasilievich "the Terrible" (1530–1584).* Gilded icons were normally used in Russian art to portray Jesus, the Virgin Mary, and the saints. This one shows the tsar who suppressed the Russian boyars and conquered Kazan and Astrakhan from the Tartars. Althought the picture follows the rather abstract conventions of iconic art, it perfectly captures Ivan's troubled, dangerous personality.

nina (oh-pritch-nee'-na). A bizarre state within a state, the oprichnina was regarded as the tsar's private property. Land and even certain streets in Moscow were assigned to it, and the original owners were settled elsewhere. The purpose was to dismantle boyar estates as well as to provide income for Ivan's court and for a Praetorian Guard of 6,000 men. Dressed in black and mounted on black horses, these *oprichniki* carried a broom and the severed head of a dog as symbols of their primary mission: to root out "treason" and terrorize the enemies of the tsar. They succeeded admirably. Although disbanded in 1572, the oprichniki represented an institutionalization of autocracy and state terror that was unique in Europe.

Russia's size and military strength made it a great power, but its autocratic system of government ensured that political effectiveness would inevitably depend on the personal qualities of the tsar. After Ivan IV, ability was conspicuously lacking. Russia turned inward for more than 100 years, to emerge once again under the not-too-gentle guidance of Peter the Great at the beginning of the eighteenth century.

The Renaissance as an Intellectual Movement (1340–1520)

The social and political transformations of the late Middle Ages were accompanied, as great changes often are, by the development of new intellectual interests. The most important of these was the **Renaissance,** or, as it was sometimes called, the New Learning. The word *renaissance* means rebirth in French. It is often applied to the entire age that marked the end of the Middle Ages and the beginning of modern times, but its original meaning was more restricted. Beginning in the fourteenth century, a number of scholars became interested in the Greco-Roman past. They sought to recover the glories of classical literature because the learning of their own day seemed to them stagnant and largely irrelevant to their needs. A later generation saw the "renaissance" of classical antiquity that they created as the birth of modern times; more recent scholarship has emphasized its continuity with the medieval past. In its original form, the Renaissance was a direct outgrowth of life in the medieval Italian city-state, and its first proponents were Italian.

The status of medieval town dwellers was unclear. Even the richest were, by feudal standards, of humble origin, yet their wealth and literacy set them apart from the peasants. Chivalric literature affected to despise them, and ecclesiastical theorists found their activities dubious if not wicked. Trade, the lifeblood of any city, was often regarded as parasitic. The merchant bought low and sold high, profiting from the honest toil of the peasant and raising prices for everyone. The need for mechanisms of distribution was not always fully understood.

Worse yet, the townsman was frequently a citizen (women, although they engaged in trade, had neither civic rights nor obligations). Under law he was compelled to vote and to hold public office if elected. Even before St. Augustine, Western Christianity had been deeply suspicious of public life, regarding it as incompatible with concern for one's soul. In short, two of the most significant features of town life were either ignored by medieval writers or condemned by them outright.

The Origins of the Renaissance in the Italian City-States.

A certain alienation from the norms of medieval culture was therefore to be expected among townsfolk even if it was not always fully conscious or easily articulated. This alienation was most intense in Italy. Italian town life had developed early (see Chapter 10). The acquisition of full sovereignty, rare in other parts of Europe, gave a peculiar intensity to political life in the Italian city-states while imposing heavy moral and intellectual responsibilities on their citizens. Extensive contact with the Muslim and Byzantine worlds may also have left the Italians more open to influences that came from outside the orbit of chivalric or scholastic ideas.

By the end of the thirteenth century, the intellectual life of the Italian towns was beginning to acquire a distinct flavor of its own. This was evident to some extent in the works of **Dante** (Don'-tay, 1265–1321). His masterwork, *The Divine Comedy,* a brilliant evocation of hell, purgatory, and paradise written in the Tuscan vernacular (the basis of modern Italian), is arguably the greatest poem ever written by a European. It is filled with classical allusions and references to Florentine politics but remains essentially medieval in inspiration. The widening gap between Italian culture and that of the scholastic, chivalric north is far more striking in the city chronicles that were becoming popular with the urban elite. Unlike northern chronicles, which were often little more than a simple record of events, they increasingly sought to analyze the causes of political and economic phenomena to provide guidance for policy makers. On a less practical level, *The Decameron,* by the Florentine **Giovanni Boccaccio** (1313–1375), was a collection of stories that portrayed the lives of city people with little reference to the conventions of chivalry.

Petrarch and Boccaccio. That Boccaccio and another Florentine, Francesco Petrarca (or **Petrarch,** 1304–1374), were among the first to develop a serious interest in the Roman past is no accident. Petrarch grew up in exile and spent most of his life at the papal court in Avignon, an existence that no doubt sharpened his personal sense of distance from chivalric and scholastic values. Believing, like other Italians, that he was descended from the ancient Romans, he began to seek out classical manuscripts and to compose works in Latin that demonstrated his affinity with the antique past. Among them were letters addressed to such ancient figures as Cicero and Livy and an epic poem, *Africa,* inspired by his reading of Virgil's *Aeniad.* His friend Boccaccio followed his lead in collecting manuscripts and compiled an encyclopedia of Greco-Roman mythology. Petrarch is probably best known today for his sonnets written in the Tuscan vernacular, but classical studies consumed most of his working life. His efforts made an undeniably vital point. To Petrarch and to many of his readers, the society of ancient Rome had more in common with that of the Italian states than did the chivalric, scholastic world of Transalpine Europe. The ancients had lived in cities and had believed that good citizenship was the highest of virtues. Accordingly, they had produced a vast body of literature on rhetoric, politics, history, and the other arts needed to produce effective citizens. Many Italians would eventually find these works to be of great practical value in the conduct of their lives.

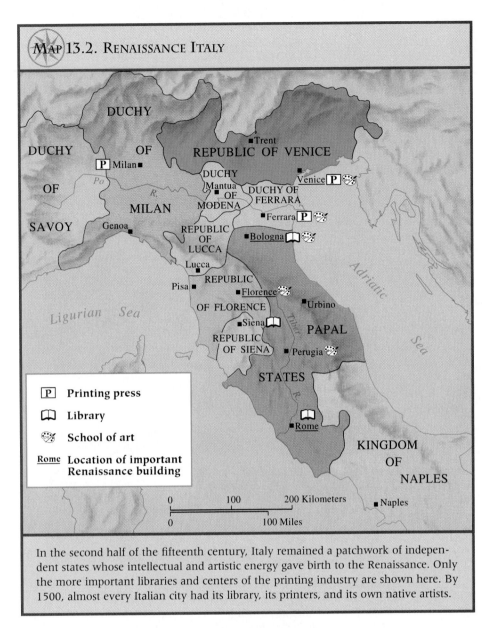

MAP 13.2. RENAISSANCE ITALY

Printing press

Library

School of art

Rome **Location of important Renaissance building**

In the second half of the fifteenth century, Italy remained a patchwork of independent states whose intellectual and artistic energy gave birth to the Renaissance. Only the more important libraries and centers of the printing industry are shown here. By 1500, almost every Italian city had its library, its printers, and its own native artists.

(Bess-air´-ee-on), and other members of the Greek delegation were able to do this for Bruni's generation and, by so doing, opened up a great literary tradition that had been lost to the West for centuries. Spurred by these developments, humanism spread from Florence and Rome to Venice and the other Italian states. By the midfifteenth century, it was attracting followers beyond the Alps.

Humanism: Its Methods and Its Goals

The early humanists cannot be associated with any fixed ideological or philosophical system. Most of them were either teachers of rhetoric or the editors of classical texts whose chief purpose was to study the classics and to apply ancient ideas and values to life in their own time. As such, they might be found on almost any side of a given issue. But for all their variety, they shared certain presuppositions that defined them as a movement. Humanists by definition believed in the superiority of ancient culture. Errors, they said, were modern. Where medieval writers had seen their world as a historical extension of antiquity, the humanists saw a radical disjuncture between ancient and modern times and regarded the interval between the fall of Rome and their revival of antique ideals as a "middle age" of barbarity, ignorance, and above all, bad literary style. Immersed in the elegance of classical Latin, they were deeply concerned with form, sometimes, according to their critics, at the expense of substance.

Because they revered the classical past, they shared a preference for argument based on the authority of ancient sources and a suspicion of formal reason that bordered on contempt. The scholastics in particular were thought to be sterile and misguided, in part because of their bad Latin, but also because the nominalist rejection of reason as a support for faith had led the philosophers into pursuits that humanists re-

The Popularization of Classical Studies. Those who did so, and who made the study of antiquity their primary task, became known as **humanists.** The term was coined by Leonardo Bruni (Lay-o-nar´-doe Broo´-nee, c. 1370–1444) to describe those engaged in *studia humanitatis,* the study of secular letters as opposed to theology or divine letters. The movement became popular in Florence during the political crisis of 1392–1402, when Bruni and other publicists used classical examples of civic virtue to stir up the public against Giangaleazzo Visconti (John-gall-ee-atz´-o Viss-cohn´-tee), despot of Milan, and his expansionist schemes. Even more important was the enthusiasm aroused by the arrival in Italy of Greek scholars who were seeking western aid against the Turks. Petrarch had known that Roman culture had Greek roots but could find no one to teach him classical Greek. Manuel Chrysoloras (Kris-a-lor´-us), Cardinal Bessarion

VERNACULAR WRITERS OF THE LATE MIDDLE AGES

The 1300s produced several great writers of vernacular poetry (poetry written in the language of their native place as opposed to Latin). Petrarch, whose picture appears at the beginning of this chapter, wrote sonnets in Italian before turning to a study of the Latin classics. Dante, a contemporary of Petrarch's father, wrote *The Divine Comedy*, the greatest of all Italian epic poems, and Boccaccio wrote *The Decameron* before joining Petrarch as one of the first humanists. In England, Geoffrey Chaucer wrote several works in Middle English, the most important of which is *The Canterbury Tales*, a group of stories that resembles *The Decameron* in spirit if not in detail.

Geoffrey Chaucer (1340–1400).

Chaucer's Pilgrims Ride to Canterbury. The Canterbury Tales, *like* The Decameron, *is a collection of stories, but in this case, the stories are told by a group of people going on a religious pilgrimage to the shrine of St. Thomas à Becket at Canterbury. The pilgrims come from every walk of life, and some of them are anything but pious in their language and behavior.*

garded as trivial. Scholastics sometimes counterattacked by accusing them of irreligion. Although humanists could be found among the critics of the church, few, if any, rejected conventional religious belief. The Renaissance moved Western society strongly toward secularism, not by attacking religion, but by reviving the ancient preoccupation with human beings and their social relationships. Humanists such as **Giovanni Pico della Mirandola** (Joe-vahn'-nee Peek'-o della Meer-an-doe'-la) asserted "the dignity of

Giovanni Boccaccio (1313–1375).

***The Beginning of* The Decameron.** *The Decameron* is a series of tales supposedly told to each other by a group of young men and women who sought shelter from the plague in the church of Santa Maria Novella, Florence. In this manuscript illumination, made for Teofilo Calcagni at the court of Ferrara in the third quarter of the fifteenth century, the participants gather for the storytelling.

Dante Alighieri (1265–1321).

***A Scene from Dante's* Inferno.** Dante's poem *The Divine Comedy* has three sections: *Inferno* (Hell), *Purgatorio* (Purgatory), and *Paradiso* (Heaven). This picture by the Renaissance painter Sandro Botticelli illustrates the eighteenth canto, or section, of the *Inferno,* which contains a description of the first two ditches in the eighth circle of Hell. In the upper ditch, the traveler (Dante and his guide the poet Virgil), pass by matchmakers and seducers who run to escape from the devils whipping them. In the lower ditch, flatterers and prostitutes are caught in excrement.

man" against preachers who saw humanity as wholly depraved (see Document 13.3), but even Pico believed that human dignity derived largely from humanity's central place in a divinely established universe. Unbelief was not at issue. The humanists believed in perfecting their minds and bodies on Earth while preparing their souls for the hereafter.

Humanist Educational Theory. Such a goal was fundamentally educational, and the humanists were

FIGURE 13.5 Portrait of the Merchant Georg Gisze
(1532) by Hans Holbein the Younger (1497–1543). Late-
medieval merchants, like lawyers, doctors, and notaries, liked
to see themselves as men of learning and culture. Many of
them embraced, and often subsidized, classical scholarship.
This portrait of a young German merchant resident in London
shows him in his office with writing implements, books, and
papers. His name appears in different styles of handwriting on
the documents tacked to the walls. Some of the objects on his
desk have symbolic meaning. The carnations, for example, are
a medieval symbol of betrothal and probably indicate that he
is engaged to be married.

predictably concerned with educational theory. Their
purpose was to create *il uomo universale* (il oo-ohm'-o
oo-ni-ver-sahl'-ay), the universal man whose person
combined intellectual and physical excellence and who
was capable of functioning honorably in virtually any
situation. It was the ancient Greco-Roman ideal,
brought up-to-date and applied to life in the Italian
city-state where the small size of the community forced
citizens or courtiers to play many roles. Although most
fully described in *The Courtier* by Baldassare Castiglione
(Bal-dus-sar'-ay Kas-tee-lee-own'-ay; published in
1528), it had long been present in the thinking of such
educational theorists as Vittorino da Feltre (1386–1446)
and Leon Battista Alberti (1404–1472).

The heart of Renaissance education was ancient literature and history (see Document 13.4). The classics were
thought to provide both moral instruction and the deep
understanding of human behavior without which correct action in the present is impossible. They were also a

guide to style. The ability to communicate is essential to
political life, and good writing comes largely from immersion in good literature. Humanists taught the art of
persuasion through an exhaustive study of rhetoric
based on the writings of Quintilian and Cicero.

Because citizens and courtiers would almost certainly participate in war, they had to study military
history and theory, the art of fortification, and ballis-
tics. Moreover, humanist educators regarded profi-
ciency with weapons and physical fitness as essential
for war and, like the ancients, regarded athletic skill
as valuable in its own right. The Renaissance man or
woman was also expected to be good company. Sports
were a social skill, as was dancing, the ability to play
musical instruments, and the possession of a trained
singing voice. Art was useful not merely for the sake
of appreciation but also as a tool of observation. Before
the camera, only drawing or sketching could preserve a
record of visual impressions—or accurately portray the
fortifications of one's enemies. Other useful subjects
included mathematics, accounting, medicine, and the
natural sciences.

The preferred means of imparting this rather daunt-
ing quantity of knowledge was in small academies or by
means of a tutor. The teacher was supposed to live with
his students and be a moral example and friend as well
as a purveyor of knowledge. Students were not to be
beaten or threatened but induced to learn by arousing
their interest in the subject at hand. These humanist
theories, and the classical examples from which they
came, remain the basis of today's liberal arts education.
They have had an enormous impact on the formation of
European youth and on the development of Western
culture. However, humanist education was intended
only for a relatively narrow social elite: the select group
that participated in public life and exercised some degree of control over its own destiny. Even women were
largely excluded, although humanists such as Leonardo
Bruni, Juan Luis Vives, and Thomas More argued that
women should be educated in much the same way as
men (see Document 13.5). Such women as Vittoria Colonna
and More's daughter, Margaret Roper, developed a reputation for classical learning. But for the most part, the
education of upper-class women continued to emphasize the domestic and social graces as it had done for
centuries.

The Spread of Humanism. The usefulness of the
Renaissance educational ideal was in part responsible
for the spread of humanism beyond the Alps. The requirements of life as a courtier or servant of the crown
in England, France, or Spain were not unlike those demanded of the upper-class Italian. Such people were
among the first non-Italians to develop an interest in
the classics, but they were quickly followed by their
princes. Isabella of Castile, for example, imported

FIGURE 13.6 *Raphael's* **School of Athens** *(1508–1511).* This monumental painting by one of the great artists of the Renaissance is a tribute to classical learning—and to the idea that antiquity had been reborn. Raphael has portrayed many of the thinkers and scientists of antiquity with the features of his contemporaries. Walking toward us in the center are Aristotle (with the beard, resembling Leonardo da Vinci) and Plato. To their right (our left) Socrates talks with his students. The old man seated below, intent on writing while a boy holds for him a tablet with the musical harmonies, is Pythagoras. Toward the center leaning on a marble block is Heraclitus (Michelangelo). To the right is Euclid (Bramante) bending over a slate and explaining a theorem, and standing behind him, Ptolemy holds a globe. Diogenes the Cynic sprawls irreverently on the steps.

Italian humanists to raise the educational standards of her court and administration. Lawyers, too, were intrigued by humanist methods. The development of philology and of the historical analysis of texts had been among the first achievements of humanist scholarship. The legal profession in France and Germany was soon divided between those who added the new techniques to their arsenals and those who refused to do so. Above all, town councils were quick to recognize the usefulness of officials trained in the new learning. It became desirable, especially in the cities of the Holy Roman Empire, to have town clerks who could communicate with one another in classical Latin and who possessed the training to interpret and decipher old documents. Usefulness aside, the presence of learned humanists within a town or principality had become a matter of prestige.

Humanism in the Universities. The universities were in general more resistant to change. They remained the strongholds of scholasticism if for no other reason than that their traditional role had been the training of theologians. Some, however, such as John Colet (Kahl'-et) Oxford and Lefèvre d'Etaples (Le-fev-

vr duh-tahp-le) at Paris, began to perceive the usefulness of humanism for the study of religious literature, which was after all another form of ancient text. Others outside the universities shared their concern. The most famous of those who turned humanist methods to the study of Scripture and of the Fathers of the church was **Erasmus of Rotterdam** (1469–1536). Believing that corrupted texts had led to false interpretations, he devoted much of his extraordinarily busy and productive life to providing authoritative editions of religious texts. Best known today for his satirical attacks on ecclesiastical ignorance and for his bitter controversy with Martin Luther over the issue of free will, he was in many ways the epitome of the humanist whose chief interests were religious. His English friend Sir Thomas More (1477–1535) combined religious with secular interests. A lawyer who ultimately became lord chancellor to Henry VIII, he is perhaps best known for *Utopia,* his vision of a perfect society that recalls Plato's *Republic.* More also applied humanist scholarship to the law and to religious questions before being martyred for his opposition to the Reformation. He was sainted by the Catholic Church in 1935. The value of humanist studies was recognized on occasion by even the most conservative of churchmen. Cardinal Francisco Jiménez de Cisneros, archbishop of Toledo, grand inquisitor, and ultimately regent of Castile, established the University of Alcalá de Henares (Al-ca-la' day Eh-nar'-ace) in 1508 to provide humanist training for the Spanish clergy. Among its first products was the *Complutensian Polyglot Bible,* printed on facing pages in Greek, Hebrew, and Latin.

The Impact of Renaissance Humanism on the Arts and Sciences

The Invention of Printing. By 1500, humanist methods and values had spread to virtually every part of Europe, thanks largely to the invention of printing with moveable type. Textiles, playing cards, and popular

PICO ON THE DIGNITY OF MAN

Giovanni Pico, Count of Mirandola (1463–1494), was something of a prodigy who, before his death at 31, wrote extensively on many subjects. Like many humanists, he was deeply interested in magic, the occult, and Neo-Platonic philosophy. In his *Oration on the Dignity of Man*, he produced what some regard as the classic Renaissance statement of human dignity and freedom. Pico does not state that man is inherently good or rational, but his *Oration* provides a vision of human potential rarely emphasized in medieval writing. The formal flowery language is typical of humanist writing.

[God] took man as a creature of indeterminate nature and, assigning him a place in the middle of the world, addressed him thus: "Neither a fixed abode nor a form that is thine alone nor any function peculiar to thyself have We given thee, Adam, to the end that according to thy longing and according to thy judgment thou mayest have and possess what abode, what form, and what functions thou thyself shalt desire. The nature of all other beings is limited and constrained within the bounds of laws proscribed by Us. Thou, constrained by no limits, in accordance with thy own free will, in whose hand We have placed thee, shalt ordain for thyself the limits of thy nature. We have set thee at the world's center that thou mayest from thence more easily observe whatever is in the world. We have made thee neither of heaven nor of earth, neither mortal nor immortal, so that with freedom of choice and honor . . . thou mayest fashion thyself in whatever shape thou shalt prefer. Thou shalt have the power to degenerate into the lower forms of life, which are brutish. Thou shalt have the power out of thy soul's judgment, to be reborn into the higher forms, which are divine.

From Pico, Giovanni, "Oration on the Dignity of Man," in E. Cassirer, P. O. Kristeller, and J. H. Randall, Jr., eds., *The Renaissance Philosophy of Man* (Chicago: University of Chicago Press, 1948).

Question: If Pico does not claim that human beings are inherently good, what is the basis of their claim to freedom and dignity?

◄FIGURE 13.7 *Erasmus of Rotterdam (1469–1536).* Erasmus was the most influential humanist of the early 1500s and arguably the greatest scholar in northern Europe. This masterful portrait by Hans Holbein the Younger shows him at work.

woodcuts had been printed from carved blocks since the beginning of the fifteenth century. Presses for oil and wine had been known for centuries; paper, since about 1200. The large-scale production of books, however, demanded moveable, reusable type that could be set to produce different texts. Between 1440 and 1550 **Johan Gutenberg** (Yo'-hahn Goo'-ten-burg) engraved hard steel punches to produce a matrix from which he could cast individual letters. He then cast the type from an alloy of lead, tin, and antimony and developed a mold in which letters of various sizes could be set for printing. As is often the case with important technologies, others developed the same process at about the same time. By the end of the century, more than 1,500 presses in every part of Europe had produced thousands of editions and literally millions of books.

Printing made it possible not only to disseminate scholarship on an unheard of scale but also to create for the first time a standardized text. The impact of humanism on the arts and sciences was therefore enormous. The humanists developed classical studies as they are known today. Aided by printing, they created the first standardized editions of classical works and distributed them widely. In the process, humanism gave birth to the disciplines of linguistics, philology (the study of words), and historical criticism.

VERGERIO ON THE VALUE OF THE LIBERAL ARTS

Peter Paul Vergerio (Vair-jair'-ee-o, 1370–1444) was a leading Renaissance educational theorist. The following is from a letter he wrote to another humanist, Ubertino of Carrara defending what we would today call a liberal arts education. Similar arguments are made today.

For no wealth, no possible security against the future, can be compared with the gift of education in grave and liberal studies. By them a man may win distinction for the most modest name, and bring honor to the city of his birth however obscure it may be. . . .

We come now to the consideration of the various subjects which may rightly be included under the name of "Liberal Studies." Among these I accord the first place to History, on grounds both of its attractiveness and its utility, qualities which appeal equally to the scholar and to the statesman. Next in importance is Moral Philosophy, which indeed is, in a peculiar sense, a "Liberal Art" in that its purpose is to teach men the secret of true freedom.

History, then, gives us the concrete examples of the precepts inculcated by philosophy. The one shows what men should do, the other what men have said and done in the past, and what lessons we may draw therefrom for the present day. I would indicate as the third main branch of study, Eloquence, which indeed holds a place of distinction among the refined Arts. By philosophy we learn the essential truth of things, which by eloquence we so exhibit in orderly adornment as to bring conviction to differing minds. And history provides the light of experience.

From Vergerio, Peter Paul, "Letter to Ubertino of Carrara," in W. H. Woodward, ed., *Vittorino da Feltre and Other Humanist Educators* (New York: Bureau of Publications, Teachers College, Columbia University, 1963, pp. 106–107).

Question: What sort of person was this education intended to produce?

Literature. In literature, however, humanist devotion to the classics retarded the development of vernacular writing (in the native language of one's country) for more than a century. In the fourteenth century, Dante, Boccaccio, and even Petrarch had written in Italian. Geoffrey Chaucer, the greatest of medieval English writers, had written his *Canterbury Tales* in Middle English. By 1400, those with literary inclinations preferred to write in Latin, often in slavish imitation of the elaborate Roman style that had developed during the Augustan Age. When vernacular literature was revived in the sixteenth century by such figures as Tasso and Ariosto (Ar-ee-ose'-toe) in Italy, Cervantes (Sair-van'-tayss) and Garcilaso de la Vega (Gar-si-lass'-o day la Vay'ga) in Spain, Rabelais (Rab-e-lay) and Montaigne (Moan-ten-ye) in France, and Marlowe and Shakespeare in England, it was transformed by classical themes and rules of composition. The fifteenth century, however, had been remarkably unproductive. Latin, in the meantime, was practically destroyed as a living language. Because the humanists insisted on weeding out all nonclassical usage, the language ceased to evolve as it had done throughout the Middle Ages when it was the day-to-day language of diplomacy and administration in both church and state. Ironically, by the middle of the sixteenth century, Latin had largely been supplanted by the various European vernaculars in every western government outside the papal states.

History and Politics. The contribution of humanism to the study of history and politics was far more posi-

tive. From the beginning, humanists had regarded history as essential to a political education. At the very least, it provided inspiring examples of civic virtue and cautionary tales that would help the citizen or courtier avoid the mistakes of the past. In the Middle Ages, the dominant form of history had been the chronicle. Outside the Italian cities, chroniclers tended to record events in their chronological order without troubling themselves greatly over historical causation or the objective accuracy of their sources. The cause of historical events was, after all, God's will. The Greeks and Romans had taken a different view. Beginning with Thucydides, the best of them had defined their topics as questions to be answered in causal terms because they believed that human nature was consistent and that history therefore repeated itself. If history was cyclical, it offered a priceless guide to action in the present, not so much because it was predictive in absolute terms but because the process of historical causation could be understood and used by the educated to their own advantage.

Machiavelli. The most effective exponent of this view during the Renaissance was the Florentine lawyer and sometime politician **Niccolò Machiavelli** (Nick'-ko-lo Mack-ee-ah-vel'-li, 1469–1527). In works such as *The Prince,* which provides advice for rulers, and *The Discourses on Livy,* which deals with politics in a republic, he attempted to establish rules for the conduct of political life based upon examples from the historical past. In the process, he freed political theory from the

LOUISE LABÉ ON THE EDUCATION OF WOMEN

Although the Renaissance ideal of education extended only to a minority of women, many saw even this as a liberating step forward in the development of women as a whole. One of them was Louise Labé (c. 1524–1566), an important French poet whose ideas in some ways foreshadow modern feminism. The following is from a dedicatory preface written to a friend. Distaffs and spindles are the implements used in spinning yarn.

Since a time has come, Mademoiselle, when the severe laws of men no longer prevent women from applying themselves to the sciences and other disciplines, it seems to me that those of us who can should use this long-craved freedom to study and to let men see how greatly they wronged us when depriving us of its honor and advantages. And if any woman becomes so proficient as to be able to write down her thoughts, let her do so and not despise the honor but rather flaunt it instead of fine clothes, necklaces, and rings. For these may be considered ours only by use, whereas the honor of being educated is ours entirely. . . . If the heavens had endowed me with sufficient wit to understand all I would have liked, I would serve in this as an example rather than an admonishment. But having devoted part of my youth to musical exercises,

and finding the time left too short for the crudeness of my understanding, I am unable in my own case, to achieve what I want for our sex, which is to see it outstrip men not only in beauty but in learning and virtue. All I can do is to beg our virtuous ladies to raise their minds somewhat above their distaffs and spindles and try to prove to the world that if we were not made to command, still we should not be disdained in domestic and public matters by those who govern and command obedience.

If there is anything to be recommended after honor and glory, anything to incite us to study, it is the pleasure which study affords. Study differs in this from all other recreations, of which all one can say, after enjoying them, is that one has passed the time. But study gives a more enduring sense of satisfaction. For the past delights us and serves more than the present.

From Labé, Louise, Dedicatory preface. From J. Aynard, ed., "Les poètes lyonnais précurseurs de la Pléide," in Julia O'Faolain and Lauro Martines, *Not in God's Image: Women in History from the Greeks to the Victorians* (London: Temple Smith, 1973, pp. 184–185).

Question: What motivates the author to encourage women's education?

---

theological principles upon which it had long been based. Although his name soon became a byword for cynicism and political manipulation, Machiavelli was in his own way an idealist. The Italian wars begun by Charles VIII of France in 1495 eventually destroyed the independence of the Italian cities, with only Venice retaining full sovereignty. Machiavelli believed that this calamity could be understood and remedied only by looking with a clear eye at the way in which politics was actually conducted.

His younger contemporary, **Francesco Guicciardini** (Fran-chess'-ko Gwee-chee-ar-dee'-nee, 1483–1540), agreed but thought that governing oneself by the kind of rules proposed by Machiavelli was impossible. As he said in his *Ricordi,* a grim collection of musings on a variety of subjects, no two situations were the same; there were always exceptions. He seems to have believed that by studying history one absorbed what he called *discretion:* the ability to react intelligently to unforeseen contingencies. His *History of Italy,* which examines the loss of Italian freedom in the years after 1494, is probably the first modern historical work and remains a useful source for the political and military history of the age.

Renaissance Philosophy. By comparison with its impact on politics and history, the humanist contribu-

tion to philosophy was indirect. The Renaissance was not a great age of formal speculation, but the course of modern philosophy would be hard to imagine without the recovery of classical works that had been lost during the Middle Ages. Much of Aristotle, most of Plato, the pre-Socratics, and many of the Epicureans and Stoics were either unknown or had been studied with little regard to their historical and intellectual context. By recovering lost works and seeking a deeper understanding of the mental world that had produced them, the humanists immeasurably broadened philosophic discourse in the West. By attacking the scholastics, they opened the way for the acceptance of ideas that lay outside the Aristotelian tradition as it was then understood. Some humanists developed an interest in the Alexandrian Neo-Platonists of the second and third centuries CE. The Neo-Platonists had adopted an extreme version of Plato's theory of forms that could be adapted to Christian mysticism. They may have done little to exploit their own discoveries, but their revival of interest in Plato made possible the great philosophical achievements of the seventeenth century.

Science. The impact of humanism on science was similar. Few humanists were scientists in the modern sense of the word. Many were devotees of what would now be called *superstition,* although the term is unhis-

POLITICAL THOUGHT IN THE ITALIAN RENAISSANCE

By removing all considerations of morality or religion from the discussion of politics, Machiavelli and Guicciardini may be regarded as the spiritual founders of political science. Their interest lay not in the way things ought to be but in what works. Machiavelli in particular was widely read in his own time, but his apparent cynicism provoked an "anti-Machiavellian" reaction, especially among sixteenth-century Spanish political philosophers who sought to develop a political theory based upon divine will and natural law.

The Political Philosophy of Machiavelli

Niccolò Machiavelli's most famous book was *The Prince*, in which he appears to favor despotic rule as a means of ridding Italy of its "barbarian" invaders. However, he was an ardent republican both in theory and in his own career as secretary to the second chancery of the Florentine republic. The following passage from *The Discourses* sets out what may be taken as his real view.

And finally to sum up this matter, I say that both governments of princes and of the people have lasted a long time, but both require to be regulated by laws. For a prince who knows no other control but his own will is like a madman, and a people that can do as it pleases will hardly be wise. If now we compare a prince who is controlled by laws, and a people who is untrammeled by them, we shall find more virtue in the people than in the prince; and if we compare them when both are freed from such control, we shall see that the people are guilty of fewer excesses than the prince, and that the errors of the people are of less importance, and may therefore be more easily remedied. For a licentious and mutinous people can be brought back to good conduct by the influence and persuasion of a good man, but an evil-minded prince is not amenable to such influences, and there is therefore no other remedy against him but cold steel.

From Macchiavelli, Niccolò, *The Discourses*, vol. I, 58, trans. Luigi Ricci; rev. E. R. P. Vincent. Modern Library Editions (New York: Random House, 1950).

Guicciardini on Political Morality

These selections from the *Ricordi* reveal how far Renaissance political thought could stray from Christian principles. Guicciardini did not intend them for publication, but their tone recalls on a more personal level some of the ideas expressed by Machiavelli in *The Prince*. With the exception of the first, Machiavelli would probably have agreed with all of them.

It is a great error to speak of things of this world absolutely and indiscriminately and to deal with them, as it were, by the book. In nearly all things one must make distinctions and exceptions because of differences in their circumstances. These circumstances are not covered by one and the same rule. Nor can these distinctions and exceptions be found written in books. They must be taught by discretion.

Political power cannot be wielded according to the dictates of good conscience. If you consider its origin, you will always find it in violence—except in the cases of republics within their borders, but not beyond. Not even the emperor is exempt from this rule; nor are the priests, whose violence is double because they assault us with both temporal and spiritual weapons.

Revenge does not always stem from hate or from an evil nature. Sometimes it is necessary that people will learn not to offend you. It is perfectly all right to avenge yourself even though you feel no deep rancor against the person who is the object of your revenge.

I would praise the man who is ordinarily open and frank and who uses deception only in very rare, important matters. Thus, you will have the reputation of being open and genuine, and you will enjoy the popularity such a reputation brings. And in those very important matters you will reap even greater advantage from deception, because your reputation for not being a deceiver will make your words be easily believed.

From *Maxims and Reflections of a Renaissance Statesman*, trans. M. Domandi (New York: Harper Torchbooks, 1965).

torical. Believing that the wisdom of the ancients was superior and being aware that Greeks and Romans had believed in divination, sorcery, astrology, and natural magic, some humanists deliberately encouraged a revival of these practices. Notions that would have been regarded as absurd in the days of Aquinas were taken seriously. Nevertheless, in their zeal to recover every aspect of the ancient past, they found and edited works that would eventually revolutionize Western thought. Galen in medicine, Eratosthenes and Aristarchus of Samos in cosmology, Archimedes in physics, and a host of other writers were rediscovered, edited, and popularized.

Mathematics. The humanists also transmitted the idea, derived ultimately from Pythagoras, that the universe

Renaissance Architecture

A revival of classical taste in architecture accompanied the revival of ancient literature. Italian architects of the 1400s studied Roman ruins in an effort to duplicate their appearance and apply their engineering principles to modern buildings. In the process, they created a classical style that replaced the Gothic and became the basis of much European (and American) public and domestic architecture until the middle of the twentieth century.

Palladio's Villa Rotunda. Andrea Palladio (1518–1580) was perhaps the greatest architect of the late Renaissance. This villa in Vicenza, Italy, represents the final stage in the Renaissance adoption of Roman architectural motifs. It inspired a host of domed country houses in Britain and the United States, including Jefferson's Monticello.

was based on number. This is the basic principle of numerology, now regarded as a pseudoscience, but it inspired such figures as **Leonardo da Vinci** (Lay-o-nar'-do da Vin'-chee, 1452–1519) to explore the mathematization of physics. Leonardo is best known today as an artist, engineer, and inventor whose ideas were far in advance of their time. His paintings, including "Mona Lisa" and "The Last Supper," are world famous and his beautifully illustrated notebooks offer a fascinating insight into one of the world's most creative minds, but he failed in his effort to express physical relationships in mathematical formulae. Galileo and others would eventually succeed, not because their mathematics were

better, but because the hypotheses on which their formulas rested were correct (see Chapter 16).

Architecture. Few of these achievements had an immediate impact on the life of ordinary Europeans. The recovery of classical antiquity was an intellectual movement created by and for a self-conscious elite, and many years would pass before it touched the consciousness of the general public. In one area, however, classical values intruded on material life, redefining the public spaces in which people moved and altering their visual perceptions of the world. Renaissance art, architecture, and city planning brought the aesthetic values

Alberti's Tempio Malatesta. An extreme example of classical imitation, the unfinished church of San Francesco at Rimini was built about 1450. Rimini was a city in the Papal States whose ruler, the infamous Sigismundo Malatesta, was a great admirer of all things Roman. At his request, Alberti transformed an existing church into a Roman temple whose facade resembles a triumphal arch. Sigismundo commissioned a statue of the Virgin Mary whose features were modeled on those of his mistress, Isotta degli Atti.

The Dome of the Cathedral of Florence. The cathedral of Florence was begun in 1296. Its mixture of gothic and classical design elements was typical of medieval Italian architecture, which never fully accepted the Gothic style. In 1420, the city commissioned Filippo Brunelleschi (1377?–1446) to design and build a dome on the Roman model. A classical scholar as well as an architect and engineer, Brunelleschi used Roman construction techniques—bricks laid in a herringbone pattern supported by stone frames—and topped the structure with a "lantern" to let in the light. The lantern was completed after his death. Domes of this kind were used in hundreds of churches until the end of the eighteenth century.

of Greece and Rome down to street level. They eventually spread from the Italian towns to the farthest reaches of Europe and America.

Italian artists had turned to classical ruins for inspiration as early as the thirteenth century. With the emergence of humanism, ancient models became universal. The architect **Filippo Brunelleschi** (Broo-nel-less'-kee, 1377–1446) measured ancient ruins to determine their proportions. He then sketched their pediments, columns, and ornamentation with the intention of adapting Roman forms to the purposes of his own day. Within a generation, churches were being built that resembled pagan temples. New construction, private and public, sported columns, pilasters, and window treatments borrowed from the porticoes of Roman buildings. It was not mere antiquarianism because Brunelleschi and his successors—Alberti, Bramante (Bra-mahn'-tay), and the sixteenth-century master Palladio (Pahl-lahd'-ee-o)—knew that modern structures were different in function from those of the past. So successful were their adaptations that Roman forms and ornamentation remained a standard feature of Western architecture until the twentieth century.

Painting and Sculpture. The revival of classical taste in painting and sculpture was equally important. Medieval artists had illustrated classical themes, and

ITALIAN RENAISSANCE PAINTING

Renaissance artists took their subjects from classical literature, but they also used classical motifs (Greek or Roman architectural details, costumes, and so on) to portray modern, medieval, or biblical themes. They avoided abstraction and introduced the use of chiaroscuro and perspective. *Perspective* is the art of depicting three dimensions on a flat plane. It makes use of the fact that planes and parallel lines appear to shrink and converge to a vanishing point or points on the horizon. The artist first establishes an arbitrary horizon line on the canvas. A vanishing point is placed at the center of that horizon to provide a fully frontal view of the subject, or two points are created, one on each side of the horizon line, as in the Bronzino portrait to provide an angled view. Filippo Brunelleschi rediscovered the mathematical rules of perspective in the early 1400s. The conventions of Renaissance art eclipsed the often abstract and static art of the Middle Ages and became the basis of European taste until the advent of impressionism, cubism, and abstract expressionism at the end of the nineteenth century.

God Creating Adam by Michelangelo Buonarroti (Mee-kel-an'-je-lo Bwo-nar-ro'-tee, 1475–1564). This detail from Michelangelo's ceiling for the Sistine Chapel shows Adam half reclining on Earth, lifting himself slightly to stretch out his arm toward the Creator. God is flying toward him and touches his finger with the divine spark, allowing him to rise and become an individual with a soul. The figures, with their heavy musculature and contorted postures, convey the drama and emotion of the moment in a way that recalls the sculptures of Hellenistic Greece, but Michelangelo's dramatic compositions also inspired the baroque artists of the 1600s.

some of them, such as Nicola Pisano (c. 1220–1278), had successfully imitated classical forms, although only in portraying scenes from the Bible. In medieval practice, tales from ancient history or mythology were normally portrayed in contemporary settings because they were intended as moral or religious allegories whose message was often unlike that of their pagan originals. To the humanists, with their archaeological view of history, this was absurd. Classical forms were appropriate to classical subjects as well as to those derived from the Bible. The imitation of classical models and the use of classical settings therefore became almost universal. Ancient ideas of beauty and proportion were adopted, especially for the portrayal of the human body.

But Renaissance art was not an exercise in antiquarianism. The technique of painting with oils, developed in the Low Countries during the fifteenth century, was

Incendio di Borgo *(Fire in the Neighborhood).* This fresco (1514–1517), composed by Raphael and executed by Giulio Romano and Giovan Francesco Penni, illustrates many of the components of Renaissance painting. It shows a fire that broke out in the *borgo* (borough) around the Basilica of St. Peter's in the year 847; Pope Leo V (847–855) extinguished the fire by making the sign of the cross. The subject is medieval, but the costumes—or lack thereof—are Roman, as is the architecture. The scene is executed using both perspective and chiaroscuro. The figure of the young man with his old father on his shoulders recalls the scene from Virgil when Aeneas carries his father Anchises from burning Troy.

soon in general use. The effort to portray the world in three dimensions, begun with the use of *chiaroscuro* (kee-ah-ro-sku'-ro) or shading by Giotto (Joe'-toe, c. 1266–1337), was brought to a triumphal conclusion with Brunelleschi's discovery of the mathematical laws of perspective (the art of making objects appear three dimensional even when portrayed on a plane surface). The application of these techniques in the paintings of Andrea Mantegna (Ahn-dray'-a Mahn-tay'-nya, c. 1431–1506) inspired other artists, and the viewing public soon came to accept foreshortening and perspective as the norm.

These techniques were new. Furthermore, Renaissance artists differed from the ancients in other ways. They were not pagans, and although they admired antiquity, they retained many of the ideas and symbols of the medieval past. Their art combined classical and Christian sensibilities in a new synthesis that shaped

FIGURE 13.8 *The* Mona Lisa, *Leonardo da Vinci (1452–1519).* Leonardo in some ways typifies the Renaissance ideal of human excellence and versatility. Scientist, mathematician, and engineer, he was also a great painter. His *Mona Lisa* is perhaps the most famous of all portraits. It is not only a subtle character study but demonstrates a masterful use of *chiaroscuro*, the use of light and shade rather than line to delineate form.

European aesthetic values until their vision was challenged by the rise of photography and nonrepresentational art in the nineteenth century. Eventually, artists such as **Michelangelo Buonarroti**, 1475–1564) would transcend the rules of classical composition, distorting the proportions of the human body to express dramatic spiritual and emotional truths. But even he and his Baroque followers in the seventeenth century remained well within the bounds of classical inspiration.

CONCLUSION

A century ago, most historians believed that the Renaissance marked the beginning of the modern world. As the full implications of the Industrial

Revolution became clear, that conviction has dimmed and the distance between twentieth-century Westerners and the preoccupations of the humanists has widened. Few today believe that the Renaissance was a true rebirth of classical antiquity or as revolutionary as its more enthusiastic supporters claimed. There had been a Carolingian Renaissance and a Renaissance of the Twelfth Century. Medieval scholars knew and quoted classical writers, but the Renaissance that began in Florence in the generation of the Black Death was far more than just another in a series of European infatuations with the antique past. By rediscovering the lost masterpieces of Greek and Roman literature, by reviving the ancient preoccupation with history, and by reexamining scientific theories ignored during the Middle Ages, the humanists redefined learning and transformed education. By the early fifteenth century, the new learning had become the dominant movement in European intellectual life. Directly or indirectly, it remade each of the arts and sciences in its own image and changed forever the way in which Westerners looked at their world.

Review Questions

- How did Ferdinand and Isabella forge a new monarchy in Spain?
- What developments enabled Charles VII and Louis XI to consolidate the French monarchy?
- What did Renaissance humanists regard as a proper education?
- How and why did humanism spread from Italy into the rest of Europe?

For Further Study

Readings

Hale, J. R., *The Civilization of Europe in the Renaissance* (New York: Atheneum, 1994). An outstanding survey of the entire period.

Hillgarth, J., *The Spanish Kingdoms, 1250–1516, vol. 2: Castilian Hegemony, 1410–1516* (Oxford: Claredon Press, 1978). The development of the Spanish Monarchy.

Lander, J. R., *Crown and Nobility, 1450–1509* (London: Arnold, 1976). The development of the English monarchy from the beginning of the Wars of the Roses through Henry VII.

Nauert, Charles G., *Humanism and the Culture of Renaissance Europe* (New York: Cambridge University Press, 1995). A sophisticated, yet accessible, analysis of humanism and its influence.

Potter, David, *A History of France, 1460–1560. The Emergence of a Nation State* (New York: St. Martin's Press, 1995).

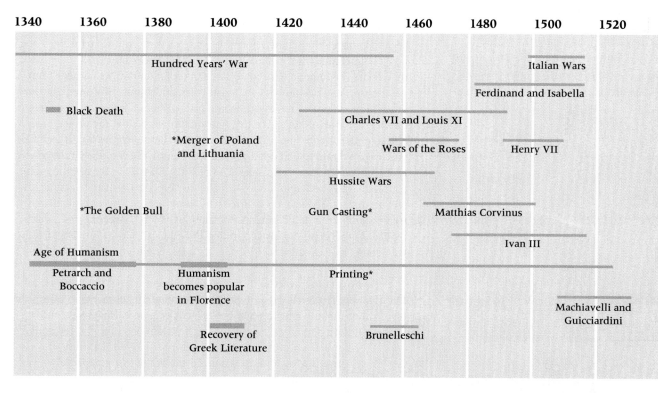

InfoTrac College Edition

For additional reading, go to your online research library at *http://infotrac.thomsonlearning.com.*

Using Key Terms, enter the search terms:
Machiavelli   *Leonardo da Vinci*

Using the Subject Guide, enter the search:
Renaissance   *humanism*

Web Site

http://www.ucalgary.ca/applied_history/tutor/endmiddle/
The End of Europe's Middle Ages. Sponsored by the University of Calgary, this site provides broad coverage of the entire period in text and includes useful links.

THE AGE OF THE RENAISSANCE

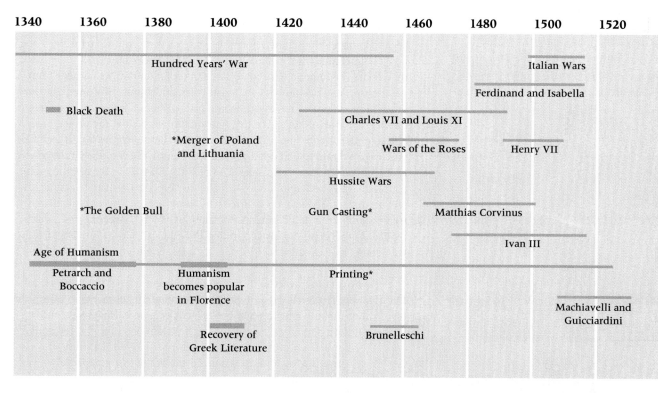

| 1340 | 1360 | 1380 | 1400 | 1420 | 1440 | 1460 | 1480 | 1500 | 1520 |

Hundred Years' War

Italian Wars

Ferdinand and Isabella

Black Death

Charles VII and Louis XI

*Merger of Poland and Lithuania

Wars of the Roses

Henry VII

Hussite Wars

*The Golden Bull

Gun Casting*

Matthias Corvinus

Ivan III

Age of Humanism

Petrarch and Boccaccio

Humanism becomes popular in Florence

Printing*

Machiavelli and Guicciardini

Recovery of Greek Literature

Brunelleschi

Visit the Western Civilization Companion Web Site for resources specific to this textbook:
http://history.wadsworth.com/hause02/

The CD in the back of this book and the Western Civilization Resource Center at *http://history.wadsworth.com/western/* offer a variety of tools to help you succeed in this course, including access to quizzes; images; documents; interactive simulations, maps, and timelines; movie explorations; and a wealth of other sources.

FOCUS QUESTIONS

- What major developments undermined the church's authority in the later Middle Ages?
- What major issues separated the reformers from those who remained Catholics?
- Why did a number of rulers and city governments support the Protestants?
- How did the reformations of the sixteenth century influence popular culture and the status of women?

Chapter 14

THE RELIGIOUS REFORMATIONS OF THE SIXTEENTH CENTURY

On April 17, 1521, a monk named Martin Luther appeared before Emperor Charles V and the princes of the Holy Roman Empire at the Diet of Worms. Four years earlier, he had attacked the church's practice of selling indulgences for cash. Although many churchmen agreed with him, the papacy condemned his position. In the controversy that followed, Luther began to attack other church doctrines and practices. After some delay, Pope Leo X condemned his teachings and ordered his books burned. The church then asked the Imperial Diet to declare Luther an outlaw. As Luther's prince, the Elector Frederick the Wise of Saxony demanded that "his" monk be permitted a hearing that, he hoped, would give Luther an opportunity to defend his views. Copies of Luther's writings were brought before the princes. An official of the Archbishop of Trier asked him if these were his books and if he was prepared to reject all or part of their contents. To everyone's amazement, Luther asked for time to consider. The next day, at 6:00 in the afternoon, he appeared again, and after a brief speech, answered in German: "I cannot and will not recant, because it is neither safe nor wise to act against conscience. Here I stand, I can do no other. God help me! Amen." Sweating and clearly shaken, Luther repeated his declaration in Latin and left the building. On the way home, an armed band of Frederick's men seized him and hurried him off to one of Frederick's castles to protect him from arrest.

For many, Luther's declaration marks the beginning of the Protestant Reformation. It was clearly one of the most dramatic moments in European history, but the movement it symbolizes had long been underway, and Luther's Reformation was but one of many. Taken together, the religious reformations of the sixteenth century shattered the unity of western Christendom and changed the life of Europe forever.

Chapter 14 begins with the problems and conflicts that confronted the late medieval church and how they led to increasingly strident demands for reform. It then examines the wide variety of religious movements that arose during the sixteenth century—Lutheran, Reformed, Calvinist, Anabaptist, and Anglican—before describing an equally important reformation within the Catholic Church. It concludes with the cultural and social consequences of religious change.

Late Medieval Demands for Religious Reform (c. 1300–1517)

The religious reformations of the sixteenth century grew out of a crisis that had been long in the making. For nearly 200 years, plague, war, and the perception of social collapse had raised the overall level of spiritual anxiety in European society while the growth of literacy narrowed the intellectual gap between the clergy and their flocks. Lay people (and many clergy) began to demand higher standards of spirituality than ever before. When the church, crippled by internal struggles of its own, failed to meet this revolution of rising expectations, calls for reform intensified. At the same time, the new assertiveness of the secular states brought their rulers into conflict with the church over rights, privileges, and revenues. The convergence of religious discontent with the interests of the state made the pressure for change irresistible.

The Conflicting Roles of the Medieval Church. The condition of the church aroused strong feelings in medieval Europe not only because almost everyone was a believing Christian but because the church as an institution was more closely integrated with the secular world than it is today. The pope claimed responsibility not only for the spiritual welfare of western Christians but also for the administration and defense of the Papal States, a territory that embraced much of central Italy. At the local level, bishops, parishes, monasteries, and other ecclesiastical foundations probably controlled 20 percent of the arable land in Europe. In less-settled areas such as the north of England, the total may have approached 70 percent. Many Europeans therefore lived on estates held by the church or had regular business dealings with those who managed them. Such contacts often caused resentment and may at times have encouraged the appearance of corruption.

Social services, too, were the church's responsibility. Clerics commonly administered hospitals, the care of orphans, and the distribution of charity and controlled formal education from the grammar school to the university. In an age when inns were few and wretched, monasteries often served as hotels, offering food and lodging to travelers in return for nominal donations.

The church's many roles made it the most important institution in Europe, but practical responsibilities bred a certain worldliness. To meet them, the church often rewarded those in whom administrative skills were more developed than spirituality. Not everyone who became a priest or nun did so from the purest of motives. Because the church offered one of the few available routes to upward social mobility, ambition or family interest caused many to become clerics without an adequate religious vocation. Some had little choice. Parents often destined their sons for the priesthood at a tender age, while unmarriageable women or those who preferred a career other than that of wife and mother had only the convent as a refuge. For women of talent and ambition, the opportunity to govern an abbey or a charitable institution was a route to self-fulfillment and public service otherwise unavailable in medieval society. For an ambitious young man without an estate, or for a scholar who wished to pursue a career at the university, the church offered the only pathway to success.

Not all late medieval clerics, of course, had worldly motives. Extreme piety and asceticism existed in close proximity to spiritual indifference and corruption. For many people in an age of great spiritual need, the contrast may have been too painful to accept. In any case, the anticlericalism that had always been present in European life ran especially high in the fourteenth and fifteenth centuries. Although by no means universal— the ties between lay people and their parish priests often remained close—it was an underlying accompaniment to the events that convulsed the church throughout this period.

The Decline of Papal Authority

Papal authority was one of the first casualties of the conflict between church and state and of the growing confusion over the temporal and spiritual roles of the clergy. A series of scandals beginning around 1300 gravely weakened the ability of the popes either to govern the church or to institute effective reforms in the face of popular demand. In 1294, the saintly Celestine V resigned from the papacy in part because he feared that the exercise of its duties imperiled his soul. His successor, Boniface VIII, had no such concerns. A vigorous advocate of papal authority, Boniface came into conflict with both Edward I of England and Philip IV of France over the issue of clerical taxation. The two kings were at war with one another, and each sought to tax the clergy of their respective realms to pay for it. When the pope forbade the practice in the bull *Clericis Laicos,* Philip blocked the transmission of money from France to Rome. (A *bull* is a papal letter, sealed because of its importance with a round leaden seal, or *bulla.* It is named after the first word or words of its text.) Boniface backed down, but Philip was not content with partial victories. In 1301, he convicted the papal legate of treason and demanded that Boniface ratify the decision of the French courts. This he could not do without sacrificing papal jurisdiction over the French church. When Boniface issued the decree *Unam Sanctam,* a bold assertion of papal authority over the secular state, Philip had him kidnapped at Anagni in 1303. Physically mistreated by his captors and furious over this unprecedented assault on papal dignity, Boniface died shortly thereafter.

The Babylonian Captivity. After the brief pontificate of Benedict IX, French influence in the College of Cardinals secured the election of the bishop of Bordeaux, who became pope as Clement V (served 1305–1314). The Roman populace was outraged. Riot and disorder convinced Clement that Rome would be an unhealthy place for a Frenchman. He decided to establish himself at Avignon (Ah-vee-nyon), a papal territory in the south of France. The papacy would remain there for 73 years.

The stay of the popes at Avignon was called the **Babylonian Captivity,** because the church appeared to have been taken captive by the French as the biblical children of Israel had been held at Babylon. It was an international scandal for several reasons. The pope was living outside his diocese, and absenteeism had long been considered an abuse by reformers. Worse yet, the pope seemed to be a mere agent of the French monarchy. This was not quite true. The Avignon popes were more independent than they appeared to be at the time, but their support of France against England in the later stages of the Hundred Years' War reinforced negative impressions. They devoted their best efforts to

strengthening papal finances and to the construction of a magnificent palace complex at Avignon. Fiscal reforms backfired politically because most countries responded to it with legislation limiting papal jurisdiction and taxation within their borders. The palace was ostentatious and fostered the idea that the popes had no intention of returning to Rome. Most people came to believe that the popes were subservient to France as well as greedy and luxurious.

The Great Schism. Criticism mounted, and in 1377, Gregory XI returned the papacy to Rome. He died the following year, and his Italian successor, Urban VI, was elected amid rioting by the Roman mob and dissension among the cardinals. Urban quickly alienated those who had elected him by his erratic behavior and by his demands for an immediate reform of the papal court. Thirteen cardinals, twelve of whom were French, left Rome. Claiming that the election had been held under duress, they elected an antipope, Clement VII. The **Great Schism** (1378–1417) had begun.

The church now had two popes. England, the Holy Roman Empire, Hungary, and Poland supported Urban VI. France, Castile, Aragon, Naples, and Scotland supported Clement. International and dynastic issues were involved, and neither claimant would step down. For nearly 40 years, each side elected its own successors while papal administration deteriorated and the prestige of the papacy itself sank to levels not seen since before the Cluniac reforms.

The most promising solution was to convene a general council of the church. In 1409, the Council of Pisa elected Alexander V, who was generally accepted throughout Europe. However, the two prior claimants,

▼FIGURE 14.1 *The Papal Palace at Avignon.*
Contemporaries saw the magnificent palace built by the popes at Avignon as a symbol of clerical greed and worldliness. It is shown here from across the Rhône River with the ruined bridge of St. Benezet (the Pont d'Avignon of the nursery rhyme) in the foreground.

arguing that the council had been called illegally by the cardinals instead of by a pope, refused to quit. There were now three popes. Finally, in 1413, Alexander's successor, John XXIII, called the Council of Constance, which declared itself superior to any pope (see Document 14.1). John, who had in the meantime been found guilty of heresy, and the Avignon claimant Benedict XIII were deposed and Gregory XIII resigned. The Council then elected Martin V to succeed Gregory, thereby preserving the legitimacy of the Roman line, which has since been regarded as official.

Conciliarism and its Legacy. The Schism was over, but the papacy had been gravely weakened in both fact and theory. The actions of the council were supported by the work of three generations of thinkers who had come to believe that councils representing the entire body of the faithful had ultimate authority over the church and that the pope was little more than a symbol of unity. This position became known as **conciliarism.** Made plausible by more than a century of papal scandals, conciliarism became a formidable obstacle to the governance of the church. Fifteenth-century popes feared with some justification that they might be deposed for any controversial act, while councils, by their nature, found making everyday administrative decisions impossible. Legally, Pope Pius II resolved the issue in 1460, when he forbade appeals to a council without papal authorization in the bull *Execrabilis*. The memory of conciliarism nevertheless would inhibit papal efforts at reform for years to come.

The Possessionist Controversy. Conciliarism also served as a focus for criticisms of the papacy that had been simmering since the Babylonian Captivity. Other complaints against the papacy, some of which were adopted by the conciliarists, grew out of the **possessionist controversy.** By the end of the thirteenth century, the Franciscan order had split into two main factions: (1) the Observant or Spiritual Franciscans, who insisted on a literal interpretation of the Rule of St. Francis, which prohibited the order from owning property, and (2) the Conventuals, who believed that the work of the order could be done only if the brothers lived an orderly life in convents and possessed the material resources with which to perform their tasks. The whole issue spoke directly to the concerns of lay people who had long resented what they saw as the materialism and excessive fiscal demands of the clergy. After much argument, John XXII condemned the Observant position. Because the Franciscan Observants had no property, they tended to find lodging on their own and were therefore not subject to the discipline of a convent. This, he thought, could only breed scandal. The Observant Franciscans responded with written attacks on the validity of papal authority, many of which would be used by later critics of the church.

The Struggle over the Forms of Piety

The issue of church governance became entangled in a growing dispute over the forms of piety. This conflict, which was about two different ways of living a Christian life, had been present implicitly in the reform movements of the twelfth century. The dominant form of piety that had emerged from the early Middle Ages was forged by the monastic tradition. It saw the clergy as heroic champions whose chief function was to serve as intermediaries between the laity and a God of judgment.

They did this primarily through the sacrament of communion (the Eucharist), which Catholics consider a sacrifice, and through oral prayers of intercession. This view, with its necessary emphasis on the public repetition of formulas, was challenged in the eleventh and twelfth centuries by Bernard of Clairvaux and other monastic theorists who sought a more personal experience of God through private devotions and mental prayer. The Franciscans adopted their views and eventually popularized them, although the process was lengthy and incomplete. The Observant Franciscans found mental prayer especially attractive because their interpretation of the Rule of St. Francis made corporate devotions difficult.

Abuses in Late Medieval Piety. To those who sought transformation of their inner life through personal contact with God, the older forms of piety were unacceptable. They came to believe that excessive emphasis on the sacraments and on oral prayer encouraged complacency as well as contractualism, the habit of making deals with God in return for special favors. The point is arguable, but in their critique of popular piety they were on firmer ground. Much late medieval piety was mechanistic and involved practices that would today be regarded as abuses. The sale of indulgences, the misuse of pilgrimages, and the proliferation of masses for the dead were all symptoms of the popular obsession with death and purgatory that followed in the wake of the bubonic plague. The sacraments of the church guaranteed salvation, but every sin committed in life carried with it a sentence to be served in purgatory. As the pains of purgatory were like those of hell, without the curse of eternal separation from God, much effort was spent in avoiding them. A mass said for the soul of the dead reduced the penalty by a specified number of years. Henry VII of England, who seems to have had a bad conscience, left money in his will for 10,000 masses. Many priests survived entirely on the proceeds from such bequests and had no other duties. An **indulgence** was a remission of the "temporal" or purgatorial punishment for sins that could be granted by the pope out of the church's "treasury of merits." Its price, too, was related to the number of years it subtracted from the buyer's term in purgatory, and an indulgence sometimes could be purchased in advance for sins not yet committed.

Clerical Ignorance. Such practices were deeply rooted in the rich and varied piety of the Middle Ages. If some religious were scandalized by them, other priests would not condemn genuine expressions of religious feeling, and still others no doubt accepted them out of ignorance. No systematic education had been established for parish priests, and thanks to absenteeism, many parishes were served by vicars or substitutes whose qualifications were minimal at best. However,

the church's critics did not reject pilgrimages, indulgences, the proper use of relics, or masses for the dead. They merely wished to ground these "works" in the faith and good intentions that would make them spiritually valid. They opposed simpleminded contractualism and "arithmetical" piety, but their concerns intensified their conflict with a church that remained immobilized by political and organizational difficulties.

Mysticism. Of those forms of piety that sought personal contact with God, the most ambitious was mysticism. The enormous popularity of mysticism in the later Middle Ages was in some respects a measure of the growing influence of women on religious life. Many of the great mystics were women. Others were men who became involved with the movement as confessors to convents of nuns. **Mysticism** may be defined as the effort to achieve spiritual union with God through ecstatic contemplation. Because the experience is highly personal, it had many variants, but most of them fell into two broad categories. The first, and probably the most common, was to experience visions or infusions of the Holy Spirit in the manner of St. Catherine of Siena (1347–1380) or Julian of Norwich (1342–c. 1416). The second, best typified by Meister Eckhardt (c. 1260–1328) and the Rhineland mystics, was influenced by the Neo-Platonic concept of ideas and aimed at a real union of the soul with God (see Document 14.2). They sought to penetrate the divine intelligence and perceive the universe as God perceives it. Both views were rooted firmly in the medieval tradition of interior piety, but Eckhardt and those like him were suspected of heresy because they seemed to deny the vital distinction between the Creator and the human soul.

The Modern Devotion. Neither form of experience was easy to achieve. Both involved a long process of mental and spiritual preparation that was described in an ever-growing literature. Manuals such as Walter Hilton's *Scale of Perfection* became extremely popular with lay people and were circulated in large numbers both before and after the invention of printing. Although mysticism was essentially private, it influenced the development of a powerful corporate movement known as the *Devotio Moderna*, or modern devotion. Its founder was Gerhard Groote (Ghro'-tuh, 1340–1384), who organized a community of religious women at Deventer in the Netherlands. These Sisters of the Common Life were laywomen, not nuns. They pledged themselves to a communal life informed by contemplation but directed toward service in the world. A parallel group for men, the Brethren of the Common Life, was founded shortly thereafter by Groote's disciple Florens Radewijns (Rah'-duh-vines). These two groups, together with the Augustinian Canons of the Windesheim Congregation, a fully monastic order also founded by Radewijns, formed the nucleus of a movement that spread rapidly through the Low Countries and western Germany. Catholic, but highly critical of the clergy, it emphasized charitable works, private devotion, and its own form of education. The goal of its adherents was the imitation of Christ. A book titled *The Imitation of Christ* by one of the Brethren, Thomas à Kempis, was a best seller until well into the twentieth century and did much to popularize a style of piety that was the opposite of contractualism.

Heresies and Other Movements

Other religious movements were less innocent, at least from the perspective of the church. Full-scale heresies emerged in England and Bohemia in response to the teachings of **John Wycliffe** (1330–1384) and **Jan Hus** (c. 1372–1415). Wycliffe was a successful teacher of theology at Oxford who became involved with politics during the 1370s. England was attempting to follow the French lead in restricting papal rights of appointment and taxation, and Wycliffe became the chief spokesman for the anticlerical views of Edward III's son, John of Gaunt. At first, Wycliffe restricted himself to the traditional arguments in favor of clerical poverty, but as his views began to attract criticism and as he began to realize that his personal ambitions would not be fulfilled, he drifted further into radicalism. In his last years, he rejected papal authority and declared that the Bible was the sole source of religious truth. Strongly influenced by St. Augustine and committed to an extreme form of philosophical realism, he supported predestination and ended by rejecting transubstantiation because it involved what he saw as the annihilation of the substance of the bread and wine. In his view, substance was by definition unchangeable, and the miracle of the mass was therefore an impossibility. This was heresy, as was his revival of the ancient Donatist idea that the value of the sacraments depended on the personal virtue of the priest who administered them.

The Lollards. Although John of Gaunt discretely withdrew his support, Wycliffe died before the church could bring him to trial. By this time, his ideas and the extraordinary violence of his attacks on the clergy had begun to attract popular attention. His followers, the Lollards, produced an English translation of the Bible and organized a march on London in 1413. Fearing that the egalitarian tendencies of the Lollards encouraged social disorder, Henry V suppressed the movement, but scattered communities preserved their traditions until the outbreak of the Protestant Reformation.

The Hussites. Because England and Bohemia were diplomatically aligned on the Great Schism, a number of Czech students left the University of Paris for Oxford after 1378. There they came in contact with the teachings of Wycliffe, and by 1400, his works were being openly

debated at Prague. Wycliffe's ideas became popular because they seemed to coincide with an already well-developed reform movement. Czech preachers had long attacked the morality of the clergy and now demanded a Czech translation of the Bible. Great resentment also existed over denying the communion to the laity in both kinds. Reserving both bread and wine for the priest while giving only bread to the laity had long been a common practice throughout Europe. The Bohemians saw it as an expression of clerical arrogance.

Although basically religious, these issues became hopelessly intertwined with the ethnic rivalry between Czechs and Germans that had troubled Bohemia for centuries. The kingdom of Bohemia had a large population of Germans who were often resented by their Slavic neighbors. Moreover, the church held nearly 40 percent of the land, and many of the leading churchmen were

FIGURE 14.2 *Jan Hus Defending His Views at the Council of Constance (1415).* In this nineteenth-century illustration, Hus defends himself before the committee of scholars appointed to look into the charges of heresy made against him. In fact, his condemnation was assured before he traveled to Constance.

German. To many, anticlericalism was therefore an expression of Czech national feeling as well as of frustrated piety. This association quickly drew the reform movement into the arena of imperial politics.

The University of Prague found itself at the center of these controversies. In 1409, King Vaclav expelled the German students and faculty and appointed Jan Hus, a Czech professor, as rector. Hus had been attracted to Wycliffe's writings by their anticlericalism, but he also saw their extreme philosophical realism as a weapon against the German theologians, most of whom were nominalists. He did not, however, reject transubstantiation and was in general more conservative than Wycliffe on every issue save that of papal authority. Hus did not think of himself as a heretic, and in 1415, he accepted an invitation to defend his views before the Council of Constance. The invitation had been orchestrated by Emperor Sigismund who offered him a safe conduct, but the promised guarantee was little more than a passport and Hus was burned at the stake on July 6.

The burning of Hus provoked a national outcry in Bohemia. Taking the communion chalice as their symbol, the Czechs broke with Rome and developed a liturgy in the Czech language. When their protector, Vaclav, died in 1419, he was succeeded as king by Sigismund. **The Hussites,** as they were now called, rose in armed revolt and resoundingly defeated the papal-imperial crusades against them in 1420, 1422, and 1431. Finally, in 1436, the Hussites secured a treaty that guaranteed them control over the Bohemian church and confirmed their earlier expropriation of church property.

Nominalism. Two intellectual movements contributed to the religious tensions and controversies of the later Middle Ages and threatened the church's authority in more subtle ways. Nominalism (see Chapter 9), which grew in popularity during the fourteenth and fifteenth centuries, tended to undermine the foundations of dogma by denying that religious teachings were susceptible to rational proof. Although never the dominant school in late medieval thought, it influenced many theologians, including Martin Luther.

Humanism. Humanism exerted an even stronger influence on religious issues. Humanists such as Erasmus criticized the moral shortcomings of the clergy and used their mastery of rhetoric to attack the scholastic philosophers. Their belief in the superiority of ancient over modern texts contributed to the idea that Scripture alone was the ultimate source of religious truth. Although many humanists, including Erasmus, remained within the old church, this concept of *sola scriptura* became central to the teachings of the reformers. Many of them, including **Huldrych Zwingli** (Hool'-drik Tsving'-lee, 1484–1531), Calvin, and Melanchthon had been trained as humanists. They used humanist methodology in their analysis of sacred texts. Humanist respect for antiquity may also have influenced the growing belief that the practices of the early church most closely approximated the intentions of Christ. They came to believe that subsequent developments, including the power of bishops and the rise of the papacy, were modern corruptions and therefore intolerable.

The Influence of Printing. After 1450, the invention of printing with moveable type (see Chapter 13) spread knowledge of these movements and criticisms to the farthest corners of Europe while encouraging the spread of literacy, especially in the towns. Handwritten books had been prohibitively expensive. Even the richest of collectors sometimes boasted of libraries that contained fewer than 200 volumes. Printing made books cheap as well as easily duplicated in large numbers. Even men and women of modest means could now learn to read, and scholars have estimated that by 1500, the literacy rate in some cities was nearly 50 percent. Religious and political tracts, the writings of the mystics, and popular sermons enjoyed great popularity.

THE PROTESTANT REFORMATIONS (1517–1555)

The reform movements that destroyed the unity of western Christendom in the sixteenth century must be seen as the products of a generalized dissatisfaction with the church. The development of printing, which made the writings of the reformers available to thousands of people, and the conjunction of religious reform with the political needs of certain states and cities transformed that dissatisfaction into the Protestant Reformations.

Martin Luther

The first and in many ways the most influential of these movements was the one created in Germany by Martin Luther (1483–1546). A monk of the Augustinian Observant order and professor of the New Testament at the University of Wittenberg in electoral Saxony,

Martin Luther, 1529

Luther experienced a profound spiritual crisis that eventually brought him into open conflict with the church. Like many of his contemporaries, Luther was troubled by an overwhelming sense of sin and unworthiness for which the teachings of the church provided no relief. Neither the rigors of monastic life nor the sacrament of penance could provide him with assurance of salvation. In the course of his biblical studies, he gradually arrived at a solution. Based on his reading of Paul's Epistle to the Romans and on his growing admiration for the works of St. Augustine, he concluded that souls were not saved by religious ceremonies and good works and pious devotions but by faith alone. Human beings could never be righteous enough to merit God's forgiveness, but they could be saved if only they would believe and have faith in the righteousness of Christ. Like Augustine, he believed that faith came not from human effort but as an undeserved gift from God.

The Issue of Indulgences. Luther believed himself transformed by this insight. Even as he formulated it, he was confronted by the issue of indulgences. In 1517, a special indulgence was made available in the territories surrounding electoral Saxony. Its purpose was to raise money for the construction of St. Peter's basilica in Rome and to retire the debt incurred by Albrecht of Mainz in securing for himself through bribery the archbishoprics of Mainz and Magdeburg and the bishopric of Halberstadt. Albrecht had committed not only pluralism but also simony (the illegal purchase of church offices). To Luther, however, this was not the central issue. To him, as to many other clerics, the sale of indulgences was a symbol of the contractualism that beset medieval piety and blinded lay people to the true path of salvation. On October 31, 1517, he posted **Ninety-Five Theses** condemning this practice to the door of Wittenberg's Castle Church.

His action was in no way unusual. It was the traditional means by which a professor offered to debate all comers on a particular issue, and the positions taken by Luther were not heretical. The Council of Trent, called by Pope Pius III in 1542 as a means of renewing the Catholic Church, ultimately condemned the sale of indulgences. However, Luther's action unleashed a storm of controversy. Spread throughout Germany by the printing press, the theses were endorsed by advocates of reform and condemned by the pope, the Dominican order, the archbishop of Mainz, and the Fugger bank of Augsburg, which had loaned Albrecht the money for the elections.

Excommunication. In the debates that followed, Luther was forced to work out the broader implications of his teachings. At Leipzig in June 1519, he challenged the doctrinal authority of popes and councils and declared that Scripture took precedence over all other sources of religious truth. In 1520, he published three pamphlets that drew him at last into formal heresy. In his *Address to the Christian Nobility of the German Nation,* he encouraged the princes to demand reform (see Document 14.3). *On the Babylonian Captivity of the Church* abolished five of the church's seven sacraments and declared that the efficacy of baptism and communion depended on the faith of the recipient, not the ordination of the priest. He also rejected transubstantiation while arguing that Christ was nevertheless truly present in the Eucharist. *The Freedom of a Christian* summarized Luther's doctrine of salvation by faith alone. Luther had not intended to break with the church, but his extraordinary skill as a writer and propagandist ignited anticlerical and antipapal feeling throughout Germany. Compromise was now impossible, and he was excommunicated on January 31, 1521.

The Diet of Worms. The affair might have ended with Luther's trial and execution, but political considerations intervened. His own prince, Frederick "the Wise" of Saxony, arranged for him to defend his position before the **Imperial Diet of Worms,** held in the city of that name in April. Luther did not defend his teachings, but as we have seen, refused to retract them in dramatic terms. The newly elected Emperor **Charles V** was unimpressed. He placed Luther under the imperial ban, and Frederick was forced to protect his monk by hiding him in the Wartburg Castle for nearly a year. Luther used this enforced period of leisure to translate the New Testament into German.

Luther and the German Princes. Frederick's motives and those of the other princes and city magistrates who eventually supported Luther's reformation varied widely. Some were inspired by genuine religious feeling

MARTIN LUTHER'S ADDRESS TO THE GERMAN NOBILITY

Martin Luther's primary concerns were always spiritual and theological, but he knew how to appeal to other emotions as well. These extracts from his *Address to the Christian Nobility of the German Nation* are a relatively modest example of the rhetoric with which he attacked the authority of the Catholic Church.

What is the use in Christendom of those who are called "cardinals"? I will tell you. In Italy and Germany there are many rich convents, endowments, holdings, and benefices; and as the best way of getting these into the hands of Rome they created cardinals, and gave to them the bishoprics, convents, and prelacies, and thus destroyed the service of God. That is why Italy is almost a desert now. . . . Why? Because the cardinals must have the wealth. The Turk himself could not have so desolated Italy and so overthrown the worship of God.

Now that Italy is sucked dry, they come to Germany. They begin in a quiet way, but we shall soon have Germany brought into the same state as Italy. We have a few cardinals already. What the Romanists really mean to do, the "drunken" Germans are not to see until they have lost everything. . . .

Now this devilish state of things is not only open robbery and deceit and the prevailing of the gates of hell, but it is destroying the very life and soul of Christianity; therefore we are bound to use all our diligence to ward off this misery and destruction. If we want to fight Turks, let us begin here—we cannot find worse ones. If we rightly hang thieves and robbers, why do we leave the greed of Rome unpunished? For Rome is the greatest thief and robber that has ever appeared on earth, or ever will.

From Luther, Martin, "Address to the Nobility of the German Nation" (1520), in trans. Wace and Buckheim, B. J. Kidd, ed, *Documents Illustrative of the Continental Reformation*, No. 35 (Oxford, England: Oxford University Press, 1911).

Question: What criticism has Luther made against the church?

rejected Catholicism and established their own churches. They confiscated church property and appointed pastors or ministers, most of whom agreed with Luther, to replace the priests. Although Luther himself did not in any way control these state churches, they became known as **Lutheran** because they generally followed his teachings on the sacraments and salvation.

The Struggle with the Emperor. The Holy Roman Emperor objected to these developments on both political and religious grounds. Charles V (1500–1558; emperor from 1519) was a devout Catholic. He also supported the ideal of imperial unity, which was clearly threatened by anything that increased the power and revenues of the princes. Only 21 at

Charles V

the Diet of Worms, he had inherited an enormous accumulation of states, including Austria, Spain, the Netherlands, and much of Italy (see Chapter 15). In theory, only the Ottoman Empire could stand against him; in fact, he could do little to stop the spread of the Reformation. When he convinced the Imperial Diet to condemn the reforming states and cities in 1529, they issued a protest that earned them the name **Protestant.** In 1531, they formed the **Schmalkaldic League** in the town of that name and defended their Reformation with varying degrees of success for the remainder of Charles's reign. When the emperor abdicated and retired to a Spanish monastery in 1557, the Reformation was still intact. His power, although great, had not been equal to his responsibilities. Pressed on the Danube and in the Mediterranean by the Turks; forced to fight seven wars with France; and beset simultaneously by Protestant princes, urban revolutionaries, and popes who feared the extension of his influence in Italy, Charles failed utterly in his attempts to impose orthodoxy. The empire remained open to religious turmoil.

The Radical Reformation

Some of that turmoil began while Luther was still hidden in the Wartburg. The reformer had believed that once the gospel was freely preached, congregations would follow it without the direction of an institutional church. He discovered that not all of the pope's enemies shared his interpretation of the Bible. Movements arose that rejected what he saw as the basic insight of the Reformation: salvation by faith alone. To many ordinary men and women, this doctrine weak-

or, like Frederick, by a proprietary responsibility for "their" churches that transcended loyalty to a distant and non-German papacy. Others, especially in the towns, responded to the public enthusiasm generated by Luther's writings. Regardless of personal feelings, everyone understood the practical advantages of breaking with Rome. Revenues could be increased by confiscating church property and by ending ecclesiastical immunity to taxation. The control of church courts and ecclesiastical patronage were valuable prizes to those engaged in state building. By 1530, several of the more important German states and a number of towns had

FIGURE 14.3 *The Lutheran Sacraments.* This altar painting from the Lutheran church at Thorslunde, Denmark, is intended as a graphic lesson in theology. Infant baptism is shown at the left. In the center, two communicants receive the sacrament in both kinds (bread and wine), while the preacher at the right emphasizes the importance of God's word. Lutheran churches recognized only Baptism and Communion as sacraments. The Catholic Church recognized five more, which Luther rejected: Penance, Confirmation, Marriage, Ordination, and Extreme Unction.

Rejecting Luther's idea of salvation by faith, they saw baptism not only as a sacrament but as the heart of the redemptive process. Salvation, they said, was purely a reward for good works. Only a responsible adult, acting in complete freedom of will, could make the decision to follow Christ. The rite of baptism, preferably by immersion in a flowing stream, was the outward sign of that decision and committed the believer to a life without sin. He or she entered a "visible church of the saints" that must, by definition, be separate from the world around it. Most Anabaptists therefore became pacifists who would accept no civic responsibilities, refusing even to take an oath in court (see Document 14.4).

ened the ethical imperatives that lay at the heart of Christianity. They wanted a restoration of the primitive, apostolic church—a "gathered" community of Christians who lived by the letter of Scripture. Luther had not gone far enough. Luther in turn thought that they were *schwärmer,* or enthusiasts who wanted to return to the works righteousness of the medieval church. Faced with what he saw as a fundamental threat to reform, Luther turned to the state. In 1527, a system of visitations was instituted throughout Saxony that for all practical purposes placed temporal control of the church in the hands of the prince. It was to be the model for Lutheran Church discipline throughout Germany and Scandinavia, but it did not at first halt the spread of radicalism.

The Anti-Trinitarians.

Because these radical movements were often popular in origin or had coalesced around the teachings of an individual preacher, they varied widely in character. Perhaps the most radical were the **anti-Trinitarians,** who rejected the doctrine of the Trinity and argued for a piety based wholly on good works. Under the leadership of two Italian brothers, Laelio and Fausto Sozzini (Sotz-zee'-nee), anti-Trinitarianism found important converts among the Polish nobility but had little influence on western Europe.

The Anabaptists.

The most numerous radicals were the **Anabaptists,** a loosely affiliated group whose name derives from the practice of re-baptizing their converts.

Persecution of the Anabaptists.

Governmental authorities saw this rejection of civic responsibility as a threat to the political order. Hatred of the Anabaptists was one issue on which both Catholics and the followers of Luther could agree, and in 1529, an imperial edict made belief in adult baptism a capital offense. Hatred became something like panic when an atypically violent group of Anabaptists gained control of the German city of Münster and proclaimed it the New Jerusalem, complete with polygyny and communal sharing of property. They were eventually dislodged and their leaders executed, but the episode, although unparalleled elsewhere, convinced political and ecclesiastical leaders that their suspicions had been correct. They executed tens of thousands of Anabaptists throughout Germany and the Low Countries, and by 1550, the movement had dwindled to a remnant. A group of survivors, afterward known as **Mennonites,** were reorganized under the leadership of **Menno Simons.** Their moderation and emphasis on high ethical standards became a model for other dissenting groups.

Zwingli and the Reformed Movement in Switzerland

Meanwhile, another kind of reform had emerged in Switzerland. Zürich (Zuer'-ik), like other Swiss cantons, was a center of the mercenary industry. By 1518, a growing party of citizens had come to oppose what they

THE ANABAPTISTS REJECT CIVIC LIFE

In 1527, a group of Anabaptists met at Schleitheim on the Swiss–German border to clarify issues connected with their teachings. The result was the *Schleitheim Confession*, a document widely accepted by later Anabaptists. This excerpt demonstrates the Anabaptist belief that Christians must separate themselves from the life of a wicked world.

Fourth. We are agreed as follows on separation: A separation shall be made from the evil and the wickedness which the devil planted in the world; in this manner, simply that we should not have fellowship with them, the wicked, and not run with them in the multitude of their abominations. This is the way it is: Since all who do not walk in the obedience of faith and have not united themselves with God so that they wish to do his will, are a great abomination before God, it is not possible for anything to grow or issue from them except abominable things. For truly all creatures are in but two classes, good and bad, believing and unbelieving, darkness and light, the world and those who have come out of the world, God's temple and idols, Christ and Belial; and none can have part with the other.

To us then the command of the Lord is clear when He calls us to separate from the evil and thus He will be our God and we shall be his sons and daughters.

He further admonishes us to withdraw from Babylon and the earthly Egypt that we may not be partakers of the pain and suffering which the Lord will bring upon them.

From all this we should learn that everything which is not united with our God and Christ cannot be other than an abomination which we should shun and flee from. By this is meant all popish and anti-popish works and church services, meetings and church attendance, drinking houses, civic affairs, the commitments made in unbelief [oaths] and other things of that kind, which are highly regarded by the world and yet carried on in flat contradiction to the command of God.

Therefore there will also unquestionably fall from us the un-Christian, devilish weapons of force—such as sword, armor and the like, and all their use for friends or against one's enemies.

From "The Schleitheim Confession," in Hans Hillerbrand, ed., *The Protestant Reformation* (New York: Harper Torchbooks, 1967, pp. 132–133).

Question: Why did the Anabaptists believe that they should separate themselves from society?

called the exchange of blood for money. The innovations of Gonsalvo de Córdoba had cost the Swiss their tactical advantage on the battlefield, and their casualties during the latter part of the Italian wars had been very heavy. Moreover, the trade had enriched a few contractors who were now thought to exert undue influence on local pol-

itics while compromising the city's neutrality through their relations with France and the papacy. One of the leading spokesmen for the antimercenary forces was Zwingli, a priest who had been a chaplain to the troops in Italy. He had received a good humanist education and, like Luther, was known for attacking indulgences and for sermons that relied heavily on the Scriptures. In 1519, the antimercenary party gained control of the Zürich city council and named Zwingli the people's priest of the city's main church, a post from which he was able to guide the process of reform.

Zwingli's Reformation. Zwingli's concept of reformation grew out of the democratic traditions of his native land. Believing that each congregation should determine its own policies under the guidance of the gospel, an idea reinforced by his humanist understanding of the early church, he saw no real distinction between church and state. Both entities elected representatives to determine policy. Both should be guided by the law of God. He therefore proceeded to reform the city step by step, providing guidance and advice on scripture but leaving the implementation of reforms to the city council.

Zwingli's Teachings. Like Luther, Zwingli was challenged at an early date by those who believed that his reforms were insufficiently thorough. In responding to such Anabaptist critics as Conrad Grebel (Gray'-bel) and Georg Blaurock, Zwingli developed teachings that differed from Luther's as well. When the Anabaptists asked how a child could be baptized if the efficacy of the sacrament depended on the faith of the recipient, Zwingli responded that the faith was that of the parent or guardian and that the sacrament was in effect a covenant to raise the child as a Christian. The rite was analogous to circumcision among the Jews. He also rejected Luther's doctrine of the Real Presence in communion and argued, after some hesitation, that for those with faith, Christ was present in spirit although not in body.

Zwingli's theologically original ideas appealed strongly to other reformers, especially in the cities of Switzerland and southwest Germany. Luther, however, rejected them at the **Marburg Colloquy** in 1529. The failure of this meeting marked the beginning of a separation between the Lutheran and Reformed traditions that persists to this day. It also coincided with the vote by the Imperial Diet to enforce the Edict of Worms against all non-Catholics. All those who protested against this measure were Protestants, but those who tended to agree with Zwingli became known as **Reformed** rather than Lutheran. In the meantime, the efforts of Zürich to export its reformation to other parts of Switzerland led to conflict with the rural cantons that wished to remain Catholic. Zwingli, who believed that his status as a minister did not exempt him from his duties as a citizen, died, sword in hand, at the battle of Kappel in 1531.

Calvin and Calvinism

Among those influenced by Zwingli's teachings was **John Calvin** (1509–1564). Calvin was born at Noyon in France, the son of a wealthy lawyer who for most of his career had been secretary to the local bishop. A brilliant student, Calvin was educated at Paris and at Orléans, where he earned a law degree. His interests eventually turned to humanism and then to theology. In 1534, he adopted the reformed faith. His conversion bore immediate fruit in *The Institutes of the Christian Religion*, a more or less systematic explanation of reformed teachings. The first edition appeared in March 1536, and although Calvin continued to revise and expand it throughout his lifetime, this early effort contained the basic elements of his mature thought.

John Calvin

Calvin's Role in the Reformation. Theologically, Calvin is best known for his uncompromising position on predestination, holding, like Zwingli, that God divides the elect from the reprobate by His own "dread decree" (see Document 14.5). Luther, like St. Augustine, believed that God predestines certain individuals to salvation but had stopped short of declaring that some are predestined to hell. To Calvin, this seemed illogical as well as a limitation on God's power. To select some is by definition to reject others. This doctrine of "double predestination," like many of his formulations on the sacraments and other issues, may be seen as refinements of ideas originally suggested by others, but Calvin was far more than a mere compiler. He made reformed doctrines more intelligible, educated a corps of pastors who spread his teachings to the farthest corners of Europe, and provided a model for the governance of Christian communities that would be influential for generations to come.

The Reformation in Geneva. The unlikely vehicle for these achievements was the small city of Geneva. When Calvin arrived there in July 1536, the city was emerging from a period of political and religious turmoil. It had long been governed by a bishop whose appointment was controlled by the neighboring dukes of Savoy. Dissatisfaction with Savoyard influence led to the belated development of civic institutions and an alliance with the Swiss cantons of Bern and Fribourg. The bishop fled. The Bernese, who had accepted the Reformation

---

DOCUMENT 14.5

JOHN CALVIN ON PREDESTINATION

The importance of John Calvin's doctrine of predestination has probably been overstated. It was neither unique to him nor the center of his own theology, which emphasized what he called the knowledge of God. Nevertheless, the power of this summary statement from the *Institutes of the Christian Religion* indicates why Calvin's teachings on predestination made an indelible impression.

As Scripture, then, clearly shows, we say that God once established by his eternal and unchangeable plan those whom he long before determined once for all to receive into salvation and those whom, on the other hand, he would devote to destruction. We assert that, with respect to the elect, this plan was founded upon his freely given mercy, without regard to human worth; but by his just and irreprehensible judgment he has barred the door of life to those whom he has given over to damnation. Now among the elect we regard the call as a testimony of election. Then we hold justification [that is, acceptance by God] another sign of its manifestation, until they come into the glory in which the fulfillment of that election lies. But as the Lord seals his elect by call and justification, so, by shutting off the reprobate from knowledge of his name or from the sanctification of his Spirit, he, as it were, reveals by these marks what sort of judgment awaits them.

From Calvin, John, *Institutes of the Christian Religion*, vol. 2, ed. J. T. McNeill, trans. Ford Lewis Battles (Philadelphia: Westminster Press, 1960, p. 931).

Questions: According to Calvin, who is saved? What happens to those who are not saved?

---

while remaining nominally Catholic for diplomatic reasons, then dispatched a French refugee, Guillaume Farel, to convert the French-speaking Genevans. Farel was a fine preacher, but he realized that he was not the man to organize a church. When Calvin stopped at Geneva on his way from Ferrara to Strasburg, he prevailed upon the young scholar to stay and assist him in the task of reformation.

Calvin's first years in Geneva were full of turmoil. Although they had no love for the pope, the Genevans resisted Calvin's attempts to reform their morals. He established the kind of godly commonwealth he sought only with great difficulty. His opponents finally discredited themselves by supporting Miguel Servetus, an anti-Trinitarian executed by the Genevan city council as a heretic in 1553. This act, now regarded as an example of gross intolerance, was universally applauded by

Catholics and Protestants and secured Calvin's position in the city until his death.

Calvin's Geneva has been called a theocracy, but Calvin believed in the separation of church and state. Neither he nor any other Genevan pastor could hold public office, and the temporal affairs of the Genevan church were guided by an elected committee or a presbytery of laymen. The city continued to be governed by its two elected councils. These bodies were empowered, as in Zürich, to enforce conformity in faith and morals. A Consistory, composed of church elders and certain municipal officials, was responsible for defining both. Geneva soon became known as a center of the Reformed movement and as a refuge for those who were persecuted elsewhere. An academy was established to train pastors who were then dispatched to create missionary congregations in other parts of Europe. They were most successful in France, in the Netherlands, and in those countries such as Hungary, Bohemia, and Poland, where resistance to German culture inhibited the spread of Lutheranism. When the reformer died in 1564, Calvinism was already a major international movement.

The English Reformation

England's revolt against the papacy was an example of reformation imposed from the top. **Henry VIII** (reigned 1509–1547) and his chief minister, **Cardinal Thomas Wolsey** (c. 1475–1530), had little use for reformed doctrines. Henry had even earned the papal title "Defender of the Faith" for publishing an attack on Luther's view of the sacraments and would probably have been content to remain in the church had he not decided to divorce his queen, **Catherine of Aragon,** the daughter of Ferdinand and Isabella of Spain.

Henry VIII, 1537

The Divorce. Catherine had suffered a series of miscarriages and stillbirths. One child, Mary, survived, but Henry feared that without a male heir the succession would be endangered. He resolved to ask for a papal annulment and to marry **Anne Boleyn** (Bull'-in), a court lady with whom he had fallen in love. His re-

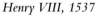

Cardinal Wolsey

quest posed serious difficulties for pope Clement VII. Emperor Charles V was Catherine's nephew. Charles vehemently opposed the divorce, and because his troops had recently sacked Rome (1527), albeit in the course of a mutiny, the pope was intimidated. Moreover, the basis of the request struck many canon lawyers as dubious. Catherine had originally been married to Henry's brother Arthur, who died before he could ascend the throne. To preserve the vital alliance with Catherine's father, Ferdinand of Aragon, Henry VII had quickly married her to his second son, but this had required a papal dispensation because marriage to the wife of one's brother is prohibited by Leviticus 18:16 and 20:21. Another biblical passage, Deuteronomy 25:5, specifically commands such marriages, but an annulment would involve repudiation of the earlier dispensation. Moreover, the fact that the marriage had endured for eighteen years raised what canon lawyers called "the impediment of public honesty."

Clement temporized. He appointed Cardinals Wolsey and Campeggio as legates to resolve the matter on the theory that their opinions would cancel each other out. Henry could not wait. In 1529, he deprived Wolsey of his secular offices and took **Thomas Cromwell** (1485–1540) and **Thomas Cranmer** (1489–1556) as his advisers. These two, a lawyer and a churchman, respectively, were sympathetic to reformed ideas and firm supporters of a strategy that would put pressure on the pope by attacking the privileges and immunities of the church in England.

The Reformation Parliament. This strategy was implemented primarily through the Reformation Parliament that sat from 1529 to 1536. Although Cromwell managed its proceedings to some extent, a consistent majority supported the crown throughout. Parliament passed a series of acts that restricted the dispatch of church revenues to Rome and placed the legal affairs of the clergy under royal jurisdiction. Finally, in 1532, Anne Boleyn became pregnant. To ensure the child's legitimacy, Cranmer married the couple in January 1533, and 2 months later he granted the king his divorce from Catherine. He was able to do so because William Warham, the Archbishop of Canterbury and a wily opponent of the divorce, had died at last (he was at least 98), permitting Henry to appoint Cranmer in his place. In September, Anne Boleyn gave birth to a daughter, Elizabeth, and in 1534, Parliament passed the **Act of Supremacy,** which declared that Henry was "the only supreme head of the Church in England."

Suppression of the Monasteries. From an economic point of view, the most important aspect of the English Reformation was Henry VIII's suppression of the monasteries. The monks were unpopular, except in the north, where monasteries dominated the economy, and Henry needed money. He had long since squandered the immense fortune left to him by his father. Beginning in 1536, Henry's government confiscated all monastic properties and dismissed the monks and nuns. Unlike priests, who retained their parishes if they accepted the Act of Supremacy, the dispossessed religious had to find places in the secular world. Vast sums flowed into the royal coffers, but unfortunately for his successors, Henry chose to sell off the monastic lands at bargain basement prices. By doing so, he enriched those who had supported him in the Reformation Parliament and satisfied his need for ready cash. His failure to incorporate these lands into the royal domain deprived the crown of renewable income that it would later need.

The Henrician Church. Henry now ruled the English church. Although he closed the monasteries and convents and adopted Miles Coverdale's translation of the Bible into English, he changed little else. The clergy remained celibate (except Cranmer, who had been secretly married before his appointment as archbishop of Canterbury), and Henry reaffirmed the principles of Catholic theology in the Six Articles of 1539. Perhaps as a result, opposition was minimal. John Fisher, Bishop of Rochester, and Sir Thomas More, the great humanist who had been Henry's lord chancellor, were executed for their misgivings, but most of political England either supported the king or remained indifferent. The Lincolnshire rebellion and the northern revolt known as the Pilgrimage of Grace were localized reactions to Henry's proposed closing of the monasteries in 1536, and he suppressed them easily.

Thomas More

The Beginnings of the Anglican Church. In 1536, Henry arranged the execution of Anne Boleyn on charges of adultery and had their marriage annulled. His third wife, Jane Seymour, gave him a male heir in 1537 but died in childbirth, and three subsequent wives failed to produce further children. Both Mary and Elizabeth were now officially illegitimate. When Henry died in 1547, Jane Seymour's son, age 10, ascended the throne as Edward VI (1547–1553) under the regency of his uncle, Edward Seymour, Duke of Somerset. Somerset was a convinced Protestant with close ties to Cranmer and the continental reformers. He and the young king, "that right godly imp," as the Protestants called him, lost little time in abolishing the Six Articles, encouraging clerical marriage, and imposing Cranmer's

FIGURE 14.4 *An Allegory of the English Reformation.* This image was intended as propaganda to support the succession of Edward VI, aged 10 and already tied to the Protestant cause. The dying Henry points to his son (who holds a scepter), as heir to his throne and Defender of the Faith (or Head of the Church of England) against the pope (forefront) who has been overcome. Against the pope's neck lies a Bible open to the words from Peter 1:24, "The word of the Lord endureth forever." On his chest are the words "All fleshe is grasse," and written along his arm is the word "Idolatry." At the bottom, monks flee.

Book of Common Prayer as the standard liturgy for English churches. An Order in Council abolished images in an act of official iconoclasm that destroyed centuries of English art.

In 1550, the equally Protestant Duke of Northumberland succeeded Somerset. He imposed a revised edition of the new liturgy and adopted the Forty-Two Articles, also written by Cranmer, as an official confession of faith. The articles proclaimed salvation by faith, reduced the sacraments to two, and denied transubstantiation, although not the Real Presence. The **Anglican,** or English state church, was now demonstrably Protestant and reflected not only the views but the masterful literary style of Thomas Cranmer.

The English Catholics. Most of the English clergy accepted the new order. Although many lay people remained loyal to the old church, they found no effective way to express their views. Aside from a brief and unsuccessful rebellion in the west of England, little resistance emerged. In 1553, Edward died at the age of 16. His sister **Mary** assumed the crown and immediately restored Catholicism with the assent of Parliament, which demanded only that she not return the lands taken from the church.

Mary Tudor, 1554

Once again, clergy and laity accepted the religious reversal, but Mary's reign was a failure. Her marriage to Philip II of Spain aroused fears of Spanish-papal domination, even among those English who were still unfavorably disposed to Protestantism. Her persecution of the reformers, although hardly the bloodbath portrayed in John Foxe's *Books of Martyrs,* the great martyrology of the English reformation, deeply offended others and earned her the historical nickname "Bloody Mary." When her sister, **Elizabeth,** succeeded her in 1558, she was able to restore a moderate Protestantism leavened by virtual tolerance for all who would acknowledge the royal supremacy. The Elizabethan Settlement, as it is called, was the foundation on which modern **Anglicanism** would be built after years of effort and struggle.

Common Features of Protestantism. Although the reforming movements that opposed the medieval church varied widely in practice and doctrine, they shared several features in common. All rejected the authority of the pope. They claimed Scripture as the sole source of religious truth and repudiated the rulings of popes, councils, and the writings of the scholastics. They also rejected much of the church's sacramental system and, with it, the traditional role of the priest as an intermediary between God and the believer. For this reason, they insisted on publishing the Bible in the vernacular language of their own countries and abandoned the use of Latin in church services. Some, but not all, believed that salvation came through faith rather than as a reward for good deeds. Views on predestination, the precise nature of baptism and communion, and other theological issues caused bitter divisions, but in some respects, the day-to-day practice of the faith marked them off more clearly than anything else from those Europeans who remained Catholic. Most objected to the use of images, services for the dead, pilgrimages, and many other manifestations of medieval piety. By 1550, one could tell by walking into a church whether it had remained Catholic or adopted reform.

THE CATHOLIC REFORMATION (C. 1490–1564)

But not all reformations of the sixteenth century were anti-Catholic. The church transformed itself as well in a movement that has sometimes been called the *Counter-Reformation.* The term is unduly restrictive. Not all of the reforms undertaken by Catholics in the sixteenth century were a response to the challenge of Luther and his fellows, and some had preceded him by decades.

Reforms Before Luther. Cardinal Francisco Jiménez de Cisneros had begun to reform the church in Spain long before Luther nailed his Ninety-Five Theses to the church door. In France, Cardinal Georges d'Amboise (dam-bwaz) introduced similar reforms between 1501 and his death in 1510. Even Wolsey had attempted to reform the English monasteries during the 1520s. The impetus behind these reforms arguably came from the secular authorities and were largely directed toward the revival of monastic life. However, each of these cardinals received broad legatine authority from several popes, and monastic reform was a central issue in the late medieval church.

Monastic Reform and the Creation of New Orders. Moreover, the reform of existing orders and the creation of new ones were often undertaken without secular involvement. The Theatines, confirmed by the pope in 1524, grew out an association known as the Oratory of Divine Love whose origins date to 1494. The Barnabites (1533–1535), Somaschi (So-mahs'-kee, 1540), and the Capuchins (Ka-poo'-chins), an order of

FIGURE 14.5 *Cranmer Burned at the Stake.* Thomas Cranmer, Archbishop of Canterbury under Henry VIII and author of the Thirty-Nine Articles and the *Book of Common Prayer,* was England's most prominent Protestant clergyman. He was burnt at the stake on March 21, 1556, after the restoration of Catholicism by Queen Mary. Cranmer had at one point recanted his Protestant beliefs under interrogation but later reasserted his Protestant beliefs. He is shown here holding the hand that signed the recantation in the fire. Such executions aroused public disapproval and gravely weakened the Catholic cause.

reformed Franciscans, were all voluntary associations of churchmen pledged to the ideal of monastic reform. Maria Laurentia Longo (d. 1542) founded the female counterpart of the Capuchins, and in 1535, Angela Merici (Mare'-i-chee, c. 1473–1540) founded the **Ursulines,** an order that would play a decisive role in the education of Catholic women for centuries. None of these foundations was related in any way to the Protestant threat. Most popes regarded the proliferation of religious orders with suspicion. Their rivalries had long been a fruitful source of trouble, and most reform-minded clerics believed in consolidation rather than in new confirmations.

The Jesuits. Of all the religious orders founded or reformed during the sixteenth century, the Society of Jesus, or **Jesuits,** played the largest part in the struggle against Protestantism, but they had been created for other purposes. Their founder, **Ignatius of Loyola** (1491–1556), was originally inspired by the idea of converting the Muslims. After a long period of educational and religious development that produced *The Spiritual Exercises,* a manual of meditation that remains the foundation of Jesuit discipline, he and nine companions formed their order in 1534. Their asceticism, vigor, and vow of unconditional obedience to the pope led to their confirmation in 1540.

Although the order did little to convert the Muslims, it achieved moderate success in Asia under the leadership of **St. Francis Xavier** (Za'-vee-er, 1506–1552). In Europe, the Jesuits became the intellectual shock troops of the Counter-Reformation. Their high standards in recruitment and education made them natural leaders to reconvert areas of Europe that had deserted to Protestantism. Jesuit missions helped restore a Catholic majority in regions as diverse as Bavaria and Poland. An important means of achieving this was through education. Jesuit academies combining humanist educational principles with religious instruction spread through the subcontinent after 1555 and served much the same purpose for men that the Ursuline academies served for women.

Reforms Directed by the Papacy. The creation of new orders was essentially spontaneous, arising from reform-minded ele-

ments within the church, but the papacy itself was not idle. Reform remained difficult, if not impossible, until the ghost of conciliarism was laid to rest, and for this reason, the popes proceeded with great caution. Clement VII, besieged by the mutinous troops of Charles V and the demands of Henry VIII, accomplished little. Paul III (reigned 1534–1549) at first sought reconciliation by appointing a commission to investigate abuses within the church. Its report, a detailed analysis with recommendations for change, caused great embarrassment when the contents leaked to the public. Then an attempt to negotiate a settlement with the Lutherans broke down at the Regensburg Colloquy in 1541. These failures encouraged a policy of repression, and in 1542, the Roman Inquisition was revived under the direction of Gian Pietro Caraffa (John Pee-ay'-tro Kar-aff'-a), an implacable conservative and one of the founders of the Theatine order. Later, as Pope Paul IV (served 1555–1559), Caraffa would conduct a veritable reign of terror against those whom he regarded as corrupt or heretical. To protect the faithful from intellectual contamination, he also established the *Index Librorum Prohibitorum,* an ever-expanding list of books that Catholics were forbidden to read.

The Council of Trent. Repression alone could not solve the problems of the church. Despite the obvious danger to papal authority, Paul III decided to convene a general council at Trent in 1542. Sessions were held from 1543 to 1549, in 1551–1552, and in 1562–1563. Much disagreement arose over goals and the meetings

FIGURE 14.6 *The Final Session of the Council of Trent (Detail), 1563.* Attributed to Titian, this painting shows the conclusion of the great council whose decrees inspired the Catholic Church until the 1960s.

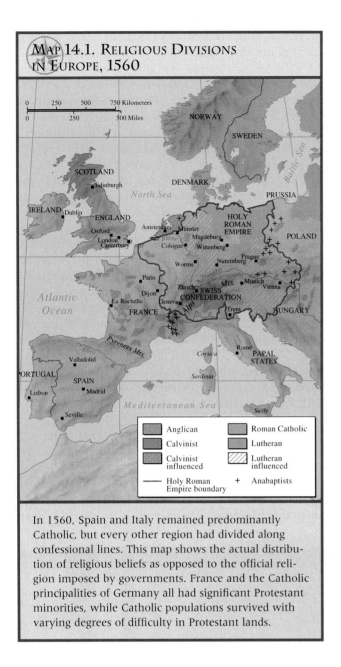

MAP 14.1. RELIGIOUS DIVISIONS IN EUROPE, 1560

Anglican

Calvinist

Calvinist influenced

— Holy Roman Empire boundary

Roman Catholic

Lutheran

Lutheran influenced

+ Anabaptists

In 1560, Spain and Italy remained predominantly Catholic, but every other region had divided along confessional lines. This map shows the actual distribution of religious beliefs as opposed to the official religion imposed by governments. France and the Catholic principalities of Germany all had significant Protestant minorities, while Catholic populations survived with varying degrees of difficulty in Protestant lands.

Knowing that many of the church's problems arose from ignorance, the delegates ordered every diocese to establish a seminary for the education of its priests. To instruct the laity, they advocated the use of catechisms, or printed sets of questions and answers about the faith. At first, poverty prevented many bishops from carrying out all of these mandates, but the Council of Trent marked the beginning of the modern Catholic Church. Its institutional principles and the forms of piety that it established were not substantially modified until Vatican Council II in 1962–1965.

THE CONSEQUENCES OF REFORM

The impact of the sixteenth-century reformations has been the subject of much scholarly debate. The religious unity of western Christendom had clearly vanished forever. Religion became yet another source of conflict among European states and helped fuel the wars of the later sixteenth and early seventeenth century. Otherwise, cities and territorial states tended to benefit from reform, for Protestantism increased their control over church patronage and revenues. Even Catholic states exhibited more independence because the papacy became more cautious in its claims than it had been in the Middle Ages. Although hardly decisive, reform was therefore an important influence on the development of the modern state.

The Economics Effects of the Reformation. The economic consequences of the Reformation are far less clear. The idea that Protestantism somehow liberated acquisitive instincts and paved the way for the development of capitalism is highly suspect if for no other reason than that capitalism existed long before the Reformation and that the economic growth of such Protestant states as England and the Netherlands can be explained adequately in other ways. In some areas, notably England, the alienation of church property may have accelerated the capitalization of land that had begun in the years after the Black Death; in others, it served primarily to increase the domain revenues of the crown. In Denmark, for example, the crown held 40 percent of the arable land by 1620, primarily because, unlike Henry VIII, the Danish kings retained church lands confiscated during the Reformation.

The Status of Women. The reformers also sought to change the status of European women. Beginning with Luther and Zwingli, they rejected the ideal of clerical celibacy and declared that a Christian marriage was the ideal basis for a godly life. They specifically attacked medieval writings that either condemned women as temptresses or extolled virginity as the highest of female callings, and they drew attractive and sentimental portraits of the virtuous wife. A chief

were often sparsely attended, but the **Council of Trent** was a conspicuous success.

Theologically, Trent marked the triumph of Thomism, the theological system established by St. Thomas Aquinas. The Council specifically rejected Luther's ideas on justification, the sacraments, and the priesthood of all believers. It reasserted the medieval concept of the priestly office and the value of good works, and made efforts at the organizational level to correct most of the abuses that had been attacked by the reformers. These included not only the clerical sins of pluralism, absenteeism, nepotism, and simony but also such distortions of popular piety as the sale of indulgences and the misuse of images. The strengthening of ecclesiastical discipline was one of the council's greatest achievements.

A Protestant View of Marriage

The Money-Changer and His Wife (1539).

The city of Strasbourg in Alsace was an important center of the Reformation. Its reformer, Martin Bucer (Bootz'-er, 1491–1551), was more generous than most in his attitude toward women. Here, he argues that under certain circumstances a woman may leave her adulterous or abusive spouse and be free to remarry. Although rejected by Catholic authorities, a number of reformed cities accepted his viewpoint and passed laws accordingly.

For the Holy Spirit says that there is neither male nor female in Christ. In all things that pertain to salvation one should have as much regard for woman as for man. For though she is bound to keep her place, to put herself under the authority of her husband, just as the church does in relation to Christ, yet her subjection does not cancel the right of an honest woman, in accordance with the laws of God, to have recourse to and demand, by legitimate means, deliverance from a husband who hates her. For the Lord has certainly not made married woman subservient to have her polluted and tormented by the extortions and injuries of her husband, but rather so that she may receive discipline from him, as if from her master and savior, like the church from Christ. A wife is not so subject to her husband that she is bound to suffer anything he may impose upon her. Being free, she is joined to him in holy marriage that she may be loved, nourished, and maintained by him, as if she were his own flesh, just as the church is maintained by Christ. . . . Again, though a wife may be something less than her husband and subject to him, in order that they be rightly joined, the Holy Spirit has declared, through its apostle, that man and woman are equal before God in things pertaining to the alliance and mutual confederation of marriage. This is the meaning of the apostle's saying that a wife has power over the body of her husband, just as a husband has power over the body of his wife (1 Corinthians 7). . . . Hence, if wives feel that their association and cohabitation with their husbands is injurious to salvation as well of one as of the other, owing to the hardening and hatred on the part of their husbands, let them have recourse to the civil authority, which is enjoined by the Lord to help the afflicted.

From Bucer, Martin, "De Regno Christi," book 2, chap. 34, in Julia O'Faolain and Lauro Martines, *Not in God's Image: Women in History from the Greeks to the Victorians* (New York: HarperCollins, 1973, pp. 200–201).

Question: According to Bucer, what is the proper relationship between husband and wife?

virtue of that ideal woman was her willingness to submit to male authority, but the attachment of the reformers to traditional social hierarchies should not be misinterpreted. The **companionate marriage** in which wife and husband offered each other mutual support was the Reformation ideal (see Document 14.6). If women were subordinate, it was, as Calvin said, because women "by the very order of nature are bound to obey." To him, other reformers, and Catholic theologians, the traditionally ordered family was both part and symbol of a divinely established hierarchy. To disrupt that hierarchy risked chaos.

The Reformation's endorsement of women may have been qualified, but it increased the status of wife and mother and placed new demands upon men, who were encouraged to treat their wives with consideration. As early as the 1520s, some German towns permitted women to divorce husbands who were guilty of gross abuse. The reformers also encouraged female literacy, at least in the vernacular, because they wanted women to read the Scriptures. The impact of these prescriptions on the lives of real women may be questioned. On the negative side, the Protestant emphasis on marriage narrowed a woman's career choices to one. Catholic Europe continued to offer productive lives to women who chose not to marry, but Protestant women could rarely escape the dominance of men. If they did, it was through widowhood or divorce, and Protestant societies offered no institutional support for the unmarried. St. Teresa of Avila

(Ah'-vee-la), Angelique Arnauld (Ar-nawd'), Madame Acarie (Ah-ca-ree), Jeanne de Chantal (Shan-tal), and the other great female figures of post-Tridentine Catholicism had few Protestant counterparts.

The Attack on Popular Culture.

From the standpoint of the reformers, whether Catholic or Protestant, such issues were of secondary importance. Their primary concern was the salvation of souls and the transformation of popular piety. They made heroic efforts to catechize or otherwise educate the laity in most parts of Europe, and after about 1570, an increasing tendency was seen toward clerical interference in lay morals. Catholic church courts and Protestant consistories sought to eliminate such evils as brawling, public drunkenness, and sexual misbehavior. Inevitably the churchmen were forced to condemn the occasions on which such activity arose. The celebration of holidays and popular festivals came under scrutiny, as did public performances of every kind from street jugglers to those of Shakespeare and his troop of actors. Dancing aroused special concern. No one worried about the stately measures trod by courtiers, but the rowdy and often sexually explicit dances of the peasants seemed, after years of familiarity, to induce shock.

Civil authorities supported this attack on popular culture for practical reasons. The celebration of holidays and popular festivals encouraged disorder. When accompanied as they usually were by heavy drinking, public amusements could lead to violence and even riots. Moreover, like street theater, most celebrations con-

tained seditious skits or pageants. They mocked the privileged classes, satirized the great, and delighted in the reversal of social and gender roles. The triumph of a Lord of Misrule, the costumed figure in street celebrations who mocked accepted standards, for even a day made magistrates nervous, and prudence demanded that such activities be regulated or prohibited outright. Popular beliefs and practices were attacked with equal vigor. The authorities rarely took action against academic magic, astrology, or alchemy—sciences that, although dubious, were widely accepted by the wealthy and educated—but they no longer tolerated folk magic. In some cases, official suspicion extended even to the traditional remedies used by midwives and village "wise women."

The Witch-Craze of 1550–1650.

The epidemic of witch hunting that convulsed Europe in the late sixteenth and early seventeenth centuries may have been related to these concerns. In the century after 1550, Protestant and Catholic governments in virtually every part of Europe executed more than 60,000 people for being witches or Satanists. Medieval thinkers such as Thomas Aquinas had denied the power of witches, but a later age thought differently. Magistrates and learned men built theories of a vast satanic plot around their imperfect knowledge of folk beliefs. Their ideas crystallized in manuals for witch hunters, the most famous of which, the *Malleus Maleficarum* (Hammer of Witches) went through twenty-nine editions between 1495 and 1669. Its authors, like most people in early modern Europe, believed that in a providential world there could be no accidents; evil required an explanation. Otherwise unexplained disasters were caused by witches who gained extraordinary powers through worshipping the devil and used those powers to injure their neighbors. The community could be protected only by burning witches alive.

In this case, ordinary people shared the concerns of the intellectual elite. Accusations of witchcraft tended to multiply in waves of hysteria that convulsed entire regions. Many of those denounced were no doubt guilty of trying to cast spells or some other unsavory act, but the victims fit a profile that suggests a generalized hostility toward women and perhaps that the persecutions were in part a means of exerting social control. The great majority of those burned were single women, old and poor, who lived at the margins of their communities. The rest, whether male or female, tended to be people whose assertive or uncooperative behavior had aroused hostility.

FIGURE 14.7 *Peasant Dance (c. 1567), Pieter Brueghel the Elder.* Religious reformers of all faiths objected to popular festivals of the kind portrayed here with its evident lack of restraint. Everyone in the village appears to be more or less drunk, perhaps especially the young couple kissing. Those who can still navigate, dance to the music of a bagpipe. An old man pulls a young woman forward, and in the background, another man urges a housewife to join the dance.

The trials subsided after 1650, but not before other traditional beliefs had been discredited by their association with witchcraft. Some of these involved "white" magic, the normally harmless spells and preparations used to ensure good harvests or to cure disease. Others were "errors," or what the Inquisition called *propositions*. This was a broad category that included everything from the popular notion that premarital sex was no sin to alternative cosmologies devised by imaginative peasants. Post-Tridentine Catholicism, no less than its Protestant rivals, discouraged uncontrolled speculation and was deeply suspicious of those forms of piety that lacked ecclesiastical sanction. Popular beliefs about the Virgin Mary, the saints, and miracles were scrutinized, while lay people claiming to have religious visions were ridiculed and sometimes prosecuted.

The efforts of the reformers, in other words, bore modest fruit. Drunkenness proved ineradicable, but some evidence is available that interpersonal violence decreased and that behavior in general became somewhat more sedate. Although lay morals and religious knowledge improved slowly if at all, the forms of piety were transformed in some cases beyond recognition.

Many ideas and practices vanished so completely that historians of popular culture can recover their memory only with great difficulty. Devotion based on personal contact with God through mental prayer became common in virtually all communions. Catholics abandoned the sale of indulgences and consciously sought to limit such abuses as the misuse of pilgrimages and relics. Protestants abandoned all three, together with Latin, vigils, the cult of the saints, masses for the dead, and mandatory fasts. By 1600, the religious landscape of Europe had been transformed, and much of the richness, vitality, and cohesion of peasant life had been lost.

CONCLUSION

After 1300, the Western church found itself under attack by the increasingly aggressive monarchies of the day and by those who demanded higher standards of piety in the face of plague and social disorder. Internal conflicts led to a series of scandals that undermined the authority of the popes and strengthened anticlerical sentiment. New spiritual and intellectual movements undermined traditional faith. Between 1517 and 1555, a series of religious movements emerged to challenge the medieval church: Lutheran, Reformed, Anabaptist, Calvinist, Anglican, and others. Several of them gained political support as both states and city governments used them to seize the church's wealth and increase their independence. Collectively, these movements are known as the Protestant Reformation, but their beliefs and organization differed widely, and

they were rarely able to cooperate with one another. At the same time, the Catholic Church reformed itself from within, partially in response to the Protestant challenge, but largely because a majority of those who remained loyal to the old church demanded reforms as well. Together, the reformations of the sixteenth century gave birth to two distinct systems of Christian thought and practice, both of which opposed many aspects of medieval piety and popular culture. In so doing, they obliterated much of the medieval past and created a religious division in Western society that continues to this day.

Review Questions

- Why did late medieval popes find it difficult to respond to demands for reform?
- How did the rise of mysticism, nominalism, and humanism influence the coming of the Reformation?
- Why was Emperor Charles V unable to halt the growth of Protestantism in the Holy Roman Empire?
- What reforms did the Catholic Church introduce during the sixteenth century?

For Further Study

Readings

Dickens, A. G., *The Counter Reformation* (New York: Norton, 1979). Still the most accessible survey of Catholic reform. Profusely illustrated.

Dickens, A. G., *The English Reformation*, 2nd ed. (University Park: Pennsylvania State University Press, 1991). A readable, clear, and balanced presentation.

Kittelson, James M., *Luther the Reformer: The Story of the Man and His Career* (Minneapolis: Augsburg, 1986). A readable and sympathetic biography.

McGrath, Alister E., *A Life of John Calvin: A Study in the Shaping of Western Culture* (Cambridge, MA: Blackwell, 1990). Probably the most accessible of the works on Calvin.

Oakley, Francis, *The Western Church in the Later Middle Ages* (Ithaca, NY: Cornell, 1979). The best survey of the late medieval church and its difficulties.

InfoTrac College Edition

For additional reading, go to your online research library at *http://infotrac.thomsonlearning.com.*

Using Key Terms, enter the search terms:

Reformation	*Counter-Reformation*
Martin and *Luther* not *King*	*John Calvin*

Web Site

http://www.fordham.edu/halsall/mod/modsbook02.html
Internet Modern History Sourcebook. Look under Reformation.

THE LATE MEDIEVAL CHURCH AND THE REFORMATION

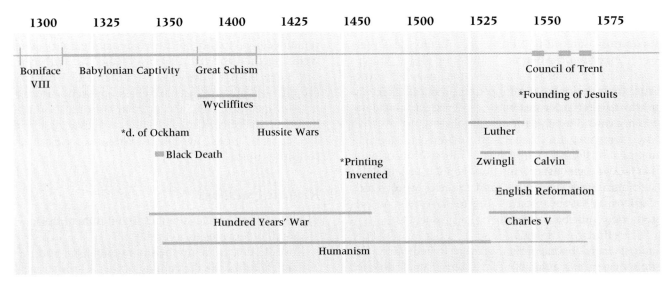

| 1300 | 1325 | 1350 | 1400 | 1425 | 1450 | 1500 | 1525 | 1550 | 1575 |

Boniface VIII

Babylonian Captivity   Great Schism

Wycliffites

*d. of Ockham   Hussite Wars

Black Death

*Printing Invented

Council of Trent

*Founding of Jesuits

Luther

Zwingli   Calvin

English Reformation

Hundred Years' War   Charles V

Humanism

Visit the Western Civilization Companion Web Site for resources specific to this textbook:
http://history.wadsworth.com/hause02/

The CD in the back of this book and the Western Civilization Resource Center at *http://history.wadsworth.com/western/* offer a variety of tools to help you succeed in this course, including access to quizzes; images; documents; interactive simulations, maps, and timelines; movie explorations; and a wealth of other sources.

Chapter 15

OVERSEAS CONQUEST AND RELIGIOUS WAR TO 1648

FOCUS QUESTIONS

- Why did Spain and Portugal embark upon the development of overseas empires?
- What caused the Revolt of the Netherlands, and how did the revolt come to involve France and England?
- What were the most important causes of the Thirty Years' War, and why did the conflict prove difficult to resolve?
- What were the major causes of the English Civil War?

*I*n the spring of 1519, **Hernán Cortés,** age 33, left Cuba without the governor's permission to conquer an empire. He brought with him 600 men, 16 horses, 14 artillery pieces, and 13 muskets. After 2 years of peril and privation, he succeeded. The Aztec Empire and all of central Mexico fell to the Spanish. Cortés had conquered a nation larger than his native Spain. Years later, Bernal Díaz del Castillo, one of his soldiers, wrote *The True History of the Conquest of New Spain* to explain how it all happened. Why would men come 4,000 miles from their homes to undertake such an improbable project? The answer, he said, was, "We came to serve God and also to get rich." It would be hard to imagine a better answer.

The voyages of exploration and conquest undertaken by Europeans in the late fifteenth and early sixteenth centuries had no real parallel in any other civilization. They arose from the expansion and consolidation of the European monarchies and from the desire to convert non-Christians to the faith. These same impulses brought nearly a century of war and suffering to Europe while visiting untold misery on the inhabitants of distant lands.

The first half of Chapter 15 tells of Europe's confrontation with a broader world: the overseas voyages undertaken by Europeans in the fifteenth and sixteenth century and the first great colonial empires they established. It then examines another conflict with non-Europeans: the struggle between the Ottoman Empire and the empire of Charles V. The second half of the chapter deals with a century of fratricidal struggles within Europe itself: the French Wars of Religion, the Revolt of the Netherlands, The Thirty Years' War, and the civil war in England. They, too, arose from a mixture of motives that Bernal Díaz would have understood.

THE FIRST EUROPEAN VOYAGES OVERSEAS

The process of overseas exploration began appropriately enough in Portugal, the first modern monarchy and a center of the fourteenth-century revolution in shipbuilding. The Portuguese state had been effectively consolidated by John I in 1385. Like other medieval rulers, he and his descendants hoped to maximize domain revenue by increasing taxable commerce. The gold and ivory of Africa were a tempting goal, but that trade was dominated by Moroccan intermediaries who shipped products from the African heartland by camel caravan and sold them to Europeans through such ports as Ceuta and Tangier. The Portuguese knew that enormous profits could be realized by sailing directly to the source of these commodities and bypassing the middlemen, who were in any case Muslims and their traditional enemies.

The Portuguese Voyages. These considerations, and a desire to find new converts for the church, inspired **Prince Henry "the Navigator"** (1394–1460) to establish a center for navigational development on the windswept bluffs of Sagres at the far southwestern tip of Europe. While Henry's cosmographers and mathematicians worked steadily to improve the quality of charts and navigational techniques, his captains sailed ever further along the African coast, returning with growing quantities of gold, ivory, pepper, and slaves. The enslavement of Africans was part of the expansionist enterprise from the start. The Portuguese ships were fast, handy caravels that combined the best features of northern and Mediterranean construction. Their instruments were improved versions of the compass, the quadrant, and the astrolabe. The compass had been introduced to the Mediterranean in the twelfth or thirteenth century, probably by the Arabs. The quadrant and the astrolabe permitted sailors to find their latitude based on the elevation of the sun above the horizon.

Before the death of Prince Henry, the Portuguese adopted the idea of sailing around the tip of Africa to India as their primary goal. By so doing they hoped to bypass the Italian–Arab monopoly and gain direct access to the spice trade. In May 1498, **Vasco da Gama** reached Calicut on the coast of India after a 2-year voyage. His arrival disturbed political and commercial relationships that had endured for centuries. Indian and Arab merchants found the newcomers rude and barbaric and their trade goods of little interest. Although the voyages of da Gama and Cabral made a profit, only the judicious use of force could secure a major Portuguese share in the trade. After 1508, **Alfonso de Albuquerque** (1453–1515) tried to gain control of the

Vasco da Gama (c. 1469–1525)

Indian Ocean by seizing its major ports. Aden and Ormuz eluded him, but Goa became the chief Portuguese base in India and the capture of Malacca (1511) opened the way to China. A Portuguese settlement was established there at Macao in 1556. The Portuguese initiated trade with Japan in 1543, and for 75 years thereafter, ships from Macao on the Chinese mainland brought luxury goods to Nagasaki in return for silver.

These achievements earned Portugal a modest place in Asian commerce. The Portuguese may have been the first people of any race to trade on a truly worldwide basis, but the total volume of spices exported to Europe did not immediately increase as a result of their activities. Furthermore, the Arab and Gujarati merchants of the Indian Ocean remained formidable competitors for more than a century.

Columbus and the Opening of America. Meanwhile, the Spanish, by sailing west, had reached America. Isabella of Castile and Ferdinand of Aragon regarded the expansion of their Portuguese rivals with dismay and believed, as Prince Henry had done, that they were obligated by morality and the requirements of dynastic prestige to spread the Catholic faith. When **Christopher Columbus,** a Genoese mariner, proposed to reach Asia by sailing across the Atlantic, they were prepared to listen. Columbus had offered the same project to the Portuguese in 1484 and was turned down. They apparently found him both demanding and ignorant. A self-educated man, Columbus ac-

FIGURE 15.1 *Christopher Columbus (1451–1506).* A fine contemporary portrait by an anonymous Spanish painter.

cepted only those theories that supported his own and underestimated the circumference of the globe by nearly 7,000 miles. The Portuguese cosmographers believed in the more accurate calculations of Eratosthenes. Because neither they nor he knew of America, they assumed that he would perish in the Atlantic several thousand miles from his goal. Columbus's first reception in Spain was no better, but he eventually gained the support of the queen and Ferdinand's treasurer, who found ways to finance the voyage with little risk to the crown.

In August 1492, Columbus set sail in the ship *Santa Maria,* accompanied by two small caravels, the *Pinta* and the *Niña.* Their combined crews totaled about ninety men. Columbus sailed southwest to the Canary Islands and then westward across the Atlantic, taking advantage of winds and currents that he could not fully have understood. Despite the season, he encountered no hurricanes, and on October 12, he sighted what he believed to be an island off the coast of Japan. It was one of the Bahamas.

Columbus made three more voyages before his death in 1506, insisting until the end that he had found the western passage to Asia. The realization that it was a continent whose existence had only been suspected by Europeans was left to others. One of them, a Florentine navigator named Amerigo Vespucci (1454–1512), gave it his name. The true dimensions of the "New World" became clearer in 1513, when Vasco Núñez de Balboa crossed the Isthmus of Panama on foot and became the first European to look upon the Pacific.

The achievement of Columbus has been somewhat diminished by his own failure to grasp its significance and by the fact that others had no doubt preceded him. The Vikings visited Newfoundland and may have explored the North American coast as far south as Cape Cod. Portuguese and Basque fishermen had almost certainly landed there in the course of their annual expeditions to the Grand Banks, but being fishermen, they kept their discoveries secret to discourage competitors and these early contacts came to nothing.

The voyage of Columbus, however, set off a frenzy of exploration and conquest. In the Treaty of Tordesillas (1494), the Spanish and Portuguese agreed to a line of demarcation established in the mid-Atlantic by the pope. Lands "discovered" to the east of that line belonged to Portugal; those to the west belonged to Spain. The inhabitants of those lands were not consulted. This left Brazil, Africa, and the route to India in Portuguese hands, but a line of demarcation in the Pacific was not defined. Much of Asia remained in dispute.

Magellan's Voyage. To establish a Spanish presence there, an expedition was dispatched in 1515 to reach the Moluccas by sailing west around the southern tip of South America. Its leader was **Fernando Magellan,** a Portuguese sailor in Spanish pay. Magellan crossed the Pacific only to be killed in the Moluccas by natives unimpressed with the benefits of Spanish sovereignty. His navigator, Sebastian del Cano, became the first captain to circumnavigate the globe when he brought the expedition's only remaining ship back to Spain with fifteen survivors in 1522. The broad outlines of the world were now apparent.

Ferdinand Magellan (c. 1480–1521)

THE TOOLS OF EXPLORATION

Improved ships and better navigational techniques made it possible for Europeans to embark on overseas explorations. Chapter 12 described the evolution of shipbuilding in the later Middle Ages. Navigation at sea depends on knowing the ship's direction and its position on the globe. The compass, which enabled mariners to find their direction at sea, had been known for centuries. Latitude, or the ship's distance from the equator, could be calculated with an astrolabe or with a cross-staff. Longitude, or east–west distance, was more difficult. Until the invention of accurate chronometers in the eighteenth century, it could only be estimated by a process known as dead reckoning.

▶ *A Portuguese Caravel of the Fifteenth Century.* Although rarely more than 70 or 80 feet in length, these vessels were extremely seaworthy and formed the mainstay of Portugal's explorations along the coasts of Africa and in the Atlantic. This one is lateen rigged for better performance to windward, but some of them carried square sails as well, usually on the foremast. The Spanish used caravels, too. This one probably resembles Columbus's *Niña*, before she was fitted with square sails for the trip across the Atlantic.

THE FIRST COLONIAL EMPIRES: PORTUGAL AND SPAIN

The Portuguese Colonies. Conquest and the imposition of European government accompanied exploration from the beginning. The Portuguese made no effort to impose their direct rule on large native populations, in part because they lacked the manpower to do so and in part because the primary purpose of Portuguese expansion was trade. Instead, they established a series of merchant colonies to collect goods from the African, Indian, or Asian interior for transshipment to Portugal in return for cash or European commodities. These colonies were rarely more than towns protected by a Portuguese garrison and governed by Portuguese law. They were not, for the most part, self-sustaining. To prosper, they had to maintain diplomatic and commercial relations with their neighbors while retaining the option of force, either for self-protection or to obtain a favorable market share in regional trade. Because Portugal's population was small, there was no question of large-scale immigration. Governors from Albuquerque onward sought to maintain colonial populations and to solidify Portuguese control by encouraging intermarriage with native peoples.

Communication between these far-flung stations and the mother country was maintained by the largest ships of the age, the thousand-ton carracks built especially for the *Carreira da India* (road to India). The voyage around the tip of Africa took months and caused dreadful mortality among crews, but profit to the crown made it all seem worthwhile. To discourage smuggling, everything had to be shipped to and from a central point—the Guinea Mines House at Lagos, near Sagres—where royal officials could inspect the cargoes of spice and silks and assess the one-third share owed to the king. In return, the monarchy provided military and naval protection for the colonies and for the convoys that served them. Colonial governors, although appointed by the crown, enjoyed the freedom that comes from being far from home. Corruption flourished, but Portuguese rule was rarely harsh.

The Astrolabe. Astrolabes have been used by astronomers since the sixth century. They are complex instruments that consist of a movable map of the stars, a series of lines indicating celestial coordinates, and a straight rule known as an *alidade*. The navigator points the alidade at the sun to determine his latitude, or distance from the equator. The astrolabe was simplified for navigational use in the fifteenth century and weighted to keep it vertical on a pitching ship, but it never achieved perfect accuracy and was difficult to use.

The Cross-staff. Cross-staffs became common in the early 1500s. They were simpler, easier to use, and more accurate than an astrolabe. The mariner figures latitude by moving a sliding crosspiece along a marked staff. When the bottom of the crosspiece is on the horizon and its upper edge is on the sun, he can read his latitude in the markings on the staff. He risks eye damage because he has to look into the sun, but the cross-staff could fix latitude to within about 1 degree of accuracy, while the astrolabe sometimes erred by as much as 5 degrees. A degree equals 60 nautical miles, or about 69 land miles.

Where controlling large tracts of land became necessary, as in Brazil, the Portuguese established captaincies that were in fact proprietary colonies. Captains-general would be appointed in return for their promise to settle and develop grants of land given to them by the crown. The model had first been used in the settlement of Madeira, a group of Atlantic islands settled by Portugal in the 1420s. Both Brazil and Madeira evolved into societies based largely on sugar plantations worked by African slaves.

The Spanish Conquests. The first Spanish attempts at colonization resembled the Portuguese experience in Brazil. Columbus had set a bad example by trying to enslave the native population of Hispaniola, the island now occupied by Haiti and the Dominican Republic. Spanish settlers made similar efforts at Cuba and elsewhere in the Caribbean without success. The Indians died of disease and overwork, fled to the mainland, or were killed while trying to resist. The Spanish then imported African slaves to work in the mines and sugar cane fields. In the meantime, the conquest of Mexico and Peru had changed the basic nature of Spanish colonial enterprise. Both regions contained populous, highly developed civilizations. For the first time, Europeans sought to impose their rule on societies as complex and populous as their own.

The various nations of central Mexico were grouped into political units that resembled city-states. Their combined population almost certainly exceeded that of Spain. By the fifteenth century, most of these peoples had become either subjects or tributaries of the warlike **Aztecs** whose capital, Tenochtitlán, was a vast city built in the midst of a lake where Mexico City now stands. Hernán Cortés could not have conquered this great empire in

Hernán Cortés

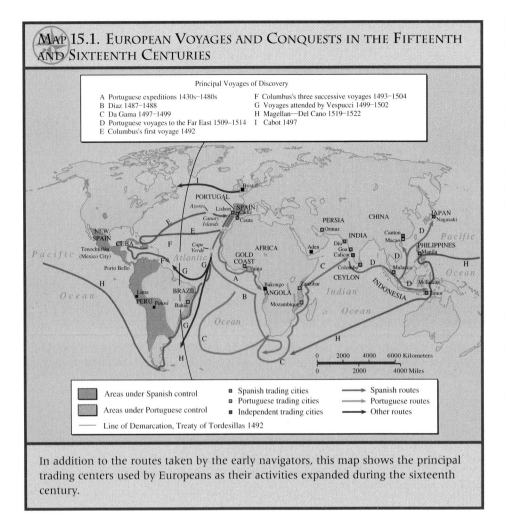

Map 15.1. European Voyages and Conquests in the Fifteenth and Sixteenth Centuries

Principal Voyages of Discovery

A Portuguese expeditions 1430s–1480s
B Diaz 1487–1488
C Da Gama 1497–1499
D Portuguese voyages to the Far East 1509–1514
E Columbus's first voyage 1492
F Columbus's three successive voyages 1493–1504
G Voyages attended by Vespucci 1499–1502
H Magellan—Del Cano 1519–1522
I Cabot 1497

Areas under Spanish control
Areas under Portuguese control
Line of Demarcation, Treaty of Tordesillas 1492
■ Spanish trading cities
■ Portuguese trading cities
■ Independent trading cities
→ Spanish routes
→ Portuguese routes
→ Other routes

In addition to the routes taken by the early navigators, this map shows the principal trading centers used by Europeans as their activities expanded during the sixteenth century.

fortune to arrive in the midst of a dynastic dispute that divided the Indians and virtually paralyzed resistance. By 1533, the Spanish, now numbering about 600, had seized the capital and a vast golden treasure, but they soon began to fight among themselves. Pizarro was murdered in one of a series of civil wars that ended only in 1548.

The Imposition of Royal Government. The rapid conquest of two great empires forced the Spanish crown to confront basic issues of morality and governance. Tension between conquerors and the crown had begun with Columbus. His enslavement of the Indians and high-handed treatment of his own men led to his replacement as governor of Hispaniola. Officials sent from Spain executed Balboa for his misbehavior in Darien. To regularize the situation, the *encomienda* system, an institution that had been used to settle Muslim regions during the Spanish Reconquest of the Middle Ages, was introduced after the conquests of Mexico and Peru. *Conquistadores* (kon-kees-ta-dor'-es; conquerors) were to provide protection and religious instruction for a fixed number of Indians in return for a portion of their labor. The system failed. The Spanish conquistadores were for the most part desperadoes, members of a large class of otherwise unemployable military adventurers that had survived the wars of Granada or of Italy. They had braved great dangers to win what they thought of as a New World and had no intention of allowing priests and bureaucrats to deprive them of their rewards.

Efforts to Protect the Indians. In the meantime, the Indians of the mainland had begun to die in enormous numbers, like those of the islands before them. Although many were killed while trying to defend themselves, most fell victim to European diseases for which they had developed no immunities. Smallpox was probably the worst. Estimates of mortality by the end of the sixteenth century range as high as 90 percent, and although all figures from this period are open

1521 without the assistance of the Aztecs' many native enemies, but his success left Spain with the problem of governing millions whose culture was wholly unlike that of Europeans.

The problem was compounded in Peru a decade later. In 1530, **Francisco Pizarro** landed at Tumbez on the Pacific coast with 180 men and set about the destruction of the **Inca Empire.** The Incas were the ruling dynasty of the Quechua people. From their capital at Cuzco they controlled a region nearly 2,000 miles in length by means of an elaborate system of roads and military supply depots. More tightly organized than the Mexicans, Quechua society was based on communal landholding and a system of forced labor that supported both the rulers and a complex religious establishment that did not, unlike that of the Aztecs, demand human sacrifice. Pizarro had the good

Francisco Pizarro

THE HAZARDS OF A LONG VOYAGE

The Straits of Magellan.

This passage, now called the Straits of Magellan and running between the southern tip of the South American mainland and the island of Tierra del Fuego, connects the Atlantic and Pacific Oceans. Its regular 100-mile-per-hour gusting winds must have terrified sailors.

This extract is taken from a firsthand account of Fernando Magellan's voyage around the world by Antonio Pigafetta, but similar conditions might be expected on any sea journey if it lasted long enough. The disease described is scurvy, which results from a deficiency of vitamin C. It was a serious problem even on transatlantic voyages. The cause was not understood until the eighteenth century, but captains could usually predict the first date of its appearance in a ship's company with some accuracy.

Wednesday, November 28, we debauched from that strait [since named after Magellan], engulfing ourselves in the Pacific Sea. We were three months and twenty days without getting any kind of fresh food. We ate biscuit, which was no longer biscuit, but powder of biscuits swarming with worms, for they had eaten the

good. It stank strongly of the urine of rats. We drank yellow water that had been putrid for many days. We also ate some ox hides that covered the top of the mainyard to prevent the yard from chafing the shrouds, and which had become exceedingly hard because of the sun, rain, and wind. We left them in the sea for four or five days, and then placed them on top of the embers and so ate them; and we often ate sawdust from boards. Rats were sold for one-half ducat a piece, and even then we could not get them. But above all the other misfortunes the following was the worst. The gums of both the lower and upper teeth of some of our men swelled so that they could not eat under any circumstances and therefore died. Nineteen men died from that sickness. . . . Twenty-five or thirty men fell sick.

From Pigafetta, Antonio, *Magellan's Voyage around the World*, ed. and trans. J. A. Robertson (Cleveland: 1902).

Question: What would cause someone to go on a long sea voyage that presented such conditions and risks?

---

to question, the conquest clearly was responsible for the greatest demographic catastrophe in historical times (see Table 15.1).

Given the state of medical knowledge, little could be done to control the epidemics, but church and state alike were determined to do something about the conquistadores. The Dominican friar **Bartolomé de Las Casas** (1474–1566) launched a vigorous propaganda campaign on behalf of the Indians that ended in a series of debates at the University of Salamanca. Basing his arguments on Aristotle, he declared that the Indians were "rational beings" and therefore could not be enslaved. Las Casas won his point. In 1542 and 1543, Emperor

Charles V (1500–1558) issued the so-called New Laws, forbidding Indian slavery and abolishing the encomienda system.

The Spanish Colonial System. The edicts for the protection of the Indians met with powerful resistance (see Document 15.2), and not until the reign of **Philip II** (1556–1598) did Spain implement the system of governance that would last throughout the colonial era. Mexico and Peru became kingdoms ruled by viceroys who were the personal representatives of the king. Like the Portuguese, the Spanish tried to limit access to its colonial trade. No foreigners could participate, and all

FIGURE 15.2 *A Sugar Mill.* European demand for sugar encouraged the colonization of Brazil and the Caribbean Islands. It also created an insatiable demand for African slaves to work the sugar plantations. In this open-air mill, slaves fed the cane into the ox-powered grinder to the right. The juice was then placed in the boiling vats (center), where it was reduced into molasses for shipment.

goods had to be shipped and received through the *Casa de Contratación,* a vast government customs house in Sevilla. From the middle of the sixteenth century, French and English adventurers sought to break this monopoly and eventually became a threat to Spanish shipping in both Caribbean and European waters. By this time, massive silver deposits had been discovered at Potosí in what is now Bolivia (1545) and at Zacatecas in Mexico (1548). Bullion shipments from the New World soon accounted for more than 20 percent of the empire's revenues, and a system of convoys, or *flotas,* was established for their protection.

The Cultural Legacy of the Conquests. The European conquests had a disastrous effect on Native Americans. The extermination of millions of people was largely unintentional, but the Spanish in particular saw American culture as a barrier to conversion and tried to destroy it. They leveled temples and built churches on the ruins. They destroyed cities and rebuilt them along Spanish lines, while extensive intermarriage between Spaniards and Americans tended to weaken the cultural identity of the latter. Religious instruction sought not only to instill Catholicism but also to obliterate traditional beliefs. This campaign against memory was remarkably successful, although many of the old ways survived as folklore or as superficially Christianized myths.

Biological Exchange. The term **biological exchange** refers to the transfer of new life forms among cultures. The introduction of European and African diseases to the New World provides a terrifying example,

but it was not fully reciprocal. Aside from a strain of syphilis endemic to the Americas, Europeans suffered few medical effects from the conquests as long as they remained in Europe. Those who came to America or visited Africa in search of slaves often died of yellow fever and other African diseases for which they had no immunity. Europeans also resisted American foods such as tomatoes, potatoes, maize, and bell peppers until the eighteenth century. Until then, biological exchange remained largely a one-way street. The colonists brought horses, cattle, and hogs to regions that lacked native sources of animal power or animal protein, but the value of these benefits has been questioned by modern ecologists and by vegetarians. Sugar, a Middle Eastern plant formerly cultivated in small quantities, became available for mass consumption in Europe when huge sugar plantations were established in the Caribbean and Brazil. The widespread availability of sugar was no

FIGURE 15.3 *An Illustration from the Works of Las Casas.* The Dominican friar, Bartolomé de Las Casas, worked tirelessly to improve the treatment of the Indians under Spanish rule. His *Very Brief Account of the Destruction of the Indies* (written 1542) provided a catalogue of atrocities that eventually helped inspire legal reform. It also provided Spain's many enemies with a propaganda tool of great value. In fact, Spanish behavior was probably little worse than that of other colonizing nations, all of whom saw indigenous peoples as a resource to exploit. In this illustration from a French edition of Las Casas's work, the Spanish roast an Indian alive over a slow fire. In the background, another has his hands cut off as a warning to others.

TABLE 15.1 POPULATION DECLINE IN CENTRAL MEXICO

Little agreement exists on the size of Mexico's pre-Columbian population. These figures are more conservative than most but reflect a stunning rate of mortality.

REGION	POPULATION 1530—1535	POPULATION IN 1568
Basin of Mexico (excluding Mexico City)	589,070–743,337	294,535–297,335
Mexico City	218,546–273,183	109,273
Morelos	460,797–614,396	153,599
Southern Hidalgo	257,442–321,802	128,721
Tlaxcala	140,000–165,000	140,000–165,000
West Puebla Above 2000 meters	160,664–200,830	80,332
Below 2000 meters	152,412–190,515	38,103
Total	1,978,931–2,509,063	944,563–972,363

Source: Adapted from William T. Sanders, "The Population of the Central Mexican Symbiotic Region, the Basin of Mexico, and the Teotihuacán Valley in the Sixteenth Century," in William M. Denevan, ed., *The Native Population of the Americas in 1492*, 2nd ed. (Madison: University of Wisconsin Press, 1992, p. 128).

Questions: Did all cities decrease in population? If not, which didn't? Why did Tlaxcala's population not decrease? What could explain the difference in the amount of decreased population in the two areas of West Puebla?

DOCUMENT 15.2

PROCLAMATION OF THE NEW LAWS IN PERU

In 1544, a new viceroy, Blasco Nuñez Vela, introduced the New Laws to Peru. The popular outrage recounted here by Francisco López de Gómara led to a serious but unsuccessful revolt under the leadership of Gonzalo Pizarro, the conqueror's brother.

Blasco Nuñez entered Trujillo amid great gloom on the part of the Spaniards; he publicly proclaimed the New Laws, regulating Indian tributes, freeing the Indians, and forbidding their use as carriers against their will and without pay. He told them, however, that if they had reason to complain of the ordinances they should take their case to the emperor; and that he would write to the king that he had been badly informed to order those laws.

When the citizens perceived the severity behind his soft words, they began to curse. [Some] said that they were ill-requited for their labor and services if in their declining years they were to have no one to serve them; these showed their teeth, decayed from eating roasted corn in the conquest of Peru; others displayed many wounds, bruises, and great lizard bites; the conquerors complained that after wasting their estates and shedding their blood in gaining Peru for the emperor, he was depriving them of the few vassals he had given them.

The priests and friars also declared that they could not support themselves nor serve their churches if they were deprived of their Indian towns; the one who spoke most shamelessly against the viceroy and even against the king was Fray Pedro Muñoz of the Mercedarian Order, saying . . . that the New Laws smelled of calculation rather than of saintliness, for the king was taking away the slaves that he had sold without returning the money received from them. . . . There was bad blood between this friar and the viceroy because the latter had stabbed the friar one evening in Málaga when the viceroy was corregidor there.

From López de Gómara, Francisco. "Historia de las Indias," trans. B. Keen. In *Latin American Civilization*, vol. 1 (Boston: Houghton Mifflin, 1974, pp. 142–143).

Question: What did the New Laws do, and how did the Spanish populace respond?

---

doubt bad for European teeth. It certainly allowed the large-scale distillation of gin and other spirits in the seventeenth century, a process that requires vast amounts of sugar. Both ranching and sugar planting had a destructive effect on native American ecologies.

Demographically, few Americans traveled to Europe and survived. Europeans and Africans emigrated (willingly or unwillingly) in great numbers to create a racially diverse population in the Americas. Africa and most of Asia remained demographically unchanged, because the permanent European presence there was comparatively small and because Asians and Europeans shared the same disease pool and therefore the same immunities. The world population of Africans and African

Americans may actually have increased despite the terrible mortality of the slave trade. The descendants of those who survived the slave ships became more numerous in the Americas, although the wretched conditions imposed by slavery kept their rate of growth far below that of Caucasians. Meanwhile, the cassava, a starchy South American root, became the staple food of West Africa and permitted a substantial increase among the populations that had eluded the slavers.

The Economic and Political Legacy of the Conquests. America's entry into the world market increased the overall volume of world trade, and its massive exports of gold and silver increased the European money supply. Early modern rulers began to think that it was better to increase revenues by seizing new territory and by expanding trade than by exploiting their existing subjects more efficiently. The idea, although popular with their subjects, was based in part on an illusion. Trade and colonies provided additional pretexts for war. Their protection demanded the establishment of fortresses and the maintenance of expensive deep-sea navies. During the sixteenth and early seventeenth centuries, the cost and intensity of European warfare reached new heights, and it was obvious well before 1600 that even if the primary cause of these conflicts was rarely colonial rivalry, their scope was becoming global.

A CLASH OF EMPIRES: THE OTTOMAN CHALLENGE AND EMPEROR CHARLES V (1526–1558)

The wars that plagued sixteenth-century and early seventeenth-century Europe were for the most part a continuation of old dynastic rivalries, complicated after 1560 by rebellion and civil war in nearly all of the major states. These struggles were pursued with unparalleled vigor even though most Europeans believed, or

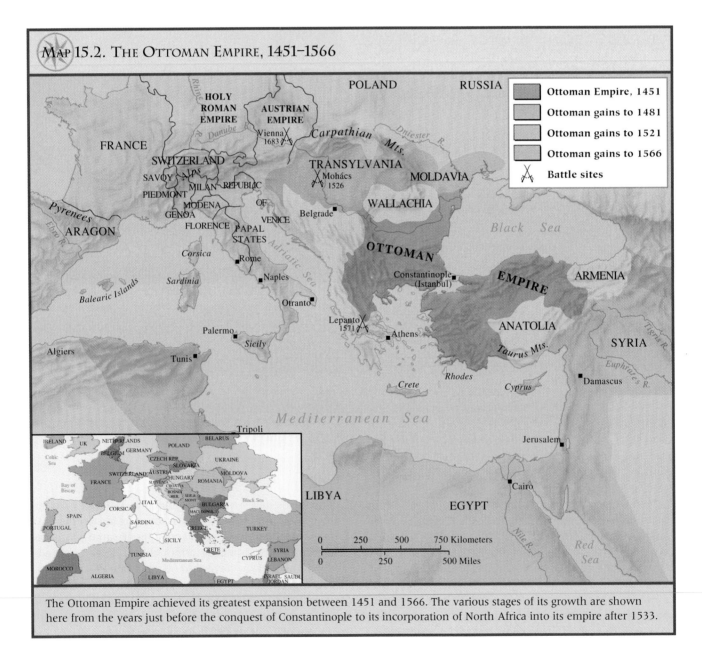

MAP 15.2. THE OTTOMAN EMPIRE, 1451–1566

Ottoman Empire, 1451
Ottoman gains to 1481
Ottoman gains to 1521
Ottoman gains to 1566
Battle sites

The Ottoman Empire achieved its greatest expansion between 1451 and 1566. The various stages of its growth are shown here from the years just before the conquest of Constantinople to its incorporation of North Africa into its empire after 1533.

FIGURE 15.4 *A Turkish Janissary.* The Janissaries, for the most part were Christian boys who had been enslaved, converted to Islam, and trained as soldiers. They formed the elite core of the Turkish army and often rose to positions of great wealth and power. The drawing is by Gentile Bellini (c. 1429–1507).

claimed to believe, that the survival of Christendom was threatened by Ottoman expansion.

The structure of the Ottoman state forced the sultans to maintain a program of conquest even after the fall of Constantinople. Their personal survival often depended on its success. Because the sultans practiced polygyny on a grand scale, inheritance was by a form of natural selection. Each of the sultan's legitimate sons was given a provincial governorship at age 14. Those who showed promise acquired more offices and more military support until, when the sultan died, one of them was in a position to seize power and murder his surviving brothers. The role of the military in securing and maintaining the succession meant that its loyalty had to be maintained at all times. The most important component of the army was the Janissaries, an infantry composed of men who were technically slaves of the sultan. Male children were taken as tribute from conquered areas, converted to Islam, and raised as soldiers. Originally, the Janissaries were forbidden to marry, but they were not immune to the attractions of wealth and power. Like the Praetorian Guard of ancient Rome, they could overthrow a sultan if their ambitions were not achieved. War

gave them booty, governorships, and new recruits. It was wise to keep them as busy as possible.

Turkish Offensives in Europe. The Turks first became a serious threat to western Europe in the reign of Süleyman I "the Magnificent" (1520–1566). In 1522, his fleet drove the Knights of St. John from their stronghold at Rhodes, thereby permitting unimpeded communications between Constantinople and Egypt. After defeating the Hungarians at Mohács in 1526, Süleyman controlled the central Hungarian plain. The Austrian Hapsburgs continued to rule a narrow strip of northwestern Hungary, but Transylvania under its *voivod* János Zapolya (d. 1540) became a Turkish tributary, Calvinist in religion, and bitterly hostile to the Catholic west. Then, in 1529 and again in 1532, Süleyman besieged Vienna. He failed on both occasions, largely because Vienna was beyond the effective limits of Ottoman logistics. But the effort made a profound impression. The Turk was at the gates.

In retrospect, the attacks on Vienna probably were intended only to prevent a Hapsburg reconquest of Hungary. They were not repeated until 1689. In 1533, the Turks launched a new offensive at sea. Fleets under the command of Khair ed-Din, a Christian convert to Islam known as Barbarossa for his flaming red beard, ravaged the coasts of Italy, Sicily, and Spain and threatened Christian commerce throughout the Mediterranean.

The Empire of Charles V. The brunt of these struggles ultimately fell on the Spanish Empire. In 1517, Charles of Hapsburg (1500–1558) ascended the thrones of Castile and Aragon to become Charles I, first king of a united Spain. He was the son of Juana "la Loca" (the Crazy), daughter of Ferdinand and Isabella, and Philip "the Handsome" (d. 1506), son of the emperor Maximilian I and Mary of Burgundy. His mother lived until 1555, but she was thought to be insane and had been excluded from the succession. From her, Charles inherited Castile and its possessions in the New World. From Ferdinand, he inherited Aragon and much of Italy, including Naples, Sicily, and Sardinia. With the death of his grandfather Maximilian in 1519, he gained the Hapsburg lands in Austria and Germany and the remaining inheritance of the dukes of Burgundy, including the seventeen provinces of the Netherlands. In 1519, he was elected Holy Roman Emperor as Charles V.

The Wars of Charles V. The massive accumulation of states and resources embroiled the young emperor in endless conflict. Although he had placed the Austrian lands under the rule of his brother Ferdinand, Charles defended Vienna in person against the Turks. Because Turkish naval efforts were directed primarily against his possessions in Spain and Italy, he thought it necessary to invade Tunis in 1535 and Algiers in 1541. Francis I of

FIGURE 15.5 *The Abdication of Emperor Charles V.* Worn out by physical ailments and a lifetime of struggle, the emperor astonished the world by abdicating his offices and retiring to a Spanish monastery. In this French tapestry, woven between 1630 and 1640, Charles begins the process by resigning as ruler of the Netherlands in favor of his son Philip II (seen here kissing the emperor's hand). Charles abdicated as king of Spain in the following year and was succeeded as emperor by his brother Ferdinand I in 1558. Charles died on September 21, 1558. The ceremony shown here took place at Brussels on October 25, 1555.

France fought seven wars with him in 30 years to make good his own claim to Naples, Sicily, and Milan. This Hapsburg–Valois rivalry (named after the families of the two rulers) was in some ways a continuation of the Italian wars at the beginning of the century, but it was fought on three fronts: northern Italy, the Netherlands, and the Pyrenees. As a devout Catholic, the emperor also tried in 1546–1547 and again in 1552–1555 to bring the German Protestants to heel but received no help from the papacy. Paul III, fearing imperial domination of Italy, allied himself with the Most Christian King of France, who was in turn the ally of the major Protestant princes and of the Turks.

The empire of Charles V was multinational, but in time its center of gravity shifted toward Spain. Charles, born in the Low Countries and whose native tongue was French, became increasingly dependent on the revenues of Castile. Spanish soldiers, trained in the Italian wars, became the core of his army. Castilian administrators produced results, not endless complaints about the violation of traditional rights or procedures,

and by 1545, his secretary, his chief military adviser, and his confessor were Spanish. Sick and exhausted, Charles began to abdicate from his various offices in 1555. In 1557, he retired to the remote monastery of Yuste in Spanish Extremadura, where he died in 1558. His son, Philip II (reigned 1556–1598), was Spanish to his fingertips. His father's abdication left him Italy, the Netherlands, and the Spanish Empire, while the Hapsburg lands in central Europe were given to Charles's brother Ferdinand, who was elected emperor in 1558.

The war between France and Spain came to an end in 1559 with the treaty of Cateau-Cambrésis, but the underlying rivalry remained. Both sides were simply exhausted. Although Philip was forced to repudiate his father's debts, the predictability of Castilian revenues and a dramatic increase in wealth from the American mines soon restored Spanish credit. The policies of the new king would be those of the late emperor: the containment of Islam and of Protestantism and the neutralization of France.

THE CRISIS OF THE EARLY MODERN STATE (1560–1660)

The wars and rebellions of the later sixteenth century must be understood in this context. The cost of war had continued to grow, forcing states to increase their claims upon the resources of their subjects. By midcentury, nobles, cities, and their elected representatives had begun to resist those claims with unprecedented vigor, especially in France and the Netherlands. They began to reassert ancient privileges to counter demands for more money or for greater royal authority. This heightened resistance was based in part on economics. A series of bad harvests attributed to the "Little Ice Age," a period of cold, wet weather that lasted from the 1550s to after 1650, worked together with monetary inflation to keep trade and land revenues stagnant. Real wealth was not increasing in proportion to the demands made upon it. Although the European elite continued to prosper by comparison with the poor, they grew ever more jealous of their prerogatives.

The controversies that arose in the wake of the Reformation made matters worse. Outside the Iberian Peninsula, the populations of most states were now bitterly divided along confessional as well as economic lines. Because nearly everyone believed that religious tolerance was incompatible with political order, each group sought to impose its views on the others. This attitude was shared by many who were not fanatics. In a society that had always expressed political and economic grievances in religious language, the absence of a common faith made demonizing opponents easy.

Reaching compromise on any issue became difficult, if not impossible.

In the light of these struggles, it appeared that the evolution of the monarchies, for all its success, had not resolved certain basic issues of sovereignty. The relationship of the crown to other elements of the governing elite remained open to question in France, England, and the Netherlands. In the Holy Roman Empire, the role of the emperor was imperfectly defined, and many of the empire's constituent principalities engaged in internal disputes. Underlying everything was the problem of dynastic continuity. The success of the early modern state still depended to an extraordinary degree on the character and abilities of its ruler. Could its basic institutions continue to function if the prince were a child or an incompetent? Some even doubted that they could survive the accession of a woman.

The French Wars of Religion and the Revolt of the Netherlands

The peace of Cateau-Cambrésis was sealed by the marriage of Isabel of Valois, daughter of Henry II of France, to Philip II of Spain. The celebrations included a tournament in which the athletic, although middle-aged, Henry died when a splinter from his opponent's lance entered the eye socket of his helmet. The new king, Francis II, was a sickly child of 15. The establishment of a regency under the leadership of the **Guise** (Geeze) family marked the beginning of a series of conflicts known as the **Wars of Religion** that lasted until 1598. The Guise came from Lorraine, a duchy technically independent of France, and were not related to the royal family. Their ascendancy threatened the **Bourbons,** a clan descended from Louis IX and headed by the brothers Antoine, King of Navarre, and Louis, Prince of Condé. It was also a threat to Henry's widow, **Catherine de Médicis** (May'-dee-see, 1519–1589), who hoped to retain power on behalf of her son, Francis, and his three brothers. Yet another faction, headed by Anne de Montmorency, constable of France, sought, like Catherine, to play the Guise against the Bourbons for their own advantage.

At one level, the Wars of Religion were an old-fashioned struggle between court factions for control of the crown, but the Guise were also devout Catholics who intensified Henry II's policy of persecuting Protestants. Most French Protestants, or **Huguenots** (Hue-ge-noze), were followers of John Calvin. In 1559, they numbered no more than 5 or 10 percent of the population, but their geographical and social distribution made them a formidable minority. Heavily concentrated in the south and west, Calvinism appealed most to rural nobles and to the artisans of the towns, two groups with a long history of political, regional, and economic grievances. The nobles were for the most part trained in the profession of arms; unhappy artisans could easily disrupt trade and city governments.

Searching for allies, the Bourbons found the Huguenots and converted to Protestantism. The conflict was now both religious and to a degree regional, as the Catholics of Paris and the northeast rallied to the house of Guise, who in turn were secretly allied with Philip II of Spain. Francis II died in 1560, shortly after Condé and the Huguenots tried unsuccessfully to kidnap him at Amboise. He was succeeded by his brother, Charles IX (reigned 1560–1574), who was closely controlled by Catherine de Médicis, but the wars went on. Although the Huguenots were not at first successful on the battlefield, they gained limited religious toleration in 1570.

Causes of the Netherlands Revolt. Meanwhile, the Netherlands had begun their long rebellion against the king of Spain. The seventeen provinces of the Low Countries were now the richest part of Europe, an urbanized region devoted to trade and intensive agriculture. Although divided by language (Dutch or Flemish was spoken in the north and west, French or Walloon—a French dialect—in the south and east), they shared a common artistic and intellectual tradition and an easygoing tolerance for foreigners and heretics. A majority of the population remained Catholic, but Lutherans and Calvinists flourished in the major cities. Government was decentralized and, from the Spanish point of view, woefully inefficient. Philip II was represented by a regent, his half-sister Margaret of Parma (1522–1586), who presided over the privy council and the councils of finance and state. Seventeen provincial estates, all of which were represented in the States General, controlled taxes and legislation. A virulent localism based on the defense of historical privilege made agreement possible only on rare occasions. Taxes were often defeated by squabbles over who should pay the largest share—nobles or townspeople. No common legal code existed, and the nobles controlled a host of independent legal jurisdictions whose administration of justice was often corrupt.

None of this was acceptable to Philip II. He was determined to reorganize the government, reform the legal system, and root out heresy by reforming the church along the lines suggested by the Council of Trent. All of these proposals struck directly at the wealth and power of the Netherlandish nobles. Philip's plan to reorganize the governing councils weakened their authority, while legal reform would have eliminated the feudal courts from which many of the nobles drew large revenues. Although his reform of the church sought to increase the number of bishops, the king was determined to end the purchase of ecclesiastical offices and to appoint only clerics whose education and spirituality met the high standards imposed by the Council of Trent. The ancient

FIGURE 15.6 *French Catholics Massacre Protestants.* This engraving by Franz Hogenberg, dated 1567, illustrates a massacre of French Protestants (Huguenots) by Catholics during the Wars of Religion. A number of such incidents culminated in the St. Bartholomew's Day massacre of 1572 in which thousands of Protestants lost their lives. Engravings of this kind were widely distributed as a kind of news release that described important events for a largely illiterate population.

custom by which nobles invested in church offices for the support of their younger sons was at an end.

Four years of accelerating protest by leading members of the aristocracy accomplished nothing. Finally, in 1566, a wave of iconoclasm brought matters to a head. The Protestants, acting in opposition to Philip's plan for ecclesiastical reform and encouraged by members of the higher nobility, removed the images from churches across the country. In some areas, iconoclasm was accompanied by rioting and violence. Although the regent's government was able to restore order, Philip responded in shock and anger. In 1567, he dispatched his leading general, the Duke of **Alba** (or Alva, 1507–1582), to put down what he saw as rebellion. Although Alba was at first successful, the harshness of his government alienated virtually every segment of opinion. When he attempted to introduce a perpetual tax in 1572, most of the major cities declared their allegiance to **William "the Silent," Prince of Orange** (1533–1584), the man who had emerged as leader of the revolt.

The Huguenot Alliance. Although William was not yet a convert to Protestantism, he attempted to form an alliance with the French Huguenots, who, under the leadership of **Gaspard de Coligny** (Gahsspar de Ko-lee-nyee), had gained new influence with Charles IX. The situation was doubly perilous for Spain because Philip II, while maintaining Alba in the Netherlands, had renewed his father's struggles with the Turk. The Mediterranean war culminated in the great naval victory of **Lepanto** (October 7, 1571), but Philip's treasury was once again exhausted. French intervention in the Netherlands was averted only by the **Massacre of St. Bartholomew** (August 23–24, 1572) in which more than 5,000 Protestants, Coligny included, were killed by Catholic mobs. The massacre revived the French civil wars and permitted Alba to retake many of the rebellious towns, but the duke was recalled in 1573 and his successors were unable to bring the revolt under control. Margaret's son, Alessandro Farnese, Duke of Parma (1545–1592), finally was able to impose Spanish rule on the ten southern provinces in 1585.

Founding of the United Netherlands. By this time, the seven northern provinces had organized into an independent republic with William of Orange as *stadtholder*, or chief executive. The United Netherlands was Dutch in language and culture. Enriched by trade, secure in its control of the sea, and defended by the heavily fortified "water line" of three broad rivers—the Rhine, the Maas, and the Waal—the new republic was almost invulnerable to Spanish attack. It was also Protestant. The government was dominated by Calvinists, and William converted to Protestantism before he was assassinated by a Spanish agent in 1584. Refugees from Spanish rule, most of them French-speaking Calvinists, poured into the north, while a number of Dutch Catholics headed south into what is now Belgium.

English Intervention. These developments critically altered the balance of power in northern Europe. Philip II was still determined to recover his lost provinces and to assist the Catholics of France in their battle against the Huguenots. The English, restored to Protestantism by **Elizabeth I** (ruled 1558–1603), were equally determined to prevent a concentration of Spanish power on the coasts of the North Sea. When Parma took Antwerp, the largest and richest city in the Netherlands in 1584, they sent an expeditionary force to support the Dutch.

Although a prosperous land of about 3.5 million people, Elizabethan England was no match for the Spanish Empire. It had the core of a fine navy but no army worthy of the name. Perpetual taxes were unknown, and the improvidence of Henry VIII had left his daughter with meager revenues from the royal domain. In the

FIGURE 15.7 *Elizabeth I.* An engraving based on three portraits of Elizabeth made at the beginning, middle, and end of her long reign. From left to right, by Hans Holbein, F. Zucchero, and Marc Garrard the Elder.

event of war, funds had to be sought from Parliament, and Parliament continually tried to interfere with the queen's policies. It was especially incensed at her refusal to marry, in part because its members thought a woman incapable of governing on her own and in part because it feared disorder if she died without an heir.

The Spanish Armada. Parliament need not have worried about Elizabeth's ability, but this last concern, at least, was real. Catholics everywhere had rejected Henry VIII's divorce. To them, Elizabeth was illegitimate, and **Mary Stuart, Queen of Scots** (1542–1587), was the true queen of England. A devout Catholic, descended from Henry VII and connected on her mother's side to

the house of Guise, Mary had been driven from Scotland in 1568 by a coalition of Protestants inspired by the Calvinist reformer John Knox and led by her kinsman the earl of Moray. Elizabeth offered her refuge but held her under house arrest for 19 years before ordering her execution in 1587. Mary was killed not only because she had plotted against Elizabeth but also because the English queen was convinced that war with Spain was inevitable. Elizabeth wanted no rival to encourage the hopes of Philip II or of her own Catholic subjects. These fears, too, were realistic, because for more than 20 years, Elizabeth had pursued a course of intermittent hostility toward Spain. She had encouraged her subjects, notably Sir John Hawkins and Sir Francis Drake, to raid Spanish colonies in the Caribbean and in 1586 sent an English force to assist the Dutch. From the Spanish point of view, the execution of Mary was the last straw. Philip responded by sending a fleet to invade England. The great **Spanish Armada** of 1588 failed, but the disaster did not end the war. Philip rebuilt his navy and tried again without success in 1595, while Drake and the aged Hawkins made another vain attempt on Havana and Cartagena de Indias in the same year.

◄FIGURE 15.8
The Spanish Armada, 1588. This painting by an unknown artist shows a critical moment in the defeat of the Spanish Armada. The Spanish fleet had anchored off Gravelines on the Flemish coast to support an invasion of England by the duke of Parma. The English sent fireships (center) into the anchorage, forcing them to scatter and to abandon the invasion.

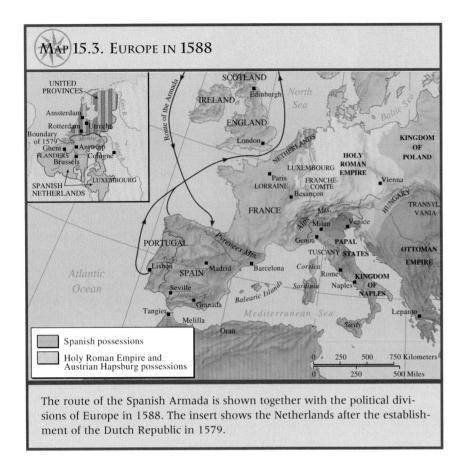

MAP 15.3. EUROPE IN 1588

UNITED PROVINCES
Amsterdam
Rotterdam Utrecht
Boundary of 1579
Ghent Antwerp
FLANDERS Cologne
Brussels
LUXEMBOURG
SPANISH NETHERLANDS

SCOTLAND
Edinburgh
IRELAND
ENGLAND
London
North Sea
Baltic Sea

Route of the Armada
NETHERLANDS
LUXEMBOURG
HOLY ROMAN EMPIRE
KINGDOM OF POLAND
Paris LORRAINE FRANCHE-COMTÉ
Besançon
Vienna

FRANCE
Alps
Milan Mts.
Venice
HUNGARY
TRANSYL VANIA

PORTUGAL
Pyrenees Mts.
Genoa
PAPAL STATES
TUSCANY
OTTOMAN EMPIRE

Lisbon
SPAIN Madrid
Barcelona
Corsica
Rome
KINGDOM OF NAPLES
Naples

Seville
Sardinia
Balearic Islands
Atlantic Ocean
Granada
Tangier
Melilla
Mediterranean Sea
Sicily
Lepanto

Oran

Spanish possessions
Holy Roman Empire and Austrian Hapsburg possessions

0   250   500   750 Kilometers
0   250   500 Miles

The route of the Spanish Armada is shown together with the political divisions of Europe in 1588. The insert shows the Netherlands after the establishment of the Dutch Republic in 1579.

The End of the Wars of Religion in France. By this time, the Spanish were at war in France as well. In 1589, the Bourbon leader Henry of Navarre emerged from the "War of the Three Henrys" as the only surviving candidate for the throne. The other two Henrys, Henry of Guise and Henry III, the last surviving son of Catherine de Médicis, had been assassinated by each other's supporters. Philip thought that if France were controlled by Huguenots, the Spanish Netherlands would be crushed between two Protestant enemies, and he sent Parma and his army into France. This expedition, too, was a costly failure, but Henry's interests turned out to be more political than religious. He converted to Catholicism in the interest of peace and ascended the throne as Henry IV (reigned 1589–1610). To protect the Huguenots, he issued the **Edict of Nantes** (Nahnt, 1598), which granted them freedom of worship and special judicial rights in a limited number of towns, most in the

Henry IV (Navarre) of France

southwest. In some respects, it created a state within a state, but the ordeal of France was over.

The Thirty Years' War

The resolution of the French wars and the death of Philip II in 1598 marked the end of a political cycle. The Netherlands continued to fight on under the leadership of William's son, Maurice of Nassau (1567–1625), a capable general who added the eastern Netherlands to the Dutch Republic. Spain and the Netherlands concluded a 10 years' truce in 1608, but it was a truce, not a treaty. Although Spain was financially exhausted, it still refused to recognize the Dutch state. War was expected to break out again when the truce expired in 1618. The war, when it came, was much more than a resumption of the Dutch Revolt. It involved all of the European states and turned central Europe into a battleground from 1618 to 1648.

The Bohemian War. The first phase of the Thirty Years' War began with a struggle for the crown of Bohemia. In 1555, the Peace of Augsburg had established the principle *cuius regio, eius religio;* that is, princes within the empire had the right to determine the religious beliefs of their subjects. Calvinists, however, were excluded from its provisions, and issues regarding the disposition of church properties and the conversion of bishops were left in dispute. Since then, two electoral principalities, the Palatinate and Brandenburg, had turned Calvinist, and several bishops had converted to Protestantism while retaining possession of their endowed lands. Violent quarrels arose over these issues, and by 1610, the empire was divided into two armed camps: the Protestant Union and the Catholic League.

The Bohemian controversy arose because Matthias, King of Bohemia in 1618, was also Holy Roman Emperor, a Catholic Hapsburg, and uncle of the future emperor **Ferdinand II** of Austria (1578–1637). Matthias was determined to preserve Bohemia for the faith and for his family, and in 1617, he secured the election of Ferdinand as his successor to the throne of Bohemia. Most of the Bohemian gentry and lesser nobility opposed this election. They were, for the most part, Calvinists or Hussites and feared persecution from the devout Ferdinand and his Jesuit advisers. On May

23, 1618, an assembly of Bohemians threw three of the Hapsburg's regents from a window of the Hradschin palace, appointed a provisional government, and began to raise an army.

The "Defenestration of Prague" was an act of war. Revolt spread to the hereditary lands, threatening not only Bohemia but also the basic integrity of the Hapsburg state. Worse yet, the King of Bohemia was an elector of the empire. If the Bohemians elected a Protestant, the Protestants would have a majority of electors just as a new imperial election appeared imminent. Matthias was in poor health and Ferdinand hoped to succeed him as king of Bohemia as well as emperor. Ferdinand needed time to muster support, but in June 1619, he invaded Bohemia with the army of the Catholic League, drawn largely from his ally, Bavaria. The Bohemians responded by offering the crown to a Calvinist prince, Frederick V (1596–1632), elector palatine and son-in-law of James I of England.

Frederick accepted, after the death of Matthias and the election of Ferdinand as emperor on August 28. It was a tragic mistake. He was supported by only a part of the Protestant Union. James I refused to help, and a diversionary attack on Hungary by Bethlen Gabor (1580–1629), the Calvinist prince of Transylvania, was eventually contained by the Hapsburgs. Finally, on November 8, 1620, Frederick and his Protestant allies were soundly defeated at the White Mountain near Prague. Frederick's cause was now hopeless. The Spanish truce with the Netherlands had expired, and the Palatinate lay squarely across the route by which Spanish troops and supplies were sent to the Low Countries. While Frederick's forces fought to preserve his claim to Bohemia, a Spanish army invaded his ancestral lands.

The Danish and Swedish Interventions. A second phase of the war began in 1625, when Christian IV of Denmark (1577–1648) emerged briefly as the champion of Protestantism. Christian's Lutheranism was reinforced by his territorial ambitions in north Germany, but he was no match for the imperial generals. By 1629, he was out of the war. His place was taken by the formidable **Gustav Adolph** of Sweden (1594–1632). Since the reign of Erik XIV (ruled 1560–1568), Swedish policy had aimed at control of the Baltic. Wars with Russia and Poland had taught Gustav the art of war and given him all of Livonia, a territory roughly equal to present-day Estonia, Latvia, and Lithuania. He now sought to defend his fellow Protestants and to establish Swedish control over Mecklenburg and Pomerania on the north German coast. His brilliant campaigns, financed in part by France, came to an end when he died victorious on the battlefield at Lützen on November 16, 1632.

The Final Phase. The last phase of the war (1535–1648) continued the Franco-Swedish alliance, but with France acting openly as the leader of the anti-imperial forces. Henry IV had died at the hands of an assassin in 1610, leaving the queen, Marie de Médicis, as regent for the 9-year-old Louis XIII (1601–1643). Her regency was unpopular, but the disasters of 1560 were not repeated. Louis seized power from his mother in 1617 and, after 1624, entrusted much of his government to Armand de Plessis, Cardinal Duke of **Richelieu** (Ree-shel-you, 1585–1642). One of the ablest statesmen of the age, Richelieu was alarmed by the Spanish–Imperial alliance and returned to the policies of Francis I in the hope of preventing the encirclement of France by the Hapsburgs. He pursued the war through surrogates until the death of Gustav Adolph forced him into the open. The Spanish were by this time

FIGURE 15.9 *The Defenestration of Prague.* In 1618, Bohemian Protestants threw two Austrian Catholic imperial regents and their secretary out of windows of the Hradschin palace in Prague, thereby setting off the first phase of the Thirty Years' War. The act intentionally copied the beginning of the Hussite revolt 200 years before. Then, the victims had been tossed from the window of Prague's town hall and landed on a mass of upthrust pikes with fatal results. In 1618, victims fell 60 feet but were uninjured. Catholic accounts stated the men were carried to the ground by angels; Protestants contended that they escaped death by landing on a pile of manure.

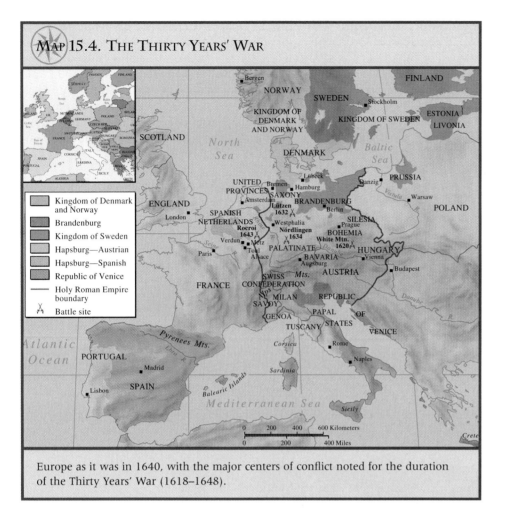

MAP 15.4. THE THIRTY YEARS' WAR

Europe as it was in 1640, with the major centers of conflict noted for the duration of the Thirty Years' War (1618–1648).

in irreversible decline, and their defeat by the French at Rocroi (1643) marked the end of their military power. A Franco-Swedish force ravaged Bavaria in 1648, and peace was at last concluded on October 24 of that year.

The Peace of Westphalia. The Treaties of Westphalia brought the Thirty Years' War to an end, leaving France the dominant power in Europe. The Netherlands, which had fought Spain in a series of bitter actions on land and sea, was at last recognized as an independent state, and the German principalities, many of which had been devastated, were restored to the boundaries of 1618. Bohemia reverted to the Hapsburgs, but imperial authority as a whole was weakened, except in the Hapsburg lands of southeastern Europe. It was a meager return for three decades of unparalleled violence.

The English Civil War

England did not participate in the Thirty Years' War because the early Stuart monarchs, **James I** (ruled 1603–1625) and **Charles I** (1625–1649), were caught in a political dilemma from which they could not es-

cape. As the son of Mary Queen of Scots, James was already King of Scotland when he inherited the English crown from Elizabeth in 1602. Scotland was poor. England, like Denmark and Sweden, was a "domain" state: the regular revenues of the crown came not from taxes, which could be levied only by Parliament, but from the royal domain. This was not necessarily a disadvantage. The Danish monarch held more than 40 percent of the arable land in Denmark and derived vast revenues from the sound tolls levied on every ship passing from the North Sea into the Baltic. The Swedish royal estate derived great wealth from export duties on copper and iron, the country's major exports. Both countries therefore exerted a political and military influence wholly disproportionate to their size.

The Financial Problem. England had no comparable sources of revenue. The failure of Henry VIII to retain monastic lands taken at the time of the Reformation left the crown without sufficient property to "live of its own." Even import and export duties, although technically part of the domain, had to be authorized by Parliament. The resulting poverty, already evident under Elizabeth, restricted the crown's ability to reward its supporters. Worse, it forced her Stuart successors to seek wealth in ways that profoundly offended their subjects (see Document 15.4). Charles in particular resorted to arbitrary fines, *quo warranto* proceedings that led to the confiscation of properties held since before the days of written titles, and the abuse of wardships. He extended ship money (a tax for the protection of the coasts) to the inland counties and then spent it for purposes other than the navy. All of these measures struck directly at property rights and aroused a firestorm of opposition.

King Charles I of England

Much of this opposition was at first centered in the legal profession where such jurists as Sir Edward Coke (Cook, 1552–1634) revived the common law as a protection against royal prerogatives, but in the end, Parliament proved to be the crown's most formidable adversary. Between 1540 and 1640, the wealth and numbers of the landholding gentry, the professions, and the merchant community had increased enormously. These elements of the English elite dominated the House of Commons, which took the lead in opposing royal policies. The Stuarts feared their disaffection and would have preferred to rule without calling Parliament. Except for relatively short periods, this was impossible. Even the smallest of crises forced the crown to seek relief through parliamentary taxation.

The Unpopularity of the Stuarts. The growing resentment in Parliament might have been better managed had it not been for the personalities of the Stuart kings. Neither James nor Charles inspired great loyalty. James was awkward, personally dirty, and a homosexual at a time when homosexuality was universally condemned. His son was arrogant and generally distrusted, and most people thought that the court as a whole was morally and financially corrupt. Although James, who annoyed his subjects with treatises on everything from the evils of tobacco to witchcraft, wrote eloquently in support of the divine right of kings, his own behavior and the devious policies of his son continually undermined the legitimacy of his family's rule.

The Religious Question. The religious question was more serious. Elizabeth, not wishing "to make windows into men's souls," had established a church that was Protestant but relatively tolerant. Some of her subjects had retained a fondness for the ideas and liturgical practices of the old church; others, known as **Puritans**, followed Calvin with varying degrees of rigor. James I accepted Calvinist doctrines. He commissioned the **King James Bible** of 1611, the translation used by English-speaking Protestants for more than 300 years, and established Protestant colonists in northern Ireland. Although he rejected all demands to abolish bishops in favor of a more democratic form of church governance, he managed to avoid an open breach with the Puritans as they grew more powerful over the course of his reign.

Charles I, however, supported the anti-Puritan reforms of Archbishop William Laud (1573–1645). Laud was what might today be called a High-Church Anglican. He rejected papal authority and clerical celibacy, but his understanding of communion, baptism, and justification (the means by which believers are saved) seemed Catholic to the Puritans, as did his fondness for elaborate church rituals. Queen Henriette Marie (1609–1669), however, heard Mass regularly as an open Roman Catholic. She was the sister of Louis

DOCUMENT 15.3

THE DEFENSE OF LIBERTY AGAINST TYRANTS

In both France and the Netherlands, the Protestants had to justify their revolt against the monarchy. One of the most important theorists to do so was Philippe du Plessis-Mornay, a councilor to Henry of Navarre, the leader of the Bourbon faction who later became Henry IV. Plessis-Mornay based his argument on an early version of the social contract theory, which argued that all rulers received their power from the people. His ideas would have a powerful impact on the political thinkers of the Enlightenment and on the framers of the United States Constitution. This is an excerpt from his treatise, *Vindiciae contra tyrannos.*

Thus, at the beginning all kings were elected. And even those who seem today to come to the throne by succession must first be inaugurated by the people. Furthermore, even if a people has customarily chosen its kings from a particular family because of its outstanding merits, that decision is not so unconditional that if the established line degenerates, the people may not select another.

We have shown . . . that kings receive their royal status from the people; that the whole people is greater than the king and is above him; that the king in his kingdom, the emperor in his empire, are supreme only as ministers and agents, while the people is the true proprietor. It follows, therefore, that a tyrant who commits felony against the people who is, as it were, the owner of his fief; that he commits lèse majesté *[treason] against the kingdom or the empire; and that he is no better than any other rebel since he violates the same laws, although as king, he merits even graver punishment. And so . . . he may be either deposed by his superior or punished under the* lex Julia *[the Roman law on treason] for acts against the public majesty. But the superior here is the whole people or those who represent it. . . . And if things have gone so far that the tyrant cannot be expelled without resort to force, they may call the people to arms, recruit an army, and use force, strategy, and all the engines of war against him who is the declared enemy of the country and the commonwealth.*

From Philippe du Plessis-Mornay, "Vindiciae contra tyrannos," in *Constitutionalism and Resistance in the 16th Century,* trans. and ed. Julian H. Franklin (New York: Macmillan, 1969).

Question: How would a king react to this document?

XIII of France and a strong personality who exerted great influence over her husband. The Puritans suspected that Charles meant to restore Catholicism. They thought that their faith, as well as liberty and property, was at risk.

The Outbreak of the Revolt. Twenty years of increasingly bitter conflict between Parliament and the crown led to civil war in 1642. The Scots rebelled in

DOCUMENT 15.4

THE ENGLISH PETITION OF RIGHT, 1628

The 1628 Petition of Right summarized Parliament's grievances against Charles I, who was trying to solve his financial problems through illegal and arbitrary means. The objections are based largely on perceived violations of the Magna Carta, also known as the Great Charter. The following are excerpts from a much longer document.

And where also, by the statute called the Great Charter of the Liberties of England, it is declared and enacted that no freeman may be taken or imprisoned, or be disseised [dispossessed] of his freehold or liberties or his free customs, or be outlawed or exiled or in any manner destroyed, but by the lawful judgment of his peers or by the law of the land. . . .

They do therefore humbly pray your most excellent majesty that no man hereafter be compelled to make or yield any gift, loan, benevolence, tax, or such like charge without common consent by act of parliament; and that none be called to make answer, or take such oath, or to give attendance, or be confined, or otherwise molested or disquieted concerning the same, or for refusal thereof; and that no freeman, in any such manner as is before mentioned, be imprisoned or detained; and that your majesty would be pleased to remove the said soldiers and mariners [who had been quartered in the counties to enforce the king's measures]; and that the foresaid commissions for proceeding by martial law may be revoked and annulled; and that hereafter no commissions of like nature may issue forth . . . lest by colour of them any of your majesty's subjects be destroyed or put to death, contrary to the laws and franchise of the land.

From Journals of the House of Lords, vol. 3.

Question: What abuses does this document address?

1638, when Charles, in his capacity as king of Scotland, tried to introduce the English *Book of Common Prayer* at Edinburgh. To pay for the Scottish war, he summoned what is called the Long Parliament because it met from 1640 to 1660. In response to his call for money, the Commons impeached Archbishop Laud and Charles's chief minister, Thomas Wentworth, Earl of Strafford. They then abolished the prerogative courts of Star Chamber and High Commission. When Charles failed in his attempt to impeach the parliamentary leaders, he fled from London. Parliament decided to raise an army in its own defense.

The Execution of Charles I.
After 3 years of hard fighting, Parliament's army defeated the royalists at Naseby (June 14, 1645), but serious divisions had appeared in the parliamentary ranks. Independents, who favored a congregational form of church government, now dominated the army. The Parliament they served was controlled by Presbyterians, who believed in a church governed by presbyters or elders rather than bishops. The Independents refused to disband without guaranteed freedom of conscience and the removal of certain Presbyterians from Parliament. The Scots, fearing a threat to the Presbyterian Church order they had just reestablished after a lapse of 30 years, became alarmed. Charles sought to capitalize on these strains by accepting the abolition of the Scottish episcopate in return for Presbyterian support, but Parliament's New Model Army, as it was called, defeated the Scots and their English allies at Preston (August 17–20, 1648). The victors now believed that compromise was impossible. In December, the army captured Charles and purged the Commons of its Presbyterian members. A court appointed by the Rump, as the remnant of Parliament was now called, sentenced the king to death. He was beheaded at Whitehall on January 30, 1649.

Cromwell's Protectorate.
For all practical purposes, the army now governed England. A republican constitution had been established, but real power lay in the hands of **Oliver Cromwell** (1599–1658), the most successful of the parliamentary generals. In 1653, Parliament named him Lord Protector of the Commonwealth of England, Scotland, and Ireland. A radical Protestant and Independent, Cromwell attempted to reform English society along Puritan lines while following a vigorous policy abroad. After subduing the Scots, he fought a naval war with the Dutch (1552–1554) and started another with Spain in 1656. The Irish Catholics, who had massacred thousands of Protestants in 1641, were ruthlessly suppressed.

Oliver Cromwell

Cromwell had refused to accept the crown when it was offered to him in 1657, but when he died in the following year, he left the Protectorate to his son Richard. Richard's rule was brief and troubled. He was forced to resign after only 9 months, and a Convention Parliament restored Charles II (1630–1685), son of Charles I, on May 8, 1660. The English had tired of Puritanism and military rule.

Charles II of England

The Price of Conflict

The Organization and Conduct of War. The wars and revolutions of the century after 1560 caused extensive disruption in almost every part of Europe, largely because of the way they were organized and fought. Armies had become vastly larger and more expensive in the course of the sixteenth century, and the wars themselves became almost interminable. Given their political objectives, it could not have been otherwise. The French Wars of Religion were a struggle between two, and at times three, irreconcilable segments of the country's elite. Most of the battles involved cavalry actions that resulted in a clear victory for one side or the other but that could not end the war. Only the total destruction of the losers could have prevented them from trying again. Neither battles nor massacres like that of St. Bartholomew could accomplish this.

In the Netherlands, the primary goal of both sides was to take and hold land or, conversely, to deny it to the enemy. After 1572, the war became a series of sieges that, thanks to the defensive value of the bastion trace, lasted months and often years. Both sides tended to avoid battles because their troops were, in the short term at least, irreplaceable. Sixteenth-century tactics demanded professional soldiers. The recruitment, training, and movement of replacements to the war zone took months, and positions under constant enemy pressure could not be left even partially defenseless.

If the war in the Netherlands was virtually static, the situation in Germany during the Thirty Years' War was too fluid. Central Europe had become a kind of power vacuum into which unpredictable forces were drawn. Bloody battles were fought only to see the victor confronted with yet another set of enemies. It is hard to imagine what, other than sheer exhaustion, might have ended the struggle. War, as Michael Roberts has said, "eternalized itself." No early modern state could afford this. Even the wealthiest European monarchies lacked the ability to recruit and maintain full-scale standing armies. They relied instead on a core of subject troops (or, as in the French Wars of Religion, troops personally and ideologically committed to a cause), supplemented by a far larger number of mercenaries. The latter were usually recruited by contractors who commanded them in the field. If the mercenaries were not paid, they left; if they stayed, they had little incentive to risk their lives unnecessarily. Their employers had little control over their actions, and even subject troops were capable of mutiny if they were left too long unpaid.

War, in other words, had become an even more chaotic business than usual. *Rank* in the modern sense meant little because officers sometimes refused to obey the orders of those who might have been their inferiors in civilian life. There were no uniforms, and weapons were not for the most part standardized. Logistics were a nightmare. The armies of the period might number anywhere from 30,000 to 100,000 combatants. They housed their troops in makeshift field shelters or quartered them on the civilian populations of the war zones, which meant that civilians might be forced to provide food and housing for months on end. The close contact between soldiers and civilians bred hostility and led to chronic breakdowns in military discipline. To complicate matters further, camp followers numbered at least three and often six for each combatant. These women and children were the support troops who made shelter, foraged for food, and nursed the sick and wounded. No army could function without them, but together with the men they made up a society that lived by its own rules with little concern for civilian norms.

The system reached a peak of absurdity during the Thirty Years' War when contractors such as the imperial general Albrecht von Wallenstein (1583–1634) offered recruits a month's pay—which they had to give back to pay for their arms and equipment—and then marched them so far from their homes that they could not easily return. From that point onward, they were expected to live off the land by looting farms and villages. Such practices account for much of the dislocation caused by the German wars. It was safer for a man's family to join him in the army than to be robbed, raped, or killed by marauding soldiers at home (see Document 15.5). Entire villages were depopulated only to reconstitute themselves wherever they found themselves when the war ended.

The Decline of Spain. When a state tried to provide adequately for its troops, the costs quickly became prohibitive and could lead to social breakdown. The fate of Spain is an example. During the 1570s, Philip II spent 140 percent of his annual revenues on warfare. The uncovered balance was provided by loans, often at high rates, from Italian or Dutch bankers. Not even the import of American silver could long sustain this kind of expenditure, and in time the economy of Castile virtually collapsed (see Table 15.2). The other Spanish kingdoms were exempt from most forms of taxation, but in Castile, taxes increased to the point that peasants had to leave the land and take refuge in the cities where the church periodically distributed grain and oil to the poor. Commerce and industry were virtually destroyed. Declining production not only reduced tax collection but increased the country's dependence on imports, which in turn lowered the value of Spanish money and worsened an inflation that had been fueled for years by silver from the Indies. When Philip II died in 1598, the population of Castile had been shrinking for nearly a decade.

To make matters worse, economic decline actually raised the costs of war by increasing the interest in government loans. Unfavorable exchange rates raised the cost of goods and services that Spain had to purchase in Germany or the Netherlands. Troops were often poorly supplied or left without pay for as much as 3 years at a time. This provoked mutinies, which prolonged the wars and raised costs even higher. Similar problems arose in other countries but were far more serious in Spain, because the military effort lasted for more than a century and a half. From the wars of Granada to the Peace of Westphalia, the Castilian economy had no opportunity to recover.

Philip III (1598–1645) and his minister, the shrewd but lethargic Duke of Lerma, tried to provide Spain with a much-needed respite from war but could not restrain the king's viceroys who launched military campaigns on their own without royal approval. When Philip IV's chief minister, the energetic Count-Duke of **Olivares** (1587–1645), tried to spread the burdens of taxation and recruitment to other Spanish realms, he faced rebellion. Portugal, which had been annexed by Philip II in 1580 after its king died without heirs, declared independence in 1640. Catalonia, on the other side of the peninsula, rebelled in the same year. The government of Olivares lacked the resources to stop them, and Portugal remains free to this day. Catalonia returned to the Spanish fold in 1652, after France emerged as a greater threat to its liberties than Castile.

The Condition of Europe. Spain may have been a special case, but the condition of Europe as a whole after a century of war and rebellion was grim. Most of the German states were a shambles, and the emperor's role had much diminished outside his hereditary lands. Although Cromwellian England briefly tapped the country's wealth in the service of the state, the restoration of Charles II revived many of the old conflicts between crown and Parliament and once again limited the king's wealth and ability to govern. France, the richest of all European states, proved more resilient, but when the 4-year-old Louis XIV ascended the throne under a regency in 1643, a series of aristocratic rebellions known as the Fronde (1648–1652) revealed that the foundations of the monarchy remained insecure.

Eastern Europe was no better. Russia had not yet emerged from its "Time of Troubles," the period of anarchy that followed the death of Ivan the Terrible in 1584. Military intervention by Poland and Sweden complicated a series of revolts led by boyars trying to reverse Ivan's policies of centralization. After 1613, the Romanov Dynasty restored a measure of stability in Moscow but faced challenges from the Old Believers, a movement that rejected all innovation in the Russian church, and from the **Cossacks,** the descendants of peasants who had fled serfdom in Poland and Russia in the sixteenth century. Establishing themselves on the Ukrainian steppes (the great plains north of the Black Sea) the Cossacks became fierce horsemen who served as a buffer against the Turks and Tartars of central Asia but violently resisted tsarist control. At midcentury, only the Dutch Republic appeared strong and stable. For Europe's monarchies it seemed that the years of turmoil had done little to resolve the problem of sovereignty.

Intellectual Achievement. Surprisingly, this age of troubles was in many places a time of intellectual, literary, and artistic achievement. A distinction must be made between those regions that were combat zones, those that remained peaceful

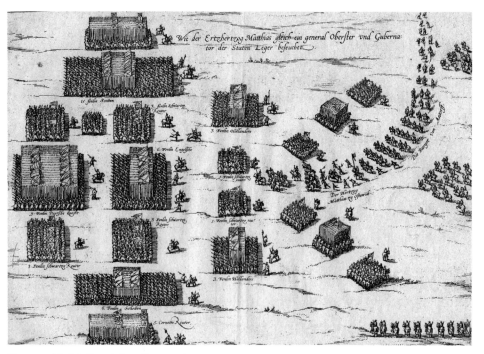

FIGURE 15.10 *Spanish Military Formations.* From the 1530s until the middle of the Thirty Years' War, the Spanish infantry was arguably the best in Europe. It used a formation based on a pike square surrounded by men armed with arquebuses, a kind of light matchlock firearm. This engraving by Franz Hogenberg (1578) shows several such formations. Some of the skirmishers shown outside the formation are *arquebusiers* who try to draw the enemy into battle. Others carry muskets, a heavier weapon whose longer range and greater firepower made it more effective against personal armor.

The novel *Simplicissimus* by Hans von Grimmelshausen (c. 1622–1674) was based in part on the author's own experiences in the Thirty Years' War. In these passages from the beginning of the book, the title character, Simplicissimus, who is not as simple as he appears, describes the sack of his parent's farm. Like the hero, people took to the roads or joined the armies to avoid such horrors.

The first thing these troopers did in the blackened room of my Dad was to stable their mounts. Thereafter, each fell to his appointed task, fraught in every case with ruin and destruction. For although some began to slaughter, cook, and roast, as if for a merry banquet, others stormed through the house from top to bottom, ransacking even the privy, as though they thought the Golden Fleece might be hidden there. Some packed great bundles of cloth, apparel, and household goods, as if to set up a stall for a jumble sale, but what they had no use for they smashed and destroyed. Some thrust their swords into the hay and straw as if they had not enough sheep and pigs to slaughter. Others emptied the feather-beds and pillows of their down, filling them instead with meat and other provender, as if that would make them more comfortable to sleep on. Others again smashed stoves and windows as if to herald an everlasting summer. They flattened copper and pewter utensils and packed up the bent and useless pieces; chests, tables,

chairs, and benches they burnt, though in the yard they could have found many cords of firewood. Finally, they broke every dish and saucepan, either because they preferred their food roasted or because they intended to have no more than a single meal there.

And now they began to unscrew the flints from their pistols and to jam the peasant's thumbs into them, and to torture the poor lads as if they had been witches. Indeed, one of the captives had already been pushed into the bread oven and a fire lit under him, although he had confessed nothing. They put a sling around the head of another, twisting it tight with a piece of wood until the blood spurted from his mouth, nose, and ears. In short, each had his own device for torturing peasants, and each peasant received his individual torture. . . . Of the captured women, girls, and maidservants I have nothing in particular to tell, for the warriors would not let me see what they did with them. But this I do know: that from time to time one could hear pitiful screams coming from different parts of the house, and I don't suppose my Mum and Ursula fared any better than the others.

From Grimmelshausen, H. J. C. von, *Adventures of a Simpleton*, trans. W. Wallich (New York: Ungar, 1963, pp. 8–9).

Question: What would cause soldiers to behave this way?

---

but that were forced to assume heavy financial burdens, and those that were virtually untouched by the fighting. Even the most devastated regions experienced peace for at least a portion of the century between 1560 and 1660; their recovery was sometimes rapid.

Art. Painting, sculpture, and architecture continued to flourish, especially in Italy and Spain. Inspired by the Catholic Reformation, artists modified the artistic conventions of the Renaissance to express emotion and religious fervor in new ways. Using color, texture, and dramatic lighting, painters tried to create a dramatic effect far removed from the serene classicism of the Renaissance. Baroque sculpture, like that of the Hellenistic age, expresses strong emotion through dramatic postures and flowing drapery. Architects placed their buildings like stage sets for maximum impact. Sculptors and painters produced interior spaces so rich and detailed that they resemble the contemporary vision of heaven. Art historians call this style **Baroque.** In the Protestant north, Dutch artists created a very different style of painting that will be discussed in Chapter 16.

TABLE 15.2 CROWN INCOME AND DEBT IN CASTILE

These figures (in millions of ducats) provide an idea of the financial burdens that war imposed on the Castilian economy. During most of this period, nonmilitary costs rarely rose above 10 percent of the annual budget.

YEAR	REVENUE	DEBT	INTEREST ON DEBT
1515	1.5	12	0.8
1560	5.3	35	2.0
1575	6.0	50	3.8
1598	9.7	85	4.6
1623	15.0	112	5.6
1667	36.0	130	9.1

Source: C. Wilson and G. Parker, eds., *An Introduction to the Sources of European Economic History* (Ithaca, NY: Cornell University Press, 1977, p. 49).

Questions: How much does the interest on debt increase during the 152 years? Why was the increase of interest on the debt detrimental?

FIGURE 15.11 *View of St. Peter's, Rome.* Baroque architects and artists sought to create a sense of drama. St. Peter's, the cathedral church of Rome and seat of the Papacy, was completed in the early 1500s. Later architects built a portico around the plaza in front of the cathedral, not only to enclose the square but to focus the visitor's eye on the façade of the church. Popes have traditionally appeared on the balcony over the main entrance to address the faithful on holidays and other important occasions. The intended effect was something like a stage set. This eighteenth-century drawing shows how it looked to an earlier generation.

Literature and Theater. In some cases, the experience of war produced literary masterpieces. The age of the religious wars was not a golden one for France, but it produced the elegant and skeptical essays of **Michel de Montaigne** (Me-shel de Mon-ten-y, 1533–1592), an antidote to sectarian madness. In Germany, the wreckage of the Thirty Years' War was nearly complete, but it was wryly chronicled in Grimmelshausen's *Simplicissimus. Don Quixote* (Kee-hoe'-tay), one of the

John Milton

greatest of all literary classics, was written by **Miguel de Cervantes** (Me-gell de Ther-van'-tes, 1547–1616), who had lost an arm at the battle of Lepanto. It is, at least in part, a satire on his countrymen's fantastic dreams of glory. The age also gave birth to at least one classic of epic poetry. In *Paradise Lost*, Cromwell's Latin secretary, **John Milton** (1608–1674), created a Puritan epic to rival the vision of Dante.

Theater flourished in Spain and England. In the time of Elizabeth I, London boasted several theaters that welcomed patrons from every class of society. Among the many authors who wrote, produced, and acted in these plays, **William Shakespeare** (1564–1616) is by far the most famous. His dramas and comedies had an impact on the development of the English language comparable to that of the King James Bible and the *Book of Common Prayer*. Puritan opposition closed the theaters until the restoration of Charles II in 1660. By the 1590s, nearly

William Shakespeare

every city in the Spanish Empire boasted its own playhouse, and traveling theater companies had become common. Like Shakespeare, **Lope de Vega** (Lo'-pay de Vay'-ga, 1562–1635) and his contemporaries wrote for a popular audience. Lope produced no fewer than 1,500 plays, of which perhaps 500 survive. In later years, royal patronage helped to create a more refined theatrical tradition that dealt in heroic themes. The works of **Calderón de la Barca** (1600–1681), who best exemplifies this genre, are still produced as well.

Political Theory. Political turmoil gave birth to political theory. The challenge of governing a vast empire filled with people who had no prior experience of European ways produced an entire school of Spanish political theorists, most of whom were associated with the University of Salamanca. Between 1530 and 1570, they worked not only to justify the conquests but to create an imperial government based on divine and natural law in opposition to the ideas of Machiavelli. As social and economic problems multiplied in Spain itself after 1590, another group of theorists known as *arbitristas* proposed reforms that strongly influenced the views of Olivares and Philip IV.

The English Civil War overturned accepted conventions of government and produced a host of books and pamphlets on every political issue. Thomas Hobbes (1588–1679) argued that political salvation lay in *Leviathan,* an autocratic superstate, while *Oceana* by James Harrington (1611–1677) reflected the republican ideals of the Commonwealth. Both works powerfully influenced the thinking of a later age.

CONCLUSION

The age of the Renaissance and Reformation marked the beginning of European conquests overseas. Their purpose in the first instance was to expand the resources available to the emerging monarchies of western Europe. The conquests were therefore an extension of the state-building process, but a religious motive was evident, too, which at times recalled the Christian triumphalism of the Crusades. To say that European expansion overseas changed the world is an understatement. Although it laid the foundations for a world market and added much to Europe's store of wealth and knowledge, it did so at a terrible cost in human misery. In Europe itself, the rivalries that encouraged overseas exploration fueled the imperial struggles of the early sixteenth century and the so-called Religious Wars of 1559–1648. The growing cost of warfare stretched the resources of princes to the breaking point. This led to massive unrest as subjects sought to recover rights and privileges lost to rulers who were desperate to pay for security. Both the subsequent revolts and the international conflict that helped sustain them were complicated by religious issues that made them extremely difficult to resolve. In the end, the wars of what has been called the Iron Age brought much of Europe to the brink of political and economic ruin.

Review Questions

- What were the most important consequences of Spanish and Portuguese expansion?
- How and why did the Ottoman Empire come into conflict with that of Charles V?
- What were the major causes of the French Wars of Religion, and why did Henry IV emerge victorious?
- What characteristics of sixteenth- and seventeenth-century warfare caused its destructive effect on the economies and political structure of states?

For Further Study

Readings
Holt, Mack, *The French Wars of Religion* (Cambridge University Press, 1995). A clear, up-to-date account.

Hughes, Ann, *The Causes of the English Civil War* (New York: St. Martin's, 1991). Clear and brief.

Parker, Geoffrey, *The Dutch Revolt* (Ithaca, NY: Cornell University Press, 1977). The best treatment of its subject.

Parry, J. H., *The Age of Reconnaissance. Discovery, Exploration and Settlement, 1450 to 1650* (London: Weidenfeld and Nicholson, 1963). Still the best survey of the subject.

Wedgewood, C. V., *The Thirty Years' War* (London: Cape, 1938). Old, but still the most readable and accessible account for the nonspecialist.

InfoTrac College Edition
For additional reading, go to your online research library at *http://infotrac.thomsonlearning.com*.
Using Key Terms, enter the search terms:
F. Magellan   *Vasco da Gama*
Elizabeth I   *Thirty Years' War*

Using Subject Guide, enter the search terms:
Christopher Columbus

Web Sites
http://www.fordham.edu/halsall/mod/modsbook.html
Internet Modern History Sourcebook. Contains a good section on the Early Modern World System
http://www.british-civil-wars.co.uk
British Civil Wars, Commonwealth and Protectorate. Biographies, timelines, military analysis, and links to sources and related subjects.

Visit the Western Civilization Companion Web Site for resources specific to this textbook:
http://history.wadsworth.com/hause02/

The CD in the back of this book and the Western Civilization Resource Center at *http://history.wadsworth.com/western/* offer a variety of tools to help you succeed in this course, including access to quizzes; images; documents; interactive simulations, maps, and timelines; movie explorations; and a wealth of other sources.

Chapter 15

Overseas Conquest and Religious War

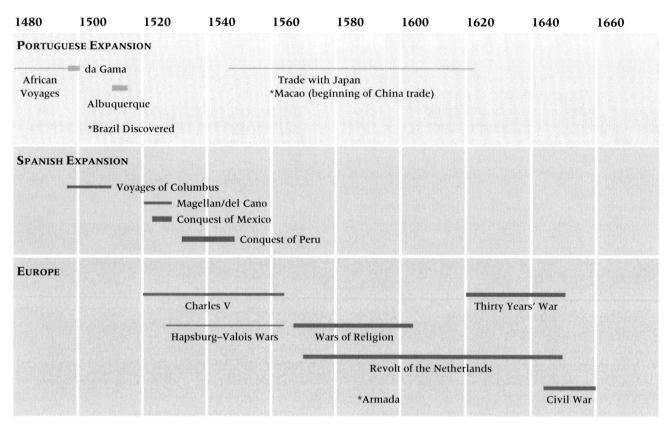

1480	1500	1520	1540	1560	1580	1600	1620	1640	1660

PORTUGUESE EXPANSION

da Gama

African
Voyages

Albuquerque

Trade with Japan
*Macao (beginning of China trade)

*Brazil Discovered

SPANISH EXPANSION

Voyages of Columbus

Magellan/del Cano

Conquest of Mexico

Conquest of Peru

EUROPE

Charles V

Thirty Years' War

Hapsburg–Valois Wars

Wars of Religion

Revolt of the Netherlands

*Armada

Civil War

Chapter 16

PREINDUSTRIAL EUROPE: SCIENCE, ECONOMY, AND POLITICAL REORGANIZATION

FOCUS QUESTIONS

- How do the assumptions and methods of modern science differ from those of ancient and medieval science?
- What specific reforms in the conduct of war and government reflected the ideals of "absolutism"?
- Why did England emerge as a major power after the revolution of 1688?
- What were the most important social consequences of economic growth in the later seventeenth century?

The Anglo-Dutch wars of 1652–1653, 1665–1666, and 1672–1673 were among the bloodiest conflicts ever fought at sea. When asked why England attacked another Protestant power, the English General-at-Sea, George Monck, answered with characteristic bluntness: "What we want is more of the trade the Dutch now have." Economic competition had surpassed religion as the driving force in international affairs. The seventeenth century saw the emergence of England, France, and the Netherlands as imperial powers. After a brief "Golden Age," the Netherlands declined, leaving France and England as dominant powers. Both countries reorganized their military and governmental systems. In France, Louis XIV created an absolutist model for a host of other states, from Spain to Austria. In England, Parliament at last wrested power from the king and developed the financial system that would eventually pay for the Industrial Revolution. For this reason, the period from the late sixteenth to early eighteenth century is often called the Preindustrial Age, but the new wealth generated by imperial and commercial expansion did not benefit everyone. Even in England, the poor grew poorer as the middle class expanded and the rich grew even richer.

Chapter 16 begins with the Scientific Revolution that weakened the hold of religion on the mind of Europe's upper classes and produced discoveries that made the Industrial Revolution possible. It then looks briefly at French, English, and Dutch expansion overseas and describes the society of the Netherlands in its Golden Age. In the aftermath of the Religious Wars that ended in 1648, the monarchies of Europe reorganized. The methods of Louis XIV and his imitators are described, together with the very different approach to war and government developed by England. This chapter concludes with economic and social change in the later seventeenth century.

The Scientific Revolution (1530–1727)

The Scientific Revolution of the late sixteenth and seventeenth centuries has no parallel among modern intellectual movements. Like the thought of ancient Greece, it changed not only ideas but also the process by which ideas are formulated. The Renaissance and the Reformation, for all their importance, had been rooted in traditional patterns of thought. They could be understood without re-ordering the concepts that had permeated Western thinking for more than 2,000 years. The development of modern science, although in some ways an outgrowth of these earlier movements, asked questions that had not been asked before, and by so doing created a whole new way of looking at the universe. Modern science and the scientific method with which it is associated may be the one body of European ideas that has had a transforming effect on virtually every non-Western culture.

Ancient and Medieval Science. In 1500, the basic assumptions of science had changed little since the days of Pliny (23–79 CE). The ancients believed in a universe organized according to rational principles and therefore open to human observation and deduction. Deduction in this case meant the logic of Aristotle, which was rooted firmly in language and the meaning of words. Ancient science therefore tended to be qualitative rather than quantitative. With few exceptions, it required neither measurement nor the construction of mathematical models. Accurate observation provided clues to the nature or essential quality of the object being observed. Reason could then determine the relationship of that object to other objects in the natural world.

This was important because the ancients believed that all parts of the universe were interrelated and that nothing could be studied in isolation. Today, this idea is called holistic or organic. It was stated expressly by Aristotle and, metaphorically, in the popular image of the individual human being as a microcosm or little world whose parts corresponded to those of the universe as a whole. It formed the basis not only of academic science but also of the applied sciences of the day: medicine, natural magic, astrology, and alchemy. The last three were partially inspired by the Hermetic tradition, a body of occult literature that supposedly derived from ancient Egypt. The church regarded the Hermetic arts with suspicion because they thought their practitioners tried to interfere with Providence, but its theoretical assumptions did not conflict with those of Aristotle. Many, if not most, of the early scientists were as interested in astrology or alchemy as they were in physics and made no real distinction between the occult and what would today be regarded as more legitimate disciplines.

Whatever their interests, ancient and medieval scientists agreed that the world was composed of the four elements—earth, air, fire, and water—and that the elements corresponded to the four humors that governed the body (blood, phlegm, yellow bile, and black bile) as well as to the signs of the zodiac. **Magic,** "the chief power of all the sciences," sought to understand these and other relationships between natural objects and to manipulate them to achieve useful results. **Alchemy** sought to change "base" metals into gold and to discover the sovereign cure for all diseases. The causes of natural phenomena were of academic but little practical interest and generally explained teleologically. That is, virtually everyone believed that the world had been created for a purpose and that the behavior of natural objects would necessarily be directed to that end. This preconception, together with the tendency to describe objects in qualitative terms, ensured that causation, too, would usually be explained in terms of the nature or qualities of the objects involved. Such ideas reflected the Christian view that divine providence governs the world.

Modern Scientific Method. Ideas of this kind are now found largely in the pages of supermarket tabloids, but they were once universally accepted by learned people. They provided a rational, comprehensive, and comforting vision of what might otherwise have been a terrifying universe. They have little in common with the principles of modern science, which substitutes measurement for qualitative description and attempts to express physical relationships in quantitative, mathematical terms. Because its vision of the world is mechanical instead of holistic and providential, modern science concentrates heavily on the causes of physical and biological reactions and tries to reject teleological and qualitative explanations. It is more likely to ask "how?" or "why?" than "what?" and has few compunctions about isolating a given problem to study it. Correspondences based on qualitative or symbolic relationships of the sort studied by magicians are ignored.

Methodologically, modern science seeks to create a hypothesis by reasoning logically from accurate observations. If possible, the hypothesis is then tested by experiment, and a mathematical model is constructed that will be both explanatory and predictive. The scientist can then formulate general laws of physical behavior without becoming entangled in the emotional overtones of language. The scientific model of the universe therefore tends to be mechanistic rather than holistic, mythological, or poetic. It is not necessarily godless, but its predictability does away with the need for divine intervention on a regular basis.

The Origins of Modern Scientific Thought

An intellectual shift of this magnitude did not occur quickly. Its roots are found in several traditions that coexisted uneasily in late medieval and Renaissance thought: the Aristotelian, the experimentalist, and the humanistic. During the sixteenth century, a process of fusion began as thinkers adopted elements of each in their attempts to solve an ever-growing list of problems. The problems arose mainly from the perception that old, accepted answers, however logical and comforting they may have been, did not square with observed reality. The answers, and the accumulation of methods by which they were achieved, laid the groundwork of modern science.

The Aristotelian tradition contributed a rigorous concern for accurate observation and a logical method for the construction of hypotheses. In the wake of nominalist criticism, many Aristotelians, especially in the Italian universities, had turned their attention to the physical sciences, often with impressive results. Their tradition remained vital in some places until the eighteenth century. Experimentalism derived ultimately from a radical offshoot of the Observant Franciscans. Believing (heretically) that God's kingdom would be established on Earth, some of

Sir Francis Bacon

them used experiment in an effort to understand the natural world. **Sir Francis Bacon** (1561–1626), the Lord Chancellor of England under James I, revived and popularized the idea of experiment without the religious overtones. Like his predecessors, he accomplished little because his hypotheses were faulty, but the elegance of his prose inspired a host of followers. His contemporary **Galileo Galilei** (1564–1642) used experiment to greater effect, although many of his best demonstrations were designed but never performed. The humanist tradition contributed classical texts that reintroduced half-forgotten ideas, including the physics of Archimedes and the heliocentric theories of Eratosthenes and Aristarchus of Samos. It also encouraged quantification by reviving the numerological theories of Pythagoras.

Copernicus. The thinkers of the sixteenth and seventeenth centuries were interested in nearly everything, but they achieved their greatest breakthroughs in astronomy and physics. The Middle Ages had accepted the ancient Ptolemaic theory that the Earth was the center of the universe and that the sun and the planets revolved around it in circular orbits. The problem lay in explaining why planets sometimes appear to move backward in their orbits (retrograde movement) and why they vary in brilliance. It seemed obvious that they must at some times be farther away from Earth than at others. But this was impossible, because if their orbits

were circular, they would always be equidistant from the Earth around which they revolved. Ptolemy solved these problems only by using an elaborate system of mathematical fictions known as epicycles. Among the many scholars who found this incompatible with reason or observable reality was the Polish humanist and mathematician **Nicolaus Copernicus** (1473–1543). As a humanist, Copernicus knew that a minority of ancients had believed that the Earth circled the sun; as a mathematician he decided to construct a mathematical model to prove their theories. His hypothesis, complete with mathematical proofs, reached print shortly after his death. The

Nicolaus Copernicus

Copernican theory that the Earth and planets revolved around the sun aroused opposition from those who believed it contrary to the Bible. Mathematicians and astronomers tended to support it, but no one regarded it as a perfect model of the universe. Copernicus had retained the idea of circular orbits, largely because he believed that the circle was the perfect geometrical figure and that God would not have created an imperfect universe. He therefore reduced the number of epicycles but did not eliminate them.

Kepler. A more plausible model of the cosmos was devised by **Johannes Kepler** (1571–1630), court astrologer to the emperor Rudolph II. Kepler's views combined mysticism, numerology, and solid observation. He believed that the Earth had a soul, but as a follower of Pythagoras, he thought that the universe was organized on geometrical principles. The Copernican epicycles offended his notions of mathematical harmony. He wanted to believe in circular orbits, but when he posited eccentric circles that did not center on the sun, he was left with a minute discrepancy in his mathematical formulas. It was a terrible dilemma: the circle may have been the perfect geometric figure,

Johannes Kepler

but he could not accept a universe founded on imperfect mathematics. In the end, he decided that planetary orbits had to be elliptical. This solution, which proved to be correct, was not generally accepted until long after his death, but Kepler did not mind. Like the number

GALILEO ON SCIENTIFIC PROOF

In this excerpt from *The Assayer*, Galileo attacks an opponent for arguing in the traditional manner by compiling lists of authorities who support his position. It not only shows the gulf that separated scientific thinking from that of the traditionalists but also provides some indication of how Galileo made enemies with his pen.

Sarsi goes on to say that since this experiment of Aristotle's has failed to convince us, many other great men have also written things of the same sort. But it is news to me that any man would actually put the testimony of writers ahead of what experience shows him. To adduce more witnesses serves no purposes, Sarsi, for we have never denied that such things have been written and believed. We did say they are false, but so far as authority is concerned yours alone is as effective as an army's in rendering the events true or false. You take your stand on the authority of many poets against our experiments. I reply that if those poets could be present at our experiments they would change their views, and without disgrace they could say they had been writing hyperbolically—or even admit they had been wrong. . . .

I cannot but be astonished that Sarsi would persist in trying to prove by means of witnesses something that I may see for myself at any time by means of experiment.

From Galilei, Galileo, "The Assayer," trans. and ed. Stillman Drake. *Discoveries and Opinions of Galileo* (New York: Doubleday, 1957, pp. 270–271).

Question: What earlier intellectual movement inspired Sarsi's form of argument, and how did it differ from Galileo's?

mystic he was, he continued searching for other, more elusive cosmic harmonies that could be described in musical as well as mathematical terms.

Galileo. Meanwhile, Galileo rejected the theory of elliptical orbits but provided important evidence that the planets rotated around the sun. A professor at the University of Padua, Galileo was perhaps the first thinker to use something like the modern scientific method. He quarreled with the Aristotelians over their indifference to mathematical proofs and denounced their teleological obsession with final causes, but like them he was a careful observer. Unlike them, he tried to verify his hypotheses through experimentation. From the Platonists and Pythagoreans, he adopted the view that the universe followed mathematical laws and expressed his theories in mathematical formulae that were intended to be predictive. His vision, however, was mechanistic, not mystical or organic.

The invention of the telescope inspired Galileo's exploration of the planets. The Aristotelians had discovered the basic principles of optics, and eyeglasses were

FIGURE 16.1 *Galileo before the Holy Office of the Vatican.* In 1633, Galileo was condemned by the papal Inquisition for publishing a defense of the Copernican system in his *Dialogue on the Two World Chief World Systems: Ptolemaic and Copernican.* By this time, many churchmen accepted Copernicanism, but Galileo had offended many, including his one-time friend, Pope Urban VIII. He had ignored the pope's request to present the Copernican theory as a hypothesis and then had Simplicio, the foolish character in the dialogue, present the pope's ideas as his own. This reconstruction of the scene, including a good likeness of Galileo at the center, was painted by J. N. Robert-Fleury (1797–1890).

introduced early in the sixteenth century. By 1608, Dutch and Flemish lens grinders were combining two lenses at fixed distances from one another to create the first telescopes. Using a perfected version of the telescope that he had built himself, Galileo turned it on the heavens. The results created a sensation. His discovery of the moons of Jupiter and the phases of Venus seemed to support the Copernican theory, whereas his study of sunspots raised the unsettling possibility that the sun rotated on its axis like the planets.

Perhaps because he was not interested in astrology, Galileo ignored the problems of planetary motion that obsessed Kepler. Instead, he concentrated on the mechanics of motion. Kepler had established the position of the planets with his Rudolphine Tables of 1627, but he had been unable to explain either the causes of their motion or what kept them in their orbits. The issue had perplexed the ancients because they believed that rest was the normal state of any object. The Aristotelians had argued that an object remains at rest unless a force is applied against it and that the velocity of that object is proportionate to the force exerted in moving it. As a result, it was hard to explain why a projectile continued to move after the impetus behind it had ceased. Galileo turned the problem on its head by proving that a body in motion will move forever unless it is slowed or deflected by an external force and that the application of uniform force results in acceleration instead of motion at a constant rate. Movement, therefore, is as natural a state as rest. Once it had been set in motion by its Creator, the universe could, in theory, go on forever without further intervention.

The Trial of Galileo.

It was a profoundly disturbing vision. To Galileo, God was the Great Craftsman who created the world as a self-sustaining and predictable machine. To those who saw the universe as an organic entity upon which God still imposed His will, such a view was not only frightening but also blasphemous. In 1632, Galileo published his *Dialogue on the Two Chief World Systems: Ptolemaic and Copernican* in Italian rather than in Latin so that it could be more widely read. It brought him before the papal Inquisition in what has become one of the most famous trials in history. The indictment of Galileo was in some respects a mistake. Many Catholics, including the Jesuits, shared his views. Others agreed with him that there was no real conflict between science and religion. In the end, his ideas were condemned not only because he defended the Copernican system and because his ideas undermined a worldview that had prevailed for nearly 2,000 years but because he had personally offended the pope. Yet the importance of this celebrated trial should not be exaggerated. Galileo's condemnation forced him to retire to his country villa; it did not prevent him or any other Italian from proceeding with research along the lines he

had suggested. Galileo was arrogant and bad-tempered with patrons and opponents alike. He was also a brilliant writer and publicist (see Document 16.1). Had his ability to attract enemies not equaled his genius, the episode might never have occurred.

Vacuums and Gases.

Galileo's vision of the universe as a kind of giant machine eventually triumphed, and the church would not again mount a frontal attack against it. **René Descartes**

René Descartes

(Day-kart, 1596–1650), the most influential philosopher of his day, based his thought on a radical separation between mind and matter that precluded holistic thinking and encouraged the analysis of nature as a kind of machine that could be understood through the application of mathematical principles. His efforts inspired others, such as Pierre Gassendi (1592–1655), who attempted to revive the atomic theories of the Epicureans. To do so, he was forced to posit the existence of a vacuum. The possibility of nothingness had been denied by virtually everyone from Aristotle to Descartes, but the results of barometric experiments by Evangelista Torricelli (Tor-ri- chel'-lee, 1608–1647) and by Blaise Pascal (1623–1662) could be explained in no other way. In 1650, Otto von Guericke (fon Gear'-i-kee, 1602–1686) ended the debate by constructing an air pump with which a vacuum could be created. These efforts in turn inspired Robert Boyle (1627–1691) to formulate his laws about the behavior of gases.

Isaac Newton.

In astronomy and physics, the scientific movement culminated in the work of **Isaac Newton** (1642–1727). A professor at Cambridge and a member of the Royal Society, Newton was in some respects an odd character who spent at least as much time on alchemy and other occult speculations as he did on mathematics and physics. In spite of this, he formulated the laws of planetary motion and of gravity, thereby completing the work begun by Kepler and Galileo and establishing a cosmology that dominated Western thought until the publication of Einstein's theories in 1904.

In his *Principia*, or *Mathematical Principles of Natural Philosophy*, presented to the Royal Society in 1686, Newton formulated three laws of motion: (1) every object remains either at rest or in motion along a straight line until it is deflected or resisted by another force (the law of inertia), (2) the rate of change in the motion of an object is proportionate to the force acting on it, and (3) to every action there is an equal and opposite reaction. These formulations accounted not only for the

FIGURE 16.2 An Experiment with a Bird in the Air Pump (1768). Scientific studies became a fad with members of the upper and middle classes. Here a disheveled "scientific gentlemen" demonstrates an air pump. He has placed a bird inside a vacuum chamber and pumped the air out of it, causing the bird to die. One woman averts her eyes, while a young girl stares in appropriate horror. Painting by Joseph Wright of Derby.

behavior of moving objects on Earth but also for the continuing movement of the planets. He then perfected Kepler's theories by demonstrating how the planets move through a vacuum in elliptical orbits under the influence of a force centered on the sun. That force was gravity, which he defined as the attractive force between two objects (see Document 16.2). It is directly proportionate to the product of their masses and inversely proportionate to the square of the distances between them. To many, these theories explained the mysteries of a universe that acted like clockwork—smooth, mechanical, and eternal. Newton, who was a deeply religious man, would not have been pleased at the use to which his ideas would soon be put by the philosophers of the eighteenth-century Enlightenment.

The Anatomical Revolution. Mechanistic views would also triumph in medicine, but the process by which they did so was more convoluted than it had been in physics. Physicians moved from mechanism to magic and back again in the course of the sixteenth century. The works of the ancient Greek anatomist Galen had long been known through Arabic commentaries and translations. Galen's views were mechanistic in the sense that he was careful to relate the form of organs to their function and had little use for magic or for alchemical cures. The recovery and translation

of original Galenic texts by the humanists popularized his teachings, and by the early sixteenth century, his influence dominated academic medicine.

Paracelsus and the Chemical Philosophy. In response, a Swiss physician and alchemist who called himself **Paracelsus** (Par-a-sel'-sus, 1493–1541) launched a frontal attack on the entire medical establishment. Declaring that "wise women" and barbers cured more patients than all of the Galenists put together, he proposed a medical philosophy based on natural magic and alchemy. All natural phenomena were chemical interactions between the four elements and what he called the three principles: sulfur, mercury, and salt—the combustible, gaseous, and solid components of matter. Because the human body was a microcosm of the universe and because diseases were produced by chemical forces acting on particular organs of the body, sickness could be cured with chemical antidotes.

This chemical philosophy was widely accepted. Its hermetic and Neo-Platonic overtones recommended it to many scholars, although those who practiced it may have killed fewer patients than their Galenist opponents. Paracelsus believed in administering drugs in small, carefully measured doses. He rejected bleeding, purges, and the treatment of wounds with poultices whose vile ingredients almost guaranteed the onset of infection. As a result, the bodies of his patients had a fighting chance to heal themselves, and he was credited with miraculous cures.

The Triumph of the Anatomists. The war between the Galenists and the Paracelsians raged throughout the midsixteenth century. In the end, the Galenists won. Their theories, although virtually useless for the treatment of disease, produced new insights, whereas those of Paracelsus did not. **Andreas Vesalius** (1514–1564) was shocked to discover that Galen's dissections had been carried out primarily on animals. Using Galenic principles, he retraced the master's steps using human cadavers and in 1543 published his *De humani corporis fabrica (On the Structure of the Human Body)*. Although

NEWTON ON GRAVITY

In the *Principia*, or *Mathematical Principles of Natural Philosophy*, Sir Isaac Newton describes his revolutionary concept of gravity and, in the process, sets forth some of his thoughts on scientific method. Note that he does not claim to understand how gravity is actually produced. That discovery was not made until the twentieth century. *Induction* is the process of reasoning from a particular phenomenon to a general principle. *Deduction* reasons from the general to the particular.

Hitherto, we have explained the phenomena of the heavens and of our sea by the power of gravity, but have not yet assigned the cause of this power. This is certain, that it must proceed from a cause that penetrates to the very centers of the sun and planets, without suffering the least diminution of its force; that operates not according to the quantity of the surfaces of the particles upon which it acts (as mechanical causes used to do) but according to the quantity of solid matter which they contain, and propagates its virtue on all sides to immense distances, decreasing always in the duplicate portion of the distances. . . .

Hitherto I have not been able to discover the cause of those properties of gravity from the phenomena, and I frame no hypothesis; for whatever is not deduced from phenomena is to be called an hypothesis; and hypothesis, whether metaphysical or physical, whether of occult qualities or mechanical, have no place in experimental philosophy. In this philosophy particular propositions are inferred from the phenomena, and afterward rendered general by induction. Thus it was the impenetrability, the mobility, and the impulsive force of bodies, and the laws of motion and gravitation were discovered. And to us it is enough that gravity does really exist, and acts according to the laws that we have explained, and abundantly serves to account for all the motions of the celestial bodies, and of our sea.

From Newton, Isaac, *The Mathematical Principles of Natural Philosophy*, book 3, vol. 2, trans. Andrew Motte (London: 1803, p. 310).

Question: Does Newton support inductive or deductive reasoning in scientific matters?

William Harvey

not without error, it was a vast improvement over earlier anatomy texts and a work of art in its own right that inspired others to correct and improve his work. The long debate over the circulation of the blood, culminating in the explanation published by **William Harvey** in 1628 (see Document 16.3), was also a Galenist enterprise that owed little or nothing to the chemical tradition.

By the time microscopes were invented in Holland at the beginning of the seventeenth century, the anatomists had seized the initiative. The new device strengthened their position by allowing them to examine small structures such as capillaries. Blood corpuscles were described for the first time, and bacteria were identified, although a full-fledged germ theory would not be verified until the nineteenth century. These discoveries made sustaining the ancient metaphor of the human body as a microcosm of the universe even more difficult.

The body was beginning to look more like a machine within a machine.

The Triumph of Science as an Intellectual System. By this time, interest in scientific inquiry had assumed the proportions of a fad. All over Europe, men of leisure and education were examining the physical world and developing theories about it. Many, including Boyle and Pascal, were also gifted writers whose work inspired others to emulate them. Science was becoming a movement, and it was only a matter of time until that movement was institutionalized. The English Royal Society and the French Academie des Sciences were founded in the 1660s, the latter under the patronage of **Louis XIV's** minister, **Jean Baptiste Colbert** (Zhan Bahp-teest Kole-bare', 1619–1683). Colbert, like England's King Charles II, was quick to perceive the possible connection between the new science and improved technologies for war, agriculture, and manufacturing. Not all of the work performed was useful, and much of it remained tied to the earlier vision of an organic, providential universe, but mechanistic and mathematical views gained ground steadily throughout the century.

As Galileo had explained to the Inquisition, there was no inherent conflict between science and religion. Few

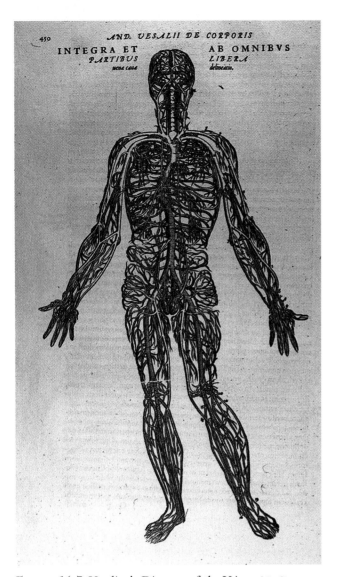

FIGURE 16.3 *Vesalius's Diagram of the Veins.* This diagram is from Andreas Vesalius's (1514–1564) *De humani corporis fabrica.* The venous system was especially important to physicians because drawing blood was the primary treatment for many ailments. As impressive as these drawings are, they contain anatomical errors. Vesalius did not understand the circulation of the blood and based some of his ideas on the dissection of animals (see the arrangement of veins at the base of the neck, which is not found in humans). However, his work, with its magnificent illustrations, is still a remarkable monument to the anatomical revolution.

people in seventeenth-century Europe abandoned their belief in God, but for the educated, science offered a new and exciting perspective on the universe. The Scientific Revolution increased the secularizing tendencies that had begun in the Renaissance and would reach a peak of sorts in the eighteenth-century Enlightenment. More concretely, it produced a body of knowledge that would prove useful in developing new technologies during the Industrial Revolution.

THE EXPANSION OF THE NORTHERN POWERS: FRANCE, ENGLAND, AND THE NETHERLANDS (1560–1660)

In the years when Galileo and others transformed European thought, seafarers from France, England, and the Netherlands continued the work of mapping the globe and exploiting its economic resources. The centralized, closely controlled empires created by the Iberian powers had been resented from the first by northern Europeans, who wished to engage in the American trade. French pirates and privateers became active in the Caribbean after the 1530s and sacked Havana in 1556. In 1565, the Spanish massacred a colony of French Protestants near the present site of St. Augustine, Florida. Neither of these failures inhibited French, English, and Dutch captains from trying to enter the Caribbean market. The Englishman John Hawkins (1532–1595) tried to break the Spanish–Portuguese monopoly by introducing cargoes of slaves in 1562 and again in 1567, but he was caught by the incoming Spanish fleet in 1567 and barely escaped with

Sir Francis Drake

his life. One of his surviving captains, Francis Drake (c. 1543–1596), raided Panama in 1572–1573 and attacked Spanish shipping in the Pacific when he circumnavigated the globe in 1577–1579.

The First English Colonies in North America. To many in England, these efforts, however inspiring, were no substitute for the establishment of permanent English colonies. Commercial interests and the growing political and religious rivalry with Spain demanded nothing less. The first English settlement in North America was planted on Roanoke Island, North Carolina, in 1585 but disappeared before it could be reinforced. Subsequent efforts at Jamestown (1607) and Plymouth (1620) were more successful. The Spanish claimed sovereignty over North America but lacked the resources to settle it or to protect it against interlopers. The Native American population was, by comparison with that of Mexico or Peru, small, scattered, and politically disunited. Obstacles to settlement were relatively easy to overcome, and by 1650, the English had established themselves at various locations along the entire Atlantic seaboard from Newfoundland to the Carolinas.

WILLIAM HARVEY ON THE CIRCULATION OF BLOOD

The English physician William Harvey (1578–1657) first described the circulation of blood. His predecessors, including Galen and Vesalius, knew that blood moved within the body but did not understand the role of the heart as a kind of pump and did not know that the same blood moves from the heart through the arteries and then returns to the heart by way of the veins. In this passage from his treatise, "On the Motion of the Heart and Blood in Animals," Harvey summarizes the most important points of his argument.

But lest anyone should say that we give them words only, and make mere specious assertions without any foundation, and desire to innovate without sufficient cause, three points present themselves for confirmation, which being stated, I conceive that the truth I contend for will follow necessarily, and appear as a thing obvious to all. First, the blood is incessantly transmitted by the action of the heart from the vena cava [a large vein that feeds the right side of the heart] to the arteries in such quantity that it cannot be supplied from the ingesta [digested food], and in such matter that the whole must quickly pass through the organ; Second, the blood under the influence of the arterial pulse enters and is expelled in a continuous, equable, and incessant stream through every part and member of the body, in much larger quantity than were sufficient for nutrition, or than the whole mass of fluids can supply. Third, the veins in like matter return this blood incessantly to the heart from parts and members of the body. These points proved, I conceive it will be manifest that the blood circulates, revolves, propelled and then returning, from the heart to the extremities, from the extremities to the heart, and thus that it performs a kind of circular motion.

From Harvey, William, "On the Motion of the Heart and Blood in Animals, 1628," Chapter IX, in *The Works of William Harvey*, trans. Robert Willis (London: 1847).

Question: Why was this discovery important to the practice of medicine?

From the standpoint of global politics and immediate gain, these North American colonies were something of a disappointment. They produced no precious metals and offered England few strategic advantages. With the notable exception of tobacco from Virginia and Maryland, they had little of value to export and quickly became self-sufficient in everything but luxury items. In the meantime, the French had established themselves in the St. Lawrence valley and were developing an important trade in furs from the North American interior. English competition in the form of the Hudson's Bay Company did not emerge until 1670.

French and English Colonies in the Caribbean.

Expansion in the Caribbean remained a primary goal. The English established a colony on the uninhabited island of Barbados in 1624 and introduced sugar in 1640. By 1660, its sugar exports made Barbados the most valuable of the English colonies and its position windward of the Spanish Main made it virtually invulnerable to Spanish attacks. (The sailing ships of the day could sail into the wind only with great difficulty.) The French established sugar colonies of equal wealth on the nearby islands of Guadeloupe and Martinique. By this time, Spanish power was in decline. In 1656, an English fleet seized Jamaica. Eight years later, the French West India Company took possession of some settlements that had been established years before by French buccaneers in the western part of Hispaniola and laid the foundations of St. Domingue, the rich slave colony that would one day become Haiti.

The French and English Colonial Systems.

The French and English, like the Spanish and Portuguese, wanted their colonial systems to be self-contained and closed to outsiders. In practice, this was as difficult to achieve, as it had been for their rivals. Both France and England governed their possessions on the proprietary model. They made huge grants of land to wealthy speculators and allowed them to serve as governors as long as they populated them with colonists. Neither country developed anything like the elaborate colonial bureaucracy of Spain. Royal authority tended to be correspondingly weak. Distance, the limitations of sailing ship technology, and the perishability of certain cargoes, notably slaves, encouraged smuggling and made it difficult to suppress. Planters and merchants of any nationality had nothing to gain from dealing exclusively with their own countrymen when others might offer better prices or more rapid delivery. Cargoes could always be landed secretly in remote coves, but much illegal activity was conducted in the open, for governors were under enormous pressure from their subjects to look the other way.

The Dutch in America.

Almost from the beginning, the chief beneficiaries of this illegal trade were the Dutch, whose maritime activities increased during their

Jamestown, 1622

FIGURE 16.4 *Jamestown, the First Permanent English Colony in America.* The first colonies in North America were little more than agricultural villages. The English colony at Jamestown in Virginia is shown as it was in 1622, 15 years after its foundation. Note the wooden palisade that protected the town from potential attacks by both Indians and the Spanish.

revolt against Spain. The Dutch had some 98,000 ships registered by 1598, but ships and trained seamen were not enough. They needed bases from which to conduct their operations. Between 1621 and 1640, the newly formed Dutch West India Company seized Curaçao, St. Eustatius, St. Maarten, and Saba in the Caribbean and established a colony called New Amsterdam on the present site of New York. From 1624 to 1654, the Dutch controlled much of the Brazilian coast, and in 1637, they captured the African fortress and slave-trading station of Elmina from the Portuguese. Brazil and New Amsterdam were expensive ventures. The Dutch, like the Portuguese, lacked the manpower to impose their rule on large geographical areas, and when the English seized New Amsterdam in 1664, the West India Company settled down to a more modest—and in the end more profitable—career as a trading company based in Curaçao and St. Eustatius.

The Dutch East India Company. Only in the East did the Dutch manage to establish something like regional hegemony. Dutch traders first appeared in East Indian waters in 1595. Bypassing India, they sailed directly to the Spice Islands (Indonesia), rounding the Cape of Good Hope and running due east in the so-called roaring forties before turning north to Java or Sumatra. The fast but dangerous trip brought them directly to the sources of the Portuguese and Indian spice trade. To improve efficiency and minimize competition, the Dutch traders organized in 1602 into the East India Company.

Under the governor-generalship of **Jan Pieterszoon Coen** (Yan Pee'-ter-sone Koon,1587–1629), the company's forces destroyed the Javan town of Djakarta and rebuilt it as Batavia, center of Dutch enterprise in the East. Local rulers were forced to restrict their trading activities to rice and other local necessities, and European competition was violently discouraged. English traders especially had been active in Asian waters since 1591. They had formed their own East India Company on Christmas Day in 1600 but lacked the ships and capital to match the Dutch. Coen expelled most of them from the region by 1620. His successors attacked the Portuguese colonies, seizing Malacca in 1641 and the Indian bases shortly thereafter, but Goa survived a Dutch blockade and remained in Portuguese hands until 1961. The Japanese trade fell into Dutch hands when the Portuguese were expelled in 1637, and for two centuries, a Dutch trading station in Nagasaki harbor provided that country's only contact with the West.

By 1650, the Dutch had become the dominant force in Europe's Asian trade. More than 100 Dutch ships sailed regularly to the East, exchanging German arms, armor, linens, and glass for spices and finished silks. Even the surviving Portuguese colonies were now forced to deal largely through Dutch intermediaries. The major exception was Macao, which continued to export Chinese silks to Spain via Manila. This monopoly was successfully challenged in the eighteenth century by the revived British East India Company and to a lesser degree by the French, but the Dutch remained in control of Indonesia until the outbreak of World War II. Like the Portuguese in Asia, however, they lacked the manpower to impose their government or culture on native peoples outside the major trading centers. They, too, tried to maintain direct control of a few strategically situated towns and relied on sea power, diplomacy, and the judicious use of force to protect their trade with native rulers.

FIGURE 16.5 *New Amsterdam.* The Dutch colony at New Amsterdam is shown as it appeared in a Dutch map of 1656. It was located at the lower end of Manhattan Island and eventually grew into the city of New York.

THE GOLDEN AGE IN THE NETHERLANDS (1598–1679)

Long-distance trade made the Netherlands an island of wealth and culture amidst the turmoil of the early seventeenth century. A century before, the city of Antwerp had dominated the economy of the region. Its merchants traded in wool from Spain and England, finished cloth from the towns of Brabant and Flanders, wine from the Iberian Peninsula, and a variety of products exported from Germany to England and Scandinavia. The city's prosperity, however, did not survive the Revolt of the Netherlands. Antwerp is located at the head of navigation on the Scheldt, a broad estuary whose western approaches are controlled by the Zeeland (Zay'-land) towns of Vlissingen (Flushing) and Middelburg. When the Zeelanders joined the Dutch revolt, they cut off Antwerp from the sea and destroyed its prosperity.

The Rise of Amsterdam. Amsterdam took its place. Set in the marshes where the Amstel River meets the IJ (eye), an inlet of the Zuider Zee (Zye'-der Zay), the city was virtually impregnable to attack by sea or land. Already the center of the Baltic trade, it grew enormously after 1585, when southern refugees poured in, bringing their capital with them. When Maurice of Nassau took the lands east of the Ijssel River from

Spain between 1591 and 1597, contact with Germany improved and Amsterdam replaced Antwerp as the conduit through which goods flowed from the German interior to the Atlantic and North Sea. The repeated failure of Spanish and Sicilian harvests in the same years made Amsterdam a dominant force in the Mediterranean trade as well. Dutch merchants had established themselves in the Baltic ports of Riga (Ree'-guh) and Gdansk (Danzig) at an early date. The Amsterdam exchange determined the price of wheat, and vast quantities were shipped southward in Dutch ships, together with timber, Swedish iron, and other northern products.

Shipbuilding, always a major industry in the ports of Holland and Zeeland, expanded with the growth of the carrying trade. Economies of scale, better access to Baltic naval stores, and the presence of a skilled maritime population enabled the Dutch to charge lower shipping rates than their competitors. With the founding of the East and West India companies, this advantage became global. The axis of the spice trade shifted from Lisbon to Amsterdam, and Dutch skippers took advantage of the delays occasioned by the flota system and by a general shortage of Iberian shipping to intrude on the commerce of the Americas. The profits from

FIGURE 16.6 *The Return of the Dutch Fleet to Amsterdam, 1599.* This painting by Andries van Eertvert (1590–1652) commemorates the return of one of the first Dutch trading voyages to the East Indies. Its success helped inspire the founding of the East India Company in 1602.

FIGURE 16.7 **The Dam at Amsterdam,** *1669, Jan van Kessel.* Much of Holland's overseas trade passed through the great city of Amsterdam. The Dam, shown here, is its central square. The palace of the stadtholders, now the Royal Palace, is on the left. The New Church, the largest of Amsterdam's Reformed churches, can be seen at right.

FIGURE 16.8 *Rembrandt van Rijn,* **Self-Portrait as a Young Man.** This is probably one of Rembrandt's many portrayals of himself in different guises and attitudes. Rembrandt is now regarded as the greatest Dutch painter of the Golden Age. In his own day, however, he often struggled to find commissions. This portrait shows his unequalled mastery of chiaroscuro as well as his ability to get to the heart of a subject's personality.

these sources generated investment capital, and Amsterdam soon became Europe's banking center as well as its commercial hub.

In these years, the modern city with its canals and high, narrow townhouses took shape. For all its wealth and beauty, however, Amsterdam was never more than the largest of several towns that supported and at times competed with each other in a variety of markets. The Dutch republic was overwhelmingly urban. A network of canals linked its cities and provided cheap, efficient transportation. Agriculturally, although a few large estates remained, most of the land was divided into relatively small plots and cultivated intensively to grow produce and dairy products for the nearby towns. Most peasants were independent farmers and relatively prosperous. Pockets of urban misery existed, but a real industrial proletariat existed only in the cloth towns of Haarlem and Leiden. Dutch society was therefore resolutely middle class. It valued hard work, thrift, and cleanliness; ostentation was suspect.

Dutch Art. A series of extraordinary painters provide a vivid picture of Dutch life in the seventeenth century. Jan Vermeer (1632–1675) portrayed bright, spotless interiors and virtuous housewives at work in an idealized vision of domesticity that was central to Dutch notions of the good life. Rembrandt van Rijn (van Rine, 1606–1669), Frans Hals (c. 1581–1666), and a host of others left brilliant portraits of city magistrates, corporate directors, and everyday drunks as well as grand illustrations of historical events. Masters like Ruisdael and van Goyen painted the brooding skies and placid landscapes of the Netherlands, and dozens of still lifes by other painters dwell lovingly on food, flowers, and other everyday objects.

Government and Politics. The political and the social structure of the republic rested on the values of the late medieval city, preserved tenaciously through the long struggle against Spanish regalism. Each town elected a council, which in turn elected representatives to the Provincial Estates. The States General was elected by the provinces. The stadtholder was not a king or even a permanent officer, but a kind of "first citizen" elected to conduct war on land in times of crisis. He was almost always, however, a descendent of William of Orange. Five admiralties, each of which was nominally independent, conducted war at sea, supplementing its own warships with heavily armed vessels leased from the East and West India companies.

Local privilege dominated the system at every level, and conflict among the various components of the body politic was normally intense. Fortunately, the leadership of the councils, states, directorships, and committees formed a kind of interlocking directorship. A great merchant, banker, or rentier might hold several elected offices in the course of a lifetime, as well as directorships in one or more of the chartered companies. The Dutch republic was an oligarchy, not a democracy, but the existence of a well-defined group of prominent citizens facilitated communication, dampened local rivalries, and helped ensure a measure of continuity in what might otherwise have been a fragmented and overly decentralized system.

National policy therefore remained consistent. It encouraged trade, even with enemies, and supported freedom of the seas long before **Hugo Grotius** (Gro'-she-us, 1583–1645), attorney general of Holland, publicized the modern concept of international law. Although aggressive in its pursuit of new markets and the protection of old ones, Dutch foreign policy was otherwise defensive.

Tension between the governing elite and the stadtholders of the House of Orange dominated internal politics. At times, the struggle took the form of religious antagonism between extreme Calvinists, who tended to be Orangists supported by the artisan class, and the more relaxed Arminians, who rejected predestination and were supported by the great merchants. Class feeling played a major part in these struggles, but by comparison with other countries, both sides remained committed to religious toleration. The government actively encouraged Jewish settlement and protected Catholics from harassment. Holland became a refuge for the persecuted, many of whom, such as Descartes and the philosopher **Baruch Spinoza** (1632–1677), a Sephardic Jew, added luster to its intellectual life. Spinoza was among the first to offend Jews and Christians alike by arguing that God was in everything (an idea known as pantheism) but lacked the capacity to act in history and had no special interest in man. The Dutch republic was an oasis of tolerance as well as prosperity.

THE REORGANIZATION OF WAR AND GOVERNMENT (1648–1715)

Most seventeenth-century states were not as fortunate as the Dutch. Between 1560 and 1648, France, Spain, England, and the German principalities all suffered in varying degrees from military stalemate and political disintegration. Public order, perhaps even dynastic survival, depended on the reorganization of war and government. The restructuring of virtually every European state after 1648 has been called the triumph of **absolutism** (see Document 16.4). The term is in some ways misleading. No government before the Industrial Revolution could exert absolute control over the lives of its subjects. To do so even approximately requires modern transport and communications. But if by *absolutism* one means the theoretical subordination of all other elements of a country's power structure to the crown, the word is at least partially descriptive. The

DOCUMENT 16.4

ABSOLUTISM IN THEORY

Jacques-Bénigne Bossuet (Jhahk Bay'-neen-yee Bo-sue-ay, 1627–1704), Bishop of Meaux (Mo), was court preacher to Louis XIV and tutor to his son. In this passage, which reveals something of his power as a preacher, he argues the case for royal absolutism on both practical and religious grounds.

The royal power is absolute. . . . The prince need render account of his acts to no one. . . . Without this absolute authority the king could neither do good nor repress evil. It is necessary that his power be such that no one can escape him, and finally, the only protection of individuals against the public authority should be their innocence. This confirms the teaching of St. Paul: "Wilt thou not be afraid of the power? Do that which is good" [Rom. 13:3].

God is infinite, God is all. The prince, as prince, is not regarded as a private person: He is a public personage, all the state is in him. As all perfection and all strength are united in God, so all power of individuals is united in the person of the prince. What grandeur that a single man should embody so much!

Behold an immense people united in a single person; behold this holy power, paternal and absolute; behold the secret cause which governs the whole body of the state, contained in a single head: you see the image of God in the king, and you have the idea of royal majesty. God is holiness itself, goodness itself, and power itself. In these things lies the majesty of God. In the image of these things lies the majesty of the prince.

From Bossuet, Jacques-Bénigne, "Politics Drawn from the Very Words of Holy Scripture," in J. H. Robinson, ed., *Readings in European History,* vol. 2 (Boston: Ginn, 1906).

Question: Why would this view of the world soon be questioned by those who had accepted the Scientific Revolution?

Spain of Philip II met this definition in the sixteenth century; after 1660, the model for all other states was the France of Louis XIV.

The France of Louis XIV

Louis XIV (ruled 1643–1715) came to the throne as a child of 4. To the end of his life he harbored childhood memories of the Frondes and was determined to avoid further challenges from the French aristocracy at all costs. He knew that

Louis XIV of France

their influence derived from the networks of patronage that had long dominated rural life and used the fact that such networks are ultimately dependent on favors to destroy them as independent bases of power. As king of a country in which perpetual taxation had long been established, Louis had more favors to hand out than anyone else. He developed the tactic of forcing aristocrats to remain at court as a condition of receiving the titles, grants, monopolies, offices, and commissions upon which their influence was based. By doing so, he bound them to himself while cutting them off from their influence in the countryside.

The Court of Versailles. This was the real purpose behind the construction of **Versailles** (Vare-sigh), a palace large enough to house the entire court while separating it from the mobs of Paris, 12 miles away. Louis adopted the sun as his personal symbol and developed an elaborate ritual centered around his own person to occupy his courtiers. Every royal action was accompanied by great ceremony, and proud aristocrats contended for the honor of emptying the king's chamber pot or handing him his shirt. The world of Versailles was cramped, artificial, and riddled with intrigue, but it was a world controlled in every particular by a king who knew what was happening under his own roof. To stay was to sacrifice one's independence; to leave was to lose all hope of honor or profit. By 1670, the French nobility had been fully domesticated.

Royal Administration. The centralization implied by Versailles extended to the royal administration, although in this case, Louis followed precedents established by Henry IV and Richelieu. Richelieu in particular had worked to replace the old system of governing through councils with ministries, in which one man was responsible to the crown for each of the major functions of government. He had also brought royal authority to the provinces by introducing *intendants,* commissioners who supervised the collection of taxes and served as a constant check on local authorities. Louis expanded and perfected this system. Intendancies transcended provincial borders, further weakening the ties of local privilege. The ministers of war, finance, foreign affairs, and even of roads and bridges reported directly to the king, who, unlike his father, served as his own prime minister. Louis may have been the Sun King, surrounded by ritual and devoted to the pleasures of the bed, the table, and the hunt, but he was a hard worker. He devoted at least 6 hours a day, 7 days a week to public business. Significantly, Louis usually drew his ministers from the *nobles de la robe,* the great legal dynasties of the French towns, not from the old nobility.

The Organization of War. Because war was the primary function of the early modern state and accounted for the vast majority of its expenditures, Louis XIV made every effort to bring the military under control. He instituted a series of reforms under the guidance of the war ministers Michel Le Tellier (Mee-shel Le Tell-yay, 1603–1685) and Le Tellier's son, the Marquis de Louvois (Loo-vwa, 1639–1691). A tableau of ranks, comparable to that used by most modern armies, established a hierarchy of command that in theory superseded civilian titles. The cost of quartering troops was allocated to entire provinces instead of to specific towns, and like military justice, financial

FIGURE **16.9** *Palace of Versailles.* This color engraving by Pierre Denis Martin shows the palace of Louis XIV as it looked in the eighteenth century. It was like a great city, inhabited by thousands of courtiers, officials, and servants, as well as a giant stage set that proclaimed the glory of the king. The vast gardens are in the distance.

arrangements for the army were placed under the control of the intendants.

On the battlefield, the French army abandoned the old combination of pike and shot in favor of volleys of musket fire from ranks that were rarely more than three deep. Based on the innovations of Gustav Adolph, this tactic required regular drills and marching in step, practices that had first been introduced by Maurice of Nassau but generally ignored by other armies. To improve discipline and unit cohesion, barracks, uniforms, and standardized muskets had all been adopted by 1691. Combined with the scientific principles of siege warfare perfected by Sébastian le Prestre de Vauban (Say'-bas-tyan Le Pre-tr de Vo-ban, 1633–1707), the reforms of Le Tellier and Louvois created what might be called the first modern army. Louis gave it ample opportunity to prove itself.

The Wars of Louis XIV. In the early years of his reign, Louis pursued an aggressive and, in the best French tradition, anti-Hapsburg, foreign policy. His invasion of the Spanish Netherlands in 1667–1668 brought him into conflict with the Dutch republic, which he tried to destroy in a bitter war that lasted from 1672 to 1679. Faced with almost certain destruction, the Dutch overthrew their government and made William of Orange (later **William III of England,** lived 1650–1702) stadtholder. Holland saved itself by flooding the countryside, and William's diplomacy brought Spain, Sweden, Brandenburg, and the Holy Roman Empire into the war. France fought them all to a standstill, but the alliance was a precursor of things to come.

Emboldened by the favorable terms he had negotiated at the Peace of Nijmegen (1679), Louis then tried to annex all territories that had ever belonged to France, whether in the Netherlands, Italy, the Pyrenees, or the Rhineland. Hostility to the Holy Roman Empire made him the only Christian prince to oppose the liberation of Hungary from the Turks (1682–1699), although it was at last achieved with the assistance of **Eugene of Savoy** (1663–1736), a prince who had been raised at his court and who became one of his most formidable enemies as the Hapsburg Empire's leading general. At the same time, Louis's revocation of the Edict of Nantes and expulsion of the Huguenots in 1685 further alienated Europe's Protestants.

The basic issue at stake in the wars of Louis XIV was not, however, religion but rather the control of property in Europe and overseas. Louis's enemies believed that he aimed at nothing less than French hegemony, and by 1689, nearly all of Europe had turned against him. For the rest of his life, he followed a basically defensive policy, but it was too late. In the War of the League of Augsburg (1689–1697), Louis fought a powerful Anglo-Dutch coalition while France suffered through one of the worst economic depressions in its

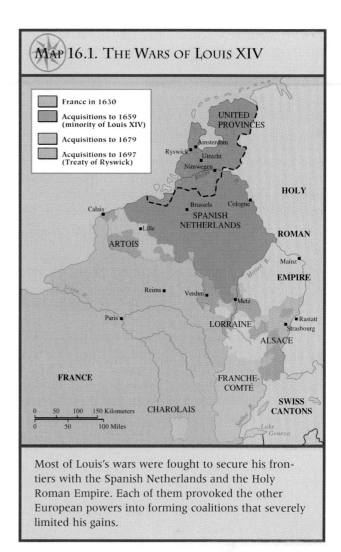

MAP 16.1. THE WARS OF LOUIS XIV

- France in 1630
- Acquisitions to 1659 (minority of Louis XIV)
- Acquisitions to 1679
- Acquisitions to 1697 (Treaty of Ryswick)

Most of Louis's wars were fought to secure his frontiers with the Spanish Netherlands and the Holy Roman Empire. Each of them provoked the other European powers into forming coalitions that severely limited his gains.

history. In the **War of the Spanish Succession** (1701–1714), an allied army commanded by an Englishman, John Churchill, Duke of **Marlborough** (Mall'-bur-ruh, 1650–1722), consistently defeated his forces. This war and its predecessor were true world wars in that they involved conflict at sea and on distant continents. Not even France could sustain such burdens indefinitely, and when the Sun King died in 1715, the country was in a severe, if temporary, decline.

The power of Louis XIV was not unlimited. Within France, local privilege still thwarted his intentions, and parlements acting as appellate courts sometimes rejected his edicts on legal grounds. Law and custom frustrated his efforts to solve basic problems of finance. Until the French Revolution of 1789, the provinces continued to pay different taxes at different rates, based largely on agreements negotiated when they became part of the kingdom in the Middle Ages. Financial administration, although no worse than in many early modern states, remained primitive. The French kings borrowed against future tax revenues, which they then farmed out to their creditors for collection. This kind of **tax-farming** by private individuals was not only inefficient but also woefully corrupt and left no room for the sophisticated financial practices being devised by Louis's Dutch and English rivals.

France as a Model for Other Princes

The Hapsburgs. Despite these shortcomings and the uneven success of Louis's foreign policy, the France of Louis XIV became a model for other princes. From Spain to the Urals, they copied his court etiquette, his system of military and administrative organization, and even the architectural style of Versailles, which became the pattern for dozens of palaces and country estates. The last Hapsburg king of Spain, Charles II "the Bewitched," died childless in 1700, and the final war of Louis's reign was waged to place a member of his own Bourbon dynasty on the Spanish throne. The new ruler, Louis's grandson Philip V (reigned 1700–1746), began a process of reform that by 1788 had created a near replica of French administration.

After 1555, the eastern Hapsburgs devoted most of their efforts to building a multiethnic empire based on Austria and Bohemia. The victory of Eugene of Savoy over the Turks in 1683 enabled them to annex most of Hungary 1699. The Austrian archduke Charles (1685–1740), although he failed to gain Spanish support as the rival of Philip V in the War of the Spanish Succession, took the Spanish Netherlands as a consolation prize at the Peace of Utrecht in 1713. This territory, present-day Belgium, was also incorporated into the Austrian Empire. After his election as emperor in 1711, Charles, now known as Charles VI, began to reform the far-flung Austrian administration on French lines.

Most of the German princes followed suit, although it could be argued that Frederick Wilhelm I of Prussia (1688–1740) had already carried reform beyond anything achieved by Louis XIV. Set without geographical defenses in the midst of the northern German plain, Brandenburg-Prussia had been devastated in the Thirty Years' War and remained vulnerable to the shifts of central European politics. A veteran of the War of the Spanish Succession, Frederick Wilhelm resolved to turn his kingdom into a military power of the first rank and ended by making its administration subservient to the army. After 1723, his government became little more than a branch of the *kriegskommisariat,* or war ministry, but his reforms laid the groundwork for Prussia's emergence as a major power.

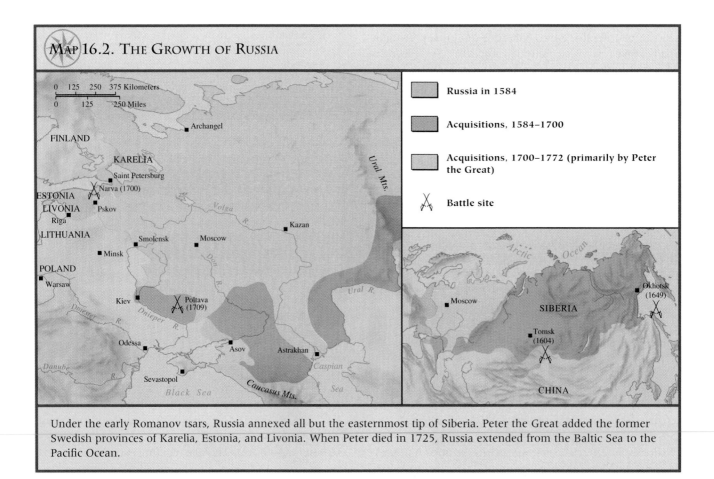

MAP 16.2. THE GROWTH OF RUSSIA

Russia in 1584

Acquisitions, 1584–1700

Acquisitions, 1700–1772 (primarily by Peter the Great)

Battle site

Under the early Romanov tsars, Russia annexed all but the easternmost tip of Siberia. Peter the Great added the former Swedish provinces of Karelia, Estonia, and Livonia. When Peter died in 1725, Russia extended from the Baltic Sea to the Pacific Ocean.

FIGURE 16.10 *Peter the Great.* One of the tsar's greatest achievements was the construction of the city of St. Petersburg, built on pilings sunk into marshy ground near the mouth of the river Neva. He is shown here in an enamel in 1723 in front of the St. Paul and St. Peter Fortress and Trinity Square in his new capital.

Russia under Peter the Great. Perhaps the most spectacular efforts at reform were undertaken by Peter I "the Great" of Russia (1672–1725). Like Louis XIV, he had survived a turbulent regency in his youth and came to the throne determined to place his monarchy on a firmer basis. Peter realized that to do so he would have to copy western models, and he spent 1697–1698 traveling incognito to France, England, and the Netherlands as part of what he called the Grand Embassy. When he returned, he immediately began to institute reforms that, although western in inspiration, were carefully adapted to Russian conditions.

Using knowledge acquired firsthand in the shipyards of Holland and England, Peter supervised the building of a navy that could control the Baltic. He destroyed the *streltsy,* or palace guard, that formed the core of the Russian army and had long been a fruitful source of plots against the tsars and replaced it by an army organized on the French model. Peter, however, raised his troops through conscription for life, a method suggested by Louvois that could not be implemented in the less autocratic atmosphere of France. The new forces served him well. In the Great Northern War (1700–1720), he broke the power of Sweden and established Russian control over Estonia, Karelia, and Livonia. To consolidate his gains and to provide Russia with an all-weather port, he built the modern city of St. Petersburg near the mouth of the Neva River and made it his capital.

Internally, Peter established a series of colleges or boards to supervise the work of thirteen new governmental departments and divided the country into fifty provinces, each with its own governor appointed by himself. He created a table of ranks for civilian officials and opened state service for the first time to men of middle-class origin. To compensate the hereditary nobility for its loss of state positions, Peter abandoned the distinction between *pomest'e* and hereditary lands and introduced primogeniture. In some cases, he resorted to large-scale distributions of land and serfs. The condition of the latter predictably worsened, and peasant rebellions during the eighteenth century were put down with memorable savagery.

The Emergence of England as a World Power

The system created by Peter the Great was more autocratic than its western models—and more permanent. It lasted without major modifications into the nineteenth century. The situation in England was very different. Although **Charles II** (1660–1685) reclaimed his father's throne in 1660, the fundamental issue of sovereignty had not been resolved. Like his predecessors, Charles did not like to call Parliament into session, and the taxpaying gentry proved as unwilling as ever to provide adequate support for the crown. Shrewd, affable, and personally popular, the new king avoided open confrontations with his subjects, but poverty limited his freedom of action. For a time he even accepted a pension from Louis XIV, who hoped for English support against the Dutch. For this reason, England did not for some time develop the administrative structures that were being adopted on the continent.

The Creation of a New English Navy. Only in the creation of a modern navy could the English keep pace. Before 1660, England, like other countries, had possessed a handful of fighting ships supplemented in time of war by contracting with private owners who provided both ships and crews for the duration of hostilities. No permanent officer corps existed, and men who owed their positions to civilian rank or to military experience on land typically commanded the fleets. Administration was minimal, often temporary, and usually corrupt. The success of 1588 and the remarkable performance of the Commonwealth navies showed that such fleets could do well if properly motivated. But the system as a whole was analogous to military contracting on land: at best inefficient and at worst uncontrollable.

Both Charles II and his brother James, Duke of York (1633–1701), had a deep interest in naval affairs, and their unswerving support of secretary of the Admiralty **Samuel Pepys** (Peeps, 1633–1703) enabled him to introduce reforms that, in effect, created the English navy. Pepys, who is probably best known today for his famous diary, created a permanent corps of naval officers who attained their rank by the passage of formal examinations. To ensure their availability when needed, the navy kept them on half-pay when not at sea. He improved provisioning and repair facilities and increased the number of royal ships under the command of a reformed Admiralty. By the end of the century, even tactics had been changed to permit better control of battle fleets.

The Glorious Revolution.

But a reformed fleet was in itself no guarantor of world-power status. As Louis XIV's minister of finance and related matters, Colbert had introduced similar measures in France only to have his plans abandoned during the fiscal crisis of the 1690s. Great ships, like great armies, need a consistent supply of money. Ironically, England achieved this only by overthrowing the men who had made the naval reforms possible. When Charles II died in 1685, his brother ascended the throne as James II. A convert to Roman Catholicism, James instituted policies that alienated virtually every segment of the English elite, and in the fall of 1688, they deposed him in favor of his daughter Mary and her husband, William of Orange. As stadtholder of the Netherlands and King of England, William III brought the island nation into the Grand Alliance against Louis XIV.

The Glorious Revolution, as it is called, changed the basis of English politics. By overthrowing one king and effectively appointing another, Parliament and those it represented had at last resolved the issue of sovereignty. Parliament and not the king would rule England. Under William and again under his sister-in-law Anne (reigned 1702–1714), Parliament showed an unprecedented willingness to open its purse and support massive outlays for war, knowing that a weakened monarchy could not use the money to subvert the freedoms of its subjects.

England's Economic Growth.

The wealth that underwrote England's command of the sea and financed the campaigns of Marlborough on land came from nearly a century of unparalleled economic growth. England's growing commercial strength was based in part on geographical advantage. Faced with the implacable hostility of Louis XIV, the Dutch had to spend much of their wealth defending their borders on land. England, an island, was spared this expense. Moreover, with their deep-water ports and location to windward of the continent, the English could disrupt Dutch trade and steal their markets by blocking access via the English Channel. The Anglo-Dutch wars of 1652–1653, 1665–1666, and 1672–1673 were fought over this issue. Dutch seamen acquitted themselves well, but the cost of battles in which more than 100 ships might be engaged on each side, together with the need to provide convoys for trading vessels even in peacetime, gradually eroded their competitive advantage (see Document 16.5).

English Finances.

Even favorable geography could not have given England a decisive lead had it not been for a system of credit and finance that became the envy of Europe. The revolution of 1688 paved the way for the land tax of 1692 and the extension of excise taxes to a wide range of consumer goods. England acquired the benefits of permanent taxation for the first time in its history. The Bank of England, established in 1694, then stabilized English finances by underwriting government war loans. In the eighteenth century, it became the first of Europe's central banks, allowing private bankers to draw on its reserve in periods of financial crisis.

TABLE 16.1 ENGLISH TRADE BALANCES

The most active phase of the War of the Spanish Succession lasted from 1701 to 1711. During that period, the English lost 1,061 merchant ships to enemy raiders, with the worst year being 1702. At the same time, the English balance of trade (surplus of exports over imports) increased enormously, owing primarily to increased exports of cloth and grain to Portugal, Holland, Germany, and Russia and to decreased imports from France and Spain. Because the increase in trade more than compensated for the subsidies sent to the continent for war, the British were, in mercantilist terms, net beneficiaries of the war. The extra-European trade balance in the table to the right refers to trade with non-European partners.

Year	Extra-European Trade Balance	Overall Trade Balance
1699–1701	£489,000	£974,000
1702	233,000	971,000
1703	515,000	1,745,000
1704	968,000	1,519,000
1706	836,000	2,705,000
1707	672,000	2,024,000
1708	630,000	2,022,000
1709	271,000	2,111,000
1710	825,000	2,486,000
1711	969,000	2,731,000

Question: How did the policies described in Document 16.5 contribute to the results shown in this table?

Adapted from Jones, D. W., *War and Economy in the Age of William III and Marlborough* (Oxford: Basil Blackwell, 1988, p. 220).

HELVETIUS ON DUTCH TRADE IN DECLINE

The problem of maintaining Dutch trade reached a crisis during the War of the Spanish Succession (1702–1713) when war closed many of traditional markets. The following memo was presented to the French Foreign Minister in 1706 by Adrianus Engelhard Helvetius, a Swiss-born physician who dealt in medical supplies and made several visits to the Netherlands as a French spy during the War of the Spanish Succession. At the time he wrote, England and the Netherlands were firm allies.

The commerce of the United Provinces in Europe has never been in worse condition than it is today. During the course of earlier wars, although Dutch vessels were also open to the attacks of privateers, at least they could take refuge in the Atlantic and in the Mediterranean ports under Spanish rule, which are now closed to them. Furthermore, even when they were completely barred from the trade of France, they still continued to ply both the Baltic trades, which they continue to enjoy, and the trades of Spain, the kingdoms of Naples and Sicily, and Spanish Flanders, which now they have good reason to miss. Not only is the market greatly reduced for their cloth, both of their own manufacture as well as that made in India and the Baltic, and for their other wares, spices, salt fish, etc., but they are also deprived of the profitable return trade in wool, wine, and necessary commodities. . . .

As a result, there are frequent bankruptcies, word of which scares people and discourages them from entrusting money to the

merchants, whose own funds are limited, as they are in the habit of doing in peacetime. This decline even effects the domestic commerce of the country, which is suffering badly, especially thanks to the cunning manipulations of the English, who take advantage of the opportunity to raise themselves upon the ruins of their allies.

The English, a people as fierce as they are capable, being convinced that the States General need their help so badly that they would not dare dispute anything with them, follow the maxim of making the Dutch pay their auxiliary troops, even when they are engaged in battle. They supply them with goods of every kind, sending cloth and Indian fabrics which are forbidden in England, butter, tallow, even manufactured candles, grain, etc., and in this they manage to make a profit on the support of troops for which they ought to be paying themselves.

From Helvetius, "Mémoire sur l'état présent du Gouvernment des Provinces Unis," in M. van der Bijl, ed., *Bijdragen en Mededeldingen van het Historisch Genootschap* 80 (1966, pp. 171–180); trans. Herbert H. Rowen, *The Low Countries in Early Modern Times. A Documentary History* (New York: Harper Row, 1972, pp. 226–227).

Question: What does Helvetius see as the primary reasons for Dutch decline?

Credit, backed by reliable taxation, paid for the fleet, Marlborough's armies, and the large subsidies that England paid to its continental allies. England, which became Great Britain when it merged with Scotland in 1707, was therefore able to expand its empire and protect its markets more easily than the Dutch, whose war fleet declined after 1673 and whose decentralized institutions blocked the formation of more effective credit mechanisms. English trade, which had been expanding steadily throughout the seventeenth century, became a flood during the War of the Spanish Succession when the British navy swept the seas of all rivals. In time, the enormous wealth derived largely from overseas markets would provide the capital for the Industrial Revolution and further strengthen English claims to great power status.

ECONOMIC AND SOCIAL CHANGE IN THE 1600S

Mercantilism. The economic policy that underlay these developments is called **mercantilism.** Mercantilism was not really a theory but rather a set of assumptions that had long been implicit in the rivalries between

states and in the beginnings of European expansion overseas. Accepted by nearly everyone, these assumptions were applied with unusual consistency by Colbert as Louis XIV's Minister of Finance. Modern economists normally define a nation's wealth as the total value of its goods and services. Mercantilists defined wealth as a nation's store of gold and silver. This was in part because cash paid for war and therefore could be translated directly into power and prestige. Because they defined wealth in monetary terms and because economic growth rates are typically slow in preindustrial societies, mercantilist theory saw the world's wealth, for all practical purposes, as a fixed quantity. Economic and military policy was therefore a zero-sum game, the purpose of which was to acquire a surplus of gold and silver at the expense of one's neighbors. The mercantilists tried to achieve this by ensuring that exports exceeded imports. A country should become as self-sufficient as possible while encouraging the development of trades that might find an external market for their products.

The Importance of Overseas Empire. To Colbert and his contemporaries in other lands, this meant protection of the home market through tariffs and the

FIGURE 16.11 *Jean Baptiste Colbert (1619–1683).* Perhaps the most gifted minister of Louis XIV, Colbert was the architect of the king's mercantilist policies and the creator of the French navy. He also supported the sciences and founded the French Royal Academy.

development of an overseas empire that could produce commodities unavailable in the mother country. Ideally, an empire should have varied components: tropical colonies to produce dyewoods, sugar, cotton, indigo, and chocolate and northern colonies to produce timber, furs, and naval stores. The colonies would produce these raw materials in return for manufactured goods from home. Every effort was made to subsidize the manufacture of luxury items that could be shipped to the colonists or sold to unwary foreigners for cash.

To protect trade and colonies, a fighting navy was essential, for the line between war and commerce was necessarily blurred. The goal of both was wealth and power, and trade was "war by other means." War, in the mercantilist view, was the normal state of things, whereas peace was an aberration, a temporary lull between periods of hostility. The European game of annexations and sieges was therefore extended to every corner of the globe. Conflicts with parochial names like the War of the League of Augsburg and the War of the Spanish Succession were actually the first world wars in history.

The Redistribution of Wealth. Expanded trade did not, however, create universal prosperity. It increased the number of professionals and created job opportunities for a growing middle class of bookkeepers, accountants, and small tradesmen, but it also concentrated immense wealth in the hands of a few. In England, some of these investors were merchants and bankers, whereas others were great landholders who invested in trade. The aristocratic prejudice against commerce largely vanished in the seventeenth century, in part because the composition of the titled nobility had changed. Families remained who could trace their ancestry to the remote feudal past, but many more had been ennobled for their services to the monarchy in more recent times. Their immediate ancestors had been lawyers or servants of the crown, and they continued to maintain close ties with the urban world from which they had come. This was as true in France or Germany as it was in England. It had always been the case in Italy, and even in Spain the fabled prohibition against *hidalgos* (literally, "sons of somebody") engaging in trade was largely ignored.

It could hardly have been otherwise. Those who turned their back on new sources of wealth eventually lost both power and status. Commerce, even if it were conducted at one remove by investing with urban bankers and merchants, had become for many aristocrats the primary source of new capital. They committed much of this new wealth to ostentation in an effort to maintain their social position and to ensure access to the royal court, but much of it was also reinvested.

Social Stratification. Capital accumulated by trade would later provide the massive sums needed for the Industrial Revolution, but it did nothing to halt the growth of rural poverty and may actually have increased it by accelerating the capitalization of land, a process that had been underway since the fourteenth century. One effect of increased trade was therefore to intensify social polarization. In the seventeenth and eighteenth centuries, the rich grew richer while the poor grew poorer.

The degradation of peasant life was most obvious in those regions that provided agricultural produce for the world market. The growing European demand for grain encouraged Russian, Polish, and Prussian landholders to impose or extend the institution of serfdom. Production for export was best achieved on huge estates whose labor force could be minutely controlled. Left to their own devices, peasants would diversify crops and develop other economic strategies to enhance their own security. To landholders, this diversion of effort prevented them from maximizing their profits. Serfdom, like New World slavery, was therefore a way to "industrialize" agriculture, but by limiting peasant survival strategies, it dramatically reduced rural standards of living while enriching those who were already wealthy.

Social stratification was almost as great in England, the center of commercial growth. The condition of English peasants may have improved for a time after the Black Death, but it declined steadily after the mid-fifteenth century. The rich were better able than the poor to invest in land, develop it, and profit from the cultivation of cash crops. Smallholders found it increasingly difficult to compete. Royal policy compounded the problem by supporting the retention of feudal ties while permitting the enclosure of common lands. This was the process, described in Chapter 12, by which landholders appropriated land previously shared by the inhabitants of an entire village.

Table 16.2 English Wages and Prices, 1541-1702

A comparison between wages and prices shows that while the former doubled between 1541 and 1702, the price of ordinary food items tripled. The result was a severe decline in the living standards of laboring families. It should be noted, however, that most contemporaries thought English workers were far more prosperous than their counterparts in France or the Netherlands, and richer still than the peasants of central and eastern Europe.

Labor	1541–1582	1583–1642	1643–1702
Weekly Wages			
Farmhand	3s. 3d.	4s. 10d.	6s. 4¾d.
Mason	4s. 10d.	6s. 5¾d.	9s. 10¾d.
Carpenter	5s.	6s. 2¾d.	10s. 2¾d.
Prices			
Wheat (quarter)*	13s. 10½d.	36s. 9d.	41s. 11½d
Barley (quarter)	8s. 5¾d.	19s. 9¾d.	22s. 2½d.
Oatmeal (quarter)	20s. 4¾d.	37s. 9¼d.	52s. 11d.
Chicken (1)	1d.	3d.	1s. 4d.
Goose (1)	4d.	1s. 4d.	3s.
Beer (barrel)	2s.		10s.

*A quarter, the standard measure for grains, equaled one-quarter of a hundredweight, or 25 pounds.
2 pence (d.) = 1 shilling (s.).
Figures adapted from Burnett, John, *A History of the Cost of Living* (Harmondsworth, UK: Pelican Books, 1969, pp. 71, 80–81).

Question: Try to calculate on a percentage basis how much wages rose between 1541 and 1702 and how much food prices rose during the same period. (*Hint:* To get the percent increase, convert monies in a given row to pence, then divide the total pence in the first column by the total pence in the last column.)

Table 16.3 English Incomes, 1688

In 1688, Gregory King (1648–1722) published his estimates of population and incomes in England. He believed that the number of merchants, shopkeepers, and artisans had increased but that the incomes of poor people had declined. The income figures are in millions of pounds sterling.

Class	Number of Families	Income	% of Families	% of Income
Nobility, gentry, officials	53,000	9.816	4	23
Merchants and traders	10,000	2.400	1	5
Freeholders and farmers	330,000	16.960	24	39
Shopkeepers and artisans	100,000	4.200	7	10
Military officers and clergy	19,000	1.120	2	2
Laborers, servants, paupers, seamen, common soldiers, etc.	849,000	9.010	62	21
Total	1,361,000	43.506	100	100

From King, Gregory, "Natural and Political Observations," in G. E. Barnett, ed., *Two Tracts by Gregory King* (Baltimore: Johns Hopkins, 1936, p. 31).

Question: In what ways do you think these figures might differ from those in a modern industrial country such as the United States?

Deprived of the marginal income that enabled them to survive, thousands of peasants surrendered their properties and left their homes with little more than the clothes on their backs.

Unemployment and Migration to the Cities.
Most found it difficult, if not impossible, to find work. The shift toward grazing reduced the demand for agricultural labor, while population growth after the midfifteenth century depressed wages. The situation worsened throughout the sixteenth and seventeenth centuries. Increased criminal activity and a growing population of "sturdy beggars" alarmed the authorities, but poor laws, based on the assumption that poverty and homelessness were the results of deliberate choice, accomplished nothing. Neither migration to America nor the expansion of urban employment fully relieved the pressure. Eighteenth-century London may have

been the commercial center of the world, but its slums became as enormous as its wealth. Unable to find work, England's dispossessed became a vast urban proletariat whose squalid, gin-soaked existence was immortalized in the drawings of William Hogarth (1697–1764) and in the novels of Henry Fielding (1707–1754).

In some regions, capitalization of the land encouraged social stratification without a major increase in trade. Spanish peasants, faced from the 1580s with heavy taxation and declining yields, borrowed money from urban investors to improve their land. When they found themselves unable to redeem their *censos* (a form of bond), the holders foreclosed and seized their property. By 1650, the population of Madrid had swelled to more than 100,000 as displaced peasants sought charity from the city's many religious houses and from an increasingly hard-pressed government. Lawyers, speculators, and officials amassed large estates but provided only inefficient absentee ownership.

The Costly Freedom of the French Peasant.

Although the French crown resisted the consolidation of properties common to virtually every other part of Europe, prosperity in the countryside remained elusive. Since the fifteenth century, French courts had generally supported peasant rights against those of the landowning nobility. The reasons were largely political—supporting the claims of peasants tended to break up concentrations of aristocratic power in the countryside—but by 1700, French peasants had become the freest in Europe.

Unfortunately, the wars of Louis XIV made them among the most heavily taxed. They had exchanged their oppressive landholders for a no less demanding king. At the same time, the increase of private ownership in an age of demographic growth led inevitably to the subdivision of properties. Partible inheritance remained the norm in France, and although more than half of the rural population owned a plot of land at century's end, it was rarely big enough to support a family. Thousands of peasants were forced into the labor market to pay their taxes at a time when wages had already begun to decline. Terrible famines in the 1690s showed that freedom in itself offered little protection against hunger.

Attitudes toward the Poor.

The growth of poverty did not go unnoticed by the more fortunate. Although in retrospect it seems obvious that it was caused by changes in economic relationships that had been aggravated by endemic warfare and the meager harvests of the Little Ice Age, contemporaries drew other conclusions. The attitude toward the poor began to change.

In medieval theory, if not always in practice, the poor were specially favored by God and entitled to charity. Begging symbolized the apostolic poverty of the friars, and the church regarded the giving of alms, whether to the church or to the poor, as a good work and a mark of piety. In the more conservative Catholic regions of southern Europe, this view persisted into modern times, but in the north, it had been replaced by fear and apprehension well before the Reformation.

The city of Augsburg adopted punitive measures against beggars and the homeless in 1459. Paris followed in 1473. In 1495, an ordinance of Henry VII of England condemned vagrants to three days in the stocks, following which they were to be whipped and returned to their place of origin. It was to be a model for later English poor laws. Charles VIII of France in the following year decreed that beggars be sent to row in the galleys. In the decades to come, such humanists as Erasmus, More, and Juan Luis Vives wrote against begging, while religious reformers like Luther, Calvin, and Zwingli agreed that there was no virtue in poverty.

To Protestant theologians, work performed in a Christian spirit was sanctifying. One of the more enlightened approaches to poverty involved the establishment of workhouses in which vagrants and petty criminals could rehabilitate themselves through labor. The Amsterdam *rasphuis* (rahsp'-house), founded at the beginning of the seventeenth century, was a model institution.

FIGURE 16.12 *Peasants in Front of Their House, Le Nain (Early 1600s).* Economic growth did not affect all segments of the population equally. The gap between rich and poor increased in many parts of Europe. These French peasants, shown before their ramshackle house, have not benefitted from the changes in the economy.

Inmates worked 12 to 14 hours a day turning logs of Brazil wood into sawdust so that the powder could be incorporated into dyes. The monotony of their day was enlivened by sermons and floggings. The city established a similar institution for poor women, who spun endless yards of thread to be sold by the city government. The idea behind all of these measures was that the poor were willfully lazy and that they could be reformed only if subjected to rigorous discipline.

The Rise of Gentility. Hostility to the poor was encouraged by their frightening numbers and by the many popular revolts that had occurred between the Black Death and the Great Peasants' War of 1524–1525. Virtually everyone understood that economic polarization posed a threat to the social order. What they did not understand was that the effects of polarization were being augmented by a redefinition of elite values that, consciously or not, dehumanized the poor in the eyes of their "betters."

The European elite had always justified their privilege by claiming some form of superiority. The knights of the first feudal age had taken pride in their strength and courage. In the absence of an immediate threat to society, their descendants had declared such qualities hereditary and enhanced them by cultivating chivalric courtesy. The early modern elite retained a self-proclaimed monopoly of these virtues and merged them with others that reflected the values of Renaissance humanism and of the late medieval urban life from which it had emerged. Refinement of taste and intellect became the new hallmarks of status.

Much of this gentility derived from a common education. Minimal acquaintance with the classics and an appreciation for classic aesthetics was essential. The gentleman or gentlewoman valued harmony, symmetry, and balance. Classical standards were reflected not only in the high-minded dramas of Racine or Calderón but in the architecture of Andrea Palladio (1518–1580). Baroque art and architecture, with its rich decoration and extravagant visual harmonies, gradually gave way to a more restrained style based on what was thought to have been the taste of ancient Rome. This Palladian interpretation of Roman aesthetics became the model for hundreds of palaces, country houses, and churches and persisted well into the nineteenth century. Its influence may be seen in the reconstruction of London by Sir Christopher Wren (1632–1723) after the great fire of 1666.

As the seventeenth century wore on, "reason," too, became important in the sense that those who wished to be thought "gentle" rejected superstition and extreme religiosity in favor of a more detached, "scientific" view of the world. The new science encouraged people to believe that the divine order was rational rather than providential or based on frequent interventions by a wrathful deity. A growing faith in the possibility of a rationally ordered society accompanied the growth of absolutism, while holistic, magical, or apocalyptic visions—and sometimes the display of emotion itself—became the province of the poor and ignorant.

Manners and Deportment. Manners and deportment were an even more important mark of status. Those who wished to be taken seriously adopted models of carriage, speech, and gesture based equally on courtly models and on the precepts of the classical rhetoricians. The stage, with its abundance of noble characters, provided instruction for those who lacked access to polite society. Table manners improved with the introduction of the fork, and books were written as guides to correct behavior. In time, the natural movements of ordinary people came to seem crude and loutish.

Clothing. Clothing, too, mirrored the growing separation between the classes as the fashions of the rich became ever more elaborate and expensive. Men in particular cultivated the art of magnificence with lace collars, massive wigs, and brocaded waistcoats that were sometimes trimmed in gold. To be seen in one's own hair was unacceptable even on the battlefield.

FIGURE 16.13 *A Country Cottage, 1665.* The size and prosperity of the middle class increased in both England and the Netherlands during the seventeenth century. This modest but elegant Dutch cottage was painted with its genteel inhabitants by Pieter de Hooch. Order and cleanliness have obviously become important values.

FIGURE 16.14 *The Triumph of Elegance.* Elegance, education, and taste replaced military values as the major claim to status. This painting by Dirck van Delen (1605–1671) shows ladies and gentlemen dancing sedately in an elegant room. Their elaborate ruffled collars were a very expensive status symbol and aroused the anger of moralists who periodically sought to ban the fashion.

Ordinary people tried to imitate the dress and bearing of the upper classes, but education, good manners, and a suit that cost as much as a middle class family's annual income were hard to counterfeit. "Presumption" of this sort was met with ridicule and often with violence, for upper-class men still carried swords or weighted canes and used them freely on those they regarded as inferior, but another mark of gentility, the idea of comfort, adapted more easily to the lives of ordinary people.

Domestic Comfort and Elegance. Magnificence in domestic architecture grew during the sixteenth century. The French royal palace known as the Louvre, the great chateaux built along the river Loire in the time of Francis I, and the country houses of Tudor England were legitimate ancestors of Versailles. But like Versailles, they subordinated comfort to grandeur. Their furniture, like that of the medieval castle, remained minimal. The great houses of the later seventeenth century were no less ostentatious, but their owners packed them with furnishings in the modern manner. Chairs, tables, carpets, and whatnots proliferated. Although rooms were still set aside for ceremonial and social functions, they were supplemented by sitting rooms and other cozy spaces for the private enjoyment of the owner's family. The sheer luxury of these interiors could not be matched by ordinary households, and tens of thousands of Europeans continued to huddle in wretched cottages, but the general level of domestic comfort rose steadily after about 1650.

Chimneys and glazed windows became common in the homes of town dwellers and in those of the richer peasants, while inventories of household goods began to show a steady increase in chairs, tables, and linens.

CONCLUSION

The political troubles of the late sixteenth and early seventeenth centuries did not preclude extraordinary developments in other areas. The Scientific Revolution changed the way Europeans thought about the physical universe. England, France, and above all, the Netherlands challenged the Iberian powers and created substantial empires of their own. In the process, they greatly expanded Europe's presence in world markets and accumulated capital in unprecedented amounts. The Netherlands emerged, however briefly, as a major power and a center of high culture. Eventually, states that had been nearly shattered by a century of war and revolution began to reconstruct themselves, reforming their governmental institutions, curbing the power of the local elite, and gaining control over the armies and navies whose independence had threatened to engulf them. The model for many of these changes was the France of Louis XIV, but the rise of England as an economic and naval power would have an even greater influence on the age to come.

Review Questions

- What did earlier intellectual movements contribute to the Scientific Revolution?
- How did the Dutch and English organize their first empires, and what accounts for the difference?
- How did the armies and navies of 1700 differ from those of 1648?
- What was the purpose of such palaces as Versailles?

For Further Study

Readings

Black, Jeremy, *European Warfare, 1660–1815* (New Haven, CT: Yale University Press, 1994). A clear, concise analysis of warfare as it developed in the seventeenth and eighteenth centuries.

Braudel, Fernand, *Civilization and Capitalism, 15th–18th Centuries,* 3 vols. trans. S. Reynolds (New York: Harper and Row, 1981–1984). Long, but filled with ideas and information on the development of the economy and material life in preindustrial Europe.

Schama, Simon, *The Embarrassment of Riches: An Interpretation of Dutch Culture in the Golden Age* (New York: Knopf, 1987). An insightful, beautifully illustrated portrait of Dutch culture at its peak.

Westfall, Richard S., *The Life of Isaac Newton* (Cambridge: Cambridge University Press, 1993). A good, recent biography of a complex figure.

Wolf, John B., *Louis XIV* (New York: W.W. Norton, 1968). A readable biography.

InfoTrac College Edition

For additional reading, go to your online research library at *http://infotrac.thomsonlearning.com*.

Using Key Terms, enter the search terms:

Copernicus	*Galileo* not *Jupiter*
Isaac Newton	*Mercantilism*
Louis XIV	*Peter the Great*

Web Site

http://es.rice.edu/ES/humsoc/Galileo

The Galileo Project. A cleverly designed site produced by Rice University covering nearly every aspect of Galileo's life and work.

EUROPE, 1600–1715

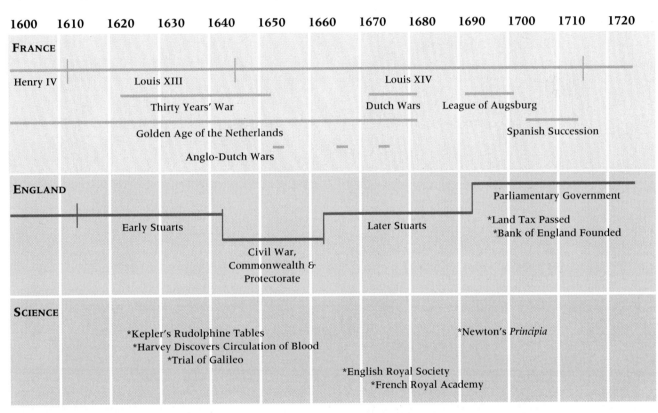

Visit the Western Civilization Companion Web Site for resources specific to this textbook:

http://history.wadsworth.com/hause02/

The CD in the back of this book and the Western Civilization Resource Center at *http://history.wadsworth.com/western/* offer a variety of tools to help you succeed in this course, including access to quizzes; images; documents; interactive simulations, maps, and timelines; movie explorations; and a wealth of other sources.

Photo Credits

Chapter 1

Page 1: Wheat/© CORBIS; 5lr: © Copyright The British Museum; 6: Courtesy the French Ministry of Culture and Communication, Regional Direction for Cultural Affairs—Rhône-Alpes region—Regional Department of Archaeology; 7: Courtesy of Mrs. Rudolf Freund, Rudolf Freund/*Scientific American*, July, 1953; 9: © Copyright The British Museum; 10: © CORBIS; 12: Courtesy LANDSAT; 14: British Museum, London, UK/Bridgeman Art Library; 19l: © Michael S. Yamashita/CORBIS; 19r; © CORBIS; 21: Deir el-Medina, Thebes, Egypt/Bridgeman Art Library; 24: © Copyright The British Museum.

Chapter 2

Page 30: The Athenian Acropolis and Agora/© CORBIS; 32: National Archaeological Museum, Athens, Greece/Bridgeman Art Library; 33: Archaeological Museum of Nauplion, Greece/Ancient Art and Architecture Collection Ltd./Bridgeman Art Library; 34: © Gian Berto Vanni/CORBIS; 35: Museo Nazionale di Villa Giulia, Rome © Scala/Art Resource, NY; 36: American School of Classical Studies at Athens, Agora Excavations (IN1997.02.0204); 40: Prometheus Being Chained by Vulcan (1623) by Dirck van Baburen, Rijksmuseum, Amsterdam (SK-A-1606); 41: © Copyright The British Museum; 42t: Muzeum Narodowe, Warsaw, Poland/Bridgeman Art Library; 42b: British Museum, London, UK/Bridgeman Art Library; 43: Musee Municipal Antoine Vivenel, Compiegne, France/Lauros/Giraudon/Bridgeman Art Library; 51: © Copyright The British Museum; 52l: Courtesy The Trireme Trust; 52tb: © John Sherwood Illsley; 53: © Copyright The British Museum

Chapter 3

Page 57: *The Wedding of Alexander the Great and Roxana*, 1810 (oil on canvas) by Baron Pierre-Narcisse Guerin/Musee des Beaux-Arts, Rouen, France/Peter Willi/Bridgeman Art Library; 58: © CORBIS; 60t: © CORBIS; 60b: hand-colored print from *Bilderbuch Fur Kinder* by Friedrich Bertuch (Munich: 1810)/private collection; 61lr: Hirmer Verlag, Munich; 62: Museo Capitolino, Rome, Italy, Giraudon/Bridgeman Art Library; 63: Fitzwilliam Museum, University of Cambridge, UK/Bridgeman Art Library; 64: Munich Kunsthistoriches; 66: British Museum, London, UK/Bridgeman Art Library; 74: Vatican Museums and Galleries, Vatican City, Italy/Lauros/Giraudon/Bridgeman Art Library; 75: *Alexander and Diogenes*, 1818 (oil on canvas), by Nicolas Andre Monsiau/Musee des Beaux-Arts, Rouen, France/Peter Willi/Bridgeman Art Library

Chapter 4

Page 78: Detail from *The Dictatorship Offered to Cincinnatus*, Giovanni Battista Tiepolo/The State Hermitage Museum, St. Petersburg, Russia; 81: © Archivo Iconografico, S.A./CORBIS; 83lr: Courtesy *Athena Review*; 84: Tripoli Museum, Libya/© Roger Wood/CORBIS; 85: Biblioteca Apostolica Vaticana, The Vatican, Italy/Giraudon/Bridgeman Art Library; 89: Louvre, Paris, France/Lauros/

Giraudon/Bridgeman Art Library; 90: © Copyright The British Museum; 93t: Engraving from *Great Men and Women* (New York: Selmar Hess, 1894)/private collection; 93b: Museo e Gallerie Nazionali di Capodimonte, Naples, Italy/Bridgeman Art Library; 96: Sousse Museum, Tunisia/© Roger Wood/CORBIS; 97: Museo Capitolino, Rome, Italy/Giraudon/Bridgeman Art Library

Chapter 5

Page 100: A Legionary in the Roman Army/© Copyright The British Museum; 105: © Copyright The British Museum; 107lr: © Copyright The British Museum; 108: © Bettmann/CORBIS; 110: Cortile Delle Corazze/M. Sarri/© Alinari Archives/CORBIS; 112tl: © Paul Almasy/CORBIS; 112bl: © Carmen Redondo/CORBIS; 112r: © CORBIS; 115: © Copyright The British Museum; 116: © Copyright 1997 Leo C. Curran (ac880902); 120: © Araldo de Luca/CORBIS; 121: courtesy The VRoma Project (www.vroma.org)

Chapter 6

Page 123: Relief showing Battle Between the Romans and the Dacians/© Gianni Dagli Orti/CORBIS; 124: Villa dei Misteri, Pompeii, Italy/Alinari/Bridgeman Art Library; 127: Forum, Rome, Italy/Index/Bridgeman Art Library; 128: "Crucifixions by the Romans," engraving by Jan Luyken, published by Wilhelmus Goeree, Amsterdam, 1690/private collection; 129: © Araldo de Luca/CORBIS; 134l: Hirmer Verlag. Munich; 134r: © Paul Almasy/CORBIS; 137: Hirmer Verlag, Munich; 138: © Sandro Vannini/CORBIS; 142: San Vitale, Ravenna, Italy/Bridgeman Art Library; 144: *St. Benedict Hands over the Rule of the New Order to the Monks of Monte Cassino*, Turino Vanni (fl.1390-1415) Galleria dell' Accademia, Florence, Italy/Bridgeman Art Library

Chapter 7

Page 152: The Coronation of Emperor Charlemagne by Pope Leo III at St. Peters, Rome, 800 CE/Bibliotheque Municipale, Castres, France/Giraudon/Bridgeman Art Library; 156: © Keren Su/CORBIS; 157: Duomo, Cefalu, Sicily, Italy/Lauros/Giraudon/Bridgeman Art Library; 159: The State Hermitage Museum, St. Petersburg, Russia; 161: engraving (after Fikentsher) from *History of the World* by J. C. Ridpath (Cincinnati: Jones Brothers, 1901)/private collection; 163: Private Collection/Bonhams, London, UK/Bridgeman Art Library; 164l: © Aaron Horowitz/CORBIS; 164r: © Fernando Alda/CORBIS; 166lr: © Copyright The British Museum; 170lr: © Copyright The British Museum; 171: © Copyright The British Museum; 174: The Bodleian Library, University of Oxford, UK (MsBodl. 218, f.62r)

Chapter 8

Page 176: Lord and Vassal/Archivo de la Corona de Aragon, Barcelona, Spain/Index/Bridgeman Art Library; 178: ©The Museum of National Antiquities, Stockholm (IN 15115); 179lr: © University Museum of Cultural Heritage, University of Oslo,

Norway; 181: The Pierpont Morgan Library, New York (MS M. 736, f.14); 182: Rijksuniversiteit Bibliotheek, Leiden; 183l: Dr. John Crook, FSA (jcrook@netcomuk.co.uk); 183r: Universitätsbibliothek, Heidelberg; 185: Universitätsbibliothek, Heidelberg; 187: photograph © Baxter 1992/private collection; 188: By permission of the British Library (Royal 2 B.VII fol.78v); 189: By permission of the British Library (Add. 19720 fol. 117v.); 194: hand-colored engraving (detail after the Bayeux Tapestry) from *The Middle Ages* by S. Hamilton (Chicago: Morehouse, 1916)/private collection; 195l: © Dr. John Crook, FSA (jcrook@netcomuk.co.uk); 195r: hand-colored engraving (detail after the Bayeux Tapestry) from *The Middle Ages* by S. Hamilton (Chicago: Morehouse, 1916)/private collection; 196: Department of the Environment, London, UK/Bridgeman Art Library; 197: MS. Cim. 4453 fol. 42r/Bayerische Staatsbibliothek, Munich, Germany/Bridgeman Art Library

Chapter 9

Page 200: King John surrenders his crown to the papal legate/ engraving from *Pictorial History of the World* by J. D. McCabe (Boston: Desmond Publishing Co., 1894)/private collection; 203: By permission of the British Library (MS. Cotton Claudius E.V, fol. 41v); 206–7: © Dr. John Crook, FSA (jcrook@netcomuk.co.uk); 208: By permission of the British Library (Royal.2.A.XXII. f.220); 209: MS. Fr 6465 Fol. 174/Bibliotheque Nationale, Paris, France/Bridgeman Art Library; 211: Palazzo Ducale, Urbino, Italy/Bridgeman Art Library; 212: The Royal Cornwall Museum, Truro, Cornwall, UK/Bridgeman Art Library; 213: Prado, Madrid, Spain/Index/Bridgeman Art Library; 214: © Dr. John Crook, FSA (jcrook@netcomuk.co.uk); 217: By permission of the British Library (Burney MS. 275, fol. 176v); 218: San Marco, Florence, Italy/Bridgeman Art Library

Chapter 10

Page 221: Departure of a Fleet of Ships (tapestry, 16th c.)/Musee d'Art et d'Archeologie, Moulins, France/Lauros/Giraudon/ Bridgeman Art Library; 222: Bibliotheque Historique de la Ville de Paris, Paris, France/Archives Charmet/Bridgeman Art Library; 223: MS. 165 fol. 48v (1409–80)/Fitzwilliam Museum, University of Cambridge, UK/Bridgeman Art Library; 224: MS. Fr 2091 fol. 125/Bibliotheque Nationale, Paris, France/Bridgeman Art Library; 226t: By permission of the British Library (The Latin/Luttrell Psalter, Add 42130 f.170); 226b: © The British Museum; 227l: By permission of the British Library (Egerton 2019 fol. 7); 227r: chromolithograph (after French miniature, 15th c) (London: McAllister & Son, 1921)/private collection; 229: The Bodleian Library, University of Oxford, UK (MS. Bodl. 264, fol. 218r); 230: By permission of the British Library (Add. 27695 fol. 8); 232: woodcuts from *Science and Literature in the Middle Ages and at the Period of the Renaissance* by Paul Lacroix (New York: D. Appleton & Co., 1878)/private collection; 234: Edifice, London; 237: woodcut (anonymous, 16th c, German)/private collection; 239: Palazzo Pubblico, Siena, Italy/Bridgeman Art Library; 242: Private Collection/The Stapleton Collection/Bridgeman Art Library

Chapter 11

Page 245: *A Frugal Meal,* By permission of the British Library (Add. 28162 fol. 10v) 246: Bibliotheque Municipale, Angers, France/ Giraudon/Bridgeman Art Library; 249: Wellcome Institute Library, London (WMS 544 fol. 65r); 251: By permission of the British Library (Sloane 1975 fol. 93); 252–253: © Dr. John Crook, FSA (jcrook@netcomuk.co.uk); 254lr: lithographs by F. Kellerhoven (after medieval French miniatures) from *Science and Literature in the*

Middle Ages and at the Period of the Renaissance by Paul Lacroix (New York: D. Appleton & Co., 1878)/private collection; 254r: Musee des Beaux-Arts, Lyon, France/Peter Willi/Bridgeman Art Library; 259: Victoria & Albert Museum, London, UK/Bridgeman Art Library; 265: MS. 76 f.2 fol.169r/Koninklijke Kabinet, The Hague, The Netherlands/Bridgeman Art Library

Chapter 12

Page 270: Death takes the Carthusian, the sergeant, the monk and the usurer, MS.279 ff.5v-6v/Lambeth Palace Library, London, UK/Bridgeman Art Library; 273: By permission of the British Library (Royal 6.E.VI fol. 301); 276: By permission of the British Library (Royal MS 18E, i.f.175); 277: woodcut by Jost Amman, ca. 1565/private collection; 278: chromolithograph from *Le Costume Historique* by Racinet (Paris: Librairie de Firmin-Didot, 1877-1886)/private collection; 279: Graphische Sammlung Albertina, Vienna; 280l: © Copyright The British Museum; 280r: Trinity College Library, University of Cambridge, UK; 281lr: Drawing © Joseph Wheatley, from *Historic Sail,* by Joseph Wheatley and Stephen Howarth (London: Greenhill Books, 2000); 284: National Gallery, London, UK/Bridgeman Art Library; 286: Private Collection/Bridgeman Art Library; 288l: MS. Fr 2643 f.165v/ Bibliotheque Nationale, Paris, France/Bridgeman Art Library; 288r: © Archivo Iconografico, S.A./CORBIS; 289l: Private Collection/The Stapleton Collection/Bridgeman Art Library; 289r: Maison Jeanne d'Arc, Orleans, France/Bridgeman Art Library; 290: © Sandro Vannini/CORBIS; 292: © Francis G. Mayer/CORBIS

Chapter 13

Page 294: Petrarch (Francesco Petrarca)/Biblioteca Nazionale, Turin, Italy/Bridgeman Art Library; 295: chromolithograph (after English miniature, 14th c) (London: George Barrie & Son, 1901)/private collection; 296: woodcut (after Amman) from *Science and Literature in the Middle Ages and at the Period of the Renaissance* by Paul Lacroix (New York: D. Appleton & Co., 1878)/private collection; 298: Capilla Real, Granada, Spain/Bridgeman Art Library; 300: State Collection, France/Bridgeman Art Library; 301: hand-colored engraving from *Les Travaux de Mars* (Paris, 1672) by Mallet/private collection; 302: Phillips, The International Fine Art Auctioneers, UK/Bridgeman Art Library; 305: Nationalmuseet, Copenhagen, Denmark/Bridgeman Art Library; 308l: engraving from *Great Men and Women* (New York: Selmar Hess, 1894)/private collection; 308r: By permission of the British Library (Royal MS 18D. i.i, f.148); 309tl: engraving by W. Hopwood (after Van Dalen) from *The Gallery of Portraits* (London: Charles Knight, 1833)/private collection; 309tr: The Bodleian Library, University of Oxford, UK (MS. Holkham misc. 49, fol. 5r); 309bl: engraving (after Botticelli) from *Great Men and Women* (New York: Selmar Hess, 1894)/private collection; 309br: By permissiion of the British Library (Add. MSS. 19720, f.214); 310: Gemaldegalerie, Berlin, Germany/Bridgeman Art Library; 311: Vatican Museums and Galleries, Vatican City, Italy/Giraudon/Bridgeman Art Library; 312: Louvre, Paris, France/Giraudon/Bridgeman Art Library; 316: © Sandro Vannini/CORBIS; 317l: Tempio Malatestiano, Rimini, Italy/ Bridgeman Art Library; 317r: © CORBIS; 318: Vatican Museums and Galleries, Vatican City, Italy/Bridgeman Art Library; 319: Vatican Library, Rome, Italy/Bridgeman Art Library; 320: Louvre, Paris, France/Giraudon/Bridgeman Art Library

Chapter 14

Page 322: Luther before the Diet of Worms (Charles V in the foreground), engraving from *Pictorial History of the World* by

J. D. McCabe (Boston: Desmond Publishing Co., 1894)/private collection; 324: © Gail Mooney/CORBIS; 328: trade card (after Leffing) Germany, 1920/private Collection; 329: © David Lees/CORBIS; 330: trade card (after Titian) Germany, 1920/private collection; 331: National Museet, Copenhagen, © Archivo Iconografico, S.A./CORBIS; 333: engraving from *Great Men and Women* (New York: Selmar Hess, 1894)/private collection; 334t: trade card (after Holbein) Germany, 1920/private collection; 334b: trade card, England, 1919/private collection; 335l: trade card (after Holbein), England, 1919/private collection; 335r: National Portrait Gallery, London, UK/Bridgeman Art Library; 336t: trade card (after Moro) Germany, 1920/private collection; 336b: Lambeth Palace Library, London, UK/Bridgeman Art Library; 337: Louvre, Paris, France/Lauros/Giraudon/Bridgeman Art Library; 339: Prado, Madrid, Spain/Giraudon/Bridgeman Art Library; 340: Kunsthistorisches Museum, Vienna, Austria/Bridgeman Art Library

Chapter 15

Page 343: Detail from *Neptune Offering Gifts to Venice*, Giovanni Battista Tiepolo (1696-1770)/Palazzo Ducale, Venice, Italy/ Bridgeman Art Library; 344: Private Collection/Index/Bridgeman Art Library; 345l: Private Collection/Bridgeman Art Library; 345r: Villa Farnese, Caprarola, Lazio, Italy/Bridgeman Art Library; 346: Drawing © Joseph Wheatley, from *Historic Sail*, by Joseph Wheatley and Stephen Howarth, (London: Greenhill Books, 2000); 347tlr: courtesy Smithsonian Institution; 347br–48: engraving from *Great Men and Women* (New York: Selmar Hess, 1894)/private collection; 349: photograph © William J. Duiker; 350t: Bibliotheque Nationale, Paris, France/Lauros/Giraudon/ Bridgeman Art Library; 350b: William L. Clements Library, University of Michigan; 353: © The British Museum; 354: Musee du Temps, Besancon, France/Lauros/Giraudon/Bridgeman Art Library; 356t: engraving by Franz Hogenberg, October, 1567/ private collection; 357t: engraving (after, from left to right, Holbein, F. Zucchero, and Garrard the Elder), London: G. Barrie & Son, 1904/private collection; 357b: © National Maritime Museum, London; 358: engraving by T Woolnoth (after Porbus) from *The Gallery of Portraits* (London: Charles Knight, 1833)/private collection; 359: Private Collection/Bridgeman Art Library; 360: trade card (after Vandyke) Germany, 1920/private collection; 362t:

trade card (chromolithograph after Walker) English, 1919/private collection; 362b: engraving by H. Bourne (after Kneller) from Becket and Loggan, *Contemporary Engravings* (London: Blackie & Son, 1860)/private collection; 364: engraving by Franz Hogenberg, July 14, 1578/private collection; 366tl: © Archivo Iconografico, S.A./CORBIS; 366tr: trade card (chromolithograph after Faithorne) English, 1919/private collection; trade card (chromolithograph) English, 1919/private collection

Chapter 16

Page 369: *The Burning of "The Royal James"* at the Battle of Sole Bank, 6th June 1672, Willem van de Velde, the Younger (1633-1707)/Rafael Valls Gallery, London, UK/Bridgeman Art Library; 371l: engraving from *Great Men and Women* (New York: Selmar Hess, 1894)/private collection.; 371tr: engraving from *Great Men and Women* (New York: Selmar Hess, 1894)/private collection.; 371br: trade card (chromolithograph), Germany, 1920/private collection; 372t: engraving by Robert Hart (after Ramsay) from *The Gallery of Portraits* (London: Charles Knight, 1833)/private collection; 372b: Louvre, Paris, France/Peter Willi/Bridgeman Art Library; 373: engraving by W. Holl (after Hals) from *The Gallery of Portraits* (London: Charles Knight, 1833)/private collection; 374: National Gallery, London, UK/Bridgeman Art Library; 375tb: engraving from *Great Men and Women* (New York: Selmar Hess, 1894)/private collection; 376l: New York Academy of Medicine; 376r: trade card (chromolithograph, after Hondius) English, 1919/private collection; 378: © Bettmann/CORBIS; 379t: © New-York Historical Society, New York, USA/Bridgeman Art Library; 379b: Johnny van Haeften Gallery, London, UK/Bridgeman Art Library; 380l: National Gallery of Ireland, Dublin; 380r: Rijksmuseum, Amsterdam, Holland/Bridgeman Art Library; 381: engraving from *Pictorial History of the World* by J. D. McCabe (Boston: Desmond Publishing Co., 1894)/private collection; 382: © Archivo Iconografico, S.A./CORBIS; 385: Hermitage, St. Petersburg, Russia/Bridgeman Art Library; 388: engraving by W. Holl (after Mignard) from *The Gallery of Portraits* (London: Charles Knight, 1833)/private collection; 390: Fine Arts Museums of San Francisco, CA, USA/Giraudon/Bridgeman Art Library; 391: Rijksmuseum, Amsterdam (SK-C-150); 392: Private Collection/ Rafael Valls Gallery, London, UK/Bridgeman Art Library

Index

Yüan Dynasty, 268–269
Yuste, monastery of, 354

Zakat, 160
Zapolya, János, 353
Zara, 208

Zeno, 74, 141
Zero-sum game, 387
Zeus, 38, 40
Ziggurat, 13
Zoroastrianism, 48–49, 161, 213
Zürich, 331–332

Zwingli, Huldrych
  celibacy, views, 338
  humanism, 328
  poverty, views, 390
  teachings, 332–333